THE
CANADIAN
POLITICAL
TRADITION

THE CANADIAN POLITICAL TRADITION

BASIC READINGS

Edited by
R.S. BLAIR and J.T. McLEOD
University of Toronto

Nelson Canada

© Nelson Canada
A Division of International Thomson Limited
Published in 1989 by
Nelson Canada
A Division of International Thomson Limited
1120 Birchmount Road
Scarborough, Ontario M1K 5G4

Originally published by Methuen Publications in 1988.

Canadian Cataloguing in Publication Data

Main entry under title:

The Canadian political tradition

ISBN 0-17-603477-3

1. Canada - Politics and government.   I. Blair,
R. S. (Ron S.).   II. MacLeod, Jack, 1932-   .

JL65 1989.C36 1989   320.971   C89-094494-6

Printed and bound in Canada
1 2 3 4 5   GP   5 4 3 2 1 0 9

Contents

Foreword

"History is past politics; politics is present history." This aphorism summarizes the dilemma faced by the student of politics. Clearly, the object is to secure an understanding of the political world today, but this cannot be attained without some reasonable comprehension of the past as well. The study of politics requires a larger perspective than a knowledge of current events. As R. MacGregor Dawson wrote, "The character of a government, like that of an individual, is shaped by the two primary forces of heredity and environment. . . ."

Thus, we believe that students should be given an opportunity to read not only contemporary writings, valuable though many of these are, but also what might be called "classic" analyses of various aspects of Canadian government and politics. This volume is distinctive in providing students with a comprehensive selection of the best writing in Canadian political science; many of these core essays have had a marked influence in shaping academic, and, ultimately, popular understanding.

The readings are grouped into four parts, each having a brief Introduction. The readings in Part 1 relate to constitutional foundations, specifically responsible government, federalism and the Canadian Charter of Rights and Freedoms. An understanding of these is a prerequisite for further study in the field, yet it is notorious how few actually understand them. In Part 2, the focus is on social factors that shape, and are shaped by, political institutions. The term social factors is employed in a broad sense, embracing not only such forces as geography and economics, but also the realm of values and ideas. The readings in Part 3 examine aspects of the linkages between society and government, most obviously parties, interest groups and the electoral process. The final section addresses the crucial question of "Who rules?" and contains a number of readings that examine the capacity of key actors in the polity to influence and decide.

The exigencies of publishing have dictated some editing of these essays, but we have attempted to keep this to a minimum.

We would like to thank the staff of Methuen Publications, and in particular Anita Miecznikowski and Cathy Munro, for their kind and efficient assistance in preparing this reader.

R.S. BLAIR
J.T. McLEOD

PART 1

THE CONSTITUTION AND FEDERALISM

Many Canadians mistakenly believe that the passage of the Canada Act and the Constitution Act in 1982 by the United Kingdom Parliament meant that their country had acquired a new Constitution. In fact, as Eugene Forsey has frequently pointed out, the "new" Constitution is simply the "old" Constitution "with knobs on." These "knobs" are very important, especially the Charter of Rights and Freedoms and the Amending Procedure, but they represent additions to the Constitution that had its birth in 1867.

Alan Cairns' essay (Reading 1) was written in 1970 when the process of constitutional review was in full swing and when a great deal of criticism was being directed against the supposed deficiencies of the "old" Constitution. Many critics appeared to equate that Constitution with a single statute, the British North America Act of 1867 (now retitled the Constitution Act, 1867). The great merit of Cairns' essay is in its argument that constitutions are "organic living institutions," not just pieces of paper frozen in time. This concept of a "living constitution" is far more meaningful than simplistic notions of static constitutions which become obsolete.

Like Caesar's Gaul, the Canadian Constitution is divided into three parts. The excerpt from Peter Hogg's brilliant textbook, *Constitutional Law of Canada* (Reading 2), provides a clear and comprehensive explanation of one of these parts, responsible government. In so doing, it shows the immense importance of convention in the actual operation of the Constitution. Convention plays a part in the working of every constitution, but it is in countries with responsible government that convention is most significant. So much is this the case that an exposition of the Constitution without reference to conventional rules would be meaningless.

Peter Russell's essay (Reading 3) provides a valuable perspective on another part of the Constitution, the Charter of Rights and Freedoms. He emphasizes that those political leaders who were advocates of an entrenched charter saw it as an instrument to foster national unity as well as to enhance the protection of rights and freedoms. With respect to the first goal, Russell argues that the role of the Supreme Court is the critical factor, since, as the final court of appeal, it will, in effect, be setting national policies. With respect to the second goal, he points out that, while this was the basis for the Charter's popularity with the general public, entrenchment in itself is no guarantee that rights and freedoms will be better protected. These are not absolutes, but, rather, are subject to limits, and the significance of the Charter is that the decisions about these limits are now being made by appointed judges and not by elected politicians.

The third part of the Constitution has to do with federalism, and Reading 4, by Donald Smiley, demonstrates that, in Canada, this involves a great deal more than legal arrangements concerning the distribution of powers. He analyzes the nature of the original Confederation settlement and argues that, since World War I, profound differences have developed between English- and French-speaking Canada as to the purposes of federalism and the proper role of the national government. Although this paper was written in the mid-1960s, Smiley's argument remains important for an understanding of contemporary federalism.

Ramsay Cook's essay (Reading 5) continues one aspect of Smiley's paper by examining how French-speaking Canadians in Quebec have viewed their place in the federal system, in particular their relationship as a minority to the English-speaking majority. In the "quest for equality," French-speaking Canadians have not been of one mind, and Cook discusses the "four general schools of thought" that can be identified as having emerged over time. Neither the Quebec referendum in 1980 nor the Constitution Act in 1982 nor even the constitutional accord of 1987 ended this debate, and it can be safely assumed that it will continue into the forseeable future.

1

The Living Canadian Constitution

ALAN C. CAIRNS

The dustbin of recent history is littered with discarded constitutions cast aside after brief and withering exposure to reality. Constitutions capable of responding and adapting to the perils of change have sufficient scarcity value to be treated with the deference appropriate to rare achievements. All the more curious, therefore, has been the detached, unappreciative Canadian attitude to one of the most durable and successful constitutions in the world.

A partial explanation is found in the nature of the British North America Act. It is a document of monumental dullness which enshrines no eternal principles and is devoid of inspirational content. It was not born in a revolutionary, populist context, and it acquired little symbolic aura in its subsequent history. The movement to Confederation was not a rejection of Europe, but was rather a pragmatic response to a series of economic, political, military and technological considerations. There was no need for the kind of political theorizing which accompanied the American experience of creating a new political entity, and which exercised a spell on subsequent generations. With the important exception of the federal system, Canada was endowed "with a Constitution similar in Principle to that of the United Kingdom." Constitutional monarchy and responsibile government in a parliamentary setting were already part of the Canadian heritage which was approvingly translated to the larger sphere of action which the new Dominion created. No resounding assertions of human rights accompanied the creation of the new polity. The British tradition precluded any approach to their protection premised on comprehensive declarations of principle.

The absence of an overt ideological content in its terms, and the circumstances surrounding its creation, have prevented the BNA Act from being perceived as a repository of values by which Canadianism was to be measured. Further, the first thirty years of its existence were troubled by depression, threats of secession, and constant bickering over its terms. These scarcely constituted the circumstances for the Act to become the symbolic focus for the nascent political system. Consequently, a conscious ideological adherence and loyalty to the BNA Act and the constitution of which it was a part never became overt integral components of the Canadian civic identity.

Abridged from Alan C. Cairns, "The Living Canadian Constitution," *Queen's Quarterly* 77, No. 4 (Winter 1970), 483-98. Reprinted by permission of the author.

An additional factor in the Canadian lack of appreciation for the constitution is a confused understanding of the meaning of age and time for institutions.

With the passage of time the intentions of the Fathers unavoidably became an increasingly artificial concept with an ever attenuated contact with reality. Their visions were responses to the problems they faced in the light of prevalent conceptions of the role of government. Many of the conditions to which they addressed themselves faded away, to be replaced by conditions they could not predict. In such circumstances deference to their intentions became impossible, for they had none. Nevertheless, the BNA Act, which represents a consolidation of some of their intentions, remains an important constitutional document. This raises the question of how relevant for a contemporary evaluation of the Canadian constitution is the fact that the BNA Act is a century old. . . .

[The fact is that] institutions do not have a natural life span. They are, when wisely constructed and carefully tended, evolving human arrangements for avoiding the ravages of time by flexibly responding to the demands which confront them. Therefore to discuss the relevance of an institution in terms of its age, defined by the lapse of time since its first beginnings, is to misconceive what an institution is.

Canadian understanding of the constitution would have been much improved had it been consistently viewed in the significant American phrase as a "living constitution."[1] The wise admonition of Holmes reveals a perspective sadly lacking in Canada:

> The provisions of the Constitution are not mathematical formulas having their essence in their form; they are organic living institutions transplanted from English soil. Their significance is vital, not formal; it is to be gathered not simply by taking the words and a dictionary, but by considering their origin and the line of their growth . . . When we are dealing with words that are also a constituent act, like the Constitution of the United States, we must realize that they have called into life a being the development of which could not have been foreseen completely by the most gifted of its begetters. It was enough for them to realize or to hope that they had created an organism; it has taken a century and has cost their successors much sweat and blood to prove that they created a nation. The case before us must be considered in the light of our whole experience and not merely in that of what was said a hundred years ago.[2]

It is the virtual absence of this understanding of a living constitution which has produced the mistaken belief that the constitution is a century old, that it has already outlived its allotted life span, and that *younger* means *better* and *older* means *worse*. Given this belief it is possible to advocate a new constitution simply because the BNA Act was drafted a century ago. The rather trite conclusion automatically follows that a constitution, or a constitutional document, so heavy with years must be out of date.

In the 1960s there has been a recurrence of the criticism of the constitution as obsolete which was so widespread in the Depression of the thirties. In that troubled decade, the constitution as judicially interpreted was roundly condemned by centralists for the barriers it placed in the way of decisive action by the federal government. The contemporary attack has different roots. One source is the spurt of nation building and constitution making which followed the demise of Western imperialism. . . . [O]nly a masochist would find [such] experience worthy of emulation.

An additional source is the French-Canadian view of recent years that the existing constitution restricts the process of nation building in Quebec. . . . Their search for a new constitution is sustained by English-Canadian writers such as Peter O'Hearn.[3] . . . Other English-Canadian support is found in politicians who capitalize on any groundswell of opinion, or who naively assume that to be progressive requires a repudiation of the past, at least at the level of oratory. They sympathize with T.C. Douglas . . ., when he states: "The time has come for Canadians to free themselves from the dead hand of the past and forge a constitution that will enable Canada to keep its rendezvous with destiny. . . . Human rights are sacred but constitutions are not."[4]

In an age when rapid obsolescence is viewed as the natural and inevitable end for every man-made product, such a thesis quickly finds attentive, receptive hearers. Superficially it has compelling force, for clearly the conditions of 1867 have passed away. It logically follows that decisions made in the light of those conditions must become increasingly irrelevant with the passage of time.

Crucial to this widespread position is the belief that the constitution is by and large what the Fathers bequeathed to us a century ago. From this perspective the constitution emerged in 1867 in the form of the British North America Act and its accompanying understandings, the product of a small political élite, the Fathers of Confederation, and barring formal amendments, is now what it was then. The confusion is subtle. To view the constitution in terms of what the Fathers intended and immediately achieved fails to see that the constitution is a continuous creation. It accords too much deference to the constitution as it existed in 1867, and too little attention to the contribution of subsequent generations to its evolution.

The Canadian constitution is the body of understandings defining the basic institutions of government and the relationships between them, plus the relationships between governments in the federal system, and between the citizens and those governments. At any given point of time the content of the constitution is a series of living practices which has been worked out by successive generations. It is a product of continuous selection, rejection, and addition. It is always, in a practical sense, contemporary. It is a living instrument of government, wider in scope than the BNA Act, and not restricted to the 1867 intentions of the Fathers. It is an evolving institution which has responded to pressures and flexibly accommodated itself to a variety of needs and changing demands.

The distinction between the constitution as an institution and the key statute that went into its formation is cogently described by Llewellyn in his discussion of the American constitution:

> The discrepancy between theory and fact found in private law is exaggerated in the constitutional field, because under a code of rigid words no easy and gradual rewording of outmoded rules in such manner as to hide the changes made in their content, is possible. The consequence is that with growing age all force in the actual words of a code withers and dies. What is left, and living, is not a code, but an institution. Many of the institution's roots trace back through time into the code. *Many do not*. But the living institution is neither the dead code nor its "interpretation." It is not even by any parthenogenesis descended from its great-grandmother code alone. It is new, it is different, it is growing; and in its blood run so many other streams that resemblance to the code is seldom strong and always confined to single traits.[5]

Evidence on the living nature of the constitution is ubiquitous. The settlement of 1867 was only a beginning. It has been under constant transformation since that time. The major evidence is as follows:

1. The instruments of federal control—disallowance, reservation, and refusal of assent by the Lieutenant-Governor—have fallen into virtual desuetude. If not entirely dead, there is no likelihood that they will ever again be used in the coercive fashion of the early post-Confederation years.

2. The transformation of Empire into Commonwealth—from "Colony to Nation"—has reduced the ties to Great Britain until all that remains is an increasingly attenuated emotional link, a similarity in the institutions of parliamentary and monarchical government, and an embarrassing leftover in the continuing (entirely formal) role of the British parliament in the amending procedure.

3. As is well known, the division of powers in the BNA Act was importantly affected by the Judicial Committee of the Privy Council. While its decisions aroused much resentment and may or may not have been appropriate to Canadian needs, it cannot be denied that they made a fundamental contribution to the constitutional evolution Canadians actually experienced.

4. The division of powers was also transformed by the massive engine of the federal spending power and the conditional grants mechanism. Once again the evaluation may be favourable or unfavourable, but it is clear that the result was marked change in the practical significance of Sections 91 and 92 of the BNA Act. Perhaps the spending power was used indiscriminately. Perhaps its use should have been (or should be) more tightly controlled, but that is not the issue here.

5. The proliferation of federal-provincial meetings of administrators and politicians, culminating in conferences of premiers and prime ministers has added, as many have pointed out, an important new mechanism of coordination for the federal system.

6. Since the onset of World War II the fiscal system has not been the

chaos of clashing taxing jurisdictions which it was in the Depression. Further, as part of a succession of fiscal agreements, huge equalization grants have been paid to the less well-endowed provinces. The original compulsory federal subsidies have been rendered financially trivial by comparison.

7. The parliamentary system has been transformed by the development of the party system, the institution of party discipline, the emergence of third parties and their recognition, the institution of research staffs for the opposition parties, etc. Recently we have been told that before our very eyes the parliamentary system is being transformed into a presidential system without the requisite checks and balances. What is relevant is that the parliamentary half of the Canadian wedding of parliamentary government and federalism has not stood still.

8. Even prior to the passage of the Diefenbaker Bill of Rights, the Supreme Court, and particularly Mr. Justice Rand, began to develop a court-supported jurisprudence for the protection of civil liberties. Basing their decisions on the flimsy constitutional basis of the preamble to the BNA Act which stated that Canada was to have "a Constitution similar in Principle to that of the United Kingdom," the court enunciated an important series of civil liberties decisions.

9. Finally, there were the formal amendments to the Act which contributed to its evolution.

Even in the cryptic fashion expressed above, these changes have been of momentous significance in the evolution of the Canadian constitution.

The agents of these changes were largely the politicians and civil servants of both levels of government responding to the demands and opportunities which the possession of office imposed on them. To examine the above list is to have it confirmed that the constitution never has been, and is not now, only what the courts say it is. The evolution of the constitution has been largely guided by successive generations of political leaders and their influential bureaucratic advisers. Admittedly they did not have a clean slate to work with. Admittedly the result has been evolution rather than revolution. Admittedly certain key parts of the constitutional framework remain, in form at least, as they were originally established in 1867. It is also true that a different beginning would have produced a different outcome, but that is true of all human experiments. The point is not that what happened in 1867 did not matter, but that the decisions then made did not constitute a cake of custom which has held subsequent generations of Canadians in unwilling thralldom in a world they never made. The point is that the constitution has worked and grown in response to the shifting conditions thrown up by the passage of time. A constitution which had accommodated for a century the often competing demands of two ethnic groups, which had survived through depression and war, the transformation of a rural society into an urban society, the settlement of the West, and the technological revolution of recent years might have been appreciated in more prosaic times for its real practical virtues, rather than, as was so often the case, being scorned for its absence of symbolic appeal, and criticized for a non-existent inflexibility. In the words of Eugene Forsey, "There is no point in change for its own sake, or just for the sake of having the very latest thing in constitutions. (What matters in a constitution is not how new it is but how good it is, how well it works.) The bigger the change, the heavier the onus upon those who propose it to prove that it is necessary, or even useful."[6]

It may be taken for granted that the Canadian constitution, like any other, prejudices some and fosters other public policy outputs. Any constitution, particularly a federal one, will regularly prevent some group of office holders from attaining some of their policy objectives. To criticize a constitution because it entails this consequence, however, is similar to criticizing the law of gravity. The more precise and relevant question is comparative, whether or not the existing constitution erects more barriers to desired governmental output than would its successor. The answer depends on the nature of the particular new constitution that is advocated. Until that information is available, it is entirely proper to note the flexibility of the existing constitution.

All of the changes noted above are obvious and well known. Why then has so little heed been paid to the message they contain about the flexibility of a living constitution? What explains the constant confusion implicit in the attacks on the constitution because of its age? First, there is sometimes failure to distinguish between the BNA Act and the constitution. Then the relative paucity of formal amendments, especially dealing with the division of powers, has produced a misleading impression of stablity belied by our actual experience even in that area. Much of the change which has occurred has not been formally designated as constitutional, and it has not been accompanied by fanfare. It has simply represented the handiwork of busy men attempting to work an ongoing system of government.

A good part of the explanation simply lies in a compartmentalization of the minds of the critics and analysts. While all the changes have been recognized and noted, they have frequently co-existed with the assumption that the constitution is a century old. The absence of the concept of a living constitution has aided in this compartmentalization. The confusion has been deliberately sewn by propagandists who have undertaken partisan attacks on the constitution because it stood in the way of their pet panacea. No century-old document (or constitution), they contend, should be allowed to stand in the way of the people. At the opposite pole, blindness on the part of some constitution-worshippers, who have been reluctant to believe that their god could be affected by anything so mundane as the passage of time, has had some influence.

Finally, the scholarship of historians and lawyers, and to a lesser extent of political scientists, has been obsessed with discovering the true meaning of 1867. Centralists and provincialists, compact theorists and their opponents, have all fought over the BNA Act in an attempt to discover its true meaning, and often to further their partisan objectives. By so doing they have exaggerated the importance of the original agreement of 1867 and have down-graded the changes it underwent in its subsequent expression.

In view of the preceding, two frequent tendencies in the discussion and evaluation of the Canadian constitution have been based on dangerous misunderstandings. It is simply mistaken to attack the existing constitution because of the age of the BNA Act, one of the key documents which went into its making a century ago. Llewellyn describes a working constitution "as being in essence not a document, but a living institution built (historically, genetically) in first instance *around* a particular document."[7] "With every passing decade," stated Carl Brent Swisher, "a constitution written long ago provides less and less guidance for its own interpretation amid patterns of social change and with sheer change in the dictionary meanings of familiar terminology."[8] It is equally fallacious to transform the constitutional settlement of 1867 into a measuring rod against which subsequent deviations can be assessed and their perpetrators chastised. Two American authors described the "intentions of the framers" as a "filio-pietistic notion that can have little place in the adjudicative process of the latter half of the twentieth century. . . . A nation wholly different from that existing in 1787, facing problems obviously not within the contemplation of the Founding Fathers, can scarcely be governed—except in broadest generality—by the concepts and solutions of yesteryear."[9] The same point was lucidly expressly by Chief Justice Hughes of the United States Supreme Court: "It is no answer to say that this public need was not apprehended a century ago, or to insist that what the provision of the Constitution meant to the vision of that day it must mean to the vision of our time. If by the statement that what the Constitution meant at the time of its adoption it means today, it is intended to say that the great clauses of the Constitution must be confined to the interpretation which the framers, with the conditions and outlook of their time, would have placed upon them, the statement carries its own refutation."[10] To attack the constitution on grounds of age is to fail to see its living nature. It is the same failure which produces the description of post-1867 changes as deviations.

This latter approach was very widespread in discussions of judicial review, particularly in criticisms of the Privy Council. Since lawyers constitute the professional group which has arrogated specialized expertise to itself in this matter they have an important responsibility for the misconceptions which heavily influence our constitutional discussion. I do not forget that one category of legal criticism of the Judicial Committee was based on the alleged failure of British judges to treat the BNA Act as a living instrument of government. It is true that to this group Lord Sankey, with his "living tree" analogy, was the closest thing to a judicial hero that is found in the law periodicals. However, the other major group of criticisms was specifically based on the unacceptable conduct of the Judicial Committee in departing either from the intentions of the Fathers, or the clear meaning of the BNA Act in which those intentions were presumably embodied. Further, the "living tree" school of Canadian criticism typically also reproached the Privy Council for leading Canada down the provincial path away from the limited, centralized federalism so wisely chosen in the sixties of the nineteenth century. This was partly because those critics willing to overtly discuss the constitution in terms of current need were usually centralists. Consequently, they could not resist appealing to the Fathers and their original creation as the touchstone of constitutional wisdom.

In general, the basic language of both constitutional case law and its Canadian critics stressed fidelity to an ancient document. O'Connor, the author of the classic fundamentalist statement that judges should apply the Act in terms of the meanings deliberately embodied in it by its creators, strongly attacked the Judicial Committee for "most serious and persistent deviation . . . from the actual text of the Act." He was highly critical of Lord Watson's "assumption of the guardianship of the autonomy of the provinces. His proper function was merely that of an interpreter of the meaning of the words of a statute."[11] This position reflected the British tradition which instructs judges to apply statutes literally. Thus, jurisprudence in Canada, both in the language of courts and that of their critics, has not devised adequate criteria to guide judges in the employment of the discretion they unavoidably possess. This has been unfortunate, for it has meant that much constitutional advocacy has been, literally, meaningless. It has also contributed to the misunderstanding of what a constitution is.

The critics of the Privy Council frequently asserted that its failure rested on an unwillingness to use the variety of historical evidence available to throw light on the intentions of the Fathers, and thus clarify obscurities in the BNA Act. This approach was always fraught with difficulties, but with the passage of time its desirability became increasingly questionable. This was recognized by Professor Strayer in a recent publication. He noted the "very limited" evidence available on the formation of the Act, and, more important, questioned its utility in principle. "Conditions have so drastically changed since 1867," he pointed out, "that the particular context in which the Act was passed may have little bearing on the context in which it is now expected to operate."

This position represents a marked change from the obsessive concern with the intentions of the Fathers in the decades prior to the abolition of appeals to the Privy Council. Yet Strayer is still caught in a historical quagmire of his own making. The obligation to appeal to the past is irresistible. His argument continues: "The more crucial question now is: What would the framers have intended had conditions been in 1867 as they are today? Even if the courts could now be induced to make use of external evidence as to the conditions of that time such evidence would be of limited value in answering this hypothetical question."[12]

Unfortunately, we are not told what evidence would be helpful. Given the impossibility of deciding how to undertake this pseudo-historical quest, one wonders why it should be undertaken at all. The assertion of Learned

Hand is as valid for Canada as for the United States: "It is impossible to fabricate how the 'Framers' would have answered the problems that arise in a modern society had they been reared in the civilization that has produced those problems. We should indeed have to be sorcerers to conjure up how they would have responded."[13]

In the evolution of a constitution, it is evident that the passage of time does and should reduce the weight to be given to the views and desires of the Fathers or of influential moulders of the constitution at other points of time. As time transforms the conditions to which the constitution must be responsive, the search is not for what was originally intended, but for what can be creatively extracted from a constitutional heritage of which the BNA Act is only a part. The search for the contemporary meaning of the constitution does not consist in minute examination of what was said or intended or achieved a century ago. Such an approach would deny to constitutional unfolding the benefits which a century of experience has given us. This generation, its predecessors and successors, partially have and certainly should view the constitution for what it is, a developing responsive tradition neither to be lightly departed from nor to be casually obeyed.

The arrangements of 1867 were never a sacrosanct body of holy writ. Approaches which so regarded them constituted a disservice to the Canadian polity and rested on a misunderstanding of the nature of a constitution. They inhibited change and thus reduced the flexibility essential for survival. Equally important, they blinded their possessors to the changes which did occur. Realistically, all working constitutions are living constitutions springing from, but not bound and gagged by, history. Inadequate recognition of this truth is a significant cause of the constitutional morass in which we now find ourselves. Cryptically we might say that the constitution has not failed us, so much as we, by our inadequate understanding of its living nature, have failed it. In a living constitution all generations are simultaneously Fathers and Sons, by necessity even if not by choice. King, Bennett, Diefenbaker, and their provincial counterparts were in their own way Fathers as were Macdonald and Cartier. Like Macdonald and Cartier they were also sons in that they built on the achievements of their predecessors. There can be no quarrel with the fact that each succeeding generation of Canadians has decided what parts of the constitution they received were viable and worthy of continued life, and which were not. However, we can quarrel with those who, either blinded by a deification of the past, resist new departures because the Fathers intended otherwise, or propose a new constitution on the mistaken grounds that the existing one, because of its time of origin, is necessarily an inflexible, incompetent instrument for new conditions. The first approach makes us prisoners of the past. The second approach deprives us of the benefits which a rich tradition provides.

To view a constitution as a living constitution has important consequences. It is to recognize that the processes of constitutional change are manifold and unpredictable. The processes of formal amendment and judicial review are neither the only nor the most important vehicles for change. The constitution is constantly interpreted and modified by the men who work it. No new division of powers can prevent the intermingling of the activities of both levels of government in modern conditions. Predictable, clear-cut procedures for change can be obtained in the area of formal amendment, but nowhere else. The Supreme Court can be revamped in various ways, but "the history of judge-made law invites no other view than this: that the parties to the original federal 'bargain' can never be certain that the words in which they have clothed their intentions can ever be more than a rough guide to political activity, or that the range of permissible activity at any time after will bear any exact relation to their intentions."[14]

The terribly difficult problem, frequently overlooked because of obsession with the written text and the more blatant methods of change by amendment and judicial review, is how to devise conventions and understandings by which the other, less obvious methods of change can be brought within a framework of constitutionalism. The main weakness, for example, of the compact theory as a set of criteria for constitutional change did not lie in its hotly contested validity, but in the restricted scope of its intended operation. Even if wholehearted agreement to its terms had existed, this would have represented no more than a control of the amending procedure, one of the least important methods of constitutional change in Canadian history.

This problem is, of course, recognized by influential Quebec spokesmen. The late Premier Daniel Johnson, for example, stated in 1967:

> Canada today is faced with a whole series of problems which the Fathers of Confederation . . . could not conceivably have foreseen. . . . Therefore, when a new problem arises in Canada, we are more and more likely to base each government's responsibilities for it, not on constitutional principles, but on considerations of the moment which, in turn, derive from a variety of factors such as relative capacity to act, financial resources or merely the political power wielded by a given area of government. Hence even though there is a written document called the British North America Act from which we may expect some light to be cast on such traditional fields as education and municipal institutions, the allocation of new tasks among governments has not been guided by this document but by decisions mainly based on exigencies of the day. . . . Our present Constitution, perhaps admirable during the age of steam trains, no longer suits Canada's needs in this era of interplanetary rockets.[15]

At the 1966 Federal-Provincial Conference on taxation, Johnson stated:

> Having reached what it considers a turning point in its history, Quebec expects some specific things from the present constitutional system. First, it wants proof that the division of powers written in the constitution is not mere window-dressing and that, accordingly, it can count on the fiscal and financial resources it requires in order to discharge its obligations properly. . . . Quebec also wants assurance that it can exercise, fully and without interference from any quarter, all its powers

under the present constitution. It wants the Government of Canada to withdraw from fields which are not federal or in which the provinces have priority.[16]

Essentially the same point was made by Professor Dubuc who asserted that a century of change had rendered the BNA Act "too far removed from the basic structure and values of . . . [contemporary] . . . society to remain the touchstone for the division of powers," with the consequence that the "most important conflicts are settled on the political level and become confrontations of power; these are the conditions of political chaos."[17]

The general cogency of these critiques can be accepted. The question, however, is what can be done about them. To Johnson and Dubuc the obvious answer is a new constitution whose division of powers reflects the worked-out results of a contemporary agreement, responding to today's conditions, as to what the responsibilities of each level of government should be. Assuming for the moment that agreement could in fact be reached on a new constitution, the contribution that this would make to the solution of the problem which troubles Dubuc and Johnson is debatable. Obviously, if Quebec were to be granted greatly enhanced jurisdictional authority, the seriousness of the problem from Quebec's viewpoint would be greatly diminished. The problem would still exist, but its scope would be less extensive. If, however, as seems more likely, a new division of powers did not deviate markedly from the existing division, we would be little better off. It is not entirely clear that an ancient division of powers is more likely to produce "decisions mainly based on exigencies of the day" than is a division freshly minted at a constitutional conference. To some extent the problem arises from the impossibility of devising a comprehensive catalogue of powers into which all proposed legislation can be easily fitted. The operations of modern governments are too complex, the future is too unpredictable, and words are too full of imprecision and ambiguity for such an achievement. Further, the very political processes which Johnson and Dubuc decry for the uncertainties they generate can be seen as the instruments to produce the concordance between the division of powers and contemporary requirements which they seek. If such processes did not exist, we would really be in a bad way. The difficult problem, as suggested earlier, is to find ways by which they can be brought within a framework of constitutionalism.

The assault on the existing constitution has led to a process of constitutional review out of which a new, or at least a drastically modified, constitution is supposed to emerge. Unfortunately, the justification for this review does not reside in any self-evident likelihood that a new and better constitution can be created. The existing constitution was caught in a barrage of criticism based on its age, which is largely a fraudulent consideration, and a confused battery of French-Canadian demands to break with the past and stake out for themselves a status in Canadian federalism superior to what was apparently possible under the constitution as they perceived it.

From the evidence which is available, there is little possibility that a new constitution will emerge. Most of the political leaders engaged in constitutional review are dutifully going through the motions with little hope or desire that any major changes will transpire. If their pessimism is correct, Canadians will be left with the existing constitution whose limited sanctity has been further eroded by the criticism to which it has been subjected in the process of review. Its claim to our continued allegiance may come to rest on the flimsy basis that it is the only constitution Canadians have.

The perspective on the constitution adopted in this essay is a reminder that a constitution is not merely a piece of paper. It is a set of relationships between governments and between governments and peoples which has become embedded in the evolving habits and values of successive generations of Canadians. Tinkering with constitutional documents in an era of *laissez faire* might have left the mass of citizenry unaffected. However, when governments increasingly involve themselves in the nooks and crannies of our lives, dramatic constitutional change presents a less attractive and less plausible face. It is only necessary to observe the difficulties of successfully introducing major policies, such as medicare or tax reform, to question the feasibility of attempting to change a large part of the very constitutional framework from which governments derive their authority and by means of which citizens deal with government.

A new constitution can be no more than a point of departure. The day after it is proclaimed its evolution away from the agreement just reached will commence. The new settlement will inevitably be subject to the informal processes of change and growth which helped "undermine" the BNA Act. The security and control of the future which can be obtained from a written document are only relative. Further, if a new constitution is created, the short-run result of its implementation inevitably will be an increase in uncertainty and insecurity until the text is fleshed out by the actions of men struggling to make it work. This, of course, is in addition to the uncertainties automatically generated by the simple fact of change from the old constitution to the new. Given these corollaries of a new constitution, we might consider whether constitutions are not like wine—much better when well aged. Perhaps, however, 1867 was not a good year for constitutions.

NOTES

1. For an excellent American discussion of the living constitution, see K.N. Llewellyn, "The Constitution as an Institution," *Columbia Law Review*, 34 (1934).
2. Cited in Archibald Macleish and E.F. Pritchard, Jr., eds., *Law and Politics: Occasional Papers of Felix Frankfurter* (New York: Capricorn Books, 1962), p. 71.
3. Peter Joseph Thomas O'Hearn, *Peace, Order and Good Government* (Toronto: Macmillan of Canada, 1964), p. 6.

4. Toronto *Globe and Mail*, 13 April 1966, p. 7.
5. Llewellyn, op. cit., p. 6 n.
6. "Constitutional Monarchy and the Provinces," *Ontario Advisory Committee on Confederation: Background Papers and Reports* (Toronto: Queen's Printer, 1967), p. 180.
7. Llewellyn, op. cit., p. 3.
8. *The Supreme Court in Modern Role*, rev. ed., (New York: New York University Press, 1965), p. 192.
9. Arthur S. Miller and Ronald F. Howell, "The Myth of Neutrality in Constitutional Adjudication," *University of Chicago Law Review*, 27 (1960), 683.
10. Cited in Paul Abraham Freund, *The Supreme Court of the United States* (Cleveland and New York: Peter Smith, 1965), p. 20.
11. *Report Pursuant to Resolution of the Senate to the Honourable the Speaker by the Parliamentary Counsel Relating to the Enactment of the British North America Act, 1867. . . .* (Ottawa: King's Printer, 1939), 11, Annex 1, p. 47.
12. Barry L. Strayer, *Judicial Review of Legislation in Canada* (Toronto: University of Toronto Press, 1968), p. 156.
13. Learned Hand, *The Bill of Rights* (Cambridge, Mass.: Harvard University Press, 1958), pp. 34–35.
14. Rufus Davis, "The 'Federal Principle' Reconsidered," in Aaron B. Wildavsky, ed., *American Federalism in Perspective* (Boston: Little Brown, 1967), p. 14.
15. *The Confederation of Tomorrow Conference: Proceedings* (Toronto: Queen's Printer, 1968), Appendix B, p. 8.
16. *The Federal-Provincial Conference, Quebec—Federal-Provincial Tax-Structure Committee* (Ottawa: Queen's Printer, 1966), pp. 56–57.
17. Alfred Dubuc, "The Decline of Confederation and the New Nationalism," in Peter Russell, ed., *Nationalism in Canada* (Toronto: McGraw-Hill for the University League for Social Reform, 1966), p. 131.

FURTHER READINGS

Ackerman, B.A., and R.E. Charney. "Canada at the Constitutional Crossroads." *University of Toronto Law Journal* 34, 2 (Spring 1984): 117–135.

Banting, K., and R. Simeon, eds. *And No One Cheered: Federalism, Democracy and the Constitution Act*. Toronto: Methuen, 1983.

Beck, S.M., and I. Bernier, eds. *Canada and the New Constitution: The Unfinished Agenda*. 2 vols. Montreal: Institute for Research on Public Policy, 1982.

Cairns, A.C. "The Politics of Constitutional Renewal in Canada." In K.G. Banting and R. Simeon, eds. *Redesigning the State. The Politics of Constitutional Change*, 95–145. Toronto: University of Toronto Press, 1985.

Cheffins, R.A., and P.A. Johnson *The Revised Canadian Constitution: Politics as Law.* Toronto: McGraw-Hill Ryerson, 1986.

Milne D. "The New Canadian Constitution." In M.S. Whittington and G. Williams, eds. *Canadian Politics in the 1980s.* 2nd ed., 312–330. Toronto: Methuen, 1984.

Smiley, D.V. "The Three Pillars of the Canadian Constitutional Order." *Canadian Public Policy* 12, Supplement (Feb. 1986): 113–121.

Stanley, G.F.G. *A Short History of the Canadian Constitution.* Toronto: Ryerson Press, 1969

2

Responsible Government

Peter W. Hogg

1. HISTORY

In the 1830s, the colonies of British North America had achieved representative government,[1] but they had not achieved responsible government. The government of each colony was "representative," because it included a legislative assembly elected by the people of the colony. The assembly had the power to make laws, to raise taxes, and to grant supply (money) to the executive. But colonial government was not "responsible" because the executive was not responsible to the assembly. Executive power was possessed by the British-appointed governor, who was responsible to the Colonial Office of the United Kingdom government, which had appointed him, instructed him, and continued to supervise his work. The governor also received advice from a local executive council whom he appointed, but the members of the executive council in each province were drawn from a wealthy elite who not only lacked the confidence of the assembly but who often actively opposed the policies determined upon by the assembly. This meant that laws enacted by the assembly would often not be enforced; policies opposed by the assembly would often be implemented; civil servants regarded as unsuitable or incompetent by the assembly would often be appointed; and colonial revenues which did not come from taxes would often be spent for purposes of which the assembly disapproved.

In every colony, there was chronic conflict between the assembly and the governor (and his executive council). In Upper and Lower Canada, these frustrations led to armed rebellions in 1837. After the rebellions, Lord Durham was appointed governor of all the British North American colonies with instructions to report upon the causes of and remedies for the colonial discontent. Lord Durham reported in 1839. He accurately identified the causes of conflict between assembly and executive, and he recommended the institution of responsible government: in Durham's view, the Colonial Office should instruct each governor to appoint to his executive council only persons who enjoyed the confidence of a majority of the assembly. This recommendation

Abridged from Peter W. Hogg, "Responsible Government," *Constitutional Law of Canada*, 2nd edition (Toronto: The Carswell Company Limited, 1985), 189-213. Reprinted by permission of the author and The Carswell Company Limited. Only selected footnotes appear in the essay.

simply applied to the colonies the same system that had recently evolved in the United Kingdom to reconcile the powers of the representative Parliament and the hereditary King. In the colonies, however, there was a further complication. How could the governor obey instructions from the Colonial Office in London as well as following the advice of his local executive council? Durham's solution was to distinguish between matters of imperial concern and matters of local concern. The only matters of imperial concern, he submitted, were constitutional arrangements, foreign affairs, external trade, and the disposal of public lands. On these matters, the governor would act on the instructions of the Colonial Office. On all other matters, the governor would act on the advice of his local executive council.

At first, the government of the United Kingdom would not accept Lord Durham's wise recommendation (although it readily accepted his foolish plan for the union of Upper and Lower Canada). But in 1846 a new Colonial Secretary, Earl Grey, did accept the recommendation and instructed the governors along the lines indicated by Lord Durham. In 1848 the new system was put to the test in Nova Scotia, when after a general election the assembly carried a vote of no confidence in the executive council. The council resigned and the governor appointed the leader of the majority party in the assembly to be premier with power to name the other members of the new council—all in accordance with the conventions of responsible government. Changes of government occurred in the same way in the united province of Canada and in New Brunswick also in 1848, in Prince Edward Island in 1851, and in Newfoundland in 1855. Responsible government was thus achieved in those provinces. British Columbia did not achieve responsible government until 1872, a year after its admission to Canada. Manitoba (created in 1870), Alberta (created in 1905) and Saskatchewan (also created in 1905) were each granted responsible government at the time of their creation.

2. LAW AND CONVENTION

In a system of "responsible government" (or cabinet or parliamentary government, as it may also be called) the formal head of state, whether King (or Queen), Governor General or Lieutenant Governor, must always act under the "advice" (meaning direction) of ministers who are members of the legislative branch and who enjoy the confidence of a majority in the elected house of the legislative branch. Responsible government is probably the most important non-federal characteristic of the Canadian Constitution. Yet the rules which govern it are almost entirely "conventional," that is to say, they are not to be found in the ordinary legal sources of statute or decided cases.

. . . [R]esponsible government had been achieved in each of the uniting colonies at the time of confederation in 1867. The intention to continue the same system after confederation was evidenced by the assertion in the preamble to the Constitution Act, 1867 that Canada was to have "a constitution similar in principle to that of the United Kingdom." Other than this vague reference, however, the Constitution Act is silent on responsible government; it confers powers on the Queen and the Governor General but makes no mention of the Prime Minister or the cabinet. Thus, s. 9 provides that the "executive government" of Canada is vested in "the Queen"; s. 10 contemplates that the Queen's powers may be exercised by a "Governor General"; and s. 11 establishes a "Queen's Privy Council for Canada" whose function is "to aid and advise in the government of Canada" and whose members are to be appointed and removed by the Governor General. The Governor General is also an essential part of the legislative branch in that a "bill" which has been enacted by both Houses of Parliament passes into law (and becomes a "statute") only after the Governor General (or the Queen) has given the royal assent to the bill (ss. 17, 55). In addition, the Governor General is given power to appoint the members of the appointive upper house, the Senate (s. 24), to summon into session the members of the elective lower house, the House of Commons (s. 38), to dissolve the House of Commons (s. 50), to withhold the royal assent from a bill passed by both Houses of Parliament or to "reserve" the bill "for the signification of the Queen's pleasure" (s. 55). The Queen herself has a discretion whether or not to assent to a bill reserved by the Governor General (s. 57), and she has the further power to "disallow" (annul) any statute enacted by the Canadian Parliament (s. 56). In each province, there is a "Lieutenant Governor" and an "Executive Council" with powers similar to those of the Governor General and Privy Council (ss. 58-68, 90). The Lieutenant Governors are appointed by the Governor General in Council (s. 58),[2] and it is the Governor General (rather than the Queen) to whom a Lieutenant Governor reserves a provincial bill, and the Governor General in Council (rather than the Queen in Council) in whom is vested the power of disallowance of a provincial statute (s. 90). There are other provisions of the Constitution Act, 1867 which confer specific powers on the Governor General or the Lieutenant Governors. Furthermore, the statute books will reveal that the Canadian Parliament and provincial Legislatures to this day usually confer major powers of government upon the Governor General in Council or the Lieutenant Governor in Council.

The Constitution Act, 1867 also tells us that Canada is a monarchy, that is to say, the formal head of state is the Queen (s. 9). The Queen has in fact delegated all of her powers over Canada to the Canadian Governor General, except of course for the power to appoint or dismiss the Governor General. Moreover, most powers of government, whether conferred by the Constitution or by ordinary statute, are conferred upon the Governor General (or the Governor General in Council) directly. It is therefore simpler, and sufficiently accurate for most purposes, to speak of the Governor General being the formal head of state. He or she is appointed by the Queen, and in colonial times of course the Queen acted on the advice of her British ministers in making the appointment. However, the imperial conference of 1926 declared that the Governor General was not the "representative or agent" of the British government, and the imperial conference of 1930 resolved that thenceforth the Governor General would be appointed by the Queen acting on the advice of the ministers of the dominion concerned.[3] Since 1930, all Canadian Governors General have been selected by the Canadian Prime Minister with the Queen merely formalizing the appointment. It is also the Canadian Prime Minister who determines the Governor General's term of office, and the Canadian Parliament which fixes his salary.

The Governor General does not use any personal initiative or discretion in the exercise of his powers of government, except for certain "reserve powers" or "personal prerogatives," which are exercisable only in exceptional circumstances, and which are discussed later in this chapter. The effect of responsible government is to transfer effective political power to elected officials.

3. THE EXECUTIVE BRANCH

(a) The Ministry

What precisely are the conventions of responsible government? For convenience of exposition, I shall concentrate on Canada's federal government, but the rules are much the same in each of the provinces (and indeed in all those jurisdictions outside Canada whose governments are responsible in the technical sense). Where there is any significant variation in provincial practice, that fact will be noted.

The narrative must start with an exercise by the Governor General of one of his exceptional reserve powers or personal prerogatives. In the formation of a government it is the Governor General's duty to select the Prime Minister. He must select a person who can form a government which will enjoy the confidence of the House of Commons. For reasons which will be explained later, the Governor General rarely has any real choice as to whom to appoint: he must appoint the parliamentary leader of the political party which has a majority of seats in the House of Commons. But it is still accurate to describe the Governor General's discretion as his own, because, unlike nearly all of his other decisions, it is not made upon ministerial advice.

When the Prime Minister has been appointed, he selects the other ministers, and advises the Governor General to appoint them. With respect to these appointments, the Governor General reverts to his normal non-discretionary role and is obliged by convention to make the appointments advised by the Prime Minister. If the Prime Minister later wishes to make changes in the ministry, as by moving a minister from one portfolio to another, or by appointing a new minister, or by removing a minister, then the Governor General will take whatever action is advised by the Prime Minister, including if necessary the dismissal of a minister who has refused his Prime Minister's request to resign.

It is basic to the system of responsible government that the Prime Minister and all the other ministers be members of parliament. Occasionally a person who is not a member of parliament is appointed as a minister, but then he must quickly be elected to Parliament. If he fails to win election, then he must resign (or be dismissed) from the ministry. The usual practice when a non-member of parliament is appointed to the ministry is that a member of the Prime Minister's political party will be induced to resign from a "safe seat" in Parliament, which will precipitate a by-election in which the minister will be the candidate from the Prime Minister's party.

(b) The Cabinet and the Privy Council

When the ministers meet together as a group they constitute the cabinet.[4] The cabinet is not mentioned in the Constitution Act, 1867, although we have already noticed that a body called the Queen's Privy Council for Canada is established by s. 11. The cabinet ministers are all appointed to the Queen's Privy Council for Canada. But the Privy Council includes many other people as well. Appointments to the Privy Council are for life, so that its membership always includes not only the ministers of the government in office, but also all living persons who were ministers in past governments. Moreover, appointments to the Privy Council are often made to persons of distinction as an honour, so that its membership will include such persons as the Duke of Edinburgh, the Prince of Wales, a British Prime Minister, a Canadian High Commissioner, or a provincial Premier; and of course such honorific appointments will be for life. The whole Privy Council would be a body of some one hundred members of widely differing political persuasions. Such a body could not, and does not, conduct the business of government. The whole Privy Council meets very rarely, and then only for ceremonial occasions.

The cabinet, which does meet regularly and frequently, is in most matters the supreme executive authority. (The "reserve powers" remain in the Governor General, and some powers are vested in the Prime Minister; these powers are discussed later.) The cabinet formulates and carries out all executive policies, and it is responsible for the administration of all the departments of government. It constitutes the only active part of the Privy Council, and it exercises the powers of that body. The Governor General does not preside over, or even attend, the meetings of the cabinet. The Prime Minister presides. Where the Constitution or a statute requires that a decision be made by the "Governor General in Council" (and this requirement is very common indeed), there is still no meeting with the Governor General. The cabinet (or a cabinet committee to which routine Privy Council business has been delegated) will make the decision, and send an "order" or "minute" of the decision to the Governor General for his signature (which by convention is automatically given). Where a statute requires that a decision be made by a particular minister, then the cabinet will make the decision, and the relevant minister will formally authenticate the decision. Of course a cabinet will be content to delegate many matters to individual ministers, but each minister recognizes the supreme authority of the cabinet should the cabinet seek to exercise it.

(c) The Prime Minister

While in most matters the cabinet is the supreme executive authority, the Prime Minister (or provincial Premier) has certain powers which he does not need to share with his colleagues. Two of these[5] are of great importance. First, there is the power to select the other ministers, and the power to promote, demote or dismiss them at his pleasure. (Technically, of course, he only has power to recommend such measures to the Governor General, but his recommendations will invariably be acted upon.) Secondly, the Prime Minister is personally responsible for tendering advice to the Governor General as to when Parliament should be dissolved for an election, and when an elected Parliament should be summoned into session.[6]

Not only are these powers important in their own right, but the Prime Minister's possession of them also ensures that his voice will be the most influential one within the cabinet. In addition, the Prime Minister enjoys the special authority which derives from his having been selected by a political party as its leader, and from his having led the party to victory in the previous election. Modern Canadian election campaigns have increasingly emphasized the qualities of the competing leaders, and this practice inevitably strengthens the position within the party of the leader of the victorious party. No doubt the extent of a Prime Minister's personal power varies from government to government, depending upon a number of factors. But in some governments a Prime Minister who chooses to take on his own initiative, or on the advice of a few ministers, decisions which would traditionally be the preserve of the cabinet is politically able to do so; and the extent to which the full cabinet plays a role in important decision-making may depend in large measure upon the discretion of the Prime Minister. In this connection it is important to notice that the Prime Minister calls the meetings of cabinet, settles the agenda, and presides over the meetings.[7]

(d) Ministerial Responsibility

There is a minister at the head of each of the departments of government. Most of the cabinet ministers have charge of at least one department. (There are usually one or more ministers without portfolio who are members of the cabinet, but who do not have charge of a department.) Each minister who does have charge of a department has the administrative duties which go with such an office. In addition, he "represents" his department in Parliament: he pilots the departmental estimates of proposed expenditures through the House, he explains and defends the policies and practices of the department, and he introduces into Parliament any bills which relate to the work of the department.[8]

A government department is, of course, administered by civil servants, who, in contrast to the minister, are supposed to be politically neutral. The senior civil servant in each department, who in Canada is usually called a "deputy minister," is the link between the minister and the civil servants. The deputy minister acts both as an adviser to the minister and as the senior administrator of the department. Of course, the minister is under no obligation to follow the advice of his deputy minister. The deputy minister is within the tradition of civil service neutrality: when the government changes, the deputy minister, like other career civil servants, will usually retain his position. However, the deputy minister is not appointed by normal civil service procedures: he is appointed by order in council on the recommendation of the Prime Minister. The appointment is normally made from within the ranks of the career civil service, and is not treated as political patronage. Nevertheless, occasionally a particular deputy minister is perceived as too closely associated with the party in power, and he may be replaced when a new government takes office.

One aspect of the political neutrality of civil servants is the convention that they are anonymous in the sense that they should not be criticized personally or otherwise held accountable in Parliament. All the acts of the department are done in the name of the minister, and it is the minister who is responsible to Parliament for those acts. In this context, the word "responsible" is often said to entail two consequences. First, the minister is supposed to explain to Parliament, when asked, the actions of his department. This is a real responsibility, in that a minister will be frequently called upon by other members of parliament to answer questions about the work of his department. Secondly, the minister is supposed to resign if a serious case of maladministration occurs within his department. This second aspect of ministerial responsibility is often asserted to exist, but is of much more doubtful strength. In a case of misconduct or serious maladministration by a minister personally, the principle would certainly apply and would require the resignation of the minister. In a case of misconduct or maladministration by a civil servant in the minister's department, a ministerial resignation is quite unlikely to follow in Canada. Accordingly, it may be more realistic (and therefore accurate) to define ministerial responsibility as not including an obligation to resign for merely departmental sins, although such resignations are often called for by the opposition and do occasionally occur.

The notion of the responsibility of individual ministers is related to, but distinct from, the notion of the "collective responsibility" of the cabinet as a whole. All cabinet ministers collectively accept responsibility for cabinet decisions. This means that a cabinet minister is obliged to give public support to any decision reached by the cabinet, even if he personally opposed the decision within the cabinet and still disagrees with it. If he does decide to express dissent in public, then he should resign; and if he does not resign he can expect to be dismissed by the Prime Minister (unless the Prime Minister decides to tolerate the offence). Even after resignation or dismissal the obligation of unanimity is supposed to continue, but the Prime Minister will normally give permission to the minister to publish his reasons for resignation.

Collective responsibility implies more than cabinet solidarity. Its most fundamental consequence is that if a cabinet decision is attacked in Parliament the issue is one of confidence in the government. As will be explained later, . . . if a government is defeated in the House of Commons[9] on an issue of confidence in the government, then the government must either resign or advise the Governor General to dissolve the House for an election. Consequently, the government will insist that its supporters in the House vote on party lines in favour of the government. Since the government is in office because it commands a majority of the members of the House, it is normally in a position to resist any opposition attack on its policies. The vigour of the doctrine of collective responsibility is what undermines the doctrine of individual responsibility. If a ministerial decision has been approved or ratified by the cabinet, then the individual minister will be protected by collective responsibility. More bluntly, one must acknowledge that if the government does not want a minister to resign, then no matter how clearly the facts would seem to warrant the minister's resignation, there is no way that the opposition can force it to happen.

4. THE LEGISLATIVE BRANCH

(a) The Parliament

The legislative power of the federal government is vested in the Parliament of Canada, which consists (in the language of s. 17 of the Constitution Act, 1867) "of the Queen, an upper house styled the Senate, and the House of Commons." There are thus three elements which must combine for passage of legislation—and the cabinet is not one of them. Nevertheless the cabinet is able to control the legislative process. In order to see why this is so, let us examine separately each element of the process.

(b) The House of Commons

The House of Commons is a body which is elected on the basis of universal adult suffrage. As such it is representative of most shades of Canadian opinion. But the Prime Minister and his cabinet (the government) are in office solely because they have the support of a majority of members in the House of Commons. In normal circumstances this support is unwavering and is available for every measure proposed by the government. Canada's political parties insist upon strict party discipline from their parliamentary members. For a variety of good reasons, party discipline is effective to the point that each member of the government party can nearly always be relied upon to support all government measures. Very rarely does an issue arise which so divides the government party that any members will vote against the government. When that happens the combined votes of the opposition parties and the government defectors may defeat the government.

A more common situation in which the government may lose the support of a majority in the House of Commons is after a close election has given neither of the two major parties a majority in the House of Commons, and the control of the House depends upon one of the major parties being able to secure the cooperation of one of the minor parties. Here the cabinet's control is much more precarious, and the minor party can bring about the defeat of the government whenever it chooses. Sometimes this situation of "minority government" can be stabilized by the major party entering into coalition with the minor party and admitting its leaders to the cabinet. Coalition governments have not been uncommon in the provinces, and in countries outside Canada, but the Canadian federal government's only experience of this kind was the "union government" which was formed during the first world war. In recent years there have been frequent minority governments in which either the Progressive Conservative Party or the Liberal Party has had to depend upon the support of a third party,[10] but there does not seem to have been any serious consideration of coalition. However, even a minority government is able to exercise very substantial control over the legislative process. The minor party is inhibited from voting against the government by the fact that, for reasons given later, a vote against the government is almost certain to force a new general election. An election is always expensive and exhausting and is not to be lightly precipitated, especially as a minor party which has overturned a government without a very good reason is almost certain to lose votes and seats.[11] On the whole then it is a fair generalization to say that all measures proposed by the cabinet are assured of passage through the House of Commons.

(c) The Senate

The second element in the legislative process is the Senate.[12] Its members are appointed by the Governor General, which of course means, by convention, the cabinet. But the Constitution Act, 1867, by ss. 21–22 and 26–28, sets limits to the numbers of senators who may be appointed, and, by s. 29, provides that once appointed a senator holds office for life if appointed before June 1965 (when compulsory retirement at age 75 was enacted), and until age 75 if appointed after June 1965. Since each government tends to appoint its own supporters to the Senate, a government which has been in office for a long time will have a majority—and sometimes an overwhelming majority—of its own party members in the Senate. After a long-standing government loses an election the new government will be faced with a Senate which is still controlled by the opposition party, and it may be a long time before deaths, retirements and resignations enable the new government to redress the unhappy balance. Even in this situation, however, the Senate will rarely reject or even amend measures proposed by the government. Although the Constitution Act, 1867 gives to the Senate the same powers as the House of Commons (except that, by s. 53, money bills must originate in the House of Commons), it is accepted by opposition as well as government senators that the appointive nature of the Senate must necessarily make its role subordinate to the elective House.[13] The result is that very few government bills are rejected or substantially amended by the Senate.

The Senate was intended to serve as a protector of regional interests, which is a traditional function of the upper house in federal systems. Its membership was drawn equally from the three original regions of Canada, namely, Ontario, Quebec and the maritime provinces. The west later became a fourth region.[14] The plan was to offset representation by population in the House of Commons with equality of regions in the Senate. With hindsight, it is obvious that this plan was fatally flawed, because the senators were to be appointed rather than elected, and appointed by the federal government rather than by provincial governments. In any event, the Senate has never been an effective voice of regional or provincial interests.

Whether it is now feasible to reform the Senate[15] so as to restore the original plan is doubtful. The difficulty is that in a system of responsible government the cabinet is responsible to the House of Commons, not the Senate. If government policy is defeated in the House of Commons, then the government must resign and make way, either for a new government that can command the support of the House of Commons, or for an election that will provide a new House of Commons. An upper house has no obvious place in this scheme of things. That is why in so many jurisdictions with parliamentary systems the upper house has been abolished or reduced to impotence. And that is why the assertions of independence by the Australian Senate that led to the dismissal of Prime Minister Whitlam in 1975 were so bitterly controversial in that country. A powerful upper house could block major government bills (as the Australian Senate did), could refuse to vote supply to the government (as the Australian Senate did), and could eventually bring the government down (as the Australian Senate did). This kind of obstruction has never occurred in Canada, although the Canadian Senate's powers are, in law, as ample as those of the Australian Senate. The restraint by the Canadian Senate is caused by its recognition that, as an appointed body, it has no political mandate to obstruct the elected House of Commons. The Australian Senate, as an elected body, is not subject to the same inhibitions. If the Canadian Senate were reformed, either by making its membership elected or by making its membership appointed by provincial governments, it would naturally want to make more use of its powers. Serious obstruction of the House of Commons could be avoided if limitations were imposed on the powers of a reformed upper house. But, to the extent that the powers of a reformed upper house are limited, so also is its capacity to assert effectively regional and provincial interests.

(d) The Governor General

The Governor General, who must complete the legislative process by conferring the royal assent, plays no discretionary role whatever. It is true, of course, that the Constitution Act, 1867, by s. 55, gives the Governor General the power to withhold the royal assent from a bill which has been enacted by both Houses of Parliament, and the power to reserve a bill for the signification of the Queen's pleasure; and by s. 56 gives to the Queen the power to disallow a Canadian statute. But the imperial conference of 1930 resolved that the powers of reservation and disallowance must never be exercised. This conference and the full acceptance of responsible government have established a convention that the Governor General must always give the royal assent to a bill which has passed both Houses of Parliament. There is no circumstance which would justify a refusal of assent, or a reservation, or a British disallowance.[16]

(e) The Cabinet

It will now be obvious that in a system of responsible government there is no "separation of powers" between the executive and legislative branches of government. The head of the executive branch, the cabinet, draws its personnel and its power to govern from the legislative branch, the Parliament; and the cabinet controls the Parliament. This contrasts with the presidential form of government in the United States, which was established at a time when the separation of the executive, legislative and judicial powers of government was regarded by influential political theorists as the ideal constitution for the preservation of individual liberty.[17] The President of the United States is not a member of the Congress, nor are the members of his cabinet; he is often not a member of the party with the majority of members in the Congress; and he is never able to exercise control over the Congress.

In Canada, the legislative programme for each session of Parliament is planned by the cabinet, and announced at the beginning of the session in the speech from the throne which is delivered by the Governor General. The speech is written by the Prime Minister. The cabinet determines the order of business in the Parliament, and generally exercises close control over the proceedings. Nearly all bills which are subsequently enacted are "government bills," that is to say, bills which have been approved by cabinet and introduced by one of the ministers. The Constitution Act, 1867, by s. 54, requires that a "money bill" must be introduced in the House of Commons only after it has been "first recommended to that House by message of the Governor General." Needless to say, it is the cabinet which prepares the message, and a minister who transmits the message to the House and introduces the bill. Other bills can be introduced in either House and by any member of parliament, but the cabinet uses its majority in the House of Commons to ensure that the bulk of the Parliament's time is devoted to consideration of the government's own legislative programme, and, except for "private bills,"[18] it is only the measures which have been approved by the cabinet and introduced by a minister ("government bills") which stand any real chance of passage.

5. DEFEAT OF THE GOVERNMENT

(a) Withdrawal of Confidence

Since the major premise of responsible government is that the cabinet (or "government" or "administration") enjoys the confidence of a majority in the House of Commons, it follows that a cabinet which has lost that confidence cannot indefinitely continue in office. This is the primary meaning of the "collective responsibility" of the cabinet to the House of Commons.

If the House of Commons passed a motion of no confidence in the government, that would be the clearest possible evidence that the government had lost the confidence of the House of Commons; but the defeat of the government on any important vote is usually regarded as a withdrawal of confidence.[19] Where the defeat is on a matter of little importance, the defeat would not need to be treated as a withdrawal of confidence. A more difficult case is where the defeat occurs on a major measure, but is the result of a "snap vote" which catches the government party with some of its supporters inadvertently absent from the House at the time of the vote. A snap vote led to the defeat in the House of Commons of a government measure in 1968, and the Pearson government decided not to treat it as a withdrawal of confidence. The government reinforced its decision and acknowledged the primacy of the House by subsequently securing the passage of a resolution to the effect that the prior defeat was not to be interpreted as a withdrawal of confidence in the government.

(b) Dissolution of Parliament

When a government measure is defeated in the House of Commons, then, subject to the comments made in the previous paragraph, the House of Commons is deemed to have withdrawn its confidence from the government. There are then only two alternatives: either the government must resign to make way for a new cabinet which will command the confidence of the House, or the House must be dissolved to make way for an election which will produce a new House of Commons.

It is the dissolution of the House of Commons which is the course normally favoured by a Prime Minister whose government has been defeated in the House, and that is the course which he will normally advise the Governor General to take. In the event of a dissolution the Prime Minister and his ministers remain in office, despite the fact that they have lost the confidence of the House of Commons. The period between the dissolution of one House of Commons and the election of another may be as long as several months, but the government must remain in office and exercise its functions: the country cannot be left without any government at all. The ensuing election may produce a new House of Commons which the government is able to control. If that happens the government will continue in office without a break. Thus, while the Constitution imposes a maximum duration for the House of Commons of five years, there is no maximum duration for any particular government— and most Canadian governments have lasted for longer than five years. It is the hope of continuance in office which makes dissolution a more attractive alternative than resignation for the government which has lost the confidence of the House of Commons.

As we shall see later, . . . it is probable that the Governor General has a reserve power to refuse to grant a dissolution to a Prime Minister whose government has lost the confidence of the House of Commons, but this has happened only once this century in Canada—in 1926. If a dissolution were refused, the Prime Minister whose government had lost the confidence of the House of Commons would have to resign, or be dismissed by the Governor General; and the resignation or dismissal of a Prime Minister involves the resignation or dismissal of the entire ministry.

(c) Resignation or Dismissal

If a Prime Minister whose government has lost the support of the House of Commons does resign (whether voluntarily or because a dissolution has been refused by the Governor General), or is dismissed from office by the Governor General, then the Governor General would have to find a member of parliament who could become Prime Minister and form a government which would enjoy the confidence of the House. In selecting a new Prime Minister, as we have already noticed, the Governor General is entitled to exercise a personal discretion.

6 THE GOVERNOR GENERAL'S PERSONAL PREROGATIVES

(a) The Principle

The Governor General has certain "personal prerogatives" or "reserve powers" which he may exercise upon his own personal discretion. Whereas in the exercise of governmental powers generally he must act in accordance with the advice of his Prime Minister or cabinet, there are some occasions on which he may act without advice, or even contrary to advice.

The definition of those occasions when the Governor General may exercise an independent discretion has caused much constitutional and political debate. But it is submitted that the basic premise of responsible government supplies the answer: so long as the cabinet enjoys the confidence of a majority in the House of Commons, the Governor General is always obliged to follow lawful and constitutional advice which is tendered to him by the cabinet. But there are occasions, as we have seen, when a government continues in office after it has lost the confidence of the House of Commons, or after the House of Commons has been dissolved. There are also occasions, for example, after a very close election, or after a schism in a political party, where for a period it is difficult to determine whether or not the government does enjoy the confidence of a majority in the House of Commons. In all these situations it is submitted that the Governor General has a discretion to refuse to follow advice which is tendered to him by the ministry in office.

When a government is in office without the support of the House of Commons, there is the makings of a constitutional crisis: not only can the government not secure the passage of any legislation, it cannot even secure parliamentary approval of supply to meet government expenditures. The crisis can be resolved or averted by a new election or by the resignation or dismissal of the ministry. But the ministry in office, which lacks the support of the House of Commons and which stands to lose most by the resolution of the crisis, is not the fittest group to determine the mode of resolution of the crisis. It is true of course that the Governor General has even less of a political base than the ministry in office, but it is for this very reason that he may reasonably be trusted to set aside partisan considerations and act impartially in the interests of the country as a whole. In this situation his role is somewhat akin to that of a judge—another non-elected official to whom we readily entrust large powers in the expectation that they will be exercised impartially.

(b) Appointment of Prime Minister

Perhaps the clearest and least controversial of the Governor General's reserve powers or personal prerogatives is the power to select a Prime Minister. This power has to be exercised whenever a Prime Minister resigns. The resignation of the Prime Minister (unless it is a personal retirement) automatically vacates all ministerial offices, and thus involves the resignation of the entire ministry or government. Resignation may occur, as we have seen, when the House of Commons withdraws its confidence from the government. The more usual case of resignation occurs after an election in which the government party has failed to obtain a majority of the seats in the House of Commons. The theory of responsible government indicates that the Prime Minister would be justified in remaining in office until the House of Commons assembles and votes against his government, but the modern practice (perhaps it is now a convention) is to resign as soon as the election results make clear that the opposition party has gained control of the House of Commons. However, if the election gave no party a clear majority, and it was not clear which major party would attract the support of minor parties or independent members, the Prime Minister would certainly be justified in awaiting a Commons vote.[20]

Once a government has resigned, for whatever reason, the appointment of a new Prime Minister has to be made by the Governor General. This decision is always a personal one in the sense that he does not act upon ministerial advice. But other conventions of responsible government have now severely limited the discretion which the Governor General really possess. He must find the person who has the ability to form a government which will enjoy the support of the House of Commons. The only person with this qualification is the leader of the party which has a majority of seats in the House of Commons. Moreover, each Canadian party has procedures for selecting its own parliamentary leader. This means that in most cases the Governor General's "choice" is inevitable.

One situation which has occurred and could again is the death or retirement of a Prime Minister in office before his party has selected a successor. In that case, when the government still retains a majority in the House, the death or retirement is personal and the government as a whole does not vacate office. The country does not lack a government, but merely a Prime Minister. How is he to be replaced? Canadian political parties do not normally choose a deputy leader or second-in-command at the same time as they select a leader. The cabinet will usually designate a minister to act as Prime Minister during the absence from Ottawa of the Prime Minister, but the Acting Prime Minister is not intended to be the successor to the Prime Minister in the event of the Prime Minister's death or retirement. Before 1896, there were a number of occasions on which a Governor General had to use his own initiative to find a Prime Minister by reason of the death or retirement of the Prime Minister in office. The situation has not recurred since 1896, because every Prime Minister since then has decently refrained from dying or retiring until his party has selected a successor. . . . If a Prime Minister did die or retire in office without a successor, it is certain the the government party would want to choose his successor by its own procedures, and would not be content to accept the Governor General's choice. Given this political fact, the Governor General would be obliged to appoint the party's choice, for only the party's choice would be successful in forming a government. The utmost initiative which I can conceive of the Governor General exercising would be the appointment of a caretaker Prime Minister for the period when the party was making its choice; but even in this circumstance it is likely that the party, perhaps by vote of its parliamentary caucus, would also wish to designate the caretaker, and, in the absence of some gross impropriety in the mode of selection, a Governor General would be obliged to defer to the party's wish.[21]

(c) Dismissal of Prime Minister

The second reserve power of the Governor General is the power to dismiss the Prime Minister. The dismissal (or resignation) of a Prime Minister automatically involves the dismissal (or resignation) of the entire ministry. Thus what is formally a dismissal of a Prime Minister is in substance the dismissal of the ministry or government.

The power of dismissal has been exercised very rarely. In Canada no federal Prime Minister has ever been dismissed, and no provincial Premier has been dismissed since 1905. In the United Kingdom no Prime Minister has been dismissed since 1783.

When does the power of dismissal arise? It is obvious that a Governor General may not dismiss a ministry because he believes its policies to be unwise, or because he believes it to be incompetent. Those are judgments which in a democracy may be made only by the people or their elected representatives. Could the Governor General dismiss a ministry because he believed its policies to be illegal? There is a New South Wales precedent for such a dismissal, but it is soundly criticized by Evatt on the ground that the Governor of New South Wales (or any other head of state) has neither the competence nor the authority to assume to adjudicate a question of law and to provide a remedy for a finding of illegality; questions of illegality are properly justiciable and remediable in the courts. There is also the recent Australian federal precedent of the dismissal in 1975 of Prime Minister Whitlam. The Whitlam Labour government had a secure majority in the lower house, but could not secure supply from the upper house. This dismissal also seems improper since its effect was to install in office a government which the Governor General knew could not command a majority in the lower house. It is true that the Governor General stipulated that the new government should be a "caretaker government" only, which would "make no appointments or dismissals or initiate new policies before a general election is held"; but to purport to bind a government to such conditions is itself an unprecedented and highly dubious exercise of vice-regal discretion.

My opinion is that the only occasion upon which a Governor General would be justified in dismissing a ministry is when the ministry has lost the support of a majority of the House of Commons. When this happens, as we have already noticed, one of two changes must occur; either the House must be dissolved for an election which will produce a new House, or the ministry must resign to make way for a new ministry which will enjoy the confidence of the existing House. If a Prime Minister who had lost his parliamentary support refused to advise dissolution and refused to resign, then the Governor General would have no alternative but to dismiss the Prime Minister and call upon the leader of the opposition to form a government. If a Prime Minister who had lost his parliamentary support advised dissolution but had his advice rejected by the Governor General (the Governor General's power to refuse a dissolution is discussed in the next section . . .) and yet the Prime Minister refused to resign, then again the Governor General would have no alternative but to dismiss the Prime Minister. In Canada neither of these series of events is likely to occur, but if it did the Governor General's action of dismissal would be necessary to force an orderly transfer of power.

(d) Dissolution of Parliament

The Constitution Act, 1867, by s. 50, provides that a House of Commons "shall continue for five years" unless it is "sooner dissolved by the Governor General." It is not the practice of Canadian federal Prime Ministers to allow the House of Commons to continue until the expiration of its five-year term. The usual practice is for the Prime Minister to select what he regards as a propitious time for an election and to advise the Governor General to dissolve the House in time for that election. In the normal situation the Prime Minister still has the confidence of the House of Commons, and he is simply seeking an earlier renewal of his government's mandate than would be provided by the eventual expiration of the House. No Canadian Governor General has ever refused a dissolution requested by a Prime Minister in command of a majority in the House, and it would probably be contrary to convention for a Governor General to do so.[22]

There is one famous Canadian precedent of a Governor General's refusal of a dissolution, but the request for a dissolution came from a Prime Minister who had lost the support of a majority in the House of Commons. In 1926, Prime Minister King's minority Liberal government lost the support of some of the Progressive, Labour and Independent members whose cooperation had provided the government with its majority.[23] Faced with an opposition motion of censure which was likely to carry (since the government had been defeated on motions to amend and to adjourn), Prime Minister King advised the Governor General, Lord Byng, to dissolve the House so as to lead to the calling of a general election. Lord Byng took the view that his personal discretion extended to the rejection of his Prime Minister's advice, and he refused the dissolution. Prime Minister King immediately resigned. Lord Byng then called upon the leader of the Conservative Party, Mr. Meighen, to form a new government. Mr. Meighen did so, but within a week his government was defeated, and so he advised Lord Byng to dissolve the House. Lord Byng accepted this advice, thereby granting to Mr. Meighen the dissolution which he had so recently refused Mr. King. In the ensuing election Mr. King's Liberal Party used the incident as an issue of Canadian independence from the Empire, and they won the election. It is clear that Lord Byng's failure to follow Prime Minister King's advice was unwise, since a dissolution in fact turned out to be necessary,[24] but there is no agreement among constitutional writers as to whether it was in violation of constitutional convention.

There have been occasional suggestions in Canada that after an inconclusive election the Prime Minister would be justified in requesting a dissolution and therefore a second election without even waiting for the Parliament to meet. This view is almost certainly wrong. The House of Commons has been elected, and it should surely be allowed to meet and see if it can transact public business. If it turned out that the House could not even elect a speaker, or if it turned out that neither the Prime Minister nor the leader of any other party could command the support of a majority of members, then there would be no alternative to dissolution; but to dissolve the House before it had even met would be an abuse of the electoral system, and one which the Governor General would surely be entitled to refuse.

(e) Appointments to Senate and Bench

The Governor General's power to appoint senators (Constitution Act, 1867, s. 24) and judges (s. 96) is of course exercised on the advice of the cabinet. In 1896, however, after Parliament had been dissolved and after a new election had decisively defeated the incumbent Conservative government of Prime Minister Tupper, the Tupper government advised the Governor General, Lord Aberdeen, to appoint a number of senators and judges. The Governor General refused to make the appointments. The Tupper government accordingly resigned (as it would have had to do anyway because of the election result). The Governor General then invited Mr. Laurier, the leader of the Liberal Party which had won the election, to form a new government. Mr. Laurier did so, and his government filled the vacancies which the previous government had attempted to fill. The action of the Governor General in this case seems to me to be both wise and in accordance with convention. It was quite improper for the Tupper government to attempt to strengthen its support in the Senate and (less obviously) the bench after it had been defeated at the polls. True, the government was still in office, but the Governor General was entitled to recognize that it was not going to have a majority in the newly-elected House of Commons. In this circumstance the Governor General had a discretion to refuse to concur in an important and irrevocable decision which could await the early and inevitable formation of a new government which was bound to enjoy a majority in the House of Commons.

(f) The Justification for a Formal Head of State

A system of responsible government cannot work without a formal head of state who is possessed of certain reserve powers. While the occasions for the exercise of these powers arise very rarely, the powers are of supreme importance, for they insure against a hiatus in the government of the country or an illegitimate extension of power by a government which has lost its political support. The strength and the weakness of responsible government lie in the executive's dependence on support in the legislature. The strength lies in its provision of an executive which is in accord with the latest expression of the electorate's wishes and which is able to execute its policies. The weakness lies in the absence of clear legal rules as to when governmental power shall be assumed or relinquished and when elections shall be held. In situations where a discredited government is reluctant to relinquish its power, or where parliamentary support is fluid, the head of state is able to resolve the impasse impartially, either through formation of a government, or through an election.

This function of the head of state is unnecessary in a presidential (or gubernatorial) form of government, where the president (or governor) is directly elected for a fixed term and is not dependent upon the support of the legislative branch. The Americans have therefore been able to unite in the one office the formal head of state and the political executive of the nation (or state). The countries which have inherited the British system of responsible government have all had to establish a dual executive in which a formal head of state presides over a government which is actually administered by political officials. While the formal head of state rarely has to exercise his reserve powers, it should not be overlooked that he also performs many formal, ceremonial and social functions which are important in the life of the nation.

(g) The Monarchy

While responsible government requires a dual executive, it does not require that the formal head of state be the Queen. This is demonstrated by countries such as India, Ireland, Israel and South Africa, which possess responsible government, but no monarchy.[25] Canada could if it chose easily become a republic by the simple device of securing an amendment of the Constitution to make the Governor General the formal head of state in his own right.[26] Many constitutional and statutory powers are in any case conferred directly upon the Governor General or the Governor General in Council, and would need no alteration. Those powers which are expressly conferred on the Queen could easily be amended to substitute the Governor General for the Queen. The personal prerogatives which are nowhere authoritatively defined, but which are exercised by the Governor General under a delegation from the Queen, should probably be explicitly conferred on the Governor General directly, although it could be argued that they are implicit in the position of a head of state in a system of responsible government. Certainly, they would not need to be defined in detail, unless that exercise was regarded as worthwhile in itself. A new mode of appointing the Governor General would have to be worked out, because at present the appointment is made by the Queen. But the Queen makes the appointment on the advice of the Canadian Prime Minister anyway, and so the real power of appointment has already been domesticated. In short, the shift from a monarchy to a republic could be accomplished with practically no disturbance of present constitutional practice. In considering the question whether Canada should make the change, the constitutional considerations may be dismissed as neutral or unimportant; obviously, such matters as tradition, sentiment and ceremony are the important considerations.

NOTES

1. British Columbia was an exception.
2. The fact that the Lieutenant Governor is to be appointed by the Governor General (the federal government) led to early controversy as to whether he was a representative of the Crown or of the federal government. The issue was important because if the Lieutenant Governor were not the representative of the Crown then the provincial government would not be entitled to the executive powers and prerogatives of the Crown; all executive powers and prerogatives would rest with the central government, unless specifically delegated to the provinces. In *Liquidators of Maritime Bank v. Receiver General of N.B.*, [1892] A.C. 437 the Privy Council, speaking through Lord Watson, emphatically rejected the view that the Lieutenant Governors (and their provincial governments) were subordinate to the Governor General (and his federal government): "a Lieutenant-Governor, when appointed, is as much the representative of Her Majesty for all purposes of provincial government as the Governor-General himself is for all purposes of Dominion government" (p. 443). It followed that the federal distribution of legislative power entailed a matching distribution of executive powers and prerogatives as well. . . . In the early years of confederation the Lieutenant Governors did also fulfil a secondary role as federal officers, but this has fallen into disuse.
3. . . . No comparable convention has been established with respect to the appointment of Lieutenant Governors. Under s. 58 of the Constitution Act, 1867, such appointments are to be made by the Governor General in Council; this power is exercised on the advice of the federal Prime Minister not the provincial Premier. The appointee will normally be a member of the political party in power in Ottawa, and the provincial Premier will normally be consulted only if he is a member of that party.
4. The ministry and the cabinet are not necessarily identical. In the United Kingdom and Australia, for example, not all ministers are members of cabinet. Whether a particular minister is admitted to the cabinet lies in the discretion of the Prime Minister. The usual Canadian practice has been for the Prime Minister to admit all ministers to the cabinet, . . . and this has been the general practice of the provincial Premiers as well.
5. Other powers which the Prime Minister may by convention exercise independently of his colleagues if he chooses are: the recommendation to the Governor General for appointment of a Lieutenant Governor or a Chief Justice, and the recommendation to the Queen for appointment of a Governor General.
6. These important powers are limited by the Constitution Act, 1982, s. 4

of which prescribes a maximum duration for the House of Commons or a provincial legislative assembly of five years, and s. 5 of which requires that there be a sitting of Parliament and of each Legislature at least once every twelve months. See also ss. 50 and 86 of the Constitution Act, 1867.

7. Criticism of the "imperial presidency" occasionally conveys the impression that the President of the United States is a more powerful figure within the American presidential system of government than is the Prime Minister (or provincial Premier) within a system of responsible government. This is incorrect. In a normal situation of majority government, the Prime Minister's leadership of the majority party in the House of Commons, reinforced by strict party discipline, and sanctioned by his power to dissolve the House, leads to a concentration of power in the hands of the Prime Minister that has no counterpart in the presidential (or gubernatorial) system.

8. In addition to his departments, a minister will often have a number of Crown corporations and regulatory agencies assigned to his ministry. These bodies are outside the departmental structure because they are intended to operate with more autonomy than a government department. However, because they are publicly funded, they have to be subjected to some degree of ministerial control; the mechanisms of that control differ greatly from one body to another.

9. The responsibility of the government and of individual ministers is to the elective lower house, and not to the Senate. A defeat in the Senate does not entail resignation or dissolution. For this reason only a few cabinet members are drawn from the Senate. . . .

10. There have been six federal minority governments: (1) 1921–22, 1923–24 and 1925–26 (King): (2) 1926 (Meighen); (3) 1957–58 and 1962–63 (Diefenbaker); (4) 1963–68 (Pearson); (5) 1972–74 (Trudeau); (6) 1979–80 (Clark).

11. Federal governments have only been defeated by a withdrawal of the confidence of the House of Commons six times since Confederation, namely, 1873 (Macdonald), 1926 (King), 1926 (Meighen), 1963 (Diefenbaker), 1974 (Trudeau) and 1979 (Clark).

12. None of the provinces now has an upper house, although Manitoba, New Brunswick, Nova Scotia, Prince Edward Island and Quebec each used to have one (a Legislative Council) and subsequently abolished it.

13. The Senate of the United States is able to function as a strong upper house, partly because it is an elected body, and also because the President is elected separately from the legislative branch for a fixed term of office: he is not dependent upon a majority in the Congress for his continuance in office. In Australia, where the Senate is also elected but the system is one of responsible government, the Senate's occasional bursts of independence (as in the denials of supply to Prime Minister Whitlam in 1974 and 1975, the latter leading to the Prime Minister's dismissal) have created almost

unbearable political tensions. . . . A strong upper house is not compatible with responsible government.

14. The Senate consists of 104 senators: Constitution Act, 1867, s. 22 (as amended in 1975). There are 24 senators from each of four regions, namely: (1) Ontario; (2) Quebec; (3) the three maritime provinces; and (4) the four western provinces. On Newfoundland's entry [in] to confederation in 1949, six senators were added to represent that province, and in 1975 the Yukon and Northwest Territories were each given one senator. Under s. 26, the number can be increased by either four or eight senators, drawn equally from the four regions, but this power has never been exercised. It has been a persistent (and plausible) claim by British Columbia that the west should be regarded as two regions, namely, the Prairie region (the three prairie provinces) and the Pacific region (British Columbia).

15. A federal proposal for reform was held to be outside the competence of the federal Parliament in *Re Upper House* [1980] 1 S.C.R. 54. Since the adoption of the Constitution Act, 1982, by virtue of s. 42(1)(b), any change in "the powers of the Senate and the method of selecting senators" requires the general amending procedure (federal Parliament plus two-thirds provinces with fifty per cent population); by virtue of s. 44, lesser changes can be made by the federal Parliament alone.

16. By s. 90 provincial legislation is also made subject to reservation and disallowance, but the power of reservation is in the Lieutenant Governor (instead of the Governor General) and the power of disallowance is in the Governor General (instead of the Queen). It is less clear whether these powers have been effectively nullified by convention.

17. . . . The independence, if not formal separation, of the judicial branch from the executive and legislative branches is, however, still generally regarded as essential to the impartial administration of justice both in the United States and in countries such as Canada which have inherited their non-federal constitutional law from the United Kingdom.

18. "Private bills," which relate to a particular person or institution, or a particular locality, are enacted by a different and simpler procedure, which does not require government sponsorship, and they are often enacted after introduction by a private member. . . . Private bills should not be confused with "private members' bills," which are bills introduced by private members. They may be either public or private bills, but when they are public bills they stand little chance of passage.

19. The rule did not used to be so strict. Many British and Canadian governments were defeated in the House of Commons last century without either resigning or advising dissolution. The reason was the looser party discipline and the number of independent members. The strict rule is more appropriate today where party discipline is tight and there are very few or no independent members. But minority government restores some of the fluidity of former times, and it may be sensible and constitutional for

a minority government to follow the earlier precedents and revert to a laxer rule as to what amounts to a withdrawal of confidence in the government. This position is cogently argued by Forsey, *Freedom and Order* (1974), 114–116; and there are precedents accumulating in its favour, e.g., the defeat of the British government on March 10, 1976; (1976) 53 The Parliamentarian 174; the defeat of the Ontario government on June 15, 1976: the *Globe and Mail*, June 16, 1976 and June 17, 1976. In neither case did the minority government resign.

20. Prime Minister St. Laurent resigned after the election of 1957 as soon as the election results showed that his Liberal party had won fewer seats than the Progressive Conservative party, despite the fact that neither party had an absolute majority. He apparently did not want to appear to be clinging to office after an electoral "defeat." But since the election results did not answer the question of who could command the support of a majority in the House of Commons, it seems to me that the Prime Minister would have been fully justified in remaining in office until the parliamentary situation was clear, which might not have been until Parliament met. It turned out, however, that the Progressive Conservative party was able to form a government which lasted for a year so that Prime Minister St. Laurent's resignation could be interpreted as an accurate reading of the parliamentary situation. Prime Minister King was faced with a similar situation after the election of 1925 in which his Liberal government won fewer seats than the Conservative party. He did not resign, and it turned out that he was able to continue in office for eight months with the support of Progressive, Labour and Independent members. Since 1957 the frequent Canadian minority governments, while by definition lacking an absolute majority, have had more government party members in the House than the major opposition party, and so the St. Laurent "precedent" has not required re-examination.

21. Three Quebec Premiers have recently died in office: Duplessis in 1959, Sauvé in 1960 and Johnson in 1968; in each case the parliamentary caucus of the governing Union Nationale party selected a successor, and presented a "petition" to the Lieutenant Governor asking him to commission the person chosen; the Lieutenant Governor complied. In the last case the Premier so chosen, Premier Bertrand, insisted upon his appointment also being ratified by a subsequent party leadership convention.

22. Forsey, *The Royal Power of Dissolution [of Parliament] in the British Commonwealth* (1943), reprinted, 1968), 146–162, takes the view that in some situations refusal of a dissolution would be appropriate, e.g., where a motion of censure is under debate in the House of Commons, or where the last election was very recent. . . .

23. The exact standings of the parties in the House of Commons were: Liberals, 101; Conservatives 116; Progressives 24; and Labour and Independents, 4.

24. The most thorough study of the King-Byng dispute is Forsey's *The Royal Power of Dissolution of Parliament in the British Commonwealth* . . . chs. 5, 6, and Forsey comes down strongly in support of Lord Byng's action. . . . My view that the dismissal was at least unwise is based on the fact that Lord Byng and Mr. Meighen must have known that Meighen would have great difficulty in forming a government because of the legal requirement of that time (it was repealed in 1931) that each minister with portfolio had to vacate his seat and seek re-election in a by-election. If Meighen had formed a ministry in the normal way he would have lost about 15 of his supporters in the House. Since he could not afford such a loss (see the voting figures: Forsey, 159), he formed a "temporary ministry" of ministers without portfolio who became "acting ministers" of the departments of government. This device evaded the necessity for ministerial by-elections, but led to a motion in the House of Commons condemning the device which passed by one vote: Forsey, 131–139. While the exact fashion of the Meighen government's downfall was obviously not forseeeable when Byng refused King's request for a dissolution, it was manifest at that time that the formation of a government by Meighen would present "unusual difficulties" (as Forsey, 135, admits). Marshall, *Constitutional Conventions* (1984), 39, suggests that convention authorizes the refusal of a dissolution only if the Governor General can rely on finding a Prime Minister who can form an alternative government; if this is correct, Lord Byng did not observe the convention.
25. Abolition of the monarchy would not entail leaving the Commonwealth. The Queen would no longer be Canada's head of state, and would play no role in the government of Canada, but she would still be recognized by Canada as the head of the Commonwealth and as the symbol of that association. This was the formula which was adopted in 1949 when India decided to become a republic within the Commonwealth; since then, of course, many of the members of the Commonwealth have become republics.
26. The Constitution Act, 1982, by s. 41, requires the assents of the federal Parliament and all provinces (unanimity procedure) for an amendment in relation to "the office of the Queen."

FURTHER READINGS

Dawson, R.M. *The Government of Canada*. 5th ed., revised by N. Ward, chapters 1–4. Toronto: University of Toronto Press, 1970.

Forsey, E.A. *Freedom and Order: Collected Essays*. Toronto: McClelland & Stewart, 1974.

Mallory, J.R. *The Structure of Canadian Government*. rev. ed., chapters 1–3. Toronto: Gage Publishing, 1984.

Special Issue on Responsible Government. *Journal of Canadian Studies* 14, 2 (Summer 1979).

Note: The following work is extremely informative on this subject; unfortunately it is not easily available:

Forsey, E.A., and G.C. Eglington. *The Question of Confidence in Responsible Government*. A study prepared for the Special Committee on Reform of the House of Commons, 1985.

3

The Political Purposes of the Canadian Charter of Rights and Freedoms

PETER H. RUSSELL

Discussion of Canada's new constitutional Charter of Rights and Freedoms should not overlook the broad political purposes which inspired Canadian politicians to propose it and induced so many Canadian citizens to support it. In the long run, it is in terms of these broad political purposes that the Charter should be, and probably will be, judged.

The political purposes of the Charter can be thought of as falling into two general categories. These two kinds of purposes are, as I shall show, closely related, although analytically distinct. The first has to do with national unity and the Charter's capacity to offset, if not reverse, the centrifugal forces which some believe threaten the survival of Canada as a unified country. This national unity function of the Charter is most relevant to explaining why politicians, especially those who led the federal government, pushed so hard for a charter. The second kind of purpose is the conviction that a charter will better protect, indeed will even "guarantee," fundamental rights and freedoms. Belief in this purpose is most relevant to explaining the widespread public support for the Charter. In this article I will examine each of these purposes in turn and the prospects of their being fulfilled by the Charter.

1. NATIONAL UNITY

To understand the national unity rationale of the Charter, it is necessary to recall the context in which the federal government made a charter its number one priority for constitutional reform.

In the mid–1960s right up to the Confederation of Tomorrow Conference organized by the Premier of Ontario, John Robarts, in the fall of 1967, the Liberal Government in Ottawa was not interested in constitutional reform of any kind. Patriation with an amending formula had been very nearly achieved in 1964. Since then only Quebec had been pushing for constitutional change. But Quebec had drastically raised the stakes. The Lesage Liberals followed by

Abridged from Peter H. Russell, "The Political Purposes of the Canadian Charter of Rights and Freedoms," *Canadian Bar Review* 61, No. 1 (March 1983), 30-54. Reprinted by permission of the author and the *Canadian Bar Review*.

Daniel Johnson's Union Nationale administration insisted that the price of Quebec's support for patriation of the Canadian Constitution would be agreement on substantive constitutional reform giving Quebec more recognition and power as the French Canadian homeland. This demand of Quebec provincial leaders for major constitutional change reflected a wholly new phase in Quebec nationalism. Historically the constitutional position of Quebec leaders had been profoundly conservative. Their prime concern had been to preserve the rights they believed had been acquired for Quebec and French Canada in the constitution of 1867. But now, under the impetus of Quebec's "quiet revolution," the province's leading politicians had become constitutional radicals. So long as these Quebec demands for radical change were the central preoccupation of constitutional debate, it was not in the federal government's interest to encourage the process of constitutional reform. The proposals likely to dominate such a debate, if they went far enough to placate Quebec nationalism, would either go too far in weakening the involvement of the federal government in the life of Quebec or else give Quebec representatives in federal institutions such a privileged place as to alienate opinion in the rest of the country. So the Pearson government at first tried to respond to Quebec through pragmatic adjustments in fiscal and administrative arrangements and took a dim view of Premier Robarts' constitutional initiative.

However, the very success of the Confederation of Tomorrow Conference in raising national expectations about both the necessity and the possibility of responding creatively to Quebec's constitutional discontents seemed to convince the Prime Minister and his Justice Minister, Pierre Trudeau, who was soon to succeed him, that a different strategy was needed. The constitutional issue could no longer be kept on the back burner. But if constitutional reform was to be seriously pursued, it was essential that Quebec's demands be countered by proposals designed to have a unifying effect on Canada. It was at this point that the federal government urged that a charter of rights be at the top of the constitutional reform agenda.

After the Confederation of Tomorrow Conference, Prime Minister Pearson suggested to the provincial governments "that first priority should be given to that part of the Constitution which should deal with the rights of the individual—both his rights as a citizen of a democratic federal state and his rights as a member of the linguistic community in which he has chosen to live,"[1] This was the position his government took at the Constitutional Conference in February 1968. Prime Minister Trudeau took exactly the same position. His government's paper prepared for the February 1969 Constitutional Conference repeated the commitment to a charter of rights as the first priority in constitutional change. "To reach agreement on common values," Trudeau argued, was "an essential first step" in any process of constitutional renewal.[2] From this point until the final enactment of the Constitution Act, 1982, giving constitutional expression to fundamental rights including language rights was the Trudeau government's first constitutional priority. And throughout, the fundamental basic rationale for this constitutional strategy was the perceived value of such a measure as a popular and unifying counter to decentralizing provincial demands in the Canadian constitutional debate.

The Charter's attractiveness to the leaders of the federal Liberal Party as the centrepiece of their constitutional strategy was decisive in improving the political fortunes of the project of entrenching rights and freedoms in the Canadian constitution. Since World War II there had been a great deal of discussion of the Bill of Rights idea both within and outside Parliament. The prime stimulus of this discussion was international—the concern for human rights arising from the war against fascism and Canada's obligations under the United Nations Declaration of Human Rights. Domestic events also stimulated interest in a Bill of Rights. At the federal level, there was regret concerning the treatment of Japanese Canadians during the war and the denial of traditional legal rights in the investigation of a spy ring following the Gouzenko disclosures in 1946. At the provincial level the persecution of Jehovah's Witnesses by the Duplessis administration in Quebec, the treatment of Doukhabors and other religious minorities in the west and the repression of trade unionism in Newfoundland were major *causes célèbres*. There was also a touch of the national unity theme in the submissions made on a number of occasions to parliamentary committees on the implications of post-war immigration. The addition of such large numbers of new Canadians with no education or experience in liberal democratic values, it was argued, meant that Canada could no longer rely on the British method of protecting civil liberties. For such a heterogeneous population a written code was needed. Liberal leaders were not moved by these arguments for a Canadian Bill of Rights. The C.C.F. was the only national party to commit itself to establishing a Bill of Rights. And it was under a Progressive Conservative government led by John Diefenbaker that a statutory Bill of Rights affecting only the federal level of government was enacted in 1960.

Pierre Trudeau, before he entered politics and joined the Liberal Party, expressed interest in a constitutional Bill of Rights. In 1965, as a legal academic writing a background paper on how to deal with the Quebec agitation for constitutional change, he placed a Bill of Rights in first place on his list of constitutional reform proposals. But the main thrust of his paper was to dissuade Quebecers from relying on constitutional reform to solve their problems of political and social modernization. His constitutional reform proposals were for "some day" in the future. Whenever a Bill of Rights was added to the constitution, he saw the abolition of the federal power of reservation and disallowance over provincial legislation as a logical *quid pro quo*. This emphasis on the connection between a constitutional Bill of Rights and the federal powers of reservation and disallowance underlines a constitutional charter's capacity for imposing national standards on the provinces. This link appeared again in the Trudeau government's 1978 constitutional initiative but was not part of the constitutional package which contained the new Charter. To have made a change in powers a *quid pro quo* for a charter of rights would not have fitted in very well with a political campaign in which the Charter was being sold as part of a "people's package" and provincial premiers were being chastised for trying to swap rights for powers. In any event, by 1967 that distant day when constitutional reforms should be undertaken had suddenly arrived. Speaking to the Canadian Bar Association as Justice Minister in 1967 Trudeau announced his government's conclusion that a constitutional Bill of Rights proposal was "the best basis on which to begin a dialogue on constitution reform between the federal government and provincial governments," and he emphasized that in taking this approach: "Essentially we will be testing—and, hopefully, establishing—the unity of Canada."

After 1967 there were factors other than constitutional strategy which provided additional reasons for adopting a constitutional charter of rights. The application of the European Convention on Human Rights to the United Kingdom, Canada's accession to the International Covenant of Civil and Political Rights in 1976 and the enactment of human rights legislation by most of the Canadian provinces increased Canadian interest in a constitutional codification of basic rights. The invocation of the War Measures Act in 1970 and the excesses of the R.C.M.P.'s Security Service stimulated civil libertarian interest in a constitutional Bill of Rights, as did the Supreme Court's generally narrow interpretation of the "Diefenbaker" Bill. But I doubt that any of these developments had much to do with the Trudeau government's commitment to the Charter—except insofar as they indicated greater public support for such a measure.

Aside from the political and strategic advantages of the Charter, it may also have had some purely intellectual or even aesthetic attractions for Mr. Trudeau and some of his colleagues. Federal government position papers put forward the view that the rational approach to the constitution was to begin with a statement of the fundamental values of the Canadian political community. This notion of constitutional rationality, of the constitution as a logical construct built on an explicit formulation of first principles, may be a manifestation of French rationalism and the civil law tradition with its penchant for deduction from codified principles in contrast with English empiricism and the inductive nature of common law. Even if there is some validity in this kind of ethnic stereotyping, it surely cannot account for the strength of the Trudeau government's political commitment to the Charter.

That commitment proved to be very strong indeed. A version of a constitutional Bill of Rights took pride of place in the Victoria Charter which Mr. Trudeau came so close to negotiating successfully with the provincial Premiers in 1971. Again in 1978 when, in response to the electoral victory of the separatists in Quebec, the federal government embarked on another serious programme of constitutional reform, a constitutional charter, albeit one which at first would not bind the provinces, was given a prominent position. But it was the inclusion of a constitutional Charter of Rights binding on the provinces in the package of constitutional change which Mr. Trudeau threatened to achieve, if necessary, unilaterally without provincial support that demonstrates how deeply he and his government believed in its benefits. At this point, when federal-provincial negotiations on the constitution were at an impasse, it would have been ever so much easier, from a political point of view, for the federal government to have proceeded simply with patriation and an amending formula. The insistence on coupling a constitutional charter with patriation shows how strongly the Trudeau government believed in the nation-building potential of a constitutional charter. They would risk dividing the country in order that it might become more united. This nation-building aspect of the Charter was the central thesis of Mr. Trudeau's final parliamentary speech on the Charter:[3]

> Lest the forces of self-interest tear us apart, we must now define the common thread that binds us together.

Will the Charter fulfill the expectations of its political sponsors in promoting national unity? In the context of the immediate exigencies of Canada's constitutional debate the Charter did provide a useful counterpoise to demands for greater provincial powers. But the national unity benefits of such a manoeuvre were discounted, if not eliminated by Mr. Trudeau's unilateralism and by the failure, in the end, to secure the Quebec government's assent to the constitutional package. The thirst for more provincial power or more effective representation in national institutions evident in Quebec and western Canada has not been quenched by "the people's package." In the long run, the Charter's efficacy in contributing to national unity will depend not on its utility to federal politicians at a particular stage in the constitutional debate but on its real potential for strengthening the Canadian political community.

The most frequently and widely acclaimed unifying effect of a charter is its capacity to serve as a unifying symbol. The symbolic function of a constitutional charter was, for instance, emphasized by the Canadian Bar Association's Committee on the Constitution:[4]

> A clear statement in the Constitution of the fundamental values all Canadians share would, we think, have an important unifying effect. It would inculcate in all citizens, young and old, a consciousness of the importance of civil liberties and an authoritative expression of the particular rights and liberties our society considers fundamental.

Lawyers and politicians seem very confident about the Charter's symbolic impact. And they may be right! Social scientists have stressed the important role that symbols play in shaping political attitudes and beliefs. Murray Edelman, for example, in his classic study of *The Symbolic Uses of Politics* goes so far as to suggest that all political constitutions are "largely irrational, in genesis and in impact." But exactly how the emotional chemistry of laws as political symbols operates, in precisely what kind of circumstances a particular set of symbols (for instance a constitutional charter of rights) will have a particular effect (for instance strengthening national unity), has not been established.

My own intuition is that if the reality of a charter is confined to the symbolic level, it is unlikely to have a unifying effect. If the Charter is no more than a fancy document that hangs on the school-room wall, that is recited in citizenship classes and eulogized in after-dinner speeches, I doubt that it will have a significant impact, of any kind, on the attitudes of citizens—except possibly to promote cynicism. This doubt is fortified by the experience of living for several years in one country, Uganda, whose constitution contained an elegant Bill of Rights but whose political leaders were not effectively constrained by any part of the constitution. To take a less extreme example, I think it unlikely that the statement of rights and freedoms in the Soviet Union's constitution does much to enhance political allegiance in that country.

Professor McWhinney contends that the Canadian Charter's symbolic power may be stultified by poor draftsmanship. He criticizes "the heavy, wooden quality" of the Charter's language and style. Its "technical lawyer's language," the "weasel-word exceptions" which qualify so many of the rights and freedoms and its excessive length will, he suggests, prevent Canada's Charter from achieving "the inspiration and grandeur of the American and French charters."[5] Personally I doubt whether less technical, and more inspiring language could by itself make much of a difference. The inspirational character of the American Declaration of Independence and the French Declaration of the Rights of Man and the Citizen derives at least as much from the historic significance of the revolutionary events with which these documents are associated as from their language. The phrasing of the United States Bill of Rights does not strike me as significantly more inspiring or less technical than the language of the new Canadian Charter. For Professor McWhinney the proviso in section 7 that an individual might be deprived of his right to life, liberty or security "in accordance with the principles of fundamental justice" is an example of the Canadian Charter's "timidity." But is this provision really so different from the United States Constitution's Fourteenth Amendment which stipulates, among other things: "nor shall any State deprive any person of life, liberty, or property, without the due process of law;"?

It seems to me that the trend in the drafting of modern bills of rights is to spell out in fairly precise language major qualifications of the various rights and freedoms. Take, for example, the European Convention of Human Rights and the International Convention of Civil and Political Rights. The rights and freedoms inscribed in both are replete with qualifications phrased in language which is certainly as prolix as anything to be found in the Canadian Charter.[6] Nor do I find the language of charters in the constitutions of such modern democratic states as West Germany, India or Ireland—all of which were, in part, intended to be nation-building instruments—either dazzling or succinct. All of these documents make tedious reading. The trend towards explicit qualification reflects, I believe, the greater sophistication of peoples who have learned through historical experience that no rights and freedoms are so "fundamental" that they can be enjoyed in an absolute sense. We may well be past that point in history where popular belief in the merits of a regime can be sustained or fortified by grandiloquent constitutional language.

There are certain parts of the Charter which are clearly intended to be unifying not only symbolically but also in terms of their real effects on government policy and citizens' rights. These are the sections dealing with mobility and language rights. The mobility rights in section 6 aim at overcoming the "balkanization" of Canada by giving citizens the right "to take up residence and to pursue a livelihood anywhere in Canada without discrimination based on the previous province of residence."[7] The language clauses, by giving formal constitutional recognition, for the first time, to English and French as Canada's Official Languages, by extending the constitutional right to use these languages to dealings with the executive branch of the federal government and with all branches of government in New Brunswick and, most importantly, by establishing minority language education rights for the English in Quebec and the French outside of Quebec, aim at giving greater reality to the ideal of the whole of Canada being a homeland for French-speaking as well as English-speaking Canadians.

For the Liberal government these sections were the heart of the Charter. Their importance is underlined by the fact that section 33 which permits the federal and provincial legislatures to override sections of the Charter does not apply to these rights. In his speech introducing the Charter to the House of Commons, Mr. Chrétien, the Minister of Justice, referred to these rights as "fundamental to what Canada is all about."[8] They express the pan-Canadian nationalism which, at the level of ideology, is the counter to the nationalism of Quebec separatism. Since entering politics in the 1960s Mr. Trudeau had, in a sense, been engaged in a rival programme of nation-building to that of Quebec indépendentistes. At the centre of this programme was the task of persuading the Québécois that they could best fulfill themselves by enjoying the opportunities flowing from membership in a Canadian community wider than Quebec. It was for this reason that these nationalist provisions of the Charter, especially the language rights, were of such great importance to Mr. Trudeau and his Quebec colleagues. They were also the only part of the whole constitutional package which, by any stretch of the imagination, Mr. Trudeau and his federalist allies could point to as fulfilling the commitment they had made during the Quebec Referendum campaign to "constitutionnal renewal."

What is the potential of these sections for realizing their nationalist objectives? So far as mobility rights are concerned, section 6 is not likely to make any great inroads on the economic balkanization of Canada. To begin with it deals only with labour mobility and not with other major obstacles to a Canadian common market such as discriminatory tax and government purchasing policies. Moreover, section 6's impact on labour mobility was severely curtailed by the qualification introduced as part of the November Accord between the federal government and nine provinces. This proviso will shield from the Charter the protective employment policies of provinces experiencing above average unemployment. Still, section 6 may turn out to be an important check on provinces like Alberta endeavouring to preserve their relative prosperity by denying provincial services to Canadians from other provinces.

The language rights relate to a more intractable dimension of the national problem—the question of identity. Here, section 23, the language of education clause, makes a more significant contribution than sections 16 to 20 which deal with the language of government. The latter do little more than elevate statutory rights into constitutional rights. Any symbolic gains for national unity that may flow from such a change are largely offset by the persistence of the government of Ontario, the province with the largest Francophone minority, in refusing to give constitutional status to bilingualism in the public life of that province. The language of education section is bound to spark controversy in the short run. In Quebec it collides directly with educational policies emanating from Franco-Quebec nationalism that deny English Canadians who move to Quebec access to the province's English schools. This collision was softened by a last minute concession that makes the rights of new Canadian citizens whose English education was obtained outside of Canada to send their children to Quebec's English schools conditional on the agreement of the Quebec legislature. The rights which section 23 extends to the small francophone minorities in the western provinces will do nothing to reduce alienation in the west where there is little respect for the fundamental nature of French-English dualism in the Canadian experience.

Nevertheless it could turn out that these divisive effects were only short term and that in the longer run were worth risking if the Charter's recognition of bilingualism makes it more likely that Canada will survive as a common homeland for English and French-speaking North Americans. But the rights contained in the Charter, even when added to all that has been done to promote bilingualism outside of the Constitution, may be too little too late to overcome the legacy of political and judicial policies which in the late 1800s and early 1900s gave priority to provincial rights over minority cultural rights and thereby prevented the building of a dualistic society on the new Canadian frontier. I suspect that if Canada overcomes Quebec separatism, it will be not so much because recognition of bilingualism in the "new" Canadian Constitution is decisive in the battle for the hearts and minds of the Québécois but because of the exhaustion of nationalist politics brought on by more compelling economic concerns.

But it is neither through the Charter's nationalist provisions nor its symbolic force that the Charter is likely to have its strongest centripetal effect on the Canadian polity. I think the Charter's nationalizing influence will be felt most through a process scarcely mentioned by its political sponsors—the process of judicial review. It is primarily through judicial decisions interpreting the Charter—applying its general terms to particular laws and government activities—that the Charter will come to play an important part in the ongoing political life of Canada.

Now it may seem rather perverse to think of judicial interpretation of the Charter as a unifying process. Judicial decisions based on the Charter will frequently be concerned with sensitive political issues and are therefore bound to be controversial. Consider, for instance, the sharp divisions of opinion within Canadian society on such issues as censoring pornography, school prayers, abortion, police powers, compulsory retirement and affirmative action. Judicial decisions on claims made under the Charter will touch on all of these issues. American experience demonstrates that judicial decisions in these areas are bound to anger the losers as much as they please the winners. Given the political sparks that judicial interpretation of the Charter will set off, why do I ascribe unifying consequences to the process of judicial review?

Judicial decisions on the Charter will be unifying in that the very debates and controversies they produce will be national and on issues that transcend the regional cleavages which are usually a feature of national political controversy in Canada. Court cases on the Charter normally will not pit region against region or the provinces against the "feds." Instead the principal protagonists will be interest groups and aggregations of individuals from all parts of Canada. For instance, litigation dealing with police powers (the first major policy field in which judicial interpretation of the Charter is likely to be of political importance) will find small "c" conservatives aligned against small "l" liberals all across the country. Although the controversy will be intense, it will be waged on a national level in the arena of national politics and on grounds that do not call into question the legitimacy of Canada as a national political community. It is in this sense that the Charter may well turn out to be a nation-building instrument.

There is an even more direct sense in which judicial interpretation of the Charter will be a nationalizing process. In interpreting the Charter, the Supreme Court of Canada, at the top of the judicial structure, will set uniform national standards—often in policy areas which otherwise would be subject to diverse provincial standards. Film censorship, school prayers and discrimination in employment practices are all clear examples. In contrast to the executive and legislative power, the judicial power in Canada is essentially unified. Policy directives flowing from Supreme Court decisions on the Charter are transmitted through a single hierarchy of appeals that binds all the courts in the land, and shapes the rights of all Canadians and the powers of all who govern.

It is true that section 33 by permitting legislatures to override certain sections of the Charter—for five years at a time—modifies judicial supremacy. However, because of the adverse political consequences that a government would usually risk in using this power, I very much doubt that it will be frequently used. In the case of Quebec, where the P.Q. Government has already purported to have used the section on a blanket basis, it has been invoked not to protect provincial policies from the impact of judicially established standards but as part of a campaign challenging the legitimacy of changes in the constitution made without the consent of Quebec's provincial government.[9] This symbolic use of section 33 will, I believe, be confined to Quebec. While this rejection of the Charter was to be expected under a Quebec government committed to Quebec's independence, it will be interesting to see whether a non-separatist Quebec government maintains this ironic "special status" of Quebec. Elsewhere there will be a great deal of political pressure exerted against a province's immunizing itself from the Charter. This is apt to be especially true where the Supreme Court has established a new national standard—for example, the standard of reasonableness which must be met by provincial censorship arrangements. There may be difficulty in securing effective compliance with the Supreme Court decisions from all those whose behavior in the field of activity concerned is supposed to be governed by the court's decision. But direct rejection by the legislature of the Supreme Court's definition of a constitutional requirement is quite another thing.

In selling the Charter, the federal government tended to ignore this dimension of the Charter. Federal representatives were at pains to point out that the Charter involves "no transfer of powers from the provinces to the federal government." These disavowals of any centralizing implications of the Charter are entirely valid providing one interprets "government" narrowly to exclude the judicial branch. However, in this day and age, it is only on the basis of a blind, and most anachronistic view of the judicial process that the policy making role of the judiciary, above all in interpreting the broad language of a constitutional Bill of Rights, could be denied. Once the discretion and choice necessarily involved in interpreting that language is recognized, the centralizing tendencies of judicial review must be acknowledged. As the Supreme Court's capacity to function as a kind of national Senate reviewing the reasonableness of provincial laws and policies becomes evident, the reality of judicial power will overtake the rhetoric of federal politicians. Among other things, this will mean that the federal government's monopoly of the power to appoint judges, not only to the Supreme Court of Canada but to all of the higher provincial courts, will be increasingly questioned. To be able to maintain that a transfer of power from politicians to judges entails "no transfer of power from the provinces to the federal government" it may become necessary to give provincial governments a share of the action in the judicial appointment process.

Such a development assumes a widening recognition of the importance of judicial power in determining the actual policy consequences of a constitutional charter. Public awareness of that power is still in the making. The popularity of the Charter was based primarily on a belief that one basic policy would flow automatically from the Charter—the better protection of fundamental rights and freedoms. It is to the analysis of that belief and the likelihood of the Charter's fulfilling it that I now turn.

2. PROTECTING RIGHTS AND FREEDOMS

"Protecting rights and freedoms" is a deceptively simple idea. Those who accept such a slogan as a fair summary of what a constitutional Bill of Rights is all about could hardly be expected to be anything other than enthusiastic about adding a charter to the Canadian Constitution. As Yvon Pinard, the government's House Leader, echoing so many of his colleagues, put it, "what is wrong with the fundamental freedoms of Canadian citizens being protected forever by the Canadian constitution?"[10] What indeed could possibly be wrong with such a project if that was basically all there was to it? Surely all of us would be mad to reject or even to question a proposal that is guaranteed to protect our individual rights and freedoms forever.

While this simplistic language undoubtedly assisted in winning public support for the Charter, it is not very helpful in understanding the real political consequences of such an instrument. The trouble with this language is that it tends to reify fundamental rights and freedoms, by treating them as things which people either possess in their entirety or not at all. But in our actual civic experience we do not encounter these rights and freedoms in such a zero-sum fashion. We enjoy more or less of them. What we have to settle about these rights and freedoms is not whether or not we will "have" them but what limits it is reasonable to attach to them and how decisions about these limits should be made.

Those parts of the Charter which deal with what might be termed universal rights and freedoms (as opposed to rights and freedoms based on the particular circumstances of Canadian history) are related to core values or ideals of all contemporary liberal democracies: political freedom, religious toleration, due process of law and social equality. In Canada for some time now there has been no serious debate about the *minimum* extent to which each of these values should be realized in the laws and practices of our state. The right to criticize the government and to organize non-violent opposition to it has been basically unquestioned since the middle of the last century. Since the Quebec Act of 1774, it has been accepted that individuals should not suffer civil disabilities because of their religious beliefs nor be forced to subscribe to the tenets of any religion. At least since the advent of legal aid, Canadians charged with a criminal offence have had access to a fair trial. As in other liberal democracies, social equality has been the last of the core values to gain effective recognition. But now there is wide-spread acceptance of the ideal that each person should be treated as an individual on his or her merits and not penalized or denied opportunities by the state because of gender, skin colour, ethnic background or other distinguishing characteristics of birth.

As we move out from the central core of these values, we encounter restrictions and limits on each, and considerable controversy about the right limits. Have we gone far enough in removing restrictions on political speech or should we go further and narrow the civil wrong of defamation when politicians are the targets of criticism, or perhaps eliminate the crime of inciting race hatred? Should the protection of political speech extend to the public exhibition of all kinds of sexual activities? Is it right to limit the freedom of broadcasters in order to nurture our national culture? Should religious freedom be extended to the point where no one should suffer an economic penalty (like closing a business on Sundays) in order to comply with a law originally introduced for religious reasons, or to the point where no one is obliged to obey a law that offends his religious or philosophic beliefs—no matter how eccentric those beliefs? How far back in the pre-trial proceedings of our criminal justice system should we extend the right to counsel? Should it apply (and in the case of indigent persons, be paid for by the state) to all offences however minor—even to infractions of parking by-laws? Should the police be able to use evidence from private premises only when they have obtained it through a judicially authorized search warrant? What about evidence they come upon by chance in effecting an arrest or responding to a citizen's complaint? Should we begin to make amends for inequalities suffered in the past by adopting laws that discriminate against males and Caucasians? Should the premises of private clubs that practice racial discrimination receive police protection? Should our courts enforce wills that discriminate on the basis of religion or race or gender? How far should we go in ensuring that all of our public facilities are fully accessible to the physically handicapped?

It is in the way we deal with these questions that the Charter will have its main effect. A constitutional charter guarantees not that there will be no limits to rights and freedoms but that a change will be made in the way our society makes decisions about these limits. At the initial level, decisions on these limits will still be made, for the most part, by the legislature and executive, although where common law remains important—for instance, contempt of court, the law of libel and the law of evidence—even the initial decisions will be judge-made rules of law. A charter introduces a second level of decision making in which decisions made at the first level are subjected to a process of judicial review triggered by litigants who claim that a particular limit is excessive or unreasonable. Not only that, but what is most dramatic about this process when it is based on a constitutional as opposed to a statutory charter—and accounts, of course, for the language of "entrenchment" and "guarantees"—is that the results of this second level of decision-making, especially when they issue from the highest court, are very difficult to change. These judicial decisions can only be altered by the difficult process of constitutional amendment,[11] by a change in judicial outlook (resulting, perhaps, from a change in the composition of the bench) or through the exercise of that unique Canadian option—the legislative override power.

Considered from this point of view, the legislative override is not as contradictory a feature of the new Canadian Charter as some of its detractors have claimed. Section 33 has been denounced as incompatible with the Charter's basic purpose:[12]

> The whole object of a charter is to say, you never opt out, they're inalienable rights. If you believe in liberty, if you believe in rights, the rights are not inalienable.

But note how this objection assumes the zero-sum, absolute nature of rights and freedoms. Once the fallaciousness of that assumption is recognized, and the hard issues concerning the proper limits of rights are acknowledged, the legislative override appears in a more acceptable light. The legislative override simply enables a legislature to put off for five years judicial review of its decision to accept a particular limit on a right or freedom.

In treating the Charter as primarily affecting the way we make decisions about the limits on fundamental rights and freedoms, I do not mean to call into question beliefs about the fundamental nature of certain rights or principles of government. I believe that the right to government based on the consent of the governed rather than on coercion, freedom from the theocratic enforcement of a particular religious creed, the right to be secure from arbitrary and unlawful deprivations of one's personal liberty or property, and recognition of the essential dignity of every human being regardless of race, colour, creed or gender are basic requirements of good government that derive from man's nature. For countries in the liberal democratic tradition these principles constitute fundamental purposes of government. As general principles, I cannot see that they are any less fundamental to liberal democracies without constitutional charters—for example, Australia, pre-charter Canada, and the United Kingdom—than they are in countries with constitutional charters—for example, Ireland, Japan, the United States and West Germany. What I am insisting upon is the difference between a right stated as a general principle and operative rules of law affecting that principle. For instance, the political traditions and practices of liberal democracies, those with and those without charters, recognize the fundamental principle of government by consent and its corollary that such consent requires, among other things, freedom to criticize the government and to persuade one's fellow citizens that the government should be changed by electoral means. But among the liberal democracies there are different rules and practices concerning the extent to which there is freedom to advocate the use of violence to change the regime to one that does not tolerate political opposition, or to the extent to which free expression should extend outside the political realm to public displays of lewd or violent acts or commentary on trials in progress. These various rules and limits affect the outer limits of fundamental rights and freedoms while preserving their inner core.

The expectation of those who supported a constitutional charter on the grounds that it would guarantee rights and freedoms might be more realistically phrased as a belief that a charter will at least work against tightening existing limits on rights and freedoms and might even lead to the reduction of some restrictions. In this way, it might be argued, a constitutional charter will preserve and possibly expand fundamental rights and freedoms.

There can be no doubt that the Charter will promote a more systematic review of public policies in terms of the rights and freedoms included in the Charter. At least initially, this review will involve more than the judiciary. Already police officials have been taking steps to bring police practices into line with the standards of due process set out in the Charter. Ministries of the Attorney General have been scouring statute books for possible breaches of the Charter. The three-year postponement of the coming into force of the equality rights in section 15 is designed to facilitate an intensive review of discriminatory aspects of law and policy so that potential conflicts with the Charter can be minimized. Even though the Charter does not contain an equivalent of section 3 of the Canadian Bill of Rights which required the Minister of Justice to scrutinize draft regulations and Bills for inconsistencies with the Bill of Rights, still it is likely that at both the federal and provincial levels legal advisers to the government will examine legislative proposals in the light of the new Charter's provisions.

But the judicial branch will be the most important forum for the systematic application of Charter standards. Judicial opinions will be authoritative on the specific meanings to be given to the Charter's general principles. In most instances judicial decisions will be final and definitive on the proper limits of rights and freedoms. Moreover, initiation of the judicial review process is essentially independent of the executive and legislative branches of government. Where constitutional rights and freedoms rather than the division of powers are at issue, the process of judicial review will normally be "turned on," so to speak, by individuals and groups, not by governments.[13] As a result the spectrum of interests that can influence the agenda of law reform is considerably widened.

Already in the first few months under the Charter private litigants have instigated judicial review of a substantial number of laws and policies. . . . I doubt that very many, indeed if any, of these matters were slated for consideration in the immediate future by the responsible legislatures. Indeed it is the unpredictable character of the law reform programme inaugurated by a constitutional charter which I find so intriguing. . . .

This opening up of the law reform process may be the major democratizing consequence of a constitutional charter. But what are the substantive results of this process likely to be? There can be no doubt that old and new restrictions on rights and freedoms are more apt to be challenged under a charter. But will the results of these challenges necessarily expand rights or freedoms or prevent their contraction? Here we must acknowledge a great deal of uncertainty. The political orientations and legal philosophies of the judiciary are not static. If American experience with constitutional "guarantees" teaches us anything it is that over the decades or even centuries of judicial interpretation we should expect periods of both judicial conservatism and judicial liberalism. Because politicians play the crucial role in the selection of judges it is unlikely that the ideological profile of the judiciary will differ dramatically from that of the countries' dominant political elite. Changes in judicial attitudes may lag behind changes in the political culture, but in the long run these attitudes will reflect major shifts in popular political orientations.

Even if Canada does experience a relatively liberal period of judicial review under the Charter, it does not follow that all of the consequences for fundamental rights and freedoms will be positive. To begin with rights and freedoms conflict with one another. A freedom may be expanded at the expense of another right. It is not difficult to think of possibilities: review of our laws concerning contempt of court may expand free speech while adversely affecting the right to a fair trial; contraction of police powers through interpretation of legal rights may better protect the rights of criminally accused while diminishing the effective protection to the right to life and personal security of the victims of crime. Nor can it be said that the rights of minorities are bound to be beneficiaries of a liberally interpreted charter. Leaving aside the question of why in a democratic society the views of minorities should be systematically favoured on basic policy questions over the view of the majority, there is the difficulty of identifying the relevant minority on the legislative issues which will be the subject of judicial review. On the pornography issue, for instance, which is the preferred minority—the conservatives who believe present restrictions provide insufficient protection of human dignity or radicals who regard these same restrictions as an illegitimate encroachment on free expression? On many of these issues to be decided under the Charter the interested public consists not of a majority and *the* minority but of a number of minorities some of which will feel benefited by and others which will feel offended by the outcome of judicial review.

Lawyers are too prone to think of rights and liberties entirely in legal terms. They are apt to ignore the possibility that judicial decisions which remove or narrow legislative restrictions on rights and freedoms can have the effect of expanding social or economic constraints. The issues raised by the Kent Commission on corporate concentration of the press provide a good illustration.[14] It is possible that the courts will find legislation enacted in response to the Kent Commission to be an unconstitutional violation of "freedom of the press and other media of communication." If this occurs, it would mean the continuation of restrictions on the expression of political opinion stemming from the concentration of ownership of the means of mass communication. Harold Innis warned Canadians some years ago of the bias which results from viewing freedom of speech through the prism of an excessive legalism.[15] It would be a pity if adoption of a constitutional charter of rights blunted our capacity to recognize that the state is not the only centre of power in our society capable of restricting freedom or equality or of abusing rights.

Here again we encounter the complexity of rights and freedom issues. Rights and freedoms do not form a simple piece of whole cloth which by some new constitutional mechanism can be made to expand in a single direction. Around any civil liberties issue there will likely be a cluster of rights and social interests some of which will be affected positively and others of which will be affected negatively by contracting a legal restriction on a particular right or freedom. This does not mean that we must be agnostic about what is the right way to treat an issue or that there is no better way than that embodied in the existing legislative arrangements. But it does suggest how facile it is to regard a broad liberal construction of a guarantee as always yielding the most reasonable balance—the result which provides the fairest treatment of rights and freedoms.

There is also the possibility that the courts will render conservative decisions—that is decisions that uphold existing laws and practices as not violating rights and freedoms or at least as not constituting unreasonable limitations on these rights and freedoms. The libertarian enthusiast of a charter of rights may think that while such decisions will be disappointing in that they represent missed opportunities for expanding rights and freedoms, still such decisions cannot reduce rights and freedoms. Conservative decisions, it might be contended, may not push out the limits on rights and freedoms but neither will they push those limits in. But this argument overlooks the way in which a decision upholding existing arrangements as constitutional can legitimize the status quo. There may be a tendency under a constitutional charter of rights and freedoms to accept as a corollary of the proposition that "if it is unconstitutional it must be wrong" the proposition that "if it is constitutional it must be right." There is an element of this in American constitutional history. The Supreme Court decision in *Plessy v. Ferguson* did not establish racial segregation in American schools, but by putting the constitutional seal of approval on separate but equal facilities it created an additional obstacle for proponents of integration. In Canada it is well within the realm of possibilities that if the Charter had been in force during the 1970 October crisis the Supreme Court would have found the restrictions imposed on civil liberties under the War Measures Act to be "reasonable" and "demonstrably justified in a free and democratic society." Such a decision would have made it even more difficult than it already is to mobilize political support for much needed reforms of Canada's emergency legislation.

The point in questioning libertarian expectations of the constitutional Charter is not to renew the debate on whether Canada should "entrench" rights. For all practical purposes that debate is over. Canada has a constitutional charter and all of us, its former opponents and supporters alike, must learn to live with it intelligently. To do this it is necessary to discard the rhetoric of the Charter's political salesmen and adopt a more realistic appraisal of the Charter's potentialities. Such an understanding requires that we bear in mind the Charter's consequences not only for policy results but also for the policy process.

The principal impact of a charter on the process of government can be neatly summarized as a tendency to judicialize politics and politicize the judiciary. The political leaders who led the campaign for the Charter gave little attention to this consequence of a charter. When they did refer to it, they did so in a very optimistic vein. Mr. Chrétien, for instance, in acknowledging the important policy questions which judges will have to decide in interpreting the language of education section of the Charter, said:[16]

> I think we are rendering a great service to Canada by taking some of these problems away from the political debate and allowing the matter to be debated, argued, coolly before the courts with precedents and so on.

Unquestionably Canada can benefit from the rationality which a thoroughly researched, well reasoned judicial decision can bring to the resolution of a difficult question of social or political justice. Such benefits will contribute to national unity if cogent judicial decisions help build a stronger national consensus on such historically divisive issues as language rights. But, while acknowledging these possible benefits, we should not lose sight of the possibility that excessive reliance on litigation and the judicial process for settling contentious policy issues can weaken the sinews of our democracy. The danger here is not so much that non-elected judges will impose their will on a democratic majority, but that questions of social and political justice will be transformed into technical legal questions and the great bulk of the citizenry who are not judges and lawyers will abdicate their responsibility for working out reasonable and mutually acceptable resolutions of the issues which divide them.

Mitigation of this danger to Canadian democracy will require, on the part of both judges and the public, a sensitivity to the hazards of a judicial imperium. It would be a tragic self-delusion for judges to believe that they can escape the dilemmas of the new power which the Charter has thrust upon them by resorting to a kind of knee-jerk conservatism. An automatic upholding of virtually everything challenged under the Charter would bestow the mantle of constitutionality on all manner of legislation, government practice and police activity. It would be equally unfortunate if Canadian judges were to go to the other extreme of "government by judiciary" and become guilty of what an American critic of the United States judiciary refers to as "a kind of moral arrogance and judicial imperialism in undertaking to solve social problems for which they lack the competence, wisdom, or, for that matter, charter to undertake."[17]

No simple recipe for avoiding these extremes can be written. But there is one change in the methodology of judicial decision making that Canadian judges should consider. That is softening, if not discarding, the taboo against the use of legislative history in interpreting the general language of the Charter. There was an extensive parliamentary discussion of the Charter. If counsel and judges mine the record of this discussion, I think there is less danger of the Canadian judiciary constituting itself a constituent assembly fabricating constituational law without reference to the expectations of the original framers. No doubt the light which the historical record casts on some points will be scant and uncertain. The trouble with such a massive constitutionalization of rights as was undertaken in the new Canadian Charter is that, despite many days of discussion in the Joint Parliamentary Committee on the Constitution and debate in the House of Commons and the Senate, some difficult points were glossed over lightly or settled in last minute, private negotiations. Still there are sections which were extensively discussed in Parliament. The concepts and purposes embodied in some of these sections evolved through well reported political negotiations outside of Parliament. A good example is section 23 on the language of education. Examination of this legislative and political background material may rarely, if ever, uncover the full range of meaning which it was intended should attach to a constitutional guarantee, but it may often be a reliable guide to what was *not* included in the intentions of the constitution makers.

A new discipline will also be required by the public that evaluates the work of judges. If Canadians are to enjoy the cool rationality which Mr. Chrétien and others believe should result from the adjudication of disputes about constitutional rights, there must be a wider public capacity for giving consideration to judicial reasons. If for the public it is only the judicial outcome— "the bottom line"—that counts, our judges will tend to become simply another group of politicians and we will realize little of the distinctive benefits to be derived from expanding the judiciary's policy-making responsibilities. On the other hand, public debate and discussion of judicial decisions must not be muted by awe of the judicial office. It must be remembered that what is at stake in applying the norms of a constitutional charter of rights to the ever-changing details of our public life is the balance to be struck among our fundamental political values. In a democracy the public should not be disenfranchised from this area of decision-making. Unfortunately, the political rhetoric of "guarantees," "entrenchment" and "inalienable rights" used to promote the Charter has left the Canadian public ill-prepared for life under the Charter.

NOTES

1. *Federalism for the Future* (1968), p. 8.
2. *The Constitution and the People of Canada* (1969), p. 14.
3. House of Commons Debates, March 23, 1981, p. 8519.
4. *Towards a New Canada* (1978), p. 15.
5. McWhinney. *Canada and the Constitution, 1979–1982*, (1982)], pp. 55–57.
6. The opposite criticism to McWhinney's is that the qualifications in the Canadian Charter are not specific enough. For instance the Canadian Charter does not contain provisions like Art. 4 of the International Convention or Art. 15 of the European Convention identifying rights and

freedoms which are not to be abridged even at times of public emergency. Instead s. 1 applies to all the rights and freedoms in the Charter, limits that are "reasonable" and "can be demonstrably justified in a free and democratic society."

7. The Hon. Jean Chrétien, House of Commons Debates, Oct. 6, 1980, p. 3286.
8. Ibid.
9. Bill 62 was introduced in the Quebec National Assembly on May 5th, 1982, just 19 days after the Charter came into force and was assented to on June 23rd, 1982. It is arguable that this blanket use of s. 33 without a separate legislative Act on each exempted piece of legislation is unconstitutional. The 5-year limitation on use of the override power suggests that it was intended the power be used only through deliberate and responsible decision-making by the legislature.
10. House of Commons Debates, Oct. 15, 1980, p. 3704.
11. Except for national language rights, all other sections of the Charter can be amended by the general procedure provided for in the Constitution Act, 1982. This procedure requires resolutions of the House of Commons and Senate (or the House of Commons alone if after 180 days the Senate has not approved a resolution) and of the legislative assemblies of at least two-thirds of the provinces that have at least 50% of the population of all the provinces. A dissenting province can opt out of an amendment affecting the rights of its legislature or government. Amendments affecting the right to use English and French require the support of the House of Commons and the legislatures of all the provinces, unless the amendment relates to one or more but not all the provinces in which case only the support of the provinces affected is required.
12. Edward Greenspan as quoted in We Feel Betrayed on Charter, National, Feb. 1982, p. 26.
13. S. 32(1) states that the Charter applies to the legislatures and governments at the federal, provincial and territorial levels so that one would expect court cases to be initiated by private parties challenging legislation or government action. However, under the reference case procedure it is possible for federal or provincial governments to request a judicial opinion on whether enacted or proposed legislation violates the Charter. Also governments can assist the initiation of court challenges under the Charter by financing interest groups and by intervening in support of interest groups as the federal government has done in the challenge launched by English parents against Quebec's Bill 101.
14. Report of Royal Commission on Newspapers (1981).
15. Innis, The Bias of Communication (1951). See especially his essay in this volume on Technology and Public Opinion in the United States.
16. Minutes of Proceedings and Evidence of the Special Committee of the Senate and of the House of Commons on the Constitution, Issue No. 48, Jan. 29th 1981, p. 110.

17. Theberge. *The Judiciary in a Democratic Society* (1979). p. 129.

FURTHER READINGS

Beckton, C.F., and A.W. MacKay, eds. *The Courts and the Charter.* Toronto: University of Toronto Press, 1985.

Cheffins, R.A. and P.A. Johnson. *The Revised Canadian Constitution: Politics as Law,* Chapter 10. Toronto: McGraw-Hill Ryerson, 1986.

Morton, F.L., and L.A. Pal. "The Impact of the Charter of Rights on Public Administration." *Canadian Public Administration* 28, 2 (Summer 1985): 221–243.

Russell, P.H. "The Effect of a Charter of Rights on the Policy-making Role of Canadian Courts." *Canadian Public Administration* 25, 1 (Spring 1982): 1–33.

——— "The Supreme Court in the Eighties—Wrestling with the Charter." In P.W. Fox and G. White, eds. *Politics: Canada.* 6th ed., 151–169. Toronto: McGraw-Hill Ryerson, 1987.

Smiley, D.V. *The Canadian Charter of Rights and Freedoms.* Toronto: Ontario Economic Council, 1981.

4

The Two Themes of Canadian Federalism

Donald V. Smiley

Canadian federal experience has centred around two major themes. The first relates to cultural dualism, the desire and ability of French- and English-speaking Canadians to survive as such and to use the governmental institutions which they respectively dominate in order to ensure this outcome. The second involves public action to meet the material expectations of individuals and groups living within an economy where burdens and benefits have been determined largely by the economic policies of successive federal administrations. Those who have concerned themselves with Canadian federalism have usually believed, explicitly or implicitly, that *either* the cultural *or* the economic problem was the major challenge which the federal system faced. Thus there are two versions of what our constitutional arrangements are all about, and these are most strikingly illustrated by the divergent perspectives of the Rowell-Sirois[1] and Tremblay Commission.[2] The former was almost exclusively concerned with the reallocation of revenues, revenue sources, and functional responsibilities between the two levels of government and did not deal in any explicit way with the impact of existing or proposed arrangements on the survival of the two cultures.[3] To the Tremblay Commission the great theme of our constitutional history since Confederation is the attempt of English-speaking Canada to subvert the original federal compact and the resistance of these attempts by French Canadians; its Report does deal in great detail with economic issues but its basic argument is that the essential and permanent value of Canadian federalism is to make possible the survival of the two cultural groups. This essay is an attempt to view Canadian federalism as both an economic and a cultural device and to analyse the past and present interrelationships of the two sets of factors.

The analysis is based upon two major assumptions:

First, federal arrangements, like other human institutions, must if they are to survive respond effectively to the demands made upon them. The political scientist has only the crudest of analytical tools to determine what the demands made upon a particular political system are, and how responsive it is to these influences. However, serious failures of a federation to meet the expectations

Abridged from Donald V. Smiley, "The Two Themes of Canadian Federalism," *Canadian Journal of Economics and Political Science* 31, No. 1 (February 1965), 80-97. Reprinted by permission of the author and The Canadian Political Science Association.

of particular groups within it may be revealed by such developments as a strong tendency toward political separation in one or more regions, the inability of any of the national political parties to comprehend the interests and aspirations of all the regions, and powerful pressures toward economic autarchy by some or all of the state or provincial governments. Other failures may be brought to the attention of the observer when one or more of the major political parties changes its policies as to the appropriate division of privileges and responsibilities between the two levels of government and when the electorate appears to tolerate these changes in direction. The long-run test of the success of a federal system is its ability to generate a continuing consensus throughout the nation that this form of government should continue; the resources of adaptability are being strained when influential groups come to attribute the deprivations they feel strongly about to the federal arrangements themselves.

Second, the adjustments of a federal system to changing demands made upon it are effected through redistributions of legislative authority, revenue sources, public revenues, and functional responsibilities between the two levels of government. Again, the survival of a federal system depends on its resources of flexibility. Thus it seems irrelevant to judge the appropriateness of current developments in a federation by reference to one's understanding of the events at the time the union was founded. In Canada, both English- and French-speaking scholars have from time to time pleaded that we go back to 1867. One version, influential in English Canada since the 1930s, asserts that the Judicial Committee of the Privy Council after 1896 distorted the clear intentions of the Fathers by restricting both the federal residual power and federal jurisdiction over trade and commerce and by extending the classes of subjects to which exclusive provincial jurisdiction over property and civil rights should apply.[4] The French-Canadian case has been that Lower Canada insisted at Confederation on a federal system as against the expressed preference of Upper Canadian and some of the Maritime leaders for legislative union, and that future developments must be judged in the light of their conformity or otherwise to the "federative compact."[5] Both arguments have been impressively buttressed by historical documentation; neither comes to grips with the more fundamental problem of who among the Canadian people find their interests and aspirations advanced, or frustrated, by current federal arrangements.

CULTURAL AND ECONOMIC ASPECTS OF THE CONFEDERATION SETTLEMENT UNTIL 1920

Although arguments from the "intentions of the Fathers" seem to me irrelevant to the solution of the problems of Canadian federalism, an understanding of those problems requires some interpretation of the kind of settlement evolved by British North American political leaders between 1864 and 1866 and given legal ratification with few substantive changes by the Parliament of the United

Kingdom. As the Confederation Debates make clear, the division of legislative powers between Parliament and the provincial legislative assemblies was not deemed as important to the Fathers as it has since become. However, the crucial significance of the actual division in later periods makes necessary some explanation of the rationale behind sections 91, 92, 93 and 95 of the British North America Act.

As I understand it, the Fathers of Confederation believed they had agreed upon a division of legislative authority between the Dominion and the provinces that was compatible with the triple objectives of effective military defence, the integrated economic development of British North America, and harmony between French- and English-speaking citizens. Apart from the physical defence of the colonies, the overriding aim of the Fathers, and more particularly those from the United Canadas, was to lay the groundwork for an integrated economic unit in the northern half of the continent, and the Dominion was given the legislative powers and revenue sources deemed necessary to ensure the success of this venture. Within a physical environment where it was expedient to qualify the prevailing ideology of *laissez-faire* by widespread public involvement in economic development, the main tasks of government as they were regarded in the 1860s were thus conferred on the federal authorities. But, as several of the Fathers in the Confederation Debates asserted, it was anticipated that in respect to such matters French- and English-speaking citizens would not be brought into conflict. . . . As Professor Donal Creighton has said of the Canadian leaders most influential in bringing about the Confederation settlement:

> . . . the political deadlock into which Canada had drifted during the fifties and sixties convinced the Conservatives that a strongly centralized federalism might even be preferable to a distracted unitary state. Federal union would permit the separation of these two categories of interest, these two sets of values, which had been brought into unnecessary and paralyzing conflict ever since the days of the British conquest. Local and cultural matters could be confided to the provincial governments; but the great affairs which from the first had been associated with the St. Lawrence, the projects of territorial expansion and material development, would be entrusted to the national government.[6]

The Tremblay Commission came to somewhat the same conclusion:

> . . . The powers [the Fathers of Confederation] entrusted to the federal government, in general, bore on subjects which did not divide the two [cultural] groups and in which they had a common interest. . . .
> . . . The central government was entrusted with the main general, military, administrative and technical services but there was reserved to the provinces all— save the few exceptions mentioned above—that concerned social, civil, family, school and municipal organization; everything which touched the human side most nearly and which most influenced the Canadian citizen's manner of living.[7]

The Canadian designers of the Confederation settlement thus believed that they had devised a set of arrangements through which the aggressive economic development of the British North American economy would be compatible with the cessation of the cultural strife which had pervaded the politics of the United Canadas, in spite of the quasi-federal conventions which had been evolved over the preceding quarter-century.[8] The broad solution was to entrust the Dominion with the authority believed necessary to effective military defence and economic development, and in respect to which no cultural cleavages were anticipated, while the provinces would have jurisdiction over those classes of subjects where legislation would have a direct cultural incidence, which, in the perspectives of a century ago, involved a relatively limited range of matters. This, so far as Canada was concerned, was the essence of the Confederation settlement; the circumstances under which Nova Scotia and New Brunswick and later the other provinces entered Confederation involved for the most part material considerations unrelated to cultural dualism.

(There was a minority created by the establishment of the new federation—the English-speaking Canadians of the new province of Quebec. This minority, or at least its leaders, had a great deal to gain in a material sense from the new arrangements. However, the Confederation Debates make clear that English-speaking Quebeckers had understandable anxieties that under the projected federal system their cultural privileges would exist only by the grace of the French-speaking majority in the province. The British North America Act as enacted contained several provisions wholly or partly relevant to this minority[9] and provided several procedures by which the power of a Dominion-wide English-speaking majority might be brought into play in its defence. For whatever reasons, such federal interventions have not proved necessary to sustain these privileges.)

Up until about the First World War the federal government confined its activities for the most part to economic development, defence, and external relations, as was contemplated at the time of Confederation. There had been, of course, several clashes in federal politics involving the two cultural groups. The hanging of Riel in 1885 precipitated one of the most serious of these. The federal authorities were put under pressure to come to the aid of French-language and Catholic schools in New Brunswick in the 1870s, in Manitoba in the 1890s, the Northwest Territories a decade later, and in Ontario in 1915–17. Cultural cleavages arose over Canadian participation in the Boer War, the establishment of a navy, and military conscription in the First World War. It is significant, however, that all of the serious clashes between French- and English-speaking Canadians at the federal level in the period prior to 1920 involved either the country's external orientation or the privileges of French-Canadian minorities outside Quebec. In these kinds of circumstances it was demonstrated conclusively that the English-speaking majority could get its way if it was determined to do so; the expectations of Lower Canadian statesmen at Confederation that the workings of the federal Parliament itself, particularly the Senate, would safeguard the interests of French Canada were belied.[10]

However, in the pre-1920 period the preoccupation of the federal government with policies of national economic integration and development and the relatively restricted expectations of the Canadian people in respect to what any level of government might appropriately do resulted in a kind of equilibrium in the federal system not unlike that contemplated at the time of Confederation.

THE EXTENSION OF FEDERAL ACTIVITIES

The establishment of federal grants-in-aid of highways, provincial employment offices, and vocational training in 1919 presaged a kind of development in Canadian federalism which challenged one of the understandings of the Confederation settlement in a most fundamental way. In the broadest of terms, it can be said that successive federal policies have reflected a consensus in English-speaking Canada that Ottawa has the moral obligation to involve itself in any matter deemed to be of great importance and to require public action, including matters within the legislative jurisdiction of the provinces. Apart from general elementary and secondary education there is now federal intervention in virtually every major provincial function—health, welfare, vocational training, hospitalization, road construction, natural resource development, and so on. Federal funds are available for a great variety of cultural activities and for amateur athletics. The universities have become increasingly dependent on federal assistance in the form of *per capita* grants, and for specific research activities and capital expansion. Increasingly, federal initiatives in programs of winter works, housing, urban redevelopment, welfare, hospitalization, and now the Municipal Development Fund have involved the federal authorities with local governments. There is no reason to think that this trend is coming to an end and one may expect in the foreseeable future new forms of federal assistance to provincial and local governments and to private individuals and groups—*perhaps* assistance for provincial prepaid medical care plans, public libraries, university scholarships, specialized welfare services, and so on. Obviously too, the financial burdens assumed by Ottawa for matters within provincial legislative jurisdiction induce the federal authorities to be less willing than they would otherwise be to withdraw wholly or partly from certain tax fields to the benefit of the provinces; there is some truth along with much exaggeration in the comments of the Tremblay Commission in relation to this matter:

> . . . the federal government, instead of leaving the field clear to the provinces in the field of direct taxation so that they can themselves collect the sums required for the discharge of their constitutional functions, is interesting itself in all these questions which are none the less of exclusively provincial concern, until, finally, it has its *interest* recognized as a *right* to busy itself with these questions.
> Then it invokes the heavy expenditures which it makes in order to maintain and even augment its monopoly in the collection of major taxes. . . .[11]

It is striking that federal involvement in a very great range of matters within the legislative jurisdiction of the provinces has not been accompanied by large-scale transfers of legislative power to Parliament either by constitutional amendment or changing patterns of judicial review. The amendments of 1940 and 1951 respectively gave Parliament the power to legislate exclusively in respect to unemployment insurance and concurrently with the provinces in relation to old age pensions. However, the second amendment was sought by the federal government only because they had made a prior decision to finance the proposed scheme of old age pensions partly from the proceeds of a special income tax levy made for that purpose; if, as in the case of family allowances, the program had been financed wholly from general revenues, no such amendment would have been necessary and so this measure does not constitute a significant shift in legislative power. Neither has judicial review opened the way to extensions of federal activity. In only two cases have the courts ruled on the constitutional validity of the exercise of the federal spending power on objects outside the legislative jurisdiction of Parliament[12] and it is impossible to predict what limits, if any, the judiciary might place on the use of this device in the future. . . . In a technical sense then, the trend towards federal spending on an increasingly wide range of matters within the legislative jurisdiction of the provinces has not been accompanied by formal constitutional changes. However, from a broader viewpoint we have evolved into a situation where action of the provincial and federal executives has in respect to many important matters superseded formal constitutional arrangements in delineating the respective roles of the two levels of government.

The exercise of the federal spending power has resulted in a situation in which the basic understanding of the Confederation settlement that, with few exceptions, the federal authorities would not involve themselves in matters with a direct cultural incidence, has been undermined. The pressures toward such federal involvement have been almost completely from English-speaking Canada and, so far as I can discover, no influential person or group outside Quebec has challenged the appropriateness of federal action in this direction. Pressures towards new federal initiatives are quite indiscriminate and English-speaking Canadians have come to look to Ottawa for leadership and money in furthering a great variety of what are regarded as worthy national purposes. In pressing for federal participation in matters within the legislative jurisdiction of the provinces Anglo-Canadians have ordinarily not felt it necessary to demonstrate the administrative or other disabilities of exclusively provincial action or the constitutional appropriateness of their proposals; the case usually goes no further than a demonstration that the subject under discussion is of great importance and *ipso facto* Ottawa should do something about it. Within the context of English-speaking Canada, this pragmatic attitude about the appropriate roles of the federal and provincial governments has added a valuable element of flexibility to the Canadian federal system. Understandably, however, the kind of development I have outlined has given rise to anxieties in Quebec.

Although the French-Canadian majority in Quebec has always resisted federal involvements in matters within the legislative jurisdiction of the provinces, successive provincial administrations have not in all cases been willing to incur the financial penalties consequent on failure to participate in federal programs. The province began to collaborate in the federal-provincial old-age pension program only in 1936, nine years after it began. The Godbout Government in 1940 agreed to a proposed amendment to the British North America Act transferring jurisdiction over unemployment insurance to Parliament, although perhaps this consent can be explained as the payment of a political debt to Prime Minister King and his federal colleagues who had intervened aggressively to help defeat the Union Nationale in the recent provincial election. In the post-war years the Duplessis administration participated in shared-cost programs related to agriculture, welfare, public health and, up to 1957, vocational training; but refused to collaborate in joint arrangements for civil defence, hospitalization, and the Trans-Canada Highway. The Union Nationale put pressure on Quebec universities to refuse federal *per capita* grants after 1952 but agreed to a proposed amendment to the British North America Act giving Parliament concurrent jurisdiction in respect to old-age pensions. Shortly after coming to power in 1960 Premier Lesage announced that it would be the policy of his administration "to take the necessary steps to accept, on a temporary basis and without prejudice to its full sovereignty, all the conditional grants it is not now receiving which are made to the other provinces by the Federal Government";[13] the Lesage Government, however, refused to co-operate with the federal Royal Commission on Health appointed in 1961.

A resurgent Quebec government pursuing aggressive policies of cultural and economic development can be expected to resist federal encroachments on matters within the legislative jurisdiction of the provinces. Any success that the Quebec administration may have in influencing the federal authorities to make significant withdrawals from the direct tax fields can only have the long-run effect of making Ottawa less willing to extend its commitments to provincial and local functions. Further, the determination and skill of the Quebec government in using its powers as positive instruments for the expansion and development of French-Canadian culture, in contrast with the conservative policies of previous administrations in that province, seem to make likely a whole range of conflicts about matters which were not in dispute when the objectives of Quebec were less sharply defined. And yet there is no evidence that English-speaking Canada will cease to look to Ottawa for leadership and financial assistance in regard to matters deemed to be of importance, including those within provincial legislative jurisdiction.

Since about 1920 then the understanding of the Confederation entente has been altered in the most basic way. By the unilateral action of English-speaking Canada the broad distinction evolved in 1864–66 between activities relating to economic integration, defence, and external policies on the one hand

and those with a cultural impact on the other has been blurred by federal involvement in a great many matters within provincial jurisdiction. So far as Quebec is concerned, the alternative to federal measures which are felt to be a direct challenge to the cultural integrity of French Canada has been a heavy financial price to government and individual citizens.

ONE NATION OR TWO?

The basic problem of our contemporary federal system is that English-speaking Canada is determined to effect its purposes through the federal government in such a way as to challenge what most French Canadians believe to be the necessary conditions of the expansion and survival of their culture. "Canadians and Canadiens" do not agree on the community to which they give their primary allegiance—Canada or French Canada—and this difference in allegiances makes impossible any agreement on the appropriate distribution of powers and privileges between federal and provincial governments. . . .

There is then a growing sense of community in English-speaking Canada, and English Canadians have in the main agreed that the purposes of this community should be advanced through the federal government. These purposes can be classified under three headings: (1) egalitarianism—the sentiment that Canadians in all provinces and regions are entitled to certain minimum standards in regard to material goods, including public services; (2) the preservation of the cultural integrity of Canada; (3) the maintenance of civil rights. These purposes are above and beyond those relating to national economic integration and development pursued through federal action from the Confederation settlement onward.

1. Egalitarianism

The existence of a modern state means much more than that the writs of one government run within its territorial limits. National associations are established for dealing with government and for other purposes, political parties almost perforce organize themselves on national lines, national systems of transportation and communication facilitate the movement of persons, goods, and information within national boundaries and inhibit to a greater or lesser extent their movement across these boundaries, and so on.[14] So far as public amenities are concerned, professional groups involved with particular public services exercise a continuing egalitarian influence by their efforts to convince the politicians and the populace that the standards of performance developed within these groups are appropriate guides to public policy. Out of these interactions develop nationalistic sentiments which lead individuals and groups in less favoured areas to compare the opportunities available to them with those found in the more prosperous jurisdictions and, if nationalism is more than a rallying cry for the underprivileged, the national government and those of the wealthier states or provinces will be disposed to make some concessions to these demands. In a federal state perhaps the best single evidence of nationalism is the disposition of influential individuals and groups to regard regional inequalities in public services as instances of unwarranted discrimination rather than of acceptable exercise of provincial, state, or local discretion. . . . Ever since Confederation the federal government has been committed to unconditional subventions to the provinces based on some standard of provincial fiscal need. However, it is only in the last decade that subsidies have been paid according to what in Harvey Perry's words is "something like a scientific formula, even though a partial one."[15] Attempts of the federal government to meet the needs of the less prosperous provinces in the tax agreements concluded in 1942, 1947, and 1952 were impeded by Ottawa's strong desire to obtain exclusive access to the income tax and succession duty fields and the consequent necessity to make concessions to the wealthier provinces. However, for whatever reason, the federal authorities from the mid–1950s onward became less convinced of the necessity of their exclusive occupation of these tax fields as a precondition of effective fiscal policies. The settlement that prevailed between 1957 and 1962 was therefore a landmark in the movement towards egalitarianism by its provision that substantial tax equalization and revenue stabilization be made to the provinces whether or not they concluded tax-rental agreements with Ottawa. The arrangements which came into effect in 1962 continued this trend and it is reasonable to expect that future federal policies will result in unconditional subsidies according to even more explicit and sophisticated criteria of fiscal need than those now used, unless the wealthier provinces are successful in confining the federal government to a much more restricted part of the direct tax field than it now occupies.

Egalitarian ends have also been advanced through federal grants-in-aid of particular provincial and local services. There has been significant progress in eliminating local and provincial residence requirements as conditions of access to public assistance and hospitalization. Standards of performance have been raised by federal action both by making adherence to these standards a condition of the payment of federal funds and by less direct methods, including the provision of grants for training purposes. By encouraging some jurisdictions to make available amenities they would otherwise choose not to provide, federal participation has encouraged a more uniform range of public services throughout the nation than would have existed without such action. The provision by Ottawa of staff, research, and advisory services related to particular services has also had an egalitarian effect as the provinces with low per capita incomes also have populations too small to support such specialized facilities. There are, however, certain features of federal grants-in-aid which work in an anti-egalitarian direction. To induce the wealthier provinces to participate, the scales of federal contributions and the comprehensiveness and rigor of federal controls over provincial performance are often determined by the interests of these provinces. Further, in some provinces, particularly the less prosperous ones, expansion in services aided by federal funds has taken place at the expense of other provincial and local functions for which no money from Ottawa is available. With all their limitations as egalitarian devices, however, grants-in-aid have played a significant role in equalizing the range and quality of public amenities throughout the nation.

From time to time also the federal government has evolved complexes of measures to meet the special needs of particular regions. The events of the 1930s in the Prairie provinces induced the federal authorities to undertake a series of measures specifically designed to assist prairie agriculture, most importantly those providing for the Prairie Farm Rehabilitation Administration and the Canadian Wheat Board. Similarly, the inauguration of the Maritime Marshland Redevelopment Administration in 1948, the Atlantic Provinces Adjustment Grants in 1958–59 and the Atlantic Provinces Development Board in 1963 provided landmarks in federal recognition of the peculiar problems of the Atlantic Region. Also the federal government has used the railroad freight-rate structure to benefit the Atlantic and Western provinces through such policies as the Crow's Nest differential, the "bridge" subsidy, assistance on feed grain shipped from the prairies to Eastern Canada and British Columbia, and prescribed rate reductions available to shippers in the Atlantic provinces.

2. The Survival and Expansion of Canadian Culture

It is perhaps in the findings of the three federal royal commissions—the Aird,[16] Massey,[17] and Fowler[18] Reports of 1929, 1951, and 1957, respectively—that the concept of an autonomous Canadian community advancing its purposes partly through the instrumentality of the federal government is made most explicit. The Massey Commission asserted: "If the federal government is to renounce its right to associate itself with other social groups, public and private, in the education of Canadian citizens, it denies its moral and intellectual purpose, the complete conception of the common good is lost and Canada, as such, becomes a materialistic society.[19] In a more explicit form the Report of the Royal Commission on Broadcasting of 1957 viewed "the preservation of a separate and distinct cultural identity in Canada" as an inherent part of the national policy, blurring over the dichotomy between culture and economic development which, as I have argued, was the basis of the Confederation settlement:

> This is not a new problem for Canada. It has become familiar through many examples over the ninety years of our national history. The very creation of the Canadian confederation and the territorial expansion of the original union across the continent were, to some extent at least, responses to pressures from the United States. The building of the first Canadian transcontinental railway was only the

first of many devices to pull together into a nation the vast expanse of Canadian territory. In different ways but with the same purpose we created a national financial structure through the chartered banking system and we sought to build up industry and trade through a protective tariff. At a later date we developed a national air-transportation system. There are many other examples of steps taken to make Canada a nation despite the forces of geography and the powerful attraction and influence of the United States. The natural flow of trade, travel and ideas runs north and south. We have tried to make some part, not all, of the flow run east and west. We have only done so at an added cost, borne nationally. There is no doubt that we could have had cheaper railway transportation, cheaper air service and cheaper consumer goods if we had simply tied ourselves into the American transportation and economic system. It is equally clear that we could have cheaper radio and television service if Canadian stations became outlets of American networks. However, if the less costly method is always chosen, is it possible to have a Canadian nation at all? The Canadian answer, irrespective of party or race, has been uniformly the same for nearly a century. We are prepared, by measures of assistance, financial aid and a conscious stimulation, to compensate for our disabilities of geography, sparse population and vast distances, and we have accepted this as a legitimate role of government in Canada.[20]

3. The Protection of Civil Rights

A third purpose which English-speaking Canada seems disposed to advance is that of the protection of the traditional Anglo-Saxon civil rights of freedom of speech, association, and worship. The moral basis of these claims was perhaps most explicitly set forth in several of Mr. Justice Rand's judgments when he was a member of the Supreme Court of Canada. The claim is that the inherent rights of Canadian citizenship include certain judicially enforceable restrictions on provincial legislative power; a dictum by Mr. Justice Abbott in the Switzman case suggests that similar prohibitions on Parliament are implied by this principle.[21] There appears to be in English-speaking Canada at least a very high degree of support for a constitutional amendment which would place traditional civil liberties beyond the reach of any level of government as an expression of the fundamental moral purposes of the Canadian community. The Duplessis administration had little regard for the protection of traditional liberties and its policies in these matters brought the aspirations of English- and French-speaking Canada into conflict; the incumbent Quebec Government may in the future be more disposed to co-operate in measures for the protection of these rights.

Although the major influences towards the use of federal institutions to achieve broad national purposes have received their main impetus from English-speaking Canadians, it would be inaccurate to say either that no French Canadians participated willingly in these purposes or that these initiatives were directed in any conscious way against the minority culture; at worst they were a reflection of what André Laurendeau has called "un impérialisme inconscient."

At different times and places Canadians of both languages have believed in a bi-cultural nation seeking its ends through the federal government. Furthermore, the extension of federal involvement has not resulted in the displacement of the provinces and institutions within provincial legislative jurisdiction from the fields of activity in which Ottawa has come to play a part; there has been an utterly pragmatic attitude about the proper roles of the two levels of government in the achievement of purposes deemed worthy. However, it is understandable that the majority in Quebec should regard these extensions of federal involvement as a threat posed from English Canada, particularly in a period where the Quebec Government itself has assumed a more positive role in the development of French-Canadian culture.

IS A NEW EQUILIBRIUM IN THE MAKING?

The analysis up to this point can be recapitulated briefly. The Confederation settlement made a rough distinction between government activities with a cultural incidence and those which had no particular relevance to the relations between English-and French-speaking Canadians. A kind of equilibrium along these lines prevailed between 1867 and 1920, with the federal government confining its activities for the most part to matters related to national economic integration, defence, and external affairs. However, from the 1920s onward English-speaking Canadians became increasingly disposed to effect what they regarded as worthy national purposes through the federal government, and as some of these purposes were very costly their implementation contributed to a higher degree of fiscal centralization than would have otherwise prevailed. The reaction of the Quebec majority to these developments has been understandably defensive. Is a new federal equilibrium possible within which the demands of the two major cultural group can be met?

The current situation has elements which may permit a reconciliation of the interests and aspirations of English- and French-speaking Canadians within the framework of existing federal institutions. A solution can be conceived whose essential element would be a different sharing of legislative powers, revenue sources, and functional responsibilities between Quebec and Ottawa than between the federal government and the other provinces; concomitant arrangements would be necessary to ensure that the government and people of Quebec would not suffer significant financial disabilities because of this "contracting out." Perhaps, too, one might contemplate a complex of financial and administrative relationships between such explicitly cultural federal agencies as the Canada Council, the National Film Board, the Canadian Broadcasting Corporation, and the National Library on the one hand and the organs of the Quebec government charged with cultural development on the other, relationships which would have no counterpart in the case of the other provinces. The French-language network of the CBC may provide a model for the internal organization of other federal agencies where the interests and attitudes of Quebec differ significantly from those of the rest of Canada.[22] The delegation section of the BNA Act proposed by the federal government in 1961 would, if enacted, provide new possibilities by which some or all of the English-speaking provinces might choose to confer certain of their legislative powers on Parliament while Quebec would retain these powers. In general then, a solution would seem possible if all the governments concerned were to recognize that in respect to many significant matters Quebec is not a province "comme les autres," and that this particularity should not impose significant financial disabilities on the people of Quebec or their provincial government.

There is some scattered evidence that Canadian federalism might develop along these lines. The federal tax abatement provisions evolved during the 1950s demonstrated that the national government could be influenced to make some concessions to individuals and provinces not entering the tax-rental agreements. On the refusal of the Quebec universities, under pressure from the Union Nationale, to accept federal *per capita* grants the federal government in 1957 decided that these moneys would be accumulated to the credit of the institutions rather than forfeited. The funds were released shortly after Duplessis' death; the Fleming-Sauvé agreement concluded between Ottawa and Quebec in 1960 provided for an extra one per cent corporate income tax abatement for Quebec in lieu of the acceptance of the *per capita* payments to the universities. The federal program of the New Democratic Party adopted at its founding convention in 1961 asserted that the best method of redistributing wealth among provinces was by federal unconditional subventions and these should eventually replace unconditional grants; it was further asserted that "in areas affecting education, language and similar rights now in the British North America Act, where a province does not participate in a grant program it will not forego its right to equivalent funds." The Liberal national program of 1962 stated that individual provinces should be allowed to withdraw without financial loss from established shared-cost programs involving regular expenditures, and that in such circumstances Ottawa should make compensation by lowering its direct taxes and increasing unconditional subventions. Such developments, which have particular relevance to Quebec, show the ability of Canadian federalism to respond to the demands of cultural dualism.

An English Canadian might expect that the kind of solution outlined above would put to rest the anxieties generated in Quebec by federal interventions in matters within the legislative jurisdiction of the provinces. It is implicit in such a solution that the federal government will retain a preferred if not dominant position in respect to more lucrative fields of direct taxation, that effective federal action can be taken to promote economic stability and growth and that the provinces, including Quebec, will remain to a significant extent dependent on federal unconditional subventions. The rationale for such arrangements might well be the basic understanding of the Confederation settlement that economic matters and those with a cultural incidence are separable, and that the integrity of the majority culture in Quebec is thus not directly challenged by federal attempts to integrate and develop the national economy, or to equalize the range and quality of public services available to residents of other provincial jurisdictions across Canada.

Recent developments in social thought and public policy in Quebec make it unlikely that this kind of solution will be acceptable to the present leadership of that province. Until recently the predominant current of French-Canadian nationalism was profoundly unconcerned with economic affairs. . . . Furthermore, successive provincial administrations were notoriously generous in conferring privileges on English-speaking capital, and undisposed to use the powers at their disposal to impede the economic domination of the French-Canadian people. In these circumstances there was little in the Quebec position to offer an effective challenge to the federal government in its historical task of integrating and developing the national economy.

The prevailing directions of thought and policy in Quebec now assert the necessity of a very large area of provincial autonomy in fiscal and economic matters as a precondition of the cultural welfare of French Canada. This point of view was presented most explicitly by the Honourable René Lévesque, Quebec Minister of National Resources, in an interview printed in *Le Devoir* of July 5, 1963. To Lévesque the economic problem was of the highest importance and in regard to this problem,

> Il faut le résoudre par tous ls moyens légitimes et dans notre cas, plus que chez beaucoup d'autres nations, le premier de ces moyens, c'est notre Etat du Québec. Faire le point de nos ressources et de nos besoins, orienter et planifier le developpement économique, amenager le territoire, assurer la mise en valeur des riches naturelles pour la nation, au bénéfice de la nation, recupérer nos droits dans le domaine de la fiscalité, etc., autant de tâches souverainement importantes, qui incombent à l'Etat.

To carry out these responsibilities, "L'Etat du Québec . . . a besoin de tous les pouvoirs, de tous les instruments, qu'un régime fédératif peut lui accorder sans cesser d'exister." In such a system the needs of the provinces are primary, those of the federal government residual; Lévesque is logical enough to apply this specifically to the function of military defence. Thus the economic autonomy of Quebec is of the utmost significance.

> Il est infiniment plus important de faire un Québec progressif, libre et fort que d'engager le plus clair de nos énergies dans l'aventure du biculturalisme. D'ailleurs, le rayonnement de la culture française au Canada, le respect de la langue française sont conditionnés d'abord par la vigeur, par l'importance économique et politiques du Québec. C'est la ce qui doit être et rester de loin notre premier souci, notre préoccupation dominante et incessante.

The forces in the Quebec Government represented by Mr. Lévesque are thus challenging in the most explicit way the basic understanding of the Confederation settlement that the federal government should have at its disposal the necessary powers to integrate and develop the national economy. This settlement assumes that one or other of the levels of government will be relatively passive in particular matters of economic direction, and sharp conflicts have arisen when particular provinces have directly challenged central aspects of national economic policies, from the disputes involving the chartering of railway companies by Manitoba in the 1890s, to the Alberta monetary experiments of the Great Depression, to the hydro-electric policies of British Columbia during the Diefenbaker administration. Quebec has never been involved in a dispute of this kind and the expectations of the Fathers of Confederation that English-speaking majorities and French-speaking minorities would not be mobilized in respect to economic matters has up to this decade proved to be reasonable. . . .

In brief, the new directions of social thought and public policy in Quebec provide a situation in which regional-economic and cultural cleavages combine to present the Canadian federal system with a kind of challenge it has not heretofore faced. It would be irresponsible to predict whether the system has the flexibility needed to evolve a new equilibrium to satisfy these conflicting demands within the framework of our traditional federal institutions.

My analysis as it applies to the contemporary Canadian situation may be summarized briefly:

1. A viable federal system must conform to the fundamental demands of both English- and French-speaking Canadians.

2. The Canadian federal system as it has evolved since about 1920, particularly in the period after the Second World War, has seen the English-speaking Canadian community advance its purposes through agencies of the federal government in such a way as profoundly to disturb the majority in Quebec. These purposes, including egalitarianism and cultural development, have included far more than the economic integration, contemplated by the Confederation settlement, which was in fact the main concern of successive federal governments until the First World War.

3. The only distribution of powers and privileges between the two levels of government which will satisfy the current demands of English- and French-speaking Canadians is one which provides for a very different sharing of these powers and privileges between Quebec and Ottawa than that which prevails between the federal administration and other provinces, with concomitant arrangements to ensure that Quebec does not suffer financially from her choices in these matters. There is some recent evidence that influential groups in English-speaking Canada would find a solution along these broad lines acceptable.

4. Public policies and social doctrines which now appear to be dominant in Quebec offer a new challenge to Canadian federalism in their assumption that a very wide measure of provincial autonomy in matters of fiscal policy and economic control are necessary preconditions of the survival and expansion of French-Canadian culture. Like English Canadians in the period after 1920,

French Canadians now appear to believe that the basic understandings of the Confederation settlement no longer conform to their basic needs.

NOTES

1. *Report of the Royal Commission on Dominion-Provincial Relations* (Ottawa, 1940).
2. *Report of the Royal Commission of Inquiry on Constitutional Problems* (Quebec, 1956).
3. For an analysis of the general perspectives of this document, see the introductory essay to *The Rowell-Sirois Report*, I, abridged by Donald V. Smiley (Toronto, 1963).
4. See *Report on the B.N.A. Act*, Senate of Canada (Ottawa, 1939).
5. *Tremblay Report*, II, sec. 2.
6. "Conservatism and National Unity," in R. Flenley, ed., *Essays in Canadian History* (Toronto, 1939), 167.
7. Vol. I, 37–8.
8. Among these were the *de facto* recognition of French as an official language, legislation which applied to only one of the sections, the bifurcation of several of the ministries, the double-majority rule, and the leadership of governments by a representative of each section.
9. English was to have equal status with French in the Legislature and courts of Quebec, Senators from Quebec were to be chosen by districts, the rights of denominational schools were secured, divorce was to be a matter of exclusive federal jurisdiction, etc.
10. Unlike most other federations the provinces have no explicit place in the workings of the federal government which has developed as a majoritarian instrument.
11. Vol. II, 222–3.
12. . . . The general position has been asserted by Professor Bora Laskin ". . . the rejection of an attack on the constitutionality of the *Family Allowances Act* lends emphasis to the view that the Courts have no concern with the disbursement of public funds which have been validly raised." *Canadian Constitutional Law* (2nd ed., Toronto, 1960), 655.
13. *Proceedings of the Dominion-Provincial Conference*, 1960 (Ottawa, 1961), 130.
14. There is a common argument that federalism is being attenuated in Canada because of the weakening of the emotional attachment of people to particular localities, economic integration on national lines, the development of transportation and communication facilities, and like factors. However, even a cursory observation indicates that the division of public responsibilities sustains, and is sustained by, a large number of vital associations at the provincial level—political parties, teachers' and trustees' organizations, labour federations, conservation groups, etc.

15. "The Historical Background and Development of Federal-Provincial Relations," *Canadian Public Administration*, March 1962, 26
16. *Report of the Royal Commission on Radio Broadcasting* (Ottawa, 1929).
17. *Report of the Royal Commission on National Development in the Arts, Letters and Sciences* (Ottawa, 1951).
18. *Report of the Royal Commission on Broadcasting* (Ottawa, 1957).
19. *Report on Arts, Letters and Sciences*, 8.
20. *Report on Broadcasting*, 9.
21. *Switzman* v. *Elbling and A.-G. Que.* 7 DLR 2d. 337.
22. It is significant that French Canadians do not appear to regard federal control over broadcasting as a significant challenge to their culture.

FURTHER READINGS

Black, E.R. *Divided Loyalties: Canadian Concepts of Federalism*. Rev. ed. Toronto: Gage, 1982.

Meekison, J.P., ed. *Canadian Federalism: Myth or Reality*. 3rd ed. Toronto: Methuen, 1977.

Sabetti, F., and H.M. Waller, eds. "Crisis and Continuity in Canadian federalism." Special issue of *Publius* 14, 1 (Winter 1984).

Smiley, D.V. *The Federal Condition in Canada*. Toronto: McGraw-Hill Ryerson, 1987.

Smiley, D.V., and R.L. Watts. *Intrastate Federalism in Canada*. Toronto: University of Toronto Press, 1985.

Stevenson, G. *Unfulfilled Union: Canadian Federalism and National Unity*. Rev. ed. Toronto: Gage, 1982.

5

French Canada and Confederation:
The Quest for Equality

RAMSAY COOK

Canadian federalism owes its originality to the fact that its components are of two different kinds. The first are territorial or political, that is, states or provinces, which now number ten. The second are sociological, that is, two nations, societies or cultural communities united by history, one of which has had its roots implanted in Canadian soil for over three and a half centuries.

–Submission of the Quebec Delegation to the
Continuing Committee of Officials of the Constitutional
Conference, July 24, 1968

Several years ago the late premier of the Province of Quebec, M. Daniel Johnson, published a small book which he entitled *Egalité ou Indépendance*—Equality or Independence. Though the book was far from free of those calculated ambiguities that are the stock-in-trade of the practising politician everywhere, Premier Johnson's general message was evident enough: unless French Canadians could be guaranteed a status of equality within Confederation, they would eventually choose to establish their own sovereign state of Quebec. The message was not entirely new, though its formulation, in the context of the 1960s, was more formidable than it had ever previously been.

Equality is a status which French Canadians have demanded almost since the day that the flag of France was replaced by the flag of England over the citadel at Quebec in 1759. It is, however, only in the last decade that significant numbers of French Canadians have begun to view an independent Quebec as a viable alternative to that apparently unending quest for equality. As we shall see, the definition of that most revolutionary of terms in modern political discourse—'equality'—has changed in many ways over the long years of debate.

Premier Johnson's title, *Egalité ou Indépendance*, accurately defined the options that are open to French Canadians in contemporary North America. Neither he nor his successor, M. Jean-Jacques Bertrand, ever conclusively excluded either of these two options, preferring instead to keep every possibility available. Others have been more willing to choose. On the one hand there are those who have declared their support for what M. René Lévesque, the leader of the *Parti québécois*, has christened *Option Québec*. For M. Lévesque equality or independence are not alternatives but rather different sides of the same coin: equality is impossible without independence. Quebec must therefore become a sovereign nation recognized, juridically, as the equal of the other sovereign nations in the world. . . .

Those who oppose the Lévesque option believe that French Canadians should remain partners in the Canadian Confederation, but with their rights as French Canadians guaranteed from Newfoundland to Vancouver Island. This position is best expressed in a book entitled *Le Fédéralisme et la société canadienne-française—Federalism and the French Canadians*—written by one-time law professor, political economist, judo expert, and skin diver, M. Pierre Elliott Trudeau, who in his current incarnation is the Prime Minister of Canada. In M. Trudeau's view, the best guarantee for the French culture in North America and the most realistic hope for a status of real equality is the continued partnership of French and English Canada within a reformed federal system.

Within these two broad groups—*les indépendantistes* and *les fédéralistes*—there are some subtle and some not so subtle differences in program. But fundamentally there are only these two options. There are still, of course, some political leaders who have not made a choice, preferring to wait and see which way their followers want to lead them. But the alternatives are clear enough.

In analysing these two options there is one very important distinction which must never be obscured—though in practice some of the disputants intentionally do so. That distinction may be stated thus: Quebec and French Canada are not interchangeable terms. Quebec is a province in which about eighty per cent of all the French Canadians live. It is also a province whose population is about twenty per cent non-French Canadian. French Canada, on the other hand, is composed of all those Canadians whose mother tongue is French and who are scattered throughout Canada—though ninety-five per cent are concentrated in New Brunswick, Quebec, and Ontario. This distinction between French Canada and Quebec may seem pedantic, but it is most assuredly not. It is, indeed, the very essence of the current debate: M. Trudeau, the federalist, demands equality for French Canadians; M. Lévesque, the indépendantiste, demands equality for Quebec. M. Trudeau views Quebec as a province within Canada; M. Lévesque views Quebec as a nation moving towards separation from Canada. In an important sense the whole history of French Canada, indeed even of Canada, is summed up figuratively in the views of these two French-Canadian politicians.

The central problem of Canadian history—more fundamental than the problem of our relations with the outside world—has been the ever-repeated effort to establish a satisfactory relationship between the English-speaking majority and the French-speaking minority. Looking at this problem from the perspective of French-Canadian history, the proposition might be stated in this fashion: the history of French Canada since 1759 has been the story of the gradual, but unceasing, movement of French Canada towards a political status which would erase finally the stigma of the Conquest. That is the central event in French-Canadian history, and the one that each successive generation of French Canadians attempts to come to terms with. Conquest implies subordination and inferiority. The cure to conquest, to subordination and inferiority, is equality. But what is the meaning of equality? That is a question that has been answered in different ways in every generation. Confederation itself was offered as an answer and during most of its first century of existence it proved, except in certain crises, a satisfactory one. But satisfaction did not mean the end of controversy; rather it meant that the controversy was never, or at least rarely, serious enough to threaten the fabric of Confederation. It is only in the sixties that the controversialists were able to drown out those who spoke in the soothing tones of satisfaction. In an age when social and political established orders are being contested throughout the post-industrial world, it comes as no surprise to anyone familiar with our history that in Canada the contestation has taken place most critically within the context of the relations between French and English Canada, between the minority and the majority.

If French Canadians had been left to themselves to decide the shape of British North America in 1867, it is doubtful if there would have been a Confederation. It was not that the Union of 1841 provided them with an ideal state that they wished never to change. It was rather that the dangers of the status quo were at least familiar; a broader union of all of the British colonies, plus the promise of a vast new empire to be added in the west, carried with it dangers unknown, but suspected. Yet French Canadians then, as always, were realists. They knew that the union could not be maintained indefinitely, that it was working its way toward total deadlock. Moreover pressure for westward expansion was growing irresistible. Within the existing union, expansion could only mean a strengthening of Canada West, with the consequent increase in the demand that representation by population replace representation by section as the basis of the union. Obviously a new constitutional formulation of the relations between the French and the English in Canada was necessary, even if not altogether desirable. But French Canadians had to be sure that any new formulation would offer better guarantees of their status than what it replaced.

For French Canada, then, the key to Confederation was the federal system. To a greater or lesser degree this was also the case for the other sections of the country, because a unitary government, whatever its theoretical advantages, could not be squared with the sectional diversities of British North America in the 1860s—or at any time since. But for French Canadians federalism was especially significant, for it gave to Quebec, where the vast majority of them lived, a government of its own—a government over which the French-Canadian majority would have complete control. It was a provincial government within a rather highly centralized federal system, but it neverhteless exercised authority over those matters that were deemed essential to the preservation of the French-Canadian culture—education, religion, civil law.

It provided something more as well: an opportunity to share at the federal level of government in the development of what was potentially an enormously rich domain. And that sharing could be done, at least to some extent, in the French language. The new constitution, for the first time since the conquest, made French one of the official languages of the country, at least in federal institutions. Nothing was said about linguistic rights at the provincial level except in Quebec, which became an officially bilingual province and where the economic power of the English-speaking minority ensured that their language would be respected. It is true that some guarantees were provided for minority schools—Protestant in Quebec, Catholic in Ontario—but here the guarantees were for religious, not linguistic, minorities, a fact which probably suggests that minorities were more concerned about potential threats to religious rights than to linguistic rights. In practice there were Catholic schools in Ontario and New Brunswick where French was the language of instruction and Protestant schools in Quebec where English had that status. But no constitutional guarantees were either asked for or given for these linguistic privileges—a serious deficiency as the future was only too quickly to indicate.

In 1867, then, French Canadians accepted a dual status within the Canadian federal system: one at the level of the central government, the other at the level of the province. In this, of course, they were no different from the other colonies that came into the new union. What distinguished them was their French cultural heritage, including a history characterized by a constant struggle to maintain that heritage. Since 1867 the great debate among French Canadians has centred on the question of which of these poles of attraction—the central or the provincial government—should be given the primary role in promoting the interests of French Canada. That debate, of course, remains unresolved today, but out of it one can discern four general schools of thought that have emerged over the past one hundred years in response to changing historical circumstances. It is through an examination of these schools that French Canada's constant quest for equality can best be exemplified.

The first school must be named after its founder: Sir George Etienne Cartier, whose role in the creation of Confederation was second only to that of Sir John Macdonald. Cartier's view was that the central government, the government at Ottawa, was the primary government in Canada and that the French-Canadian presence could and should always be vigorously exerted there. This he believed could be done as long as French Canadians stood together united as a bloc that, working in co-operation with groups of English Canadians, could maximize their position. The French-Canadian bloc would always be strongly represented in any cabinet and, provided it was willing to make those accommodations necessary to the workings of democratic politics, its interests and those of the country would be advanced. It is important to realize that when Cartier spoke of bloc politics he was not thinking of a French-Canadian or a Catholic party. Indeed, that was the very antithesis of his conception, for that would emphasize the minority position of the French Canadians or the Catholics by automatically creating an English-Canadian or Protestant party. Instead, he felt that a French-Canadian bloc should work in co-operation with English Canadians within the structure of one of the religiously and racially neutral Liberal and Conservative parties. The school of Cartier is the school to which all of his successors as leaders of the French Canadians at Ottawa have adhered, regardless of political party: Laurier, Lapointe, and St. Laurent.

The school of Cartier was not, of course, an institution that every French Canadian was prepared to support. There have always been those who have argued that in the crunch of national crisis Cartier's strategy was bound to fail. That is to say, the kind of national crisis which in fact divided Canadians along ethnic and religious lines. In such a crisis the French Canadians would always and inevitably find themselves in the minority. That meant that they should fall back upon the bastion where their own majority ruled: the government of the Province of Quebec. This school drew intellectual sustenance from the arguments put forward in 1865 by the French-speaking opponents of Confederation, notably the brilliant *rouge* leader, Antoine-Aimé Dorion. Dorion had argued in the Confederation debates that the new union was a serious potential threat to the French-Canadian culture because it was not a real federation but rather a unitary government with a few federalist frills added to mollify the French Canadians. In this highly centralized arrangement, French Canada would always be subject to the will of the English-speaking majority and consequently in danger. Cartier had brushed these arguments aside, insisting that the French-Canadian presence in Ottawa would always protect the minority's rights.

Within fewer than twenty years after Confederation, a series of events took place that caused some French Canadians to wonder whether Dorion had not been a better prophet than Cartier. The major event in this development was the decision of the Macdonald government in 1885 to allow Louis Riel's death sentence to be carried out. French Canadians had come to identify their cause with that of the Western Métis leader, and to fear that his fate, symbolically at least, was their fate so far as French-Canadian rights outside of Quebec were concerned. After months of emotional debate Riel was hanged. No French Canadian had quit his post in the federal cabinet, and the French-Canadian bloc in the Ottawa parliament had not been able to maintain that unity which was supposed to be the guarantee of French Canada's interests. And even if it had, the unity of English Canada would likely have proven complete enough to override the French-Canadian will. The response to this situation came from a provincial politician—one who had opposed Confederation in the first place, and who now led the provincial Liberal party. His name was Honoré Mercier, and he called upon his compatriots to cease their fratricidal quarrels and unite with him in a *parti national* to defend the bastion of Quebec against the threatening power of Ottawa. His proposal was to defend French-Canadian rights through the defence of provincial rights. In Mercier, then, we see the beginnings of an identification of French Canada and Quebec—though this identification was never fully made, nor was it Mercier's intention that it should be. Instead, Mercier joined hands with the Premier of Ontario, Oliver Mowat, and some other proponents of provincial rights to give practical expression to the theory that Confederation was a "compact" of the provinces, that the provinces and not the central authority were supreme in the system, and that they could act to modify the constitution. It was Mercier and Mowat who called the first Interprovincial Conference in 1887, a conference that was designed at once to restrict the powers of the central government and to extract more money from Ottawa for the provinces.

In taking the stance that he did, Mercier won the right to the title of father of the second school of thought: the provincial rights school. Since Mercier, no Quebec government has ever failed to pay lip-service to the doctrine of provincial autonomy and to warn its electorate of the dangers inherent in the ever-extending tentacles of Ottawa's centralizing ambitions. And nothing, historically, has contributed more to the Quebecker's suspicion that Ottawa was unsympathetic to his interests than the events of the two great wars, and specifically the adoption of the policy of conscription for overseas service. Conscription was imposed against the nearly unanimous will of the French Canadians in 1917. Both the provincial Liberals of Alexandre Taschereau and Maurice Duplessis's Union Nationale party were able subsequently to hide corruption, maladministration, and do-nothingism behind the mantle of defending Quebec French Canadians against the power of Ottawa by merely reminding the electorate of 1917. When it appeared that this tactic had about run its course, the events of World War II once again forced Ottawa to adopt a limited measure of conscription. The act restored Duplessis to power and helped to set the process of identifying Quebec with French Canada on a new and powerfully driven course.

Nevertheless, the doctrine of provincial autonomy, which could protect those French Canadians in Quebec but offered no support to the minorities outside the reserve, was never accepted as the only weapon in French Canada's constitutional armoury. It was a preoccupation with this difficulty—the problem of the diaspora—that led to the development of a third school of thought, the one which must be called the school of Henri Bourassa.

The implications of the provincial rights doctrine were plainly written in the great controversies that surrounded the attacks upon French and Catholic rights outside of Quebec. Of these controversies the most significant were in Manitoba in the 1890s and in Ontario in the second decade of this century. In 1890 the Manitoba government abolished both the French language from the public business of the province and separate schools from the educational system. In 1912–13 Ontario passed a controversial regulation that appeared, at least, to limit rather seriously the use of French as a language of instruction in Ontario schools. To reduce a complicated story to its essence, both of these provinces, with a fairly complete degree of success, stood behind the doctrine of provincial rights in educational matters and refused to respond to any form of pressure to restore the aggrieved minority's rights. Thus provincial rights was discovered to be a two-edged sword which could be used to defend Quebec against Ottawa, but which also could be called into battle by other provinces eager to defy a central authority attempting to protect minority rights.

In response to this dilemma Bourassa developed a theory of Canada which, while not rejecting the theory of the compact of the provinces, added to it a new dimension. Bourassa argued that while Confederation was the creation of the provinces and was therefore the result of a provincial compact, it was also a compact in an even more important sense. Confederation, he held, was the creation of two distinct ethnic groups, and it represented an agreement or *entente* or compact between the French and the English to live together in an equal partnership that recognized Canada as a bilingual and bicultural community. And Bourassa meant that this agreement covered all of Canada. Since there was no evidence of such an explicit agreement in the dusty legal documents of Confederation, Bourassa contended that it rested not on one specific constitutional declaration but upon evolving historical experience consecrated by morality. It was a moral compact whereby each partner would recognize the equal rights, privileges, and duties of the other. It followed from this conception, of course, that those provinces which had acted in a fashion detrimental to the rights of the minority had contravened the very fundamental agreement upon which the union of 1867 had been constructed. Since the cultural compact was sanctioned by morality, it need hardly be added that it took precedence in Bourassa's mind over the mere constitutional and legal claims that formed the basis of the provincial rights argument.

Unfortunately, in political communities legal rights are more readily enforceable than rights based on claims of morality. During Henri Bourassa's public career, therefore, conflicts between provincial rights and minority rights ended almost without exception in victory for the former. Bourassa's concept of the morally guaranteed cultural compact of Confederation remained, then, little more than an ideal to be aimed at, to be one day transformed into a legally enforceable reality.

Bourassa remained optimistic to the end of his life that his concept of Canada as an association of equal cultures would some day be achieved. But even in his own time there were those who condemned it as utopian and called for French Canadians to look to their one corner of safety, and to transform it gradually into a true *patrie* that would one day assume the status of full nationhood. Bourassa's grandfather, Louis-Joseph Papineau, the leader of the Rebellion of 1837, might be named father of this school. But his school died with him and had to be refounded, in a form which he would not have accepted, in the late nineteenth century by an idiosyncratic journalist named Jules-Paul

Tardivel. This man, half French and half American by birth, spoke not a word of French until he migrated to Quebec to complete his education. Thereafter he became a leading spokesman of Quebec nationalism in its ultramontane and conservative form.

For Tardivel a nation was a religiously and culturally homogeneous community. Canada could not therefore be a nation; French Canada could. As a good, conservative Catholic he could not advocate the forceful destruction of Confederation. He could merely begin the long process of public education which he hoped would eventually open the eyes of his compatriots to the truth that Confederation was a fool's paradise and would eventually either undermine their language and religion or be broken up, giving them their own nation on the banks of the St. Lawrence. . . . Tardivel's message was simple enough: Bourassa's conception of a Canadian nation founded upon two distinct cultures was a foolish, unfulfillable dream. Equality could never come that way, but only through the establishment of a *Nouvelle-France* built upon the foundations that had been shaken but not destroyed in 1759. Thus Tardivel's school is the *indépendantiste* one, a school which has never, until recently, had a large following. But it has nevertheless been a school which, since Tardivel, has never completely closed its doors. Not all of its present-day, secular-minded adherents would willingly recognize the editor of *La Verité*, and the author of *Pour La Patrie*, as their intellectual father. But in reality, little has been added by today's theorists of Quebec's claims to independence that was not long ago explained by Jules-Paul Tardivel.

These, then, schematically at least, are the ways that French Canadians have viewed their place in Confederation over the past century. Of course, these are basic positions, and variations within schools have existed. Laurier was more favourably disposed to a decentralized federalism than Cartier, though Laurier's French-Canadian successor as Prime Minister of Canada, Louis St. Laurent, was probably nearer Cartier than Laurier in this matter. Yet all three, along with Lapointe and others, emphasized the need for a strong French-Canadian presence at Ottawa. Similarly, there are variations within the other schools. . . .

Nevertheless, it would be misleading not to remark that some of the standard positions have undergone changes in recent years that may almost be said to create new schools entirely. Let me just say something further in conclusion about the way in which these schools have become mixed together in the last decade in ways that modify some of the distinctions which I have suggested.

The school of Tardivel is present today in M. Lévesque's *Parti québécois*. But that school has lost its religious underpinnings, and also dropped Tardivel's conservative, agrarian social philosophy. Instead it espouses a moderate brand of democratic socialism. Moreover, it is a party which is unwilling to commit itself to a complete divorce from Canada, for it proposes that since we must continue to occupy the same geographic house, we might just as well share the economic plumbing; in short, it proposes a divorce that calls for cohabitation, but separate beds. M. Lévesque wants to maintain some sort of common market for economic purposes, and to establish a minimum of common political machinery to operate it. But the arrangement would begin with the recognition of sovereignty on both sides. Yet despite these minor limitations, and added doubts that such an arrangement could have any permanence, the Lévesque position stands in the line of direct descent from Tardivel.

Tardivel, however, has also contemporary followers who accept part of the master's basic philosophy, but not all of it, for they have at the same time attended the school of Bourassa. These people argue that French Canada is a nation, and that Quebec is the homeland of that nation. Since Quebec is the homeland of a nation, and also the only province where the French Canadian is in a majority, it must be accepted as a province *pas comme les autres*— not like the others. In reality, this implies that Quebec is the nation-state of French Canada and must therefore be granted powers more extensive than the powers of other Canadian provinces, for English Canadians have their nation-state in the government at Ottawa. The extent of special status for Quebec varies with the spokesman—and sometimes with the audience—but this is a position which is accepted these days, in varying degrees, by both the major provincial parties, and such influential opinion-makers as the newspaper *Le Devoir*. The roots of the special-status concept may be found in Tardivel. But the proponents of this position also contend that since about twenty per cent of French Canadians live outside Quebec, and further that twenty per cent of Quebec itself is non-French, a system of bilingual institutions should be maintained throughout Canada. This, then, is a variation on the philosophy of Bourassa.

But Bourassa's position is best and most fully represented today by those French Canadians who follow Prime Minister Trudeau. Like Bourassa, these men are convinced that Canada is a single political nation, based upon a federal system of government and the co-existence of French- and English-speaking cultural groups. They wish to guarantee that both French- and English-speaking Canadians will have their rights guaranteed throughout Canada. In place of Bourassa's moral compact, they offer an entrenched Charter of Human Rights that would guarantee linguistic rights in addition to the normal civil rights. They accept much of the Mercier school's insistence upon the autonomy of the provinces, but they also support Cartier's conviction that a strong French-Canadian presence at Ottawa is necessary to assure the rights of their people, and never has that presence been stronger than today. Finally, they reject Tardivel's claim that Quebec and French Canada can be interchanged, even to the extent of refusing to concede that Quebec should have a "special status." Their belief is that once Quebec is recognized, even in a limited fashion, as the nation-state of French Canada, the road to complete independence is opened and paved. That, they believe, is the road to the formal independence of banana republic status.

And so the debate continues. But its goal remains the same: for the French Canadian, survival and equality. For the past century the Confederation of 1867 provided the framework within which that goal was striven for. No one can claim that the goal was fully achieved, nor can it be fairly asserted that no progress was made. But today Canadians are committed to the proposition that a new constitution must be elaborated. The process will be long and often tedious. No one can predict its final outcome. But one observation can perhaps be offered with some security. That quest for equality which has characterized so much of French Canada's history will not be concluded by the mere promulgation of a new constitution, for, after all, every generation dreams of new forms of equality. *Egalité ou Indépendance?* Independence is easy—how many nations have achieved it since 1945? But equality? How many peoples have achieved that in all of recorded history?

FURTHER READINGS

Gagnon, A.C., ed. *Quebec: State and Society.* Toronto: Methuen, 1984.

McRoberts, K., and D. Posgate. *Quebec: Social Change and Political Crisis.* Rev. ed. Toronto: McClelland & Stewart, 1980.

McWhinney, E. *Quebec and the Constitution, 1960–1978.* Toronto: University of Toronto Press, 1979.

———. *Canada and the Constitution, 1979–1982.* Toronto: University of Toronto Press, 1982.

Whitaker, R.A. "The Quebec Cauldron." In M.S. Whittington and G. Williams, eds. *Canadian Politics in the 1980s.* 2nd ed. 33–57. Toronto: Methuen, 1984.

PART 2

IDEAS
AND
SOCIETY

It is often said that there is nothing so invincible as an idea whose time has come. If the study of politics is the study of power, there are few things as powerful as beliefs. The eighteenth century Scottish philosopher David Hume referred to the "empire of opinion" as the most important factor in securing political obedience and loyalty. Usually, political conflict is caused by struggles over wealth or legitimacy, but that conflict invariably is expressed in terms of ideas, beliefs and ideologies.

A political ideology is a set of ideas or principles used to explain, exhort or justify public behaviour. Since the French Revolution of 1789 there has been a proliferation of ideologies, usually put forward as "-isms": conservatism, liberalism, socialism, Marxism, fascism, nationalism and others. These are not mere slogans which express preferences, but beliefs which cause action and change.

"Regionalism" is another concept of some consequence in larger countries. In Canada, regionalism is both a fact of our political experience and an idea about the existence of communities within the state. Most commentators agree that, compared to (say) the United States, regional identities are much stronger in Canada. Mr. Joe Clark, when he was leader of the Conservative party, popularized the concept of Canada as a "community of communities." The make-up of our major political institutions, including the cabinet, pressure groups, and the parties reflect the regional nature of the country, and many Canadians think of themselves primarily as Maritimers, Westerners, Northerners, or Québécois, often with a wry glance at relatively privileged Ontarians. The article by Ramsay Cook at the end of Part 1 raised the question of whether Quebec should be regarded as the homeland of a separate cultural-linguistic "nation" or the most distinctive of several regions of Canada. Whichever way one views French Canada, it is clear that both nationalism and regionalism are salient factors in our politics, and both factors are emphasized in Reading 6, excerpted from *A Future Together*, The Report of the Task Force on National Unity, 1979.

In Reading 7 interregional tensions within the federal system are examined in the context of western alienation. Doug Owram's essay illustrates how, since the 1870s, the western provinces have to some degree resented and protested their unsatisfactory place in Confederation.

It would be difficult to understand Canadian politics without a grasp of basic economic forces and ideas which moulded the nation, particularly Sir John A. Macdonald's "National Policy," as adopted and only slightly adapted by Laurier. The three-pronged policy of tariff protection, railroad construction, and western settlement provided much of the economic bone and sinew which shaped our existence. In Reading 8, D.V. Smiley's brilliant, synoptic article employs a political economist's range of expertise to show how Canada was "born in original economic sin" and how orthodox liberal economists to this day reject the political assumptions which underlay the broad strategy of nation building. Most students will find that this essay repays rereading; it raises very basic issues concerning the nature of free markets, government intervention, foreign investment, and regional economic disparities, issues which show no signs of disappearing.

Our attention is thus thrown back to the abiding problems of "what is a nation?" and how should we view "nationalism?" Admitting that the idea of nation is a "difficult concept," Alexander Brady, in Reading 9, discusses the founding of Canada as a pluralistic political nationality, the urge toward exclusive *survivance* and separatism in Quebec, and the possibility that bilingual programs may foster a new pan-Canadian identity.

George Grant's book of 1965, *Lament for a Nation*, from which Reading 10 is taken, addressed "The Defeat of Canadian Nationalism" but paradoxically helped rekindle among English-speaking Canadians an assertive and anti-American economic nationalism. Professor Grant is a Christian philosopher and a tory or red tory, but also a pessimist concerning the likelihood of distinctive national identities being able to persist. You cannot expect to have, Grant argues, both separateness and the "progress" of homogenizing technological advance. In an age of "progress," conservatism is impossible, and thus the conserving of Canada through nationalism may be an impossibility.

It may also be undesirable, as former Prime Minister Trudeau asserts in Reading 11. Mr. Trudeau champions "Reason over Passion," calls nationalism emotional, tribal, and reactionary, and insists that internationalism (or cosmopolitanism) and federalism (permitting unity plus diversity) are rational, and therefore always preferable to nationalism. Like Ramsay Cook, Mr. Trudeau often quotes Lord Acton:

> A great democracy must either sacrifice self-government to unity or preserve it by federalism. . . . The co-existence of several nations under the same State is a test, as well as the best security of its freedom. It is also one of the chief instruments of civilization. . . . The combination of different nations in one State is as necessary a condition of civilized life as the combination of men in society.

Throughout his book, *Federalism and the French Canadians*, Mr. Trudeau argues from the individualist-liberal position that nationalism breeds conformity and loss of choice and liberty.

The starkly contrasting views of Grant, the nationalist tory, and Trudeau, the quintessential liberal anti-nationalist, remind us that the Canadian political culture appears to reflect a wider diversity of ideologies than that of the United States. Political culture, as defined by the *International Encyclopedia of the Social Sciences*, is "the set of attitudes, beliefs and sentiments which give order and meaning to a political process . . . the product of both the collective history of a political system and the life histories of the members of the system. . . ."

Consider some of the differences between Canada and the United States. "Canada and the American Value System," an article published by Seymour Martin Lipset in 1965, built upon the earlier writings of de Tocqueville and Bryce and observed that Canadians, compared to Americans, tend to be less violent, less risk-taking, more deferential to authority, less egalitarian and, in their economic development, placed less emphasis on rugged-individualist private enterprise and more on public enterprise. Whereas the United States was born of revolution, both English and French Canada began as counter-revolutionary societies. Canada is described, in short, as less liberal than the United States. It is a cliché that, in contrast to the American founding myth of natural rights to "life, liberty and the pursuit of happiness," Canada's founding document speaks of "Peace, Order, and Good Government."

Harvard Historian Louis Hartz, in *The Founding of New Societies* and *The Liberal Idea in America*, assessed the value system of the United States in terms reducible to the model or paradigm of liberalism: reason, liberty, equality, competition, and the primacy of the individual. By contrast, the political culture of South America was described by Hartz in terms of the tory paradigm: tradition, authority, hierarchy, co-operation, and the primacy of the organic community. In the Hartzian analysis, North America is seen as a liberal "fragment" of northern Europe, reflecting early notions of capitalism and democracy, while the South American fragment reflects the values of southern Europe, mainly Spain and Portugal, which were pre-capitalist, pre-democratic, feudal (or tory) societies.

Gad Horowitz is the leading exponent of Hartz in Canada. Reading 12 is Horowitz's, now classic, 1966 article in which he contrasts Canada and the United States, examines the "different position and character" of liberalism in the two countries, considers the tory element in early French Canada and in the United Empire Loyalists, and argues that the persistence of socialism in Canada is related to the relative strength of the "tory touch." The chief implication of Horowitz's provocative work is that the major differences between Americans and Canadians are due to the non-liberal elements in our political culture.

6

The Anatomy of Conflict

THE TASK FORCE ON CANADIAN UNITY

We believe that the heart of the present crisis is to be discovered in the intersecting conflicts created by two kinds of cleavages in Canadian society and by the political agencies which express and mediate them. The first and more pressing cleavage is that old Canadian division between "the French" and "the English." We will consider the present configuration of this historic problem of Canadian duality in a moment. The second cleavage is that which divides the various regions of Canada and their populations from one another. Regionalism, like duality, also has an extended lineage in Canadian social, economic and political life, and we pursue this matter subsequently as well.

Both duality and regionalism, then, are deeply rooted in our history and are major elements in the social and economic foundation of Canada. The shape of these two structural forces of Canadian life has altered quite rapidly in the past quarter of a century as power has shifted within and between various groups and as their aspirations have changed. Canada is in no sense unique in experiencing such stresses; indeed, a survey of the international scene will reveal that "national unity" is a rather scarce commodity in the world community. However, it is the particular expression of these stresses in Canada that has brought us to our present pass, where the existing constitutional and political arrangements no longer adequately reflect or express the main social and economic forces which are at work in the country.

In our judgement, the first and foremost challenge facing the country is to create an environment in which duality might flourish; the second is to provide a fresher and fuller expression of the forces of regionalism in Canada's constitutional system and power structure. We wish to emphasize that it is in the context of the *present* crisis that we assign priority to these two, and we do so for a very simple reason. Each, if ignored or left unsatisfied, has the power to break the country, and each must accept the other if a new period of harmony is to be achieved. . . .

But what, more precisely, do we mean when we speak of duality and regionalism?

Abridged from The Task Force on Canadian Unity, "The Anatomy of Conflict," *A Future Together: Observations and Recommendations*, catalogue number CP32-35/1979 (Ottawa: Supply and Services, 1979), 21-32. Reprinted by permission of the Minister of Supply and Services Canada.

DUALITY

To take French-English duality first, it could signify the thesis of the two founding peoples, the two-nations theory, the notion of the British North America Act as a pact between two peoples, the simple existence of two languages in Canada, or the distinction between Quebec society on the one hand and the rest of Canada on the other.

None of these, and no other, so far as we know, has received unanimous support. The native peoples (the country's real founders) understandably find the two-founding-peoples concept of duality offensive. English-speaking Canadians find it difficult to conceive of two nations and doubt whether there was a pact in 1867. Québécois believe that any attempt to consider French-speaking Quebec simply as a branch of French Canada belittles its role. Francophones outside Quebec and anglophones within Quebec are wary of any undue emphasis on the cleavage between Quebec and the rest of the country because it has the effect of submerging them within each majority society.

It is clear to us that duality is a multifaceted concept. The general understanding of it can be expected to alter as the society which it describes evolves, and the particular dimension which is emphasized will vary according to one's preoccupations, experience and situation in the country.

Our use of the concept of duality in this report will reflect this variety, and the reader will observe that we find several different dimensions of it worthy of consideration. The historic relationship between French- and English-speaking peoples in the upper half of North America has been problematic for centuries, and the conflicts between the two have been fed from many sources and sustained in many areas of life: in religious practices, cultural outlook, at work, in school, in patterns of settlement, in the exercise of political power, and in many other ways as well. . . .

Our report thus seeks to reflect the complex and multifaceted character of duality, but the reader will also find that it is shaped by a certain emphasis and preoccupation which we wish to make clear at this point. The dominant interpretation of duality which commends itself to the Task Force, and which we think must receive the attention of the country as a whole, is that which bears most directly on the crisis as it manifests itself today. While we freely acknowledge that duality is many-sided, we would nevertheless insist that to confront the heart of the issue today is to address one main question, namely, the status of Quebec and its people in the Canada of tomorrow. While the origins of the crisis are many, its resolution must necessarily be primarily political and constitutional in nature, and aimed at securing if possible a satisfactory position for Quebec and its people within Canada as a whole.

Our understanding of duality is shaped by this perception, and our emphasis in the balance of this report will be on Quebec's political and constitutional position and the relationship which in our judgement should prevail between the Québécois and other Canadians. . . .

QUEBEC

We contend, therefore, that the essential condition in recognizing duality within Canada at the present time is to come to terms with modern Quebec. Quebec will continue to be the pillar of the French fact in all of North America; it will perform this function inside the Canadian federal system or outside it. So the challenge is not to try to confer on Quebec a role that it has in any case played for centuries, but to demonstrate that it is a role which can be played more effectively within a restructured federal system which is expressly cognizant of Quebec's distinctiveness and its sources.

One can readily identify several factors which have led to the emergence of a distinct society in modern Quebec. We have identified six: history, language, law, common origins, feelings and politics—which, together with others, have led to the development of a distinct society in modern Quebec.

The first, then, is history—the legacy of over three hundred years of the continuous development of a people. During much of this period, but particularly after Confederation, it was possible to speak of a single French-Canadian community which extended to many parts of what is now Canada and to which Quebec contributed a substantial portion of the leadership and the vision to sustain it. French Canada, like English Canada, was knit together from distinct regional societies which, over time, came to think of themselves, for at least some purposes, as one. However, the changes in Canadian social structure since the Second World War have drastically weakened the organic links between these communities. What now is emerging from the old French Canada is a strong and vital Quebec, and many more vulnerable smaller and weaker French-Canadian communities in other provinces, each of which has been forced by circumstances and a constant threat of assimilation to set its own course independently of, and sometimes in opposition to, developments within Quebec. This process, rooted in the history of Canada generally, would by itself designate Quebec as the most viable and important locus of the French culture in North America; yet there are other, equally important, factors.

The second important factor is language. Quebec is home to over 85 per cent of all citizens who speak French, and 81 per cent of Quebec's population is French-speaking. Current demographic data for Canada as a whole reveal a growing linguistic territorial concentration which is rendering Quebec increasingly French and the rest of the country, excluding New Brunswick, increasingly English.

A third factor is Canada's legal duality. Quebec was authorized by the Quebec Act of 1774 to retain its French civil laws. One year before Confederation, the civil laws were codified along the lines of the *Code Napoléon*. Amended from time to time since then, the civil code is the basis of Quebec's private law while the other provinces have lived under the English common law tradition, thus producing two distinct legal systems.

A fourth factor contributing to Quebec's unique character is the distinctive ethnic group or people which French Canadians form. The majority of these are persons whose families came to North America several centuries ago. While the more recent arrivals from France have been somewhat less likely to settle in Quebec, a majority still does so. This means that in addition to the linguistic distinctiveness of the province may be added the fact that the ethnic origins of its majority are shared. Quebec is simply not a multicultural society in the same sense as many other parts of Canada. Although it has become more ethnically diverse in the last few decades, particularly in the Montreal area, Quebec is and will remain predominantly French in language and in ethnicity; it is unique in Canada on both of these counts.

There remain two other factors which must be added. The legacy of history, a shared language and common origins are all important social facts in their own right, but they say nothing about the feelings of Québécois, a fifth factor which marks Quebec off from the other provinces. The shared desires, aspirations and even the fears of the collectivity provide perhaps the most compelling evidence in support of Quebec's cultural distinctiveness.

For the longest part of Quebec's history one theme dominated the cultural life of the collectivity. That theme was *survivance*, or sheer survival. This overriding concern for the maintenance of the way of life of a people coloured the relationship between Quebecers and their compatriots, and it continues to do so. Yet only an insensitive observer of the life of the province could fail to note a substantial shift in approach in which that collectivity's concern for survival is now expressed by the thoroughly contemporary and dynamic pursuit of its own development, or what has been often described as *épanouissement* (literally, "blooming," "blossoming").

Psychologically, the transition from *survivance* to *épanouissement* has been accompanied by a remarkable alteration in Quebecers' attitudes toward themselves. This may be described as the shift in self-perception of French-speaking Quebecers from a Canadian minority only grudgingly accepted in many parts of Canada to a Québécois majority, increasingly confident and determined to secure its future.

This transformation is reflected in the very vocabulary that Quebecers have used to describe themselves. Originally, the French-speaking people of Quebec called themselves *Canadiens* and referred to the English-speaking people as *les Anglais*. In the middle and late nineteenth century, they began calling themselves *Canadiens français* to distinguish themselves from English-speaking Canadians. In recent years, however, more and more have adopted the name and identity of *Québécois*, underlining this sense of themselves as a majority, as a people.

Parallel to this development, French Canadians elsewhere in Canada increasingly have come to see themselves as a part of their provincial communities rather than as members of a comprehensive French Canadian society. They describe themselves as *Franco-Ontariens*, *Franco-Manitobains*, *Fransaskois*, and collectively as *les francophones hors Québec*, outside of Quebec.

These changes suggest the sixth and final factor contributing to the distinctiveness of the province of Quebec—namely, the changing meaning of politics to a society in transition. The psychological passage from minority to majority has been marked by the wholesale appropriation of the state for this cultural struggle. The last several decades have produced leaders in Quebec, as elsewhere, who are prepared to employ the resources of the provincial state to achieve collective goals and to promote rapid social and economic development.

History, language, law, ethnicity, feelings and politics render Quebec at once a society, a province and the stronghold of the French-Canadian people. Taken together, these factors produce in the Québécois a vision of Quebec as the living heart of the French presence in North America; collectively they are as strong or as weak as Quebec is: no more, no less. It is this reality with which other Canadians and the Canadian federal system must come to terms. For the people of Quebec, the question that remains to be answered is whether they can better serve their future within Canada and its federal system or whether they would do better standing on their own.

REGIONALISM

What of regionalism, which we have identified as the second line of cleavage in Canadian society which needs attention in the present crisis? Two observations come immediately to mind.

First, one cannot begin to consider regionalism as a force in Canadian life without recognizing the interrelationships which exist between it and the concept of duality. Regionalism and duality are not isolated phenomena. They are ways of describing the same realities from different perspectives. They interpenetrate and influence each other to such a degree that duality can be regarded, in a sense, as a regional phenomenon, while, as we have seen, many of the regions incorporate elements of duality.

Second, very little investigation is required to reveal that, as in the case of duality, there is a multiplicity of meanings and associations that can be attached to the notion of regionalism in Canada.

For a start, most Québécois we observed, are inclined not to see regionalism as a very significant factor in Canadian life; they view Canada essentially in terms of the relations between French and English-speaking Canadians or between Quebec and the rest of Canada. As a result of this dualistic outlook, they are sometimes tempted to think of English-speaking Canada as one monolithic entity.

However, English-speaking Canada is a much less monolithic and homogeneous society, and a much more diverse and complex one, than the Québécois often assume it to be. This complexity needs to be taken into account in the analysis of Canadian problems and in the search for solutions, because it determines the way in which English-speaking Canadians look at their country and in which they react to stresses like those of the present.

Indeed, the regional nature of English-speaking Canada complicates its perception of French-speaking Canada, just as the comparatively homogeneous and concentrated character of Quebec society complicates its perception of the rest of the country. Because many English-speaking Canadians think of their country as a cultural and geographic mosaic, they tend to regard French-speaking Canadians as members of one of the many minority groups that make up the Canadian mosaic. They do not spontaneously think of their country in a dualistic way, though some have begun to do so over the course of the last decade or so.

It is not an easy matter, then, to settle on a single notion of regionalism in Canada or one definition of a region. Some economists have identified the thirteen major urban systems of Canada as the most plausible economic regions of the country. A similar perspective treats regionalism as an intra-provincial phenomenon and distinguishes between the populous, industrialized regions of a province (for example, British Columbia's lower mainland, southwestern Ontario or Montreal Island) and those other parts of the province which are economically and socially distinct.

The regions of Canada can also be seen as four or five units composed of various combinations of the following: the Atlantic region, Quebec, Ontario, the Prairies and British Columbia (or sometimes the West and the North). These ways of looking at the country are sometimes useful in economic analysis and at the federal level when for certain purposes of administration the provincial boundaries are less important.

The Task Force, like many other national bodies, was appoined on a regional (as well as on a dual) basis, and we will employ the four or five-region approach from time to time in our report. If we do not do so more often, it is because this approach has two drawbacks. First, the interests of the individual provinces within these regions are not always identical: those of Newfoundland, for example, are distinct from those of New Brunswick, just as those of Manitoba are more similar in some ways to those of the central provinces than to Alberta.

In the second place, regional communities require an institutional framework if they are to become viable units which can express themselves and organize their collective life in an effective manner. For that reason, it seems to us that the provinces and the northern territories are the basic building blocks of Canadian society and the logical units on which to focus a discussion of Canadian regionalism, even though they may not always be the most "natural" regions from an economic or other point of view. They are, nevertheless, the political frameworks through which the various regional communities express and will continue to express themselves. We see no trends which allow us to believe that the people of any Canadian province are ready to abandon their traditional provincial units in favour of larger regional structures, even though in some cases, and especially in the Maritimes, groups of provinces are prepared to cooperate to an increasing extent in common endeavours for the common good.

In this report, then, we will use the concept of regionalism in more than one way. Sometimes we will use it to mean economic and geographic regions transcending provincial boundaries. But more often we will use it to designate the provinces themselves. The provincial political institutions are the primary frameworks through which regional populations can organize and express themselves, and their existence serves in turn to develop the social networks and interests based on them, thus reinforcing the provincial focus of regionalism. . . .

Our conclusion, then, with respect to regionalism parallels our judgement about duality in two ways. First, we accept both of them as basic social and political realities, but we also recognize the legitimate claims of both and the potential they offer to enrich and diversify Canadian life. In other words we accept their existence; we also recognize their value. Second, just as we contend that, for a complex variety of reasons, duality must today be approached primarily (although not exclusively) through the medium of Quebec's relations with the rest of Canada, we also believe that regionalism in Canadian life is expressed primarily (although, again, not exclusively) within the framework of the provinces, and we regard the provincial and territorial governments as critical agents in articulating the concerns and aspirations of these regional communities.

REGIONALISM IN ENGLISH-SPEAKING CANADA

Because of the concentration in the following pages on the regional and cultural diversity of English-speaking Canada, we sense that it would be possible for us to appear to downplay consideration of some commitments which are shared by the vast majority of English-speaking Canadians. So that there is no doubt as to the views of the Task Force on these common commitments, we shall give them our full attention here.

We believe that central to an understanding of English-speaking Canadians is the fact that they share elements of what could be called a common "political culture." That is, most English-speaking Canadians are strongly committed to the maintenance of a united country from sea to sea, to the political institutions and traditions which sustain a parliamentary form of democratic government, and to a federal system. There are quite naturally significant variations of opinion on each of these items, but we nevertheless observed a widely shared commitment to them among the great majority of English-speaking Canadians.

We would not want to leave our readers with the impression that these commitments are to be found uniquely among English-speaking Canadians; many French-speaking Canadians are as strongly committed to a united Canada, federalism and parliamentary government as long as there are reforms. Nevertheless, it is important to take into account the relative unanimity with which support for the basic aspects of our federation, though not its current operation, is voiced throughout English Canada.

Despite these shared commitments, and the network of political, economic and cultural institutions which link and bind together English-speaking Canadians in all parts of the country, the current crisis of Canadian unity has not had the effect of eliciting from anglophones throughout Canada a single, unified response. The Task Force is of the view that this lack of unanimity of opinion among English-speaking Canadians on the present crisis and on many other matters is quite natural.

We would identify five principal sources of diversity in English-speaking Canada: geography, history, economics, ethnicity and federalism itself.

To take geography first, the size and physical character of what is now Canada has always been a major force acting upon the peoples inhabiting this part of the world. It is an old cliché to say that Canada was knit together in defiance of geography—a view that, as some writers have pointed out, must be qualified by the unifying role of our waterways—but however it is qualified, the fact remains that Canadian unity has always had to struggle against physical barriers which divide its territory into at least five distinct geographical areas, and subdivide these into many more.

The second source of diversity, history, supplements the first. For much of our past, the ties between the regions have been very tenuous, if they existed at all. Geography and history combined to produce patterns of settlement which have played a continuing role in shaping the regional character of the country. If one studies the so-called "Vinland Map," one of the earliest European maps to show the coastline of northeastern North America, one is struck by the fact that "Vinland" appears as the last of a string of islands extending westward from northern Europe. This striking visual image expresses what is a fundamental reality for much of early Canadian history: the various regions of what is now one country were settled and developed by Europeans rather as "islands" unto themselves, largely unrelated to their neighbours, but linked by the sea to the mother countries and to other parts of the world. Before Confederation, the regions of present-day Canada were rather like a bunch of balloons, unattached to each other but held, by separate strings, in one hand.

Among its other accomplishments, Confederation associated the English-speaking people of four provinces in a single state, and provided a set of indigenous institutions having a claim on their loyalties larger than the colony or province. Loyalties to the province, which are particularly marked throughout Canada, antedate loyalty to the federation for English Canadians just as they do for French Canadians. Evidence that these pre-existing loyalties were never to be lightly discarded by English-speaking Canadians is plentiful in our history, as is suggested by the fact that the original Confederation agreements hardly received what one might call "massive" public support. There are many residents of the Maritime provinces today who preserve a good deal of skepticism about whether the political union called Canada has evolved in quite the way their representatives at the Charlottetown, Quebec and London conferences had intended.

To many foreign observers, the fact that Confederation is widely evaluated from the particular point of view of how given provinces have fared over the years is a remarkable feature of Canadian life. In other countries, cleavages such as social class, religion, race or creed have been of decisive importance to the collective or political lives of their citizens. In Canada, how much the people of any given province or region have participated in the benefits of the federation, or shared in its costs, has been at the forefront of our politics. And, we believe, this historically based reality is equally prevalent today. For many, perhaps most, English-speaking Canadians, a key element in how they evaluate their federation lies in the treatment it accords, or is felt to accord, their province, its natural resources, its industries, its population, and their particular priorities.

As these words suggest, a third source of regionalism, resulting from both history and geography, is economics. Because of the physical distinctions and distances between its various regions, the country has developed a somewhat unbalanced economic structure. Because the provinces are unequally endowed with natural resources and population, because basic industries vary greatly from one region to another, because geography grants them unequal access to both domestic and foreign markets, the level and character of economic development is very uneven across the country. This unequal distribution of economic well-being has traditionally been an important factor contributing to regional discontent and continues to weaken Canadian unity today.

A fourth source of the cultural and regional diversity of English-speaking Canada is ethnicity. The dual nature of our population was of course demonstrated in our earliest census. However, even if the "English" half of the duality were today still comprised almost exclusively of those of British origin, as it was in 1871, cultural differences even within it would nevertheless be quite pronounced. For one thing, British origin groups together the Irish, English, Scots and Welsh—peoples who historically have only rarely been found in complete agreement. For another, the vast expanse of Canadian territory, the fragmented nature of our economy, the unequal endowment of the provinces, and even such minor factors as variation in climate would soon assert themselves by producing, as such factors produce in every large country, tangible differences in the pace of everyday life, in occupation and, eventually, in identity.

Of course, the facts of the matter are that English-speaking Canada has become much more diverse in terms of ethnicity. Canadians of ethnic origins other than French or British have been part of the country virtually since its creation. They have settled vast parts of its territory, have contributed to its development, and continue to blend their efforts with one another and with all other Canadians to produce better lives for themselves and their children. In cultural terms, the importance of this influx has been enormous.

In coming to Canada, members of the other ethnic groups were not able, of course, to transport their complete culture from their native lands. They brought instead habits, practices, languages, traditions and outlooks, many of which were not common to the majority of those they encountered in Canada. In these cultural heritages, incomplete as they necessarily were, arriving immigrants and their offspring found and find a measure of identity and, very frequently, a source of pride. They also found in Canada a country which was not expressly dedicated to developing a common culture into which they were called upon to fit. Rather, they found a country whose very existence was predicated on the idea that it was not necessary to have a single language and culture to have a united people.

Wherever and whenever they arrived, immigrants from around the world have conducted their lives in Canada as part of a regionally diverse society. In some cases, they were able to influence the development of a city or province virtually from the start. In others, they were able to contribute perhaps less basically to their immediate surroundings. All of those who came have contributed something to Canada, and most of these contributions enlivened the cultural atmosphere of English-Canadian towns and cities, and continue to do so. This has been anything but an evenly distributed process, and it has meant more to some regions than others. But the result is that "English" Canada is composed of many communities and groups who have in common principally the fact that they now share a language and a commitment to Canada.

In summary, ethnicity may not be the decisive factor that guaranteed the cultural diversity of English Canada, but it has been a major factor in reinforcing this diversity. It has interacted with regionalism in several ways, in different times and places, with the result that the two factors are so fused in their effect that they may never be fully disassembled.

We turn now to the fifth factor which produces the cultural diversity of English Canada—federalism itself. While Canada may be a union of peoples or nationalities, it is a federation of provinces. From the start, territory was seen to be the natural basis of division for purposes of creating a wider political union. We have already mentioned some historical reasons for this choice. We now wish to discuss the consequences.

The British North America Act of 1867 grants, or has been interpreted to grant, quite substantial powers to the provincial governments of Canada. They are reasonable at the present time for many of the most basic and costly services governments anywhere are called upon to deliver to citizens: health care, social services and education, to name a few. In giving provinces these weigthy responsibilities, the BNA Act served to reinforce Canadian regionalism by permitting the development of provincial political institutions of sufficient size, authority and importance to undertake, in addition to the provision of certain services, a more general role of expressing regional views without regard to jurisdiction. Aggressive, well-staffed provincial governments have come, in other words, to represent the people of the provinces they serve in a number of ways, and not solely in the ways set out as provincial responsibilities in our constitution.

This is certainly the case in Quebec. The provincial government there has become the main instrument of Québécois aspirations. In English-speaking Canada, several provinces have taken similar, if less dramatic, initiatives to support and encourage what amounts to little less than the development of provincial societies. Some observers believe that strong provincial governments have been at the forefront of this process, have actually created the demand for increased provincial government activity. Others believe that the provincial governments of English Canada have been responding to deeply felt desires of their citizens for government that is close to the people.

Whatever the exact sequence (and it may vary in different provinces), the fact remains that the formal institutions of Canadian federalism have been a significant factor supporting the development of a regionally diverse English-Canadian society. This is a process which has come to fruition only in the last few decades. The provincial governments of many provinces in English-speaking Canada join the government of Quebec in calling the central government to account for its interventions in what they consider their own spheres of jurisdiction and for the more general treatment of the people of their province by federal authorities.

These five factors—geography, history, economics, ethnicity, and the formal institutions of Canadian federalism—have, then, helped to create and sustain a vigorous regionalism in English-Canadian life, and they will no doubt continue to do so in the future.

FURTHER READINGS

Bell, D.V. "Regionalism in the Canadian Community." In Fox, P.W. ed. *Politics: Canada*, 126–134. Toronto: McGraw-Hill Ryerson, 1982.

Bercuson, D.J., ed. *Canada and the Burden of Unity*. Toronto: Macmillan, 1977.

Economic Council of Canada. *Living Together: A Study of Regional Disparities*. Ottawa: Supply and Services Canada, 1979.

Gibbins, R. *Regionalism: Territorial Politics in Canada and the United States*. Toronto: Butterworths, 1983.

Hodgetts, J.E. "Regional Interests in a Federal Structure." *C.J.E.P.S.* 32, 1 (February, 1966): 3–14.

Marchak, P. "The Two Dimensions of Canadian Regionalism." *Journal of Canadian Studies* 15, 2 (Summer, 1980): 88–97.

Simeon, R. "Regionalism and Canadian Political Institutions." *Queen's Quarterly* 82, 4 (Winter, 1975): 499–511.

Simeon, R., and D.J. Elkins. *Small Worlds*, Chapter 2. Toronto: Methuen, 1980.
Wade, M., *Regionalism in the Canadian Community, 1867–1967*. Toronto: University of Toronto Press, 1969.

7

Reluctant Hinterland

Doug Owram

A paradox seems to exist in western Canada. On the one hand, the region has never been so prosperous. Migrants from other parts of the nation flood in to take advantage of job opportunities and financial potential unparalleled in the rest of Canada. Two of the provinces, Alberta and British Columbia, have recently surpassed Ontario in terms of average per capita income. The West is booming and it has become recognized throughout Canada as the great growth sector of the nation. On the other hand, western discontent is as great as at any time in its history. . . .

In many ways, . . . the obviously unhappy mood of the West is totally explicable. Changing economic indices have affected the details of western grievance but they have not altered the substance of an historical sense of injustice. For, as will be argued, western grievance has not been about money. Money, the standard of living, and other economic matters have all fueled the anger of Westerners through the years but these subjects are not really at the base of the western sense of grievance. Rather, such financial issues must be included with such diverse matters as the cultural centralism of the Canadian Broadcasting Corporation, bilingualism, markings on RCMP patrol cars, and accusation of paternalism hurled against the East. Beneath them all lies a more general concern in western Canadian thought and action. Western Canada, it has been charged through the past decades, has not received and is not receiving adequate attention from national policy makers, whether the governmental or private sectors. The West's basic complaint concerns a hinterland status which seems to encompass everything from economics to culture and which leaves elsewhere the key powers of decision in these areas. The demand that this be changed underlies much of the region's quest for change.

To understand the reasons for this attitude it is necessary to turn not to earlier history of the West but to the ideas and attitudes of mid-nineteenth century central Canada. This was the period when the idea of opening the West to settlement first became seriously established. Centred in Toronto and in other parts of Canada West a powerful expansionist movement began in 1856. Behind the movement was a whole complex of ideas concerning the

Abridged from Doug Owram, "Reluctant Hinterland," in *Western Separatism: The Myths, Realities and Dangers*, ed. Larry Pratt and Garth Stevenson (Edmonton: Hurtig Publishers Ltd., 1981), 45-64. Reprinted by permission of the publisher future of Canada. Included among these was a strong sense of the necessity for a new area which would further the growth of the towns and cities along the Great Lakes-St. Lawrence system. Montreal and especially Toronto merchants, businessmen, and editorialists thought it imperative to develop a new and larger market for goods if, as the Toronto *Globe* put it in 1856, the city was "ever to rise above a fifth-rate American town." The idea of a vast agricultural region buying from the East while pouring its produce through the Great Lakes system became a dominant theme of Canadian development for the next century.

From this well known fact many writers have jumped to the conclusion that this simply proves that the West was always intended as a sort of colonial hinterland in permanent economic vassalage to the dominant urban centres of Canada. This is too simplistic an argument. After all, had this been the intention nobody would have come West from Ontario, preferring instead to remain in the position of exploiter rather than exploited. Yet, for the first twenty years or more Ontario was the major source of western immigrants. Even after new sources of immigration began to develop in the mid-1890s, central Canada continued to send thousands of its people westward in the search for a better life.

The picture of deliberate exploitation does not take into account the fact that there were very different assumptions in existence concerning the relationships of the various sectors within the economy in the Confederation era. These assumptions, in turn, accurately mirrored Canada at the time of expansion. Canada, in the later nineteenth century, was primarily a rural society based on an agricultural economy. The agricultural sector was at the centre of Canadian economic life and it was both argued and believed that a well-developed and well-run farm provided a secure, rewarding, and healthy way of earning a living. The commercial and manufacturing sectors were, it was true, an important component of Canadian activity, but ultimately it was thought they depended on a strong agricultural base. Moreover, it was also believed that (setting aside the few spectacular success stories of businessmen millionaires) most Canadians had a better chance of success on the farm. While always somewhat exaggerated, this assessment should not be dismissed as pure myth. The established Ontario farmer of the 1870s, and for many decades thereafter, probably had greater material success and certainly a higher position in society than the unskilled worker or even the skilled artisan of the city.

If the agricultural sector was both important and attractive then it followed that a region centred on agriculture could become as prosperous and as important as a region with a significant commercial or manufacturing component. The vast West with its hundreds of thousands of acres of prime wheat-growing land promised to become, as the pamphlets of the day put it, "the granary of the empire." Such a region would be central to the Canadian economy and could thus expect to reap commensurate rewards. In short, the idea of an agricultural region fed by a metropolitan one did not, in itself, imply an inferior standard of living or economic influence for the former. In fact, there was considerable concern expressed in Ontario during the 1870s and 1880s, because the prairie wheat farmers were beginning to displace the traditional Ontario dominance in that crop. A region without an agricultural base was, in the nineteenth century, thought an undesirable, if not crippling, phenomenon.

Nor did the concept of an agricultural region imply political subordination. In an age when eighty-two per cent of the population of Canada was rural it was quite feasible that a rural population might assert control over Canadian political decisions. Further, by the time Canada annexed the West in 1870, it had so convinced itself of the region's drawing power that figures were tossed around rather freely by the publicists and promoters of the age. Talk of several million people in the region by the turn of the century was common. Such growth predictions implied that the West would soon become the centre of population in Canada with the political clout necessary to guarantee that the interests of the new region would be heard at the national level.

Thus, in terms of both the material possibilities for the individual and the eventual political power of the region, the West was not really seen as a permanent hinterland to an Ontario-Quebec industrial economy. It was assumed, it was true, that several decades would be necessary for the development of the region. In the longer term, however, the writers of the age of Confederation casually assumed a new and major power would develop in the West—a power so potentially great that it was even predicted that some day Winnipeg might become the capital not just of Canada but of the whole British Empire.

Obviously neither the assumption of economic security nor that of political power has proven correct. Yet neither should the idea be dismissed too readily as completely false. The West has, at various periods in its history, seen itself on the edge of becoming a central part of the Canadian economic scene. In the wheat boom years surrounding the turn of the century and again in the mid-twenties, western wheat prices and yield seemed to indicate a new and more prosperous way of life. In the 1970s, other natural resources, oil, natural gas, uranium, and timber, have once again given the region hope that the long-delayed expectations may finally be realized.

Ultimately, however, the economic hopes of the region have always proved delusory. The boom of the Laurier years was followed by the recession of 1912–15, and, after, a war-spurred boom followed by bad years from 1919–22. The prosperous twenties were followed by disastrous depression years. It is not surprising therefore that for all the wealth of the region, there is a sense of underlying insecurity among Westerners. Boom in the past has always been followed by bust, and the fear is that the cycle will be repeated.

As it was in the case of the economy, so it has been in the case of political power. For a while it appeared as though the region might eventually become a decisive power bloc within Canada. With the boom of the Laurier years, the population growth rate of the West far outstripped that of the East. From a mere fifteen Members of Parliament of 1891, the region expanded its representation to twenty-seven seats by 1904, fifty-six by 1917, and sixty-eight by 1925. The 1931 census brought another redistribution and the West was given seventy-four seats, more than Quebec and within striking distance of the number held by Ontario. Nearly one third of all House of Commons seats in Canada in the next federal election would be from the West. If such growth had continued, the West would have been more powerful than the combined provinces of Ontario and Quebec by the third quarter of the century.

Even as the 1931 census was being taken, however, the beginnings of drought, dust storms, and the collapse of the international price for wheat, signalled a reversal of the trend. Over the next decade, thousands left the land. By 1951, Saskatchewan, the province hardest hit by the Depression, saw its population drop by 100,000. In the meantime, Ontario's had grown by over a million. Overall, the region's growth rate fell well behind the national average for the period to 1960 in spite of strong growth in British Columbia. By the 1950s, the prairie provinces had fewer seats in the House of Commons than they had a generation earlier—even though the House had been enlarged. Even by 1980, after a considerable period of prosperity and rapid growth, the overall power of the West only approximates the position it had in 1931.

Nor is it possible for many Westerners to see the last half century as a mere interruption in the growth of political power. Were the Depression the only circumstance involved, such a view might be possible, but the relative power of central Canada and the West has been determined not merely by economic cycles but by the fact that the rural-agricultural nation of the nineteenth century has become the urban-industrial one of the twentieth century. A population resting on agricultural or, for that matter, on many, primary resources is not going to surpass the industrial heartland of a nation with more than three quarters of its population living in cities. The West has had to face the fact that the majority of Canadians will live elsewhere, and therefore, that political control of the nation will also lie elsewhere. Equally, at least until the post-OPEC world, the West also had to accept the fact that financial and economic power rested in Toronto and Montreal. Head offices of banks, insurance companies, and, of course, manufacturers were rarely seen on the Prairies. Vancouver, it was true, did possess a certain metropolitan status, but it too remained tributary to the major financial centres of Toronto and Montreal.

With population and finance centred elsewhere other things followed. The cultural institutions of the nation—the CBC, major arts, and theatre companies remained in the East. Tastes were determined in Toronto (on the way through from New York or London) and the populations of Ontario and Quebec, if they thought of the West at all, conjured up hazy visions of rural rustics or reactionary cowboys. The West, in short, was a hinterland in cultural, economic, and political terms.

. . . Most of the complaints emanating from the West over the years are really directed at this hinterland status. Demographic distribution precluded industrial development, added to freight rate charges, and forced a reliance on primary resources. In turn, a primary resource base tended to maintain a dispersed population and to be vulnerable to violent economic swings. Such large-scale forces thus lie at the root of prairie grievance and they cannot be easily, or perhaps ever, remedied. All of this is perfectly true but the point is that the West did not really expect to be a hinterland and has never viewed its future in terms of a continuation of that hinterland status. Politicians, newspaper editors, and commentators have all noted that the West has been demanding a more active role in Confederation. This is more than a cliché. It is a reflection of the long-standing desire to move from hinterland to metropolitan status.

The difficulties inherent in this situation have been made greater by the cultural makeup of the West and, especially, of the prairie provinces. In the nineteenth century, old cultural elites with established national connections and national aspirations, asserted their right not only to dominate the region itself, but to play a major role in Canada as a whole. However, it was difficult to maintain power from small frontier communities on the periphery of the nation, and as the years passed and connections became more tenuous a sense of "unease" increased. The elite was never really powerful or influential where it counted—in Toronto, Montreal, and Ottawa. Further creating a distinct western culture was the establishment of new and distinct ethnic and cultural groups after the turn of the century. These new immigrants had no connection with eastern Canada and, in spite of assimilation, viewed Canada through regional eyes. They were Canadians but they were distinctly western Canadian. To them the central Canadian obsession with, for example, French-English relations, seemed irrelevant and potentially dangerous to their own interests. The West was thus never completely a cultural by-product of the East and, especially after 1920, the East often seemed somewhat parochial in its obsessions and old fashioned in its concerns. The new West very much thought of itself as Canadian. It had, however, defined the idea of Canada in western terms.

All of this would tend to suggest that western complaints have been misdirected. The only realistic target of blame would seem to be those earlier generations of politicians and promoters who promised too much. After all, neither other Canadians nor the Canadian government can be blamed for basic geographical and economic forces. Or can they? For it is another argument of western grievance that the region is a hinterland not due to historical accident but because it suited the nation to keep it that way.

In the years immediately following its transfer to Canadian control, the entire prairie West was developed under very strict guidance from Ottawa. The government of the North-West Territories, the North-West Mounted Police, the land system, and the financial resources were all centred in the nation's capital. Manitoba, it was true, had been created as the "postage stamp" province as a result of the Métis resistance there, but even in this case, lands and natural resources were left under Dominion control. Given the daily range of services, from police to land, under the control of the Dominion government, nobody in the West could doubt where the real power for the development of the region lay.

There were two major reasons for this centralization of control. First, the development of the West was seen as part of a national economic necessity too important to be left to the haphazard agencies that might spring from the local communities. Secondly, Canadians had a strong desire to avoid what they perceived to be the rather lawless and anarchic social behaviour of the American frontier. Moreover, they accepted the importance of their region to the nation as a whole and felt that the nation as a whole should have a say in developing that region. That is, it should have a say until the region was populous enough and developed enough to assume control of local matters for itself. In legal matters, as in other matters, it was expected that the West would be treated as a hinterland only for a fairly short and transitory frontier period.

It was not long before complaints began to be heard about federal control over the West. At first, the question was not so much one of the principle of control as it was of details. Land registration delays, the progress of surveys, the route of the railway, and even the North-West Territories' enforcement of prohibition began to rankle local officials and to gain expression in the emerging newspapers of the region. By the 1880s more and more doubts began to be expressed as to whether the Canadians who remained in the East truly understood what was expected of government policy in the West. Prime Minister John A. Macdonald, who more and more rather disturbingly referred to the West as a "crown colony," seemed to view the inferior relationship of the region as a very long-term thing. A feeling of betrayal was building and, as early as 1884, the Edmonton *Bulletin* could charge that "papers and politicians in the East have utterly false ideas as to the relationship of the North-West to Canada as a whole." The same year saw growing discontent among all groups in the region and though the whites in the North Saskatchewan area generally did not support Riel's 1885 uprising, there were a good many who sympathized with the Métis feeling of anger and frustration toward a distant and seemingly uncaring government.

The disillusionment which the West felt in these years was not simply with government policies, though they were a part of the process. Rather, every development and every institution seemed to be directed not towards aiding the West to achieve its full place within the nation but towards exploiting the possibilities of the region for corporate profit or eastern interests. The Canadian Pacific Railway, so desperately needed by the prairie West and British Columbia, is a perfect example. Even before it was finished, the tremendous land grants received by the "Syndicate" building the railway and the monopoly clause which prevented any competing line between the railway and the border for twenty years became a source of western concern. The corporation was so necessary to the West that it became a threat. Its power over the determination of transportation charges and its ability, as later events would show, to save or destroy the year's work of a farmer through the allocation of box cars, made it an object of suspicion and even hatred. The policy of the railway to cover the unprofitable parts of the line through charges to the prairie producer further entangled the issue and has led to the whole western concern with freight rates—a subject so complex that the mythology is practically impossible to sort from the facts.

As with the CPR, so it was with other institutions. Banks, land companies, implement firms, and others all naturally sought to participate in the development of this newest region of Canada. Most of these institutions, and certainly all the major ones, had their headquarters in the East as had been expected. Yet as the years went by there was a growing feeling, partly justified and partly not, that the equal partnership was not that equal. Instead, many of these corporations seemed to be exporting their profits to central Canada and acting as a drain on the West. In the nineteenth century, with the notable exception of the CPR, such comments were still relatively rare but they foreshadowed an avalanche of complaints that were to come in later years.

The initial response of the West to this growing dislike of the way the region was being developed was to concentrate on gaining greater political autonomy. Through the early 1890s, territorial politicians of the North-West Territories government vied with the federally appointed lieutenant governor for control. The obvious federal reluctance to grant concessions indicated a certain continued colonialism at the centre but then, in 1896, the new government of Wilfrid Laurier acceded to the growing chorus of voices from the West and granted full responsible government to the North-West Territories. A locally elected politician, and not the governor, would henceforth be the head of government for the region. The West had won from Ottawa what British North America had won from Great Britain a half century before. There was thus a natural hope that the attitude of the new government would lead to a more flexible policy toward western Canada.

The question of the attitude of the Laurier government was to prove especially important because the next few years brought tremendous growth to the Territories. The post-1896 immigration and the beginning of the wheat boom meant that the West, while finally hoping that its day might have come, was also faced with tremendous problems in terms of finances and services for the ever larger population. The financial system of territorial government quickly proved inadequate, and the voices which a few years before had been calling for a responsible government now began to call for full provincial status. In 1900, Territorial Premier F.W.G. Haultain, backed by a resolution of the Legislative Assembly, asked the federal government to create a new province or provinces in the West. After three years of avoiding any answer, the Laurier government disappointed many in the region with its refusal to consider the question. For the next two years a major political battle raged in which the arguments on both sides resembled those used earlier on the question of responsible government. Finally, in 1904, Laurier yielded and promised provincial status. In 1905, the two new provinces of Alberta and Saskatchewan were created.

This final achievement of local control for the region was, ironically, the source of another western grievance. Laurier, under the prompting of Clifford Sifton, his Minister of the Interior, decided to retain for the Dominion control over all lands and natural resources in the new provinces. Not until 1930, a quarter of a century later, were the three prairie provinces finally given what every other province in the Dominion already possessed. Whether true or not, it is one of the traditions of western rhetoric to the present day that the only reason the lands and resources were transferred then was that Ottawa thought there was nothing worth keeping.

The refusal of Ottawa to turn over the lands is an important political event in the history of western alienation. From the national point of view it was thought essential that this crucial western resource remain in Dominion hands. From the point of the three prairie provinces, the refusal to make them equal with the original provinces of the nation was, as the Calgary *Herald* put it in 1905, "autonomy that insults the West." A growing suspicion seemed, by this action, to be confirmed. The West was, many argued, Canada's colony and its resources were, in the name of the nation, being exploited without giving the West a fair return. The memory of this national action has become one of the repeatedly used symbols of western grievance.

All the complaints mentioned so far, even the withholding of Dominion lands from provincial jurisdiction, must be subordinated in the litany of western complaints to those directed against another federal policy. When John A. Macdonald returned to office in 1878, after a term in opposition, he did so advocating what he termed the National Policy. The policy was a natural extension of earlier assumptions about the importance of the West and of the necessity of manufacturing in Ontario. It included a rapid completion of the Pacific railway, promotion of immigration to the West, and, most importantly, a policy of protective tariffs to encourage Canadian manufacturing development. The immigrants would not come for several years and the CPR was complete by 1885, but for at least the next half century the protective tariff became the basis of Canadian economic development.

The history of the tariff and the controversies that have surrounded it are extremely complex. Moreover, in the last decade or so the West's attitude has become much more ambiguous. British Columbia has, since the Second World War, had considerable interest in protecting some local industries, and in Alberta, the booming petrochemical industry means that not all Westerners are free traders in all things. In fact, cogent arguments have been presented to the effect that the tariff structure of Canada has not had the negative impact which has so often been stated. What is important, however, is not just what the tariff did or did not do, but how Westerners have perceived it. Their perception was straightforward, consistent, and vocal. The West, dependent on an export economy selling at world prices, gained no protection and could gain no protection from a policy of tariffs. It could, however, be forced to bear the costs of one. The picture of protected Canadian industries enjoying advantages at the expense of the western consumer and farmer was the final "proof" that economic inequality was not the result of circumstance but of deliberate government policy. Ontario and Quebec had used the influence they possessed at Ottawa to obtain for themselves a permanently preferential position in the Canadian economy.

While complaints about the tariff structure of the nation stretch back to the nineteenth century and were an important issue in the general elections of 1891 and 1911, the issue really came to the fore in the West during the depression decade of the 1930s. It was one thing to bear the costs in times of prosperity when, it could be argued, this was part of the mutual partnership between East and West, but it was quite another to bear it when the West was devastated economically. All four western provinces complained of the costs of the tariff to the Royal Commission on Dominion Provincial Relations as an unfair burden on one region of the country for the sake of another. The Alberta submission probably summed up the sense of injustice best when it charged that "the tariff, during the Depression at least, was in the nature of a subsidy to maintain higher standards of living than could be afforded in the areas paying for it." To further emphasize the point all the provinces drew on the work of political scientist Norman Rogers who in 1934 wrote that only two provinces in Canada—Ontario and Quebec—benefitted from the effects of the tariff. Rogers had written the work while at Queen's University but it was an especially useful study by the time of the Commission as he was then a member of the federal cabinet. The result, western studies unanimously concluded, was both to force their region into economic subservience to the manufacturing regions of Canada and to ensure that for all its potential the West would continue to have an inferior economic position in Canada. "The people of British Columbia," that Province warned "have to exert greater effort in order to create exchange values than would be the case if they were free to purchase these goods in the markets in which they sell."

Overall, if one were to generalize on the nature of these historical complaints concerning the West's position in Canada—and there are others than those mentioned above—it would be that the West has never been allowed to fulfill its own potential because, for reasons of their own, forces in central Canada have never been willing to relinquish their privileged position. Moreover, there has existed a suspicion and a charge from the territorial years that the national government is, in fact, merely the representative of those central Canadian interests. Premier Allan Blakeney of Saskatchewan restated a common western charge when he said that "We in the West find it passing strange that the national interest emerges only when we are talking about western *resources* for eastern *benefits*."

This western sense of exclusion has helped to create some of the more interesting, and exotic, political protest movements in Canadian history. The late W.L. Morton, Canada's leading historian of the West, has organized this tradition of political protest into three phases which he terms collectively "the bias of prairie politics." Until 1905, this bias was reflected in what he terms the politics of colonial protest when, as has been discussed, the West sought first local autonomy and then provincial government. The second phase, running from 1905 through to the Depression, he terms the politics of agrarian protest. This period saw the growth of the great prairie farm organizations such as the United Farmers of Alberta and farmer co-operatives such as the Grain Growers Grain Company. It was also in these years that the farmers turned to direct political action electing, in 1921, a surprising sixty-five Members of Parliament under the banner of the newly formed Progressive Party. At the same time, the United Farmers of Alberta swept the Liberals out of office at the provincial level. It was the last time the Alberta government would be in the control of one of the traditional parties until 1971. In other provinces, the traditional parties survived, but only by quickly donning the appearance of the farmers' government. The prairie West had shown just how powerful the voice of the farmer was in the region.

The final phase of prairie politics Morton sees as utopian politics. The Social Credit Party is the most obvious example of a Utopian Party in the West, but the rise of the Co-operative Commonwealth Federation was in many ways a more complex form of utopianism—especially as interpreted in the rural areas of the depression-ridden West. The utopian parties, unlike the agrarian, sought to remedy *all* the ills of society through programs of reform— whether monetary or social—and thereby usher in the brighter future not just for the West but for all Canada.

By the time Morton wrote his article in 1955, much of the utopianism and radicalism of the 1930s was fading. Under Ernest Manning, Social Credit had been converted from an advocate of drastic monetary reform and apocalyptic moral judgements to a rurally based Conservative Party with only mild hints of populism to connect it to its founding days. The NDP has moved closer to the mainstream of Canadian thought, though in part because that thought has altered. Nevertheless, terms in office in, first, Saskatchewan and then Manitoba and British Columbia tended to temper the rhetoric of the Regina Manifesto. Thus, the radicalism of earlier western parties has pretty much disappeared in recent years. Equally, utopianism has faded with the dreams of the social-credit dividends and other ideas of instant solutions to serious problems.

From this it might be argued that the distinctive "bias" of Canadian politics was fading by the 1950s and has disappeared since that time. It has, in fact, been well argued that prairie regionalism is itself fading and that the collapse of distinct political movements in the recent years is simply one aspect of that broader assimilation into the mainstream of Canadian society. Yet, as the same author admits, alienation has not declined and in that, if in nothing else, there is a distinct regional orientation to western politics. There has been no diminution of what this author terms the "political ideology of regional discontent." Thus, the bias of prairie politics remains. It has just metamorphosed once more. This most recent phase of political bias has turned toward provincial rights to protect the region against outside exploitation. Such provincialism was present to some extent in the politics of Social Credit, but, ultimately, early Social Credit looked to a national and monetary solution rather than a federal one. In recent years, however, Westerners have increasingly looked to their provincial boundaries as a means of protecting them.

This retreat behind the ramparts of provincial rights parallels a similar move in Quebec in the later nineteenth century and was undertaken for the same basic reason. Western Canadians in the last years have felt themselves surrounded by a generally unsympathetic and occasionally actively hostile Canadian majority. One way to thwart the national majority was to turn to means of limiting that majority by dividing its jurisdiction into its provincial components. This approach, in turn, reveals a significant and in some ways unfortunate shift in the long-standing sense of western grievance against the rest of the nation. Until the 1930s, western political protest tended to focus on either political structures or, more often, on "special interests." These special interests, whether banks, railway companies, or whatever, were perceived as using their power and their influence to affect national policy in their favour and against the interests of the West. The political response, therefore, tended to be framed in terms of reform. Programs to nationalize the CPR, reform the monetary system, smash the bankers, control the Grain Exchange, or whatever, all concentrated on attacks on systems thwarting the functioning of democracy. Reform of the system was the answer to western grievance because once the reforms were instituted, the grievances would disappear. Thus, for all the connections to regional protest, the CCF consistently called for a centralized socialist state within Canada rather than a more loosely defined one.

Since the Second World War, however, a different perception has crept over many western observers and has changed the way in which political protest is expressed in the West. Rather than see the problem as lying with special interests, the West has more and more come to believe that the problem is more fundamental than that. Regional self-interests do differ and that fact leads to different expectations not just among elites but among the average voter as well. The real threat to the West, this chain of argument goes, comes from the consumer and worker in central Canada. The essential problem is not the money system or capitalism but the nature of democracy itself and especially the age-old problem of what has been termed the "tyranny of the majority."

The last two decades of federal elections provide a clear illustration of the problem. In the 1958 election, the West returned to one of the traditional parties in Canada after years of voting for third parties. The role of the West in electing John Diefenbaker's Conservatives was part of a national trend and not a specifically regional movement. Thus, the West seemed both to be integrated into national voting patterns and to have in office a prime minister from Saskatchewan who would pay careful attention to the concerns of the region. A sympathetic government in Ottawa and the more prosperous western economy of the post-war years seemed finally to herald an opportunity to remove some of the traditional sense of alienation.

The opportunity was never realized. The Diefenbaker government, it was true, remained popular in the West. Sales of wheat to China and specific western programs on the part of the government further cemented support for Diefenbaker in at least the prairie provinces. The problem was that the government did not remain popular elsewhere in Canada. Administrative, political, and economic problems caused the voters of the larger cities to turn away from the Conservatives. Diefenbaker's view of individual over group rights and his vision of "one Canada" met with little acceptance in Quebec. In 1962, his government was reduced to a minority position and in 1963, thrown out of office.

The 1963 election simply provided further evidence that the West could not, in itself, determine the direction of national policies. In every prairie province, the Conservatives remained the most popular party. Even if British Columbia is included in the assessment, the Conservative Party remained the clear choice of voters west of the Ontario border, electing forty-seven Members of Parliament to ten for the Liberals. The new government of Lester Pearson was not even the second choice of western Canada as the New Democratic Party elected eleven Members of Parliament. Four years later, Diefenbaker was rejected by his own party in a move that, whether accurately or not, many Westerners saw as a rejection of their region and their region's values at the national level. . . .

With the national majority controlled elsewhere, it is natural that the region should turn within itself for protection. The provinces and their powers within a federal state thus become the bulwark against another more powerful region. This, in turn, further fragments the national sense of purpose. Provincial politicians, for their part, both respond to voters' concerns and play on those concerns in order to strengthen their own position. Canada has always been a difficult country to govern but it threatens at the present to become impossible to do so.

At the beginning of this paper a paradox was noted between th wealth of the West and its strong sense of grievance in the last few years. Yet this very wealth has facilitated the tendency of the provinces of the region to assert themselves against Ottawa. It is, after all, very difficult for a province to assert its provincial rights too strongly if it cannot afford them. The strong anti-federal rhetoric often employed by Alberta's Social Credit government in the 1930s, for example, contrasted rather sharply with the plea that the federal government take areas within the province's jurisdiction. The problem was that the exercise of those powers provincially was rapidly bankrupting the province. On one occasion when Alberta did resist federal dictation on a debt-refunding scheme the Dominion's response was simple. It stood by and watched as the province was forced into partial default on its loans. Poverty, whether in individuals or governments, leads to dependence.

In spite of the added encouragement given to provincialism by the prosperity of the West, the basic complaints of the region are amazingly constant. The West is still viewed as being in a disadvantaged position in terms of national economic policies and political actions. Subsidies of oil prices are, to many, simply an extension of the National Policy of protection in a new form. The West is still paying for the sake of the centre. Aid to troubled central Canadian industries is viewed with scepticism as a move based more on political expediency than on economic good sense. The West is prosperous but there is a deeply held feeling that prosperity owes nothing to either the attitudes of central Canadians or to the policies of the federal government.

In another sense the prosperity of the region is irrelevant to the mood of the West. It has been argued through this paper that western alienation and sense of grievance has not been about material benefits as such, though those benefits form an important part of the argument. Rather, the West's main complaint has been about unequal treatment within Confederation and about politics thought to be designed to keep the region in a subordinate position relative to Ontario and Quebec. The West has never felt in control of its own destiny. None of the wealth of recent years has eased this feeling. In fact, the tremendous wealth of the region merely sharpens the contrast with the political powerlessness that exists on the national level. The recent tendency of the federal government towards unilateralism, on both energy and consti-tutional questions, accentuates an already-strong sense of insecurity. Without political power, this line of reasoning seems to go, there is nothing that can protect the wealth that exists. The national government can, if it so wishes, drain the West of its wealth and leave it both economically and politically impoverished within a few years. Such a conclusion seems far-fetched and even deliberately alarmist but, given the growing alienation and suspicion of recent years, it is not surprising some should reach it.

The new wealth of the West, combined with the growing tensions between regions in Canada, has also led to the new phenomenon of large-scale meetings in favour of western separatism. The idea of separation from Canada cropped up in the past from time to time but, until the last year or so, was never a respectable idea for even a small minority of western Canadians. The West

was, in its early days, too much a frontier region to consider going it alone
and then, through the 1930s and for a time after, too poor to make such an
option worth considering. The new wealth of the region has changed this
and many Westerners, especially in Alberta, believe that being part of Canada
imposes a financial obstacle to the West's further prosperity. Oil prices at less
than half of world value prove a powerful rallying cry in the producing provinces.
Given the economic burden on top of all the other problems of Confederation,
separatists argue, why not go it alone?

As of the time of writing, western separatism remains the cause of a
small, if vocal, minority—justifiably criticized for its authoritarian and racist
overtones. Western Canadians have always sought a larger role for themselves
in Canada and are unlikely to turn their backs quickly or easily on a nation
that they have always felt is as much their as anyone else's. Nevertheless, it
would be dangerous for Canadians to ignore the existence of separatism. Support
for the movement, at least at the superficial level, has grown rapidly in the
West in the wake of recent federal actions. There is at present a mood which,
given further provocation, could become so angered at national dictation to
the region that, regardless of the circumstances, it might turn on the nation
itself. It is unlikely, but the consequences of such an event are so great that
it would be folly to dismiss the mood as mere "hysteria." After all, hysterical
or not, emotions have often proved to be powerful and often dangerous catalysts
for action.

What then is the solution to a sense of regionalism and alienation within
the West that matches and threatens to surpass anything known in the past?
The first step toward a solution must be to recognize that there is no easy
solution and that western discontent has deep roots and will not be removed
by one or even several specific policy decisions. Nevertheless, the necessity
in the present era may not be to find ultimate solutions, but to find a way
to ease tensions and to begin to give the West a feeling of control of its own
destiny, and of a fair voice in Canada as a whole, while simultaneously preserving
the nation and avoiding further drift to the "fortress province" mentality which
is so common today.

The first requirement is for a change in attitude. This is unfortunate
because it is perhaps the most difficult change of all. A tremendous gap of
perception of the problems of regionalism in Canada exists today between
the centre and the West. This gap of perception must be overcome on both
sides. Those in central Canada must attempt to overcome the tendency of some
Ontario politicians to see their regional interest as national while perceiving
all other regional interests as dangerous to the nation. The West will continue
to insist that power flow westward with the wealth, and central Canada, while
its dominance is not really threatened, must be willing to share influence and
decision making with the West to a degree commensurate with new circumstances. The federal government, so often accused of being an agent of the
central provinces, must recognize its responsibility to transcend regional

interests and to try to heal the splits that have opened rather than yield to the temptation of playing upon them for partisan advantage.

The West also has to undergo a re-evaluation of its attitude. Both the provincial governments and the people they represent must recognize that they have gained tremendous wealth and, yes, power, in the past decade. It should not be surprising to them if other parts of the nation feel uneasy and insecure about a future in which so much of the wealth is being created elsewhere while industry, a traditional base of employment for millions of Canadians, undergoes shock after shock in the central provinces. The West, therefore, should be willing to consider ways of using its wealth to promote its own interests but at the same time to promote the interests of all Canada.

If the first problem is attitudinal, the second one is institutional. The problem of the protection of regional concerns in the face of a national majority has, as mentioned, led to a turning inward to provincial rights. Yet this turn to provincial rights presents its own difficulties. With an excessive orientation to provincial rights in the name of regional protection there is a danger that the national government will be paralyzed, left unable to move in any direction without trespassing on the provincial jurisdiction. To remedy this, some means must be found to allow regional involvement in the federal government, thereby strengthening the national institution that has the responsibility of acting for all Canada while helping to assure that such national power will not be used to ride roughshod over regional interests. . . . [T]he Canadian federal government, in terms of its own institutions, is one of the most centralized of the western world's federal states. Such centralism further accentuates the western sense of alienation from the national government and ultimately serves to weaken rather than to strengthen the Canadian federation.

One possibility for institutional adjustment lies in reform of the Canadian Senate. Created in 1867 as a guardian of regional interest, the Senate quickly turned instead into a very useful place to reward the political faithful. Representing nothing more than a non-popular arm of the federal government, it never fulfilled the regional function intended for it. If, however, a new means of obraining Senators were found, the body might gain new life and purpose. It might also serve to assist in integrating both the West and the East into national politics in such a way as to give both a sense of political equality within Canada.

Two alternative proposals for Senate reform are often argued. One supports appointment of Senators directly by the provinces (sometimes reserving a certain share for the federal government). This would make the Senate a truly representative guardian of provincial interests, but may not halt the growth of provincialism as this new Senate would be, after all, a creature of the provinces. Another proposal would see the Senate elected on a regional basis directly by the public. The people of the regions would thus have additional power in Ottawa rather than their provinces. Neither proposal is perfect and both raise questions about the role of the second house in a parliamentary system. Further investigation of any such idea would be required before a final decision would be possible, but it might be worthwhile to consider the proposal. The federal government will not like it because it will lose control of the body. The provinces will not like it because it might tend to compete with them as the representatives of regional interests. Yet, the very opposition the idea is likely to create from existing institutions may perhaps be an indication of the useful role such a body could play as a counterbalance within the federal system.

Reform of the Senate, or of the Supreme Court, Wheat Board, or whatever, should not be seen as a panacea for the problems facing the West and the nation. Regional tensions in Canada will not disappear in the foreseeable future no matter what institutional alterations take place. The challenge for the present decade is to transform what has become a dangerous and hostile series of confrontations between a federal government with little understanding of the West and a West with little sympathy for the federal position into a more constructive balance of forces which will channel the regional tensions of the nation along positive lines. Perhaps, in the process, though this is an admittedly optimistic hope, the West will finally take its greater role within Canada.

FURTHER READINGS

Bercuson, D.J., ed. *Canada and the Burden of Unity.* Toronto: Macmillan, 1977.

Elton, D., and R. Gibbins. "Western Alienation and Political Culture." In R. Schultz, O. Kruklak and J. Terry, *The Canadian Political Process*, 82–97. Toronto: Holt, Rinehart and Winston, 1979.

Fox, P.W., ed. *Politics: Canada*, "Regionalism," Section 5. Toronto: McGraw-Hill Ryerson, 1982.

Morton, W.L. "The Bias of Prairie Politics." In A.B. McKillop, ed. *Contexts of Canada's Past: Selected Essays of W.L. Morton*, 149–160. Toronto: Macmillan, 1980. (Carleton Library No. 123).

Pratt, L., and G. Stevenson. *Western Separatism: The Myths, Realities and Dangers.* Edmonton: Hurtig, 1981.

Roberts, S. "How the West Was Lost." *Policy Options.* 2, 2 (May, 1981): 30–31.

Smith, E.D. "The Third Canada." *Policy Options* 2, 2 (May, 1981): 27–29.

8

Canada and the Quest for a National Policy

DONALD V. SMILEY

The most persistent expression of the nationalist impulse in Canada has been economic. There have been, and are, other manifestations of Canadian nationalism—the imperial movement so ably analysed by Carl Berger,[1] cultural nationalism whose most lucid rationale is in the Report of the Royal Commission on the Arts, Letters and Sciences, pressures for a Canadian role in military and diplomatic affairs more independent of Britain and later the United States. Yet economic nationalism persists. . . .

The turning away of Canadians from their preoccupation with cultural duality in the early and mid-1970s has led to a renewed quest for a "new national policy.". . .

The term "national policy" has been used in three somewhat different ways in Canada.

First, the National Policy—by tradition dignified by capital letters when used in this sense—has referred to the explicitly protectionist direction of Canadian commercial policy taken by the Macdonald Conservatives after they were returned to power by the general election of 1878.

Second, "national policy" has been taken to mean what W.A. Mackintosh designated as the "three basic national decisions" of the new Dominion of Canada to (1) acquire and subsequently settle and develop Rupert's Land and the Northwest Territory as a Canadian frontier region, (2) cause the construction of a transcontinental railway wholly on Canadian territory, (3) effect the industrialization of the Canadian heartland through protective tariffs. In this essay, the trilogy will be designated as "the Macdonald-Laurier national policy."

Third, and more broadly, "national policy" has referred to the continuing complex of policies undertaken by successive Canadian governments to establish and sustain a national economy in significant degrees both integrated and autonomous. Writing in 1952 Vernon Fowke said, ". . . the term 'national policy' includes collectively the group of policies which were designed to transform the British North American territories of the mid-nineteenth century into a political and economic unit. As thus defined, the national policy was fully formulated in its main outlines prior to Confederation which was its main

Abridged from Donald V. Smiley, "Canada and the Quest for a National Policy," *Canadian Journal of Political Science* (March 1975), 40-55. Reprinted by permission of the author and The Canadian Political Science Association.

constitutional instrument."[2] In somewhat similar fashion W.T. Easterbrook and Hugh C.J. Atiken orient their *Canadian Economic History* published in 1956 around this nation-building theme and state in the preface, "If this book has a central focus, it is the part which business organizations, big and small, working in cooperation with government, have played in creating a national economy in Canada."

THE MACDONALD-LAURIER NATIONAL POLICY AND ITS PASSING

The political and economic structures both shaped and envisioned by the Confederation settlement of 1864-7 were preeminently the manifestations of an impulse to establish a transcontinental economy in the remaining British territories of North America. The story is well known of how the dominant business interests of British North America were frustrated from pursuing their objectives, first within an imperial framework by the dismantling of the British protective system and later within a continental one by the actions of the government of the United States. In collaboration with the colonial political leadership these interests thus turned to the creation of a transcontinental northern economy in a classic instance of what Hugh G. Aitken has called the "defensive expansionism" which has characterized much of the nation-building process in Canada. Within this emergent structure the significance of the Galt-Cayley tariff of 1848-9 in the province of Canada should not be under-estimated. There was here the successful assertion of colonial fiscal autonomy as a concomitant of responsible government in the face of hostility from important commercial and political interests in both the United Kingdom and the United States. This measure also presaged the future in its defence by Galt on explicitly protectionist grounds and on the grounds that the public revenues which would be so derived were necessary for the improvement of transportation facilities in Canada.

So far as the design of new political institutions was concerned, the Confederation settlement was relatively conservative. It was rather in those parts of the settlement bearing directly on the economic integration of the remaining British territories in North America where the Fathers showed a high degree of imaginative purpose. There were here two major tasks: the more proximate one of the integration of the Canadian and Maritime economies and the acquisition and subsequent development of a western hinterland. The BNA Act accordingly provided the legal modalities for the future incorporation into the Dominion of the remaining British territories in North America. Section 121 decreed a free trade area within Canada by stipulating that "All Articles of the Growth, Produce, or Manufacture of any one of the Provinces shall, from and after the Union, be admitted free into each of the other Provinces." Section 147 committed the Dominion within six months of union to begin a railway linking Halifax with the St Lawrence River and to complete this project "with all practicable Speed." Section 91 gave Parliament the power to legislate for the peace, order, and good government of Canada except for those matters reserved explicitly and exclusively to the provinces, and the enumerated headings of this section—along with Dominion paramountcy in respect to agriculture and immigration, both matters concerned directly with economic development—specified most of those powers believed necessary to the economic integration of the projected nation. Finally, the powers given to the federal authorities to reserve and/or disallow provincial legislation under sections 55 and 90 conferred on the Dominion a means for overcoming obstruction to national economic policies.

The Macdonald-Laurier national policy as it emerged out of the Confederation settlement was crucial to Canadian nationhood. In a negative sense, as R. Craig Brown has pointed out, Canadian nationalism could not be based on appeals to a common language, a common history, or a common cultural tradition, so what was substituted was a "political nationalism . . . expressed in terms of tariffs and railways."[3] More particularly, in the early formative years of Confederation the national policy conferred on one set of Dominion institutions and on one political party, the Macdonald Conservatives, the responsibility for attaining objectives which most Canadians came to believe essential to their welfare—and in the buoyant years of the fulfilment of the national policy from 1896–1911 the Laurier Liberals owed a large measure of their success to their adoption of the Conservative political formula. Further, the national policy—to the extent that it was successful—steadily enhanced the interdependence of the scattered provinces and regions of Canada.

Yet in the acquisition and subsequent development of the vast area between the Great Lakes and the Rockies the national policy was mercantilist, and it is a characteristic of this form of political and economic organization that the hinterland develops a pattern of interests contrary to those of the metropolitan centre. Chester Martin asserted of the transfer of Rupert's Land and the "North-Western Territory" to Canada in 1870, "it transformed the original Dominion from a federation of equal provinces each by a fundamental section (109 of the British North America Act) vested with control of its own lands, into a veritable empire in its own right, with a domain of public lands five times the area of the original Dominion, under direct federal administration."[4] The mercantilist nature of the relations between the central Canadian heartland and the western hinterland under the national policy can be mentioned briefly:

- metropolitan policies confined the hinterland to the production of a small number of staples;
- metropolitan policies required the hinterland to buy the manufactured products of the heartland;
- the hinterland and the heartland were physically linked by transportation

facilities established and characteristically operated for the benefit of the latter;

- capital development in the hinterland was carried out through institutions centred in the heartland;
- many of the critical aspects of the heartland-hinterland relations were carried out through the instrumentalities of large business organizations protected by the imperial authorities from foreign or hinterland competition;
- there was a continuing pattern controlling the political authorities of the hinterland in the interests of the heartland.

It may plausibly be argued that the national policy was crucial to Canadian nationhood in sustaining a value system differentiating Canada from the United States. In one sense, the national policy was emulative of American achievements: the grand design was to create a *second* transcontinental nation in North America, and the ways in which this was done through the trilogy of policies relating to tariffs, railways, and immigration/settlement were to a large degree patterned after what had happened and was happening in the Republic. Further, again in Craig Brown's terms, the commitment of the national policy was to industrialism and industrial expansion at the time when the nationalisms of the larger western nations, including of course the United States, were economic in their emphasis and strongly influenced by the requirements of what was perceived as Darwinian competition. However, from another perspective the national policy was crucial in perpetuating a Canadian value system diverging from that dominant in the United States. S.D. Clark wrote in 1964, "the Canadian political community was not the creation of a people seeking a distinctive national identity. It was the creation of certain business, political, religious and cultural interests, seeking the establishment of a monopolistic system of control. Geography, which favoured individual enterprise and limited political interference in the conduct of economic, social and religious affairs over a large part of the continent, favoured on this part of the continent large-scale bureaucratic forms of organization and wide-spread intervention by the state."[5] In Clark's analysis Canadian development has been essentially bureaucratic-elitist, American the result of individual enterprise, and these two patterns gave rise to very different value systems. Much of Clark's argument is based on the difference between the Canadian and American frontiers and the differing relations between these frontiers and their respective metropolitan centres. The American part of the continent was staked out in the main by individual farmers, the demands of nation-building did not require that these successive agricultural frontiers be subjected to stringent metropolitan controls, and American capitalism has been pervasively influenced by these individualistic origins. In contrast, "Canada has been what the late H.A. Innis called a 'hard frontier.' The exploitation of her resources has required large accumulations of capital, corporate forms of business enterprise, and state support.

. . . The effect has been to weaken the development within Canadian society of capitalist, urban, middle class social values and forms of social structure."[6]

The objectives of the Macdonald-Laurier national policy had been achieved by about 1914, although some scholars have seen the completion of its objectives as explicitly recognized in 1930 by the transfer to the prairie provinces of control over their natural resources. By the beginning of the First World War all but a small part of the arable lands in Canada were under cultivation: in the postwar period the major objective of federal policies towards agriculture was not as before in the direction of expansion but rather aimed at sheltering the industry from the vagaries of world prices. The country had now not one but three transcontinental railroads and, as was the case with agriculture, the problem confronting the federal government was not expansion but rationalization and actions to minimize the high fixed costs of railway transportation resulting from the exuberant development of preceding decades. Although immigration revived in the prosperous decade after the war, and 1,141,834 immigrants came to Canada in the years 1919–29 inclusive, in the four years 1910–13 a total of 1,394,753 such persons had come and in each of these latter years there was a larger number of immigrants than had entered Canada in any previous year.

The ending of the First World War found the government of Canada without a coherent set of national economic objectives. The "new industrialism" based on minerals, pulp and paper, and hydroelectricity turned the emphasis on economic development away from the western provinces and integration on an east-west axis to the Canadian Shield and integration between the provinces and contiguous parts of the United States. Significantly, the new priorities both in economic development and other matters were for the most part within provincial rather than federal jurisdiction.

The Great Depression again revealed Canada's vulnerability to adverse economic circumstances in the outside world. However, unlike such periods in the past, the national government evolved no coherent responses to those challenges. In his 1952 article Fowke saw during the interwar years a groping towards "a new national policy"—the extension of federal responsibilities for welfare, the establishment of the Bank of Canada very near to the time that regulation of the national economy according to Keynesian prescriptions became possible, new policies for agriculture to shield farmers from the disturbances of an economy which had become predominantly industrial and commercial. Yet even together these new directions were inadequate substitutes for the nation-building elements of the older national policy.

It is of course arbitrary to assign a particular date to the ending of the Macdonald-Laurier national policy and even in the past quarter-century there has been a continuing though piecemeal development of the east-west infrastructure which was the essential element of this policy and of Canadian nationhood. Thus since the Second World War have come the Trans-Canada highway and the Trans-Canada pipeline, the St Lawrence seaway, two national television networks, two national airlines, and a system of airport facilities. Yet paradoxically, perhaps, most of these developments, as was the case with some of the elements of the Macdonald-Laurier national policy, have contributed to both east-west and north-south integration. Easterbrook and Aitken said of the St Lawrence seaway:

> The creation in Canada of a transcontinental national economy was essentially the end-product of a series of forced extensions of the east-west axis until it reached the Pacific Coast, the impelling motive being the determination to counteract the decisive north-south pull of the United States. In a sense the construction of the St. Lawrence Seaway is a continuation of this same national policy. But whereas formerly the St. Lawrence River carried Canada's foodstuffs and raw materials to Europe, now a large part of the traffic which passes along it consists of exports of raw material to the United States . . . The St. Lawrence River, traditionally the symbol of Canada's economic orientation to Europe, now serves in part at least to strengthen Canada's ties with the United States.[7]

Similarly, the Trans-Canada pipeline was built to carry Alberta natural gas to both eastern Canada and the United States, Canadian television networks devote a large part of their time to programs produced in that country, and the Canadian civil aviation system contributes to both national and continental integration, as will the Mackenzie Valley pipeline if it is built.

THE SURROGATES FOR A NATIONAL POLICY

National policy in the Canadian context is developmental: it is action by the national government both to stimulate economic activity and to shape the structure of the economy. In the past generation there have been two alternative formulations of the appropriate role of the federal government in economic matters which ignore this developmental dimension and thus may reasonably be regarded as surrogates for a national policy. The first formulation was explicitly set out in the Report of the Royal Commission on Dominion-Provincial Relations published in 1940, the second in the White Paper on Employment and Income and the "Green Book" proposals to the Dominion-Provincial Conference on Reconstruction, both of the latter documents issued by the federal government in 1945.

The Rowell-Sirois Report proposed important changes in the distribution between the Dominion and the provinces of tax sources, revenues, and responsibilities. The federal government was to have exclusive access to personal and corporate income taxes and to inheritance taxes and was to assume responsibilities for deadweight provincial indebtedness and relief for unemployed employables. The master-objective was interprovincial fiscal equalization, a regime in which all provinces would always be in a position to cause to be provided, as they chose, financial and local services at average Canadian levels without subjecting their residents to provincial and local taxation at rates above the national average. To the extent that from time to time particular provinces would be unable to do this they would receive from Ottawa unconditional National Adjustment Grants paid according to the recommendations of a Fiscal Commission independent of the federal government.

A trenchant criticism of the Rowell-Sirois formula was made by Harold Innis. Innis' essential point was that the Commission had failed to provide a solution for the "disequilibrium" in the Canadian economy which had resulted from the national policy. His view of the economic requirements of Canadian nationhood as these had emerged in the 1930s included sophisticated compensatory measures to aid those provinces and regions disadvantaged by the national policy, along with measures to increase economic productivity and to distribute more equitably the fixed costs of the transportation system. By these tests, the Commission's recommendations were defective. In Book I of its Report—as well as in the study by W.A. Mackintosh published under its auspices—Canadian economic development had been analysed historically within the framework of the national policy. The Commission had heard and later considered the claims of the Maritime and western provinces as these claims were pressed in terms of relief from particular disabilities of national policies in respect to transportation and the tariff. Yet when it came to its recommendations the Commission opted squarely for interprovincial equalization based on fiscal need rather than compensation for these alleged disabilities. The Commission's reasons for this choice were both constitutional and practical. From the constitutional standpoint, it was argued that the Dominion was accountable to Parliament and to the Canadian people rather than the provinces as such for the burdens and benefits resulting from national economic policies. In practical terms, the complexity and interrelatedness of these policies made impossible any precise measure of their provincial incidence.

Subsequent events have validated Innis' analysis of the deficiencies of interprovincial fiscal equalization as the sole federal instrument for dealing with the economic circumstances of the provinces. In comparison with other federal states such equalization is highly developed, although contrary to the Rowell-Sirois recommendations it has come to be based on revenue equalization alone and does not take into account the needs of the provinces or the differing provincial costs of funding them. Yet intractable regional differences remain. Further, there has been little development of sophisticated techniques either to measure the provincial and regional incidence of national economic policies or to compensate provinces disadvantaged by these policies.

The preoccupations of the Second World War and the opposition of several of the provinces prevented the implementation of the Rowell-Sirois recommendations. However, just at the end of the war Ottawa committed itself to a new Grand Design in economic matters in the White Paper on Employment and Income and in the series of proposals put before the Dominion-Provincial Conference on Reconstruction. These new formulations were based squarely on the Keynesian imperative that the chief economic role of national governments was to ensure appropriate levels of aggregate demand through generalized fiscal and monetary policies and through lowering barriers to international trade and investment. Undoubtedly, the Keynesian analysis was highly attractive to federal policy-makers at that time and J.K. Galbraith has said that "Canada was perhaps the first country to commit itself unequivocally to a Keynesian economic policy"[8] Unlike other economic theories this analysis contained fairly precise directions for implementation. Keynesianism purported to show how the economy could effectively be managed without any significant extension of public ownership or the complex structure of controls which had prevailed under wartime conditions—and without any explicit widening of the constitutional powers of the national government. Because the thrust of the Keynesian formulation was that peacetime capitalist economics faced chronic deficiencies of aggregate demand, the 1945 proposals included an important role for the federal authorities in public investment and, in cooperation with the provinces, in establishing and sustaining a Canadian welfare state.

The kind of development projected in the White Paper and Green Book proposals provided a relatively coherent basis for federal policy in the succeeding decade. Fowke wrote critically in his 1952 article, "at times within the past ten years it has been a question whether all peacetime policy might not be subsumed under the head of full employment policy. When baby bonuses and agricultural price support legislation are in danger of being regarded as being mere instruments of the maintenance of full employment it is possible to suggest at least a temporary distortion of the national perspective."[9] The Royal Commission on Canada's Economic Prospects in its Report made in 1957 discussed the "Role of Government" mainly in terms which gave little important place to public action in shaping the structure of the economy and dealt with these responsibilities under the tripartite headings of "maintaining economic stability," commercial policies towards the liberalization of international trade, and meeting the needs of the economy for trained manpower and research.

A sophisticated rationale for the Canadian variant of the Canadian welfare state was made by Maurice Lamontagne, then chairman of the department of economics at Laval University, in a paper published in 1953. Lamontagne's analysis was concerned with the past, present, and future role of government in Canada. The earliest period of evolution was that of the "first industrial revolution" based on coal, steam, and steel and ending about the First World War. Despite the preference of most Canadians for private enterprise, the conditions of the country required a broader developmental role for government than had been necessary in other western nations. The second technological revolution was founded on oil and water-power and on metals which were substitutes for steel, on new forms of transportation, and on mass production. In contrast with the first industrial revolution and in comparison with other nations, Canada was now in a peculiarly favourable position. Thus in the present Canadian setting the large-scale involvement of government in economic development was not necessary. The major role of the state lay in "maintaining short-run economic stability" through the instruments of "monetary policy, international trade policy, fiscal policy and public debt management." The activities of government in health, welfare, and education had of course increased and were expected to do so in the future. However, in the now beneficent Canadiant environment the active role of the public authorities in economic development could be regarded as finished.

The Keynesian prescription as it was received in Canada was agnostic about the structure of the economy and the interprovincial distribution of economic activity. Innis had written in 1943, "each region has its conditions of equilibrium in relation to the rest of Canada and to the rest of the world, particularly in relation to Great Britain and the United States. Manipulation of a single instrument such as monetary policy implies a highly elaborate system to determine how far transfers between regions and provinces are necessary. Otherwise full employment will become a racket on the part of the central provinces for getting and keeping what they have . . ."[10] The counter-assertions of more recent economic analysis have been that the inappropriate use of generalized fiscal and monetary policies has resulted in the recrudescence of federal-provincial conflict from the late 1950s onward and that the disposition of successive federal governments to turn to more particularistic economic policies has been an inadequate substitute for measures to ensure appropriate levels of aggregate demand. It is not within my competence to assess the relative merits of the aggregate-demand and structuralist arguments, although it is interesting that by 1960 Lamontagne himself, now economic adviser to the leader of the opposition, was arguing the regional and industrial incidence of "stagnation, inflation and unemployment" and cautioning against "attempts to solve such economic problems as if they had the same causes and the same intensity throughout the country and as if they could be effectively met by the same policies in all industries and all regions."

THE OPPONENTS OF THE NATIONAL POLICY: THE ECONOMIC LIBERALS

The chief ideological opponents of the Canadian quest for a national policy have been economic liberals. Abraham Rotstein has written that "the economic liberals have never forgiven the country for having been conceived in original sin. The National Policy, whether for good or ill, rejected laissez-faire and pivoted on the tariff. The aim was to provide a material base for Confederation by subordinating the economic to the political." John Dales has assented to Rotstein's assertion in these terms: "Sir John A. Macdonald gave us our first national policy and our first lesson in the irrelevance of economics . . . Macdonald was the first great Canadian non-economist."[11]

Dales has directly attacked both the national policy and the dominant trends of Canadian historical and economic analysis which have seen this policy as essential to nationhood. "I do not believe that economic policies can *create* a nation . . . I am prepared to believe that the existence of Canada can be explained on the basis of geography, political decisions, military events or historical evolution—on almost any basis indeed, *except* economic policy . . . I take the *existence* of Canada and Canadian nationalism to be independent of Canada's economic policies"[12] (emphasis Dales'). Nationalism is to Dales the pride that the citizens of a country take in its various achievements and is affected by its economic policies only as they contribute to or detract from this pride.

On the basis of his economic analysis Dales has concluded that the national policy has "*increased* our National Income and *reduced* our standard of living," i.e., that tariff and immigration policies in particular have resulted in a larger GNP and population and a lower per-capita income than would otherwise have occurred.[13] This has been detrimental to both the economic and political quality of Canadian life. Lower per-capita income has led to the more able and aggressive citizens emigrating and in general to inferior economic performance. Immigration has been used as an alternative to upgrading the skills of the domestic labour force and has resulted in lower payments for skills, both domestic and imported. Low incomes lead to low per-capita saving, resulting both in a high proportion of foreign as against domestic capital and low per-capita levels of social capital in such amenities as universities, libraries, and parks. The national policy has also complicated and degraded the political process. "Federal politics in Canada often seems to be a confused game of regional blackmail in which the victims believe they should bribe others to participate in a game in which they, as well as everyone else, are losers . . . The National Policy, bequeathed to us by Macdonald, ought to be dismantled, if only in the interests of reducing political frictions and simplifying Canadian politics."[14]

Dales challenges directly the political and economic historians who have propounded the view that the Macdonald-Laurier national policy was essential to Canadian nationhood. These historians and others have been misled by "crude hero worship, or an unconscious human predisposition to human explanations of history" towards a belief that economic development in Canada is to be attributed to "Macdonald's wise nation-building policies."[15] the truth is that in the nineteenth century these policies were a failure and the rapid economic development which occurred after 1900 was in no sense a result of them. In general, "economic man does not need to be prepared by government policy before he reacts to opportunities for making profits . . . It is high time that someone should write the history of Canada since Confederation as a triumph of the forces of economic and political development over the national policies of Macdonald and his successors."[16]

Harry Johnson's critique of Canadian economic nationalism has been directed towards existing and projected policies rather than those of the past. But, like Dales, Johnson argues that nationalistic policies do not contribute to Canadian political independence: ". . . neither imports of American goods nor imports of American capital acquire voting rights, so Canadian independence as embodied in the independence of Parliament can hardly be threatened that way."[17] The argument that closer economic inegration with the United States need lead to political absorption "seems to me to assume a degree of economic determinism in politics going beyond anything the facts of history would warrant."[18] As in Dales' formulation, enhanced Canadian economic performance would have, if anything, a positive effect on Canadian nationhood. ". . . I would expect that closer economic integration [with the United States], by enabling Canadians to have a standard of living closer to that of the United States would make them better able and more willing to use the political sovereignty of their country to pursue political and social policies appropriate to their own conceptions and requirements."[19] Johnson's major economic prescriptions are those of other liberals—the effective use of generalized fiscal and monetary policies; the floating exchange rate; policies to encourage competition; the lowering of restrictions to unilateral trade even if, in the Canadian case, this is done by unilateral action. He has deplored the turning away of Canadian economic policy from the generally liberal directions it took in the immediate postwar period to particularistic solutions, including those of economic nationalism. Much of Johnson's approach is summed up in his remark on one occasion that bad economists take up sociology.

Johnson's social perspective is a celebration of what he has called the "opulent society." In his application of classical economic theory to this society he has argued that both consumption and labour should appropriately be regarded as capital. Thus, "while it is not true . . . that the masses are becoming capitalists in the sense of owning and controlling the means of production, it is true that they are becoming capitalists on an increasing scale in two other ways—as owners of consumption capital, and as possessors of educated skills. Thus though the productive structure remains hierarchical, the political and social systems may nevertheless move in the direction of a democratic and free society."[20] Writing some years later, Johnson saw the progress of industrialism as moving from an "ownership-based" to a "knowledge-based" capitalism. Enjoyment of these possibilities "demands a transformation of traditional status-oriented societies into mobile competitive societies, in which rewards follow from contribution rather than status, and a transformation of geographically and ethnically defined exclusive groups into sub-units of a world-wide human culture."[21] Progress is represented by the United States. Canada, unfortunately, has resisted these trends both because of our British and French inheritances and because "our immigration policies have for the most part favoured European immigrants without forcing them through a melting-pot process."[22] Johnson's commitments are so stated: "by the 'wave of the future' I mean a society in which a person is valued, not for what he is by birth or property right, but for what he can do by ability and training, and is not discriminated against—or in favour of—by criteria irrelevant to current performance ability and outside his own original powers of choice."[23]

The carrier of liberal values is of course the multinational corporation, and in his recent writings, Johnson has examined the claims of this form of organization as against those of the nation-state. He wrote in 1970, "the nation-state is an agency of social conservatism and of the use of power to coerce the . . . majority for the benefit of the educated minority. The corporation is an agency of both efficiency and regulated change; but it has to live within the limits set by national states, and it has no obligation to humanity beyond these limits. Our problem is that the nation-state looks backward with deep nostalgia and the corporation looks forward with heavy blinders. How can we combine the economic efficiency of the corporation with the human responsibilities of the nation-state?"[24] Yet in a more recent article Johnson has answered his own question: "the multinational corporation, precisely because it is a threat to the sovereignty and independence of the nation-state, may well be the harbinger of further evolution of human society toward a more humane, equitable and non-discriminatory civilization."[25]

Johnson has formulated a coherent liberal philosophy based on norms of individual development and social life. There is nothing in this philosophy of the sonorous mush of recent Canadian Liberalism to the effect that this doctrine is a "middle way" between the extremes of laissez-faire and socialism. Johnson's thought is a reminder that liberalism in any rigorous form is, like Marxism, essentially millennial.

THE POLITICAL THEORY OF CANADIAN ECONOMIC NATIONALISM

Any serious contemporary justification of economic nationalism must contain some defence of the claims of the nation-state as against those of the multinational enterprise. Western political theory for centuries revolved around the competing claims of church and state and in the decades immediately ahead it is likely that a primary axis of controversy will be the legitimacy of the state and that of the multinational business corporation. As we have seen, an essential part of the social philosophy of Harry Johnson is a defence of the multinational corporation as the carrier of modernization and the "opulent society." The counter-claims of the nation-state have come into Canadian discussion largely through the application by Abraham Rotstein of the thought of Karl Polanyi to current Canadian circumstances.

Polanyi's remarkable *The Great Transformation* published in 1944[26] is an analysis of the economic development of the western world from the late eighteenth century onward which diverges radically from the alternative formulations of liberalism and Marxism. Unlike most other economic historians, Polanyi was a student of anthropology and his abiding preoccupation was the relation between economy and society. From this perspective, the establishment of the "self-regulating market economy" in the western world was both revolutionary and unprecedented. In all other human societies the economy has been "submerged in social relationships"; only in modern times has society been subordinated to the demands of the market. The inexorable workings of the market economy have meant that land, labour, and money be treated as commodities, although they could be so regarded only by a set of justifying fictions which Polanyi took to be both morally and analytically indefensible.

In Polanyi's view, the expansion of the market economy has been profoundly destructive of the "human and natural substance of society." The human degradation in this expansion was not manifested primarily in economic exploitation but rather in the liquidation of the social institutions within which social existence is imbedded. The most crucial deprivations were thus social and cultural rather than in a narrow sense economic.

The development of the market economy gave rise to various counter-movements aimed at protecting the social fabric against disruption—the early resistance to the enclosure movement by the English monarchy and bishops, the resistance of landed interests to industrialization in the late eighteenth century; the Owenite movement; Chartism; the cooperative and trade union movements; central banks protecting national currencies against the instabilities of the automatic gold standard. Most of these influences were directed towards positive action by the public authorities. Although such pressures have characteristically reflected the interests of particular social classes, in a very real sense they have also embodied a more general public interest in social stability and cohesion.

Rotstein's application of the Polanyi analysis sees technology operating under the aegis of the multinational enterprise as the major force making for social disruption in the contemporary world. Within this framework, nationalism is a conservative reaction to technological change and the national imperative is to secure the powers of government against the multinational corporation.

The Polanyi-Rotstein formulation is a sophisticated rationale of what Gad Horowitz has called "red toryism." This formulation conforms to the classic requirements of an ideology in explaining how a particular set of human circumstances came about, providing a standard for the critical judgment of these circumstances and issuing a call to change them. From this perspective the state emerges as the conservator of social, cultural, and institutional values and not as in Marxism the executive committee of the ruling class, or in liberalism—in its normative dimensions—the protector of individual rights. Yet it is important to note that red toryism, in this variant at least, emphasizes the communitarian aspect of socialism and neglects its egalitarian imperatives; there is little recognition of the exploitive as well as integrative nature of public authority. Rotstein in particular takes a particularly favourable view of the contemporary nation-state in both its domestic and international dimensions: "The bourgeois nation-state of the nineteenth century stood for private property and the enforcement of contract. In our own day it is giving way to the nation-state committed on the domestic scene to full employment, to increased equality and social welfare, to the mediation of the disruptive effects of technological change and to the fostering of the cultural values of the nation. On the international scene the nation-state becomes increasingly committed to foreign aid, to the tasks of peace-keeping and to other forms of international cooperation."[27]. . .

An essential part of the Polanyi thesis is that the market economy inappropriately treats land, the natural inheritance of a society, as if it were a commodity produced for sale. Although he did not proceed explicitly within the Polanyi formulation, Donald Creighton in a polemical essay written in 1971 came to broadly the same conclusion in providing an ideological justification for the conservation of Canadian natural resources under Canadian control. These resources are, in Creighton's terms, the "birthright" of Canadians and Canadians have a profound "instinct" to defend this natural inheritance. "These natural resources are not looked upon as ordinary assets—things the Canadians have built or acquired themselves. They are regarded as part of the original endowment of nature, as the birthright of Canada."[28] The enemy is continentalism based on our "manic obsession" with economic growth and our sharing of the America illusion that "progress consists in the conquest of nature for the satisfaction of human wants." But, "all that technology has done so far is to ransack the treasures of a finite world; and all that the sale of our resources could do would be to strengthen the American military and industrial machine." In general, "the only power strong enough to prevent the destructive onward march of economic and military imperialism is the national state."[29]

Red toryism provides a particularly convenient ideological support for contemporary Canadian economic nationalism. By its emphasis on the communitarian aspects of socialism and conservatism and its neglect of the contradictory answers of these ideologies to the matter of equality, it gives a common rallying-ground to persons of these very different persuasions. By its portrayal of liberalism as the enemy it provides a justification for Canadian resistance to various manifestations of American influence as the United States is characteristically portrayed as a community monolithically committed to Lockean liberalism and the American multinational corporation as the carrier of values which are at once liberal, technological, and disruptive of community. Red toryism also attempts to break the historic affinity of Canadian leftists for the American experience. According to the earlier perspectives, American values are more universalistic and egalitarian than Canadian and those who have asserted the superiority of the latter have usually done so from a conservative perspective. The red tory ideology on the other hand provides a reasoned position for those Canadians who wish to be both socialists and nationalists.

TOWARDS A NEW NATIONAL POLICY (?)

. . . [I]t is possible to delineate broadly an emergent national policy in process of being accepted by the government of Canada and embodied piecemeal in legislation and administrative measures. Often this new formulation goes by the designation of "industrial strategy." The thrust of this emergent industrial strategy and the older national policy coincide in that both are directed towards deliberate action by the federal government to structure the national economy.

Before there is a consideration of the new national policy, it is perhaps useful to refer in passing to two formulations which from different perspectives deny the possibility of Canadian integration through such a policy. George Grant's general argument is well known: the ongoing development of liberalism and technology leads inexorably to the destruction of community, including national communities, and to the "universal and homogeneous state." Yet Hugh C.J. Aitken in his *American Capital and Canadian Resources* describes the processes of continental integration in what is for me more convincing detail than does Grant, and for those who wish to preserve Canada this book, along with *Lament for a Nation* and Goldwin Smith's *Canada and the Canadian Question*, is among the most pessimistic analyses of the Canadian situation ever made. In Aitken's argument, the ongoing development of continental economic integration poses for Canadians the contradictory alternatives of material prosperity and autonomy in economic matters. While there are policies by which Canadians might choose to preserve a significant range of such autonomy, it is unlikely that they will accept the material burdens inherent in these choices, particularly in the light of the increasing powers of the provinces and the interests of provincial governments in those forms of economic development which strengthen continental integration. However, Canada, and to a much more limited degree the United States, is denied the material benefits of an integration which is both economic and political because of the opposition of powerful interests in both countries. Canada can have little influence over American economic policies except in those circumstances where Canadian interests can ally themselves with important domestic interests in the United States. In general terms, Canadian integration and autonomy through a "new National Policy" is impossible. The older national policy was directed towards east-west integration through the development of staples produced mainly for European markets. Today, however, "Canada's new staples are marketed mainly in the United States . . . The frontier of settlement is no longer a frontier of settlement producing agricultural staples for Europe; it is a frontier of capital-intensive resource industries producing raw materials for the United States. Development therefore to the extent that it is based on those staples, must be in the direction of continental integration along north-south lines."[30] This circumstance, along with other dimensions of Canadian dependence involving American capital and technology, makes Canadian economic autonomy impossible—at least at the price Canadians are likely to be willing to pay.

The master-prescription of the emergent national policy is for a Canadian economy with a highly developed capacity for indigenous innovation. The most authoritative statements of this prescription have been made in the Report of the Senate Special Committee on Science Policy, several reports of the Science Council of Canada and studies published under the Council's auspices and, in part, the Gray Report on Direct Foreign Investment in Canada. Among politicians, the most persistent exponents of the new national policy have been Senator Maurice Lamontagne and the Honourable Alastair Gillespie. . . .

The new currents look at the national economy from a very different perspective than has been common before. In the recent past several economic indicators, applied either alone or in combination, would have been deemed adequate to measure national economic performance—indicators related to per capita GNP, economic growth, rates of productivity, balance of payments, unemployment, price stability, etc. The general progress of the economy towards development would be charted in terms of the relative growth of secondary and tertiary industry as against primary industry. Current preoccupations with the "quality of life" and current attempts to develop new social indicators will likely result in subjecting the economy to tests related to, for example, aesthetic considerations, satisfactions experienced through consumption and employment, environmental pollution, and the conservation of non-renewable resources. The new industrial strategy applies the following tests to the national economy.

First, a modern economy is characterized by a highly developed capacity for innovation. Pierre Bourgault has given this definition, "technological innovation can be defined as the application of scientific and technological knowledge in a new way with commercial success . . . Innovation is considered to include all of the steps from research, through development, produce or process engineering and marketing, to the point of commercialization."[31]

Second, in a modern national economy innovation comes about through indigenous action rather than outside influences. Thus, according to this test, a national economy would be ranked as underdeveloped if the major impulses for change come from outside the country even though the nation were urbanized, industrialized, and prosperous. . . .

The major and interdependent prescriptions of the emergent national policy are these:

1/ There should be major cooperative effort involving industry, the universities, and government in applying organized intelligence to industry and thus to enhance the performance and innovative capacity of the national economy.

2/ First priority is to be given to the rationalization of the secondary manufacturing sector to increase the relative importance of this sector in the economy and make it internationally competitive.

3/ To the extent that the national economy continues to rely on the export of natural resources, these resources should be exported in a state more nearly finished than is now the case.

4/ There should be an ongoing redefinition of certain activities and industries (e.g., aerospace and computers) which are in the forefront of technological advance as key sectors to be reserved for Canadian ownership and control.

5/ Better industrial performance it to be encouraged by the lowering of tariffs through bilateral agreement with the United States or multilaterally.

6/ There should be positive attempts to mobilize Canadian savings for investment in Canada to decrease the existing levels of foreign direct investment.

These new directions point to very different patterns of Canadian-American economic relations than have up to now evolved. The new national policy implies a shift towards Canadian control over the national economy, particularly in respect to those aspects of activity featured by technological innovation, and Cordeil has said bluntly, "in earlier times, colonial or dependent status was manifest in the export of raw materials and the import of finished products. Today, a kind of 'colonial status' may consist of the import of technology in the context of direct foreign investment."[32]. . .

EVALUATION AND CONCLUSIONS

The emergent national policy is in several important respects congruent with both past Canadian experience and how an increasing number of Canadians are beginning to view the national economy. Like the older national policy, it gives the federal government a crucial role in economic development. In terms of S.D. Clark's interpretation of Canadian experience and the Canadian value system, it is based on the harmonious interaction of government, business, and university elites. In most of its manifestations, specifically those coming from the Science Council and the Senate Special Committee on Science Policy, it purports to be non-ideological and ignores serious consideration of its impact on the distribution of material and other burdens and benefits among different elements of the Canadian community. It attempts to shift the emphasis in the continentalist-nationalist debate from the form that it has often taken to the effect that integration can be opposed on only non-economic grounds and suggests that continentalism is not unequivocally to Canada's material advantage. Finally, in its focus on efficiency in the use of resources rather than growth the new national policy can be made congruent with an emergent conservationist ethic, an ethic which some Canadians see as potentially at least a major differentiating element between Canadian and American value systems.

The Canadian quest for a new national policy was in the past and remains a defensive response to the economic nationalism of other countries. In the context of contemporary Canadian debate this is often forgotten. Both those who welcome and those who deplore the penetration of Canada by the American multinational corporation appear to believe that economic integration on a continental basis is possible by this means. On the one side a somewhat uncritical Marxism postulates those corporations as nothing more than the decisive component of American imperial power, a formulation blind to the complexities of American national purposes and of the relations between the public authorities of the United States and its business community. More influentially in the Canadian context, the often elegant formulations of economic liberals about the alleged material benefits of continental economic integration usually assume uncritically an arms-length relation between American business and American government. In contrast to these crudities of Marxism and liberalism, it seems reasonable to assume that the continuing existence of two sovereign states imposes crucial constraints on Canadian-American economic integration. . . .

The major deficiency of the new national policy is that it fails to come to grips with the federal dimension of Canada and in particular to provincial economic nationalisms and the complications of the federal-provincial division of powers over economic matters. The general answer of the Confederation settlement and the Macdonald-Laurier national policy was clear—the federal authorities were to wield the major powers over economic development and to act decisively against whatever provincial obstructions might arise in the exercise of these powers. Despite these intentions, as the recent research of Christopher Armstrong and H.V. Nelles has shown,[33] provincial economic nationalism developed in Ontario from the late nineteenth century onward, and there have been other manifestations of this phenomenon in the Alberta of the 1930s and Quebec since 1960. The response of the proponents of the new national policy to the contemporary recrudescence of provincial economic nationalisms has been weak and is typified by the patently unrealistic recommendation of the Science Council of Canada for a National Resources Management Authority to "develop and coordinate long-range policies for integrated management of resources and the environment."[34] Similarly, the Report of the Senate Special Committee on Science Policy, one of the most authoritative formulations of the new national policy available, concluded unconvincingly, "a new National Policy based on a high flow of innovation contains no inherent bias against any region, particularly if it is coupled with a realistic strategy for regional expansion."[35]

The Western Economic Opportunities Conference held in Calgary on 24–6 July 1973 revaled in a clear-cut way some of the conflicts between the emergent new national policy and Canadian regionalism. In his opening statement to the Conference, Prime Minister Trudeau contrasted the "old national policy" based on "a Central Canadian 'metropole' with an agricultural and resource 'hinterland' in the West" with current needs for a "new national policy" of "more balanced and diversified regional growth throughout the country." Yet as these meetings progressed the Western premiers were able to make a strong case that at least some elements of federal industrial strategy had the effect of perpetuating if not exaggerating the historic dominance of the Canadian heartland. . . .

The industrial strategy of the western provinces is thus for a larger and more diversified manufacturing sector in that region. Events since the Calgary Conference show that Alberta is willing to exploit the very considerable bargaining power it has through its ownership of most of the Canadian supply of petroleum and natural gas in pursuit of this strategy. The emergent national policy has not yet come to terms with western regionalism.

Like its predecessor, the new national policy is based on the harmonious interaction between government and the dominant economic institutions of the Canadian community in achieving national goals. There is a continuing mercantilist pattern in Canadian economic history. Under the new circumstances, both domestic and international, the most critical elements to be harnessed in pursuit of national objectives are the universities and those elements of the business sector subject to rapid technological change. There is evidence that Canadian universities have not the will, nor perhaps the ability, to maintain any pretensions they may have developed as centres of autonomous intellectual inquiry and will offer little resistance to being coopted in the attainment of goals as set by the public authorities. The extent of cooperation from the private sector will of course depend on measures to lessen foreign control over business corporations. Yet any mercantile system is vulnerable to its subordinate areas mounting an effective challenge to metropolitan control. Western Canada appears now in the process of sustaining such a challenge in regard to such central elements of the older national policy as banking and transportation. Whether this region will successfully frustrate the new technological mercantilism is still in doubt.

NOTES

1. *The Sense of Power: Studies in the Ideas of Canadian Imperialism 1867–1914* (Toronto, 1971).
2. "The National Policy—Old and New." *Canadian Journal of Economics and Political Science* 18 (1952): 271-86.
3. "The Nationalism of the National Policy," in *Nationalism in Canada*, ed. Peter Russell (Toronto, 1966), 162.
4. *"Dominion Lands" Policy*, ed. and intro. Lewis H. Thomas, Carleton Library Series (Toronto and Montreal, 1973), 9.
5. "Canada and the American Value System," in S.D. Clark, *The Developing Canadian Community* (Toronto, 2nd ed., 1968), 232.

6. "The Limitations of Capitalist Enterprise in Canadian Society," in ibid., 248.
7. *Canadian Economic History* [(Toronto, 1956)], 556–7.
8. "How Keynes Came to America," in [J.K.] Galbraith, *Economics, Peace and Laughter* (New York, 1971), 51.
9. "The National Policy", 285.
10. "Decentralization and Democracy," in Harold A. Innis, *Essays in Canadian Economic History*, ed. Mary O. Innis (Toronto, 1956), 371.
11. "Canada's National Policies" in Dales, *The Protective Tariff in Canada's Development* (Toronto 1966), 144.
12. "Protection, Immigration and Canadian Nationalism" in *Nationalism in Canada*, 164–5.
13. Ibid., 168
14. Ibid., 171
15. *The Protective Tariff*, 153.
16. Ibid., 153–4.
17. "Problems in Canadian Nationalism" in *The Canadian Quandary* (Toronto 1963), 14.
18. Ibid.
19. Ibid., 15.
20. "The Political Economy of Opulence," [in *The Canadian Quandary*], 251–2.
21. "Canada and Contemporary Society," Convocation Address, Carleton University, 22 May 1970 (mimeo), 5.
22. "Gordon to Watkins to Uselessness," Speech delivered to the Ontario Institute of Management Consultants, 12 May 1971 (mimeo), 1.
23. Ibid.
24. *"Canadian Contemporary Society,"* 8.
25. *The Economic Benefits of the Multinational Enterprise*, 167.
26. (Boston). For a more summary statement of Polanyi's views see his essay "Our Obsolete Market Mentality" in *Business and Government in Canada* ed. K.J. Rea and J.T. McLeod (Toronto 1979), 362–74.
27. *The Precarious Homestead*, [(Toronto, 1973)], 35–6.
28. "Continentalism and the Birthright of Canada" in Creighton, *Toward the Discovery of Canada* (Toronto 1972), 287.
29. Ibid., 292.
30. [Hugh C.J. Aiken, *American Capital and Canadian Resources* (Cambridge, Mass., 1961)], 136.
31. *Innovation and the Structure of Canadian Industry*, [(Ottawa, 1972)], 22.
32. *The Multinational Firm*, [*Foreign Direct Investment, and Canadian Science Policy* (Ottawa, 1971)], 24.
33. See the results of this work in their article "Private Property in Peril: Ontario Businessmen and the Federal System 1898–1911" in *Enterprise*

and National Development, ed. Glenn Porter and Robert Cutt (Toronto 1973), 20–38; and Nelles' article "Empire Ontario: The Problems of Resource Development" in *Mowat's Ontario*, ed. Donald Swainson (Toronto 1972), pp. 189–210; and Nelles, *The Politics of Development: Forests, Mines and Hydro-Electric Power in Ontario 1849–1941* (Toronto 1974).

34. *Natural Resource Policy Issues in Canada* (Ottawa 1973), 8.

35. *Report*, Vol. II, 597.

FURTHER READINGS

Aitken, H.G., ed. *The State and Economic Growth*, 79–114. New York: Social Science Research Council, 1959.

Easterbrook, T., and M. Watkins eds. *Approaches to Canadian Economic History*, Part Four. Toronto: McClelland & Stewart, 1967.

Innis, H.A. *Essays in Canadian Economic History*. Toronto: University of Toronto Press, 1956.

Levitt, K., *Silent Surrender*. Toronto: Macmillan, 1970.

Molot, M.A., and G. Williams. "The Political Economy of Continentalism." In M. Whittington and G. Williams, eds. *Canadian Politics in the 1980s*. 2nd ed., 81–104. Toronto: Methuen, 1984.

Pammett, J., and B. Tomlin, eds. *The Integration Question*. Toronto: Addison-Wesley, 1984.

Russell, P., ed. *Nationalism in Canada*. Toronto: McGraw-Hill, 1967. (Particularly the essays by Dales, Brown, Rotstein, and Watkins.)

Safarian, A.E. *Foreign Ownership of Canadian Industry*. Toronto: McGraw-Hill, 1966.

———. "Some Myths About Foreign Investment." *Journal of Canadian Studies* 6 (August, 1971): 3–21.

———. *Foreign Direct Investment: A Survey of Canadian Research*. Montreal: Institute for Research on Public Policy, 1985.

9

The Meaning of Canadian Nationalism

Alexander Brady

Nationalism is a difficult concept. Its difficulty lies partly in the fact that every nationality is *sui generis*, the result of a special environment and history, and partly in the wide variety of subjective meanings given it by individuals. The term usually refers to that intense feeling of community in a people derived from their historical experiences which differentiates them from other and neighbouring peoples. In at least one respect all nationalities are alike: they live by a sense of their history and by an aspiration to mould their own future. A nationality grows out of prolonged social and political co-operation among a people sharing a common homeland, obeying the same laws, respecting the same customs, and cherishing the same values. It survives through a continuing will to sustain these intimate bonds. This J.S. Mill had in mind when he said that the strongest factor in shaping the feeling of nationality was an "identity of political antecedents: the possession of a national history, and consequent community of recollections: collective pride and humiliation, pleasure and regret connected with the same incidents in the past."

Mill generalised from the case of European nations fashioned over centuries by an historical process. History in fact created a national sentiment among Germans and Italians before they achieved independent statehood. This sentiment inspired their struggles for political freedom and unity. Canadian nationality was different. The term had little meaningful application before Confederation, when the Founding Fathers proclaimed their ambition to establish a new nation out of weak and struggling colonies. Unlike the contemporary Italians and Germans who created a state to express a nationality already existing, the Canadians created a state to make a future nationality possible. Yet it would be a mistake to assume that they had begun this task only in 1867. Already they had an attachment to laws and institutions in common, and understood the meaning of political collaboration. Indeed their ambition to make a new nation resulted from having lived closely together in North america as subjects of the British Crown and independent of the United States. As colonists they were hardly conscious of ancient traditions and long-established folk ways indigenous to the country. Their leaders, unlike the exponents of nationality in Europe, did not enlist the aid of romanticism.

Abridged from Alexander Brady, "The Meaning of Canadian Nationalism," *International Journal* 19, No. 2 (Summer 1964), 348-63. Reprinted by permission of the publisher.

Renan defined nationality as an attachment to a collective soul. Nothing so ethereal entered into the thinking of Canada's Fathers. They were merely conscious that in achieving self-government they had been active partners in furthering important common purposes. In acquiring in the Empire the title deeds of autonomy they had asserted their sense of a separate identity and as colonists enhanced their stature. They took genuine pride in their parliamentary institutions. It is true that these were a legacy from Britain, but they tailored the inheritance to their own needs. The establishment of a federal state was simply a means for achieving what seemed solid material advantages, such as the protection of their institutional inheritance from attrition, and the pre-empting of half a continent from American expansion.

The Fathers of Confederation had large and liberal views on nationality that would have warmed the heart of Lord Acton if not of J.S. Mill. They readily accepted in their new nation differences of language, religion and culture. None expressed this more explicitly than George-Etienne Cartier: "We would form a political nationality with which neither the national origin, nor the religion of any individual would interfere. It was lamented by some that we had this diversity of races and hopes were expressed that this distinctive feature would cease. The idea of unity of races was utopian—it was impossible. Distinctions of this kind would always exist."[1] Cartier employed the term race, not in its usual twentieth century connotation, but merely to mean an ethnic grouping of people. His argument on the matter lacked precision, but his pluralistic views on the nature of nationality resembled those in Acton's famous essay published three years before the Confederation Debates. Both employed the term "political nationality" to embrace peoples of diverse cultures within one state.

This type of nation was made possible by the previous collaboration of the French and English. For eighty years after the American Revolution the history of Canada, excluding the Maritime colonies, was primarily that of a small bi-cultural community concentrated in a relatively narrow tract of the St. Lawrence valley between the lower river settlements in the east and Lake St. Clair in the west. This territory of little more than 50,000 square miles was the strategic base from which the nation-building forces in British North America ultimately stemmed. The people in the region at first, however, had difficulty in achieving integration among themselves. From the British conquest until the middle of the nineteent century the French outnumbered those of English speech. They had received protection in the Quebec Act of 1774 for their religion, laws and customs, and were thus enabled to survive as a distinct and cohesive community. Early British rulers may have complacently assumed that in the passage of time the French would be assimilated to the English, but such hopes were illusionary. In 1831, in his American travels, Tocqueville briefly visited Quebec and tossed off a confident opinion: "Lower Canada will end by becoming a people entirely French. But it will never be a numerous people. Everything around them will become English." The French island in an Anglo-Saxon sea existed and was destined to endure because it was large enough and integrated enough for purposes of survival.

Moreover its own self-consciousness was fostered under the representative institutions provided by the Constitutional Act from 1792–1840. In this era of emergent nationalism in Europe, the social and political conditions in Lower Canada were remarkably well calculated to arouse in the French a sense of nationality: they constituted a decisive electoral majority, dominated the legislature, but were denied the real seats of power in the government, which were firmly held by an English minority from whom they were alienated by differences of history, language, customs and values. Under the parliamentary regime they struggled for what they considered legitimate constitutional liberties, and when denied them the less patient spirits embarked on rebellion.

The experiences of militant agitation for political liberties left a lasting impression on the French and especially on what they thought of themselves. Even before François-Xavier Garneau in 1845 began to publish his *Histoire du Canada* they saw themselves as the heirs of French civilization engaged in a heroic contest for freedom and survival as an ethnic entity. Garneau, inspired by the romantic historiography of contemporary France, provided additional literary fuel for the enduring fire of national feeling. French-Canadian nationalism is, therefore, an early nineteenth century product. It is older than Canadian nationalism.

The crucial chapter of events which made possible the broad pan-Canadian nationality extolled by Cartier began under the Union Act of 1840 in the party alliances and compacts of French and English politicians. Baldwin and Lafontaine were the precursors of a great and creative political process which laid the foundations for modern Canada. Economic forces and external pressures weighed heavily with the men who made the political decisions. The old colonial empire had dissolved with the triumph of free trade in Britain, and new and critical adjustments were needed in the colonial economy. The St. Lawrence valley, occupied jointly by the English and French, was too restricted an area for a growing people. The extension of settlement from the lowlands to the north and north-west was blocked by the Pre-Cambrian Shield, with its granite ridges, harsh winters, scanty soil, and broken water-courses. Deprived of an agrarian frontier comparable to the Mississippi valley, Canada not merely failed to retain all immigrants who entered its ports but also all its own natural increase. Hence French Canadians migrated from their ancestral parishes to New England and youths from the farms of Ontario crossed the boundary to help clear the forests of Michigan or establish homesteads in Iowa.

The solution for this cramping predicament was the expansion of Canada, which implied the building of a continental nation, capable of surviving alongside the United States. Confederation, which brought it into being, rested on two facts: first, the agreement of the French and English to replace the union of 1840 with a system that would give greater political satisfaction to each and also improve their common economic prospects; secondly, the inclusion of other British territories in North America. The nation projected in 1867 faced immense difficulties. At the outset the attachment of the various communities beyond the St. Lawrence valley to the concept of a common nationality was tentative and cautious. Before Confederation the Maritimes and British Columbia had their own ambitions for the future, and only slowly reconciled themselves to a union with Canada. National political leaders often confronted a stubborn and sullen regional spirit that made cordial relations between Ottawa and the provincial governments difficult. A local politician remarked on the adhesion of British Columbia to Confederation: "No union on account of love needs to be looked for. The only bond of union . . . will be the material advantage of the country and pecuniary benefit of the inhabitants. Love for Canada has to be acquired by the prosperity of the country and from our own children." The words were candid, but the sentiment was common. The spirit of union weakened whenever economic prospects diminished. The secession movement of Nova Scotia in the 1880s and the strong periodic dissidence of the West all testify to the early pains of nation-building. In the different geographic sections federal union was commonly judged by its material benefits, and in the first thirty years these were not impressive. Canada was then being steadily drained of people by her powerful neighbour. In the 1880s for every 1,000 births at home, more than 700 residents migrated to the United States. National pride could not be augmented by the fact that in 1901 slightly more than one-fifth of all native-born Canadians lived in the republic. "The Americans may say with truth," wrote Goldwin Smith, "that if they do not annex Canada they are annexing the Canadians." Writing gloomily to Blake in 1891 Laurier remarked: "We have come to a period in the history of this young country when premature dissolution seems to be at hand."

The twentieth century, however, brought a profound change in material achievements and national consciousness. Economic growth stimulated by the extension of railways, the settlement of the west, the inflow of capital and people, and the exploitation of mineral and forest wealth, helped to cultivate the feeling of a common national interest. Faith in the country found a stimulant in each burst of prosperity. Hardly less important was Canada's participation in the two World Wars. Both at the time strained acutely the relations between the English and the French, but on the different regions of English Canada they had an integrating and nationalizing influence. They stimulated industrialism, diversified the economy, and pervasively affected Canadian thought and sentiments by breaking down colonial inhibitions fostering the growth of a sense of corporate pride in the nation's identity.

Yet despite all these integrating influences regionalism still remains a divisive force in Canada's nationhood, and we mean by regionalism a complex of economic interests and stereotyped conceptions dominant in a geographic area. Local politicians are prone to identify the special concerns of their region with the national purposes of the country. The constant debate in party conclaves and the federal parliament never finally settles the issue as to what is of value to the whole and what to the part. The early term National Policy applied to the protective tariff provides a classic illustration. The spokesmen for the industrialists in the central provinces might assume fiscal protection to be an essential instrument in building the nation by fostering a transcontinental economy largely independent of its neighbour. It was not so obvious, however, to Saskatchewan grain growers that the integrity of Canada's nationhood necessitated duties on the machines they imported. They assumed no less confidently than the eastern industrialists that they represented the real interests of the nation and that the eastern industrialists were a selfish sectional interest. Nevertheless, fortunately in these regional contests we need not be constantly afraid that the survival of the federation is at stake. A working consensus in each case is evolved through the national parties and the federal executive. It may often be reached mysteriously and with difficulty, but it is reached.

The issue of Quebec might also be considered regional, but its dimensions and quality are different from all other regional issues. It touches the heart of Canadian nationality, and to it we must devote the remainder of this article.

Since 1867 nationalism in the sense of a consciousness of their nationality has been active in various forms in the life of French Canadians. English Canadians have generally been reluctant to acknowledge the fact of French Canadian nationality much as Englishmen had been indisposed to acknowledge the fact of Irish nationality in the nineteenth and early twentieth centuries. But the phenomenon cannot be destroyed by failing to call it by its name.

French Canadian nationalism has reflected two major strains of thought not always clearly disentangled: the separatist and non-separatist. The separatists, who hitherto have represented never more than an unimportant minority, would divorce the French of Quebec from the rest of Canada. They summarily reject the notion of a pan-Canadian nationality in which the French are participants, and see the cultural integrity of their community only in political independence. The non-separatistis, although differing widely among themselves, represent the creed that has traditionally won most allegiance over the French Canadian mind. They are not out to destroy Confederation but to adapt its framework and laws in order to secure the survival of French culture as a distinct and living organism within Canada's body politic. Their basic belief is that their cultural nationality may with wise safeguards endure indefinitely as a special entity in the federal state.

In the 1880s this nationalism had an eloquent proponent in Honoré Mercier, Premier of Quebec 1886–91, whose principal themes were to recur frequently in the arguments of his successors during the next half century: a concern for the cultural rights of French Canadians in provinces outside Quebec; an antagonism to the centralization of power in Ottawa; a concomitant attachment to provincial autonomy especially when Quebec was involved; a conviction that Roman Catholicism and French Canadian nationalism were inseparably wedded; and a hostility to any Canadian involvement with Britain or British imperialism that might require tribute in blood and money. Mercier's most dramatic espousal of the French cause outside Quebec was his criticism of the arrogant and shabby treatment of the Métis in the West, who were French in blood and Catholic in faith. Riel died on the scaffold, he told his compatriots, because of English prejudice and Orange fanaticism. The charge might be a simplification of the facts, but unquestionably it expressed the anguish of French Canadians at what they interpreted as injustice to their kin. In his attack on federal centralization Mercier had a reliable ally in Oliver Mowat of Ontario.

In the latter part of the nineteenth century French ecclesiastical leaders were hardly less conspicuous than politicians in championing nationalist ideas. A traditional theme in clerical addresses before the St. Jean-Baptiste Society (founded in 1834) was the special and providential mission of French Canadians as protectors in North America of Roman Catholicism and its ways of life. To keep the people French was to keep them Catholic. The language in particular was a guardian of the faith. This view was reduced to the simplified thesis that without religion, the language would disappear; without the language, religion would disappear. The two cherished values of the French Canadians were thus inseparable. Both must survive or none would survive.

In the 1880s and 1890s the clerical leaders had abundant opportunity to do battle for faith and nation, and especially in the dominion's newest province of Manitoba. In 1870 when this province entered federation its French and English inhabitants were nearly equal in numbers, and the French members of the federal government were keenly interested in its institutions. Under the Manitoba Act denominational or separate schools on the lines of those in Quebec were recognized and both French and English were accepted as official languages. But in the next twenty years immigration to the province from Ontario, Britain and elsewhere augmented the proportion of Protestants and English and reduced the French Catholics to a minority. In 1890 the legislature of the day passed two enactments: one replaced the separate schools with a public system, non-sectarian, and sustained by taxes on real property; and the other established English as the sole official language. The Manitoba school question was explosive not merely in provincial but national politics. The French had looked on Manitoba as the property of both peoples to be developed according to the institutions and practices of both. Their ideal was now shattered. To the French bishops in particular the school and language legislation appeared as a betrayal of liberties formerly enjoyed and a denial of something essential for the cultural survival of their flocks. They were not least provoked by the argument for the new enactments: denominational schools were thought to divide the people, and hence to be unsuited for furthering a commercial society and a united Canada. But the French had helped their own defeat by a failure to migrate to the West in sufficient numbers at a time when they freely migrated to New England.

The issues of the late nineteenth century were carried over into the early twentieth, when the dominant exponent of French Canadian nationalism was Henri Bourassa, who wrote and spoke with fascinating eloquence. He came closest, it has been said, "to being the French Canadian equivalent of a charismatic leader."[2] The tenor of his nationalist argument did not differ greatly from Mercier's, but the circumstances and environment of the time differed. In Bourassa there is more concentration on the danger of Canada's involvement in imperialism, with her participation in the South African war taken by him as the first unfortunate and warning example. On this issue he was the proponent of a pan-Canadian nationality, in which the two peoples would be united but not fused, and attached to one country free of imperial entanglements. *La Patrie* was not Quebec or Ontario but Canada. Bourassa's faith in a pan-Canadian nationhood, however, was severely shaken by the unwillingness of most provinces to concede the educational and linguistic rights to the French minority to which he believed them entitled. He here experienced the frustrations of most French Canadian nationalists since 1867. The fierce controversy over the educational provisions in the autonomy bills for Saskatchewan and Alberta brought him into the midst of the battle. With his characteristic fervour he argued the thesis that separate schools were needed in the West in order to make it a land to which the French might migrate without suffering attrition in their rights. They should not be made to feel that "Quebec is our only country, because we have no liberty elsewhere." For him a common Canadian nationality could exist only in the tolerant acceptance of differences between the two peoples and in the fact that the whole of Canada belonged to both.

This projected ideal of a Canadian nation expressed in terms of cultural dualism accepted across the country conflicted with the hard circumstance that in Canada's federation, except for some specific guarantees in the British North America Act, education was a provincial power, and in the final analysis provincial electorates and their representatives determined the extent to which if at all separate and French language schools should exist. Bourassa found it difficult to accept the course counselled by Laurier, namely, that the French must make gains solely by their own efforts within the provincial framework and through the process of democratic persuasion. They could not enjoy and cherish the full rights of provincial autonomy in Quebec and at the same time circumscribe them elsewhere in Canada. As for the French language it was not protected by the British North America Act in any province outside Quebec. Its wide employment in public instruction could be secured only through the good will of provincial educational authorities and the enlightenment of provincial opinion.

Long before Bourassa's death in 1952 his ideas on nationalism had lost much of their appeal to the younger generation of Quebec. This was due partly to the decline of his own confidence in the importance of language and culture (the growing intensity of his Catholicism tempered his nationalism) and partly to the fact that national ideas in his province were rapidly acquiring a new economic and social orientation. The old order in which he had grown up was undergoing profound change as a result of three successive events: the depression of the 1930s, the Second World War, and the accelerated pace of industrialization. . . .

The most fundamental dynamic of change in French Canada's thinking . . . was the industrialization of Quebec, stimulated by the second World War but destined to come in any case in view of its rich resources and large labour supply. The progress of industrialism tended to shift the pivot of social power and influence from a rural to an urban population and especially to a new middle class of salaried white-collar workers who saw the old issue of cultural survival in special terms. They began to question more deeply and urgently than ever before the facts and assumptions of Quebec life: the clerical control of education, the commanding position of the English in the board rooms of the large corporations, the authority of the old French élites who had run the province on long-established lines.

It may seem ironic that while a fresh ferment of ideas was becoming manifest in the French community, Quebec was ruled by Maurice Duplessis, a masterful political boss with quick brain and iron will, who lacked sympathy with new ideas, but possessed an uncanny skill in imposing his stamp on politics and in exploiting the weaknesses of his electorate. In the style of nationalist politicans he made federal centralization the enemy to fight and provincial autonomy the fortress to defend. Yet he repressed wherever possible the urgings of the younger nationalists who were eager to modernize and rehabilitate Quebec society in order to endow it with more useful vitality. Indirectly although not by design he helped the new nationalism by encouraging foreign investment in Quebec's natural resources, which in turn stimulated industrialization.

The death of Duplessis in 1959 released a torrent of new sentiments and ideas. Some found expression in small miscellaneous groups and separatists who sought the complete independence of Quebec and managed to win abundant press publicity. But more important and outside the lunatic fringe has been the surge of fresh social ideas with a nationalist colouring that influence public men and inspire the Liberal party that came to power in 1960. These ideas issue in a variety of policies designed to make Quebec a society no less modern than any other in North America or in the contemporary world. Their proponents appreciate that in comparison with Ontario their province in some matters has been lamentably backward. Despite the gradual development of industrialism, for example, it was only in 1943 after fifty years of abortive efforts that attendance at primary school was made compulsory by statute. The nationalists now eagerly tackle the problems that accompany industrialism— the control and ownership of public utilities, public health, housing in city slums, industrial law, technical education, employment, and the achievement of a balanced and viable economy.

Thus a French Canadian nationalism with social and economic undertones has modified the political versions derived from the last century. Its implications for the broader nationality of Canada are far-reaching. It is hardly surprising that most of its exponents seem bent on improving the material lot of their own ethnic community with scant interest in the country as a whole. For them the pan-Canadian concept of nationality which once fired the imagination of Henri Bourassa has lost much of its relevance. They are too fully absorbed in the large tasks of transforming Quebec and becoming masters in their own house to assess the practical effects of their accomplishments on the remainder of Canada. Their policies involve much action by the provincial government, heavy investment and expenditure, and consequently a larger share of tax revenues, with profound consequences for the existing federal system. This is not necessarily fatal to Canadian nationhood. Adjustments in the federal structure and reallocations in finance are not excessive prices to pay for the survival of a dual cultural nation. English-speaking Canadians have too complacently assumed that their conception of the federation is the only feasible one. Most of the provinces are large territories with varied resources and diverse needs, and it is desirable that they should have ample room for their own free initiative in economic and social plans rather than be homogenized by the policies of the central government. At any rate it is only in a federation permitting such initiative that Quebec could ever feel at home.

The French Canadians do not merely want scope to achieve social reform in their homeland. They want ungrudging recognition for their language as the central element in their culture. This aspiration is an integral part of their nationalism. The language issue involves more than status. It has many practical aspects. The French have long correctly believed that they lacked equal access with the English to the higher executive positions in the great corporations of Montreal. Part of their handicap is the fact that their mother tongue is French. The businessmen occupying these posts are disposed to favour those whose mother tongue is English on the assumption that misunderstandings are thereby avoided and efficiency furthered. They fear that the subtle nuances of another language and culture bring a disruptive element into the process of making executive decisions. The French, on their side, are sometimes partly responsible for the discrimination from which they suffer by a reluctance to serve in the branch offices outside Quebec of large Montreal companies. A deep attachment to their own ethnic group inhibits them from accepting the conditions that modern corporate enterprise imposes. A like situation, although less pronounced, is discernible in the higher echelons of the federal civil service.

Acceptance of the principle of bilingualism and determination to apply it will ultimately enlarge understanding in these sensitive sectors of national life. But a willing compliance with bilingualism can not be a swift solution of all the delicate problems that arise in the relations between the representatives of the two cultures. Bilingualism among special elite groups needs abundant time and trial to yield its lessons. . . .

As we have seen, French Canadian nationalism in the late nineteenth and early twentieth centuries was deeply concerned with the language and educational rights of the French minorities in the provinces outside Quebec. Although it lost the major battles then fought, it is for manifest reasons still resolved to struggle for the establishment of these rights. In some nationalist circles in Quebec there is a tendency to write off the minorities as doomed to absorption into the English-speaking society. But such pessimism is not shared by the people concerned. Administrative arrangements and compromises on language and education have been worked out in the different provinces, and, although they have never been entirely satisfactory to the French groups, they at least give them some assistance in the struggle to preserve their culture. The minorities themselves have shown considerable initiative and energy in self-help by organizing and sustaining schools, colleges, convents, newspapers, radio stations, and miscellaneous professional and cultural organizations.

In all this the Roman Catholic Church and not least the parish as a centre of association have played a leading role. A portion of these French minorities lose their language and their faith, but the bulk have exhibited a will to retain their distinctions, and are particularly successful where they dwell together in rural communities.

The minorities receive constant cultural encouragement and nutriment from Quebec, but their outlook is not identical with that of the Quebec French, especially with the ardent nationalists who extol a splendid isolation or a rigid provincialism. They have a vested interest in a strong central government in Ottawa since they know that restrictions on their liberties in the past have come from provincial and not federal enactments. They also know that some of their cultural benefits since 1945 have resulted from the actions of certain agencies of the federal government, such as the National Broadcasting Corporation, the National Film Board, and the Canada Council. . . .

French Canadians in Quebec who are not separatists, however deeply absorbed in their own provincial development, can never cease to have an interest in the minorities in the other provinces. Their measure of loyalty to Canada as a whole is inevitably affected by the extent to which their language and culture are secured by law in every part of the country. They cannot ignore the force in Bourassa's plea that their dignity as Canadians would always be abridged if they were compelled to feel that only in Quebec could they enjoy full liberty. It is in their interest . . . to foster the survival of French culture in the minorities. It is hardly less in the interest of all Canadians who believe in the dual national state and the continuance of Confederation.

The English-speaking community forms the other part of the bi-cultural Canadian nation, but defies easy description. It was not a monolith in 1867 and is not a monolith today. Aside from being fragmented in the different regions and provinces, it has multi-ethnic origins since it contains not merely the different elements from Britain and Ireland, but the bulk of the people from nations other than Britain and France who made Canada their home and constitute considerably more than a fifth of the population. It is a kind of melting-pot like American society, although less formally committed to the ideal of a melting-pot. Compared with the French community it appears less integrated, less homogeneous in culture, and less conscious of an ethnic purpose. Moreover it has not experienced the ascendancy of a single and powerful church, but rather the influence of many churches, especially the Protestant communions and sects, each animated by its own special outlook on formal religion and social endeavours.

English-speaking Canada differs most sharply from French in the intimacy of its relations with the United States. Sharing a common tongue, it is more directly and constantly exposed to the immense volume of cultural influences transmitted through American newspapers, magazines, radio and television. That some of these influences are good and some bad hardly needs argument. What most disturbs many reflective Canadians is that their very magnitude threatens to reduce English Canada to the permanent status of a cultural colony, with an incomplete life of its own, dependent on the larger and wealthier country for its standards, ideas, techniques, and manners. They are worried by the question posed years ago by André Siegfried: "With an American culture whose centre of gravity lies outside Canada's frontier, is it possible to found a lasting Canadian nation?" Only time, as Siegfried would admit, will give the final answer. But at present one cardinal fact needs emphasis: the more fully and sympathetically the English Canadians commit themselves to the experiment of a bi-cultural and bi-lingual nation, the more significant and enduring is the national achievement. Through wider recognition of the French as a part of the nation the English may strengthen and enrich their own culture, thus benefiting not only the French but themselves.

The French, for their part, benefit no less from the attempt to preserve a genuine pan-Canadian nation. More of them today than ever before seem seriously to contemplate separating from the English in order to achieve an independent national state exclusively their own. But any such separation, apart from obvious ill economic effects, would almost certainly threaten the creative and liberal elements in their life and limit the effectiveness of their role in English-speaking North America. In wrenching themselves apart from the English they would necessarily look inward, strive to exclude alien elements of culture, lean toward a hyperpatriotism, and in trying to conserve a separate identity adopt aggressive measures that would undermine their liberalism. Nationalist fanaticism never hesitates to sacrifice individual liberty.

Separation would, therefore, impoverish the cultures of both English and French, whereas determination to refashion a broad Canadian nationality, recognising the transcendent bonds of unity between its parts, would challenge all the progressive attributes of the two peoples, and not least their capacity for tolerance. Success in this endeavour would provide some equipoise to the power of the United States. It would also further the original aim of

Confederation: to found in the northern half of the continent a nation different from the republic, combining without fusing French and English cultures, and perpetuating the parliamentary inheritance.

NOTES

1. *Parliamentary Debates on the subject of the Confederation of the British North American Provinces* (Quebec, 1865), p. 60.
2. Jean-C. Bonenfant and Jean-C. Falardeau, "Cultural and Political Implications of French Canadian Nationalism," *Annual Report of the Canadian Historical Association*, 1946, p. 66.

FURTHER READINGS

Cook, R. *Canada, Quebec, and the Uses of Nationalism.* Toronto: McClelland & Stewart, 1986.

———. *The Maple Leaf Forever.* Toronto: Macmillan, 1971.

———. *Canada and the French-Canadian Question.* Toronto: Macmillan, 1966.

Forsey, E.A. "Canada: Two Nations or One?" *C.J.E.P.S.* 30, 1 (February, 1964): 485–501.

Fox, P.W. ed. *Politics: Canada,* Sections 5 and 6. Toronto: McGraw-Hill Ryerson, 1982.

Lévesque, R. *My Quebec.* Toronto: Methuen, 1979.

McRoberts, K., and D. Postgate. *Quebec: Social Change and Political Crisis.* Toronto: McClelland & Stewart, 1980.

Russell, P., ed. *Nationalism in Canada.* Toronto: McGraw-Hill, 1967.

Trudeau, P.E. *Federalism and the French Canadians.* Toronto: Macmillan, 1965.

Whitaker, R. "The Quebec Cauldron." In M. Whittington and G. Williams, eds. *Canadian Politics in the 1980s.* 2nd ed., 33–57. Toronto: Methuen, 1984.

10

Lament for a Nation:
The Defeat of Canadian Nationalism

GEORGE GRANT

The impossibility of conservatism in our era is the impossibility of Canada. As Canadians we attempted a ridiculous task in trying to build a conservative nation in the age of progress, on a continent we share with the most dynamic nation on earth. The current of modern history was against us.

A society only articulates itself as a nation through some common intention among its people. The constitutional arrangements of 1791, and the wider arrangements of the next century, were only possible because of a widespread determination not to become part of the great Republic. Among both the French and the British, this negative intention sprang from widely divergent traditions. What both peoples had in common was the fact they both recognized, that they could only be preserved outside the United States of America. The French were willing to co-operate with the English because they had no alternative but to go along with the endurable arrangements proposed by the ruling power. Both the French and the British had limited common ground in their sense of social order—belief that society required a high degree of law, and respect for a public conception of virtue. Both would grant the state much wider rights to control the individual than was recognized in the libertarian ideas of the American constitution. If their different conservatisms could have become a conscious bond, this nation might have preserved itself. An indigenous society might have continued to exist on the northern half of this continent.

To see why this intention failed in Canada, it is necessary to look more closely at the origins of both the French and the British traditions to see what has happened to them. To start with the British, it would be foolish to over-emphasize the niceties of theory among those who came to the St. John Valley or Upper Canada in the late eighteenth and early nineteenth centuries. It is difficult to put into words the conservatism of the English-speaking peoples in the Atlantic colonies or Upper Canada. The manifold waves of differing settlers must not be simplified into any common pattern. Much of English-speaking conservatism was simply a loyalty based on the flow of trade, and therefore destined to change when that flow changed. To repeat, Diefenbaker

Abridged from George Grant, *Lament for a Nation: The Defeat of Canadian Nationalism* (Toronto: McClelland & Stewart, 1965), 68-87. Reprinted by permission of the author.

spoke with telling historical sense when he mentioned the Annexation
Manifesto in his last speech to Parliament before the defeat of his government
in 1963. He pointed out the similarity between the views of the Montreal
merchants in 1849 and the wealthy of Toronto and Montreal in 1963. In neither
case did they care about Canada. No small country can depend for its existence
on the loyalty of its capitalists. International interests may require the sacrifice
of the lesser loyalty of patriotism. Only in dominant nations is the loyalty of
capitalists ensured. In such situations, their interests are tied to the strength
and vigour of their empire.

This does not imply that the nationalism in English-speaking Canada was
simply a front for interest. Many of its elements were shaped by that strange
phenomenon, British conservatism, which led the settlers to try to build on
the northern half of this continent an independent society. British conservatism
is difficult to describe because it is less a clear view of existence than an appeal
to an ill-defined past. The writings of Edmund Burke are evidence of this.
Yet many of the British officials, many Loyalists, and later many immigrants
felt this conservatism very strongly. It was an inchoate desire to build, in these
cold and forbidding regions, a society with a greater sense of propriety than
the United States. The inherited determination not to be Americans allowed
these British people to come to a *modus vivendi* with the more defined desires
of the French. English-speaking Canadians have been called a dull, stodgy, and
indeed costive lot. In these dynamic days, such qualities are particularly
unattractive to the chic. Yet our stodginess has made us a society of greater
simplicity, formality, and perhaps even innocence than the people to the south.
Whatever differences there were between the Anglicans and the Presbyterians,
and however differently their theologians might interpret the doctrine of
original sin, both communities believed that the good life made strict demands
on self-restraint. Nothing was more alien to them than the "emancipation
of the passions" desired in American liberalism. An ethic of self-restraint
naturally looks with suspicion on utopian movements, which proceed from
an ethic of freedom. The early leaders of British North America identified
lack of public and personal restraint with the democratic Republic. Their
conservatism was essentially the social doctrine that public order and tradition,
in contrast to freedom and experiment, were central to the good life. The
British Crown was a symbol of a continuing loyalty to the state—less equivocal
than was expected from republicans. In our early expansions, this conservative
nationalism expressed itself in the use of public control in the political and
economic spheres. Our opening of the West differed from that of the United
States, in that the law of the central government was used more extensively,
and less reliance was placed on the free settler. Until recently, Canadians have
been much more willing than Americans to use governmental control over
economic life to protect the public good against private freedom. To repeat,
Ontario Hydro, the CNR, and the CBC were all established by Conservative
governments. The early establishment of Ontario Hydro succeeded because

of the efforts of an administrator, a politician, and a journalist, all of whom wrapped themselves in the Union Jack in their efforts to keep the development of electric power out of the hands of individual freedom.

English-speaking Canadians had never broken with their origins in Western Europe. Many of them had continuing connections with the British Isles, which in the nineteenth century still had ways of life from before the age of progress. That we never broke with Great Britain is often said to prove that we are not a nation but a colony. But the great politicians who believed in this connection—from Joseph Howe and Robert Baldwin to Sir John A. Macdonald and Sir Robert Borden, and indeed to John G. Diefenbaker himself—make a long list. They did not see it this way, but rather as a relation to the font of constitutional government in the British Crown. Many Canadians saw it as a means of preserving at every level of our life—religious, educational, political, social—certain forms of existence that distinguish us from the United States.

To repeat what has been said earlier about the tragedy of Green and Diefenbaker, the end of the Canadian experiment was involved in the collapse of Western Europe, particularly in the disappearance of the British political tradition. Since 1945, the collapse of British power and moral force has been evident to nearly all the world. Its present position is the end-process of that terrible fate that has overtaken Western civilization in the last century. When the British ruling class rushed headlong into the holocaust of 1914, they showed their total lack of political wisdom. As much as anybody, they had been corrupted by the modern mania. Whatever the courage of Churchill in 1940, it must be remembered that he was one of those in the Liberal Cabinet of 1914 who pushed their nation into the intemperance of the earlier disaster. The best British and Canadian youth had their guts torn out in the charnel house of the First World War. To write of the collapse of Western Europe is not my purpose here, but one small result was to destroy Great Britain as an alternative pull in Canadian life.

The history of conservatism in Great Britain has been one of growing emptiness and ambiguity. A political philosophy that is centred on virtue must be a shadowy voice in a technological civilization. When men are committed to technology, they are also committed to continual change in institutions and customs. Freedom must be the first political principle—the freedom to change any order that stands in the way of technological advance. Such a society cannot take seriously the conception of an eternal order by which human actions are measured and defined. For some individuals it remains a heavenly insurance policy. Without the conception of such an order, conservatism becomes nothing but the defence of property rights and chauvinism, attractively packaged as appeal to the past. Great Britain was the chief centre from which the progressive civilization spread around the world. Politically it became the leading imperial power of the West. As Plato saw with unflinching clarity, an imperialistic power cannot have a conservative society as its home base. From Hooker to Coleridge, the English conservatives had less and less influence in their own society. The thinkers who increasingly influenced their society were the liberals, with their clear advocacy of freedom and the knowledge that history was on their side. Practical conservatives continued to exert influence. But the classes and institutions to which they belonged have disappeared. The more honest have simply fought rearguard actions; the more ambitious have twisted conservatism into a façade for class and imperial interests. By the second half of the nineteenth century, appeals to such institutions as the monarchy and the church become little more than the praising of formal rituals, residual customs, and museums. Politicians from Disraeli to Macmillan have applied the term "conservative" to themselves; this was hardly more than a nationalist desire to take as much from the age of progress as they could. Indeed, they were less and less competent to do even this. Canada exported to Great Britain a series of extreme buccaneers who assumed the name "British conservative" during its degenerate era.

British conservatism was already largely a spent force at the beginning of the nineteenth century when English-speaking Canadians were making a nation. By the twentieth century, its adherents in Britain were helping to make their country an island outpost in the American conquest of Europe. Was British conservatism likely, then, to continue as a force to make English-speaking Canada independent? If not, what would? The Laurentian Shield and the Eskimos? British tradition has provided us with certain political and legal institutions, some of which are better than their American counterparts. Our parliamentary and judicial institutions may be preferable to the American system, but there is no deep division of principle. Certainly none of the differences between the two sets of institutions are sufficiently important to provide the basis for an alternative culture on the northern half of this continent.

For all the fruitfulness of the British tradition in nineteenth-century Canada, it did not provide any radically different approach to the questions of industrial civilization. Canadians in particular felt the blessings of technology in an environment so hard that to master it needed courage. But conservatism must languish as technology increases. It was not conceivable that industrial society would be organized along essentially different principles from those to the south. Try to imagine whether Toronto could be a quite dissimilar community from Buffalo or Chicago, or Vancouver from Seattle, and this is to answer the question. What other kind of industrial civilization is likely to appear anywhere on earth, let alone on the northern frontier of Manifest Destiny?

Because of the British tradition, socialist movements have been stronger in Canada than in the United States. But socialism has been a weakening force in Canadian life since 1945. To repeat a previous generalization: democratic socialism is not, as it believed itself to be, the high crest of the wave of the future, but rather a phenomenon from the nineteenth century. Since 1945, the forces that will shape our future in the West show themselves to be bureaucratic state capitalism. The only time when democratic socialism was strong in

Canadian industrial society was in Ontario during the utopian days at the end of the Second World War. But the Frost and Robarts régimes have shown what a feeble and transitory phenomenon that was. In Ontario, some form of planned economy was the only conceivable alternative to Americanization. But to have anticipated a socialist Ontario was to hope rather than to predict. Certainly its leadership could not have come from the good-natured utopians who led our socialist parties. They had no understanding of the dependence of socialism and nationalism in the Canadian setting. Their confused optimism is seen in the fact that they have generally acted as if they were "left-wing" allies of the Liberal party. Socialist leadership in Canada has been largely a pleasant remnant of the British nineteenth century—the Protestant tabernacle turned liberal. Such a doctrine was too flaccid to provide any basis for independence.

To turn to the more formidable tradition, the French Canadians are determined to remain a nation. During the nineteenth century, they accepted almost unanimously the leadership of their particular Catholicism—a religion with an ancient doctrine of virtue. After 1789, they maintained their connection with the roots of their civilization through their church and its city, which more than any other in the West held high a vision of the eternal. To Catholics who remain Catholics, whatever their level of sophistication, virtue must be prior to freedom. They will therefore build a society in which the right of the common good restrains the freedom of the individual. Quebec was not a society that would come to terms with the political philosophy of Jefferson or the New England capitalists.

Nevertheless, indigenous cultures are dying everywhere in the modern world. French-Canadian nationalism is a last-ditch stand. The French on this continent will at least disappear from history with more than the smirks and whimpers of their English-speaking compatriots—with their flags flying and, indeed, with some guns blazing. The reality of their culture, and their desire not to be swamped, cannot save them from the inexorable facts in the continental case. Solutions vary to the problem of how an autonomous culture can be maintained in Quebec. But all the answers face the same dilemma: Those who want to maintain separateness also want the advantages of the age of progress. These two ends are not compatible, for the pursuit of one negates the pursuit of the other. Nationalism can only be asserted successfully by an identification with technological advance; but technological advance entails the disappearance of those indigenous differences that give substance to nationalism. The solutions to this dilemma, which were attempted in the last few years, illustrate its nature.

One solution was the régime directed by Duplessis. No province in Canada gave more welcoming terms to American capital than the government of Duplessis. At the same time, in questions of education, provincial autonomy, etc., Duplessis followed policies that won support from the rural episcopate. It is all very well for a practising politician to base his régime on the combined support of St. James St. and the traditional Church. The people would depend on the corporations for their employment, while accepting the paternal hand of the cleric in the parish and in the school. Did the clerics think this was the best way for their people to learn to live with industrialism? Surely they recognized that such a régime could not last; it would produce new classes in society ultimately more hostile to Catholicism than to capitalism.

René Lévesque's solution to the problem, unlike Duplessis's liaison with American capitalism, seems to attempt to build a semi-socialist society within the bounds of the province. The idea is to guarantee that the managerial élite be men of French culture and that the control of the economy rest firmly in native hands. In such a scheme the continuance of Confederation is simply a question of convenience. If French civilization can be protected as a province within Confederation, then all well and good. If it cannot be, then separatism becomes a necessity. Lévesque's brilliant description of Laurier as "a black king" shows the seriousness of his intention.

There are two main difficulties in a semi-socialistic solution. The first of these is symbolized by the presence of Eric Kierans and George Marler as Ministers in the same government as Lévesque. The two men well represent the new and the old establishments of English-speaking Montreal. Provincial control of economic development is not only useful for French-Canadian nationalism but also for international capitalism. Any federal system of government strengthens the power of the corporations. The division of powers weakens the ability of public authority to control private governments; the size of the provinces allows them to be controlled by private economic power. The espousing by American or Canadian "conservatives" of greater authority for the local states has always a phoney ring about it, unless it is coupled with an appeal for the break-up of continental corporations. Decentralized government and continental corporations can lead in only one direction. In his criticism of Walter Gordon's budget in 1963, Kierans made a violent attack against any curbing of foreign investment as being a deterrent to economic growth. As a Minister of the Quebec government, he accepts the thesis that economic growth is chiefly a responsibility of provincial governments. As regards provincial responsibility, Lévesque and Kierans are in agreement, but their motives for espousing responsibility are quite different. The motive of quick industrializing is surely likely to come in conflict with the motive of nationalism.

The financial pages of every newspaper are filled with announcements of French-speaking appointments to management. Continental capitalists have learnt that they are going to be in trouble if such appointments are not made. But when French nationalists derive satisfaction from these appointments, they would do well to remind themselves of the ancient adage: "I fear the Greeks, especially when they come with gifts." Corporations make concessions about management personnel for the sake of better relations with the alien community. These do not involve the basic control of the economy. Here the lines of battle will surely be drawn. How long will the people of Quebec be willing to pay the economic price of rejecting the terms laid down by big business for the development of power at Hamilton Falls? . . .

The concession over French managerial personnel points to a greater chink in the national armour. Lévesque presumably believes that the indigenous control of the French-Canadian economy will be maintained by the vote. Governments will retain final control of their economies through socialistic measures by seeking electoral support. But is it to be expected that the new managerial élites will sustain their French culture for very long? If they work for continental corporations, will they not identify themselves with those corporations and vote for governments not interested in preserving national control of the economy? This is what happened in Ontario in the 1940s and 1950s. Even when much of the economy is socialized, the managers will gradually become indistinguishable from their international counterparts. To run a modern economy, men must be trained in the new technology over human and non-human nature. Such training cannot be reconciled with French-Canadian classical education. An élite trained in the modern way may speak French for many generations, but what other traditions will it uphold? The new social sciences are dissolvents of the family, of Catholicism, of classical education. It is surely more than a language that Lévesque wishes to preserve in his nation. New Orleans is a pleasant place for tourists. The dilemma remains. French Canadians must modernize their educational system if they are to have more than a peon's place in their own industrialization. Yet to modernize their education is to renounce their particularity. At the heart of modern liberal education lies the desire to homogenize the world. Today's natural and social sciences were consciously produced as instruments to this end.

In the immediate future, the wilder of the nationalist French-Canadian youths may hope to build some kind of Castro-like state in Quebec. As traditional Catholicism breaks up, there will be some exciting moments. A Catholic society cannot be modernized as easily as a Protestant one. When the dam breaks the flood will be furious. Nevertheless, the young intellectuals of the upper-middle class will gradually desert their existentialist nationalism and take the places made for them in the continental corporations. The enormity of the break from the past will arouse in the dispossessed youth intense forms of beatness. But after all, the United States supports a large beat fringe. Joan Baez and Pete Seeger titillate the *status quo* rather than threaten it. Dissent is built into the fabric of the modern system. We bureaucratize it as much as everything else. Is there any reason to believe that French Canada will be different? A majority of the young is gradually patterned for its place in the bureaucracies. Those who resist such shaping will retreat into a fringe world of pseudo-revolt.

What does Lévesque think is the place of Catholicism in the continuing French fact? The young French Canadians who desire a better society, because they grew up under Duplessis, believe in both nationalism and social freedom. Their liberalism is openly anti-Catholic and even existentialist or Marxist.

Others accept Catholicism but are determined that the Church should be disestablished. But the old Church with its educational privileges has been the chief instrument by which an indigenous French culture has survived in North America. Liberalism is the ideological means whereby indigenous cultures are homogenized. How then can nationalism and liberalism merge together into a consistent political creed?

In 1918, Bourassa put the purposes of French-Canadian existence in clear words:

> Notre tâche à nous, Canadiens-français, c'est de prolonger en Amérique l'effort de la France chrétienne; c'est de défendre contre tout venant, le fallût-il contre la France elle-même, notre patrimoine religieux et national. Ce patrimoine, il n'est pas à nous seulement: il appartient à toute l'Amérique catholique, dont il est le foyer inspirateur et rayonnant; il appartient à toute l'Eglise, dont il est le principal point d'appui dans cette partie du monde; il appartient à toute la civilisation française, dont il est l'unique port de refuge et d'attache dans cette mer immense de l'américanisme saxonisant.[1]

Here is a national intention, beautifully expressed.

Bourassa's clarity about this intention was not matched by his understanding of what the twentieth century was going to be. He considered North America to be essentially *saxonisant* and dominated by an explicitly Protestant ethos—the "time is money" theology of a debased and secularized Calvinism. He lived in a world in which the British Empire still appeared a dominant force. Presumably he still thought of Latin America as in that twilight period of subservience to North America, which extended from the beginning of the nineteenth century. Above all, Bourassa does not seem to have been aware of the effect of homogenization—what industrial civilization would do to all countries and all religions. Industrial culture had arisen in Protestant societies and was the very form of *américanisme saxonisant* that surrounded his nation. Bourassa seems therefore to have identified the two, rather than to have recognized that technological culture was a dissolvent of all national and religious traditions, not simply an expression of one of them. There is little of Gandhi's rejection of industrialism in his writings, but rather the positive assumption that the culture of Quebec was French Christianity. Nationalism was for him something essentially conservative—the maintenance in his part of the world of the true way of life against the heresy of *Américanisme saxionisant*. This was a wasting and tragic dream for our dynamic era. Nevertheless, despite his unawareness of the dynamism of the twentieth century, he was surely right when he said that Catholicism as well as Frenchness was necessary to make Quebec a nation.

Dynamic civilization has spread like oil over the surface of the world during the half-century since Bourassa wrote. The twentieth century is not something that belongs essentially to *l'americanisme saxionisant*. It is no longer potential but actual in Quebec. Indeed, a wider question arises here: What is the status of Catholicism in the age of progress? Will a liberalized Catholicism accept industrialism and still be able to shape it to a more human end? In Quebec, Catholicism will no longer be "*Je me souviens*," but a Catholicism appropriate to a vital present. Lay education will not destroy the Church, but enable her to become the spiritual leader of a free people. Accepting the age of progress, the Church will give leadership to a more humane industrialism than has arisen elsewhere in North America. It will provide the spiritual basis for a continuing Franco-American civilization.

The possibility of such a Catholicism in Quebec cannot be discussed apart from the relation of Catholicism to technology throughout the world. That intricate question cannot be discussed at length in this writing. Suffice it to say that, although the recent statements of the Papacy seem optimistic about the Church's ability to live with our age, it is still an open question whether Catholicism will be able to humanize mass Western society or be swept into the catacombs. What happens to the Catholic view of man, when Catholics are asked to shape society through the new sciences of bio-chemistry, physiological psychology, and sociology? These sciences arose from assumptions hostile to the Catholic view of man. Whatever the historical outcome, the ability of Catholicism to sustain a continuing Franco-American civilization appears dubious. If liberal Catholicism arises in Quebec, will it not be similar to the Catholicism of Cushing and Spellman, which is well-established within the assumptions of the American Empire? Such a religion may have the same name, but it will be very different from the one Bourassa envisaged. The Church in America does not question the assumption of the society that permits it, except in the most general way. With this kind of Catholicism, industrialized Quebec would hardly be distinguishable from the rest of North America. Yet this is what the leading liberal clerics and laity seem to be establishing in the province. With such a moral heart, Quebec will soon blend into the continental whole and cease to be a nation except in its maintenance of residual patterns of language and personal habit.

Lévesque, at least, appears to be aware how difficult it will be to preserve the French fact on this continent. The French-Canadian liberals who plead for the continuance of Confederation and the extension of co-operative federalism seem to be more naïve. The confusion of these French-Canadian liberals is evident in a recent pronouncement by seven French-Canadian intellectuals under the title "An Appeal for Realism in Politics.[2] This pronouncement is considered by its authors to be a Canadian—not a French-Canadian—manifesto. It is an appeal for the continuance of Confederation against the various parochialisms that threaten it. It puts forward the hope for a vital federalism that will accept the cultural diversity of Canada but will not be economically nationalist. It is not my purpose here to discuss its detailed proposals, but to quote its philosophical justification as an example of the present thought of French-Canadian liberal intellectuals. At the end of the manifesto, two reasons are given why the writers refuse to be "locked into a constitutional frame smaller than Canada." The second reason for this is described in the following language:

> The most valid trends today are toward more enlightened humanism, toward various forms of political, social, and economic universalism. Canada is a reproduction on a small and simpler scale of this universal phenomenon. The challenge is for a number of ethnic groups to learn to live together. It is a modern challenge, meaningful and indicative of what can be expected from man. If Canadians cannot make a success of a country such as theirs, how can they contribute in any way to the elaboration of humanism, to the formulation of the international structures of tomorrow? To confess one's inability to make Canadian Confederation work is, at this stage of history, to admit one's unworthiness to contribute to the universal order.

Leaving aside such questions as what makes a trend "valid" and what are the conditions of human enlightenment, the point at issue is that the authors assert their faith in universalism and in the continued existence of Canada at one and the same time. The faith in universalism makes it accurate to call the authors liberal. But how can a faith in universalism go with a desire for the continuance of Canada? The belief in Canada's continued existence has always appealed against universalism. It appealed to particularity against the wider loyalty to the continent. If universalism is the most "valid modern trend," then is it not right for Canadians to welcome our integration into the empire? Canadian nationalism is a more universal faith than universalist, why should one stop at that point of particularity?

Many French-Canadian liberals seem to espouse "enlightened humanism" and universalism as against the parochial Catholicism that inhibited them personally and politically when it ruled their society. They seem to expect liberalism to purge Catholicism, but to maintain within itself all that was best in the ancient faith. In this manifesto, for example, the authors espouse the continuance of indigenous cultures and regret the victimizing of the "Indians, Métis, Orientals, Doukhobors, Hutterites, and dissidents of all kinds" in our past. They call for the democratic protection of such cultures. But do they not know that liberalism in its most unequivocal form (that is, untinged by memories of past traditions) includes not only the idea of universalism but also that of homogeneity? The high rhetoric of democracy was used when the Doukhobors were "victimized" under a French-Canadian Prime Minister. If the writers are to be truly liberal, they cannot escape the fact that the goal of their political philosophy is the universal and homogeneous state. If this is the noblest goal, then the idea of Canada was a temporary and misguided parochialism. Only those who reject that goal and claim that the universal state will be a tyranny, that is, a society destructive of human excellence, can assert consistently that parochial nationalisms are to be fought for. My purpose is not to debate at this point the question whether the "universal" values of liberalism lead to human excellence. What is indubitable is that those values go with internationalism rather than with nationalism. In this century, many men have known that the choice between internationalism and nationalism is the same choice as that between liberalism and conservatism. In a Canadian setting, internationalism means continentalism. French-Canadian liberalism does not seem to be the means whereby this nation could have been preserved.

All the preceding arguments point to the conclusion that Canada cannot survive as a sovereign nation. In the language of the new bureaucrats, our nation was not a viable entity. If one adds to this proposition the memory of the Liberals' policies, then one can truly say that the argument in their favour succeeds. They have been the best rulers for Canada because they have led the majority of us to accept necessity without much pain. *Fata volentem ducant, nolentem trahunt.* Fate leads the willing, and drives the unwilling. The debt that we owe the Liberals is that they have been so willing to be led. The party has been made up of those who put only one condition on their willingness: that they should have personal charge of the government while our sovereignty disappears.

Canada has ceased to be a nation, but its formal political existence will not end quickly. Our social and economic blending into the empire will continue apace, but political union will probably be delayed. Some international catastrophe or great shift of power might speed up this process. Its slowness does not depend only on the fact that large numbers of Canadians do not want it, but also on sheer lethargy. Changes require decisions, and it is much easier for practising politicians to continue with traditional structures. The dominant forces in the Republic do not need to incorporate us. A branch-plant satellite, which has shown in the past that it will not insist on any difficulties in foreign or defence policy, is a pleasant arrangement for one's northern frontier. The pin-pricks of disagreement are a small price to pay. If the negotiations for union include Quebec, there will be strong elements in the United States that will dislike their admission. The kindest of all God's dispensations is that individuals cannot predict the future in detail. Nevertheless, the formal end of Canada may be prefaced by a period during which the government of the United States has to resist the strong desire of English-speaking Canadians to be annexed.

NOTES

1. See H. Bourassa, *La Langue, gardienne de la Foi* (Montreal, 1918). Freely translated: "Our special task, as French Canadians, is to insert into America the spirit of Christian France. It is to defend against all comers, perhaps even against France herself, our religious and national heritage. This heritage does not belong to us alone. It belongs to all Catholic America. It is the inspiring and shining hearth of that America. It belongs to the whole Church, and it is the basic foundation of the Church in this part of the world. It

belongs to all French civilization of which it is the refuge and anchor amid the immense sea of saxonizing Americanism."
2. This manifesto was published concurrently in French in *Cité Libre*, Montreal, and in English in *The Canadian Forum* (May, 1964), Toronto. [One of its signators was P.E. Trudeau.]

FURTHER READINGS

Christian, W., and C. Campbell. *Political Parties and Ideologies in Canada*, Chapters 4 and 6. Toronto: McGraw-Hill Ryerson, 1974.

Cook, R. "Loyalism, Technology, and Canada's Fate." In R. Cook, *The Maple Leaf Forever*. Toronto: Macmillan, 1971.

Forbes, D., ed. *Canadian Political Thought*, Part III. Toronto: Oxford University Press, 1985.

Grant, G. *Lament for a Nation*. Toronto: McClelland & Stewart, 1965.

———. *Technology and Empire*, Toronto: Anansi, 1979.

Kroker, A. *Technology and the Canadian Mind: Innis, McLuhan, Grant*. Montreal: New World Perspectives, 1984.

Taylor, C. *Radical Tories*, Chapters 3 and 6. Toronto: Anansi, 1982.

11

Separatist Counter-Revolutionaries

PIERRE ELLIOTT TRUDEAU

> We are against the leaders who are of the left
> and who hide behind Marxist-Leninist ideology
> but who make it represent chauvinism. . . .
> They now offer a reactionary thesis founded
> on a union of peoples based on racism and nationalism.
>
> –N. Khrushchev, *La Presse*, April 10, 1964

THE DICTATORS

I get fed up when I hear our nationalist brood calling itself revolutionary. It conceives of revolution as a deep upheaval, but forgets that this is also characteristic of counter-revolution.

Fascism and Naziism overturned quite a few things. Notably, they replaced democratic institutions with a totalitarian system. It is true that democracy under Victor Emmanuel III and in the Weimar Republic was not a terrific success. Parliamentary democracy had shallow roots in post-Versailles Italy and Germany, the idea of a liberal state being accepted only slowly by countries of which one had long been subjected to authoritarian Catholicism and the other had grown up under Prussian militarism. At the national level, ineffectualness and corruption were playing havoc, and the government often seemed incapable of making the transition from deliberation to action.

But nevertheless the idea of liberty was honoured in these democracies. A great many men still believed that a rational political order should get its bearings from open discussion rather than a fanatical refusal of dialogue; should be founded on a consensus rather than on intolerance; should come to power through elections rather than subversion and violence.

True, freedom is often less efficacious than authority as the basis of short-term organization. And reason is often not so strong as emotion as a public driving force. That is why the progress of democracy was slow in those countries. Then other men came along claiming exclusive possession of political truth.

Abridged from Pierre Elliott Trudeau, "Separatist Counter-Revolutionaries," *Federalism and the French Canadians* (Toronto: Macmillan of Canada, 1968), 204-12. Copyright © 1968 by P.E. Trudeau. Reprinted by permission of Macmillan of Canada, A Division of Canada Publishing Corporation.

That, obviously, freed them from the need to seek that truth by means of the public confrontation which democracy provides. So as soon as they could they replaced the parliamentary system with so-called plebiscitary democracy; they abolished the opposition and installed the single-party system; they murdered liberty and enthroned themselves as dictators. All this was done in the name of the nation, whose rights (weren't they?) were superior to those of the individual, be he alien, Jew, or simply dissident.

These dictators were called Hitler and Mussolini. There were others called Stalin, Franco, and Salazar. It cannot be denied that they all claimed to be serving the destiny of their respective national communities; further, three of them called themselves socialists. But who would call the whole of their work revolutionary? They upset a great many institutions, they even opened the way for some material progress; but they abolished personal freedom, or at least prevented it from growing; that is why history classes them as counter-revolutionaries.

FREEDOM

And so I get fed up when I hear our nationalist brood calling itself revolutionary. Quebec's revolution, if it had taken place, would first have consisted in freeing man from collective coercions: freeing the citizens brutalized by reactionary and arbitrary governments; freeing consciences bullied by a clericalized and obscurantist Church; freeing workers exploited by an oligarchic capitalism; freeing men crushed by authoritarian and outdated traditions. Quebec's revolution would have consisted in the triumph of the freedoms of the human being as inalienable rights, over and above capital, the nation, tradition, the Church, and even the State.

But this revolution never took place. Certainly there have been men in Quebec to work for it and to advance freedom and democracy over the last century, but the collective power always finished by reducing them to impotence: interdicts by the Church against an Asselin or a Buies, racial proscriptions against a Rabinovitch or a Roncarelli, government arbitrariness against a Picard or a Guindon, police truncheons against the strikers of Asbestos or Louiseville.

Nevertheless, around 1960 it seemed that freedom was going to triumph in the end. From 1945 on, a series of events and movements had combined to relegate the traditional concepts of authority in Quebec to the scrap-heap; the post-war stirrings, "Refus Globale," Asbestos, the unions, the judicial victories of Frank Scott and of Jacques Perrault, *Cité Libre*, the defeat of the Union Nationale, just to give some diverse examples. So much so that the generation entering its twenties in 1960 was the first in our history to receive fairly complete freedom as its lot. The dogmatism of Church and State, of tradition, of the nation, had been defeated. Authority had returned to its proper place in a free system. A lawyer could head the Lay Movement without losing his clients. Professors could say "no to the Jesuits" without being barred from the university. Comedians or movie producers could subscribe to Marxism without being discharged by the government corporations. Students could try to impose their views on educational institutions without being kicked out. The Family itself had lost its power over young men and young women.

In 1960, everything was becoming possible in Quebec, even revolution. In fact revolution would probably not have been necessary, so wide open was the road to power for all who had mastered the sciences and the techniques of the day: automation, cybernetics, nuclear science, economic planning, and what-not else. A whole generation was free at last to apply all its creative energies to bringing this backward province up to date. Only it required boldness, intelligence, and work. Alas, freedom proved to be too heady a drink to pour for the French-Canadian youth of 1960. Almost at the first sip it went at top speed in search of some more soothing milk, some new dogmatism. It reproached my generation with not having offered it any 'doctrine'—we who had spent the best part of our youth demolishing servile doctrinairism—and it took refuge in the bosom of its mother, the Holy Nation.

As a friend wrote me recently, for religious sectarianism was substituted national sectarianism. The separatist devout and all the other zealots in the Temple of the Nation already point their fingers at the non-worshipper. And a good many non-believers find it to their advantage to receive their nationalist sacrament, for they hope thus to attain sacerdotal and episcopal, if not pontifical, office, and to be permitted thereby to recite prayers, to circulate directives and encyclicals, to define dogma, and to pronounce excommunication, with the assurance of infallibility. Those who do not attain the priesthood can hope to become churchwardens in return for services rendered; at the very least they will not be bothered when nationalism becomes the state religion.

NEO-CLERICALISM

The new clerical party, which already had is popes and its nuncios, has just found a Torquemada. After all, the new separatist counter-revolution must have its little Inquisition, mustn't it? Otherwise, what use are those lists of the proscribed that have been circulating for quite a while? I was sad to learn that François Hertel had volunteered for this task. I would not have thought that this man, whom I have long respected because he used to have the rare courage to reject all forms of conformity, would wind up as a churchmouse in the separatist chapel.

So now from Paris, beyond the reach of our criminal courts but not of our contempt, he writes: "Assassinate for me a traitor who's really one of our people. It would be a good job. For instance relieve poor Laurendeau of the existence that seems to bore him so much," . . . and so forth. To address such words to a public preparing to sacrifice all values—especially personal freedom and safety—to the idol of collectivity, and which has already begun to take terrorists for heroes and martyrs, is the act of a dangerously irresponsible man.

But the ultimate in irresponsibility is to publish these words in *Le Quartier Latin* (April 9, 1964) as "an extraordinary document", what's more, alongside other documents inciting to murder. Of course, I should have expected anything from a newspaper director who recognizes the single-party system as an acceptable course for the Quebec of tomorrow.

The more so because this same director, in this same student newspaper, had printed two days previously another 'document' on the subject of freedom of the press which proved precisely that he held that freedom of little account. I refer to an article headed "Mr. Gérard Pelletier and the Freedom of the Press" in which Professor Jean Blain writes: "In the name of the freedom of the press he [Pelletier] refuses me freedom to express myself." That is a falsehood. As *Le Devoir* of April 8 reported, Pelletier offered to print Professor Blain's statement complete in the letters columns of *La Presse*, and it was the professor who refused. *Le Quartier Latin* could have learned this fact if it had any regard for an elementary principle of justice: "hear the other side." But a certain Goebbels had already proved that justice and truth count for little when it is a case of nationalist auctioneering.

As for the root of the Pelletier-Blain argument, what can I say to people who have never read John Stuart Mill, *On Liberty*? "The beliefs which we have most warrant for have no safeguard to rest on, but a standing invitation to the whole world to prove them unfounded." No man can demand freedom of speech if he finds it a matter of indifference that public debate and free confrontation should be brushed aside as a means of arriving at political truths; these ideas are indissolubly linked. Now *Parti Pris*, according to Professor Blain himself, is based on "refusal of dialogue." Indeed, Pelletier, in the last edition of *Cité Libre*, brought out the totalitarian character of *Part Pris* thinking. And for greater certainty, in the April number of that counter-revolutionary review, on page 51, there is a confession that "there is a necessary totalitarianism.". . .

But it is not only the students, those *petits-bourgeois* of tomorrow, who embrace counter-revolutionary sectarianism. Naturally there are also the *petits-bourgeois* of today. Mr. Jean-Marc Léger, who has always had the courage and the consciousness of his nationalism—and I cannot say the same for those who looked down on him from a great height fifteen years ago but who have come today to think like him because they want to be 'liked by youth'—Mr. Léger called at the Saint-Jean-Baptiste conference for "the creation of a climate of national fervour in the schools," and, to achieve this, "forbidding French-speaking parents to enter their children in English-speaking establishments in Quebec" (*Le Devoir*, March 16, 1964). It goes without saying that this neo-clericalist thinking was welcomed by our newspapers, and nobody seemed to be alarmed that education in Quebec might pass from religious confessionality to compulsory linguistic confessionality. . . .

PERSECUTION

For humanity, progress is the slow journey towards personal freedom. Those responsible for a sudden reversal of this course can be defined as counter-revolutionaries.

Certainly there are historical cases in which personal freedom has scarcely been protected at all by established institutions; it has been possible, then, for a genuine revolutionary to stress collective freedom as a preliminary to personal freedom: Castro, Ben Bella, Lenin.

But when personal freedom exists, it would be *inconceivable that a revolutionary should destroy it* in the name of some collective ideology. For the very purpose of a collective system is better to ensure personal freedom. (Or else you are fascist.)

That is why in Quebec today you have to speak of separatist counter-revolution. True, personal freedom has not always been honoured in Quebec. But, I repeat, we had pretty well reached it around 1960. Thanks to English and Jewish lawyers (ah, yes!), thanks to the Supreme Court in Ottawa, personal freedom had at last triumphed over the obscurantism of Quebec's legislators and the authoritarianism of our courts. . . . Thanks also to those diverse movements and events I mentioned earlier, there was scarcely a sector of Quebec life in which personal freedom at all levels of the population was not making sure progress and in which censorship, interdiction, authoritariansim, clericalism, and dictatorship were not in clear retreat.

But now, today, scarcely a week passes without a handful of separatist students coming to tell me they are against democracy and for a single-party system; for a certain totalitarianism and against the freedom of the individual. In this they are in the pure tradition of all that our society has always produced that was most traditionalist, most clerical, most monolithic, most reactionary. They want to return our people to the mentality of a state of siege.

The fact is that at bottom the Separatists despair of ever being able to convince the public of the rightness of their ideas. That long work of education and persuasion among the masses undertaken by the unions for many decades, done by the Social Crediters themselves for thirty years—for this the Separatists have neither the courage, nor the means, nor, especially, that respect for the other man's freedom which is essential in undertaking it and leading it to success.

So they want to abolish freedom and impose a dictatorship of their minority. They are in sole possession of the truth, so others need only get into line. And when things don't go fast enough they take to illegality and violence. On top of everything, they claim to be persecuted. Imagine that, the poor little souls. There are numbers of them in the editorial rooms of our newspapers, they swarm at the C.B.C. and the National Film Board, they press with all their weight (?) on the mass media, but still they find the place given them in this society unfair.

Because a few of their people have been bothered because of their ideas (so they say), they want to be done with peaceful and constitutional methods. They proclaim to the newspapers that from now on they will go underground. These terrorized terrorists will be led by a Mr. X. And, in courageous anonymity, they will sow their ideas while waiting to set their bombs.

No kidding! In the province of Quebec the Jehovah's Witnesses and the Communists, two tiny minorities, have been mocked, persecuted, and hated by our entire society; but they have managed by legal means to fight Church, government, nation, police, and public opinion. Union men, in spite of being kicked out of their jobs for union activity, have never thought to destroy personal freedom but, on the contrary, have always made themselves its defenders, as also champions of the democratic cause.

But our nationalists—of whom the "experts" claim there is one dozing in the heart of every French Canadian—they despair of ever legally getting their "message" accepted by a majority of French Canadians. They cry persecution to justify going underground as fugitives from reality.

THE WIGWAM COMPLEX

The truth is that the separatist counter-revolution is the work of a powerless *petit-bourgeois* minority afraid of being left behind by the twentieth-century revolution. Rather than carving themselves out a place in it by ability, they want to make the whole tribe return to the wigwams by declaring its independence. That, of course, will not prevent the world outside from progressing by giant's strides; it will not change the rules and the facts of history, nor the real power relationship in North America.

But at least inside the tribe the counter-revolutionaries will be kings and sorcerers. They will have legal authority to declare war (making it will be a different story), to name (*bourgeois*) plenipotentiaries, to open (*bourgeois*) banks, and to impose tariffs favourable to the *petite bourgeoisie*. They will also be able to transfer the title to property and to declare that from now on foreign industries will belong to the tribal *bourgeoisie*. The tribe risks being gravely impoverished; but what matters, of course, is that the counter-revolutionaries shall not be.

Some of the counter-revolutionaries deceive themselves by dressing up in Marxist-Leninist disguise, as has already been done by those African chieftains whom, indeed, they take as models. But all this masquerade has been admirably described by Frantz Fanon in *Les damnés de la Terre*, which nevertheless our counter-revolutionaries say is the book they keep beside their beds. (This makes me think they read no more in bed than elsewhere; so I shall do them the favour of quoting at some length from this book published by Maspero in 1961 and of which they have perhaps only leafed through the chapter on violence.)

A national *bourgeoisie* never cases to demand nationalization of the economy and the commercial sectors. . . . For it, nationalization means very precisely the transfer to the native population of the favours inherited from the colonial period. (p. 115) . . . It uses its class aggressiveness to corner the positions formerly held by the foreigners. . . . It will fight pitilessly against those people who 'insult the national dignity'. . . . In fact its course will become more and more coloured with racism. (p. 118) . . . Everywhere that this national *bourgeoisie* has shown itself unable to expand its view of the world sufficiently, we witness a return toward tribal positions; we witness, with rage in our hearts, the embittered triumph of ethnics. (p. 120) Internally . . . the *bourgeoisie* chooses the solution that seems easiest to it, that of the single party. . . . The single party is the modern form of dictatorship, without mask, without disguise, without scruple, cynical. (p. 124) . . . All ideological activity is limited to a succession of variations on the right of peoples to dispose of themselves. (p. 128) . . . At the institutional level it [the national *bourgeoisie*] skips the parliamentary phase and chooses a dictatorship of the national-socialist type. (p. 129) . . . This tribalization of power brings with it, naturally, regionalist thinking, separatism. (p. 137)

Separatism a revolution? My eye. A counter-revolution; the national-socialist counter-revolution.

FURTHER READINGS

Christian, W. and C. Campbell *Political Parties and Ideologies in Canada*, Chapter 3. Toronto: McGraw-Hill Ryerson, 1974.

Cook, R. *The Maple Leaf Forever*. Toronto: Macmillan, 1971.

―――. *Canada, Quebec and the Uses of Nationalism*. Toronto: McClelland & Stewart, 1986.

Forbes, D. *Canadian Political Thought*, 326–351. Toronto: Oxford University Press, 1985.

Gwyn, R. *The Northern Magus*, Chapter 3. Toronto: McClelland & Stewart, 1980.

Newman, C.M. *Grits*, Chapter 2. Toronto: Macmillan, 1982.

Trudeau, P.E. *Federalism and the French Canadians*. Toronto: Macmillan, 1968.

12

Conservatism, Liberalism, and Socialism in Canada: An Interpretation

GAD HOROWITZ

1 / INTRODUCTION: THE HARTZIAN APPROACH

In the United States, organized socialism is dead; in Canada socialism, though far from national power, is a significant political force. Why this striking difference in the fortunes of socialism in two very similar societies?

Any attempt to account for the difference must be grounded in a general comparative study of the English-Canadian and America societies. It will be shown that the relative strength of socialism in Canada is related to the relative strength of toryism, and to the different position and character of liberalism in the two countries.

In North America, Canada is unique. Yet there is a tendency in Canadian historical and political studies to explain Canadian phenomena not by contrasting them with America phenomena but by identifying them as variations on a basic North American theme. I grant that Canada and the United States are similar, and that the similarities should be pointed out. But the pan-North American approach, since it searches out and concentrates on similarities, cannot help us to understand Canadian uniqueness. When this approach is applied to the study of English-Canadian socialism, it discovers, first, that like the American variety it is weak, and second, that it is weak for much the same reasons. These discoveries perhaps explain why Canadian socialism is weak in comparison to European socialism; they do not explain why Canadian socialism is so much stronger than American socialism.

The explanatory technique used in this study is that developed by Louis Hartz in *The Liberal Tradition in America*[1] and *The Founding of New Societies*.[2]

The Hartzian approach is to study the new societies founded by Europeans (the United States, English Canada, French Canada, Latin America, Dutch South Africa, Australia) as "fragments" thrown off from Europe. The key to the

Abridged from Gad Horowitz, "Conservatism, Liberalism, and Socialism in Canada: An Interpretation," *Canadian Journal of Economics and Political Science* 32, No. 2 (May 1966), 143-71. Reprinted by permission of the author and The Canadian Political Science Association.

understanding of ideological development in a new society is its "point of departure" from Europe: the ideologies borne by the founders of the new society are not representative of the historic ideological spectrum of the mother country. The settlers represent only a fragment of that spectrum. The complete ideological spectrum ranges—in chronological order, and from right to left—from feudal or tory through liberal whig to liberal democrat to socialist. French Canada and Latin America are "feudal fragments." They were founded by bearers of the feudal or tory values of the organic, corporate, hierarchical community; their point of departure from Europe is before the liberal revolution. The United States, English Canada, and Dutch South Africa are "bourgeois fragments," founded by bearers of liberal individualism who have left the tory end of the spectrum behind them. Australia is the one "radical fragment," founded by bearers of the working class ideologies of mid-nineteenth-century Britain.

The significance of the fragmentation process is that the new society, having been thrown off from Europe, "loses the stimulus to change that the whole provides."[3] The full ideological spectrum of Europe develops only out of the continued confrontation and interaction of its four elements; they are related to one another, not only as enemies, but as parents and children. A new society which leaves part of the past behind it cannot develop the future ideologies which need the continued presence of the past in order to come into being. In escaping the past, the fragment escapes the future, for "the very seeds of the later ideas are contained in the parts of the old world that have been left behind."[4] The ideology of the founders is thus frozen, congealed at the point of origin.

Socialism is an ideology which combines the corporate-organic-collectivist ideas of toryism with the rationalist-egalitarian ideas of liberalism. Both the feudal and the bourgeois fragments escape socialism, but in different ways. A feudal fragment such as French Canada develops no whig (undemocratic) liberalism; therefore it does not develop the democratic liberalism which arises out of and as a reaction against whiggery; therefore it does not develop the socialism which arises out of and as a reaction against liberal democracy. The corporate-organic-collectivist component of socialism is present in the feudal fragment—it is part of the feudal ethos—but the radical rationalist-egalitarian component of socialism is missing. It can be provided only by whiggery and liberal democracy, and these have not come into being.

In the bourgeois fragment, the situation is the reverse: the radical rationalist-egalitarian component of socialism is present, but the corporate-organic-collectivist component is missing, because toryism has been left behind. In the bourgeois fragments "Marx dies because there is no sense of class, no yearning for the corporate past."[5] The absence of socialism is related to the absence of toryism.

It is *because* socialists have a conception of society as more than an agglomeration of competing individuals—a conception close to the tory view of society as an organic community—that they find the liberal idea of equality

(equality of opportunity) inadequate. Socialists disagree with liberals about the essential meaning of equality because socialists have a tory conception of society.

In a liberal bourgeois society which has never known toryism the demand for equality will express itself as left-wing or democratic liberalism as opposed to whiggery. The left will point out that all are not equal in the competitive pursuit of individual happiness. The government will be required to assure greater equality of opportunity—in the nineteenth century, by destroying monopolistic privileges; in the twentieth century by providing a welfare "floor" so that no one will fall out of the race for success, and by regulating the economy so that the race can continue without periodic crises.

In a society which thinks of itself as a community of classes rather than an aggregation of individuals, the demand for equality will take a socialist form: for equality of condition rather than mere equality of opportunity; for cooperation rather than competition; for a community that does more than provide a context within which individuals can pursue happiness in a purely self-regarding way. At its most "extreme," socialism is a demand for the *abolition* of classes so that the good of the community can truly be realized. This is a demand which cannot be made by people who can hardly see class and community: the individual fills their eyes.

2 / THE APPLICATION TO CANADA

It is a simple matter to apply the Hartzian approach to English Canada in a pan-North American way. English Canada can be viewed as a fragment of the American liberal society, lacking a feudal or tory heritage and therefore lacking the socialist ideology which grows out of it. Canadian domestic struggles, from this point of view, are a northern version of the American struggle between big-propertied liberals on the right and *petit bourgeois* and working-class liberals on the left; the struggle goes on within a broad liberal consensus, and the voice of the tory or the socialist is not heard in the land. This pan-North American approach, with important qualifications, is adopted by Hartz and McRae in *The Founding of New Societies*. English Canada, like the United States, is a bourgeois fragment. No toryism in the past; therefore no socialism in the present.

But Hartz notes that the liberal society of English Canada has a "tory touch," that it is "etched with a tory streak coming out of the American revolution."[6] The general process of bourgeois fragmentation is at work in both English Canada and the United States, but there are differences between the two fragments which Hartz describes as "delicate contrasts,"[7] McRae as "subtle" and "minor."[8] Put in the most general way, the difference is that while the United States is the perfect bourgeois fragment, the "achetype" of monolithic liberalism unsullied by tory or socialist deviations, English Canada is a bourgeois fragment marred by non-liberal "imperfections"—a tory "touch," and therefore a socialist "touch." The way Hartz and McRae would put it is that English Canada and the United States are "essentially" alike; differences are to be found but they are not "basic." Surely, however, whether one describes the differences as delicate, subtle, and minor or as basic, significant, and important depends on one's perspective, on what one is looking for, on what one wishes to stress. Hartz himself points out that "each of the fragment cultures . . . is 'unique,' a special blend of European national tradition, historical timing,"[9] and so on. He is "concerned with both general processes and the individuality of the settings in which they evolve."[10] Nevertheless, his main focus is on the uniformities, the parallel lines of development discovered in the comparative study of the United States and English Canada. This follows quite naturally from his *world* historical perspective, his emhasis on the three-way contrast of feudal, liberal, and radical fragments. From this perspective, the differences between English Canada and the United States are indeed "subtle" and "minor." But they are not absolutely minor: they are minor only in relation to the much larger differences among feudal, bourgeois, and radical fragments. If one shifts one's perspective, and considers English Canada from within the world of bourgeois fragments, the differences suddenly expand. If one's concern is to understand English-Canadian society in its uniqueness, that is, in contrast to American society, the differences become not "delicate" but of absolutely crucial importance.

Hartz's pan-North Americanism is a matter of perspective: he recognizes the un-American characteristics of English Canada, but considers them minor in relation to the much larger differences between bourgeois and other fragments. McRae's pan-North Americanism, however, is not merely a matter of perspective, for he seems to consider English Canada's un-American characteristics to be absolutely "minor." For McRae, they are minor not only from the world perspective, but from the narrower perspective which considers the bourgeois fragments alone.

Take as an example the central concern of this study—the differing weights of Canadian and American socialism. . . . The CCF failed to become a major party in urban Canada, but it succeeded in becoming a significant minor party—a success denied to the American socialists. . . .

The most important un-American characteristics of English Canada, all related to the presence of toryism, are: (*a*) the presence of tory ideology in the founding of English Canada by the Loyalists, and its continuing influence on English-Canadian political culture; (*b*) the persistent power of whiggery or right-wing liberalism in Canada (the Family Compacts) as contrasted with the rapid and easy victory of liberal democracy (Jefferson, Jackson) in the United States; (*c*) the ambivalent centrist character of left-wing liberalism in Canada as contrasted with the unambiguously leftist position of left-wing liberalism in the United States; (*d*) the presence of an influential and legitimate socialist movement in English Canada as contrasted with the illegitimacy and early death of American socialism; (*e*) the failure of English-Canadian liberalism to develop into the one true myth, the nationalist cult, and the parallel failure to exclude toryism and socialism as "un-Canadian"; in other words, the legitimacy of ideological diversity in English Canada.

From a world perspective, these imperfections in English Canada's bourgeois character may appear insignificant. From the point of view of one who is interested in understanding English Canada not merely as a bourgeois fragment, but as a unique bourgeois fragment, the imperfections are significant.

3 / THE PRESENCE OF TORYISM AND ITS CONSEQUENCES

Many students have noted that English-Canadian society has been powerfully shaped by tory values that are "alien" to the American mind. The latest of these is Seymour Martin Lipset, who stresses the relative strength in Canada of the tory values of "ascription" and "elitism" (the tendency to defer to authority), and the relative weakness of the liberal values of "achievement" and "egalitarianism."[11] He points to such well-known features of Canadian history as the absence of a lawless, individualistic-egalitarian American frontier, the preference for Britain rather than the United States as a social model, and generally, the weaker emphasis on social equality, the greater acceptance by individuals of the facts of economic inequality, social stratification, and hierarchy. One tory touch in English Canada which is not noted by Lipset, . . . is the far greater willingness of English-Canadian political and business elites to use the power of the state for the purpose of developing and controlling the economy.

Lipset accepts the notion, common among Canadian historians, that the Loyalist emigrés from the American revolution were a genuine tory element; that their expulsion from the United States to Canada accounts for the development of the United States in a liberal direction and of English Canada in a conservative direction. English Canada's "point of departure," in this view, is not liberal but conservative. The idea is that English Canada was founded by British tories whose purpose was to build a society which would be not liberal like the American but conservative like the British. . . .

Canada is not a feudal (tory) fragment but a bourgeois (liberal) fragment touched with toryism. . . .

. . . Let us put it this way: pre-revolutionary America was a liberal fragment with insigificant traces of toryism, extremely weak feudal survivals. But they were insignificant in the *American* setting; they were far overshadowed by the liberalism of that setting. The Revolution did not have to struggle against them, it swept them away easily and painlessly, leaving no trace of them in the American memory. But these traces of toryism were expelled into a *new* setting, and in this setting they were no longer insignificant. In this new setting, where there was no pre-established overpowering liberalism to force them into insignificance, they played a large part in shaping a new political culture, significantly different from the American. As Nelson wrote in *The American Tory*, "the Tories' organic conservatism represented a current of thought that failed to reappear in America after the revolution. A substantial part of the whole spectrum of European . . . philosophy seemed to slip outside the American perspective."[12] But it *reappeared* in Canada. Here the sway of liberalism has proved to be not total, but considerably mitigated by a tory presence initially and a socialist presence subsequently. . . .

. . . In Canada, the Family Compacts were able to maintain ascendancy and delay the coming of democracy because of the tory touch "inherited in part from American Loyalism, which restrained egalitarian feeling in Canada."[13]. . .

. . . The early power of whiggery serves to emphasize the importance of the tory touch in English Canada. . . .

In the United States, the masses could not be swayed by the Federalist-Whig appeals to anti-egalitarian sentiments. In Canada the masses *were* swayed by these appeals; the role of the Compacts was to save "the colonial masses from the spectre of republicanism and democracy."[14] What accounts for this is the tory presence in English-Canadian political culture—the "greater acceptance of limitation, of hierarchical patterns."[15]. . .

The next step in tracing the development of the English-Canadian political culture must be to take account of the tremendous waves of British immigration which soon engulfed the original American Loyalist fragment. Here McRae's concern is to argue that the liberal ideology of the Loyalist fragment had already "frozen, congealed at the point of origin"; that the national ethos had already been fully formed (an American liberalism not "exactly" like American liberalism); that the later waves of immigration played no part in the formation of English-Canadian political culture; that they found an established culture, and were impelled to acclimatize to it. It is important for McRae to prove this point, for while there is room for the argument that the Loyalists were American whigs with a tory touch, the later British immigrants had undoubtedly been heavily infected with non-liberal ideas, and these ideas were undoubtedly in their heads as they settled in Canada. The political culture of a new nation is not necessarily fixed at the point of origin or departure; the founding of a new nation can go on for generations. If the later waves of immigration arrived before the *point of congealment* of the political culture, they must have participated actively in the process of culture formation. If this be so, the picture of English Canada as an almost exactly American liberal society becomes very difficult to defend. For *even if* it be granted that the Loyalists were (almost exactly) American liberals, it is clear that later participants in the formation of the culture were not.

Between 1815 and 1850 almost one million Britons emigrated to Canada. The population of English Canada doubled in twenty years and quadrupled in forty. The population of Ontario increased tenfold in the same period—from about 95,000 in 1814 to about 950,000 in 1851. McRae himself admits that "it would be inaccurate to say that this wave of migration was absorbed into the original fragment: an influx of these proportions does not permit of simple assimilation."[16] Nevertheless, he concludes that "despite the flood tide of immigration . . . the original liberal inheritance of English Canada survived and dominated."[17] According to McRae, the universal urge to own property and the classlessness of North American society had such a powerful impact on the immigrants that they simply "forgot their old notions of social hierarchy" and became American liberals.[18] Surely this argument is an instance of stretching the facts in order to fit a theory! Do people simply "forget" their old notions so quickly and so completely? Is it not possible that the immigrants, while they were no doubt considerably liberalized by their new environment, also brought to it non-liberal ideas which entered into the political culture mix, and which perhaps even reinforced the non-liberal elements present in the original fragment? If the million immigrants had come from the United States rather than Britain, would English Canada not be "significantly" different today?

The difficulty in applying the Hartzian approach to English Canada is that although the point of departure is reasonably clear, it is difficult to put one's finger on the point of congealment. Perhaps it was the Loyalist period; perhaps it was close to the mid-century mark; there are grounds for arguing that it was in the more recent past. But the important point is this: no matter where the point of congealment is located in time, the tory streak is present before the solidification of the political culture, and it is strong *enough* to produce *significant* "imperfections," or non-liberal, un-American attributes of English-Canadian society.

My own opinion is that the point of congealment came later than the Loyalists. . . .

The indeterminate location of the point of congealment makes it difficult to account in any *precise* way for the presence of socialism in the English-Canadian political culture mix, though the presence itself is indisputable. If the point of congealment came *before* the arrival of the first radical or socialist-minded immigrants, the presence of socialism must be ascribed primarily to the earlier presence of toryism. Since toryism is a significant part of the political culture, at least part of the leftist reaction against it will sooner or later be expressed in its own terms, that is, in terms of *class* interests and the good of the community as a corporate entity (socialism) rather than in terms of the individual and his vicissitudes in the competitive pursuit of happiness (liberalism). If the point of congealment is very early, socialism appears at a later point not primarily because it is imported by British immigrants, but because it is contained as a potential in the original political culture. The immigrants then find that they do not have to give it up—that it is not un-Canadian—because it "fits" to a certain extent with the tory ideas already present. If the point of congealment is very late, the presence of socialism must be explained as a result of *both* the presence of toryism and the introduction of socialism into the cultural mix before congealment. The immigrant retains his socialism not only because it "fits" but also because nothing really *has* to fit. He finds that his socialism is not un-Canadian partly because "Canadian" has not yet been defined.

Canadian liberals cannot be expected to wax enthusiastic about the non-liberal traits of their country. They are likely to condemn the tory touch as anachronistic, stifling, undemocratic, out of tune with the essentially American ("free," "classless") spirit of English Canada. They dismiss the socialist touch as an "old-fashioned" protest, no longer necessary (if it ever was) in this best (liberal) of all possible worlds in which the "end of ideology" has been achieved. The secret dream of the Canadian liberal is the removal of English Canada's "imperfections"—in other words, the total assimilation of English Canada into the larger North American culture. But there is a flaw in this dream which might give pause even to the liberal. Hartz places special emphasis on one very unappetizing characteristic of the new societies—intolerance—which is strikingly absent in English Canada. Because the new societies other than Canada are unfamiliar with legitimate ideological diversity, they are unable to accept it and deal with it in a rational manner, either internally or on the level of international relations.

The European nation has an "identity which transcends any ideologist and a mechanism in which each plays only a part."[19] Neither the tory, nor the liberal, nor the socialist, has a monopoly of the expression of the "spirit" of the nation. But the new societies, the fragments, contain only one of the ideologies of Europe; they are one-myth cultures. In a new setting, freed from its historic enemies past and future, ideology transforms itself into nationalism. It claims to be a moral absolute, "the great spirit of a nation."[20] In the United States, liberalism becomes "Americanism"; a political philosophy becomes a civil religion, a nationalist cult. The American attachment to Locke is "absolutist and irrational."[21] Democratic capitalism is the American way of life; to oppose it is to be un-American.

To be an American is to be a bourgeois liberal. To be a French Canadian is to be a pre-Enlightenment Catholic; to be an Australian is to be a prisoner of the radical myth of "mateship"; to be a Boer is to be a pre-Enlightenment bourgeois Calvinist. The fragments escape the need for philosophy, for thought about values, for "where perspectives shrink to a single value, and that value becomes the universe, how can value itself be considered?"[22] The fragment demands solidarity. Ideologies which diverge from the national myth make no impact; they are not understood, and their proponents are not granted legitimacy. They are denounced as aliens, and treated as aliens, because they *are* aliens. The fragments cannot understand or deal with the fact that *all* men are *not* bourgeois Americans, or radical Australians, or Catholic French Canadians, or Calvinist South Africans. They cannot make peace with the loss of ideological certainty.

The specific weakness of the United States is its "inability to understand the appeal of socialism" to the third world.[23] Because the United States has "buried" the memory of the organic medieval community "beneath new liberal absolutisms and nationalisms"[24] it cannot understand that the appeal of socialism to nations with a predominantly non-liberal past (including French Canada) consists precisely in the promise of "continuing the corporate ethos in the very process" of modernization.[25] The American reacts with isolationism, messianism, and hysteria.

English Canada, because it is the most "imperfect" of the fragments, is not a one-myth culture. In English Canada ideological diversity has not been buried beneath an absolutist liberal nationalism. Here Locke is not the one true god; he must tolerate lesser tory and socialist deities at his side. The result is that English Canada does not direct an uncomprehending intolerance at heterodoxy, either within its borders or beyond them. (What a "backlash" Part-Pris or PSQ-type separatists would be getting if Quebec were in the United States!) In English Canada it has been possible to consider values without arousing the all-silencing cry of treason. Hartz observes that "if history had chosen English Canada for the American role" of directing the Western response to the world revolution, "the international scene would probably have witnessed less McCarthyite hysteria, less Wilsonian messianism."[26]

Americanizing liberals might consider that the Pearsonian rationality and calmness which Canada displays on the world stage—the "mediating" and "peace-keeping" role of which Canadians are so proud—is related to the un-American (tory and socialist) characteristics which they consider to be unnecessary imperfections in English-Canadian wholeness. The tolerance of English-Canadian domestic politics is also linked with the presence of these imperfections. If the price of Americanization is the surrender of legitimate ideological diversity, even the liberal might think twice before paying it. . . .

. . . My argument is essentially that non-liberal British elements have entered into English-Canadian society *together* with American liberal elements at the foundations. The fact is that Canada has been greatly influenced by both the United States and Britain. This is not to deny that liberalism is the dominant element in the English-Canada political culture; it is to stress that it is not the sole element, that it is accompanied by vital and legitimate streams of toryism and socialism which have as close a relation to English Canada's "essence" or "foundations" as does liberalism. English Canada's "essence" is both liberal and non-liberal. Neither the British nor the American elements can be explained away as "superstructural" excrescences.

4 / UN-AMERICAN ASPECTS OF CANADIAN CONSERVATISM

So far, I have been discussing the presence of toryism in Canada without referring to the Conservative party. This party can be seen as a party of right-wing or business liberalism, but such an interpretation would be far from the whole truth; the Canadian Conservative party, like the British Conservative party and unlike the Republican party, is not monolithically liberal. If there is a touch of toryism in English Canada, its primary carrier has been the Conservative party. It would not be correct to say that toryism is *the* ideology of the party, or even that some Conservatives are tories. These statements would not be true even of the British Conservative party. The primary component of the ideology of business-oriented parties is liberalism; but there are powerful traces of the old pre-liberal outlook in the British Conservative party, and less powerful but still perceptible traces of it in the Canadian party. A Republican is always a liberal. A Conservative may be at one moment a liberal, at the next moment a tory, and is usually something of both.

If it is true that the Canadian Conservatives can be seen from some angles as right-wing liberals, it is also true that figures such as R.B. Bennett, Arthur Meighen, and George Drew cannot be understood simply as Canadian versions of William McKinley, Herbert Hoover, and Robert Taft. Canadian Conservatives have something British about them that American Republicans do not. It is not simply their emphasis on loyalty to the Crown and to the British connection, but a touch of the authentic tory aura—traditionalism, elitism, the strong state, and so on. The Canadian conservatives lack the American aura of rugged individualism. Theirs is not the characteristically American conservatism which conserves only *liberal* values.[27]

It is possible to perceive in Canadian conservatism not only the elements of business liberalism and orthodox toryism, but also an element of "tory democracy"—the paternalistic concern for the "condition of the people," and the emphasis on the tory party as their champion—which, in Britain, was expressed by such figures as Disraeli and Lord Randolph Churchill. John A. Macdonald's approach to the emergent Canadian working class was in some respects similar to that of Disraeli. Later Conservatives acquired the image of arch reactionaries and arch enemies of the workers, but let us not forget that "Iron Heel" Bennett was also the Bennett of the Canadian New Deal.

The question arises: why is it that in Canada the *Conservative* leader proposes a New Deal? Why is that that the Canadian counterpart of Hoover apes *Roosevelt*? This phenomenon is usually interpreted as sheer historical accident, a product of Bennett's desperation and opportunism. But the answer may be that Bennett was not Hoover. Even in his "orthodox" days Bennett's views on the state's role in the economy were far from similar to Hoover's; Bennett's attitude was that of Canadian, not American, conservatism. Once this is recognized, it is possible to entertain the suggestion that Bennett's sudden radicalism, his sudden concern for the people, may not have been mere opportunism. It may have been a manifestation, a sudden activation under pressure, of a latent tory-democratic streak. Let it be noted also that the depression produced two Conservative splinter parties, both with "radical" welfare state programmes, and both led by former subordinates of Bennett: H.H. Stevens' Reconstruction party and W.D. Herridge's New Democracy.

The Bennett New Deal is only the most extreme instance of what is usually considered to be an accident or an aberration—the occasional manifestation of "radicalism" or "leftism" by otherwise orthodox Conservative leaders in the face of opposition from their "followers" in the business community. Meighen, for example, was constantly embroiled with the "Montreal interests" who objected to his railway policies. On one occasion he received a note of congratulation from William Irvine: "The man who dares to offend the Montreal interests is the sort of man that the people are going to vote for."[28] This same Meighen expressed on certain occasions, particularly after his retirement, an antagonism to big government and creeping socialism that would have warmed the heart of Robert Taft; but he combined his business liberalism with gloomy musings about the evil of universal suffrage—musings which Taft would have rejected as un-American. Meighen is far easier to understand from a British than from an American perspective, for he combined, in different proportions at different times, attitudes deriving from all three Conservative ideological streams: right-wing liberalism, orthodox toryism, and tory democracy.

The Western or agrarian Conservatives of the contemporary period, John Diefenbaker and Alvin Hamilton, who are usually dismissed as "prairie radicals" of the American type, might represent not only anti-Bay Street agrariansim but *also* the same type of tory democracy which was expressed before their time by orthodox business-sponsored Conservatives like Meighen and Bennett The populism (anti-elitism) of Diefenbaker and Hamilton is a genuinely foreign element in Canadian conservatism, but their stress on the Tory party as champion of the people and their advocacy of welfare state policies are in the tory democratic tradition. Their attitudes to the monarchy, the British connection, and the danger of American domination are entirely orthodox Conservative attitudes. Diefenbaker Conservatism is therefore to be understood not simply as a Western populist phenomenon, but as an odd *combination* of traditional Conservative views with attitudes absorbed from the Western Progressive tradition.

Another aberration which may be worthy of investigation is the Canadian phenomenon of the red tory. At the simplest level, he is a Conservative who prefers the CCF-NDP to the Liberals, or a socialist who prefers the Conservatives to the Liberals, without really knowing why. At a higher level, he is a conscious ideological Conservative with some "odd" socialist notions (W.L. Morton) or a conscious ideological socialist with some "odd" tory notions (Eugene Forsey). The very suggestion that such affinities might exist between

Republicans and Socialists in the United States is ludicrous enough to make some kind of a point.

Red toryism is, of course, one of the results of the relationship between toryism and socialism which has already been elucidated. The tory and socialist minds have some crucial assumptions, orientations, and values in common, so that from certain angles they may appear not as enemies, but as two different expressions of the same basic ideological outlook. Thus, at the very highest level, the red tory is a philosopher who combines elements of socialism and toryism so thoroughly in a single integrated *Weltanschauung* that it is impossible to say that he is a proponent of either one as *against* the other. Such a red tory is George Grant, who has associations with both the Conservative party and the NDP, and who has recently published a book which defends Diefenbaker, laments the death of "true" British conservatism in Canada, attacks the Liberals as individualists and Americanizers, and defines socialism as a variant of conservatism (each "protects the public good against private freedom").

5 / THE CHARACTER OF CANADIAN SOCIALISM

Canadian socialism is un-American in two distinct ways. It is un-American in the sense that it is a significant and legitimate political force in Canada, insignificant and alien in the United States. But Canadian socialism is also un-American in the sense that it does not speak the same language as American socialism. In Canada, socialism is British, non-Marxist, and worldly; in the United States it is German, Marxist, and other-worldly.

I have argued that the socialist ideas of British immigrants to Canada were not sloughed off because they "fit" with a political culture which already contained non-liberal components, and probably also because they were introduced into the political culture mix before the point of congealment. Thus socialism was not alien here. But it was not alien in yet another way; it was not borne by foreigners. The personnel and the ideology of the Canadian labour and socialist movements have been primarily British. Many of those who built these movements were British immigrants with past experience in the British labour movement; many others were Canadian-born children of such immigrants. And in British North America, Britons could not be treated as foreigners.

When socialism was brought to the United States, it found itself in an ideological environment in which it could not survive because Lockean individualism had long since achieved the status of a national religion; the political culture had already congealed, and socialism did not fit. American socialism was alien not only in this ideological sense, but in the ethnic sense as well; it was borne by foreigners from Germany and other continental European countries. These foreigners sloughed off their socialist ideas not simply because such ideas did not "fit" ideologically, but because as foreigners they were going through a general process of Americanization; socialism was only one of many ethnically alien characteristics which had to be abandoned. The immigrant's ideological change was only one incident among many others in the general process of changing his entire way of life. According to David Saposs, "the factor that contributed most tellingly to the decline of the socialist movement was that its chief following, the immigrant workers, . . . had become Americanized."[29]

A British socialist immigrant to Canada had a far different experience. The British immigrant was not an "alien" in British North America. The English-Canadian culture not only granted legitimacy to his political ideas and absorbed them into its wholeness; it absorbed him as a person into the English-Canadian community, with relatively little strain, without demanding that he change his entire way of life before being granted full citizenship. He was acceptable to begin with, by virtue of being British. It is impossible to understand the differences between American and Canadian socialism without taking into account this immense difference between the ethnic contexts of socialism in the two countries.

The ethnic handicap of American socialism consisted not only in the fact that its personnel was heavily European. Equally important was the fact that it was a *brand* of socialism—Marxism—which found survival difficult not only in the United States but in all English-speaking countries. Marx has not found the going easy in the United States; but neither has he found the going easy in Britain, Canada, Australia, or New Zealand. The socialism of the United States, the socialism of De Leon, Berger, Hillquit, and Debs, is predominantly Marxist and doctrinaire, because it is European. The socialism of English Canada, the socialism of Simpson, Woodsworth, and Coldwell, is predominantly Protestant, labourist, and Fabian, because it is British.

The prevalence of doctrinaire Marxism helps to explain the sectarianism of the American Socialist party. The distinctive quality of the sect is its "other-worldliness." It rejects the existing scheme of things entirely; its energies are directed not to devising strategems with which to lure the electorate, but to elaborating its utopian theory. Daniel Bell describes the American Socialist party as one "whose main preoccupation has been the refinement of 'theory' at the cost, even, of interminable factional divisions."[30] "It has never, even for a single year, been without some issue which threatened to split the party."[31] For Bell, the failure of American socialism is its failure to make the transition from sect to party, to concern itself with popular issues rather than theoretical disputes. The unfortunate decisions made by the party—especially the decisions to oppose the two world wars—were a result of this sectarianism, this refusal to compromise with the world.

The CCF has not been without its otherwordly tendencies; there have been doctrinal disagreements, and the party has always had a left wing interested more in "socialist education" than in practical political work. But this left wing has been a constantly declining minority. The party has expelled individuals and small groups—mostly Communists and Trotskyites—but it has never split. Its life has never been threatened by disagreement over doctrinal matters. It is no more preoccupied with theory than the British Labour party. It sees itself, and is seen by the public, not as a coterie of ideologists but as a party like the others, second to none in its avidity for office. If it has been attacked from the right for socialist "utopianism" and "impracticality," it has also been attacked from the right [sic] for abandoning the "true" socialist faith in an unprincipled drive for power.

The contrast between American Marxist socialism and Canadian non-Marxist socialism, and the weakness of Marxism not only in America but in all other English speaking countries, at first led me to think that Hartz's "single factor" explanation of the illegitimacy of American socialism might be overdone. This question arose: was it socialism *per se* that could not live in the United States, or only Marxist socialism? What if American socialism had looked to Britain rather than Germany, if it had been "empirical" rather than doctrinaire Marxist? The answer that suggested itself was that if American socialism had not been handicapped by its Marxian character—if it had been handicapped only by the fact that America had not known toryism and therefore would not listen to socialism—it might have been able to live a little longer and might not have died such a horrible death.

What this line of reasoning ignored was the fact that there *was* an impact in America of British socialist thought which was, however, even weaker than the Marxist impact. Why, in America, an English-speaking country, should the British influence on socialism have been so much weaker than the German? Precisely because the "single factor" explanation is *not* overdone. Socialism could not attain any degree of strength in America, for the Hartzian reason, except for a short while as a socialism *in* America but not *of* America, that is to say, except among unassimilated foreign groups. There *was* an unassimilated continental European group; there was never an unassimilated British group. The British influence was therefore much weaker than the Marxist.

At first I thought that since Marxism fails not only in the United States but in all English-speaking countries, *peculiarly American* characteristics cannot be the explanation of its failure in the United States. This is true; the peculiarly American characteristics account for the failure of *all* socialisms, *even* English-speaking socialism, in the United States. The failure of Marxian socialism is less complete and less rapid than the failure of the others precisely because of the peculiar American cultural characteristics which mean doom for all socialisms *except* those sustained by immigrants prior to their Americanization. The strength of Marx relative to other socialisms in America is a confirmation of the Hartzian hypothesis.

6 / CANADIAN LIBERALISM:
THE TRIUMPHANT CENTRE

Canadian Conservatives are not American Republicans; Canadian socialists are not American socialists; Canadian Liberals are not American liberal Democrats.

The un-American elements in English Canada's political culture are most evident in Canadian conservatism and socialism. But Canadian liberalism has a British colour too. The liberalism of Canada's Liberal party should not be identified with the liberalism of the American Democratic party. In many respects they stand in sharp contrast to one another.

The three components of the English-Canadian political culture have not developed in isolation from one another; each has developed in interaction with the others. Our toryism and our socialism have been moderated by liberalism. But by the same token, our liberalism has been rendered "impure," in American terms, through its contacts with toryism and socialism. If English-Canadian liberalism is less individualistic, less ardently populistic-democratic, more inclined to state intervention in the economy, and more tolerant of "feudal survivals" such as monarchy, this is due to the uninterrupted influence of toryism upon liberalism, an influence wielded in and through the conflict between the two. If English-Canadian liberalism has tended since the depression to merge at its leftist edge with the democratic socialism of the CCF-NDP, this is due to the influence which socialism has exerted upon liberalism, in and through the conflict between them. The key to understanding the Liberal party in Canada is to see it as a *centre* party, with *influential* enemies on both right and left.

Hartz's comparison of the Liberal Reform movements of the United States and Europe casts light on the differences between American and English-Canadian liberalism. Hartz defines Liberal Reform as the movement "which emerged toward the end of the nineteenth century to adapt classical liberalism to the purposes of small propertied interests and the labouring class and at the same time which rejected socialism."[32] The fact that European Liberal Reform was confronted with the significant socialist challenge meant (*a*) that liberals, influenced by socialist theory, tried to "transcend the earlier individualism "the need for collective action to solve the class problem,"[33] and (*b*) that liberals, faced with powerful enemies on both the left and the right, presented an ambivalent conservative-radical image; they attacked the tories and the *status quo*, but they also defended the *status quo* from its socialist enemies.

American liberals, impervious to the socialist challenge and therefore unaffected by socialist ideas, remained "enslaved" to individualism. . . .

. . . In English Canada Liberal Reform, represented by King's Liberal party, has had to face the socialist challenge. Under socialist influence, it abandoned its early devotion to "the lofty principles of Gladstone, the sound economics of Adam Smith, and the glories of laissez faire."[34] King's *Industry and Humanity* and the Liberal platform of 1919 mark the transition of English-Canadian Liberalism from the old individualism to the new Liberal Reform.

King's Liberal Reform, since it had to answer attacks from the left as well as from the right, projected a notoriously ambivalent conservative-radical image:

> Truly he will be remembered
> Wherever men honor ingenuity
> Ambiguity, inactivity, and political longevity.

When he faced Bennett and Meighen, King was the radical warrior, the champion of the little people against the interests. When he turned to face Woodsworth and Coldwell, he was the cautious conservative, the protector of the *status quo*. He

> . . . never let his on the one hand
> Know what his on the other hand was doing.[35]
>
> . . . .

Hartz points out that this "pragmatism" of the New Deal enabled it to go farther, to get more things done, than European Liberal Reform. "The free-wheeling inventiveness typified by the TVA, the NRA, the WPA, the SEC"[36] was nowhere to be found in Europe. Defending itself against socialism, European Liberal Reform could not submerge questions of theory; it had to justify innovations on the basis of a revised liberal ideology; it had to stop short of socialism openly. The New Deal, since it was not threatened by socialism, could ignore theory; it "did not need to stop short of Marx openly"; hence it could accomplish more than European Liberal Reform.

King had to face the socialist challenge. He did so in the manner of European Liberal Reform. No need to worry about abandoning individualism; Locke was not Canada's national god; like European liberalism, Canadian liberalism had been revised. The similarity of socialism and Liberal Reform could be acknowledged; indeed it could be emphasized and used to attract the socialist vote. At the same time, King had to answer the arguments of socialism, and in doing so he had to spell out his liberalism. He had to stop short of socialism openly. Social reform, yes; extension of public ownership, yes; the welfare state, yes; increased state control of the economy, yes; but not too much. Not socialism. The result was that King, like the European liberals, could not go as far as Roosevelt. . . .

. . . Like the Europeans, and unlike Roosevelt, he had to defend private property, he had to attack excessive reliance on the state, he had to criticize socialism as "impracticality" and "utopianism." "Half radical and half conservative—a tired man who could not make up his mind"—is this not the living image of Mackenzie King?

"In America, instead of being a champion of property, Roosevelt became the big antagonist of it; his liberalism was blocked by his radicalism."[37] In

Canada, since King had to worry not only about Bennett and Meighen and Drew, but also about Woodsworth and Coldwell and Douglas, King had to embark upon a defence of private property. *He* was no traitor to his class. Instead of becoming the antagonist of property, he became its champion; his radicalism was blocked by his liberalism.

An emphasis on the solidarity of the nation as against divisive "class parties" of right and left was "of the very essence of the Reformist Liberal position in Europe." "Who," asks Hartz, "would think of Roosevelt as a philosopher of class solidarity?"[38] Yet that is precisely what Roosevelt would have been if he had had to respond to a socialist presence in the American political culture. And that is precisely what King was in fact in Canada. His party was "the party of national unity." One of the most repeated charges against the CCF was that it was a divisive "class party"; the purpose of the Liberal party, on the other hand, was to preserve the solidarity of the Canadian people—the solidarity of its classes as well as the solidarity of French and English. . . .

The Liberal party has continued to speak the language of King: ambiguous and ambivalent, presenting first its radical face and then its conservative face, urging reform and warning against hasty, ill-considered change, calling for increased state responsibility but stopping short of socialism openly, speaking for the common people but preaching the solidarity of classes.

In the United States, the liberal Democrats are on the left. There is no doubt about that. In Canada, the Liberals are a party of the centre, appearing at times leftist and at times rightist. As such, they are much closer to European, especially British, Liberal Reform than to the American New Deal type of liberalism.

In the United States, the liberal Democrats are the party of organized labour. The new men of power, the labour leaders, have arrived politically; their vehicle is the Democratic party. In English Canada, if the labour leaders have arrived politically, they have done so in the CCF-NDP. They are nowhere to be found in the Liberal party. The rank and file, in the United States, are predominantly Democrats; in Canada at least a quarter are New Democrats, and the remainder show only a relatively slight, and by no means consistent, preference for the Liberals as against the Conservatives.

In the United States, left-wing "liberalism," as opposed to right wing "liberalism," has always meant opposition to the domination of American life by big business, and has expressed itself in and through the Democratic party; the party of business is the Republican party. In Canada, business is close to both the Conservatives and the Liberals. The business community donates to the campaign funds of both and is represented in the leadership circles of both. . . .

The Liberal party in Canada does not represent the opposition of society to domination by organized business. It claims to be based on no particular groups, but on *all*. It is not against any particular group; it is for *all*. The idea that there is any real conflict between groups is dismissed, and the very terms "right" and "left" are rejeted: "The terms 'right' and 'left' belong to those who regard politics as a class struggle. . . . The Liberal view is that true political progress is marked by . . . the reconciliation of classes, and the promotion of the general interest above all particular interests."[39]

A party of the left can be distinguished from parties of the centre and right according to two interrelated criteria: its policy approach, and its electoral support.

Policy Approach

The policy approach of a left party is to introduce innovations on behalf of the lower strata. The Liberals, unlike the liberal Democrats, have not been a party of innovation. As a centre party, they have allowed the CCF-NDP to introduce innovations; they have then waited for signs of substantial acceptance by all strata of the population, and for signs of reassurance against possible electoral reprisals, before actually proceeding to implement the innovations. By this time, of course, they are strictly speaking no longer innovations. The centre party recoils from the fight for controversial measures: it loves to implement a consensus. Roosevelt was the innovator *par excellence*. King, though he was in his own mind in favour of reform, stalled until public demand for innovation was so great and so clear that he could respond to it without antagonizing his business-sponsored right wing. He rationalized his caution into a theory of democratic leadership far different from Roosevelt's conception of the strong presidency:

> Mackenzie King's conception of political leadership, which he often expressed, was that a leader should make his objectives clear, but that leadership was neither liberal nor democratic which tried to force new policies . . . on a public that did not consent to them.[40]
>
> He believed that nothing was so likely to set back a good cause as premature action.[41]

This was the official Liberal explanation of King's failure to embark on any far reaching programme of reform until 1943. King himself undoubtedly believed that his caution was based at least in part on a "democratic" theory of leadership. But his diaries suggest that the reforms came when they did because CCF pressure became so threatening that it could no longer be ignored by King's right-wing colleagues, so threatening that King felt able to surrender to it without jeopardizing the unity of his party. The bare facts are these: In August, 1943, the CCF became the official opposition in Ontario. In September, 1943, the CCF overtook the Liberals in the Gallup poll (Canada: CCF 29%, Liberals 28%; Ontario: CCF 32%, Liberals 26%; The West: CCF 41%, Liberals 23%). King's reaction is summed up in the following quotation from his diary: "In my heart, I am not sorry to see the mass of the people coming a little more into their own, but I do regret that it is not the Liberal party that is winning that position for them. . . . It can still be that our people will learn their lesson in time. What I fear is we will begin to have defections from our own ranks in the House to the CCF."[42] Almost immediately after the release of the September Gallup Poll, the Advisory Council of the National Liberal Federation, meeting at King's request, adopted fourteen resolutions "constituting a programme of reform . . . of far reaching consequences." King wrote in his diary: "I have succeeded in making declarations which will improve the lot of . . . farmers and working people. . . . I think I have cut the ground in large part from under the CCF. . . ."[43] "The great numbers of people will see that I have been true to them."[44]

The Liberal slogan in the campaign of 1945 was "A New Social Order for Canada." The election of June 11 returned King to power with a drastically reduced majority. The CCF vote rose from 8.5 per cent to 15.6 per cent, and its representation in the Commons from 8 to 29. But King's swing to the left had defeated the CCF's bid for major party status. The CCF's success was much smaller than it had expected. The success was actually a defeat, a disappointing shock from which socialism in Canada has not yet recovered.

The Liberal-CCF relationship in 1943–1945 is only the sharpest and clearest instance of the permanent interdependence forced upon each by the presence of the other, a relationship which one student describes as "antagonistic symbiosis." The Liberals depend on the CCF-NDP for innovations; the CCF-NDP depends upon the Liberals for implementation of the innovations. When the left is weak, as before and after the Second World War, the centre party moves right to deal with the Conservative challenge; when the left is strengthened, as during the war and after the formation of the NDP, the centre moves left to deal with that challenge.

In a conversation between King and Coldwell shortly before King's death, King expressed his regrets that Coldwell had not joined him. With Coldwell at his side, he would have been able to implement reforms which were close to his heart; reforms which had either been postponed until the end of the war or not introduced at all. He said the CCF had performed the valuable function of popularizing reforms so that he could introduce them when public opinion was ripe. Coldwell replied that it was impossible for him to join King, especially in view of the people who surrounded King. There, in a nutshell, is the story of the relationship between the Liberal party and the CCF-NDP. The Liberals, says King, are too conservative because the left has not joined them. The left has not joined them, replies Coldwell, because they are too conservative.

King wanted to show the people that he was "true to them." He was saddened that the CCF and not the Liberals were fighting the people's battles. But he could not move from dead centre until CCF power became so great that the necessity of moving was clear, not only to himself but to all realistic politicians. King's best self wanted to innovate; yet he saw the Liberal party not as a great innovating force but as the party which would implement reforms once they had been popularized by the CCF. Yet he wanted to absorb the CCF. The lot of the centrist politician is not a happy one. . . .

The absence of Lockean "monotheism" strengthened socialism in Canada. Socialism was present in the political culture when liberalism began to concern itself with the problems of the industrial age; liberalism was therefore forced to react to the socialist challenge. In doing so, it was cast in the mould of European Liberal Reform (centre) parties—ambivalent, radical and conservative, alternating attacks on the *status quo* with defence of the *status quo.* Socialism had sufficient strength in English Canada to force liberalism into the European rather than the American position—centre rather than left. King's liberalism was therefore not capable of reacting to the depression in a Rooseveltian manner. As a result, socialist power grew.

Socialism was not powerless, so there was no New Deal. There was no New Deal, so socialism grew more powerful. Socialism grew more powerful, so King reacted with "A New Social Order for Canada." The centre and the left dance around one another, frustrating one another and living off the frustration; each is locked into the dance by the existence of the other.

I have been stressing the strength of Canadian socialism in order to make clear the differences between the Canadian and the American situations. Of course this does not mean that the differences between Canada and Europe can be ignored. Canadian socialism has been strong enough to challenge liberalism, to force liberalism to explain itself, and thus to evoke from it the same sort of centrist response as was evoked in Europe. But socialism in Canada has not been strong enough to match or overshadow liberalism. The CCF became a significant political force, but except for the years 1942–45 it never knocked on the gates of national power.

In Europe, the workingman could not be appeased by the concessions of Liberal Reform. The centre was squeezed out of existence between its enemies on the right and on the left. In Canada, the centre party's concessions were sufficient to keep the lower strata from flocking en masse to the left. The concessions were not sufficient to *dispose* of the socialist threat, but they were sufficient to draw the socialists' sharpest teeth. In Canada the centre party emerged triumphant over its enemies on the right and on the left. Here, then, is another aspect of English Canada's uniqueness: it is the only society in which Liberal Reform faces the challenge of socialism *and* emerges victorious. The English-Canadian fragment *is* bourgeois. The toryism and the socialism, though significant, *are* "touches."

Electoral Support

There is a dearth of information about the influence of class on voting behaviour in Canada, but there are strong indications that the higher strata are more likely than the lower to vote Conservative, the lower strata are more likely than the higher to vote CCF-NDP, and that both groups are about *equally* attracted to the Liberals. This would, of course, confirm the picture of Conservatives as the right, NDP as the left, and Liberals as the "classless" centre. This is in sharp contrast to the situation in the United States, where the lower strata prefer the Democrats, the higher prefer the Republicans, and there is no centre party.

Although this picture of the relationship between class and voting is broadly true, it is also true that class voting in Canada is, generally speaking, overshadowed by regional and religious-ethnic voting. In some parts of Canada, e.g. Ontario, class voting is as high as in the United States or higher. Nevertheless, in Canada *considered as a whole* class voting is lower than in the United States; non-class motivations appear to be very strong. Peter Regenstrief suggests that one factor accounting for this is the persistent cultivation by the Liberal party of its classless image, its "abhorrence of anything remotely associated with class politics," its refusal to appeal to any class *against* any other class.

What this points to again is the unique character of English Canada as the only society in which the centre triumphs over left and right. In Europe the classless appeal of Liberal Reform does not work; the centre is decimated by the defection of high-status adherents to the right and of low-status adherents to the left. In Canada, the classless appeal of King centrism is the winning strategy, drawing lower-class support to the Liberals away from the left parties, and higher-class support away from the right parties. This forces the left and right parties themselves to emulate (to a certain extent) the Liberals' classless strategy. The Conservatives transform themselves into Progressive Conservatives. The CCF transforms itself from a "farmer-labour" party into an NDP calling for the support of "all liberally minded Canadians." The Liberal refusal to appear as a class party forces both right and left to mitigate their class àppeals and to become themselves, in a sense, centre parties.

Class voting in Canada may be lower than in the United States not entirely because regional-religious-ethnic factors are "objectively" stronger here, but also because King Liberalism, by resolutely avoiding class symbols, has *made* other symbols more important.

> He blunted us.
> We had no shape
> Because he never took sides,
> And no sides,
> Because he never allowed them to take shape.[45]

NOTES

1. New York: Harcourt, Brace (Toronto: Longmans), 1955, hereafter cited as *Liberal Tradition.*
2. New York: Harcourt, Brace (Toronto: Longmans), 1964, hereafter cited as *New Societies.*
3. Hartz, *New Societies*, 3.
4. Ibid., 25.
5. Ibid., 7.
6. Ibid., 34.
7. Ibid., 71.
8. [I]bid., 239.
9. Ibid., 72.
10. Ibid., 34.
11. In *The First New Nation* (New York, 1963), esp. chap. 7.
12. William Nelson, *The American Tory* (New York, 1961), 189–90.
13. Hartz, *New Societies*, 91.
14. Ibid., 243.
15. Lipset, *The First New Nation* 251.
16. [*New Societies*], 246.
17. Ibid., 247
18. Ibid., 246.
19. Ibid., 15.
20. Ibid., 10.
21. Hartz, *Liberal Tradition*, 11.
22. Hartz, *New Societies*, 23.
23. Ibid., 119.
24. Ibid., 35.
25. Ibid., 119.
26. Ibid., 120.
27. Historic toryism finds expression today in the writings of Conservatives like W.L. Morton, who describes America as a liberal society integrated from below, by a *covenant* of brothers, and Canada as a monarchial society held together at the top, integrated by *loyalty* to the Crown. (*The Canadian Identity* (Toronto, 1961), 99–114.) In another of his writings Morton stresses the tory belief in personal leadership, in loyalty to leaders and his readiness to let them govern. ("Canadian Conservatism Now," in Paul Fox, ed., *Politics: Canada* (Toronto, 1962), 287.) He takes an organic view of society, stresses the values of authority and tradition, rejects the liberal values of individualism and egalitariansim. He calls for the rejection of the "dangerous and improper idea of the electoral mandate" (ibid., 289). He calls for the "creation of a Canadian system of honours" (ibid., 290). And he exhorts Canadian Conservatives frankly and loyally to accept the welfare state, since "laissez faire and rugged individualism" are foreign to "con-

servative principles" (ibid., 289). Canadian and British tories are able to rationalize their parties' grudging acceptance of the welfare state by recalling their precapitalist collectivist traditions. Can one conceive of a respected spokesman of traditional Republicanism denouncing "rugged individualism" as un-Republican?

28. Roger Graham, *Arthur Meighen* vol. II (Toronto, 1963), 209.
29. *Communism in American Unions* (New York, 1959), 7.
30. "The Background and Development of Marxian Socialism in the United States," in D. Egbert and S. Persons, eds., *Socialism in American Life* (Princeton, 1952), 401.
31. Ibid., 221.
32. *Liberal Tradition*, p. 228.
33. Ibid., 231.
34. Bruce Hutchison, *The Incredible Canadian* (Toronto, 1952), 6.
35. F.R. Scott, "W.L.M.K.," *The Blasted Pine*, ed. F.R. Scott and A.J.M. Smith (Toronto, 1962), 28.
36. *Liberal Tradition*, 271.
37. Ibid., 267.
38. Ibid.
39. J.W. Pickersgill, *The Liberal Party* [(Toronto, 1962)], 64.
40. Ibid., 26–27.
41. J.W. Pickersgill, *The Mackenzie King Record* (Toronto, 1960), 10.
42. Ibid., 571.
43. Ibid., 601.
44. Ibid., 635.
45. Scott, *The Blasted Pine*, 27.

FURTHER READINGS

Bell, D. "Political Culture in Canada." In M. Whittington and G. Williams, eds. *Canadian Politics in the 1980s.* 2nd ed., 155–174. Toronto: Methuen, 1984.

Bell, D. and L. Tepperman. *The Roots of Disunity, A Look at Canadian Political Culture.* Toronto: McClelland & Stewart, 1979.

Christian, W. "Ideology and Canadian Politics." In J.H. Redekop, *Approaches To Canadian Politics.* Toronto: Prentice-Hall, 1978.

Christian, W., and C. Campbell. *Political Parties and Ideologies in Canada.* Toronto: McGraw-Hill Ryerson, 1974.

Forbes, D. ed. *Canadian Political Thought.* Toronto: Oxford University Press, 1985.

Horowitz, G. "Notes on: 'Conservatism, Liberalism, and Socialism in Canada'." *C.J.P.S.* 11, 2 (June, 1978): 383–399.

Preece, R. "Tory Myth and Conservative Reality: Horowitz Revisited." *Canadian Journal of Political and Social Theory* 2, 1 (1978): 87–98.

Wiseman, N. "The Pattern of Prairie Politics." *Queen's Quarterly* 88, 2 (Summer, 1981): 298–315.

PART 3

PEOPLE AND POLITICS

In this section we consider the dynamic processes and institutions which provide the main "linkages" of people and their ideas to the formal political system.

Democracy has been described as government by public opinion, and today that opinion is being measured constantly by pollsters. During elections, the publication of poll findings may influence the very voting intentions which purportedly are being measured. Even if poll results are accurate within a range of plus or minus four percent, nineteen times out of twenty (as pollsters claim) that margin of error casts doubt on their utility in forecasting close elections. Some European countries ban the publication of polling results during campaigns. Considerations such as these raise important questions as to the role of polling in democracies, questions addressed by Leon Dion in Reading 13.

The party system, fundamental as it is to an understanding of politics in a parliamentary system, is the subject of Readings 14 and 15. F.H. Underhill offers a synoptic review of "The Nature and Function of Political Parties," an essay which, since 1956, has stood the test of time. Underhill usefully highlights the concepts of brokerage politics, compromise, concurrent majorities, and the possibility of single-party dominance. A heavily edited version of a chapter from *The Vertical Mosaic* puts forth John Porter's view that our national parties have been obsessed by the "integrative function," a function he contends might better be performed by parties polarized on a left-right ideological cleavage.

Because parliamentary government is party government, the selection of party leaders is of obvious significance in our system, and in Reading 16 D.V. Smiley illustrates how leadership conventions, not notably successful in formulating party policy, may be élitist, reinforce non-parliamentary cults of personality, and tend to reward political inexperience.

The shortcomings of the electoral system and its implications for the party system are examined by Alan Cairns in Reading 17, a seminal article published in 1968 which has changed many perceptions of our voting arrangements. Cairns points out that the electoral system magnifies party strength in some regions and diminishes it in others, distorting both popular support patterns and regional representation. As a result, Canada is marked by a divisive and sectional, rather than an integrative and nationalizing, style of politics. This essay points to the desirability of a scheme of proportional representation which might assist parties in becoming more truly national.

It is always salutary when scholarship challenges the conventional wisdom and causes us to re-think accepted certitudes. Reading 18, a recent (1986) paper by Nelson Wiseman questions the reliability, significance, and usefulness of much of the data generated by Canadian National Election Studies. It identifies biases in the voting survey data and reveals gaps between people's reported behaviour and their actual behaviour.

Reading 19 by Hugh Thorburn confronts us with the problem of the huge and growing power of interest groups. Policy making in Canada is dominated not only by relations between governments within the federal system, but also by consultation and negotiation between private interest groups or pressure groups and governments. It is impossible to exaggerate the importance of this activity. Whether we are members of a particular segment of society such as doctors or students, or whether we are women or consumers who see ourselves as members of the more general society, various groups will try to organize and articulate our interests and press them on governments, which in turn must weigh and balance these clamourings if they want to avoid losing votes. In recent years much discussion has been focused on means of identifying and regulating the activities of pressure groups, for it is clear that such informal but powerful group actions figure prominently in the formulation of public policy.

13

Democracy as Perceived by Public Opinion Analysts

Leon Dion

The political ideas of public opinion analysts—pollsters as well as theoreticians—have often been submitted to rather harsh criticisms from political philosophers and scientists. On occasion, however, the analysts have reciprocated by accusing the latter of being poorly acquainted not only with the techniques and purpose of polling but also with the basic political assumptions that underlie their work. Public opinion analysts in the United States present themselves as champions of democracy; as a consequence, it is only natural that they should above all resent criticisms asserting that they hold naïve, false, or even subversive notions concerning democracy.

In the present article, I intend to explore the ideological conceptions of American public opinion analysts concerning the position and function of polling in a democracy. Reference to their critics will be made only when one or another public opinion analyst is known to have explicitly answered a specific point. Since many contemporary analysts acknowledge their debt to Bryce's *The American Commonwealth*, I shall start by presenting the pertinent views of the British author concerning public opinion; second, I shall summarize the views which present polling as a new technique of democratic government; third, I shall consider what public opinion analysts have to say about the impact of polling on the democratic process as such. Finally, I shall conclude by indicating how public opinion analysts view their research in relation to political theory in general.

I

Political scientists sometimes express the view that A. Lawrence Lowell is the forerunner of public opinion analysis as a supreme guide to policy because he was among the first to advocate the application of statistics to politics. It is, however, noteworthy that American public opinion analysts seldom acknowledge their dependence on *Public Opinion and Popular Government*,

Abridged from Leon Dion, "Democracy as Perceived by Public Opinion Analysts," *Canadian Journal of Economics and Political Science* 28, No. 4 (November 1962), 571-84. Reprinted by permission of the author and The Canadian Political Science Association.

written in 1913, in which Lowell presented his own conception of public opinion. It is true that Lowell in his book asserts that the essence of popular government "may be said to consist in the control of political affairs by public opinion," but his treatment of public opinion remains throughout moralistic. To him, public opinion analysis does not lend itself to the quantitative approach. Rather he holds that public opinion is a proto-metaphysical notion which bears no necessary relation to the "will of all," nor even to that of the majority. In accordance with Rousseau, he distinguishes between "real" public opinion and majority views as revealed by the ballot. To him, "real" public opinion expresses a genuine consensus of the body social in regard to questions pertaining to the basic assumptions of government whether or not, on any given issue, it coincides with the views of the majority. As a consequence of this theoretical position, analysts of public opinion cannot claim Lowell as an authority because, although he might have agreed that polling represents one of the techniques of ascertaining the distribution of views on a given issue, he would certainly have denied, as some present-day political scientists still do, that polling in fact measures public opinion.

Inversely, public opinion analysts have quite often claimed Lord Bryce as their chief authority. Bryce was not the first, of course, to associate the idea of democracy with the rule of public opinion, but to him public opinion remained primarily a statistical category. Even more important, he was among the first, if not in fact the very first, to raise the question of the possibility of devising techniques to ascertain public opinion at will on day-to-day issues. As is well known, the celebrated author of *The American Commonwealth* maintained that modern democracy underwent a developmental process of four stages, each involving a gradual shaping and assertion of public opinion. In the first, characterized by the rule of a dominant group, public opinion remains static and passive; in the second, the masses begin to assert their political rights and there occurs a split between their opinions and those of the rulers; in the third, legislative assemblies have been created and public opinion becomes an active and creative factor of public policy through the periodic election of representatives who are accountable to the people. And then he went on:

> A fourth stage would be reached if the will of the majority of citizens were to become ascertainable at all times, and without the need of its passing through a body of representatives, possibly even without the need of voting machinery at all. In such a state of things the sway of public opinion would have become more complete, because more continuous, than it is in those European countries which . . . look chiefly to Parliaments as exponents of national sentiment. The authority would seem to remain all the while in the mass of the citizens. Popular government would have been pushed so far as almost to dispense with, or at any rate to anticipate, the legal modes in which the majority speaks its will at the polling booths; and this informal but direct control of the multitude would dwarf, if it did not supersede, the importance of those formal but occasional deliverances made at the elections of representatives.[1]

In the second edition of *The American Commonwealth* (1893) he referred to the tendency on the part of ministers and legislators "to look incessantly for manifestations of current popular opinion, and to shape their course in accordance with their reading of those manifestations." But "how is the drift of public opinion to be ascertained except by counting votes?" he asked. "How without the greatest inconvenience, can votes be frequently taken on all the chief questions that arise?" Although he saw the advantages of introducing techniques of direct democracy such as primaries, referendum, initiative and recall, he was not as confident of the virtues and practicability of such devices as were the American progressives. Then he referred to "unbiased persons" who through "long practice" and "sympathetic touch" have developed a "flair" in "sizing up" the attitudes and proclivities of their fellow citizens. Furthermore, supplementing the technique of direct mass observation which he found was used by a great many politicians, he inquired about the possibility of devising "machinery for weighing or measuring the popular will from week to week or month to month." Although he thought that such a technique was not likely to be invented he made it clear that, if such a development should ever happen, it should benefit from full legal recognition. In that eventuality, the course of democratic government, shaped as it would be according to the findings of the new technique, would become completely responsive and accountable to "public opinion."

It is clear from his writings on the subject, that Bryce envisioned a device which would reveal the exact statistical distribution of views on a given issue after the manner of, but more rapidly than, elections which, in his view, simply resulted in the elucidation of majorities and minorities. When he envisioned a possible "fourth state of democracy," therefore, he had in mind a regime which would give greater effect to the supremacy of numbers in political life. As he himself asserted, it is not so much wisdom which characterizes public opinion as it is power—the power derived from the adding of "ayes" and "noes." To him, indeed, public opinion was simply "the aggregate of the views men hold regarding matters that affect or interest the community." Thus when he asserts that "in no country is public opinion so powerful as it is in the United States" he wishes to convey his conviction of a supposed greater sway of the sheer weight of numbers in the political life of that country than anywhere else. I think it fair to conclude that Bryce's doctrinal assumption was that wherever there is a majority "public opinion" on a given issue it should be made a law as soon as it is definitely ascertained through an adequate technique.

Bryce's conception of public opinion raises some of the most momentous problems confronting present-day students of political theory, sociology, and psychology. There is not even general agreement among scholars about the meaning of "public opinion"; the degree to which the technique of sampling polls really measures opinions remains a disputed matter; the relation of public opinions to basic attitudes, ideologies, and the social structure—in a word, the nature of public opinion as a social and political process—is still almost an uncharted field of research. Such being the situation, it is only to be expected that most public opinion analysts refrain from passing definite judgment on the question whether the technique of sampling polls, as practised since 1935, gives implementation to Bryce's hypothetic "fourth stage of democracy." Indeed, in their more sober moments, even the most enthusiastic pollsters, George Gallup included, would tend to answer in the negative. Nevertheless, Bryce furnished the model to which public opinion analysts relate their own reasoning in political theory.

Undoubtedly with a view to propagandizing the importance of scientific sampling polls, Gallup in his earlier writings repeatedly expressed his conviction that polling gave implementation to Bryce's "fourth stage of democracy." In that vein he wrote: "the polls substitute direct factual reporting for intuition as a guide to public opinion . . . The sampling referendum, then, is a modern answer to Bryce's problem." And again: "With the emergence of the sampling referendum in our day, the solution to the problem of measuring public opinion—the problem which Montaigne had thought insoluble and Bryce thought difficult, appears to be in sight." However, most authors have not followed Gallup in his bold and somewhat intemperate assertions. They have usually expressed their convictions in a more general manner and given the impression that Bryce's question remains to them an open problem after all: "The public opinion poll is one of the most important social inventions since the invention of the secret ballot," says F.S. Chapin. Or, in the words of Charles W. Smith:

> Public opinion is today a sovereign force. The task of democratic institutions is to provide effective machinery for the translation of the public will into action and to make public opinion worthy of its power . . . If a really accurate method for measuring public opinion could be devised and made use of, it would lead to a new era of democratic control in human affairs . . . By offering [the citizens] an opportunity to get political scores every few days, straw polls transform the election from one game into a world series.[2]

II

Whatever individual differences there may be among public opinion analysts on the over-all importance of polling, they all agree that the new technique is called upon to exercise a unique function in our big, complex, and warlike contemporary societies. Polling, according to its advocates, will help leaders in the shaping of public policies; it will make up for some of the evident deficiencies and shortcomings of the ballot; it will give greater sway to the rule of the majority.

Although few public opinion analysts have given evidence of an extensive knowledge of the apparent intricacies of modern society, many of them have contributed some thought on the subject. They generally contend that the traditional techniques of democracy might have been reasonably efficient in the era of face-to-face relationships permitted by the simple and decentralized structures of traditional society. At the same time they affirm that from the moment these primary relationships disappeared, the old techniques were no longer sufficient to accomplish their ascribed functions. They had to be supplemented by the new technique of polling which, as Gallup asserted in 1939 and 1940, in some degree artificially restores the condition of face-to-face relationship and thus procures for policy makers and other persons involved in public affairs inestimable benefits. Writing in 1940, Gallup asked: "Can democracy develop new techniques to meet the impact of this strange new decade?" And then, by reference to war conditions, he answered his own question in the affirmative:

> When the shadow of war fell upon Europe in 1939 a reliable instrument was ready to test American reactions . . . No longer was it necessary as in 1914 to guess about public opinion or to look to editors and pressure groups in an attempt to discover what the people as a whole were thinking. As a matter of fact sentiment had been measured and recorded for many months past on the question of America's role in case war did break out . . . The mood of the people, the precise strength of isolationist sentiment on one hand, and interventionist sentiment on the other, were charted.

According to Gallup, polling constitutes an invaluable technique wherever the interests or opinions or activities of large groups of people need to be assessed: "Continuous polls constitute a kind of public intelligence service in the field of social groups and opinions, and will indicate in a measurable way tendencies which would otherwise be the subject of speculation and guesswork." At about the same time, Harold F. Gosnell and Paul T. Cherington were similarly expressing their belief in the reliability of sampling polls as an instrument of democracy under the conditions of our big societies.

Indeed, public opinion analysts have, on occasion, expressed the conviction that sampling polls present a more accurate picture of public opinion than elections themselves. As usual, Gallup led the way by arguing that polls had the advantage over the ballot which is "slow, costly, and inconclusive," since by sampling, "pollsters are building a miniature electorate." We live under a crazy system," exclaimed Thomas A. Bailey, "we hold elections and then try to guess what they mean, which is a thorough[ly] unscientific procedure. Until such time as we are willing to have true referenda on specific issues, we shall have to seek the truth, not in election returns, but in unofficial public opinion polls." H.H. Field and G.M. Connelly were even more sanguine in stating their views:

> Many opinion analysts contend that scientific surveys are the most reliable expression of public opinion. They claim that surveys are not subject to political machine manipulations in getting out a disproportionately large Republican or Democratic vote, to 'short pencil artists', to dead persons' voting, to gerrymandering, to the effect of the weather keeping the elderly and infirms from the polls,

nor to the poll tax. Experts maintain that scientific surveys represent all types of persons in the degree to which they exist in the entire population, while the elections seldom do. It is common for less than half of the registered voters to go to the polls, not to mention the unregistered.

In a more cautious way William Albig wrote: "... as the poller's original purpose is the recording of public opinion, and, if in preelection polls he develops a skill which correctly reports that public opinion, then it is true that the polls may perhaps reflect the wishes of the electorate more accurately than the elections." Such being the alleged superiority of opinion polls over the ballot, one might expect that pollsters, following the suggestion made by Bryce, would propose that the former be substituted for the latter as a method of assessing public policy and choosing the representatives of the people. However, to my knowledge, in spite of many accusations to that effect, nobody in the United States has ever made such a proposal.

One of the most beneficial results of sampling polls, according to their advocates, consists in the fact that they ascertain majority opinions on a great many day-to-day issues about which elections or referenda cannot conveniently be taken. Thus, sampling polls should greatly extend the power of majority rule. But is the virtue of majority rule such that its indefinite extension in the determination of public policy is desirable? Should it be regarded in all cases as "the ultimate tribunal for social and political issues" as Gallup sometimes thought it should be? Should we, again with Gallup, formulate the wish that "polls of the future will be so accurate that the legislators will automatically follow their dictates?" More cautiously, Harry Field and Paul Hazarsfeld have contended that polls results should be "the final judge on matters of policy" but "... only when all the pertinent facts have been widely discussed, so that it can be reasonably certain that interrogator and respondent are talking about the same thing."[3]

Such a contention is based on the assumption that, as Gallup asserts, "the democratic way of life rests firmly on the premise that the surest touchstone of political action is the actual experience of the citizens." Relying on polling evidence, Gallup has quoted with approval Theodore Roosevelt's view that, "day in and day out the plain people will make fewer mistakes in governing themselves than any smaller group will make in governing them." De Witt Clinton Poole commented that if the "collective judgment" of the people has been found to be sound to an extraordinary degree it may be because there is a "value judgment" implicit in the views of "the greatest number"—a value judgment which is the best that can be found "on any given problem at any given time." Relying on his own data Gallup stated in 1949: "In my opinion the public has not only been right on most, if not all the issues of the last 14 years, but it has been ahead of our legislative leaders." And Paul T. Cherington, while deploring the fact that "the plans of the evil or the emotional or the short-sighted" to prevent the free expression of the "average public intelligence" often succeed, none the less took solace in the hope that these plans "will sooner or later be called to halt by the penetrating wisdom of *vox populi*, speaking through 'chisquares,' 'medians,' and 'cumulative means,' 'standard deviations,' and other strange statistical gadgets." Possibly not every student of public opinion will concur in the view that poll results confirm that the "plain people's judgment" on public issues is generally "more enlightened" than the judgment of legislators or experts. But the pollsters can point to some evidence indicating that this is often (though certainly not always) the case in the United States. To their detractors, pollsters retort not without justification that they should rather rejoice over what purports to be a scientific confirmation of a basic democratic dogma than lament over the alleged fact that, in the words of Edward L. Bernays, "we are no longer led by men. We are led around by polls." Furthermore, such a tragic view of the situation is groundless since no public opinion analyst or pollster, with the possible exception of Gallup in his earlier writings, has ever suggested that poll results on public opinion should be made mandatory by law.

From the evidence so far presented there appears to be little support for those critics, such as Lindsay Rogers, who attribute to pollsters and some analysts of public opinion the dark design of perverting the representative institutions of government in the United States. Does polling "tend toward an indesirable system of pure democracy," as O.R. McGuire has contended? It is true that Gallup, in his early writings, repeatedly referred to polling as constituting a "sampling referendum," a "big New England continuous town meeting," and so on. It is also true that some of the more fervent of Gallup's disciples sometimes uncritically repeat these earlier boastings of the master, when, writing from the vantage point of greater experience and knowledge, they should know that polling has not at all recreated in modern society the social conditions of a New England town meeting. When Morris L. Ernst and David Loth beg permission to dissent from pollsters on this ground (among others), they can easily be excused because, in truth, they have nothing to dissent from. . . . Gallup himself implicitly recanted his own earlier remarks on the subject when he declared: "The fears entertained by some critics in the early days of scientific polling that these procedures would lead to pure democracy and subvert democracy have been allayed."[4]

Although none of the current theories of representation—the delegate, the mandate, the pressure group, the functional (or corporate) theories—exactly correspond to the actual political processes they are intended to interpret, there appears to be no justification in advocating a "public opinion" theory of representation. It is true that pollsters and some theoreticians of public opinion tend to place "public opinion" instead of "the people" at the centre of the scene, but in so far as their own political views are concerned I think it is only fair to conclude, from the evidence presented above, that they do not advocate that public opinions (as manifested through polling techniques) should be made politically authoritative and mandatory. When they speak of "government by public opinion" they do not really mean that public opinion in any strict or scientific sense of the expression is or should be the real basis of democratic government or even the chief authoritative source of public policy. As currently used, "government by public opinion" either means in fact government by "the people," or it does not mean government at all but merely refers to the contribution of opinion polls to representative government. It is not only pollsters and theorists of public opinion who are guilty of such a loose use of the expression "public opinion." Political scientists themselves are increasingly prone to refer to democracy as government by public opinion— as if the jungle of semantic confusion which they call "political thought" were not thick enough already. Thus do they create fresh obstacles in the way of the emergence of a political science in the full sense of the term.

III

While public opinion analysts do not claim the existence or even the desirability of government by "public opinion" they are none the less firmly convinced that the technique of polling can contribute a good deal to the democratic governmental process. I shall present here a few of the many arguments they have developed in order to justify their claims.

First, they point out, with some justice, that the simple fact that the polling technique was unknown to the Founding Fathers of the American constitution should not be considered a sufficient ground for opposing its use now. Furthermore they can point with satisfaction to an abundant literature in current political science purporting to show that modern democracy, "considered as the machinery of popular power" has been "a relative failure." To those critics who oppose polling on the ground that it tends to increase the power of numbers in public affairs they retort that, to the contrary, polling submits the sham pretences of vociferous or aggressive small groups to public exposure while at the same time constituting the only technique by which minority movements of protest or insurgency can ascertain their real strength. And to those who accuse polling of subverting representative government, they answer that, far from doing that, polling by presenting data on the distribution of opinions according to occupation, age, sex, religion, and so on in fact offers useful clues which help to supplement our present system of territorial representation with some degree of functional representation.

Second, the partisans of polling maintain that sampling poll results represent one more way, in addition to the right of petition, initiative, and referendum (in such states where these are enforced), elections, the sending of letters and telegrams, and so on, in which the people can talk to their government. To some, indeed, the polling of opinions may well constitute the most satisfactory way for the people to express themselves in these days when "government has become increasingly important in the life of the individuals, whereas at the same time it has become increasingly more inaccessible and more difficult to influence." Polling, according to this view, may well represent the only sure way of ascertaining the voice of the plain people and, conversely, of curbing the influence of private interests and pressure groups and other manifestations of undemocratic trends which operate by devious ways and unregulated methods.

Third, according to its advocates, polling furnishes to the persons invested with the responsibilities of government—the president, the judges, the representatives as well as the administrators—one of the surest techniques of assessing what goes on in the minds of the people on any issue and at all times. According to Cartright, all public policies are affected with a "human element" which may account for the success or failure of any particular measure, and it is one of the functions of polling to reveal this "human element." Of course, legislators have other means of taking the people's pulse: they read newspapers and their own correspondence, and they search for "typical" people, but these methods are erratic as compared to poll results. "The poll," says Benjamin H. Williams, "gives to legislative and administrative officers in relatively accurate form a summary of public opinion on pertinent issues. Without some organized type of survey the official is forced to make his estimates of public sentiment to a large extent from fragments of information . . . The poll, in making available the opinion of a representative cross-section, has given the official a more dependable guide than he previously possessed." Pollsters point to increasing evidence of interest in polling on the part of legislators and administrators. Critics of polling, on the other hand, see danger of subservience to poll results on the part of decision makers. They anticipate that in this manner "political courage and leadership" will be destroyed; that there will develop a "leadership of obedience to polls"; that "popular ignorance and prejudice" will triumph over "expertise," and so on. Students of public opinion analysis are aware that there may exist some danger in that direction, but they also point to a good deal of evidence showing that, occasionally, knowledge of the true stand of public opinion has liberated legislators and administrators from dependence upon powerful private interests, who were claiming that the measures they advocated were desired by a majority of the population. Whichever view we take we can all agree with Elmo Roper when he says: "It is one thing to have the tools to gauge public opinion accurately and another to use this knowledge intelligently and for the betterment of mankind. It would be a sad day indeed for this country if our statesmen were to follow slavishly the voice of the majority as if it were the voice of God."[5] At all events it appears that polling, as now practised, is a useful tool in assessing the circular process that is supposed to exist in a democracy between decision-makers and the people.

In his more general statements on the impact of polling on the democratic process, Gallup feels certain that, by presenting day-by-day reports on what people are thinking on a wide range of issues as well as by assessing more basic attitudes, polls fill unique functions. "It is my sincere belief," he said in 1949, "that polls constitute the most useful instrument of democracy ever devised . . . Polls on public opinion provide almost our only check today on the increasing strength and influence of pressure groups. They provide the only sensible way of defining the mandate in any election. Finally they make possible the exploration of areas of ignorance."[6] According to Charles W. Smith, polling, by providing the possibility for public opinion to guide "the government in an almost day-by-day process . . . makes less likely the possibility of violent revolution. The little fluctuations eliminate the need for the big ones. Government by public opinion gives elasticity to political institutions." And Bernard Berelson has pointed out that polling, by ascertaining the state of mind and behaviour of the people renders it possible to assess the degree of conformity of popular convictions to democratic theory: "The tools of social research have made it possible, for the first time, to determine with reasonable precision and objectivity the extent to which the practice of politics by the citizens of a democratic state conform to the requirements and the assumptions of the theory of democratic politics . . ."[7]

Are sure arguments as these merely *post hoc* rationalizations by people who have succeeded in erecting a "business concern" worth over one hundred million dollars a year to its owners? Does polling give a false picture of representative democracy by exaggerating the degree of control that is in the hands of the people? Does it tend to corrupt the minds of people and leaders alike, under the pretence of educating them for democracy? Is it first and basically just a manipulative device which could conceivably have disastrous effects in the hands of shrewd or fraudulent propagandists—a technique which is endowed with such a degree of public interest that it should not be left to the exclusive control of a few individuals? These and similar criticisms, which tend to negate the claims of public opinion analysts, are often asserted in one form or another.

As an answer to some of his early critics Gallup had this to say about polling as a "tool":

> What is becoming clearer with each passing day is that techniques like the press, the radio, or the polls of public opinion are instruments which may be used either to make democracy work better or to enchain it in its own fetters. Undoubtedly, they are "instruments of power," but in the last analysis it is not those who administer them, but the public itself, which sets the limits within which they can operate. The limitations and shortcomings of polls are the limitations and shortcomings of public opinion itself.[8]

Furthermore, fully recognizing that the use of polling is a matter in which a public interest is and ought to be involved, Gallup and other pollsters have repeatedly agreed that a rigorous private code of ethics should regulate the polling business. They even concede that a government agency could be charged with the supervision of the operation of polling institutes; what they stubbornly oppose is the transformation of the present private polling institutes into government-operated organizations. And they back up their stand on this issue by pointing to abdundant data taken from their own polls indicating that the great majority of the American people oppose the idea of governmental control in the field of opinion-polling (except, of course, in the limited and mostly informative way in which it has been practised by federal bureaus and departments since the beginning of the Second World War).

IV

It has been said that Bryce's enduring prestige among American academic people and publicists is due to the fact that he gave an extraordinarily accurate picture of prevalent views on the "democratic way of life" and representative government as it is idealized by the common people in the United States. Inasmuch as this interpretation is true, and as Bryce's *American Commonwealth* has been used as a kind of model by public analysts, I think it would be accurate to say that public opinion analysts themselves, in their conception of democracy, reflect to a high degree popular views concerning democratic values, attitudes, and behaviour.

Public opinion analysts have often been accused by political theorists of developing their operational concepts and of shaping the categories and indices they use in the working out of samples and questionnaires on the basis of naïve and unrealistic assumptions. . . .

. . . To the accusation that public opinion analysts used crude methods of analysis, that their measuring scales had such little theoretical value that polling results bore only a slight relation to attitudes and opinions as these were defined by rigorous scientists, that pollsters were not even in a position to ascertain scientifically the significance of a given distribution of views as shown by polling results, and so on, Stuart C. Dodd could only agree that "in our polling we have been concerned very largely with measuring people's attitudes, opinion, behavior and conditions as they are, and have been content on a descriptive level—simply stating what the conditions are in the sample of the public that we have observed." But again J.E. Bachelder came to the defence of the pollsters. After having stated that theorists and practicians were worlds apart and that their conceptions did not converge, he went on: ". . . pollsters complain that the social sciences have failed to give them hypotheses, good definitions of concepts . . . What controlled laboratory experiments do we have in the field of socio-psychology, psychology, et cetera, to help us with the exact measurement of an opinion?"[9]

. . . Years have passed since these tokens of good intentions were offered and expressions of regret made for not being "more theoretical" and "more philosophical." The least one can say is that no noticeable rapprochement has occurred between the theoretical social sciences on the one hand and the empirical work of public opinion analysis on the other. On the contrary, it appears that the distance between the two levels of research has increased, at least in the United States, during the last decade. One does not have to agree with everything that Howard B. White wrote on the subject in a recent article to recognize that American faculties of political science and sociology are being submitted to ever increasing pressure on the part of polling interests, especially in the fields of market analysis and electioneering, to divert their attention and interest from theoretical and value problems and to draw them into purely empirical and "value-free" preoccupations. There is even a pressure to encourage them to substitute "the engineering of consent" for civic education as a central preoccupation in academic curricula. If such trends should be permitted to develop unchallenged, the end-result might well be the abolition, for all practical purposes, of value preoccupation in the teaching of political science in the United States. The matter appears the more important if one reflects on how much public opinion in the United States has come to be artificially created through manipulation by technicians of advertising, public relations, and so on. Thus, one could conceive an end-result of a "value-less" science of politics facing a correspondingly "value-less' public mind, and the problem of measuring "values" would have found a radical, but unfortunate, solution.

In spite of all acts of faith in democratic values, public opinion analysts tend to show far greater devotion in practice to "objective" science. This attitude on their part is only natural. What I question, however, is their right to decide how polling technique should be used in a democracy. I question further their right to decide what constitutes the essence of democracy. I have shown that there is no real indication of "subversive" intent in their perceptions of democracy, but since they themselves proclaim that they cannot include their own democratic convictions in their measuring scales, they should be willing to concede that the political significance and democratic use of their tool remains for other people to decide. For, as A. Girard asserted "opinion analysis is not an instrument for action, but a means of gathering information."[10] And if polling is above all a means of gathering information, it might be useful to recall that "public opinion, this anonymous power, is often a political force, and this force is not dependent on any constitution."[11]

NOTES

1. [James Bryce,] *The American Commonwealth*, III (1888), chap. 77, 144.
2. George Gallup and Saul Forbes Rae, *The Pulse of Democracy: The Public Opinion Poll and How it Works* (New York, 1940), 32. . . . Charles W. Smith, *Public Opinion in a Democracy: A Study in American Politics* (New York, 1939), 10, 393, 394.
3. [Harry] Field and [Paul] Lazarsfeld, *The People Look at Radio* (Chapel Hill, N.C., 1940), 76.
4. Gallup in Foreword to [John F.] Fenton, *In Your Opinion* [(New York, 1960)], viii.

5. . . . Elmo Roper, *You and Your Leaders: Their Actions and Your Reactions* (New York, 1957), 276.
6. Gallup, "The Future Trends of Opinion Sampling," [in S. Meier and Harold W. Saunders, eds., *The Polls and Public Opinion* (New York, 1949)], 218.
7. Smith, *Public Opinion in a Democracy*, 11; [Bernard] Berelson, "Democratic Theory and Public Opinion," *Public Opinion Quarterly*, XV, no. 3, 1952, 313–30.
8. Gallup and Rae, *The Pulse of Democracy*, 282.
9. [Stuart C] Dodd, discussing a paper by Samuel A. Stouffer on the subject of "Basic Social Science Research," [in Meier and Saunders, eds., *The Polls and Public Opinion*], 19–20; [J.E.] Bachelder, ibid., 172.
10. "La méthode des sondages," in C. Berger *et al.*, *L'Opinion publique* (Paris, 1957), 255.
11. Alfred Sauvy, ibid., 6.

FURTHER READINGS

Albig, W. *Modern Public Opinion*. New York: McGraw-Hill, 1956.

Boorstin, D.J. *The Image: A Guide to Pseudo-Events in America*. New York: Harper and Row, 1964.

Brooks, J.E. "Democratic Justification in the Anglo-American Polities: A Quantification of Inconsistency Between Mass Public Opinion and Public Policy." *Western Political Quarterly* 38, 2 (June, 1985): 250–261.

Gallup, G.H. *The Sophisticated Poll-Watcher's Guide*. Princeton, N.J.: Princeton University Press, 1972.

Lippman, W. *Public Opinion*. New York: Macmillan, 1960.

Whalen, H. "The Rewards and Perils of Polling." In Fox, P., ed. *Politics: Canada*, 230–252. Toronto: McGraw-Hill Ryerson, 1982.

Wolfe, M. "Opinion Surveys: The Hidden Dangers." *Saturday Night* (June, 1978): 15–20.

14

Canadian Political Parties

FRANK H. UNDERHILL

1. THE NATURE AND FUNCTION OF POLITICAL PARTIES

Political parties are essential instruments in the working of democratic representative government.

As is well known, they began to develop in the British parliament long before the arrival of democracy. Then, with the rise of the modern electorate in the nineteenth century, party organization spread itself from parliament to the voters outside. If public opinion, upon which democratic government is supposed to be based, is to express itself in any coherent and intelligible form, the public must be able to make intelligible choices among competing candidates and competing policies. The function of parties in democratic societies is to frame the issues about which choices can be made. Party has become the method of organizing voters and politicians so that public policy can be carried on with the approval of the public—or, to speak more precisely, with the approval of the majority of the public and the acquiescence of the minority or minorities.

Before we turn to consider the history of Canadian parties, let us pause to indulge in a few reflections about the nature and function of political parties in general.

Parties in the Plural

First of all, it has been demonstrated to us in this last generation that political parties in the plural are essential for the preservation of free society. Whenever totalitarian regimes have established themselves, the first thing they have done is to crush all rival parties and to concentrate all the power of the state and all the instruments of political propaganda in the hands of one party. Free government means that minorities or dissident elements in the community

Abridged from Frank H. Underhill, *Canadian Political Parties* (Ottawa: Canadian Historical Association, 1957), 3-19. Reprinted by permission of The Canadian Historical Association.

must have the opportunity to protect their interests and express their views. And ultimately this means a freely existing opposition party or several opposition parties.

The acid test of freedom in a state is whether power and office can pass peaceably from one political party to another. "Her Majesty's Opposition" is just as necessary to free government as "Her Majesty's Government." There is no need to argue this point any more. People who are still capable of believing in the freedom of the citizens of the so-called "People's Democracies" are too innocent for politics.

Two-party or Multi-party System?

As to whether a system of two parties or one of more than two parties is preferable, there is not the same agreement in our western world. All English-speaking countries have tended towards the two-party system, though Canada can hardly be said to have conducted her politics since 1921 in a two-party framework. In western European countries, except Britain, there has always been a multiplicity of parties. Perhaps it is only British and American snobbery that makes most of us think that a two-party system is proof of a greater political maturity in the communities that have it; but most students of politics in Britain, the Dominions and the United States are agreed on its superiority— though one sceptical Englishman has spoken of the two-party system as "that great Utopia of English-speaking political scientists."

It is superior not because there are only two sides to every question[1]— there are usually more than two—but because a two-party system, however it may on occasion distort issues, enables them to be presented to the mass electorate in a plain "yes or no" form. As between a well organized government party and a well organized opposition party, every question gets thrashed out until it can be presented to the voters as a simple practical choice. Do you favour candidate A or candidate B, policy *a* or policy *b*? The voter then knows what he is voting for; and the successful party can be held responsible for its policies. In a multi-party or group system the voter is liable to be confused by a variety of competing claims; and the government may be formed as a coalition of groups *after* the election takes place. This is what ordinarily happens in France—with the result that the voter has difficulty in placing responsibility when things go wrong.

A solid party government with a cohesive majority is also likely to be more stable than a coalition of groups; it is often more courageous because of its secure hold on office, and it has the opportunity to be more far-seeing.

But a two-party system cannot be created simply by wishing for it. There must be in the community the conditions that make for two moderate parties, each with a broad national appeal.

Moderate Parties

This is another important point about a two-party system. Because each party is aiming at a majority of votes, it must appeal more or less effectively to all sections in the community. This makes for moderation and for the avoidance of ideological, class or racial appeals. Small groups are apt to take up extreme positions because they know that their appeal is to a narrow body of partisans. In a two-party community the leader of each party is trying to find policies that will unite as many groups and individuals in his party as possible and will win over as many as possible from the rival party. His language, his bearing, his whole appeal must be such as will remind his followers constantly of what they have in common, so that they will hold together in spite of class, racial or sectional differences among them. Thus the two-party system has acted as a great unifying agency in countries such as Canada and the United States which haven't any very deep underlying unity to begin with.

But there is, of course, a bad side to this achievement of moderation by being all things to all men. A disillusioned English student of politics expressed it pithily when he remarked that the successful party leader is the man who can dangle the largest possible number of carrots in front of the noses of the largest possible number of donkeys. To hold a party together by bribing first one interest-group and then another is not an inspiring form of statesmanship. This is the besetting weakness of our great North American composite parties.

Here we come upon a paradox about the two-party system. It is likely to work best when there are more than two parties. What helps to keep the leaders of the two major parties from sinking into mere brokers among competing interest-groups is the constant springing up of new minor parties. These bring fresh ideas into politics; they ventilate the grievances of hitherto neglected groups; they reintroduce passionate sincerity and idealism into the political arena, even if these qualities do not penetrate into the smoke-filled rooms where party decisions are made. And, generally, they keep the major parties on their toes.

In a healthy democracy, however, minor parties come and go without upsetting the fundamental unity of the community. We need to understand that democracy will not work unless the things that unite the citizens of a given country are more important and are consciously felt to be more important than the things that divide them. British democracy is the best example of this. As a British leader once remarked, the voters in Britain can afford to fight vigorously and vehemently over their differences because they are all conscious that fundamentally they are united. If conflicts of economic interests, or racial or religious rivalries, divide a people too deeply, the democratic process of discussion and voting will not work. This means that in a healthy democracy the bulk of the people are grouped closely just to the right or to the left of centre, and that there are comparatively few extremists. Here is the condition that makes moderate parties possible.

This vital fact about democratic politics can be represented in a couple of diagrams. In a country such as Britain, if we believed what party politicians say about each other at election time, the political condition of the community would be represented as in Diagram A.

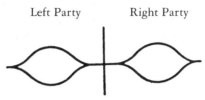

The Left and the Right parties would have hardly anything in common or any common meeting ground. Party controversy wouldn't be far removed from civil war. Actually, the division of opinion in a healthy community is as represented in Diagram B.

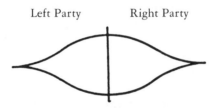

The bulk of the Left party and the bulk of the Right party are concentrated about the centre. Away out at the extreme right are a few Colonel Blimps, and away out at the extreme left are a few communist revolutionaries. But the great majority of those left of centre are not widely separated from the great majority of those right of centre; that is, they are all moderates. This is what makes it possible for politics to be carried on by the methods of discussion, adjustment and compromise.

It is impossible to over-emphasize the importance of all this. Compromise by party leaders is not necessarily unprincipled. It may represent the highest principle—the principle of keeping one's country as united as possible. A stiff attachment to doctrinaire ideas or to special interests may be the quickest way to split a community fatally. Parties should differ on real issues, or else politics becomes disgusting. But a happy country is one in which they do not differ on fundamental issues about which compromise is impossible. In a healthy democracy people should agree about ends but differ about means.

Democracy Inside the Party

We started with the assertion that political parties are essential instruments in the working of *democratic* representative government. But a party in its own inherent structure tends to be an oligarchy. It consists primarily of a small group of insiders who are trying to persuade a great mass of voters to entrust them with political power. In modern times political parties have found it necessary to adopt at least a front of democratic practice, to devise a ritual of democratic participation in their activities. The sincerity of these efforts varies from time to time and from party to party.

It was the Americans in the early nineteenth century, in the Jacksonian era, who first tried to democratize their parties by making use of the party convention to choose candidates and draw up platforms. The intention was to take control of the parties out of the hands of pseudo-aristocratic oligarchies or of inner groups of professional politicians.

The party convention spread northward to Canada when the Upper Canadian Grits held a convention in 1859. They held another in 1867 to adopt policies for the new Dominion of Canada. Their successors, the federal Liberal party, held another in 1893. Down to the death of Laurier the Liberals chose their leaders in party caucus; but in 1919 Mackenzie King was chosen leader in a party convention, and in 1948 Mr. St. Laurent was chosen in the same way. The Conservatives did not adopt the party convention for these purposes until 1927 when R.B. Bennett was chosen to succeed Arthur Meighen. Since then they have held several conventions. The N.D.P. with a highly-developed system of regular conventions, special conferences, lectures, summer-schools, study groups, has carried furthest in Canada this attempt to make the political party into a genuinely democratic form of association.

Most Canadian political scientists appear to be very sceptical about the effectiveness of the professedly democratic machinery in the two old Canadian parties. A famous Swiss student, a good many years ago, enunciated what he called the iron law of oligarchy in political party organizations, i.e. the irresistible tendency of parties towards oligarchical control. He based his conclusions upon a study of European socialist parties who had gone further than any North American party in their efforts to organize democratic mass movements. The iron law of oligarchy operates, of course, not merely in political parties, but also in churches, trade unions, sports clubs, social organizations of all kinds; in fact, wherever the apathy of the mass of the membership throws real responsibility into the hands of a few devoted workers and eventually throws real control into their hands also. This is the insoluble problem of democracy, which nevertheless we must always keep trying to solve. . . .

II. THE HISTORY OF CANADIAN PARTIES

Canadian Conditions

. . . [T]he British-American colonies before 1867 and Canada after 1867 tended to reproduce British party divisions. The British party system was part of the inheritance of the colonies, along with British laws and British parliamentary institutions.

Down to the end of the First World War Canadian politics was conducted upon this two-party system; and the Canadian parties called themselves by the British names, Liberal and Conservative. In the years just before 1914 it may have been difficult to state precisely just what Canadian Liberals were trying to liberate or Canadian Conservatives to conserve. In fact, ever since Confederation there had been critics who maintained that there was no natural basis in Canadian society for this pseudo-British way of dividing political opinion. But the two parties with their British names and their British cabinet system of running parliament and politics appeared to answer Canadian needs fairly satisfactorily.

On the other hand, the Canadian community differs in some essential features from the British. There is no class in Canada like the British landed aristocracy; and the Canadian farmer, owning and working his own family farm, has no real parallel in British agriculture. The existence of two main communal groups, the French and the English, is a unique feature of the Canadian community which makes any kind of political unity much more difficult than in a country which is racially, religiously and linguistically so homogeneous as Britain. In the twentieth century, also, new ethnic elements, non-French and non-English, have become part of Canada. But while Canada has these divisions which Britain lacks, class divisions have never become so deep or rigid here as in Britain. The British class system was the main reason in the nineteenth century why Britain had two main parties rather than several groups in politics.

The geographic extent of our country extending across a continent from Atlantic to Pacific is another distinguishing element in our Canadian society. It makes for sectional divisions such as hardly exist in a small crowded island like Britain. We have a federal rather than a unitary constitution because of these divisions within our Canadian community. In most of these features we are more like the United States than like Britain. Like our American neighbours we are a new people whose chief work has been the filling up of great empty spaces with new white population, clearing forests, tilling new soil, building railways across virgin territory, developing newly discovered natural resources. All these factors affect the working of politics and the way in which political parties perform their function of organizing public opinion.

Our North American environment makes for fundamental resemblances between Canadian and American politics. Our cabinet system of parliamentary government makes for parties on the British model. And like most other Canadian institutions and habits, our Canadian parties show this constant interplay between North American environment and British inheritance.

British American Parties Before 1867

Parties in the British North American colonies began to emerge in the generation after the War of 1812, as the struggle to obtain colonial self-government developed. The Conservatives, the Tories, were the spokesmen of the leading families who surrounded and influenced the governor from Britain, the elite among the United Empire Loyalist settlers, the chief professional and business men, most of them members of the Church of England, strong in their anti-American feelings, tending to erect themselves into a colonial aristocracy, suspicious of the equalitarian tendencies of the frontier democracy all around them, equating democracy with the Jacobinism of the French Revolution or the unruly Jacksonian upheavals in the American republic. Their belief that in every healthy stable society there is a natural governing class, and that in their colony they themselves constituted this class, was most incisively expressed for them by Sir Francis Bond Head in his *Narrative* when he burst out against Lord Durham's criticisms of the Family Compact in Upper Canada:

> It appears from Lord Durham's own showing that this Family Compact is nothing more nor less than that 'social fabric' which characterizes every civilized community in the world . . . 'The bench', 'the magistrates', 'the Clergy', 'the law', 'the landed proprietors', 'the bankers', 'the native-born inhabitants', and 'the supporters of the Established Church' [these were the social groups which Durham had defined as composing the Family Compact] form just as much a family compact in England as they do in Upper Canada, and just as much in Germany as they do in England . . . The party, I own, is a comparatively small one; but to put the multitude at the top and the few at the bottom is a radical reversion of the pyramid of society which every reflecting man must foresee can end only by its downfall.

Colonial Tories saw themselves also as the specially-appointed guardians of the British connection.

Reformers in the English-speaking colonies had much greater difficulty in organizing their efforts than had the Tories, who were already in power and whose centre of influence was the colonial capital. The Reformers tended to equate themselves with the British Whigs and Radicals who had ousted the British Tories in 1830 and passed the Great Reform Bill of 1832. But in isolated farms and little villages the pioneer settlers were not primarily interested in politics and were difficult to rouse. The exception was in Lower Canada where race, religion and language formed a bond of union that quickly gave the opposition in the legislature under Papineau an overwhelming majority. In the English settlements it is noteworthy how many of the early Reform leaders were journalists. The newspaper provided its publisher with the best instrument available for agitation, political education and party organization, and gave such men as Howe, Mackenzie and Brown their start.

Some of the Reformers, including Papineau, began to look to the example of the American Revolution. William Lyon Mackenzie in Upper Canada, just before taking up arms, issued a draft constitution on the American model for the state of Upper Canada. The chief idea of these leaders was to make all offices elective, so as to get control of Assemblies and Councils and impose their will on governors.

But men like the Baldwins in Upper Canada and Howe in Nova Scotia preferred British models. Already by the late 1820s the Baldwins were expounding what became famous as Responsible Government. Let the appointed British governor be instructed to carry on government in accordance with the advice of local advisers who could control a majority in the colonial assembly; the removal of irresponsible advisers would settle all colonial grievances.

The failure of the rebellions in 1837 and the acceptance of Responsible Government in the next dozen years is a turning point in Canadian history. British Americans, French as well as English, rejected the Jacksonian democracy which was sweeping over the United States, along with its manhood suffrage. They accepted the leadership of moderate Whigs or Tories on the model of Great Britain, where manhood suffrage and complete Chartist democracy were also rejected at this time.

There is not room here to follow out the party developments under Responsible Government in all the British American colonies. Generally speaking the British two-party system was copied as an essential part of British cabinet government. But it took time for the two parties to establish themselves. Let us concentrate on the party system in the colony of Canada after 1840.

Responsible government implies well-organized parties because everything depends upon a party being able to maintain a stable majority in a representative assembly. What impressed Lord Sydenham, the first governor under the Union, was the chaotic condition of local politics. He didn't think Canadian politicians capable of forming stable parties. So he made *himself* the centre around which a cabinet would cohere. It was the function of a new coalition between French and English Reformers to prove the governor wrong in his judgment. But it took them several years to do so. The LaFontaine-Baldwin coalition didn't quite become a party in their day, and it broke up quickly when they retired in 1851. Nevertheless it is one of the great achievements in Canadian political history. It was the beginning of organized party government.

The LaFontaine-Baldwin coalition was also the first example of what has become the most striking and distinctive feature of our Canadian politics—the bi-racial party which for the moment overcomes differences between French and English and brings them together inside one party to conduct a government on principles on which they can agree. This first example was followed by the Liberal-Conservative party of John A. Macdonald and George E. Cartier in the 1850s—a coalition of French Canadians under Cartier with Church support, the English Canadians in Montreal business and in the Eastern Townships, the Upper Canadian Tories led by the moderate Macdonald, and a good many Upper Canadian Baldwin Reformers.

This coalition gradually solidified into a party under the skilful leadership of Macdonald and Cartier. It managed to hold office for most of a period of forty years from the mid-fifties to the mid-nineties. Under Macdonald the Upper Canadian Tories learned to abandon their high-and-dry anti-democratic and anti-French Family-Compactism and to become part of a genuinely popular party. Under Cartier the French Canadians abandoned their opposition to Montreal business and joined in a programme of railway building and economic expansion. The function performed by this French-English Liberal-Conservative coalition was taken over by Laurier's Liberal party after 1896, and by the King Liberal party after the bitter cleavage over conscription in 1917.

Apparently French and English have discovered that the only effective way in which the deep racial differences in Canada can be overcome is through a bi-racial party of this kind under a sort of joint leadership: LaFontaine-Baldwin, Macdonald-Cartier, Laurier-Fielding, King-Lapointe, St. Laurent-Howe. Apparently also the Canadian community is incapable of supporting two effective bi-racial parties at the same time. So the political scene is apt to be dominated for a generation or more by one of these parties until it has exhausted its capacity for leadership, when another party of the same bi-racial composition takes its place in control of government.

It was through this technique of the bi-racial party that the French Canadians undid the conquest of 1763. It was thus that they achieved equality with the English Canadians. One hundred years after the Treaty of Paris they were sitting in the Canadian legislature as the major group in the governing party. This bi-racial party has become the main instrument through which they defend their interests as a minority within the Canadian community. It is their way of enforcing the principle of "concurrent majorities," enunciated by John C. Calhoun in the United States before the Civil War when he was trying to find a constitutional safeguard to protect the minority interests of the South in the American federal system. Since the 1840s the representatives of the French Canadians have sat in the legislature for the most part to the right of Mr. Speaker, i.e. they have formed part of the government. They protect their interests from within the cabinet rather than as an opposition party outside. No more striking proof of the French-Canadian political aptitude could be given than this success of theirs in always being in the government.

It is to be noted also that the policies adopted by Sydenham, LaFontaine and Baldwin, Macdonald and Cartier, and their modern successors, in order to overcome French-English animosities, have nearly always been the same. Whatever sentiments, ideals or interests may divide the two main communal groups in Canada, they have in common an interest in material economic expansion. "My politics is railways," said a prominent member of the Liberal-Conservative coalition in the 1850s. Confederation in 1867 was an effort to provide that each communal group should look after its own cultural interests in the provincial sphere, while the federal government should concentrate upon the great economic nation-building enterprises which they had in common. Macdonald and Laurier always tried to keep economic expansion before the minds of the voters as the best way of keeping their minds off the racial and religious differences which were apt to divide them so bitterly.

Over against the Liberal-Conservative government of the 1850s there emerged two opposition groups, the Grits of Upper Canada and the *Rouges* of Lower Canada. They combined for a moment in the summer of 1858 to form the Brown-Dorion government, and for a little longer in the early 1860s to form the Sandfield Macdonald-Dorion government. But they never quite coalesced into a solid party before 1867. Taking in allies from the Maritime provinces after Confederation, they were to become the Reform or Liberal party of Mackenzie, Blake and Laurier.

The Grits took their nickname from the hard gritty sand which was sought by masons to make good mortar in house-building. Their centre of strength was in the rapidly growing area to the west of Toronto. When George Brown joined them with his powerful newspaper, the Toronto *Globe*, and gave them a vigorous crusading leadership, they took a decidedly anti-French, anti-Catholic colour, because Brown found himself thwarted by the solid French block in the legislature. The separation of Church and State, and Representation by Population, became their main demands. "Rep by Pop" meant increased power for the Grit sections of Upper Canada. Since these areas were mainly agricultural, Grittism meant also an attack upon the vested interests of Montreal big business—banks, industrialists, wholesale merchants, railway magnates— who supported the Liberal-Conservatives.

The other group on the left, the *Rouges*, never achieved in their community the strength of the Grits in Upper Canada. They were led by professional men who had absorbed some of the ideas of the revolutionary Paris of 1848; and their chief attack was upon the control of their French-Canadian community by the Church. The struggle which they initiated between liberalism and clericalism had its effect in preventing the growth of a strong Liberal party in Quebec for a whole generation after Confederation.

From Confederation to the First World War

Confederation was brought about, so far as the province of Canada was concerned, by a coalition of the Macdonald-Cartier Conservatives with Brown's Grits. The *Rouge* group refused to join in the movement. Before July 1, 1867, Brown had led most of his followers out of the coalition. Macdonald formed the first federal government by constructing a cabinet out of his own Conservatives, allies whom he had found in the Maritimes—some of these had been previously Conservatives and some Reformers—and a few Upper Canadian Grits. There were a few years of party confusion; but by the time of the second election in 1872 a straight party fight took place between a Conservative government and a Reform or Liberal opposition.

Macdonald held office continuously from 1867 to his death in 1891, except for the five years 1873–1878; and his party continued in office till 1896. In this Macdonald era the Conservatives earned their electoral success by their vigour and boldness in building up the new nationality of which the framework had been set in the British North America Act. They brought into the new Dominion the Hudson's Bay territories in 1870, British Columbia in 1871 and Prince Edward Island in 1873. The Intercolonial Railway was built. And what was at the time almost a fantastically ambitious project was launched—that of connecting the Pacific province with the East by a transcontinental railway. This was finally carried out, after the upset over the Pacific Scandal, in the 1880s. In his second term of office, Macdonald also inaugurated the "National Policy" of high tariff protection in order to build up a well rounded national economy. These adventurous and imaginative policies made the Conservative party the nation-building party of this first generation after Confederation.

Grits and *Rouges* combined in opposition after 1867, choosing Alexander Mackenzie as their leader. Their weakness was partly the old one of clerical opposition to them in Quebec and partly the difficulty of finding allies in the outlying provinces. When Mackenzie came into office in 1873 he was unfortunate enough to begin his administration just as a great depression broke upon the world. He was unable to make progress with the Pacific railway, and he passed up the opportunity to adopt a protectionist policy, thereby losing support among ambitious industrialists. Under Edward Blake, who succeeded Mackenzie as leader in 1880, the party, back in opposition, opposed the new C.P.R. syndicate and seemed to have little faith in the future of the country. They denounced the Macdonald government's close alliance with a great transportation corporation, and its habit of lavishing grants of land, forest and mining resources to speculative entrepreneurs. But they had no real alternative to this capitalist process of economic development. Blake, however, began to reorient his party's outlook in two fields: he tried to overcome the Brown anti-French tradition and sided with Quebec on the Riel issue; and he abandoned the Cobdenite anti-tariff ideas which were also an inheritance from the Grits, announcing his acceptance of a moderate tariff not too different from the N.P. He did not succeed in carrying his party with him in these two attempts, and it was left for Laurier to reap where he had sown.

This political alignment between two parties, which had established itself in the province of Canada before 1867, only took root very gradually in the outlying parts of the Dominion after 1867. Out in the far west the eastern Canadian divisions had really not much place. What the West needed was government assistance, and the voters tended to send government supporters to Ottawa. When Goldwin Smith visited the Pacific on the new C.P.R. line in the 1880s, he asked one British Columbia citizen what his politics was and received the answer, "Government appropriations." Provincial politics in

British Columbia was not organized on a Liberal vs. Conservative basis till the turn of the century. In the Territories government was carried on by non-partisan administrations until the creation of the provinces of Alberta and Saskatchewan in 1905. But sometime between the 1880s and the early 1900s one could say with confidence that every little Canadian boy and girl was now being born either a little Liberal or else a little Conservative.

The Macdonald regime began to disintegrate after the crisis over the execution of Riel in 1885. The old French-English bitterness flared up again, and the flames were kept burning by the Jesuit Estates Act in Quebec and the schools question in Manitoba. Macdonald's successors after 1891 showed little of his skill in manoeuvre and manipulation. When the Liberals under Laurier ousted the Conservatives from power in 1896, they took over into their party many of the *Bleus*, the moderate Conservatives of Quebec, thereby achieving substantial support in Quebec and making the Liberal party the party of French-English cooperation.

With this as his base of operations, Laurier now made his party a national party in the same sense that Macdonald's Conservatives had been. After burning his fingers badly by espousing Unrestricted Reciprocity with the United States in 1891, he reverted in the budget of 1896 to a policy of moderate protection. In substance he accepted the Conservative National Policy, modifying it by a preference to British imports. His government also embarked on an ambitious railway-building policy, with two new transcontinental lines; and thereby he built up an alliance of the Liberals with ambitious railway promoters of exactly the same kind as that of Macdonald with the C.P.R. And in the favourable economic conditions of the early 1900s the Liberals succeeded in something beyond Macdonald's achievements by bringing into the country a great stream of immigration. In the magnificent Wheat Boom days the Liberals seemed clearly the nation-building party.

Laurier's efforts to keep English and French working together in this exhilarating experience of economic expansion—the twentieth century belongs to Canada, he boasted—was thwarted by a new cause of cleavage between the two groups, the question of Canada's relations with the Empire. Beginning with the Boer War in 1899, the two races took opposite sides on this issue; and when the strain of the Great War of 1914 made itself felt, they divided in the bitter quarrel over conscription in 1917. The Liberal party itself broke apart in this crisis, and the 1917 election produced the worst of all possible political alignments in Canada, a government supported by a large majority of English Canadians and opposed almost unanimously by the French Canadians.

Since the First World War

The coalition of Conservatives with English-speaking Liberals which Borden had formed in 1917 went to pieces after the war. Mackenzie King, chosen Liberal leader in 1919, reunited the Liberal party as a party with substantial support from both racial groups; while the Conservatives, having offended Quebec in 1885 and repeated the offence in 1917, failed to recover their old position as a nation-wide party. In spite of the growth of French-Canadian nationalist movements in the depression of the 1930s, the Liberals maintained their hold on Quebec in federal elections steadily from the 1920s to the 1950s. This enabled them to remain in office from 1921 to 1957, with only a short break of a few weeks in 1926 and a longer one of five years from 1930 to 1935. By their success in winning votes in substantial numbers in all parts of Canada they proved themselves a national party in the same sense that the party of Macdonald and the party of Laurier were.

The new feature in politics since the end of World War I has been the rise of a number of protest parties. Down to 1918 Canadian politics had been run on a two-party basis. No third-party movements had ever got going with enough strength to challenge the two established parties, Liberal and Conservative. But beginning with the 1920s there broke out a series of political protest movements which destroyed the solidity of the classical two-party system.

In the first post-war election of 1921 a Progressive revolt among the farmers of Ontario and the Prairie provinces sent to the House of Commons 65 members, who became at one bound the second party in the House. Prime Minister King did his best to woo the Progessives back into the Liberal party, from which most of them had broken away. The Progressives themselves were never quite sure what the function of their movement should be. The result was that they had pretty nearly disappeared by the end of the decade—though Alberta was ruled by the United Farmers of Alberta (U.F.A.). In the 1930 federal election it looked as if the old two-party system had been restored.

But the Great Depression after 1929 still further upset the orderly working of Canadian politics. In 1932 the Cooperative Commonwealth Federation (C.C.F.) came into existence as a socialist party, gathering to its support the hardier Progressives on the prairies and a sprinkling of middle-class enthusiasts across the country. Whether it could win the support of the organized trade unionists, as the labour party had done in Britain, remained for the next twenty-five years a question to be decided. In 1935 the Social Credit movement swept over Alberta, ousting the U.F.A. provincial government, and sending another minor party delegation to Ottawa. The depression also threw up a confusion of nationalist movements in Quebec, out of which finally emerged the Union Nationale party led by Maurice Duplessis; after capturing the provincial government Duplessis declined to carry his movement into the federal sphere.

For a considerable time none of the new movements from the West—Progressive, C.C.F. or Social Credit—made any effective impact upon Quebec or upon the Maritime Provinces. Ontario, after having a farmers' government for a short time in the early 1920s, returned pretty well to the two old parties, though the C.C.F. at times succeeded in electing a substantial group to the provincial legislature. In 1944 the C.C.F. also captured the province of Saskatchewan, where it remained in power for twenty years; and in 1952 Social Credit added British Columbia to Alberta. In the federal sphere, however, neither the C.C.F. nor Social Credit has been able to grow into a nation-wide movement—this in spite of the fact that in 1962 the C.C.F. presented itself in a new incarnation as the New Democratic Party in a drive to attract labour and middle-class voters, and also in spite of the fact that Social Credit in the 1963 federal election won a block of seats in Quebec.

In 1957 the long Liberal domination of federal politics, which had lasted since 1935, was brought to an end by a revived Conservative party under a new leader, Mr. John Diefenbaker. Mr. Louis St. Laurent, who had succeeded Mackenzie King in 1948 as Liberal leader and Prime Minister, now retired. The new Liberal leader, Mr. Lester B. Pearson, was decisively beaten in a general election in 1958 at which Mr. Diefenbaker won the largest majority of seats ever attained by any Canadian political leader since Confederation.

In the 1962 election, however, the Conservatives only managed to hold on to office as a minority government. There followed two more general elections, in 1963 and 1965, which produced minority Liberal governments. By the middle sixties, therefore, it seemed that neither of the two major parties was able to win majority support from the Canadian electorate, and that none of the minor parties was likely to grow into a major party. The result was a general feeling of frustration. At the same time an increasingly dynamic French-Canadian nationalism in Quebec challenged the whole structure of Confederation. Furthermore, the steady urbanization of Canadian society—the drift of population, economic power and intellectual leadership to the big cities—was transforming the social basis of Canadian politics. . . .

NOTES

1. We must never forget that famous American who declared that the reason for a two-party system is not that there are two sides to every question but that there are two sides to every office—an inside and an outside.

FURTHER READINGS

Brodie, M.J. and J. Jensen. "The Party System." In M. Whittington and G. Williams. *Canadian Politics in the 1980s.* 2nd ed., 252–270. Toronto: Methuen, 1984.

Engelmann, F. and M. Schwartz. *Canadian Political Parties.* Toronto: Prentice-Hall, 1975.

McLeod, J. "Party Structure and Party Reform." In A. Rotstein, ed. *The Prospect of Change,* 1–22. Toronto: McGraw-Hill, 1965.

Perlin, G. *The Tory Syndrome.* Montreal: McGill-Queen's Press, 1980.

Thorburn, H. ed. *Party Politics in Canada.* Toronto: Prentice-Hall, 1985.

Whitaker, R. *The Government Party*. Toronto: University of Toronto Press, 1977.

Winn, C., and J. McMenemy. *Political Parties in Canada*. Toronto: McGraw-Hill Ryerson, 1976.

15

The Canadian Political System

JOHN PORTER

THE POLITICAL SYSTEM

Canada has no resounding charter myth proclaiming a utopia against which, periodically, progress can be measured. At the most, national goals and dominant values seem to be expressed in geographical terms such as "from sea to sea," rather than in social terms such as "all men are created equal," or "liberty, fraternity, and equality." In the United States there is a utopian image which slowly over time bends intractable social patterns in the direction of equality, but a Canadian counterpart of this image is difficult to find.

The question which we are seeking to explore here is what does a political system do, what is its function in the total society? Clearly the function of the economic system is to produce a society's wealth. But the function of a political system cannot be so clearly stated. Although there is unlikely to be agreement among social scientists, the view taken here is that the political system is the one through which the society as a group can achieve its major goals and values, if it has any.

Undoubtedly major goals and values can be stated only in very general terms such as progress, a high standard of living, equality. Often these major values can be traced to some charter instrument such as a bill of rights or a constitution which has acquired, over time, a charismatic aura. These values will be reaffirmed periodically through social movements, such as Jeffersonian liberalism in the United States. They will also appear as recurring themes in a society's liberature. Because values and goals will be cast in general terms they can be appropriated by both conservative elements supporting the *status quo* and utopian liberal elements seeking social change. Freedom can be seen as "wearing a crown" and also as being achieved by the breaking of imperial ties. However, unless there are values general to the society, it is difficult for the society to make judgments about its progress, although reference can be made to standards and values of other societies.

In a discussion of the political system of the United States, Talcott Parsons

Abridged from John Porter, "The Canadian Political System," *The Vertical Mosaic* (Toronto: University of Toronto Press, 1965), 366-79. Copyright © University of Toronto Press, 1965. Reprinted by permission of University of Toronto Press. Only selected footnotes appear in the essay.

has suggested that the value system centres on what he calls "instrumental activism."[1] The values against which actions are judged are cast in terms of economic adaptation or mastery of the physical conditions of life. There are general goals also of progress and improvement in which economic production is the main instrument of advance. It is the task of the political system and the leadership roles within it to mobilize the society's resources to these broad ends. In a differentiated pluralistic society there will not be general agreement on the means to be employed to reach these general values. There will, however, be some agreement on the ground rules. There are constitutional ground rules, but at the same time there is a body of political conventions which political parties observe, one of the most important being that the political party in power permits its rivals to exist. The two-party system is a functionally appropriate way of mediating the "conservative" and "progressive" social forces.

In his discussion of right and left in American politics Parsons argues that the focus of the American right is the organization of the free enterprise economy. The "right" becomes politically conservative because positive political action is seen as a threat to this free enterprise economy. The "left" on the other hand focuses on positive political action and is favourable to reform, to control of the economy, to the promotion of welfare, and to intervention in foreign affairs. These right and left foci distinguish in general terms the Republican and Democratic parties. Both parties seek to mobilize support. They alternate in office so that there is a swinging back and forth between the two dominant trends, but some dynamic development is achieved, because although the pressure for change comes from the left, and change is bitterly opposed by the right, the right, when it gets into office, does not destroy the advances made by the left. Although not all will agree that the Republican and Democratic parties are so distinguishable, it would be difficult to refute their respective foci to the right and left, the conservative and the progressive. The important point here is that in political systems and through political parties there is a polarization of the progressive and conservative forces, even though in the United States there is still a general acceptance of the view that the major goals of the society are achieved through the economic system rather than the political.

This brief outline of Parsons' analysis of the political dynamic in the United States is not intended to suggest that a similar political process takes place in Canada. All too often Canadian social scientists draw analogies from American experience. Rather, Parsons' account is a model of a political dynamic which results from a polarization of the right and the left. A similar model could be built from British experience. Marx, of course, also presented a model except that, for him, the polarization was so complete that mediation within the same normative order was impossible.

NATIONAL UNITY:
CANADA'S POLITICAL OBSESSION

It would probably be safe to say that Canada has never had a political system with this dynamic quality. Its two major political parties do not focus to the right and the left. In the sense that both are closely linked with corporate enterprise the dominant focus has been to the right. One of the reasons why this condition has prevailed is that Canada lacks clearly articulated major goals and values stemming from some charter instrument which emphasizes progress and equality. If there is a major goal of Canadian society it can best be described as an integrative goal. The maintenance of national unity has overridden any other goals there might have been, and has prevented a polarizing, within the political system, of conservative and progressive forces. It has never occurred to any Canadian commentators that national unity might in fact be achieved by such a polarization. Rather a dissociative federalism is raised to the level of a quasi-religious political dogma, and polarization to right and left in Canadian politics is regarded as disruptive. Consequently the main focus of Canadian politics has been to the right and the maintenance of the *status quo*. The reason that the Liberal party in Canada was in office so many years until 1957 was not because it was a progressive party, but because it served Canada's major goal of national unity.

The major themes in Canadian political thought emphasize those characteristics, mainly regional and provincial loyalties, which divide the Canadian population. Consequently integration and national unity must be a constantly reiterated goal to counter such divisive sentiments. The dialogue is between unity and discord rather than progressive and conservative forces. The question which arises is whether the discord-unity dialogue has any real meaning in the lives of Canadians, or whether it has become, in the middle of the twentieth century, a political technique of conservatism. Canada must be one of the few major industrial societies in which the right and left polarization has become deflected into disputes over regionalism and national unity.

Canada's major political and intellectual obsession, national unity, has had its effect on the careers of men who take on political roles. It has put a premium on the type of man whom we shall label the administrative politician and has discounted the professional political career in which creative politicians can assume leadership roles. Creative politics at the national level has not been known in Canada since before World War I when the westward thrust to Canada's empire was still a major goal. Since the empire of the west was secured national goals of development have not been known.

Creative politics is politics which has the capacity to change the social structure in the direction of some major social goals or values. By mobilizing human resources for new purposes, it has the initiative in the struggle against the physical environment and against dysfunctional historical arrangements. Creative politics requires a highly developed political leadership to challenge entrenched power within other institutional orders. It succeeds in getting large segments of the population identified with the goals of the political system and in recruiting their energies and skills to political ends.

THE SUFFRAGE AND SOCIAL RIGHTS

Politics in industrial societies becomes polarized into conservative and progressive forces in part because the political system is the only system in which all members of the society participate. Not all have ownership rights in the economic system and there are great inequalities among those that do, because votes in the economic system are not one per person but one per share. In the political system all share a common status of citizenship. With universal adult suffrage the right to participate in the political system has led to the emergence, in the twentieth century, of social rights. The development of social rights has meant a very slow but gradual erosion of privilege.

Social rights are the claims on the social system of all members of the society to a basic standard of living and to equal opportunities for education, health, and so forth. To achieve social rights governments have sponsored activities ranging from educational to medical and health insurance. In most industrial societies there is disagreement about how far these social rights should extend. For some, welfare measures are indispensable for the good life; for others they are seen as bringing about human and social rot. The fact remains, however, that ever since the propertyless and the underprivileged have been enfranchised political elites have been able to acquire power by offering piecemeal extensions of welfare. In Canada, as in other industrial societies, there has been some extension of social rights, although, because generally they fall within the sphere of the provinces, they are by no means uniform throughout the country. Their haphazard development has come about more by the "demonstration effect" of their existence in other countries, than because they have formed the social philosophy of either of the two political parties which have been in power at the federal level. These two parties have also been adept at incorporating in their own programmes, but not always in legislation, some of the progressive ideas of the minor parties.

The right to participate in Canada's political system is not one that was given quietly or easily. The history of the franchise is extraordinarily confused because of the varying provincial franchises which were used in federal elections between 1898 and 1917.[2] Discussions about who should be enfranchised centred around the amount of property that was deemed necessary to give a person full political rights of citizenship. In a proposed federal statute in 1870 which would have established an income qualification of $400 a year, day labourers were to be excluded even though they might have earned $400 because, as Macdonald put it, "they had no abiding interest in the country."[3] . . .

. . . Because of the limitation of the franchise, the first federal election with some semblance of manhood suffrage was 1900 and with universal suffrage, 1921. Professor Ward has calculated that in the election of 1911 one-quarter of the total population was enfranchised, and in 1921 about one-half of the total population.[4] It is interesting that the arrival of universal suffrage coincided with the end of the historic two-party system that had existed previously.

Universal suffrage frees the political institutions from control by a class which benefits from a limited franchise. It therefore makes possible the building up of the political system into a system of power to counter the power of other institutional elites. The political system and its elite could become the dominant power system within the differentiated society. Universal suffrage alone does not bring this about. There must as well be, through political leadership and a social orientation to politics, a clarification of goals and a feeling of collective participation by the members. One of the reasons why this sense of collective participation has not yet developed in Canada is because the universal political right to participate is only decades old. In Canada, too ... the general level of education is too low to allow for intelligent participation. The absence of political orientation in labour organization is also a factor in weakening the political system.

There is another reason, too, why the political system has been incapable of generating its own power, that is, the belief that that government is best which governs least. In this ideology of western capitalism there is an express denial of the social benefit of political power. Historically, the erosion of autocratic political power came with the rise of entrepreneurial capitalism and the doctrine of *laissez faire*. The democracy of universal suffrage could mean political power which is collective rather than autocratic. This kind of political power can be seen in the continuing dialogue in most industrial societies between conservative and progressive forces.

Robert Lynd in his analysis of power in American society makes the distinction between "liberal democracy" which "yokes together a professedly democratic social structure and political system with a capitalist economy," and "a version of democracy in which social structure and all institutions would have coherence in expressing and implementing democratic values."[5] This second he distinguishes from "liberal democracy" as a "thoroughgoing democracy" or a "society committed throughout to democratic ends.". . .

In Canada, . . . such a political system is a long way from emerging. Our task is to try to discover how at present the political elite functions in relation to the elites of other institutional orders. . . .

MAJOR PARTIES:
THE CONSERVATIVE TONE

The most significant characteristic of the two parties which have held power at the national level in Canada is the fact that they share the same conservative values. Both have at times been responsible for reform legislation which might suggest progressive values, but these steps to the left have been taken more with a spirit of opportunism than from a basic orientation to social progress and change. The Progressive Conservative party has been ingenious enough to incorporate the political dynamic within its name. As some of its opponents have suggested it is neither conservative nor progressive, but has remained opportunistic. Both parties have produced successive contingents of administrative politicians. The political dialogue, if it can be called such, in which they participate is not related to any basic class differences in the society from which the conservative-progressive dynamic might arise. It is not that Canadian social structure is so static that it has no immanent potential for dynamic politics; it is rather that Canada's basically opportunistic parties have not harnessed this potential in the political system. They have either ignored these basic social differences or covered them up in the pretence that they do not exist.

Both politicians and intellectuals, on those occasions when they deal with political issues, have defined the political task, not in terms of creative policies, but rather in terms of interstitial compromises between competing interests. In his introduction to Mackenzie King's diaries, Mr. J.W. Pickersgill states that "Mackenzie King genuinely believed and frequently said that the real secret of political leadership was more in what was prevented than what was accomplished."[6] Mr. Pickersgill did not elaborate on his own further statement, "yet his objectives were by no means negative," except to say that, between the Liberal convention of 1919 and the end of his political career, Mackenzie King had reached his destination.

According to Canada's two most outstanding political scientists, J.A. Corry and R.M. Dawson, Canada's two indistinguishable political parties are functionally appropriate for Canadian society. The views of these two men are important because it is mainly through their writings, and their students who have become teachers, that later generations of Canadian students are introduced to Canada's political system. Corry sees party politicians as brokers of ideas selecting among those that are current in the society the ones that appeal to the largest calculable number of voters.[7] They are brokers in another sense, too. They arrange deals between different sections of opinion, or interest groups, by working out the necessary compromises. If these are the tasks of political parties and political leaders their function is not to provide a conservative-progressive dialogue in terms of general social values, but simply to make available an "alternative" government. Elections become choices between one set of brokers and another. In a democracy there must be an alternative government to keep the incumbent government aware of its responsibilities.

Corry makes the point that, if this alternative party was an ideological one deeply committed to principles, the social divisions which would follow would be so great that it would be difficult, if not impossible, to keep the nation together. Yet to obscure social divisions through brokerage politics is to remove from the political system that element of dialectic which is the source of creative politics. The choice between genuinely radical and genuinely conservative traditions could mean a period of creative politics followed by a period of consolidation as conservatives and radicals oscillated in and out of office. That at least would provide a two-party system suitable to parliamentary institutions, the debating of values, and the clarification of social goals.

To make brokerage politics work it is necessary at election time to rouse the voters from political somnolence and try to make them identify with one of the parties. When parties are without distinguishable social values voters have no commitments other than those arising from uncritical family traditions or habit. Consequently the parties require at election time an enormous "once for all" organization which takes large sums of money. On the whole these sums are not obtained from thousands of small individual contributions, but instead are obtained much more efficiently from wealthy benefactors. Because the parties do not differ in principle, the wealthy benefactors support both main parties. It is often suggested, . . . that corporate benefactors, in particular, give 60 per cent of their contribution to the party in power and 40 per cent to the party that might succeed to power. In any case, the war chests of the two parties both seem to be full, allowing them to charter aircraft, print mountains of literature, rent fleets of limousines, and buy extensive advertising space on television and radio and in the newspapers. Millions of dollars spent on political education could be a good thing for the functioning of the political system, but when it is concentrated in a few weeks before elections and on devices scarcely designed to educate, the function is questionable.

Corry accepts as inevitable these aspects of brokerage politics because in his view the role of the politician is simply to reflect the selfish aims of the various sections of the society and to make compromises between them. He recognizes that there are some unattractive features of this system but his strongest words of indictment are: "It would not be correct to say that party policy has been uninfluenced by contributions to party funds"; and "The parties deceive the public, but so do propagandists of every kind."[8] Corry's conclusion about the party system is that ". . . the evils in the party system are the outcome of general human frailties. Indeed it is hard to see how the parties which must woo the electorate with success can do other than reflect its vices and its virtues."[9] He sees little need for political education and political leadership.

Dawson, too, recognized and accepted the facts of Canadian political life, although he suggested that historically there have been differences between the parties which still influence their attitudes.[10] The Conservatives have been more conscious of the Empire tie, while the Liberals have been more nationalistic; the Conservatives have been a high tariff party and the Liberals a freer trade party; the Conservatives have been more concerned with strengthening the powers of the central government while the Liberals have been more anxious to maintain provincial rights; the Conservatives have been the party of free enterprise, while the Liberals have professed "to take the lead in public ownership and progressive social legislation."[11] Dawson claimed that these tendencies or biases still exist within the parties, although he admitted that their records on these issues have been confused and inconsistent.

Dawson also concluded that "a national party must take as its primary purpose the reconciliation of the widely scattered aims and interests of a number of areas."[12] Elections then are fought on minor issues and often the distinction between the parties is nothing more than a choice between personalities. "Finally the opportunism—and one may fairly say, the inescapable opportunism—embedded in the Canadian party system tends to minimize the importance of the platform and emphasize the importance of the party leaders. . . ."[13]

For more than thirty years, Frank H. Underhill has asked provocative questions about the Canadian political system. In his collected essays, *In Search of Canadian Liberalism*, he expresses conflicting views. One is the view of the orthodox political scientist: "a political party that aspires to the responsibility of government must not be a class party, but must be a loosely knit representative collection of voters from all groups." "National unity is preserved by having every interest-group effectively inside the party which controls the government."[14] These quotations are from an essay written in 1950 praising the contributions of Mackenzie King to Canada. In other essays, too, he seems to feel that there is an inescapable logic in having, in the North American situation, all-embracing parties where the tensions within the society are resolved within the parties rather than between the parties.

On the other hand Underhill feels the need for creative leadership in political life. This can occur only when politicians have a vision that is greater than the sum of the special interests of particular groups. Underhill has deplored the lack of conservative thought in the Conservative party and of liberal thought in the Liberal party. He admired Franklin D. Roosevelt and regretted that Canada never had a New Deal. In 1932 Underhill pointed out the inadequacy of the Canadian party system: "a party which depends for success upon the different and often contradictory appeals which it must make to different sectional interests will become dependent upon and responsive to those interest-groups which are best organized and most strategically located for applying effective pressure upon the party leaders."[15] The two groups which could apply the most pressure he thought were the Catholic church in Quebec and big business. The real function of the two-party system since the Laurier era "has been to provide a screen behind which the controlling business interests pull the strings to manipulate the Punch and Judy who engage in mock combat before the public."[16]. . .

By 1960 the two major parties were still trying to function as brokers.

Not even a moderate polarization had taken place. Consequently dynamic politics to mobilize the creative energies of the society were still absent.

PARTIES OF POLITICAL PROTEST

In some respects the emergence of minor parties in the provinces can be viewed as populist protest against the established order. As a result of the social changes which have taken place in the country . . . there has always been a large number of people who experience deprivation. It is their feelings which can be exploited by the minor parties at the provincial level. These populist reactions can also be seen at the federal level with the Progressives, the Social Credit, and the C.C.F. (New Democratic) parties. The existence of these minor parties has meant that only rarely does the victorious party acquire a majority of the popular vote. Mr. Diefenbaker's appeal in 1958 can also be interpreted as a populist one. His vision caught the imagination not only of the deprived, but also of the not so deprived but financially insecure, the heavily mortgaged suburban homeowner. Because the appeals of the minor parties run the range of the rational-irrational continuum, from social democratic humanism to reactionary fundamentalism, as a political force they are fragmented even though they appeal to the same social groups.

The electoral success of the minor parties has been confined to the provinces. . . .

. . . What little polarization there has been in Canadian politics has remained within the provinces rather than within the national system. . . .

NOTES

1. Talcott Parsons, "Voting and the Equilibrium of the American Political System," in E. Burdick and A.J. Brodbeck, *American Voting Behavior* (Glencoe, Ill., 1959), 80ff.
2. This brief review of the federal franchise is based on Norman Ward, *The Canadian House of Commons: Representation* (Toronto, 1950), 211ff.
3. Ibid., 213.
4. Ibid., 236.
5. Robert S. Lynd, "Power in American Society," in A. Kornhauser, ed. *Problems of Power in American Democracy* (Detroit, 1957), 6.
6. J.W. Pickersgill, *The Mackenzie King Record*, vol. I (Toronto, 1960), 10.
7. J.A. Corry, *Democratic Government and Politics* (Toronto, 1946), Chap. VI.
8. Ibid., 138, 139.
9. Ibid.
10. R.M. Dawson, *The Government of Canada* (Toronto, 1948), 501ff.
11. Ibid., 506.

12. Ibid., 508.
13. Ibid., 510.
14. Frank H. Underhill, *In Search of Canadian Liberalism* (Toronto, 1960), 136–37.
15. Ibid., 167.
16. Ibid., 168.

FURTHER READINGS

Brodie, M., and Jensen. J. *Crisis, Challenge and Change: Party and Class in Canada.* Toronto: Methuen, 1980.

Horowitz, G. "Toward the Democratic Class Struggle." In T. Lloyd and J. McLeod. *Agenda: 1970,* 241–255. Toronto: University of Toronto Press, 1968. Reprinted in R. Schultz, O. Kruklak and J. Terry. *The Canadian Political Process.* Toronto: Holt, Rinehart and Winston, 1979.

Manning, E.C. *Political Realignment.* Toronto: McClelland & Stewart, 1967.

Taylor, C. *The Pattern of Politics.* Toronto: McClelland & Stewart, 1970.

Young, W. *The Anatomy of a Party: The National C.C.F., 1932–1961.* Toronto: University of Toronto Press, 1979.

16

The National Party Leadership Convention in Canada: A Preliminary Analysis

Donald V. Smiley

Canada is the only country in the British parliamentary tradition which chooses its party leaders through representative party conventions called for that purpose. Like most political innovations in democratic societies, the national leadership convention was established in Canada through pragmatic responses to pressing circumstances.

The situation faced by the Liberal party after the death of Sir Wilfrid Laurier in February 1919 made the choice of a leader by the traditional caucus procedure inexpedient. There was no individual who had clearly established his prior claims to the leadership. The conscription election of 1917 had shattered the party and had resulted in a situation in which 62 of 82 Liberal MPs were from Quebec. There were further defections from traditional Liberal support in the recent moves of farmers in Ontario and the Prairies toward independent political action. These circumstances and the rapid disintegration of the wartime Unionist coalition required the Liberals almost to recreate the party around a new platform and a new leader if Liberalism was again to be a serious political force in the affairs of the Dominion. The party had experienced two earlier representative conventions, although in neither 1859 nor 1893 had the leadership been at stake. From the election of 1917 until his death Laurier had been preoccupied with the future leadership of the party and it was his view that the choice should be made by a party convention rather than the caucus. However, it seems that he believed that the national meeting should be preceded by conventions in every province, and had this been done the Canadian leadership convention would have evolved very differently. In its composition the 1919 convention followed very closely the pattern established in 1893 with two groups of delegates—those chosen by each Liberal riding association and *ex officio* delegates such as Liberal MPs, Senators, MLAs, defeated candidates, and other party officials. Voting for the

Abridged from Donald V. Smiley, "The National Party Leadership Convention in Canada: A Preliminary Analysis," *Canadian Journal of Political Science* 1, No. 4 (December 1968), 373-97. Reprinted by permission of the author and The Canadian Political Science Association.

leadership was by individual secret ballot and was to proceed until one candidate had a majority of all votes cast.

The Conservative party chose one more leader by the caucus method—Arthur Meighen in 1920. However, after the party's defeat in the 1926 general election and the subsequent resignation of Meighen, the Conservatives in turn faced circumstances which seemed to make the holding of a leadership convention expedient. No individual had emerged as the obvious choice of the party. The previous general election had given a result which made the caucus unrepresentative of two major sections of the country—there were only four MPs from Quebec and four from the Prairie provinces. In its composition and procedures the Conservative convention of 1927 also observed fairly closely the precedents established by the Liberals in 1919.

These two conventions were both held when the respective parties were in opposition and both were followed by the accession to power of the party in the general elections of 1921 and 1930 respectively. These electoral successes no doubt had a good deal to do with legitimizing the convention system among party activits and in frustrating any moves to return to selection by caucus (although in 1941 under unusual circumstances Arthur Meighen was chosen as leader by a special conference of 150 members of the Dominion Conservative Association). Subsequently, the Liberals held national leadership conventions in 1948, 1958, and 1968, and the Conservatives in 1938, 1942, 1948, 1956, and 1967.

The national leadership convention thus became the established institution by which the leaders of the two Canadian major parties are chosen. Recent events seem to have gone some way in establishing that a leader so selected can be so replaced. The actual holding of the Conservative convention in September 1967 resulted from a bitter intra-party conflict culminating in November 1966 in the election of a national president pledged to a leadership convention in the next calendar year. Despite this decision by the extra-parliamentary Association of the national party, Mr. Diefenbaker was able for a time to rally a majority of the Conservatives in the House of Commons behind him and thus in effect to assert temporarily that his position as leader of the opposition was a parliamentary office. But later, despite apprehensions among some that he might do otherwise, he recognized the legitimacy of the procedure that was to depose him by attending the convention, placing his name in nomination, recognizing the new leader on his election and a few days later resigning as leader of the opposition.

Although the Liberals have never faced a parallel situation the constitution of the Liberal Federation of Canada appears to provide a method by which a leader can be replaced against his will. The relevant sections read:

G. Conventions shall be held at least every two years.

H. A resolution calling for a Leadership Convention shall be placed automatically on the Agenda of the Biannual Convention next following a Federal General

Election. If such a resolution is duly adopted by secret ballot the Executive Committee shall call a Leadership Convention to take place within one year.

The way in which the Liberal changeover was made in 1968 may become the normal pattern when a party leader retires voluntarily. Prime Minister Pearson gave formal notice of his decision to retire in a letter to the president of the Liberal Federation of Canada dated December 14, 1967. The "convention call" to the relevant party officials and organizations was issued on January 1, 1968, by the president, acting on behalf of the party's Executive Committee, and Mr. Pearson. The outgoing Prime Minister and the new party leader began the processes of the changeover immediately after the convention, and completed them in just two weeks. Only once before—in 1948—had a leadership convention been held when the party involved was in power: in this instance Mackenzie King remained as prime minister for more than three months after Mr. St. Laurent was chosen as leader by the Liberal convention, thus demonstrating in a symbolic way at least the distinction between the office of prime minister and that of party leader.

The Conservative leadership convention of September, 1967, and that held by the Liberals seven months later followed closely in their composition and rules of procedure the traditions which had been established in previous conventions. However, certain new elements were present in these gatherings suggesting that a new kind of institution is emerging. I shall call these changes a development toward "openness" in five dimensions.

First, . . . in both parties there were more serious candidates for the leadership than ever before. I . . . define arbirtrarily a "serious candidate" as one who receives more than 10 per cent of the votes cast on the first ballot.

Second, the major candidates conducted elaborate campaigns throughout Canada. This had not usually been so in the past. . . .

Third, there was much more extensive coverage by the mass media of candidates' campaigns and the conventions than ever before. The last months of 1967 and the spring of 1978 may come to be regarded as the period of the television breakthrough in Canadian politics. . . . In the past, politicians had been seen on the television screens almost exclusively in interviews and in set speeches conducted under the relatively restrictive rules of the Board of Broadcast Governors for political broadcasting. Now they were appearing as they actually went about making major political decisions. There was correspondingly wide coverage of the conventions by radio and newspapers, including for the first time media-sponsored public-opinion and delegate polls on candidates for the leadership. For a few months at least, politics became the major Canadian indoor sport, and just at the time that the Minister of Justice was boasting that certain proposed amendments to the Criminal Code would get the government "out of the bedrooms of the nation" he and his fellow-politicians were getting into the nation's TV rooms as never before.

Fourth, it seems likely that the 1967 and 1978 leadership conventions involved the rank-and-file of the parties in a more influential way than in previous such gatherings. The intense candidate competition led to intense delegate competition in constituency, youth, and women's party organizations. The increasing affluence of Canadian society perhaps made it possible for young people and other ordinary party members to attend conventions to a greater extent than in the past. The national parties themselves went to some lengths in arranging inexpensive housing for delegates and in giving travel subsidies to those from remote areas. . . . [I]t would have been contrary to common understandings of the convention process for constituency organizations to instruct their chosen delegates to vote for a particular candidate or, to an even greater degree, to request or require any commitment from delegates who had declared themselves as to what they would do when and if their favourite was eliminated.

Fifth, both the rules governing the conventions and the convention officials were generous to token candidates. . . .

. . . Canadian political parties in selecting their leaders in the foreseeable future will not only have to work within the framework of the convention system as it was established in 1919 and 1927 but also according to the new traditions of "openness." It will likely be politically impossible, for example, to hold conventions to anoint the choices of outgoing party leaders as happened with the Conservatives in 1942 and the Liberals in 1948 and 1958. A party which does not find more than two or three contenders, even if genuine, will probably be embarrassed. It seems likely that in the immediate future the New Democratic Party will miss great opportunities to publicize itself unless its leadership is changed by procedures which duplicate at least on a smaller scale those of its political rivals.

DELEGATES, PARTY LEADERS, AND CANDIDATES: VOTING BY SUCCESSIVE SECRET BALLOTS

The Canadian party convention can be understood only against the background of its two basic voting rules: (*a*) voting is by secret individual ballot; (*b*) successive ballots are held at short intervals until one candidate has a majority of all votes cast. These procedures predetermine the patterns of relations within the convention and those established prior to it—relations between candidates and delegates, between delegates and provincial and other party leaders, and between candidates themselves. The secret, individual ballot most clearly distinguishes the Canadian leadership convention from its American counterpart. The definitive study of United States national party conventions asserts: "For many purposes, the working unit . . . is the state delegation rather than the individual delegate. The ordinary delegate seldom takes an individual part in the deliberations except in meetings of state delegations."[1] It is quite otherwise in Canada. The individual delegate in the privacy of the voting cubicle is supreme and he must be deferred to as such.

The Canadian type of balloting gives a powerful incentive for candidates and their supporters to seek the favour of individual delegates wherever this may be found. Alan C. Cairns has conclusively demonstrated that the Canadian electoral system reinforces regionalism and encourages regional appeals in federal politics, in some cases by virtually shutting out a party from parliamentary representation in a province or region in which it has significant electoral strength and in others by giving a party a regional dominance in the House of Commons quite disproportionate to its voting support. The convention voting-rules work in the other direction. The vote of each delegate counts equally, quite independently of the choices made by others from his riding, province, or region. When this factor is combined with the heterogeneity of the activists in each party in terms of age, ideology, regional and linguistic identification, and other determinants of candidate preference there are powerful influences on each candidate to make an inclusive appeal to all significant groupings, factions, and tendencies in the party.

The first aim of each candidate for the party leadership is thus to encourage individual delegates to support him and to declare their support so as to influence others. But his subsidiary goal must be to gain the tolerance of candidates overtly pledged to other contenders. The expectation that the leadership will be decided only after several ballots makes candidate strategy enormously more complex than it would otherwise be. If delegate X is committed openly to candidate Y_1 his support may be needed on the second ballot—or even more crucially, on the fifth—by candidates Y_2, Y_3, and Y_4, when Y_1 has been eliminated from the contest, either by the voting-rules or his own voluntary withdrawal. Thus every delegate is in a sense "up for grabs" by every serious candidate.

What might be called the successive-ballot expectation leads to an enormous uncertainty in the approach of candidates to individual delegates— a situation in which the delegate has all the advantages. There are many incentives for delegates to commit themselves openly to particular candidates prior to voting but few to give any indication of how they will act if their preferred contender is eliminated. Some delegates may make such first-ballot declarations in the processes of being chosen by their respective constituency or other party organizations. Others no doubt make commitments in gratitude for past, or in hope of future, favours. During the convention itself, organizers for various candidates attempt to establish their supporters as a cohesive bloc by informally commandeering sections of the convention hall, providing entertainment and refreshments for committed delegates, and so on, and it takes a delegate with a highly developed sense of inner-directedness to resist such pressures. Perhaps most importantly of all, a delegate cannot influence others to support his preferred candidate unless he declares himself. There are, on the other hand, positive disincentives for delegates to give any prior indication of how they will act as voting proceeds. Candidates and their supporters strive to create the impression that they are winners and any open discussion of successive preferences is of course an admission of possible defeat. Candidate-blocs are undoubtedly in many cases deeply divided about second and later preferences and the discussion of these matters would endanger unity.

There are thus many influences against delegates giving overt indications of their behaviour as voting proceeds. Furthermore, their voting behaviour is highly unpredictable. Canadian parties do not sustain stable factions: candidates' appeals are inclusive and play down divisions, and thus delegates give their first, second, and successive preferences for quite different reasons. Another element of uncertainty is the extent to which delegates will take their cues as balloting proceeds either from candidates who are eliminated or from provincial or other party leaders.

The voting rules of the Canadian conventions make the influence of provincial leaders over delegates less crucial than in the United States where voting is open and recorded by states. At the Conservative leadership convention Premier Robarts of Ontario did not declare himself for any candidate— something that would have happened in an American convention only under the most unusual circumstances. It is significant in this connection that Canadian conventions have not seen anything like American "native-son" candidates— i.e. candidates whose strength is limited to their state but who barter the support of cohesive state delegations as balloting proceeds. However, at the western regional convention of Liberals held some weeks before the 1968 convention, there were some desultory discussions on the possibility of a western candidate running with a Prairie and BC bloc of votes. The party influentials involved in this discussion could not agree on a candidate or apparently, on whether such a move was appropriate, and the scheme was quickly abandoned.

The expectation that several ballots will be needed to select a leader creates the corresponding expectation among candidates that they may need the support of other contenders as successive votes are taken. There are the utmost difficulties in negotiating such alliances before voting commences. The inherent uncertainties of the situation seem to preclude bargains among candidates, except of the most oblique and open-ended variety—uncertainties relating, for example, to the relative standing of candidates as voting proceeds and to the ability of eliminated contenders to deliver their supporters. The mythology of the convention favours "no deals," and even the rumour of such arrangements gives candidates so involved unfavourable publicity. Thus such bargaining as takes place must occur for the most part under the extraordinarily distracting conditions of the convention floor as balloting proceeds.

The voting rules of the Canadian leadership convention preclude the deliberate creation of the kind of presidential coalition that is so central to American national politics. The Canadian candidate strives not so much for a coalition of party forces, but for an aggregate of individual delegate support on the first and subsequent ballots, and a significant proportion of this aggregate must be won under circumstances of uncertainty, distraction and publicity.

THE NATIONAL LEADERSHIP
CONVENTION AND PARTY LEADERSHIP

Canadian national politics is profoundly personality-oriented. Peter Regenstreif is perceptive on this matter.[2] According to his analysis "there is relatively little of a long-term group basis to party affiliation that operates to stabilize voters behind a party." The national organization of Canadian parties is "weak and inarticulate" and leadership is crucial in attaining the degree of party cohesion necessary to fight elections successfully and to operate parliamentary institutions. There is, of course, the direct and immediate impact of American presidential politics. The mass media in Canada as elsewhere present a highly personalized view of the political process; in particular, newspapers have almost entirely ceased to be party organs as they were in previous periods and the working reporter is enormously more influential in presenting his perceptions of politics, so long as he makes his copy exciting. It may be too that the biographical character of most contemporary English-Canadian historiography disposes those within that linguistic community to view politics in personalized terms.

In any analysis of the relation between the party convention method of choosing party leaders and the character of that leadership there are two questions. First, does the convention system result in different kinds of leaders being chosen from what would occur under the caucus system? Second, what is the impact of convention-choice on the leadership role itself?

One can only conjecture about whether different leaders would have been chosen if caucus selection had been perpetuated in the major Canadian parties. On the basis of the experience of Australia, New Zealand, and the United Kingdom, as well as that of Canada prior to the establishment of the convention system, it seems likely that parliamentary caucuses would have been more disposed to choose leaders with long records of federal elective office. Of the ten leaders chosen by convention, three (Bracken, Drew, and Stanfield) were provincial premiers with no federal legislative experience; three others (King, St. Laurent, and Trudeau) had six years or less in the House of Commons; and only two—Manion and Diefenbaker—were in relative terms parliamentary veterans with 21 and 17 years respectively as MPs. In general, leadership conventions have been more open than caucus-selection, thereby making it possible for leaders to be chosen from among other groups than those with long experience in the federal Parliament.

The widespread reporting of recent conventions adds another degree of openness by making it possible for men who have not been national figures previously to become serious contenders for the leadership in a very short time. The experience of 1967 and 1968 is instructive here—six months before the conventions neither Stanfield nor Trudeau was well known even among the activists of their respective parties. It is significant too that both were very late entrants to the leadership contest. There has been a good deal of speculation about the role of the media in the Trudeau victory. According to one extreme version, the media rather than the delegates chose the Liberal leader. The situation was obviously more complicated. One newspaperman, Anthony Westell, has declared that reporters were hearing about the "Trudeau boom" from the grass-roots some time before they were willing to give it credence or publicity.[3] On the other hand, by the time that the convention assembled, the newspapers and television, through the polls they sponsored and other reporting, were picturing the Minister of Justice as front-runner. The impact of the media on the results of the Conservative convention of 1967 is even more difficult to assess. Mr. Stanfield was not a colourful figure, and before the convention Mr. Roblin was most commonly portrayed by the media as the leading contender. However, observers of the convention seem to agree that a crucial point in the convention was the very favourable impression made on both the 400-odd delegates on the Policy Committee and the reporters present by Mr. Stanfield on his Tuesday night speech. Joseph Wearing in a perceptive account of the convention commented, "Next day the three Toronto newspapers agreed that Mr. Stanfield had made the most impressive performance the evening before and this undoubtedly had a considerable impact on the minds of the undecided. In fact, from that point on, the three Toronto newspapers were the only media the delegates could pay much attention to and the Toronto papers said that Stanfield was winning."[4]

The impact of the convention-system on the role of the party leader can be looked upon in two dimensions—the relationship between the leader and his parliamentary colleagues and between the leader and the public.

It is reasonable to assume that because the party leadership in Canada is conferred by an extra-parliamentary body the individual so chosen has an influence over his party colleagues in the House of Commons that he would not possess if the caucus selection method were used. One writer has said of Mackenzie King, "On the rare occasions when the parliamentary caucus began to growl, when the party has been in opposition and the going has been hard, he has more than once silenced the parliamentary wolves by emphasizing that he is the representative and leader of the party as a whole, not merely of the parliamentary group. What the parliamentary group did not create, it may not destroy, at least not without ratification by the party 'grass roots.' The leader may appeal beyond the caucus to the party membership."[5] (Mr. Diefenbaker's experience after the November 1966 party convention seems to demonstrate that a leader cannot successfully rely on the support only of the preponderance of his party colleagues in the House of Commons if he has lost the support of those dominant in the extra-parliamentary party.) It may also be true that the acceptance in this decade of the tradition that party leaders are not only chosen by convention but may be so replaced further strengthens a leader in relation to caucus. Thus a leader under sustained attack by his parliamentary colleagues might claim with some justification that the failure of the extra-parliamentary organization of his party to move toward his replacement constitutes an implicit vote of confidence. However, the normal workings of parliamentary government would make it virtually impossible for a prime minister to be sustained in office if he lost the support of his colleagues in the House of Commons and retained the support of the party outside, although an opposition leader might for a time do so.

In any consideration of the impact of the convention system on the role of party leaders the question may be asked as to whether the system is influencing Canadian politics toward a presidential-plebiscitary kind of leadership and away from the normal practices of parliamentary government. Miss Mary Southin, a Vancouver Conservative lawyer, has made a root-and-branch attack on party leadership conventions in Canada and recommended a return to choice by caucus.[6] She asserts, "The American system leads inevitably to presidential tyranny of numbers." But in the United States the president's power may in some crucial circumstances be restrained by Congress. In the Canadian system, according to Miss Southin's argument, the normal traditions of party solidarity leave us without even this restraint. Further, parliamentary government is based on the collective accountability of the cabinet to the House of Commons and is incompatible with a situation in which the prime minister is not effectively accountable to his supporters in the House.

Miss Southin's strictures have a good deal of point. There are several deep-seated characteristics of the Canadian political system which make it peculiarly vulnerable to plebiscitary leadership. Howard Scarrow has lucidly summarized. these interrelated traits as ". . . the absence of policy conflict, the non-partisan posture of organized interest groups, the dominance of non-economic correlates of partisan preference, low image differential, low party identification, low policy polarization among respective [party] supporters and wide swings of the electoral pendulum."[7] Peter Regenstreif has pointed out the absence of "stable group moorings to political parties" and a situation in which "social reference affiliations are weak mediators of political loyalties."[8] Thus there are few of the social and political restraints to a highly personalized leadership where the individual relates himself to the political system directly through the leader without the mediations of family and group affiliations, political parties, members of Parliament, the House of Commons, and so on. The way in which the convention system works reinforces these tendencies. The creation of a presidential coalition in the United States is a deliberate aggregation of important party and other interests. As we have seen, the successful candidate campaign in Canada relates the contender to the individual delegates in a more direct way. . . .

In the spring of 1968 the close association between two national leadership conventions and a general election has in the most basic way resulted in at least the temporary dominance of the plebiscitary as against the parliamentary elements in the Canadian political system. Under the normal workings of parliamentary institutions the party leader, whether a prime minister or otherwise, is in a fundamental sense *primus inter pares*. A national party convention is on the other hand a highly publicized trial by combat where there are no equals, only a victor and the vanquished. A general election succeeding quickly after two such conventions is almost inevitably regarded by both politicians and public as not the choice of a House of Commons but a personalized conflict between party leaders.

THE LEADERSHIP CONVENTION AND THE PARTY SYSTEM

The holding of a leadership convention reactivates a Canadian political party at the constituency and national levels, although the provincial associations as such are not so deeply involved. A large number of party activists are brought together to make a decision recognized by all to have great consequences for the party and the country. The extensive reportage of the convention and the candidate campaigns preceding it allow the party almost to monopolize public attention and push its competitors for the moment off the political stage.

The institution of the leadership convention serves to strengthen the extraparliamentary organizations of the national party. The major Canadian parties had their origins in Parliament and extra-parliamentary national organizations were at first, and until recently, dominated by parliamentary leaders. The activity of holding a leadership convention strengthens these national organizations and gives them a degree of autonomy both vis-à-vis parliamentary caucuses and the provincial associations.

The events surrounding a leadership convention reactivate the riding associations also. We have few studies of these local bodies and circumstances undoubtedly vary from region to region, but it appears that for the most part these groups are confined to relatively pedestrian tasks during election campaigns and between elections find little of great interest or consequence to do; for many reasons riding organizations do not ordinarily play active roles in the formulation of public policy, the activity most likely to be attractive to the kinds of people the parties are allegedly anxious to attract into their ranks. However, in their nominating roles of choosing candidates to contest parliamentary seats and as delegates to leadership and other national conventions, the constituency parties come into their own. The 1967 and 1968 conventions were particularly crucial in revitalizing the riding associations because both parties decided that local delegates should be chosen according to the boundaries set up by the 1966 redistribution and the necessity of choosing such delegates forced the constituency bodies to reorganize themselves within the new territorial limits.

The holding of a national leadership convention exposes a party to the risks [of] future disunity. For whatever reasons, the heterogenous Liberal and Conservative parties have never sustained stable internal factions, and intra-party conflict on ideological or other lines has never been legitimized or institutionalized. Interestingly, none of the ten leadership conventions has resulted in a break-away party like the Roosevelt Progressives of 1912, the La Follette Progressives of 1924, or the Dixiecrats of 1948 where important party groups have refused to accept the leadership choices of American national conventions. The voting rules of the Canadian convention appear to inhibit the development of certain kinds of cleavages which would be difficult to repair. These rules predispose candidates toward inclusive appeals, appeals which are so framed as not to exclude the possibilities of support on the first or subsequent ballots of any important sentiments or interests within the party. The creation of an American presidential coalition almost inevitably excludes certain important party groupings; Canadian circumstances are otherwise. In a nationally televised press interview the day after his selection as Liberal leader Pierre Elliott Trudeau was able to turn a good deal of the discussion to party unity, a matter which he declared was a "first priority" in his attention. Mr. Trudeau's judgment, I believe an accurate one, was that the scars of the convention were for the most part personal rather than ideological in nature and affected supporters of unsuccessful candidates rather than the candidates themselves.

Under the existing circumstances of crisis between English- and French-speaking Canadians, what did the 1967 and 1968 conventions do for this critical dimensions of national unity? Paradoxically, the selection of Mr. Trudeau by the Liberals may have broken what some regarded as a fixed tradition in that party that an English-speaking leader should be succeeded by one from the [other] linguistic community. Although Trudeau's decision to enter the race was apparently motivated in part by his judgment that *some* French-speaking contender should run, he asserted again and again that he should not be regarded as *the* French-Canadian candidate, and there was here the clear implication that this affiliation did not give him any claims to the leadership that he would not otherwise have had. The rationale of the open leadership convention is contrary to such deliberate alternation and it seems unlikely that this procedure will in the future be effectively asserted for or against any Liberal candidate. It is significant that in both the 1967 and 1968 conventions Quebec support was widely scattered among contenders. This has not always been so in the past. The secrecy of the ballot precludes certainty on this point, but it seems probable that French Canadians were fairly solidly behind King in 1919, Manion in 1938, and St. Laurent in 1948—and against Diefenbaker in 1956. Although Quebec support was divided in the two most recent conventions, it is likely that Stanfield had on all ballots a smaller proportion of Quebec votes than in the convention as a whole and that in Trudeau's case the reverse was true. Another factor of great significance is that in neither convention did Quebec provincial party organizations participate. Premier Daniel Johnson is alleged to have favoured Roblin for the Conservative leadership but it is unlikely that he exerted himself in his favour. The Conservatives as such do not exist at the provincial level in Quebec and many if not most of the Quebec delegates to the Conservative convention represented little in the way of effective party organization or influential political sentiment. This is, of course, a situation which has existed in the Conservative party for a generation. However, at the 1968 Liberal convention the provincial Quebec Liberals carried through the logic of the formal separation of the federal and Quebec parties established in 1964. Mr. Lesage and his lieutenants did not attend the convention and the provincial caucus did not name the delegates to which it was entitled under the constitution of the national party. Thus the 1967 and 1968 conventions saw a rigorous separation of federal and Quebec politics which does not prevail in respect to the other provinces, a kind of *statut particulier* in partisan-political matters.

John Meisel has pointed out that the Canadian party system has failed to contribute "to the development of a national political culture."[9] It has not in his terms effectively promoted "a sense of national community."[10] A strong case can be made that, more than other Canadian political institutions, the party leadership convention works in the direction of nationalizing Canadian politics. There is here a common national experience in having several thousand partisans assemble under circumstances of great publicity to make a single choice—a choice which has up to now been accepted by all the important elements of the parties themselves in each of the ten conventions that have been held. As I have pointed out, the convention voting rules predispose candidates against regional, indeological, or other divisive appeals. Although these circumstances undoubtedly inhibit constructive and pointed debate on national issues, leadership conventions seem to work toward alleviating some of the deficiencies in our political system about which Meisel is concerned.

THE NATIONAL LEADERSHIP
CONVENTION AND PARTY POLICY

The various leadership conventions have proceeded quite differently in terms of formulating platforms or statements of party principle. Thus no firmly established traditions have evolved as to the role of these conventions in the processes by which party policy is made. . . .

During the past decade the sources of policy inputs in the Canadian political system have become much more fragmented than in the King–St. Laurent period. In the war and post-war period down to the defeat of the Liberals in 1957 the policy centre of national politics was the cabinet working in collaboration with its like-minded senior advisers in the civil service. The new circumstances have given rise to several new and as yet unco-ordinated sources of policy direction; federal-provincial conferences, policy committees of the parliamentary caucuses, the Quebec Liberal caucus, "thinkers" conferences and national party conferences not involved with party leadership questions, royal commissions, so-called "task forces," etc. The circumstances of the national leadership convention and in particular the inevitable preoccupation of all those concerned with the choice of a leader would seem to preclude the major parties in the future from attempting serious platform-making at these meetings. Further, the constitutions of these parties provide for regular meetings with precisely the same composition as the leadership convention and able to discuss party organization and policy free of the distractions of choosing a leader. The decision of the organizers of the 1968 Liberal convention that this gathering should not even go through the motions of adopting a platform or statement of party principles seems not to have occasioned criticism, or even much notice, from any quarter. It may well be that an important precedent has here been set.

THE NATIONAL LEADERSHIP CONVENTION: ARE THE TWO PARTIES DIFFERENT?

There has been a great deal of discussion among students of Canadian politics about the differences between the Liberal and Conservative parties. Such discussion proceeds in terms of (*a*) characteristics of electoral support—class, occupation, religion, etc.; (*b*) voter-support in terms of characteristics of ridings and as translated into parliamentary seats; (*c*) long-term ideological and policy commitments; (*d*) public perceptions of the parties. Although there are difficulties in summarizing these analyses succinctly the general outlines are clear—the two major parties do not differ profoundly in the social characteristics of their supporters, their orientations to public policy, or how they are perceived by citizens.

With the importance of leadership in the Canadian party system it is interesting to see how the parties behave in national leadership conventions. Liberal and Conservative conventions do not differ profoundly in composition and procedure. The Conservatives have, however, a tendency to engage in bitter public quarrels at their conventions which is less pronounced in the other party. The Conservative conflicts have indeed been dramatic—Meighen's defence of his 1923 Hamilton speech at the 1927 Convention, the consternation caused by Bracken in 1942 in his insistence that the party change its name and accept what was regarded by some as a radical platform before he would place his name in nomination, the bitter dispute centring about Diefenbaker's decision in 1956 that he would not have a French Canadian second his nomination, and Diefenbaker's attempt to have the 1967 convention reject the "two-nations" policy. The Liberals have been able to avoid such open controversies, although in 1948 C.G. Power used the occasion of his candidacy to deliver a sermon to the party on what he believed were the principles of Liberalism and in 1958 the plenary session of the convention rejected a resolution of the platform committee related to party organization.

When one examines the leadership choices of the Liberal and Conservative parties several important differences emerge. First, and most obviously, two of the four Liberal conventions have chosen as leader French-speaking Roman Catholics from Quebec, while all the six Conservative leaders so chosen have been English-speaking, five of them Protestants and one (Manion) a Roman Catholic. In none of the Conservative conventions has any French-Canadian put his name in nomination. Second, at each of their six conventions the Conservatives have chosen leaders who were veterans of elective office; but at each of the four Liberal conventions a leader with a relatively short service as an MP has been preferred over contenders with an extended period of legislative office. The dates of the first election to legislative office of each of the Conservative and Liberal leaders chosen by convention are given in Table 1.

Third, in the six Conservative conventions three provincial premiers (Bracken, Drew, and Stanfield) have been chosen as party leaders while two others (Bennett and Diefenbaker) were former provincial leaders. None of the four Liberal leaders chosen by convention had run for provincial elective office.

Fourth, the Conservatives have chosen three of their leaders (Bennett, Bracken, and Diefenbaker) from the Prairie provinces, one (Stanfield) from the Maritimes, and two (Manion and Drew) from Ontario. Of the four Liberal leaders two (King and Pearson) came from Ontario and two (St. Laurent and Trudeau) from Quebec. The central Canadian orientation of the Liberals was graphically demonstrated in the 1968 convention in which all the five leading candidates on the first ballot held seats in the House of Commons from Ontario and Quebec—four of them from Montreal and Toronto. On the other hand, of the five first ballot leaders at the 1967 Conservative convention two were from the Prairies, one from British Columbia, one from Nova Scotia, and only one from Ontario.

Fifth, the Conservatives have shown a predilection for political professionals, the Liberals for those who have been co-opted into politics after other careers.

Table 1
Legislative Background of Leaders

Conservative conventions

1927	Bennett	elected to Legislature of NWT in 1898
1938	Manion	elected to House of Commons in 1917
1942	Bracken	elected to Manitoba Legislature in 1922
1948	Drew	elected to Ontario Legislature in 1938
1956	Diefenbaker	elected to House of Commons in 1940
1967	Stanfield	elected to Nova Scotia Legislature in 1949

Liberal conventions

1919	King	elected to House of Commons in 1908 (over Fielding, elected to Nova Scotia Legislature in 1882)
1948	St. Laurent	elected to House of Commons in 1942 (over Gardiner, elected to Saskatchewan Legislature in 1914)
1958	Pearson	elected to House of Commons in 1948 (over Martin, elected to House of Commons in 1935)
1968	Trudeau	elected to House of Commons in 1965 (over Winters, elected to House of Commons in 1945)

It is broadly accurate to say that all six of the Conservative leaders chosen by convention were men to whom politics was a preoccupation throughout their adult life. Three of the Liberal leaders (St. Laurent, Pearson, and Trudeau) had been co-opted into political life after pursuing other careers. While Mackenzie King's career is in a sense *sui generis* he had been a civil servant and management consultant prior to his election as party leader. It is interesting here to note that apart from Trudeau's few months between the election of 1965 and his appointment as parliamentary assistant to the prime minister the next year none of the Liberal leaders had ever sat in the House of Commons as a private member.

Sixth, conservative conventions have tended to result in rather sharper breaks with the person and policies of the past leader than have those of the Liberals. In only one Conservative convention—that of 1942—has the retiring leader had an influential voice in the choice of his successor. Although there is still some doubt as to whom Laurier would have wished to succeed him, King possessed a decisive advantage in the 1919 convention in that he had run for election as a Liberal in 1917 while his major opponent, Fielding, had joined the Unionists. In 1948 St. Laurent was the choice of King and in 1958 St. Laurent appears to have favoured Pearson. While Prime Minister Pearson remained neutral before and during the 1968 convention, he had advanced Trudeau very rapidly after the latter's election to the House of Commons in 1965, first as one of his Parliamentary Assistants and later as Minister of Justice.

Seventh, although one should not generalize too broadly from the 1967 and 1968 conventions, it appears that the Conservatives in their choice of leaders have a mildly patrician bias, while the Liberals are more open to upwardly mobile individuals. It is indeed remarkable how similar were the backgrounds of the three Conservatives (Stanfield, Roblin, Fulton) who led on the first and subsequent ballots—members of families with reportedly significant means and long records of political service in their respective provinces, education in private schools and universities, legal training, etc. There seems to be little of this patrician element in the senior ranks of the Liberal party.

The paths to the top leadership are thus significantly different in the two major parties. An analysis of these paths is far beyond the limits of this paper, but it might be said in passing that Conservatives have been more prone than Liberals to withhold their full support from their leaders. The obvious explanation is, of course, that since the convention system was established the Conservatives have been out of power roughly four-fifths of the time. There are probably other factors involved. The focus of the Liberal party is more distinctly toward the national political arena than that of the Conservatives. It may be that the processes of co-option in the Liberal party accumulate more outstanding political debts to the leader, create more anticipations of future preferment, and cause dissidents to retreat to their other careers rather than do battle with the existing leadership as would those more committed to politics. It is also possible that the groups from which the Liberals recruit their leaders have an ethic of bureaucratic solidarity which is carried over into political life. At any rate, Mr. Diefenbaker showed he possessed an accurate knowledge of the history and predispositions of his party which extended prior to his own period as leader, when at the end of the Conservative convention of 1967 he adjured the delegates to give their support to the leader they had just chosen.

THE NATIONAL LEADERSHIP CONVENTION: SOME SUGGESTIONS FOR CHANGE

The national leadership convention has become the established procedure for choosing leaders of the Canadian parties. In making recommendations for change in this institution I am working on the assumption that the convention system coming to us from the 1919 and 1927 meetings and its evolution toward openness in the two most recent conventions are now permanent features of Canadian politics. It seems most improbable that we can return to caucus selection no matter its advantages. And in the other direction, the traditions of Canadian politics appear to preclude the establishment of an American-type primary system, although there will undoubtedly be developments in the role that party members, however defined, and the public will play in the process of leadership choice.

The Financing of Candidate Campaigns

There has been a good deal of speculation about the size and sources of candidate campaign expenditures in the 1967 and 1978 leadership contests. Mr. Eric Kierans has said that he spent more than $100,000, most of it his own money, on his very modest campaign for the Liberal leadership and there have been guesses about the cost of the more extensive campaigns of other candidates which range from $200,000 upward. Whatever the reasons, most of the serious candidates in the two conventions were men who are reportedly of considerable private means. The chief advantage for such a person is probably not his personal resources so much as his family, business, and social connections with others in favoured circumstances and as Miss Mary Southin has pointed out ". . . a rich candidate who gets contributions from other rich men is less likely [than others] to have obligations to them. His contributors may well be his friends socially as well as politically."[11] The tradition in Canadian party finance has been to divorce the "bagman" function from those running for elective office. It may be supposed that fund-raising for a leadership candidacy is a more personalized matter, perhaps involving the candidate himself more directly and at least raising for him the temptations of incurring explicit or implict obligations to his benefactors. At any rate, it may be guessed that in financing their 1967 and 1968 leadership campaigns cabinet members and private MPs have accepted moneys and services which under prevailing political ethics they would not have done in their purely parliamentary roles. It is possible that, when we are on the verge of mitigating some of the abuses in party finance along the lines proposed by the 1966 Report on the Committee on Election Expenses, a new set of difficulties is arising with respect to party conventions.

It is probably unrealistic to contemplate measures toward the full disclosure of the sources and expenditures of candidates campaign funds, at least until such a principle is firmly established with respect to party finance. The chances for progress seem to lie in two directions:

1. The provision by the parties themselves of certain facilities for candidates either free or at less than cost. Such facilities might relate to mailing, transportation, candidate offices, etc. The difficulty here is that such provisions might encourage token candidacies. In my opinion, little would be lost by the establishment of convention rules much more restrictive in this direction than those which have been used in the past, perhaps requiring candidates to have their nomination papers signed by fifty delegates who have not so signed those of other contenders, or by extending facilities only on the payment of a deposit

which would be refunded if the candidate received, say, ten per cent of the delegate votes of the leading candidate on the first ballot.

2. Party ground rules for candidate finance. It should be possible, once a convention is called, for the national convention committee or some other organization of the national party to try to evolve minimum ground rules for the raising and expenditure of candidate campaign funds in collaboration with the actual or prospective candidates or their representatives. The best chances of success would appear to be in the limitation of campaign expenditures at the conventions themselves. An observer cannot fail to note the extravagant expenditures on costly gimmickry, bands, hospitality suites, etc., and this extravagance is undoubtedly contagious, particularly in delegations whose expectations of success is in decline. It seems likely that much of the expense incurred fails to alter the voting results in any significant way and candidates have good reason to limit it by mutual agreement.

Provisions for Voting on Second and Subsequent Ballots

At each successive ballot delegates must cast a vote based on different premises from the preceding ballot. The most important of these changing premises relate to: (*a*) the relative voting strengths of the candidate on the preceding ballot; (*b*) a different set of candidates as some are eliminated by the voting rules or their own decisions: (*c*) the declarations of support for different candidates by those from whom delegates take their cues, and most importantly from eliminated candidates. In casting their first ballot all but a few delegates are undoubtedly merely registering preferences which they have made before proceeding that day to the convention hall. However, under the circumstances in which the 1967 and 1968 conventions were held delegates had to make succeeding choices quickly and under conditions of almost incredible distraction, and in many cases without full information about how those of their fellows whose judgment they trust have reacted to the changing situation.

To encourage a higher degree of delegate rationality it is recommended that after the results of the first ballot the convention be adjourned until the next day. It is further suggested that on the first and subsequent ballots any candidate who fails to secure as many as one-third of the votes of the leading candidate be eliminated. These rules taken together would give delegates and candidates an opportunity to evaluate their positions after rigorous shakedowns of the contenders and in the light of more adequate information than was available at the recent conventions of how others are reacting.

Two further reforms are suggested: First, there should be a prohibition of bands and candidate demonstrations in the convention hall during the voting period. Second, within the period of an hour after the results of the second and subsequent ballots are announced eliminated candidates and provincial party leaders should have the opportunity through the convention communication system to indicate their voting intentions. . . .

CONCLUSIONS

The conventions of 1967 and 1968 indicate profound changes in the structure and functioning of the major Canadian parties. What seems to be developing are organizations which do not conform to Duverger's influential classification of cadre and mass parties.[12] At key intervals surrounding the choices of a national party leader and of party representatives to contest seats in Parliament, there is an enormouse increase in party activity. However, many of those who participate most actively in these nominating processes are not motivated toward a similar degree of participation in other party activities, including election campaigns, and at both local and national levels the Liberals and Progressive Conservatives tend to revert to many of the characteristics of cadre parties. These parties are extraordinarily volatile and because a large proportion of their members are not committed firmly either to the party or toward electoral success they may prove increasingly difficult to control by national, provincial, and local party hierarchies.

The new kinds of political mobilization are at present directed towards personalities rather than ideologies. The voting rules of the convention predispose serious candidates against ideological stances which are divisive within the parties and there are few significant ideological differences between the major parties. Peter Regenstreif's survey of delegates to the Conservative and Liberal conventions indicates that the personal qualities of the candidates rather than issues were decisive in determining delegate preferences. Canadian parties thus appear to be evolving in very different directions from those in the United States. Frank J. Sourauf has analysed the increasing importance of ideology in American politics in this decade and has concluded:

> Many of the conditions necessary for the development of an ideological politics have been clearly present in American society since World War II. Rising educational levels, an expanded network of mass communications media, and increased leisure time all go to provide the necessary political skills and opportunities. In addition, the parties themselves have needed the kinds of skills that the ideologues possess as mass-media campaigning and coffee-hour socializing replace the canvassing and club rooms of the earlier politics. In these and many other ways we have been developing a politics of middle-class, intellectual, professional, increasingly sophisticated citizens for whom politics is only an avocation—and a somewhat genteel avocation at that. Not surprisingly, then, this new breed of political activist has brought to the party and to politics in general involvements in issues, causes and even an occasional crusade.[13]

Although the underlying conditions mentioned by Sorauf occur in both countries, the new Canadian political activists have as yet been little disposed to "issues," "causes," or even "occasional crusades." Nothing like the Vietnam war or racial relations has ideologically polarized Canadian society and, as is well known, Canadians are less prone to discuss the general role of government in ideological terms. However, the provision in the constitutions of both major parties for regular national conventions other than those convened to choose party leaders makes it at least possible that issue politics will be more important in the future. An indication of what may happen with some frequency occurred when western delegates at the convention of the National Liberal Federation in the fall of 1966 were able to mobilize majority support for a resolution calling for a North American free trade area. Within a few days Prime Minister Pearson and his Minister of Finance had repudiated this proposal, obviously with some embarrassment. The national party conventions of the next two years will indicate whether the extra-parliamentary parties will become more involved with policy, as these meetings will presumably be held under circumstances where there is neither a general election nor a leadership contest in the offing.

The open party convention contributes an influential nationalizing influence to the Canadian political system. Regionalism and localism are endemic to almost all important aspects of Canadian life and many of our political institutions and procedures reinforce these territorially based particularisms—the electoral system, the composition of the federal cabinet, a decentralized federalism, and the over-representation in the Senate and the House of Commons of the least cosmopolitan provincial and local communities. The national leadership convention, on the other hand, has had an important though inevitably sporadic integrative effect.

NOTES

1. Paul T. Daniel, Ralph M. Goldman, and Richard C. Bain, *The Politics of National Party Conventions* (Washington DC, 1960), 355.
2. *Parties and Voting in Canada: The Diefenbaker Interlude* (Toronto, 1965), 24 and 68–9.
3. "Is Charisma the Key to Solving the Trudeau Mystery?" Toronto *Globe and Mail*, Feb. 12, 1968.
4. "A Conference for Professionals: The P.C.s in Toronto," *Journal of Canadian Studies*, 2, no. 4 (Nov. 1967), p. 8.
5. [J.W.] Lederle, "The Liberal Convention of 1919 [and the selection of Mackenzie King, *Dalhousie Review*, XXVII (1948)], 86.
6. "Why Do We Need a Leadership Race?" Vancouver *Sun*, March 26, 1968.
7. "Distinguishing between Political Parties—the Case of Canada," *Midwest Journal of Political Science*, no. 1 (Feb. 1965), 73.
8. *Parties and Voting in Canada*, 6 and 24.
9. Recent Changes in Canadian Parties," in Hugh G. Thorburn, ed., *Party Politics in Canada*, 2nd ed. (Scarborough, Ont., 1967).

10. "Conclusion: An Analysis of the National (?) Results," in [John Meisel, ed.,] *Papers on the 1962 Election* [(Toronto, 1965)], 287–8.
11. "Why Do We Need a Leadership Race?"
12. Maurice Duverger, *Political Parties*, trans. Barbara and Robert North (New York, 1954), 63–71.
13. "The Rise of Ideology in American Political Parties," in C.J. Wingfield, ed., *Political Science: Some New Perspectives* (El Paso, 1966), 73–4.

FURTHER READINGS

Courtney, J.C. *The Selection of National Party Leaders in Canada.* Toronto: Macmillan, 1973.

Lele, J., *et al.* "The National Party Convention." In H. Thorburn, *Party Politics in Canada*, 89–97. Toronto: Prentice-Hall, 1985.

Leduc, L. "Party Decision-making: Some Empirical Observations on the Leadership Selection Process." *C.J.E.P.S.* 4, 1 (March, 1971): 97–118.

Punnett, R.M. "Selection of Party Leaders: A Canadian Example." *Journal of Commonwealth Political Studies* 8 (March, 1970): 54–69.

Wearing, J. "The Trudeau Phenomenon." *C.J.P.S.* 2, 3 (September, 1969): 369–372.

17

The Electoral System and the Party System in Canada, 1921–1965

ALAN C. CAIRNS

This paper investigates two common assumptions about the party system: (i) that the influence of the electoral system on the party system has been unimportant, or non-existent; and (ii) that the party system has been an important nationalizing agency with respect to the sectional cleavages widely held to constitute the most significant and enduring lines of division in the Canadian polity. Schattschneider, Lipset, Duverger, Key and others have cogently asserted the relevance of electoral systems for the understanding of party systems. Students of Canadian parties, however, have all but ignored the electoral system as an explanatory factor of any importance. The analysis to follow will suggest that the electoral system has played a major role in the evolution of Canadian parties, and that the claim that the party system has been an important instrument for integrating Canadians across sectional lines is highly suspect. . . .

THE BASIC DEFENCE OF THE SYSTEM
AND ITS ACTUAL PERFORMANCE

If the electoral system is analysed in terms of the basic virtue attributed to it, the creation of artificial legislative majorities to produce cabinet stability, its performance since 1921 has been only mediocre. Table 1 reveals the consistent tendency of the electoral system in every election from 1921 to 1965 to give the government party a greater percentage of seats than of votes. However, its contribution to one party majorities was much less dramatic. Putting aside the two instances, 1940 and 1958, when a boost from the electoral system was unnecessary, it transformed a minority of votes into a majority of seats on only six of twelve occasions. It is possible that changes in the party system and/or in the distribution of party support will render this justification increasingly anachronistic in future years.

Abridged from Alan C. Cairns, "The Electoral System and the Party System in Canada, 1921–1965," *Canadian Journal of Political Science* 1, No. 1 (March 1968), 55-80. Reprinted by permission of the author and The Canadian Political Science Association.

Table 1
Percentage of votes and seats for government party, 1921–1965

	% Votes	% Seats		% Votes	%Seats
1921	40.7	49.4 (L)	1949	49.5	73.7 (L)
1925*	39.8	40.4 (L)	1953	48.9	64.5 (L)
1926	46.1	52.2 (L)	1957	38.9	42.3 (C)
1930	48.7	55.9 (C)	1958	53.6	78.5 (C)
1935	44.9	70.6 (L)	1962	37.3	43.8 (C)
1940	51.5	73.9 (L)	1963	41.7	48.7 (L)
1945	41.1	51.0 (L)	1965	40.2	49.4 (L)

*In this election the Conservatives received both a higher percentage of votes, 46.5%, and of seats, 47.3%, than the Liberals. The Liberals, however, chose to meet Parliament, and with Progressive support they retained office for several months.

Note: The data for this and the following tables have been compiled from Howard A. Scarrow, *Canada Votes* (New Orleans, 1963), and from the *Report of the Chief Electoral Officer* for recent elections.

If the assessment of the electoral system is extended to include not only its contribution to one-party majorities, but its contribution to the maintenance of effective opposition, arbitrarily defined as at least one-third of House members, it appears in an even less satisfactory light. On four occasions, two of which occurred when the government party had slightly more than one-half of the votes, the opposition was reduced to numerical ineffectiveness. The coupling of these two criteria together creates a reasonable measure for the contribution of the electoral system to a working parliamentary system, which requires both a stable majority and an effective opposition. From this vantage point the electoral system has a failure rate of 71 per cent, on ten of fourteen occasions.

This unimpressive record indicates that if other dysfunctional consequences of the electoral system exist they can be only marginally offset by its performance with respect to the values espoused by its advocates. In this paper discussion of these other consequences is restricted to the effect of the electoral system in furthering or hindering the development of a party system capable of acting as a unifying agency in a country where sectional cleavages are significant. Or, to put the matter differently, the stability which is of concern is not that of the cabinet in its relations to the legislature, but the stability of the political system as a whole. Has the electoral system fostered a party system which attenuates or exacerbates sectional cleavages, sectional identities, and sectionally oriented parties?

THE EFFECT ON MAJOR
AND MINOR PARTIES

Table 2 indicates an important effect of the electoral system with its proof that discrimination for and against the parties does not become increasingly severe when the parties are ordered from most votes to least votes. Discrimination in favour of a party was most pronounced for the weakest party on seven occasions, and for the strongest party on seven occasions. In the four elections from 1921 to 1930 inclusive, with three party contestants, the second party was most hurt by the electoral system. In the five elections from 1935 to 1953 inclusive the electoral system again worked against the middle ranking parties and favoured the parties with the weakest and strongest voting support. In the five elections from 1957 to 1965 inclusive there has been a noticeable tendency to benefit the first two parties, with the exception of the fourth party, Social Credit in 1957, at the expense of the smaller parties.

Table 2
Bias of electoral system in translating votes into seats

Year	\multicolumn{10}{c}{Rank order of parties in terms of percentage of vote}

Year	1		2		3		4		5	
1921	Libs.	1.21	Cons.	0.70	Progs.	1.20				
1925	Cons.	1.017	Libs.	1.015	Progs.	1.09				
1926	Libs.	1.13	Cons.	0.82	Progs.	1.55				
1930	Cons.	1.15	Libs.	0.82	Progs.	1.53				
1935	Libs.	1.57	Cons.	0.55	CCF	0.33	Rec.	0.05	Socred	1.68
1940	Libs.	1.43	Cons.	0.53	CCF	0.39	Socred	1.52		
1945	Libs.	1.24	Cons.	1.00	CCF	0.73	Socred	1.29		
1949	Libs.	1.49	Cons.	0.53	CCF	0.37	Socred	1.03		
1953	Libs.	1.32	Cons.	0.62	CCF	0.77	Socred	1.06		
1957	Libs.	0.97	Cons.	1.087	CCF	0.88	Socred	1.091		
1958	Cons.	1.46	Libs.	0.55	CCF	0.32	Socred	0		
1962	Cons.	1.17	Libs.	1.01	NDP	0.53	Socred	0.97		
1963	Libs.	1.17	Cons.	1.09	NDP	0.49	Socred	0.76		
1965	Libs.	1.23	Cons.	1.13	NDP	0.44	Cred.	0.72	Socred	0.51

Independents and very small parties have been excluded from the table.

The measurement of discrimination employed in this table defines the relationship between the percentage of votes and the percentage of seats. The figure is devised by dividing the former into the latter. Thus 1—(38% seats/38% votes), for example—represents a neutral effect for the electoral system. Any figure above 1—(40% seats/20% votes) = 2.0, for example—indicates discrimination for the party. A figure below 1—(20% seats/40% votes) = 0.5, for example—indicates discrimination against the party. For the purposes of the table the ranking of the parties as 1, 2, 3 . . . is based on their percentage of the vote, since to rank them in terms of seats would conceal the very bias it is sought to measure—namely the bias introduced by the intervening variable of the electoral system which constitutes the mechanism by which votes are translated into seats.

The explanation for the failure of the electoral system to act with Darwinian logic by consistently distributing its rewards to the large parties and its penalties to the small parties is relatively straightforward. The bias in favour of the strongest party reflects the likelihood that the large number of votes it has at its disposal will produce enough victories in individual constituencies to give it, on a percentage basis, a surplus of seats over votes. The fact that this surplus has occurred with only one exception, 1957, indicates the extreme unlikelihood of the strongest party having a distribution of partisan support capable of transforming the electoral system from an ally into a foe. The explanation for the favourable impact of the electoral system on the Progressives and Social Credit from 1921 to 1957 when they were the weakest parties is simply that they were sectional parties which concentrated their efforts in their areas of strength where the electoral system worked in their favour. Once the electoral system has rewarded the strongest party and a weak party with concentrated sectional strength there are not many more seats to go around. In this kind of party system, which Canada had from 1921 to Mr. Diefenbaker's breakthrough, serious discrimination against the second party in a three-party system and the second and third party in a four-party system is highly likely.

Table 3
Minor parties: percentage of seats and votes

	Progressives		Reconstruction		CCF/NDP		Soc. Credit		Créditiste	
	votes	seats	votes	seats	votes	seats	votes	seats	votes	seats
1921	23.1	27.7								
1925	9.0	9.8								
1926	5.3	8.2								
1930	3.2	4.9								
1935			8.7	0.4	8.9	2.9	4.1	6.9		
1940					8.5	3.3	2.7	4.1		
1945					15.6	11.4	4.1	5.3		
1949					13.4	5.0	3.7	3.8		
1953					11.3	8.7	5.4	5.7		
1957					10.7	9.4	6.6	7.2		
1958					9.5	3.0	2.67	—		
1962					13.5	7.23	11.7	11.3		
1963					13.1	6.4	11.9	9.1		
1965					17.9	7.9	3.7	1.9	4.7	3.4

Table 3 reveals that the electoral system positively favours minor parties with sectional strongholds and discourages minor parties with diffuse support. The classic example of the latter phenomenon is provided by the Reconstruction party in the 1935 election. For its 8.7 per cent of the vote it was rewarded with one seat, and promptly disappeared from the scene. Yet its electoral support was more than twice that of Social Credit which gained seventeen seats, and only marginally less than that of the CCF which gained seven seats. The case of the Reconstruction party provides dramatic illustration of the futility of party effort for a minor party which lacks a sectional stronghold. The treatment of the CCF/NDP by the electoral system is only slightly less revealing. This party with diffuse support which aspired to national and major party status never received as many seats as would have been "justified" by its voting support, and on six occasions out of ten received less than half the seats to which it was "entitled." The contrasting treatment of Social Credit and the Progressives, sectional minor parties, by the electoral system clearly reveals the bias of the electoral system in favour of concentrated support and against diffused support.

DISTORTION IN PARTY PARLIAMENTARY REPRESENTATION

No less important than the general differences in the way the electoral system rewards or punishes each individual party as such, is the manner in which it fashions particular patterns of sectional representation within the ranks of the parliamentary parties out of the varying distributions of electoral support they received. This sectional intra-party discrimination affects all parties. The electoral system consistently minimized the Ontario support of the Progressives which provided the party with 43.5 per cent, 39.7 per cent, and 29.4 per cent of its total votes in the first three elections of the twenties. The party received only 36.9 per cent, 8.3 per cent, and 10 per cent of its total seats from that province. Further, by its varying treatment of the party's electoral support from Manitoba, Saskatchewan, and Alberta it finally helped to reduce the Progressives to an Alberta party.

An analysis of CCF/NDP votes and seats clearly illustrates the manner in which the electoral system has distorted the parliamentary wing of the party. Table 4 reveals the extreme discrimination visited on Ontario supporters of the CCF from 1935 to 1957. With the exception of 1940 CCF Ontario voting support consistently constituted between 30 and 40 per cent of total CCF voting support. Yet, the contribution of Ontario to CCF parliamentary representation was derisory. During the same period there was a marked overrepresentation of Saskatchewan in the CCF caucus. The 1945 election is indicative. The 260,000 votes from Ontario, 31.9 per cent of the total CCF vote, produced no seats at all, while 167,000 supporters from Saskatchewan, 20.5 per cent of the total party vote, were rewarded with eighteen seats, 64.3 per cent of total party seats. In these circumstances it was not surprising that observers were led to mislabel the CCF an agrarian party.

The major parties are not immune from the tendency of the electoral

Table 4
Percentage of Total CCF/NDP Strength,
In Seats and Votes Coming from Selected Provinces

	NS	Que.	Ont.	Man.	Sask.	Alta.	BC
1935 votes	—	1.9	32.7	13.9	18.8	7.9	24.8
seats	—	—	—	28.6	28.6	—	42.9
1940 votes	4.5	1.9 15.6	15.6	27.0	8.9	26	
seats	12.5	—	—	12.5	62.5	—	12.5
1945 votes	6.4	4.1 31.9	12.5	20.5	7.0	15.4	
seats	3.6	—	—	17.9	64.3	—	14.3
1949 votes	4.3	2.3	39.2	10.6	19.5	4.0	18.6
seats	7.7	—	7.7	23.1	38.5	—	23.1
1953 votes	3.5	3.7	33.4	10.1	24.6	3.7	19.7
seats	4.3	—	4.3	13.0	47.8	—	30.4
1957 votes	2.4	4.5	38.7	11.6	19.8	3.8	18.6
seats	—	—	12.0	20.0	40.0	—	28.0
1958 votes	2.7	6.6 37.9	10.8	16.3	2.8	22.2	
seats	—	—	37.5	—	12.5	—	50.0
1962 votes	3.8	8.9	44.0	7.4	9.0	4.1	20.4
seats	5.3	—	31.6	10.5	—	—	52.6
1963 votes	2.6	14.6	42.6	6.4	7.3	3.4	21.5
seats	—	—	35.3	11.8	—	—	52.9
1965 votes	2.8	17.7	43.0	6.6	7.6	3.2	17.3
seats	—	—	42.9	14.3	—	—	42.9

Note: Percentages of votes do not total 100 horizontally because the table does not include Newfoundland, Prince Edward Island, New Brunswick, or the territories where the CCF/NDP gained a few votes but no seats.

system to make the parliamentary parties grossly inaccurate reflections of the sectional distribution of party support. Table 5 makes it clear that the electoral system has been far from impartial in its treatment of Liberal and Conservative voting support from Ontario and Quebec. For fourteen consecutive elections covering nearly half a century there was a consistent and usually marked overrepresentation of Quebec in the parliamentary Liberal party and marked underrepresentation of Quebec in the parliamentary Conservative party, with the exception of 1958. For ten consecutive elections from 1921 to 1957 Ontario was consistently and markedly overrepresented in the parliamentary Conservative party, and for eleven consecutive elections from 1921 to 1958, there was consistent, but less marked, underrepresentation of Ontario in the parliamentary Liberal party. Thus the electoral system, by pulling the parliamentary Liberal party toward Quebec and the parliamentary Conservative party toward Ontario, made the sectional cleavages between the parties much more pronounced in Parliament than they were at the level of the electorate.

Table 5

Liberals and Conservatives: Percentage of Total Parliamentary Strength and
Total Electoral Support from Quebec and Ontario

	Conservatives				Liberals			
	Ontario		Quebec		Ontario		Quebec	
	seats	votes	seats	votes	seats	votes	seats	votes
1921	74.0	47.1	—	15.5	18.1	26.6	56.0	43.8
1925	58.6	47.4	3.4	18.4	11.1	30.1	59.6	37.8
1926	58.2	44.9	4.4	18.7	20.3	31.7	46.9	33.4
1930	43.1	38.9	17.5	24.0	24.2	33.7	44.0	30.6
1935	62.5	43.1	12.5	24.7	32.4	34.4	31.8	31.5
1940	62.5	48.6	2.5	16.4	31.5	34.4	33.7	31.2
1945	71.6	52.7	3.0	8.3	27.2	34.6	42.4	33.3
1949	61.0	43.6	4.9	22.6	29.0	31.9	35.2	33.2
1953	64.7	44.2	7.8	26.0	29.8	32.6	38.6	34.2
1957	54.5	42.9	8.0	21.7	20.0	31.1	59.0	38.1
1958	32.2	36.2	24.0	25.7	30.6	33.3	51.0	37.8
1962	30.2	36.9	12.1	21.6	44.0	39.2	35.0	28.6
1963	28.4	37.8	8.4	16.0	40.3	39.1	36.4	29.3
1965	25.8	37.4	8.2	17.3	38.9	38.6	42.7	30.0

The way in which the electoral system affected the relationship of Quebec
to the parliamentary wings of the two major parties is evident in the truly
startling discrepancies between votes and seats for the two parties from that
province. From 1921 to 1965 inclusive the Liberals gained 752 members from
Quebec, and the Conservatives only 135. The ratio of 5.6 Liberals to each
Conservative in the House of Commons contrasts sharply with the 1.9 to 1
ratio of Liberals to Conservatives at the level of voters.

Given the recurrent problems concerning the status of Quebec in Canadian
federalism and the consistent tension in French-English relations it is self-
evident that the effects of the electoral system noted above can be appropriately
described as divisive and detrimental to national unity. Brady and Siegfried,
among others, have stressed the dangers which would arise should the lines
of partisan division coincide with the "lines of nationality and religion,"[1] the
very direction in which the electoral system has pushed the party system. This
consequence has been partially veiled by the typically plural composition of
the government party. In parliamentary systems, however, the composition
of the chief opposition party, the almost inevitable successor to governmental
responsibilities over time, is only moderately less significant. The electoral
system has placed serious barriers in the way of the Conservative party's
attempts to gain parliamentary representation from a province where its own
interests and those of national unity coincided on the desirability of making
a major contender for public office as representative as possible. The frequent

thesis that the association of the Conservatives with conscription in 1917 destroyed their prospects in Quebec only becomes meaningful when it is noted that a particular electoral system presided over that destruction.

The following basic effects of the electoral system have been noted. The electoral system has not been impartial in its translation of votes into seats. Its benefits have been disproportionately given to the strongest major party and a weak sectional party. The electoral system has made a major contribution to the identification of particular sections/provinces with particular parties. It has undervalued the partisan diversity within each section/province. By so doing it has rendered the parliamentary composition of each party less representative of the sectional interests in the political system than is the party electorate from which that representation is derived. The electoral system favours minor parties with concentrated sectional support, and discourages those with diffuse national support. The electoral system has consistently exaggerated the significance of cleavages demarcated by sectional/provincial boundaries and has thus tended to transform contests between parties into contests between sections/provinces. . . .

PARTY SYSTEM AS A NATIONALIZING AGENCY

. . . One of the most widespread interpretations of the party system claims that it, or at least the two major parties, functions as a great unifying or nationalizing agency. Canadian politics, it is emphasized, are politics of moderation, or brokerage politics, which minimize differences, restrain fissiparous tendencies, and thus over time help knit together the diverse interests of a polity weak in integration. It is noteworthy that this brokerage theory is almost exclusively applied to the reconciliation of sectional, racial, and religious divisions, the latter two frequently being regarded as simply more specific versions of the first with respect to French-English relations. The theory of brokerage politics thus assumes that the historically significant cleavages in Canada are sectional, reflecting the federal nature of Canadian society, or racial/religious, reflecting a continuation of the struggle which attracted Durham's attention in the mid-nineteenth century. Brokerage politics between classes is mentioned, if at all, as an afterthought.

The interpretation of the party system in terms of its fulfilment of a nationalizing function is virtually universal. Close scrutiny, however, indicates that this is at best questionable, and possibly invalid. It is difficult to determine the precise meaning of the argument that the party system has been a nationalizing agency, stressing what Canadians have in common, bringing together representatives of diverse interests to deliberate on government policies. In an important sense the argument is misleading in that it attributes to the party system what is simply inherent in a representative democracy which inevitably brings together Nova Scotians, Albertans, and Quebeckers to a common assemblage point, and because of the majoritarian necessities of the parliamentary system requires agreement among contending interests to accomplish anything at all. Or, to put it differently, the necessity for inter-group collaboration in any on-going political system makes it possible to claim of any party system compatible with the survival of the polity that it acts as a nationalizing agency. The extent to which any particular party system does so act is inescapably therefore a comparative question or a question of degree. In strict logic an evaluation of alternative types of party systems is required before a particular one can be accorded unreserved plaudits for the success with which it fulfils a nationalizing function.

Assistance in grappling with this issue comes from an examination of a basic problem. In what ways does the party system stimulate the very cleavages it is alleged to bridge? The question can be rephrased to ask the extent to which an unvarying sectionalism has an autonomous existence independent of the particular electoral and party systems employed by Canadians. The basic approach of this paper is that the party system, importantly conditioned by the electoral system, exacerbates the very cleavages it is credited with healing. As a corollary it is suggested that the party system is not simply a reflection of sectionalism, but that sectionalism is also a reflection of the party system.

The electoral system has helped to foster a particular kind of political style by the special significance it accords to sectionalism. This is evident in party campaign strategy, in party policies, in intersectional differences in the nature and vigour of party activity, and in differences in the intra-party socialization experiences of parliamentary personnel of the various parties. As a consequence the electoral system has had an important effect on perceptions of the party system and, by extension, of the political system itself. Sectionalism has been rendered highly visible because the electoral system makes it a fruitful basis on which to organize electoral support. Divisions cutting through sections, particularly those based on the class system, have been much less salient because the possibility of payoffs in terms of representation has been minimal.

PARTIES AND CAMPAIGN STRATEGY

An initial perspective on the contribution of the parties to sectionalism is provided by some of the basic aspects of campaign strategy. Inadequate attention has been paid to the extent to which the campaign activities of the parties have exacerbated the hatreds, fears, and insecurities related to divisive sectional and ethnic cleavages.

The basic cleavage throughout Canadian history concerns Quebec, or more precisely that part of French Canada resident in Quebec, and its relationships with the rest of the country. The evidence suggests that elections have fed on racial fears and insecurities, rather than reduced them. The three post-war elections of 1921, 1925, and 1926 produced overwhelming Liberal majorities at the level of seats in Quebec, 65 out of 65 in 1921, 59 out of 65 in 1925, and 60 seats out of 65 in 1926. The Conservatives' weakness in Quebec derived from identification with conscription, the hanging of Riel, and the punitive treatment they received from the electoral system. . . . In view of the ample evidence documented by Graham and Neatby of the extent to which the Liberal campaigns stirred up the animosities and insecurities of French Canada, it is difficult to assert that the party system performed a unifying role in a province where historic tensions were potentially divisive. The fact that the Liberals were able to "convince Quebec" that they were its only defenders and that their party contained members of both ethnic groups after the elections scarcely constitute refutation when attention is directed to the methods employed to achieve this end, and when it is noted that the election results led to the isolation of Canada's second great party from Quebec.

More recent indications of sectional aspects of campaign strategy with respect to Quebec help to verify the divisive nature of election campaigning. The well-known decision of the Conservative party in 1957, acting on Gordon Churchill's maxim to "reinforce success not failure," to reduce its Quebec efforts and concentrate on the possibilities of success in the remainder of the country provides an important indication of the significance of calculations of sectional pay-offs in dictating campaign strategy. The logic behind this policy was a direct consequence of the electoral system, for it was that system which dictated that increments of voting support from Quebec would produce less pay-off in representation than would equal increments elsewhere where the prospects of Conservative constituency victories were more promising. The electoral results were brilliantly successful from the viewpoint of the party, but less so from the perspective of Quebec which contributed only 8 per cent of the new government's seats, and received only three cabinet ministers.

In these circumstances the election of 1958 was crucial in determining the nature and extent of French-Canadian participation in the new government which obviously would be formed by the Conservatives. Group appeals were exploited by the bribe that Quebec would get many more cabinet seats if that province returned a larger number of Tory MPs. Party propaganda stimulated racial tensions and insecurities. . . .

The significance of Quebec representation in explaining the nature of the Canadian party system has often been noted. Meisel states that the federal politician is faced with the dilemma of ignoring the pleas of Quebec, in which case "he may lose the support of Canada's second largest province without the seats of which a Parliamentary majority is almost impossible. If he heeds the wishes of Quebec, he may be deprived of indispensable support elsewhere."[2] Lipson describes Quebec as the "solid South" of Canada whose support has contributed at different times to the hegemony of both parties, a fact which is basic in explaining the strategy of opposition of the two major parties. An important point is made by Ward in his observation that Liberal dominance in Quebec contributes to "internal strains in other parties." He adds the fundamental point that it is the electoral system which "by throwing whole blocks of seats to one party" fosters for that party a "special role as protector of the minority," while other parties are baffled by their inability to make significant breakthroughs in representation. Prophetically, as it turned out, he noted the developing theory that opposition parties should attempt to construct parliamentary majorities without Quebec, thus facing French Canadians with the option of becoming an opposition minority or casting themselves loose from the Liberals.[3]

Ward's analysis makes clear that the special electoral importance of Quebec and the resultant party strategies elicited by that fact are only meaningful in the context of an electoral system which operates on a "winner take all" basis, not only at the level of the constituency but, to a modified extent, at the level of the province as a whole. It is only at the level of seats, not votes, that Quebec became a Liberal stronghold, a Canadian "solid South," and a one-party monopoly. The Canadian "solid South," like its American counterpart, is a contrivance of the electoral system, not an autonomous social fact which exists independent of it. . . .

Quebec constitutes the most striking example of the sectional nature of party strategy, electoral appeals, and electoral outcomes. It is, however, only a specific manifestation of the general principle that when the distribution of partisan support within a province or section is such that significant political pay-offs are likely to accrue to politicians who address themselves to the special needs of the area concerned, politicians will not fail to provide at least a partial response. The tendency of parties "to aim appeals at the nerve centers of particular provinces or regions, hoping thus to capture a bloc geographical vote,"[4] and to emphasize sectional appeals, are logical party responses within the Canadian electoral framework.

ELECTORAL SYSTEM AND PARTY POLICY

. . . The inquiry can be extended by noting that the electoral system affects party policies both directly and indirectly. The direct effect flows from the elementary consideration that each party devises policy in the light of a different set of sectional considerations. In theory, if the party is viewed strictly as a maximizing body pursuing representation, party sensitivity should be most highly developed in marginal situations where an appropriate policy initiative, a special organizational effort, or a liberal use of campaign funds might tip the balance of sectional representation to the side of the party. Unfortunately, sufficient evidence is not available to assert that this is a valid description of the import of sectional considerations on party strategies. The indirect effect of the electoral system is that it plays an important role in the determination of who the party policy makers will be.

The indirect effect presupposes the preeminence of the parliamentary party and its leaders in policy making. Acceptance of this presupposition requires a brief preliminary analysis of the nature of party organization, especially for the two major parties. The literature has been unanimous in referring to the organizational weakness of the Liberals and Conservatives. Some of the basic aspects and results of this will be summarily noted.

The extra-parliamentary structures of the two major parties have been extremely weak, lacking in continuity and without any disciplining power over the parliamentary party. The two major parties have been leader-dominated with membership playing a limited role in policy making and party financing. Although there are indications that the extra-parliamentary apparatus of the parties is growing in importance, it can be safely said that for the period under review both major parties have been essentially parliamentary parties. . . .

. . . Thus, the contribution of the electoral system to the determination of the parliamentary personnel of the party becomes, by logical extension, a contribution to the formation of party policies. Scarrow has asserted that "it is the makeup of the parliamentary party, including the proportional strength and bargaining position of the various parts, which is the most crucial factor in determining policy at any one time."[5] While this hypothesis may require modification in particular cases, it is likely that historical research will confirm its general validity. For example, the antithetical attitudes of Conservatives and Liberals to conscription in both world wars were related not only to the electoral consequences of different choices, but also reflected the backgrounds and bias of the party personnel available to make such key decisions. The generally much more solicitous treatment of Quebec and the French Canadians by the Liberals than by the Conservatives is similarly explicable. It is not accidental that bitter criticisms of family allowances as bribes to Quebec came from the Conservatives, while the recent emphasis on unhyphenated Canadianism has also been a Conservative contribution.

The significance of the electoral system for party policy is due to its consistent failure to reflect with even rough accuracy the distribution of partisan support in the various sections/provinces of the country. By making the Conservatives far more of a British and Ontario-based party, the Liberals far more a French and Quebec party, the CCF far more a prairie and BC party, and even Social Credit far more of an Alberta party up until 1953, than the electoral support of these parties "required," they were deprived of intra-party spokesmen proportionate to their electoral support from the sections where they were relatively weak. The relative, or on occasion total, absence of such spokesmen for particular sectional communities seriously affects the image of the parties as national bodies, deprives the party concerned of articulate proponents of particular sectional interests in caucus and in the House, and, it can be deductively suggested, renders the members of the parliamentary party personally less sensitive to the interests of the unrepresented sections than they otherwise would be. As a result the general perspectives and policy orientations of a party are likely to be skewed in favour of those interests which, by virtue of strong parliamentary representation, can vigorously assert their claims.

If a bias of this nature is consistently visited on a specific party over long periods of time it will importantly condition the general orientation of the party and the political information and values of party MPs. It is in such ways that it can be argued that the effect of the electoral system is cumulative, creating conditions which aggravate the bias which it initially introduced into the party. To take the case of the Conservative party, the thesis is that not only does the electoral system make that party less French by depriving it of French representation as such, but also by the effect which that absence of French colleagues has on the possibility that its non-French members will shed their parochial perspectives through intra-party contacts with French co-workers in parliament. . . .

While a lengthy catalogue of explanations can be adduced to explain the divergent orientations of Liberals and Conservatives to Quebec and French Canada the electoral system must be given high priority as an influencing factor. A strong deductive case therefore can be made that the sectional bias in party representation engendered by the electoral system has had an important effect on the policies of specific parties and on policy differences between parties. Additionally, the electoral system has helped to determine the real or perceived sectional consequences of alternative party policy decisions. . . .

In some cases the sectional nature of party support requires politicians to make a cruel choice between sections, a choice recognized as involving the sacrifice of future representation from one section in order to retain it from another. This, it has been argued, was the Conservative dilemma in deciding whether or not Riel was to hang and in determining conscription policy in the First World War. Faced with a choice between Quebec and Ontario, in each case they chose Ontario. It should be noted that these either/or sectional choices occasionally thrown up in the political system are given exaggerated significance by an electoral system capable of transforming a moderate loss of votes in a section into almost total annihilation at the level of representation. If only votes were considered, the harshness of such decisions would be greatly mitigated, for decisions could be made on the basis of much less dramatic marginal assessments of the political consequences of the alternative courses of action.

ELECTORAL SYSTEM AND PERCEPTIONS
OF THE POLITY

A general point, easily overlooked because of its elementary nature, is that the electoral system has influenced perceptions of the political system. The sectional basis of party representation which the electoral system has stimulated has reduced the visibility of cleavages cutting through sections. The effect of this on the perceptions and conduct of political activists has already been noted. Academics have also been misled and frequently have imputed a monolithic partisan unity to the sectional particularisms of Canadian society. The resultant misconception has identified particular sections with particular parties and particular parties with particular sections. . . .

. . . A hasty survey of political literature finds Quebec portrayed as "the solid Quebec of 1921," western Canada described as "once the fortress of protest movements," since transformed "into a Conservative stronghold," eastern Canada depicted in the 1925 election as having "punished King for his preoccupation with the prairies," and the Conservative party described in 1955 as "almost reduced into being an Ontario party,"[6] when in the previous election 55.8 per cent of its voting support came from outside that province.

The use of sectional terminology in description easily shades off into highly suspect assumptions about the voting behaviour of the electorate within sections. One of the most frequent election interpretations attributes a monolithic quality to Quebec voters and then argues that they "have instinctively given the bulk of their support" to the government[7] or it is claimed that "the voters of Quebec traditionally seem to want the bulk of their representation . . . on the government side of the House. . . ."[8] Several authors have specifically suggested that in 1958 Quebec, or the French Canadians, swung to Diefenbaker for this reason. . . . A recent analysis of New Brunswick politics argues that the strong tendency for MPs from that province to be on the government side of the House "must be" because "it seeks to gain what concessions it can by supporting the government and relying on its sense of gratitude."[9]

The tendency of the electoral system to create sectional or provincial sweeps for one party at the level of representation is an important reason for these misinterpretations. Since similar explanations have become part of the folklore of Canadian politics it is useful to examine the extremely tenuous basis of logic on which they rest. Quebec will serve as a useful case study. The first point to note is the large percentage of the Quebec electorate which does not vote for the party which subsequently forms the government, a percentage varying from 29.8 per cent in 1921 to 70.4 per cent in 1962, and averaging 48 per cent for the period 1921 to 1965 as a whole. In the second place any government party will tend to win most of the sections most of the time. That is what a government party is. While Quebec has shown an above average propensity to accord more than fifty per cent of its representation to the government party (on eleven occasions out of fourteen, compared to an average for all sections of just under eight out of fourteen) this is partly because of the size of the contingent from Quebec and its frequent one-sided representation patterns. This means that to a large extent Quebec determines which party will be the government, rather than exhibiting a preference for being on the government or opposition side of the House. This can be tested by switching the representation which Quebec gave to the two main parties in each of the eleven elections in which Quebec backed the winner. The method is simply to transfer the number of seats Quebec accorded the winning party to the second main party, and transfer the latter's Quebec seats to the former. This calculation shows that had Quebec distributed its seats between the two main parties in a manner precisely the opposite to its actual performance it would have been on the winning side on seven out of eleven occasions anyway. It is thus more accurate to say that parties need Quebec in order to win than to say that Quebec displays a strong desire to be on the winning side.

One final indication of the logical deficiencies of the assumption that Quebec voters are motivated by a bandwagon psychology will suffice. The case of 1958 will serve as an example. In 1957 when there was no prediction of a Conservative victory, Quebec voters gave 31.1 per cent of their voting support to the Conservative party. In 1958 that percentage jumped to 49.6 when predictions of a Conservative victory were nearly universal. On the reasonable assumption that most of the Conservative supporters in 1957 remained with the party in 1958, and on the further assumption, which is questionable, that all of the increment in Conservative support was due to a desire to be on the winning side, the explanation is potentially applicable to only one Quebec voter out of five.

In concluding this critical analysis of a segment of Canadian political folklore it is only necessary to state that the attribution of questionable motivations to Quebec or French Canada could easily have been avoided if attention had been concentrated on voting data rather than on the bias in representation caused by the single-member constituency system. The analysis of Canadian politics has been harmfully affected by a kind of mental shorthand which manifests itself in the acceptance of a political map of the country which identifies provinces or sections in terms of the end results of the political process, partisan representation. This perception is natural since elections occur only once every three or four years while the results are visible for the entire period between elections. Since sectional discrepancies between votes and seats are due to the electoral system it is evident that the latter has contributed to the formation of a set of seldom questioned perceptions which exaggerate the partisan significance of geographical boundaries.

ELECTORAL SYSTEM, SECTIONALISM, AND INSTABILITY

Individuals can relate to the party system in several ways, but the two most fundamental are class and sectionalism. The two are antithetical, for one emphasizes the geography of residence, while the other stresses stratification distinctions for which residence is irrelevant. The frequently noted conservative tone which pervades Canadian politics is a consequence of the sectional nature of the party system. The emphasis on sectional divisions engendered by the electoral system has submerged class conflicts, and to the extent that our politics has been ameliorative it has been more concerned with the distribution of burdens and benefits between sections than between classes. The poverty of the Maritimes has occupied an honourable place in the foreground of public discussion. The diffuse poverty of the generally underprivileged has scarcely been noticed.

Such observations lend force to John Porter's thesis that Canadian parties have failed to harness the "conservative-progressive dynamic" related to the Canadian class system, and to his assertion that "to obscure social divisions through brokerage politics is to remove from the political system that element of dialectic which is the source of creative politics."[10] The fact is, however, that given the historical (and existing) state of class polarization in Canada the electoral system has made sectionalism a more rewarding vehicle for amassing political support than class. The destructive impact of the electoral system on the CCF is highly indicative of this point. It is not that the single member constituency system discourages class based politics in any absolute sense, as the example of Britain shows, but that it discourages such politics when class identities are weak or submerged behind sectional identities.

This illustrates the general point that the differences in the institutional contexts of politics have important effects in determining which kinds of conflict become salient in the political system. The particular institutional context with which this paper is concerned, the electoral system, has clearly fostered a sectional party system in which party strategists have concentrated on winning sections over to their side. It has encouraged a politics of opportunism based on sectional appeals and conditioned by one party bastions where the opposition is tempted to give up the battle and pursue success in more promising areas.

A politics of sectionalism is a politics of instability for two reasons. In the first place it induces parties to pay attention to the realities of representation which filter through the electoral system, at the expense of the realities of partisan support at the level of the electorate. The self-interest which may induce a party to write off a section because its weak support there is discriminated against by the electoral system may be exceedingly unfortunate for national unity. Imperfections in the political market render the likelihood of an invisible hand transforming the pursuit of party good into public good somewhat dubious.

Secondly, sectional politics is potentially far more disruptive to the polity than class politics. This is essentially because sectional politics has an inherent tendency to call into question the very nature of the political system and its legitimacy. Classes, unlike sections, cannot secede from the political system, and are consequently more prone to accept its legitimacy. The very nature of their spatial distribution not only inhibits their political organization but induces them to work through existing instrumentalities. With sections this is not the case.

Given the strong tendency to sectionalism found in the very nature of

Canadian society the question can be raised as to the appropriateness of the existing electoral system. Duverger has pointed out that the single-member constituency system "accentuates the geographical localization of opinions: one might even say that it tends to transform a national opinion . . . into a local opinion by allowing it to be represented only in the sections of the country in which it is strongest." Proportional representation works in the opposite manner for "opinions strongly entrenched locally tend to be broadened on to the national plane by the possibility of being represented in districts where they are in a small minority." The political significance of these opposed tendencies "is clear: proportional representation tends to strengthen national unity (or, to be more precise, national uniformity); the simple majority system accentuates local differences. The consequences are fortunate or unfortunate according to the particular situation in each country."[11]

SECTIONALISM AND DISCONTINUITIES IN PARTY REPRESENTATION

It might be argued that the appropriate question is not whether sectional (or other) interests are represented proportionately to their voting support in each party but simply whether they are represented in the party system as a whole proportionately to their general electoral strength. This assertion, however, is overly simple and unconvincing.

An electoral system which exaggerates the role of specific sections in specific parties accentuates the importance of sectionalism itself. If sectionalism in its "raw" condition is already strong, its exaggeration may cause strains beyond the capacity of the polity to handle. By its stimulus to sectional cleavages the electoral system transforms the party struggle into a struggle between sections, raising the danger that "parties . . . cut off from gaining support among a major stratum . . . lose a major reason for compromise."[12]

This instability is exacerbated by the fact that the electoral system facilitates sudden and drastic alterations in the basis of party parliamentary representation. Recent changes with respect to NDP representation from Saskatchewan, Social Credit representation from Quebec, and the startling change in the influence of the prairie contingent in the Conservative party, with its counterpart of virtually eliminating other parties from that section, constitute important illustrations. The experience of Social Credit since 1962 and more recent experience of the Conservative party reveal that such changes may be more than a party can successfully handle.

Sudden changes in sectional representation are most pronounced in the transition from being an opposition party to becoming the government party. As Underhill notes, it is generally impossible to have more than one party with significant representation from both French and English Canada at the same time. That party is invariably the government party. This has an important consequence which has been insufficiently noted. Not only are opposition parties often numerically weak and devoid of access to the expertise that would prepare them for the possibility of governing, but they are also far less national in composition than the government party. On the two occasions since the First World War when the Conservatives ousted Liberal governments, 1930 and 1957, their opposition experience cut them off from contact with Quebec at the parliamentary level. Even though the party was successful in making significant breakthroughs in that province in 1930 and especially in 1958, it can be suggested that it had serious problems in digesting the sudden input of Quebec MPs, particularly in the latter year.

The transition from opposition to government therefore is a transition from being sectional to being national, not only in the tasks of government, but typically in the very composition of the party itself. The hypothesis that this discontinuity may have serious effects on the capacity of the party to govern is deserving of additional research. It is likely that such research will suggest a certain incongruity between the honorific status symbolically accorded Her Majesty's Loyal Opposition, and an electoral system which is likely to hamper the development in that party of those perspectives functional to successful governing.

THE ELECTORAL SYSTEM AS A
DETERMINANT OF THE PARTY SYSTEM

Students of Canadian politics have been singularly unwilling to attribute any explanatory power to the electoral system as a determinant of the party system. Lipson has argued that it is not the electoral system which moulds the party system, but rather the reverse. Essentially his thesis is that parties select the type of electoral system most compatible with their own interest, which is self-perpetuation. He admits in passing that once selected the electoral system "produces a reciprocal effect upon the parties which brought it into being."[13]

Lipson's interpretation is surely misleading and fallacious in its implication that because parties preside over the selection, modification, and replacement of particular institutions the subsequent feed-back of those institutions on the parties should not be regarded as causal. In the modern democratic party state, parties preside over the legal arrangements governing campaign expenses, eligibility of candidates, the rules establishing the determination of party winners and losers, the kinds of penalties, such as loss of deposits, which shall be visited on candidates with a low level of support, the rules establishing who may vote, and so on. Analysis is stifled if it is assumed that because these rules are made by parties the effect of the rules on the parties is in some sense to be regarded as derivative or of secondary interest or importance. Fundamentally the argument concerns the priority to be accorded the chicken or the egg. As such it can be pursued to an infinite regression, for it can be asserted that the parties which make a particular set of rules are themselves products of the rules which prevailed in the previous period, which in turn. . . . It might also be noted that parties which preside over particular changes in electoral arrangements may be mistaken in their predictions about the effect of the changes. It is clear that the introduction of the alternative ballot in British Columbia in 1952 misfired from the viewpoint of its sponsors, with dramatic effects on the nature of the provincial party system which subsequently developed.

The only reasonable perspective for the analyst to adopt is to accept the interdependence of electoral systems and party systems and then to investigate whatever aspects of that interdependence seem to provide useful clues for the understanding of the political system. . . .

. . . To say . . . that parties are products of societies is not to deny that they are products of institutions. The only defensible view is once again to accept the interdependence of political and other institutions which comprise society and then to establish the nature of particular patterns of interdependence by reasearch.

Confirmation of the view that electoral systems do have an effect on party systems is provided by logic. To assert that a particular electoral system does not have an effect on a particular party system is equivalent to saying that all conceivable electoral systems are perfectly compatible with that party system. This is surely impossible. Any one electoral system has the effect of inhibiting the development of the different party systems which some, but not necessarily all, different electoral systems would foster. To accept this is to accept that electoral systems and party systems are related.

APPROACHES TO A THEORY
OF THE PARTY SYSTEM

This paper has suggested that the electoral system has been an important factor in the evolution of the Canadian party system. Its influence is intimately tied up with the politics of sectionalism which it has stimulated. Sectionalism in the party system is unavoidable as long as there are significant differences between the distribution of party voter support in any one section and the distribution in the country as a whole. The electoral system, however, by the distortions it introduces as it transforms votes into seats produces an exaggerated sectionalism at the level of representation. In view of this, the basic theme of the paper in its simplest form, and somewhat crudely stated, is that statements about sectionalism in the national party system are in many cases, and at a deeper level, statements about the politics of the single-member constituency system.

The suggested impact of the electoral system on the party system is relevant to a general theory of the party system but should not be confused with such a general theory. The construction of the latter would have required analysis of the import for the party system of such factors as the federal system, the relationship of provincial party organizations to the national party, the nature of the class system, the underlying economic and cultural bases for sectionalism, a parliamentary system of the British type, and many others. For this discussion all these have been accepted as given. They have been mentioned, if at all, only indirectly. Their importance for a general theory is taken for granted, as is the interdependencies they have with each other and with the electoral system. It is evident, for example, that the underlying strength of sectional tendencies and the weakness of class identification are interrelated with each other and with the electoral system as explanations of sectionalism in Canadian politics. For any one of these to change will produce a change in the outcomes which their interactions generate. We are not therefore suggesting that sectional tendencies are exclusive products of the electoral system, but only that that system accords them an exaggerated significance.

Concentration on the electoral system represents an attempt to isolate one aspect of a complex series of interactions which is only imperfectly understood and in the present state of our knowledge cannot be handled simultaneously with precision. In such circumstances the development of more systematic comprehensive explanations will only result from a dialectic between research findings at levels varying from that of individual voters through middle-range studies, such as Alford's recent analysis of class and voting, to attempts, such as those by Scarrow and Meisel, to handle a complex range of phenomena in one framework.

We can conclude that the capacity of the party system to act as an integrating agency for the sectional communities of Canada is detrimentally affected by the electoral system. The politicians' problem of reconciling sectional particularisms is exacerbated by the system they must work through in their pursuit of power. From one perspective it can be argued that if parties succeed in overcoming sectional divisions they do so in defiance of the electoral system. Conversely, it can be claimed that if parties do not succeed this is because the electoral system has so biased the party system that it is inappropriate to call it a nationalizing agency. It is evident that not only has the electoral system given impetus to sectionalism in terms of party campaigns and policy, but by making all parties more sectional at the level of seats than of votes it complicates the ability of the parties to transcend sectionalism. At various times the electoral system has placed barriers in the way of Conservatives becoming sensitively aware of the special place of Quebec and French Canada in the Canadian polity, aided the Liberals in that task, inhibited the third parties in the country from becoming aware of the special needs and dispositions of sections other than those represented in the parliamentary party, and frequently inhibited the parliamentary personnel of the major parties from becoming attuned to the sentiments of the citizens of the prairies. The electoral system's support for the political idiosyncracies of Alberta for over two decades ill served the integration of that provincial community into the national political system at a time when it was most needed. In fact, the Alberta case merely illustrates the general proposition that the disintegrating effects of the electoral system are likely to be most pronounced where alienation from the larger political system is most profound. A particular orientation, therefore, has been imparted to Canadian politics which is not inherent in the very nature of the patterns of cleavage and consensus in the society, but results from their interplay with the electoral systm.

The stimulation offered to sectional cleavages by the single-member constituency system has led several authors to query its appropriateness for national integration in certain circumstances. Lipset and Duverger have suggested that countries possessed of strong underlying tendencies to sectionalism may be better served by proportional representation which breaks up the monolithic nature of sectional representation stimulated by single-member constituency systems. Belgium is frequently cited as a country in which proportional representation has softened the conflict between the Flemish and the Walloons, and the United States as a country in which the single-member constituency system has heightened cleavages and tensions between north and south. Whatever its other merits, the single-member constituency system lacks the singular capacity of proportional representation to encourage all parties to search for votes in all sections of the country. Minorities within sections or provinces are not frozen out as they tend to be under the existing system. As a consequence sectional differences in party representation are minimized or, more accurately, given proportionate rather than exaggerated representation—a factor which encourages the parties to develop a national orientation.

NOTES

1. A. Brady, *Canada* (London, 1932), 13–14; A. Siegfried, *The Race Question in Canada* (Toronto, 1966), 114.
2. John Meisel, "The Stalled Omnibus: Canadian Parties in the 1960s," *Social Research*, 30 (1963), 383–4.
3. N. Ward, "The National Political Scene," in [Mason] Wade, ed., *Canadian Dualism* [(Toronto, 1960),] 266, 272.
4. H.A. Scarrow, "Distinguishing between Political Parties—The Case of Canada," *Midwest Journal of Political Science*, IX (1965), 72.
5. [Ibid.], 69.
6. W.L. Morton, *The Kingdom of Canada* (Toronto, 1963), 450; R. Cook *et al., Canada; A Modern Study* (Toronto, 1963), 254; Neatby, *King: The Lonely Heights*, 74, and Underhill, "Canadian Liberal Democracy in 1955," 40.
7. F.H. Underhill, *The Image of Confederation* (Toronto, 1964), 54.
8. [J.T.] McLeod, "Party Structure and Party Reform," 10. [In A. Rotstein, ed., *The Prospect of Change* (Toronto, 1965).]
9. H.G. Thorburn, *Politics in New Brunswick* (Toronto, 1961), 176.

10. [John Porter, *The*] *Vertical Mosaic* [(Toronto, 1965),] 373–4.

11. [M. Duverger,] *Political Parties* [(London, 1965),] 383.

12. S.M. Lipset, *Political Man* (New York, 1963), 13.

13. [Leslie Lipson,] "Party Systems in the United Kingdom and the Older Commonwealth [: Causes, Resemblances, and Variations," *Political Studies* VII (1959),] 20–1.

FURTHER READINGS

Irvine, W.P. "Reforming the Electoral System." In H. Thorburn, *Party Politics in Canada*, 128–140. Toronto: Prentice-Hall, 1985.

Lovink, J.A. "The Impact of the Electoral System on the Party System in Canada." *C.J.P.S.* 3, 4 (December, 1970): 497–516.

Pammett, J.H. "Elections," in M. Whittington and G. Williams, eds. *Canadian Politics in the 1980s*. 2nd ed., 271–286. Toronto: Methuen, 1984.

Simeon, R. "Regionalism and Canadian Political Institutions." *Queen's Quarterly*. 82, 4 (Winter, 1975): 499–511.

Winn, C., and J. McMenemy, eds. *Political Parties in Canada*, Chapters 4, 5, 7. Toronto, McGraw-Hill Ryerson, 1976.

18

The Use, Misuse, and Abuse of the National Election Studies

Nelson Wiseman

This paper questions the reliability, significance, and usefulness of much of the data generated by the National Election Studies conducted soon after recent Canadian federal elections (in 1965, 1968, 1974, 1979, and 1980). It is not intended to be an assault on the use of survey research in studying politics. It represents, rather, a call for more rigorous and critical analyses of survey research. It points to biases in the data that have provided the foundations for much of the recent empirical work in Canadian politics. The National Election Studies, funded by the Canada Council and more recently by the Social Science and Humanities Research Council, require substantial resources—the 1974 study consumed just under 40 percent of the total awarded by the Canada Council for political science research that year. Are these studies repaying the effort and resources expended?

It is remarkable that although dozens of academic papers and books now rely on the survey data generated by these studies there has been little critical examination of the quality of the output and the assumptions underlying them. In contrast to the United States and Britain, Hugh Whalen notes that "the operational character and performance of Canadian mass opinion research has never been subjected to a critical examination by any disinterested authority" and the contribution of Canadian academics who have specialized in the area "has been minimal on the central problems of investigative technique even though some of them have published widely in fields where opinion poll results are a primary data consideration."[1] Canada's political scientists have eagerly accepted and employed the reported findings of the National Election Studies and have constructed theories about Canadian electoral behaviour, partisan identities, and political culture based on them. The most accessible and widely cited account of a single election study is the report on the 1974 election, *Political Choice in Canada*.[2] It has been described as "the most extensive treatment of Canadian voting behaviour and partisanship currently available" in Canada.[3] This paper argues—using *Political Choice in Canada* as a primary reference

Abridged from Nelson Wiseman, "The Use, Misuse, and Abuse of the National Election Studies," *Journal of Canadian Studies* 21, No. 1 (Spring 1986), 21-35. Reprinted by permission of the author and publisher.

point—that at least some of the most important "findings" of the National Election Studies are misleading, naive, and contrary to common sense.

REPORT vs. REALITY

Survey research promises to help explain phenomena that aggregate data analysis cannot. Aggregate data, for example, may tell us that from one election to the next one party's vote increased and another party's vote decreased. But it cannot tell what specific groups of voters switched their vote, the direction of the switch, or why they switched. The charming and scientific appeal of the sample survey—determined by the abstract and neutral statistical laws of probability theory—is the promise to reveal how individuals and groups of individuals behave politically. But does it deliver?

The 1974 study was based on interviews with a national sample of 2,562 members of the electorate in the three months following the July 1974 election. The margin of error for such a sample is narrow: between 1 and 3 percent in 19 of 20 cases. Thus we may have a high measure of statistical confidence that the results are representative of the electorate as a whole. But can we rely on what the respondents say? The principal investigators in the 1974 study, and others who have used their data, have accepted the responses at face value. They have accepted these responses even though some of the most crucial statistics are contradicted by readily available alternative data—the official election results—on the actual behaviour, rather than the self-reported behaviour, of the respondents. The problem here is not necessarily that the sample is unrepresentative (although it may be) of the Canadian electorate. If every voter could have been interviewed, there is little reason, according to probability theory, to suspect that the responses would have differed from the findings reported in the survey. The problem is deeper and more serious. The findings are unrepresentative of the reality of actual behaviour. It is with political reality and political behaviour, not statistical probability and "survey behaviour," that the student of politics must first come to terms.

Table 1
1974 Vote (%)

	Actual	Survey*
Liberal	43%	53.4%
Progressive Conservative	35	31.1
NDP	15	12.1
Social Credit	5	3.3
Others	1	–

*Others and spoiled ballots excluded.

Sources: Clarke et al., *Political Choice in Canada*, Table 12.2, p. 361: and *Report of the Chief Electoral Officer, 1974* (Ottawa, 1975). Table 6, p. xix.

Table 1 compares the 1974 survey results with the actual 1974 election results. It shows a substantial gap between what people did and what they said they did. The Liberal vote is overreported and support for the other parties underreported in the survey. Only 43 percent actually voted Liberal yet 53 percent said they did. This suggests a fundamental flaw in the post-election survey method as an accurate barometer of actual political behaviour. The authors of *Political Choice in Canada* ignore this glaring problem with reported data. The distortion between report and reality is reinforced and replicated when the reported behaviour of specific groups of voters is contrasted to what we know of their actual behaviour. The following are examples of reported voting behaviour contained in *Political Choice:*

Report	*Reality*
1. The Liberals captured 68% of the "upper and upper middle class," 53% of the "middle class," and 51% of the "working class" vote.	1. The Liberals captured 43% of the total vote
2. The Liberals captured the votes of 52% of those between the ages of 18 and 29, 54% of those between 30 and 59, and 53% of those over 60.	2. The Liberals captured 43% of the total vote.
3. The Liberals captured the votes of 53% of professionals, business-men and managers, 55% of those in clerical and sales positions, 53% of skilled labourers, and 57% of unskilled labourers.	3. The Liberals captured 43% of the total vote.
4. The Liberals captured 46% of farmer's votes, more than any other party.	4. The Liberals did not win a rural constituency on the prairies.

Further evidence of the unreliability of reported data is the gap between reported turnout at the polls and actual turnout. In Newfoundland, for example, the 1974 survey reported that 80 percent voted in the election. Only 57 percent did. Turnout was overreported in every province. Similar distortions between report and reality exist in the other National Election Studies. The 1968 study, for example, found that 60 percent of those between the ages of 21 and 45 voted Liberal as did 54 percent of those between 46 and 59 years of age and 52 percent of those 60 and over. In reality, only 46 percent of the electorate voted Liberal.

The principal investigators of the 1974 study further complicate and distort our understanding of electoral behaviour by having asked the 1974 respondents to recall how they voted in earlier elections. They proceed to make claims about changes in political behaviour based on patently unreliable reports. Table 2 compares the 1974 survey results (regarding behaviour in the 1972 election) with the actual 1972 results. The gaps here between reported vote and actual vote are even more dramatic than in Table 1. The popular vote difference in the election between the Liberals and Conservatives was a narrow 4 percent (39 vs. 35 percent) and produced 109 Liberal seats to 107 Conservative seats. But when the people spoke to the surveyors in 1974, they claimed by an almost two to one margin to have voted for the Liberals over the Conservatives (54.5 vs. 28.3 percent) in 1972. Less than half of the Social Credit vote is accounted for (8 vs. 3.8 percent). The authors of *Political Choice* do not come to grips with this problem. Rather, they try to explain it away by noting that "the fact that these two elections [1972 and 1974] were relatively close together, coupled with the fact that the direction and magnitude of recall error can be reasonably anticipated, will allow us to proceed [to explain the vote switching pattern between 1972 and 1974]."[4] Nowhere in *Political Choice*, however, is recall error calculated, nor is any compensation made for it.

Table 2
1972 **Vote** (%)

	Actual	Survey*
Liberal	39%	54.5%
Progressive Conservative	35	28.3
NDP	18	13.2
Social Credit	8	3.8
Others	1	—

*Excludes those who claimed not to have voted and those who claimed not to have been eligible to vote in 1972.
Sources: Clarke et al., *Political Choice in Canada*, Table 12.2, p. 361: and *Report of the Chief Electoral Officer, 1972* (Ottawa, 1973), Table 6, p. xix.

The authors of *Political Choice* take their survey data on reported vote in the 1972 and 1974 elections at face value and use them to explain who switched their votes and which way. One of their "findings" is "that the net result of the pattern of switching from 1972 to 1974 was actually *away* from the Liberals." They attribute the majority Liberal victory of 1974 to the reported high vote for the Liberals by both those who claimed not to have voted in 1972 and those who were not eligible to vote. "In summary," the authors assert, "the data from the 1974 survey do not support the commonly held notion that it was a large scale migration of 1972 Conservative or NDP voters that best accounts for the 1974 Liberal victory."[5] They dismiss such notions as "shorthand explanations" and "oversimplification" because they are based on aggregate data. Their alternative interpretation based on survey data—that new voters and transient voters (those who vote in some elections but not in others) produced the Liberal majority victory of 1974—is stimulating and provocative. It would be, if accurate, a significant contribution to our understanding of the 1974 election. However, the data, when reported and actual voting are compared, do not support this interpretation. A more judicious reading of the data in Tables 1 and 2 is that reported vote is unreliable, misleading, and of questionable use. The reason why it appears that more people switched away from the Liberals than to them is that the reported vote for 1972 is more inaccurate than the reported vote for 1974. Whereas the Liberal vote actually rose between 1972 and 1974 (from 39 to 43 percent), the survey data indicate that the Liberal vote declined (from 54.5 to 53.4 percent). The same faulty procedures are employed by the principal investigators of the National Election Studies in analyzing vote switching in the 1979 and 1980 elections.

Such distortions in reported and recalled voting behaviour are confirmed by studies conducted in other countries. They are not mitigated by the creation of panels, i.e., reinterviewing respondents in later years as was done with about half the 1974 sample after the 1979 and 1980 elections. In the Netherlands, for example, the same panelists interviewed eighteen months apart produced a 24 percent level of inconsistency with their original reported vote behaviour. Such a high level of recall error is over and above the error between reported vote and actual vote and, as shown in Table 1, this may be substantial. The authors of *Political Choice* undertook the task of accounting for their data and, in so doing, claimed to account as well for the real world. Sometimes explaining the one is the same as explaining the other, but not always, and not here— for the correspondence between the two is crucial.

The discrepancies between the reality of voting behaviour on the one hand and reported behaviour on the other suggests that there may be no advantage, but perhaps a disadvantage, in conducting the National Election Studies surveys after elections. The 1974 survey study clearly did not represent the reality of the election and ought not to have had the word "election" in it. Both the election and the survey are separate, quite different, snapshots of public opinion and voting behaviour. A more instructive use of panels would have been to interview the same respondents just before and just after the election. Perhaps a more informative and certainly less expensive method of determining how specific groups of voters behaved (e.g., French Canadians, the upper class, farmers, etc.) would have been to use aggregate data by correlating census data with voting data, by superimposing voting polls onto census tracts.

There are a number of reasons why people misreport their behaviour. They may confuse their current preferences with their past behaviour. The overreporting of the Liberal vote in the 1974 post-election survey is compatible with Gallup polls reporting that Liberal popularity rose in the post-election period. At the same time that the 1974 post-election survey was being conducted, Gallup found that Liberal popularity rose from 43 percent (in the election) to 48 percent and Conservative popularity dropped to 28 from 35 percent. These findings are closer to the actual vote in 1974 (although Gallup did not ask people how they had voted) than the reported vote as indicated in Table 1. Thus, many people may have skewed their reported behaviour toward their current opinion when they were surveyed for the National Election Study. Another explanation for misreporting is that the electorate, being human, may overreport its turnout and behaviour at the polls because of a "social desirability bias."[6] That is, some people may want to give the impression that they did the right thing, that they exercised their civic duty, that they participated in the election just as they are now participating in the survey about the election. Perhaps some people overreported having voted for the Liberals because they wanted to be identified with the winning side, i.e., the "bandwagon" effect. Whatever the reason, the fact remains that many voters misreported the partisan direction of their voting behaviour as Tables 1 and 2 show. If there is so much confusion, distortion, invention, misrepresentation, and amnesia on the simple questions of turnout and reported vote, we must expect similar if not greater human failings in reporting more elusive matters such as people's party identification, interest in politics, etc.

Political Choice's theoretical contribution to the study of Canadian voting behaviour is the construction of a typology of voters based on measuring the "stability," "intensity," and "consistency" of partisanship or party identification. Respondents were asked how stable their identification had been with a party over the years, how intensely they identified with their party (very strong, fairly strong, weak), and whether they identified with the same party in both federal and provincial politics, i.e., consistency. From these variables the authors create two new abstract categories of voters: durable partisans (those with "very strong" or "fairly strong," stable, and consistent partisan ties) and flexible partisans (those with an unstable partisan identification and/or inconsistent identification in federal and provincial politics, and/or "weak" intensity of partisanship). What can all these abstract categories of feelings and behaviour teach us if, as we have seen, independent data show reported data to be so far off the mark? This is especially the case with one of the pillars of the typology of partisanship—stability—which is based wholly on recall information. Although the authors note that "in Canada, there has been a continuing dispute over the utility of the concept of party identification," they provide and analyze 43 tables of data dealing with partisanship. The grounds for this are that "the relatively high levels of instability of party identifications in Canada [the variable wholly determined by unrealiable recall data] suggest that a detailed investigation of the partisan attachments of Canadian voters is in order."[7]

An alternative approach might have measured what people reported of their identification with parties against what people know of parties. For example: the overwhelming majority of respondents, 92 percent, reported specific partisan attachments at the provincial and federal level. But what does this mean in light of people's limited awareness of the parties? Many people may never have thought of themselves as having a partisan identity until the survey asked them about it. A "Canadian Awareness Test" administered to 3,100 community college students in Manitoba revealed that only 54 percent knew what party was in power provincially. The dynamics and mechanics of the survey interview format, including the questions, assume a certain knowledge of political parties exists and the task is merely to gain information respecting individual feelings and behaviour vis-à-vis parties. Respondents could have answered "don't know" or "no opinion" to the survey questions, but few did. This is human and makes it difficult to measure biases imposed by the survey technique.

In the United States the concept of partisanship has been employed in helping to explain voting behaviour. Partisanship there is reinforced for voters by the requirement that they register to vote as partisans—as Democrats, Republicans, or Independents. In other countries, such as Canada, where no such requirement exists, the use of the concept is problematic and partisan identification has been found to be remarkably unstable and empirically barely distinguishable from vote preference. An example of the volatility of party identification even in the United States is a 1973 experiment conducted by the National Opinion Reseach Center. It found that in identical questions, put 30 minutes apart, the partisan identification of 10 percent of the respondents changed. An alternative, less costly, and more efficient source of information on partisanship in Canada would have been to gather data from political parties on their actual membership, something that exists in Canada but not in the United States.

The real world of political behaviour in *Political Choice* is largely in the psyche, not in society. The authors devote a number of chapters to analyzing "perceptions," "consciousness," "images," and "orientations." Only one chapter, in contrast, is sociological, looking at social cleavages. There is a preference in *Political Choice* for studying what people say about politics, rather than who they are in politics (e.g., French Canadians, the upper class, farmers, etc.) or what they know of politics. It is difficult to test whether people's reported psychological dispositions and opinions are what people say they are, but we know from elementary principles of psychology that just as there may be a gap between people's reported and actual behaviour, there may also be a gap between reported and actual opinions. For example: soon after the 1974 election, as Liberal popularity rose in the polls, the rate of inflation also rose and gained increasing media attention. Thus, when the 1974 data show that 57 percent of the respondents reported that inflation was an important issue for them in the campaign, they may simply have skewed their responses to their then current opinion and the new reality of higher inflation.

The problems with employing reported and recalled data apply in all kinds of surveys according to methodological research on interviewing and surveying. Voting surveys do not escape them. The paradox of *Political Choice* and many of the studies based on the same data is that they take, essentially, a psychological approach to studying politics yet they are largely apsychological. They ignore or gloss over that what people say, and what they do and think may not correspond. When *Political Choice* was reviewed in the *Canadian Journal of Political Science*, the reviewer noted "as rather odd that in a book about voting behaviour and elections in Canada nobody votes until page 86." The contention of this paper is stronger: little substantial analysis of actual voting behaviour is to be found anywhere in *Political Choice*. What is offered is a faulty reported vote that is repeatedly and uncritically used as a reliable data set.

SAMPLE DESIGN AND INTERPRETATION

We must be sensitive to methodological issues and problems when we use survey data because they have substantive implications for analysis and interpretation. It is instructive therefore to consider some technical features of the 1974 sample. A simple random sample would have given every voter on the electoral lists an equal chance of being selected. Canada, however, is so large and diverse that it would be prohibitively expensive and time consuming to construct a simple random sample. In 1974, as in the other election studies, the sample was a multi-staged, stratified, clustered one that increases the statistical margin of error as compared to a simple random sample. Although this may not lead to a dramatically higher margin of error for Canada as a whole, it has substantial implications for understanding the politics of particular regions. For example, no one was interviewed in the northern portions of Quebec, Ontario, Manitoba, Saskatchewan, Alberta, and British Columbia, nor in the Yukon or Northwest Territories. Thus the majority of native Canadians— Indians, Métis, Inuit—were excluded. Therefore, we cannot learn much about the politics of natives or northerners, and they determine the outcome of elections in a number of provincial constituencies, especially in Western Canada. *Political Choice* offers a detailed analysis of how Canadians perceive the North without pointing out that no northerners were surveyed.

Circumscribed sampling points to questions about the reliability of the provincial samples. The principal investigators of the National Election Studies described regional and provincial differences in political behaviour as "one major theoretical focus" of the sample's 1974 design. They claimed "explicit attention has been given to providing regional subsamples of adequate size for meaningful analysis." In practice, when combined with the imperative of clustering respondents, this meant sampling in only four federal constituencies in each of Manitoba, Saskatchewan, Newfoundland, and New Brunswick. In Manitoba, for example, only 113 respondents were interviewed in 19 polling divisions, all in the southern part of the province. These procedures are statistically acceptable, but are they reliable or in touch with political reality? When one examines how the 113 Manitobans reported voting in the 1972 and 1974 federal elections, it becomes clear that the same problem with using reported data for Canada as a whole applies to Manitoba as well. It is also a case of reported error compounded by a larger sampling error produced by the small size of the provincial sample. Reporting on their 1972 vote, for example, the surveyed Manitobans claimed to have voted 40 to 35 percent in favour of the Liberals over the Conservatives. In actual fact, Manitobans voted 42 to 31 percent in favour of the Conservatives over the Liberals. Similarly, a plurality of the Saskatchewan respondents in 1974 said they voted Liberal that year. In reality, the Liberals ran third behind both the Conservatives and NDP. In Quebec, where the 1974 sample was a relatively substantial 702 respondents, 70 percent claimed to have voted Liberal, but only 54 percent did. In Alberta, a plurality of the 1974 sample claimed to have voted Liberal in 1972, but the Liberals won no seats and captured only 25 percent of the vote. The Conservatives, with 58 percent of the vote, captured all the seats.

It is important to draw attention to the small sizes of many of the provincial samples (in 1974: 113 in Manitoba, 102 in each of Newfoundland, Prince Edward Island, and Saskatchewan). Surveying 113 Manitobans is quite different from a statistical point of view than surveying 2,562 Canadians. The margin of error grows from somewhere between 1 and 3 percent to somewhere possibly between 5 and 15 percent. Moreover, the answers to many questions were "no opinion," "don't know," "no answer,"and "not applicable" responses. This means the sample analyzed was smaller still and the margin of error wider yet in many cases. For example, when the 113 Manitobans were asked whether they had always voted for the same party in federal elections, only 50 said they had. When the follow-up question to this group of 50 was put ("which party is that?"), the response fell within a margin of error so large as to render any analysis hopelessly questionable. Moreover, some of the responses were nonsensical non sequiturs. Of those Manitobans who claimed to have always voted for the same party, 4 percent (or two of them) didn't know which party it was!

Small provincial samples have been employed in making relatively large interpretive claims about the Canadian polity. The misuse and abuse of the National Election Studies in explaining variations among provinces and within provinces is carried to its logical absurd conclusion in a comparative study of the provincial party systems by one of the principal investigators of the 1974 study.[8] The author provides four tables based on the Manitoba data that relate partisanship to various sociodemographic variables. The tables show religion and language correlated in a statistically significant way with partisanship. The partisan identities of Roman Catholics are contrasted with those of non-Roman Catholics. The number of Manitoba Roman Catholics responding to this survey question was 16. Similarly, in comparing the party preferences of Anglophone and non-Anglophone Manitobans, we find that the number of non-Anglophones surveyed was 23. To base scientific analysis or interpretation on such sample sizes is to make much ado about next to nothing. Statistical theory requires that if one wants to be as accurate about the opinions of Manitoba's Roman Catholics as one is accurate about the opinions of Canadians as a whole, one must survey roughly as many Manitoba Roman Catholics as one surveys Canadians. Moreover, the Manitoba sample was not as representative of Manitoba society as it could have been. The census reported that 25 percent of Manitobans were Roman Catholics and that 33 percent had a mother tongue other than English, but only 19 percent of the sample was Roman Catholic and only 25 percent had a mother tongue other than English. It is difficult to check how representative the sample is of the Canadian electorate because many of the social categories employed in the survey do not correspond to the Census (e.g., the Census lumps non-voters between 15 and 17 years of age with voting 18 and 19 year olds).

When problems of sample design are overcome, problems of interpretation remain. Survey data do not speak for themselves and interpretation of them is as much art as it is science. In any field, they should be used along with other data. They should be integrated with existing knowledge in the field to help build theory, to test existing theories, to help avoid misinterpretation, and to help construct the best possible interpretation of political behaviour. Alternative interpretations and misinterpretations are possible, and the survey researcher should employ non-survey material to help understand and interpret the phenomena being studied.

Interpretations of survey data should strive to combine findings. Too many survey studies treat the responses to questions in an isolated manner, failing to use the findings in one case to illuminate those in another. An example of this is the report in *Political Choice* on regional consciousness and its implications. This is also an example of how different observers looking at the same data may come to contradictory conclusions. Respondents were asked to define their own region in Canada. In Canada as a whole, 30 percent claimed they did not think of Canada in regional terms and another 11 percent did not know what region they lived in. Although 59 percent responded by citing a region, the authors focus on the lack of uniform responses: in Saskatchewan, for example, 33 percent said they lived in Western Canada, 2 percent said Saskatchewan, and 30 percent said the Prairies. Similar results were obtained for Manitoba, Alberta and British Columbia. This could be taken as an indication of a relatively high level of regional consciousness. But the authors of *Political Choice* offer a different interpretation because there is no agreement on what the region is, i.e., the Prairies or Western Canada. "This lack of agreement on regional boundaries," they conclude, "makes it unlikely that regional consciousness will provide a major explanatory variable in the definition of Canadian party politics and in the explanation of Canadian electoral behaviour...."[9] They suggest that, on the basis of these findings, "provincial governments may experience difficulties in being perceived as defenders of regional interests."

This interpretation is contradicted both by the findings and by political reality. Provincial governments *have* been perceived as defenders of regional interests. Direct evidence of this is in a finding that is reported but not related creatively to this issue of regional consciousness. When people were asked which level of government they felt closer to—federal or provincial— respondents in every province except one (Ontario) felt closer to their provincial government. The ratios are remarkably high and consistent. In British Columbia, Prince Edward Island, and Alberta people felt closer to their provincial government than to the federal government by ratios of 78 to 13, 77 to 14, and 71 to 20 percent respectively. (Residual percentages felt equally close to both levels of government.) This information, however, is not used to clarify the findings on the strength of regional consciousness. The fact that respondents may not agree on the definition or boundaries of their region (Prairies vs. Western Canada, Maritimes vs. Eastern Canada, etc.) is not as important as the fact that most respondents do define a region they call their own. Using different but closely related terms such as Prairies and Western Canada is of secondary, not primary significance. The strength and consistency of feelings towards federal and provincial governments indicate that, despite the methodological problems, the National Election Studies contain some useful data that provide for insights into the dynamics of Canadian politics. This is but one example. There are others. The authors of *Political Choice*, however, deal with all their data democratically and indiscriminately, as being of equal and high reliability, when some, such as reported voting behaviour, are clearly less reliable.

POLITICAL CULTURE

A particularly ambitious undertaking based on data generated by the National Election Studies is the endeavour to depict and compare provincial or regional political cultures. It is an example of how issues of methodology, interpretation, and conceptualization intersect. There are over 250 available definitions and uses of the concept of culture. The literature tells us culture is pervasive and, like the air we breathe, something of which we are barely aware. We notice it best when we compare two different cultures or move from one culture to another. Culture is rooted in a specific group or nation and is cross-generational. It does not come and go like fashion. It is reliavely stable and enduring. Studies purporting to deal with political culture, therefore, must strive to bring an historic, dynamic perspective to their analysis.

The approach among Canadian political scientists that has come to dominate the study of Canadian political culture was developed by Gabriel Almond and Sidney Verba in *The Civic Culture*.[10] Virtually every major academic survey conducted in Canada since 1965, including all of the National Election Studies, has asked the same kinds of questions as formulated by Almond and Verba. The approach is individualistic in that, although culture is recognized as a collective phenomenon, it becomes—through the use of surveys—an aggregation of individual values, beliefs, attitudes, and opinions. The political culture of a society is measured and expressed as a statistical average or as majority opinion. The questions have emphasized "efficacy" (i.e., confidence in one's ability to influence political decisions), "trust" in government, and involvement in political activity.

Two of Canada's leading political scientists, Richard Simeon and David Elkins, have extracted data dealing with these questions in the 1965, 1968 and 1974 National Election Studies with the aim of determining differences among provincial political cultures.[11] Building on the cross-national, cross-cultural work of Almond and Verba, they depict British Columbia, Ontario, Manitoba and Anglophone Quebec as "citizen societies" where there are relatively high levels of trust in political leaders and institutions and whose citizens have a relatively strong sense of efficacy. In contrast, at the other end of a spectrum, the Atlantic provinces and Francophone Quebec are described as "disaffected societies" where there is more distrust of government and a relative feeling of political impotence. Simeon and Elkins claim significant and "striking differences" in political culture from province to province and that these differences persist over time. They recognize it is not clear what the differences signify and they note that differences may be linked to various factors: ritualistic responses, unique historical patterns in each province, differences in respondents' personality characteristics, socioeconomic and demographic factors, transitory political events, etc. They acknowledge the difficulty of knowing what the questions respecting "efficacy" and "trust" are measuring. They point out that none of the survey questions used in the National Election Studies to measure efficacy and trust differentiate between levels of government. Is it not reasonable to expect, in light of the dramatic differentials in the 1974 findings on how "close" Canadians feel to their respective federal and provincial governments, that levels of efficacy and trust toward these different governments would also be different? After all, what can "trust" in government mean when feelings toward one's governments are so different?

Nevertheless, it is the "findings" of this study, rather than its limitations, that have attracted attention. *Political Choice*, for example, begins its analysis of regional consciousness by citing Simeon and Elkins's comparative findings that provincial political cultures in Canada are "so divergent as to rival differences between countries elsewhere in the globe."[12] Specifically, what Simeon and Elkins found with respect to political efficacy and in comparison to Almond and Verba's findings was that "the gap between the two Canadian extremes, Newfoundland and British Columbia, appears to be even larger than that between Italy and the United States."[13] This is a bold and heady claim.

"Political culture," however defined, persists over a substantial period of time; hence the power and significance of the concept. Do variables such as "efficacy" and "trust" meet this test? The evidence suggests not. An American study reveals that between 1964 and 1980 the percentage of Americans who agreed that "you cannot trust the government in Washington to do what is right most of the time" increased from 22 to 73 percent.[14] When this "finding" is combined with Almond and Verba's "findings" for Italy and the United States in the early 1960s, the logical conclusion is amazing. It is that the political culture of the United States in the early 1980s is more like that of Italy in the early 1960s than like that of the United States in the early 1960s. This is patently ridiculous. It throws into doubt the efficacy and trustworthiness of concepts such as "efficacy" and "trust" in defining political culture.

It is logical for political scientists in the United States to study political culture there with mass surveys containing questions dealing with efficacy, trust in government, and involvement in political activity. They deal with democracy, a theme that runs back to the American Revolution. Canadian history and literature, however, suggest that Canadian political culture—both English and French—has had less to do with democracy and equality and more to do with survival. Surveys cannot inform us of such differences in political cultures nor can they reach very far back in history. The differences suggest that culture is not *answers* to unvarying questions but the nature of the *questions* themselves. In Iran, for example, a reasonable question might be: "Are people pious or godless?" One could, of course, extract answers to this question from respondents in say, Britain, but what would it tell us about British political culture? Questions with respect to efficacy, trust, and political involvement are examples of studying Canadian political culture in terms of American political culture and its preoccupations.

How striking are the differences from province to province? Simeon and Elkins claimed to obtain nearly identical results from the 1965, 1968 and 1974 data sets. However, in response to the efficacy measurement question, "People like me don't have any say about what the government does," 38 percent of the Newfoundland sample agreed with this statement in the 1965 survey and 38 percent of the British Columbia sample agreed with the identical statement in 1968.[15] In one swoop, this undermines the interpretation of significant provincial differences. The results vary so much from one survey to the next that they raise more questions about what "efficacy" questions indicate or measure. For example: the 38 percent of the Newfoundland sample in 1965 who agreed with this statement grew to 54 percent in the 1968 sample and to 67 percent in the 1974 sample. Conversely, in New Brunswick the pattern was the opposite: 73 percent of the sample agreed with the statement in 1965, 61 percent in 1968, and 51 percent in 1974. In Nova Scotia the drop was from 64 to 44 percent.[16] This undermines the interpretation of the persistence of differences over time. This yo-yo pattern is not compatible with the enduring and relatively stable nature of culture. With respect to trust in government, Simeon and Elkins depict Newfoundland as a disaffected province, yet more of its respondents were in the "high trust" category than in any other province. Simeon and Elkins found [it] "puzzling" that levels of political activity in the Atlantic provinces were the same as elsewhere in the country. In the light of their findings on trust and efficacy, they expected lower levels of political activity in a disaffected Atlantic region. One indicator of political activity was reported voter turnout. Ironically, had the actual turnout for Newfoundland

(57 percent in 1974) been consulted, rather than the reported turnout (80 percent), the findings would have been more consistent with the expectations.

In contrast to Simeon and Elkins's findings, other researchers (including a principal investigator of the 1974 study) using the same data have concluded "that the cultural orientations of Canadians, regardless of province of residence, are more notable for their similarities than their differences." The extent to which variations exist "frequently can be better explained by socioeconomic and demographic factors than by provincial residency."[17] Simeon and Elkins controlled for socioeconomic and demographic factors and found that provincial differences existed independent of them. Once again: contradictory interpretations of the same data.

One reason for these different interpretrations may be that some of the sample sizes are very small, too small to be of much interest statistically. Can one base meaningful interpretations on them? The 1968 Newfoundland sample was 48 respondents; New Brunswick's was 76. The socioeconomic and demographic factors being controlled for are even smaller: there were fewer than five cases of members of the combined "upper" and "upper middle class" in the Newfoundland, New Brunswick, Manitoba or Saskatchewan samples.[18] Nevertheless, the data generated by these small samples have attained high stature. One comparative analysis of Atlantic Canadian political culture contrasts the "hard" data provided by the National Election Studies to the "soft" data provided by historical analysis.

The criticisms in this paper are more fundamental than a call for refinements and improvements in survey methodology. One could prescribe corrective procedures that might include using pre-election surveys with post-election surveys, comparing survey results with actual behaviour, improving the questions, and constructing larger and more representative provincial samples. Such prescriptions, however, dwell on mechanics when our primary concern is meaning. Opinion formation and opinion change are highly complex subjects. Surveys are but one imperfect tool in understanding them. Surveys are useful and may help us understand how ordinary citizens think about politics, but we should never lose sight of the limitations of surveys, no matter how refined the technology. A self-professed objective of survey-based voting studies is to formulate meaningful and reliable interpretations of political behaviour. Scientifically significant interpretations require high levels of abstraction and generalization. What significant interpretations of political behaviour have the National Election Studies actually provided? The concluding sentences of the abridged edition of *Political Choice*, written during the Clark Conservative interregnum of 1979, note then current comments by pundits on the "death of the Liberal party" and "a generation of Conservative governments." "We cannot state categorically," write the principal investigators just months before the Liberal victory of 1980, "that they [the pundits] are wrong."[19] What, then, can they state categorically? What concluding statement do the investigators offer based on their massive, intensive, expensive voting study? "For much of the Canadian electorate, the vote decision is a matter of political choice."[20] This is tautological.

The survey researcher is explicitly interested in research methodology. No one, therefore, should be more familiar with the flaws and limitations of surveys. The survey researcher must be candid about discrepancies in the data, about questionable and mistaken analyses, and about mishaps in research design. Unfortunately, to justify an expensive research effort, the survey researcher may feel pressured to "massage the data," to squeeze positive findings—even startling new laws of behaviour—from weak correlations, small numbers, and ambiguous questions. We are learning together, survey researchers and non-survey researchers alike, that voting, which on the surface is so straightforward, is actually a complex overdetermined activity. We may pretend we have explained why people vote the way they do. But the hard evidence to date, if the National Election Studies are to serve as a reference point, is meagre. We have learned how little we know.

NOTES

1. Hugh Whalen, "The Rewards and Perils of Polling," in Paul Fox, ed., *Politics: Canada*, 5th ed. (Toronto: McGraw-Hill Ryerson, 1982), pp. 234–35.
2. Harold D. Clarke, Jane Jenson, Lawrence LeDuc and Jon H. Pammett, *Political Choice in Canada* (Toronto: McGraw-Hill Ryerson, 1979).
3. Michael S. Whittington and Glen Williams, eds., *Canadian Politics in the 1980s*, 2nd ed. (Toronto: Methuen, 1984), p. 286.
4. Clarke et al., *Political Choice*, p. 359. The actual vote for 1974, as opposed to the reported vote, appears in two tables (Table 4.1 pp. 96–7 and Table 12.1 p. 358) of the 136 tables and 27 figures provided in *Political Choice*. The authors do not explain the inconsistency between these two tables and their other tables.
5. Clarke et al., *Political Choice*, pp. 361, 364.
6. Stuart Oskamp, *Attitudes and Opinions* (Englewood Cliffs, N.J.: Prentice-Hall, 1977), pp. 83–84.
7. Clark et al., *Political Choice*, pp. 137–38.
8. Jane Jenson, "Party Systems," in David J. Bellamy et al., eds., *The Provincial Political Systems* (Toronto: Methuen, 1976), ch. 9.
9. Clarke et al., *Political Choice*, p. 64.
10. Gabriel Almond and Sidney Verba, *The Civic Culture* (Princeton: Princeton University Press, 1963).
11. Richard Simeon and David J. Elkins, "Provincial Political Cultures in Canada," in David J. Elkins and Richard Simeon, *Small Worlds* (Toronto: Methuen, 1980), ch. 2.
12. Clarke et al., *Political Choice*, p. 40.

13. Simeon and Elkins, p. 40.
14. Seymour Martin Lipset and William Schneider, *The Confidence Gap* (New York: Free Press, 1983), Figure 1-1, p. 17.
15. Simeon and Elkins, Table 3, p. 41.
16. Ibid.
17. Allan Kornberg, William Mishler, and H.D. Clarke, *Representative Democracy in the Canadian Provinces* (Scarborough, Ont.: Prentice-Hall, 1982), p. 88.
18. Simeon and Elkins, Table 11, p. 53.
19. Clarke et al., *Political Choice*, abridged ed. (Toronto: McGraw-Hill Ryerson, 1980), p. 274.
20. Ibid., unabridged ed., p. 393.

FURTHER READINGS

Clarke, H.D., *et al. Political Choice in Canada.* Toronto: McGraw-Hill Ryerson, 1979.

Clarke, H.D., *et al. Absent Mandate: The Politics of Discontent in Canada.* Toronto: Gage, 1984.

Courtney, J.C., *Voting in Canada.* Toronto: Prentice-Hall, 1967.

Pammett, J.H. "Elections." In M. Whittington and G. Williams, *Canadian Politics in the 1980s.* 2nd ed., 271–286. Toronto: Methuen, 1984.

19

Interest Groups in
the Canadian Federal System

Hugh G. Thorburn

Policy making in Canadian government is dominated by two separate processes of consultation and negotiation: one between private interest groups and individual governments, and a second between governments themselves— federal to provincial and, less frequently, provincial to provincial. . . .

THE DYNAMIC OF
INTEREST GROUP CONSULTATION

Canada had its beginnings in a situation of close relationships between private interest groups and the colonial governments. In the United Province of Canada, before Confederation, commercial capitalist interests sponsored the development of railways and canals, which formed the infrastructure for the developing colony. A desire to expand the horizons of the colonies west into the Prairies and east to the Maritimes, combined with fear of the United States after the Civil War, were major incentives for the enlargement of the colonies into the new Dominion of Canada via Confederation. Representatives for such interests as the major banks, railways, shipping interests and trading companies had, from the very beginning, ongoing relations with the governments in British North America. Policy making was shared between these people and the elected politicians sitting in the cabinets of Canada and the provinces. Therefore, the pattern of what was later known as elite accommodation, or pressure group politics, was a thriving arrangement from the very beginnings of Canada's history as a nation. Governments were closely involved in the financing and planning of railways and other major projects of development. Connections were forged between these capitalist interests and the political party leaders of Canada, and through them with the governments, provincial and federal. Such well known events as the Pacific Scandal in the 1870s bear witness to the close collaborative or patronage arrangements that existed at that time.

Abridged from Hugh G. Thorburn, *Interest Groups in the Canadian Federal System* (volume 69 of the Research Studies for the Royal Commission on the Economic Union and Development Prospects for Canada), 3-15. Reprinted by permission of the University of Toronto Press. Only selected footnotes appear in the essay.

With the passage of time, the relatively informal personal relations that developed between leading politicians and their higher civil servants, on the one hand, and the business leaders, on the other, hardened into a more bureaucratic relationship. As governments built up larger administrative structures in order to deliver services to the community, interest groups in the areas of activity that were closest in relation to these governmental initiatives were called into being. Close clientele relations developed between individual departments of government and the communities they served, typified by the close collaboration existing between the Canadian Federation of Agriculture and the federal and provincial departments of agriculture. Similar relationships developed in other major sectors, such as forestry, mining and secondary manufacturing. Policies relating to the support of these industries and their protection through tariffs and import regulations of various kinds were elaborated through consultation by government representatives with the spokesmen for these substantial interests. Relations with other major concentrations of capital in such institutions as the banks, insurance companies, railways and grain trading companies were established with governments in order to influence policy as it affected individual private concerns.

Businesses saw the advantage of organizing associations, permitting them to collaborate in their consultation with governments. Permanent organizations with specialist staff were built up to carry on liaison with government in the most propitious manner possible.

These representations were carried on not only with government leaders, such as ministers and their senior civil service associates, but also extended to committees of Parliament and the provincial legislatures and often involved representations to private members of Parliament, both on government and opposition sides. It was generally conceded that the groups had a right to be heard before policy affecting them was finalized by either order of government, provincial or federal.

Communities of interest developed, composed of politicians, bureaucrats and interest group representatives organized along functional lines. Associations, some pan-Canadian, some regional or local, each devoted to advancing the substantive concerns of its members, worked together where their interests coincided, and in opposition to one another when they diverged. Their concern was to influence policy along with other matters: legislation, the formulation of regulations, day-to-day administration and the general attitudes of government. Government came to rely for information upon these groups as a major input in the policy-making process. Their relationship, therefore, was not an adversarial one but one of collaboration in a common enterprise. The support of the groups could at times extend beyond the supply of information and advice to other considerations affecting the well-being of the political parties and personalities concerned.

The result was a kind of parallel process in government. On the one hand, there was the representative system which saw members of Parliament elected in their constituencies to sit in the legislative assemblies and hold the government responsible. While legislation was usually government initiated, the majority party would have to give its assent if it was to be enacted. The opposition soon developed the habit of systematic criticism of and at times obstruction to these initiatives. The dynamics of the system involved a continuous campaign by the opposition to show up the inadequacies of the government, and a corresponding attempt by government members, under cabinet leadership, to show up the opposition as incompetent, irresponsible and ill-informed. The electors were called upon at fairly regular intervals of about four years to decide which side would form the government in the ensuing period.

Parallel to this was the government to private interest relationship, which was much less widely known but was nonetheless important. Through this arrangement, advice, supplemented by at times considerable pressure, was focussed upon the government to induce it to adopt the policies favoured by individual groups. The government, therefore, was subjected to these two processes of advice and pressure, and it had to make its way between them. At times the representations would be parallel and consistent; at other times they would go in two or more directions, and the government would either have to reconcile the various positions in some kind of compromise or make hard choices between them. The task of the government then was a more difficult and complex one than appeared to the casual eye of the citizen, who was much more aware of the representative, official structures than of the more informal and less conspicuous interest group process.

Interest groups began to receive serious scholarly attention in the mid-1960s, and since that time the body of interest group literature has grown. Most of this work, however, is made up of case studies, with very little theoretical work to support it.

Most definitions of interest groups stress the link between a socially based interest and the attempt to influence public policy. David Truman's oft-cited definition saw interest groups as a "shared attitude group that makes certain claims through or upon other groups in society. . . . If and when it makes its claims through or upon any of the institutions of government, it becomes a political interest group."[1] A more useful definition for analytical purposes is provided by A. Paul Pross: "Interest groups are organizations whose members act together to influence public policy in order to promote their common interest."[2]

The major concern of political scientists has been with the extent of these groups' influence over government policy making. This "communication function" is determined by the structure of the group, the functioning of the group and its access to government. Structure refers to the degree of organizational sophistication. A group that is highly institutionalized will possess the resources to establish a permanent staff that can seek to influence government on a continual basis and offer advice on a wide variety of issues.

On the other hand, groups with only loose and volatile structures are more likely to have to resort to public confrontational approaches. This is the case especially for issue-oriented groups. This approach helps to compensate for small and fluctuating memberships.

Interest groups provide a forum where their members can compare and exchange information about common problems and about the effects of proposed government action or changing social conditions. Shared attitudes emerge about the suitability of various government actions and the need to influence government in these directions. Finally, a precondition of influence is the communication of these shared attitudes to the appropriate decision makers. Therefore, securing access is a vital part of exercising influence on government. Access can occur at a number of points in the political system: the bureaucracy, the cabinet, members of Parliament, and officials of political parties. Not all access points are valued equally, but groups will try to maintain as many contacts as their resources will allow.

Access alone will not ensure that a group will be successful in influencing government. The communication of group concerns is of little impact unless decision makers can be induced to accept the interest group recommendations and support them. For their part, governments have two primary interests in pressure groups. They value the information that groups are able to provide, and they seek out the legitimacy that interest group support can give to their policies. Continued access to the centre of power depends on the degree to which a group can fulfill these needs reliably and well. The size of the membership, the control of financial resources, the monopoly of technical knowledge, the prestige of the groups' leaders and the willingness of the group to cooperate and avoid outright confrontation are important elements in gaining recognized status within government. David Kwavnick observes that within the labour movement, the competition for recognition from government is at least as important to the major labour unions in Canada as defending the immediate interests of their members. This process has led some analysts to conclude that groups closely involved with government eventually become dependent on the state:

> Group involvement in the policy discussions not only expands the range of information available to government—it can be used to neutralize group objections to proposed legislation and to engate support for it. Government thus finds in the pressure group system a device for testing policy proposals and a means of eliciting support for them.[3]

This close relationship, according to Pross, can enhance the position of cooperative groups since they are guaranteed a measure of collaborative influence over policy decisions that affect their interests, but the groups must be willing to accept short-term defeats for continuing favourable relations in the long run. Appeals to Parliament, especially the opposition, or to the public at large, could jeopardize their privileged position with government. This arrangement may also serve the important function of keeping the political system abreast of changes within the social system, thereby promoting political stability:

> The successful performance of this last function, however, will depend on the sensitivity of the governmental and pressure group sub-systems to changes in their own immediate environments. Closed and captive agencies and groups through their failure to absorb external demands, may compound rigidities existing elsewhere in the system.[4]

Pross offers a useful conceptual approach to understanding the role of interest groups in the political system. He ranges them on a continuum from institutionalized groups to issue-oriented ones. The underlying assumption of this approach is that "the organizational characteristics of a given group may have a great deal to do with the extent to which it performs recognized functions." His model incorporates the interrelationship between the structure and functioning of a group.

Institutional groups are:

> Groups that possess organizational continuity and cohesion, commensurate human and financial resources, extensive knowledge of those sectors of government that affect them and their clients, stable memberships, concrete and immediate operational objectives that are broad enough to permit each group to bargain with government over the application of specific legislation or the achievement of particular concessions, and a willingness to put organizational imperatives ahead of any particular policy concerns.[5]

Issued-oriented groups, as one would expect, have the reverse characteristics:

> Groups whose primary orientation is to issues, rather than to organizational continuity and cohesion; minimal and often naïve knowledge of government; fluid membership; a tendency to encounter difficulty in formulating and adhering to short-range objectives; a generally low regard for the organizational mechanisms they have developed for carrying out their goals; and, most important, a narrowly defined purpose, usually the resolution of one or two issues or problems, that inhibits the development of "selective inducements" designed to broaden the group's membership base.[6]

The implication of this approach is that the

> . . . capacity to act in pressure group politics is determined by the interaction of large-scale political forces and the internal characteristics of individual groups. That is, the nature of the policy process in a given political system, its political culture, power structure, and so on define the general conditions of pressure group behaviour, but the actions of a specific group depends on the group's capacity to utilize internal resources.[7]

The advantage of the organizational base model is that it allows us to compare how different groups respond to different environments and to relate this behaviour to the structures and process of the policy system. At the theoretical level, the model shows that institutionalized groups have the financial and human resources necessary to participate in a system that encourages sustained collaboration between government agencies and their "recognized" client groups; on the other hand, issue-oriented groups can be effective in a competitive and open decision-making situation in which they can compensate for their insignificant size and lack of cohesion by rallying public opinion behind them. Their weak organizational base and narrow scope make them less valuable to governments as a steady and reliable source of information and legitimation, but they do serve an important warning function in any political system:

> In general systemic terms, issue-oriented groups enhance the adaptive capacity of the overall system, permitting a responsiveness to emergent issues that is not easily achieved by more cumbersome mechanisms of political communication. . . . Their chief advantage lies in their flexibility. Because they develop extremely quickly and are unencumbered by institutionalized structures, they are excellent vehicles for generating immediate public reaction to specific issues. Because their stake in the future is usually limited, they can indulge in forms of political communication that institutional groups are reluctant to use. This is particularly true in Canada where established groups tend not to resort to publicity for fear of disturbing relations with administrative agencies.[8]

In this sense, issue-oriented groups can act as a social barometer which forces decision makers to recognize the legitimacy of socially divisive issues that would otherwise be neglected. For example, the present increased political willingness to address the problem of drinking when driving is primarily due to the public concern generated by the efforts of the families of accident victims.

Pross's model can also be employed to analyze how the relationships between interest groups and government change over time. For example, a shift from a closed and secretive political system to one that is open and competitive would enhance the organizational advantages of issue-oriented groups. This, in fact, appears to be happening in Canada (as well as other Western countries) since the 1970s.

Prior to 1975, writing on Canadian pressure group politics demonstrates a general acceptance of the elite accommodation model as an accurate and complete description of pressure group behaviour. Essentially, this model posits a system of mutual accommodation between government and interest groups, in which social and economic elites alone determine the interest of society in informal, secretive, face-to-face contact between the upper echelons of government (ministers and their bureaucracies) and interest groups. Robert Presthus describes the Canadian political process as one in which "political leaders, including the senior bureaucracy, could and did define and seek the public interest without much need for explanation of their actions or for participation by the general public." Pross attributes this situation to two main factors: (1) the closed, hierarchical nature of Canadian political structures, especially the bureaucracy and the party system; and (2) the limited extent to which the Canadian political system is based on a pluralistic, competitive approach to decision making:

> Some competition exists, of course—intergovernment rivalry arises out of the current exercise of power or the unclear definitions of jurisdiction—but within each government there is relatively little of the functional rivalry which typifies inter-agency competition in the United States. Similarly, the fact that the executive operates within a cabinet and parliamentary system of government means that rivalries between legislators cannot be readily exploited.[9]

As a result, access to key decision makers has played a more important role in interest group activity than popularizing issues:

> The Canadian political system, then, tends to favour elite groups, making functional accommodative, consensus-seeking techniques of political communication, rather than conflict-oriented techniques that are directed towards the achievement of objectives through arousing public opinion.[10]

Obviously, such a system of decision making strongly favours institutionalized groups over issue-oriented ones. Presthus outlines the most significant features of elite accommodation: (1) a built-in disposition toward support of the status quo because it restricts meaningful participation to established groups with a direct substantive interest in the process; (2) the tendency to define problems as essentially technical with the implication that political considerations are illegitimate and certainly divisive (the result is the uncoordinated incremental expansion of governmental and private programs without adequate direction by government); and (3) the crystallization of existing patterns of resource allocation, "which makes the introduction of new scientific, technical and economic directions difficult as they strike against established influence structures, based largely on long-standing, functionally determined, agency-clientele relationships."[11]

James Gillies argues that a relationship of mutual accommodation, where business and government worked together to plan the economy, was facilitated during the 1940s, 1950s and 1960s by their shared belief in how the goals of society (i.e., economic growth and prosperity) could be achieved. Since World War II, the issue-by-issue approach has been the most frequent strategy used by business to influence government. This approach is one in which:

> . . . business reacts to individual initiatives of the government as those initiatives are introduced. The ones that are perceived to be detrimental to the corporation or an industry—and the public interest—are opposed. It implies no grand strategy; it is simply, as it states, an approach that calls for dealing with issues as they develop.[12]

This approach rests on three major assumptions: first, that a close interrelationship with the bureaucracy, the executive and the legislature is the most effective means of influencing government and preventing the formulation of policies that are hostile to the interests of business:

> Indeed, trade association officials stress that one of their major duties is to keep close to the members of the bureaucracy so that they may spot the early evolution of ideas and inform their members about any developments that may influence their activities.[13]

Second, it assumes policy flows from the bottom up and that the transmission of appropriate and useful information will stop an inappropriate policy from being enacted. Finally, it assumes that government accords business a special, privileged position over other interests, and therefore that the exercise of persuasion is a sufficient instrument for achieving its policy goals.

During the 1940s and 1950s, elite accommodation was facilitated by the growth of the bureaucratic state. Politicians took an incremental approach to the expansion of government activity after the Second World War; so responsibility for the planning and implementation of the massive intervention of the state was mainly left to the experts within the line departments. Government expansion occurred in an incremental, uncoordinated fashion, as each of the government agencies distributed resources according to its own professional norms. Therefore, the most important groups during this period were special interest groups whose concerns corresponded to the functions of separate government agencies. The special interest groups could offer officials the expertise and information necessary for the development of policy initiatives in return for policy input. Because most shared the same professional values as the government officials, cosy "clientele" relationships developed, where groups and government officials mutually agreed upon the appropriate form of action.

Despite this fundamental change in the role of the state in society, the policy-making structures of government remained relatively uncomplicated and informal:

> There were no committees of cabinet, except for the Treasury Board which was established by statute, and individual ministers operated in a highly independent manner. Any coordination that had to be undertaken was handled by deputy ministers in a very informal fashion and in those days of less complex government, the system worked effectively. Individual ministers were powerful and ran the departments without advice, let alone interference from anyone.[14]

Strong ministers such as C.D. Howe worked with their constituencies (in Howe's case the industrial community) and developed policies in collaboration with the groups and, it was assumed, in the interests of the country. No conflict was perceived between the private and the public interest. However, by the end of the 1960s, broad social changes and the continued growth of government led to a fundamental rebuilding of the policy-making structures at the federal level and in some of the provinces.

Pross cites three factors as the source of the emergent pattern in which institutionalized groups are "exposed to heightened public scrutiny and are more dependent on public opinion": (1) changes in the government policy-making structure designed to bring about central control over policy making; (2) the proliferation of interest groups, especially citizens' groups, in response to the growth of government and the increased exposure of the activities of institutionalized groups; and (3) the advent of television, which allowed groups to mobilize public support for their cause.

Changes in the policy making structure began on a small scale in the early 1960s as governments became dissatisfied with the lack of political control over the growth of their expenditures and activities. However, the major restructuring of the system came after 1968, when Prime Minister Trudeau introduced a centralized cabinet committee system as a means of directing policy making within the cabinet as a whole. Hugh Faulkner observes that these structural changes give the appearance that ultimate power is highly concentrated within the policy process when, in practice, it is highly dispersed. One reason for this is that policy making from its earliest stages now involves coordination between a number of departments:

> The new policy and expenditure management system . . . ensures that ministers must process any initiative that involves expenditures (which includes tax expenditures) through their cabinet colleagues. This process integrates policy decisions into the government priorities framework, tightens up decision-making by juxtaposing policy options and expenditures and strengthens the pattern of collegial authority over policy development and expenditure management. The effect is to limit the capacity of an individual minister to respond to interest groups. To take an initiative in one area means that another area is going to be affected. Trade-offs will be required, so that the other area has to be massaged as well. Consequently, interest groups must now be prepared to deal with the whole range of cabinet, including the cabinet committees, the membership of which has only recently become public information.[15]

This, of course, spreads a group's resources even thinner than before, as more contacts are necessary to petition government effectively.

The problem for groups is compounded because the federal example was followed at the provincial level. Ontario and Quebec adopted the same type of committee structure a few years later, and the other provinces too made similar adjustments in their structures.

Perhaps more important than the cabinet committee system itself has been the concomitant growth and development of central agencies. The Privy Council Office and its close affiliate, the Federal-Provincial Relations Office, have become crucial to the policy-making process, having assumed responsibility for advising cabinet on the integration of policy recommendations into the general framework of government objectives. Gillies and Pigott argue that the shift in influence from departments to the central agencies of government has seriously affected the ability of established groups to penetrate the decision-making process. Despite the important policy-making role played by the Privy Council Office, its officials "simply do not see their function as dealing with individual legislative thrusts, but as coordinating various inputs into the policy-making process." While the traditional channels of involvement are no longer adequate:

> . . . special interests do not have a satisfactory method of inserting their input into the determination of the public interest in anything like as meaningful a fashion as was once the case.[16]

Finally, the increased complexity of the policy-making process, due to the increasing speed and unpredictability of social and technological change, has meant that government has had to try to improve its mechanisms for interest group involvement and employ new techniques to facilitate the process. Since the 1970s, there has been a formalization of consultative devices, as the government attempted to augment its information coming from society to adapt to changing conditions. One such development was the increase in the use of white papers. Audrey D. Doerr observes that since the advent of the Trudeau administration, the white paper has been used by the federal government "to promote and stimulate broad public debate among interested groups and individuals, so that the government can receive direction from those people who will be most affected by the policies." However, she notes that examples of public responses, by and large, represent the articulate and financially well-endowed sectors of the community which have an enhanced capacity to participate and perceive a sense of efficacy in participation. Government has addressed this problem of underrepresentation with some success through financial assistance to groups with limited resources, such as welfare groups and consumer associations. The formalization of the process has had the twin advantages of opening-up the process to anyone determined enough to participate and, exposing who the vested interests are in a given policy area by making them operate through public structures.

This development of central agencies has been paralleled by similar arrangements at the provincial level, especially in Quebec and Ontario. Also, coloured papers (white papers, green papers, etc.) have been employed at that level to facilitate public discussion of policy issues with groups. This has, of course, greatly added to the burden of groups, just as it has increased their opportunities—opportunities more easily exploited by the larger and richer institutionalized groups.

A larger problem cited by Doerr is the lack of appropriate machinery to conduct debates with the general public. One promising step taken recently to improve this situation was the appointment of seven special parliamentary committees, or parliamentary task forces, which travelled the country providing early access to government policy proposals for the public, special interest groups and Parliament. Hugh Faulkner claims that the crucial issue in dealing with government overload is the absence of a legitimate process for defining the public interest in an ongoing manner, not the excessive control of big business. He considers the introduction of the parliamentary task force mechanism the most progressive change to date.

A major consequence of these changes in consultative mechanisms is that groups are now expected to prepare formal presentations and to formulate detailed recommendations in a form that allows the government to compare the demands relating to government priorities of one group with those of another. All groups and individuals are now on a more equal footing in that greater emphasis is placed on the quality of group management, rather than on size or economic resources. This enhances the opportunities for smaller groups and individuals to participate in the policy-making process. As Faulkner, an ex-federal cabinet minister, has observed:

> . . . one of the ironies of the contemporary pressure group scene is that the influential interest groups today seem to be less satisfied with the results of their efforts than some of the less powerful.[17]

The combined impact of the insularity of the Privy Council Office and the need for agencies and their associated interest groups to compete for scarce resources through open structures has forced institutionalized groups into the public arena and increased the public awareness of their activities. As a consequence, there has been a proliferation of citizens' groups established to counter the demands of vested interests. This has been expecially true in those sections of the community that previously had no means of organization:

> . . . both agencies and groups discovered that by going public they have alerted other interests to the nature of the debates that are in progress and so have encouraged their participation and perhaps the formation of new groups.[18]

In many cases, the formation of these groups has been facilitated by government funding.

In 1981 the Institute of Public Administration held a seminar on interest groups and government. As *rapporteur*, Paul Pross outlined the two schools of thought into which explanations for the proliferation of groups fall. There are those who support general environmental explanations, and those who argue that the expansion of group activities constitutes a "reactive spiral." The latter claim that the development of relations between groups and government has occurred incrementally and disjointedly and, in the process, has expanded both state activity and the constellation of formal groups which surround the state. Khayyam Paltiel, as reported by Pross, argued that:

> . . . the state itself is progenitor and prime mover in both the fostering of intervention and the formation of groups. Étatisme . . . is inspired from within the machinery of government, but must be buttressed and made legitimate by individuals and groups who are part of the general public. Hence the emergence

of bureaucratic patronage and the fostering of supportive groups—to which other groups respond from a more traditional, individualistic ideological base.[19]

Others attribute an active role to the state but steer clear of the *dirigiste* tendencies of Paltiel's explanation. Here the state is seen as fostering group activity in response to the public's expectation that certain groups should not be excluded from the process, rather than as a means of promoting support for its own initiatives. Women's groups and native groups, for example, are said to have been sponsored because government needed to hear from these sectors of the community before determining its policies.

These explanations are in many ways compatible with the environmentalist argument, which also views the proliferation of groups as an incremental response to both state activity and involvement of other pressure groups. The crucial difference is that environmentalists claim that the elaboration of government-group relations is not merely an extension of past relations but represents a fundamental change of the Canadian state into what is called the *dirigiste* state. Dominique Clift, in the same seminar, asserted that the Canadian state, now dominated by a "dynamic" public sector, co-opts what elements of the public it can and destroys those that oppose it. Clift describes it as a state in which "the kind of consensus that guides contemporary society comes not from the people, but is sponsored by the state itself."

Paltiel's moderately *dirigiste* argument seems particularly persuasive. The need for government to deal with increasingly rapid and complex social change appears to have outdistanced the capacity of existing consultative mechanisms. As a result, there has been a tendency for such devices to become political tools for building the necessary support for decisions that have already been made by government. This is not entirely manipulative, for government may not always get the support it is looking for. However, as Doerr suggests, society will have to learn quickly if it is to participate meaningfully in policy formulation in the future.

A third factor that has influenced the environment within which pressure groups must now operate is the social impact of television. Television solved the problem of communication between interest groups and people in densely populated areas and gave groups the opportunity to mobilize a more general public reaction to political issues. Issue-oriented groups have benefited most from this development; they have been able to compensate for their small and loosely organized membership by attracting public support. In fact, television can destabilize the position of established groups, which have always been able to rely for their strength on their firmly grounded status. Now established groups are compelled to cater to public opinion, as well as to the views of their membership in couching their demands. For example, Paul Pross commented:

A.E. Diamond, president of the Canadian Institute of Public Real Estate Companies, recently offered an illustration of this process when he asserted that the CIPREC must "make the public more aware of the difficulties faced by developers" in order to challenge the power that various pressure groups have captured over the development process.[20]

While television can focus public attention on an issue, it cannot act as a source of detailed demands. The complexity of most public policy and the resources needed to monitor the process mean that institutionalized groups are still in a better position to participate effectively in the complex structures of policy making. However, as indicated above, even institutionalized groups are experiencing great difficulty influencing government. Overall, a consequence of the recent changes in the policy-making environment of pressure groups seems to be an opening up of the process to greater public debate, though this has not necessarily been translated into policy outputs. There is reason to believe that this increased group activity masks the greater autonomy of the state to decide the course of government action.

NOTES

1. D. Truman, *The Governmental Process* (New York: Knopf, 1951), 37.
2. A.P. Pross, "Pressure Groups: Adaptive Instruments of Political Communication," in Pross, ed., *Pressure Group Behaviour in Canadian Politics* (Toronto: McGraw-Hill Ryerson, 1975), 2.
3. Ibid., 6.
4. Ibid., 7.
5. A.P. Pross, "Pressure Groups," In D.J. Bellamy, J.H. Pammett, and D. Rowat, eds., *The Provincial Political Systems* (Toronto: Methuen, 1976), 133.
6. Ibid.
7. Ibid.
8. Pross, "Pressure Groups: Adaptive Instruments of Political Communication," op. cit., 12.
9. Ibid., 18-19.
10. Ibid., 19.
11. R. Presthus, *Elite Accommodation in Canadian Politics* (Toronto: Macmillan, 1975), 351.
12. J. Gillies, *Where Business Fails: Business-Government Relations at the Federal Level in Canada* (Montreal: Institute for Research on Public Policy, 1981, 48.
13. Ibid.
14. J. Gillies, and J. Pigott, "Participation in the Legislative Process," *Canadian Public Administration* 25 (1982): 261.
15. J.H. Faulkner, "Pressuring the Executive," *Canadian Public Administration* 25 (1982): 243.
16. Gillies and Pigott, op. cit.: 263.

17. Faulkner, op. cit. 245.
18. A.P. Pross, "Governing Under Pressure: The Special Interest Groups," *Canadian Public Administration* 25 (1982): 177.
19. Ibid., 172.
20. A.P. Pross, "Canadian Pressure Groups in the 1970s: Their Role and Their Relations with the Public Service," *Canadian Public Administration* (1975): 127.

FURTHER READINGS

Gillies, J. *Where Business Fails: Business-Government Relations at the Federal Level in Canada.* Montreal: Institute for Research on Public Policy, 1981.

Pross, P. "Pressure Groups: Talking Chameleons." In M. Whittington and G. Williams, *Canadian Politics in the 1980s.* 2nd ed., 287–311. Toronto: Methuen, 1984.

———. ed. *Pressure Group Behaviour in Canadian Politics.* Toronto: McGraw-Hill Ryerson, 1975.

———. *Group Politics and Public Policy.* Toronto: Oxford University Press, 1986.

Rea, K.J., and N. Wiseman. *Government and Enterprise in Canada*, Part 6. Toronto: Methuen, 1985.

Research Branch, Library of Parliament, Ottawa. "Pressure Groups in Canada." *The Parliamentarian* 51, 1 (January, 1970): 11–20.

Stanbury, W.T. "Lobbying and Interest Group Representation in the Legislative Process." In W. Neilson and J.C. MacPherson, eds. *The Legislative Process in Canada: The Need for Reform*, 167–207. Montreal: Institute for Research on Public Policy, 1978.

———. *Business-Government Relations in Canada*, Chapters 7, 8, 9. Toronto: Methuen, 1986.

Thompson, F., and W.T. Stanbury. *The Political Economy of Interest Groups in the Legislative Process in Canada.* Toronto: Butterworths, 1979.

PART 4

GOVERNMENT AND POWER

Who governs? One of the oldest questions in the study of politics. Aristotle developed a famous typology purporting to explain who really governed in different kinds of polity, and we continue to explore the question to this day. Of course, the question is misleading if we think that we can actually identify a single individual or institution that holds all power and makes every decision. Even the most important officeholders are severely limited in their capacity to act on their own. We live in a "polyarchy," to use Dahl's term, and power and decision-making capacity are very widely dispersed in modern, highly complex governments. In this Part the Readings deal with the place of various elements of the governmental order in the process of governing.

Reading 20 does not tackle this question directly, for Eugene Forsey's aim is to prove that minority government is neither exceptional, nor bad, nor transient. Since this paper first appeared, minority governments have been formed in Canada on three further occasions, and there is every reason to expect that this will happen again. Clearly, the existence of majority or minority government has large consequences in terms of how power is exercised in the Canadian system of responsible government, where the political executive must always maintain the confidence of a majority of the members of the House of Commons.

In Reading 21, Paul Thomas provides a sophisticated analysis of the House of Commons. This essay is a valuable corrective to the frequent claims that the House is nothing more than a rubber stamp and that its members are virtual automatons controlled by their leaders. Thomas lays great stress upon the crucial importance of party in understanding the behaviour of the House. The degree to which the House possesses influence, and the limits to that influence, can only be comprehended in terms of party. This paper was written at the end of 1984, just as the Special Committee on House of Commons Reform was being established. As a result of that Committee's recommendations, a number of major reforms have been implemented, especially with respect to committees, but the validity of Thomas' argument remains unimpaired.

For a long time, one of the most remarkable features of cabinet government in Canada was the lack of any formal procedures and support organization.

Although this began to change at the beginning of World War II, it was in the 1960s that some of the most important developments occurred, especially after Mr Trudeau became prime minister. The aims were various, but they included a strengthening of the principle of collective responsibility of cabinet, a curb upon bureaucratic power, and a more efficient and rational decision-making process. The result is that, today, Canada has the most structured central government machinery of any "Westminister" system.

In Reading 22, Gordon Robertson provides an explanation (with particular reference to the changes in the Privy Council Office) of these important developments. Because of his position as secretary to the cabinet at that time, Robertson was supremely qualified to write on this subject. Yet his paper is also instructive in that we are now aware that the expectations, particularly about improved decision making, proved to be overly sanguine. Moreover, and ironically, it is clear that these changes have considerably enhanced the power of senior officials in the central agencies.

The basic structures established in those years have been modified by subsequent prime ministers to suit their own needs and purposes, but the essential scheme remains intact. Reading 23, by Ian Clark, deals with the manner in which Prime Minister Mulroney organized the decision-making system, and the author provides, in addition, a valuable summary of previous developments. Since the article was written, further changes have been made (in the cabinet committee system, for example), as was to be expected. One important question raised by these changes, none of which have involved any formal constitutional amendments of course, is whether or not full cabinet remains at the centre of decision making.

One much-repeated theme in the past few decades is that the position of the prime minister has become so exalted vis-à-vis the other members of cabinet that it is now appropriate to talk of prime ministerial rather than cabinet government. This view is not particular to Canada. The excerpt from Patrick Weller's study (Reading 24) places this issue in comparative perspective and, as he writes, "allows us to get away from normative ideas of how prime ministers ought to behave."

The next Reading (25) deals with the world of the bureaucracy. In our system of government, the links between elected politicians and appointed public servants are very close, and it is clear that the senior members of the public service (and perhaps especially the "Superbureaucrats" in the central agencies) are highly influential. In this essay Kenneth Kernaghan examines the nature of bureaucratic power in the context of cabinet-parliamentary government. He shows how the traditional distinction between politics and policy, on the one hand, and administration, on the other, has been replaced by a more complex pattern of interdependence. In turn, this leads Professor Kernaghan to a reconsideration of the doctrine of the political neutrality of public servants.

The period since 1945 has been marked by the emergence of a complex network of intergovernmental relations. This has occurred, in part, because of the increasing interdependence of the two orders of government, but also because of the growing importance of provincial governments. Donald Smiley has coined the term "Executive Federalism" to describe this phenomenon, and another leading student of the subject, Richard Simeon, examines it in Reading 26. Any student of Canadian government today knows that the sometimes conflictual realm of intergovernmental relations must be seen as an important part of the decision-making process. Simeon explains why this is so and what the nature of the machinery of collaboration and co-ordination is; he provides, as well, an assessment of its efficacy. Once again, it is worth noting that these highly important developments have occurred without any formal constitutional change.

The judiciary forms a distinct branch of government and it may seem surprising that, in the past, Canadians have tended not to think of judges as policy makers at all. Perhaps the entrenchment of the Charter of Rights and Freedoms has now advanced general awareness of the great importance of the judiciary in this respect, but the role is by no means a new one. Peter Russell's analysis of the Supreme Court opinion in the *Anti-Inflation Reference* of 1976 (Reading 27) deals with the nature of judicial review of the distribution of legislative powers. Whilst this case study reveals the importance of judges as policy makers, it also points to the limitations of the process of judicial review in the context of Canadian federalism.

20

The Problem of
"Minority" Government in Canada

Eugene A. Forsey

During the election of April, 1963, Liberal speeches and editorials tended to depict minority government (that is, government by a cabinet with less than half the seats in the House of Commons) as a nameless, faceless horror, the political fate that is worse than death. The authors of these productions are now hard at work trying to prove themselves wrong. They may not find it easy. For they face three deeply rooted popular notions on the subject; indeed, it was precisely because these notions were so widespread and so deeply rooted that the appeal to vote for a winner proved so powerful.

The first is that minority governments are altogether exceptional, abnormal, almost unheard of, except, of course, among benighted continental Europeans and other "lesser breeds without the Law." This is simply not so. We have had relatively few minority governments, colonial, Dominion, or provincial, in Canada; but Britain, Australia, and New Zealand have had plenty. Britain, from 1834 to 1931, had sixteen, which held office for a total of thirty-two years out of the ninety-seven. In Australia, before federation, minority governments were the rule rather than the exception in New South Wales, South Australia, and Tasmania till the 1890s, and in Victoria till the 1880s (New South Wales often had three or four governments in a single Parliament, South Australia four or five), and there have been plenty of minority governments in the states since federation. The Commonwealth itself had nothing but minority governments (six of them) from its inception till 1909, and another as recently as 1941-43. Minority governments were the rule also in New Zealand till the 1890s (one Parliament saw six governments). So it can scarcely be maintained, rationally, that minority government is something monstrous and unnatural, foreign to the whole spirit of British parliamentary institutions.

Indeed, it is the relative rarity of minority governments in Canada that is exceptional. Even if we go back to the very beginnings of responsible government in British North America, we have had only about half-a-dozen

Abridged from Eugene Forsey, "The Problem of 'Minority' Government in Canada," *Canadian Journal of Economics and Political Science* 30, No. 1 (February 1964), 1-11. Reprinted by permission of the author and The Canadian Political Science Association.

in the provinces (pre-Confederation or post-), and only four in the Dominion.
. . . Only . . . three of these [in the provinces] were what might be called
"normal" minority governments, resulting from elections in which no party
got a clear majority; the other three were freaks.

All four Dominion minority governments have been "normal," in this
sense: they have been the result of elections in which no party got a clear
majority. The first of them, King's first administration from December 29,
1921, to June 28, 1926, led, in this respect, an "off-again, on-again, out-again,
in-again, gone-again, Finnegan" life. From December 29, 1921, to December
1922, it was a minority government, with 117 seats out of 235. Then two
Progressives crossed the floor, to give it 119. From December 1922 to December
1923, therefore, it was a majority government. Then it lost two seats in by-
elections, which cut its strength back to 117 again. So from December 1923,
to November 1924 it was a minority government again. Then it gained a seat
in a by-election, which brought it up to 118. So from November 1924 to October
29, 1925, it was once more a majority government. Then the general election
gave it only 101 seats out of 245. So from October 29, 1925, to June 28, 1926,
it was a minority government once again. The second minority Dominion
government was Meighen's, which held office from June 29 to September 25,
1926. During the three days when it faced Parliament, it had 115 seats out
of 245, Meighen having automatically vacated his seat (under the law as it
stood till 1931) on accepting the salaried office of prime minister. The third
of these governments was Mr. Diefenbaker's, which held office from June 21,
1957 to April 22, 1963. It began as a minority government, with 112 seats
out of 265. Then, on March 31, 1958, the general election made it a majority
government, with 208 seats;and so it continued (with from 203 to 209 seats)
until the general election of June 18, 1962, cut its strength to 116 and made
it a minority government again, as it remained till it left office (the general
election of April 8, 1963, having reduced its seats to 95). The fourth minority
Dominion government is, of course, Mr. Pearson's present administration, with
129 seats out of 265.

Of these four governments, King's, in 1923 and 1924, was "minority" in
hardly more than form. True, it had only 117 Liberals, one less than a clear
majority. But of the rest of the Chamber, some sixty-odd were "Progressives,"
who were easy marks for King's blandishments. Most of them were ex-Liberals;
some of them abhorred the very name of "party" as the Devil . . . ; nearly
all were political innocents, and independent to the point where leader and
chief whip voted against each other. At the end of that Parliament, King could,
with truth, say that it would go down in history as "the Parliament of large
majorities."

So, for practical purposes, we have had three provincial minority governments, none of them holding office for as much as two years, and four
Dominion, three of them holding office for less than a year and the fourth
having only just taken its place on the Treasury benches. It is hardly surprising

that the Canadian public, for the most part totally unaware of the long history of minority government elsewhere in the Commonwealth, considers it exceptional and abnormal. But, plainly, it is not; and we may be entering on a period when it will become as much a commonplace here as it has often been in Britain, Australia, and New Zealand.

The second popular Canadian notion about minority government is that it is necessarily bad: incompetent, weak, indecisive, if not worse. The minority governments of Palmerston, Disraeli, Salisbury, Gladstone, and Asquith, whatever else they may have been, were certainly not incompetent, weak, or indecisive. Nor were our provincial minority governments. I know too little about Australian and New Zealand history to say how far any of those adjectives could justly be applied to any of the scores of minority governments which administered their affairs over many decades; but, obviously, neither Australia nor New Zealand, during their long periods of minority government, fell "through hideous ruin and combustion down/To bottomless perdition." On the contrary, they seem to have survived remarkably well.

Nor is this altogether surprising. "Depend upon it," said Dr. Johnson, "when a man knows he is to be hanged in a fortnight, it concentrates his mind wonderfully." When a government knows it may be hanged in a fortnight, the knowledge may broaden its mind wonderfully. Having to get support from outside its own party may not only help a government to do good and sensible things but also prevent it from doing bad and foolish things. This, as King once pointed out, is just as important, and may even be more so. The idea that "doing something" is always good, doing nothing always bad, that action is always better than inaction, is a strange, but apparently powerful delusion. A government with a clear majority may go lickety-split in the wrong direction. A government without a clear majority is more likely to stop, look, and listen. I am not, of course, arguing that minority government necessarily means good government. I am simply arguing that it does not necessarily mean bad government.

The third popular notion about minority government is that it cannot last. Clearly, this is false. Sometimes minority government has succeeded minority government, year after year, Parliament after Parliament, as, conspicuously, in Australia and New Zealand. Sometimes a single minority government has lasted for years, as Asquith's did from 1910 to 1915. If the people of Canada persist in electing Parliaments in which no party has a clear majority, and if all the parties refuse to consider a coalition (as they very properly may), then there are certain habits of thought, or feeling, which we shall have to change.

The first is, that any government defeat in the House of Commons necessarily means either the government's resignation or a fresh election. This is not so. Of course, defeat on a motion of censure or want of confidence, or on any measure which the government considers vital to its policy, is decisive; and any government is free to consider even a very minor defeat decisive, as Lord Rosebery did in 1895. But the history of British governments in the nineteenth century is studded with defeats which the government concerned simply accepted. . . . In our own country, Sir John A. Macdonald's first government was defeated over and over again in its four years of office: three times in 1868, three times in 1869, three times in 1870, and twice in 1871. It was defeated on its estimates, on government bills, on motions to refer papers to a select committee, on the tariff (where the House insisted on repealing the duties on no less than fifteen items, including coal, coke, wheat, and flour). It neither resigned nor asked for dissolution.

Of course, the main reason why British governments in the nineteenth century (especially the first half or three-quarters of it) and Macdonald's in the early years after Confederation did not regard defeats in the Commons as necessarily decisive, was that parties were then much less well organized. There were a good many more or less Independent members: what Sir John called "loose fish." We seldom have any loose fish nowadays. Individual members very rarely shift from side to side on particular votes. But we do have loose shoals of fish: parties which shift from side to side on particular votes. In the days of the individual loose fish, if governments had thought they must resign every time they were defeated in the House on more than a snap vote, there would have been incessant changes of government. If governments had thought they must have a fresh election every time they were defeated in the House, there would have been incessant elections. Instead, governments often took the commonsense course of neither resigning nor dissolving. They just let the House have its way.

With loose shoals of fish, if the electors persist in returning Parliaments with no clear majority for any party, governments may have to make up their minds to do the same. We shall certainly have to get rid of the notion that every defeat in the House means a fresh election. "No Constitution," said Lord Balfour, "can stand a diet of dissolutions." The official theory of the Liberal party, at times, anyhow, has seemed to be that elections are held to give some party a clear majority, and that if one election does not do it, there must be another at the earliest possible moment. The electors have just done their sum wrong and must be made to do it over again until they get it right. Of course they will get it right at the second try. They did in 1926, didn't they? But 1926 was really the third try: the electors had failed their second try in 1925. And now they have failed their second try again, in 1963. Are we to go on spanking them by a series of general elections, once every ten months or so, till they pass?

But "nobody will deliberately vote for minority government." Of course not. Most people presumably vote for the party they think best in the hope that it will get a clear majority to carry out the policies they favour. But no one except a clairvoyant can tell beforehand whether any party will get a clear majority. Voters who want a Liberal government with a clear majority will vote Liberal, those who want a Conservative government with a clear majority will vote Conservative, and so on. But there may not be enough voters of any one kind to give any party a clear majority; and the supporters of all four parties may persist, election after election, in voting for the party they think best. They may refuse to be bullied, by a series of elections, into voting for anyone else. They may stubbornly insist that they are grown-up people, free citizens, and have, accordingly, the right to vote as they see fit, and go on voting as they see fit.

And they will be right. If that means minority government, then the politicians will just have to lump it. They have no right to inflict on us the conspicuous waste of a series of general elections just because we elect a Parliament that does not suit them. It is our Parliament, not theirs. They are our servants, not our masters.

Elections are held to choose a Parliament to transact public business, and Parliament should transact that business until it becomes unable to do so, or until some great new issue arises on which it is imperative to consult the people, or until the Parliament's utility is exhausted by efflux of time. . . . In a Parliament which is recently elected, if one government cannot carry on with the existing House, and an alternative government is possible, and there is no great new issue of public policy, then the government which cannot carry on should resign and make way for one that can.

Elections are not picnics. They should take place only for serious reasons of public policy and this principle should operate with special force in a country where the existence of ten provincial legislatures means a large number of elections even in the ordinary course. As Asquith, a parliamentarian and constitutional lawyer of unexcelled authority, said in 1923: "The notion that a Ministry which cannot command a majority in the House of Commons . . . is invested with the right to demand a dissolution is as subversive of constitutional usage, as it would, in my opinion, be pernicious to the general and paramount interests of the nation at large."[1]

If it turns out that we are entering on a more or less prolonged period of minority government, a "period of precarious majorities," either our political leaders will have to learn self-restraint about wasting our time and substance in needless elections, or we shall have to find some means of imposing restraint on them. The means is ready to hand: the reserve power of the Crown, in very special circumstances, to refuse a prime minister's request for dissolution. "This," to quote Asquith again, "does not mean that the Crown should act arbitrarily and without the advice of responsible Ministers, but it does mean that the Crown is not bound to take the advice of a particular Ministry to put its subjects to the tumult and turmoil of general elections so long as it can find other Ministers who are prepared to give it a trial."[2] . . .

It is often glibly asserted that King's victory in 1926 destroyed this reserve power of the Crown in Canada. But King was very careful to say, repeatedly, that there could be circumstances in which the governor general would be justified in refusing dissolution; and he accepted the subsequent declaration of the Imperial Conference that the relations between the governor general and his ministers were "in all essential respects" the same as between the king and his ministers. In Britain the power to refuse certainly still exists. Sir Winston Churchill said so in 1944; so did Lord Attlee in 1952 and again in 1959; and in 1924 George V granted a dissolution to Ramsay MacDonald, only after he had made certain that neither Baldwin nor Asquith was prepared to form an alternative government. If the Queen can refuse dissolution, the governor general can too.

People who say he cannot can never really have thought out the consequences. If the governor is a mere rubber stamp, bound to grant dissolution automatically, certain results must follow as the night the day. First, a prime minister who fails to get a clear majority at one election can, on the rubber stamp theory, have another forthwith, without even allowing the new Parliament to meet. Only one prime minister in Commonwealth history [William Lyon Mackenzie King] ever dared to claim such a right, even in theory, and even he did not have the gall to try it in practice. Or, if the prime minister who has just failed to get a majority graciously consents to allow the new Parliament to meet, he can, on the rubber stamp theory, kill it any time it seems likely to vote against him. Or, if he allows it to vote, and it votes against him, he can then appeal to the people, even though the Parliament may be only a few weeks old, even though there is no new issue and even though an alternative government without an election is perfectly possible. And, of course, if he does not get a clear majority at the fresh election, he can, on the rubber stamp theory, put the country through the whole merry-go-round all over again, as often as he pleases.

It is no use saying that the necessity of getting Parliament to vote Supply will trip will trip him up. Governor general's special warrants will look after that; for, on the rubber stamp theory, the governor cannot refuse to sign the warrants. It is no use saying that the electors will deal with the culprit. On the rubber stamp theory, they cannot. If they defeat him, he can have a fresh election forthwith, or at any later date that suits him, and can repeat the performance as often as he likes. In other words, no Government could be removed from office except by its own consent or by revolution. And this is the theory which some people call "democratic!"

If the election of 1926 really did destroy the reserve power to refuse dissolution in Canada (which I deny), then we had better consider reviving it, if necessary by amending the British North America Act. The framers of the Irish constitution deliberately inserted in it a provision that the president may "in his absolute discretion refuse to dissolve" Parliament on the advice of a prime minister who has been defeated in the House. We may have to do likewise.

But can we trust a Canadian governor general's impartiality? If the Irish can trust an Irish president they elect, why cannot we trust a Canadian governor general we appoint? Some people are afraid that admitting, or conferring, a reserve power, would place too much power in the hands of the governor general. Anyone who is worried about this has just forgotten our whole political tradition, and the basic principle of parliamentary government, that the Crown cannot act except on the advice of responsible ministers. No monarch, no governor general, will ever exercise his reserve power if he can avoid it. He will always accept the advice of the prime minister unless it involves a flagrant outrage upon the constitution; and even then he will be able to refuse only if he can find an alternative prime minister willing to take responsibility for the refusal, and able to command a majority in Parliament. . . . The reserve power is precisely that: a power held in reserve, for use only when it offers the sole protection against the divine right of prime ministers.

Generally, ministers remember that they are not the people's masters but the Queen's servants, answerable to the Queen's faithful Commons; bound to let Parliament meet, bound to let it vote, bound to abide by its decision unless there are substantial reasons of public policy for appealing to the electorate. But if they do not, only the Crown can prevent Parliament from degenerating into a mere recording machine for the Prime Minister, and elections into mere plebiscites whose verdict the Prime Minister accepts only if it suits him. A political order, or rather disorder, in which Parliament exists, debates, votes, only at the pleasure of a jack-in-office, is a snare and a delusion. In Pym's words, "Parliaments without parliamentary liberty are but a fair and plausible way into bondage. Freedom of debate being once foreclosed, the essence of the liberty of Parliament is withal dissolved."[3]

We are sometimes told that the only sage rule is that "the Crown must always follow the advice of its ministers." Safe? Suppose Mr. Diefenbaker, on April 9, had asked the Governor General to dissolve the new Parliament forthwith. Will anyone in his senses say that the Governor would have been bound to consent, that a fresh election in such circumstances would have been "democratic"? Parliamentary government means more than just counting heads instead of breaking them. It also means using them. . . . If we use our brains we can survive any amount of minority government, even thrive on it. If we are not, we may have to resign ourselves to an almost continuous performance of listening to campaign speeches, watching campaign TV, and trudging through polling booths till, in sheer weariness or despair, we scrap parliamentary government and summon some Canadian de Gaulle to rescue us from the consequences of our failure to understand our "mighty heritage."

It may be objected that what I am suggesting would make Canada the ghost of the deceased French Third and Fourth Republics, sitting crowned upon the graves thereof; that we should have a succession of minority governments in a single Parliament, with the electors debarred from pronouncing judgment except once in every five years, no matter what happened. Not at all. In the first place, very few (if any) governments in the Third and Fourth Republics were minority governments; they were coalitions, which is a different story altogether. In the second place, I am not proposing to deprive the prime minister, even a defeated prime minister, of the right to get a dissolution of Parliament in proper circumstances. I am not, in other words, proposing fixed dates for elections, as in the United States, or, in practice, the French Third Republic. That would be revolutionary, and, to my mind, stupid. All I am saying is that the prime minister's right to a dissolution is not absolute, that there are certain circumstances in which it does not, and manifestly should not, exist, and that, in such circumstances, the Head of State has , and should have, power to refuse. With the long Commonwealth, as well as Canadian, tradition, in which the Crown and its representatives normally accord dissolution without question (though there have been half a hundred refusals), there is not the slightest danger that the prime minister will find himself powerless. The danger is all the other way. It is precisely because the danger is all the other way that it is necessary to insist that there is a danger and that it must be guarded against.

There is one other and final objection to minority government which merits a moment's consideration: that it may have worked well enough in the nineteenth century, and may work well enough now in Australian states or Canadian provinces, but that it will not work in the twentieth century for a national government; that the problems have become so big and so complex that only a government with a clear majority can hope to solve them, or even enable us to live with them without intolerable strain and danger. From this, of course, it follows that, if a minority government does appear, it must be got rid of as fast as possible, at any cost. For their own good, the electors must be spanked into giving some party a clear majority, no matter how many spankings it takes.

To this, I think, there are three replies. The first is that it overlooks the possibility of coalitions. If things are really as bad as they are alleged to be, surely two or more of the parties may be induced to sink some of their differences and join in a "government of national safety"? The second, and more fundamental, reply is to question whether the main policy decisions are really so much bigger than in the last century, and whether the extra complexities are not pretty well looked after by a far bigger and more expert civil service than nineteenth-century governments had at their disposal. . . . My third reply, more fundamental still, is that spanking the electors into giving some party a clear majority shows contempt for ordinary people, for the human personality, and involves the substitution of uncontrolled (and therefore despotic) plebiscitary government for parliamentary; that I do not believe our problems can be solved only at such a price, or solved at all at such a price; and that, even if I did, I should think it too high to pay.

We may have to learn to live with minority government. It may prove unsatisfactory (majority government also has been known to be). It may have certain inconveniences. It will certainly be nerve-racking at times, especially for those who have to run it. But it may turn out to give us quite tolerable or even very good legislation and administration. And it may confer on us some incidental benefits not to be despised.

First, it could restore some of the lost power of the House of Commons and of individual members. We might once again have real debates, speeches which changed votes, government by discussion. Second, it might force us to look at our system of government, learn about it, think about it. It might remind us, for example, that we live in a parliamentary monarchy; that the Queen is part of Parliament; that she is, indeed, legally, the sole source of its existence and authority; that the Senate and the House of Commons are, in law, simply the representatives of her people whom she has summoned "to have their advice"; that the Houses cannot meet save at her summons. A little reflection might show us that this is of some practical importance: that if the Queen, on the advice of her ministers, fails to summon Parliament promptly after an indecisive election, the members, even duly gazetted and sworn, cannot (as I have heard proposed) meet and transact business on their own: the House of Commons is not equipped with a self-starter. It might suggest that, as the Queen can act only on the advice of ministers, it is important to make sure that those ministers are responsible, answerable, accountable, to the House of Commons and, secondarily, to the people, and removable by the House of Commons or the people; and it might show us that in certain circumstances only the Queen (or her representative) can ensure that responsibility and removability.

It might also remind us that we are part of the Commonwealth; that behind our own constitution and its history lie the British constitution and its history; that our system of government is essentially British; that British experience may therefore be highly relevant to our problems; that Australia and New Zealand share this British heritage, and that their experience also may therefore be highly relevant (and that we ought, accordingly, to know more about it than most of us do).

It might induce in us a salutary doubt whether some old precedents are quite as obsolete as we may sometimes have supposed. Precedents, after all, grow out of particular situations. Sometimes these situations disappear for good; but sometimes they disappear and then re-appear, in the same or an altered form (as the "loose fish" disappeared, then re-appeared as loose shoals of fish); and the precedents which grew out of the original situations, and became obsolete when those situations disappeared, may become relevant again and take a new lease on life.

Finally, minority government may bring home to us that what is constitutional depends ultimately on what is reasonable, on the application of what Sir Robert Borden (too optimistically, I fear) called "the commonplace quality of common sense." Behind the precedents, behind the dicta of authorities, lies reality. As long as any one party has a clear majority, we can get along fairly well on cliches, rules-of-thumb, the wooden application of time-honoured phrases. When no party has a clear majority, this will no longer do: it produces, as was abundantly evident in 1926, and evident enough in this last year, the most fantastic confusions and absurdities. Faced with a House of minorities, we have to look at the realities the phrases were intended to explain, the problems they were meant to settle. We have to ask ourselves whether a particular phrase, however venerable, is really relevant in new, unfamiliar situations. We have to use our minds, rendering "the debt of our reason we owe unto God."

Minority government can be not a "problem" but an opportunity, not a threat but a promise.

NOTES

1. *The Times*, Dec. 19, 1923.
2. Ibid.
3. Quoted in Arthur Beauchesne, *Rules and Forms of the House of Commons of Canada*, 3rd ed. (Toronto, 1943), 91.

FURTHER READINGS

Geller-Schwartz, L. "Minority Government Reconsidered." *Journal of Canadian Studies* 14, 2 (Summer 1979): 67–79.

Herman, V. and J. Pope. "Minority Governments in Western Democracies." *British Journal of Political Science* 3, 2(1973): 191–212.

Jackson, R.J., and M.M. Atkinson. *The Canadian Legislative System*. 2nd, revised ed., Chapters 5 and 8. Toronto: Macmillan, 1980.

McLeod, J.T. "Living in a House of Minorities." *Canadian Forum* 43 (June 1963): 49–51.

21

Parliamentary Reform
Through Political Parties

PAUL G. THOMAS

INTRODUCTION

Central to an understanding of the modern House of Commons—its functions, organization, procedures, and much of the activity of its members—is party. . . . The arrangements within the Canadian cabinet-parliamentary system elevate parties over individual politicians. Most of the actions by individuals are, in fact, forms of party behaviour. Members of Parliament are involved in numerous relationships, but the primary one is with their political parties. Ambitious individuals get ahead by acquiring a party label through nomination, seeking election largely on the basis of the party's and the leader's appeal, and striving to advance within the ranks of the parliamentary party. Despite the fundamental importance of political parties to our political system, their parliamentary organizations and operations have received surprisingly limited analysis to date.

. . . Any major organizational or procedural reforms to the House of Commons are bound to fail (or at least to disappoint) if they ignore the factor of partisanship which is central to the daily functioning of the House of Commons. Concern has been expressed, for example, about upgrading Parliament's capacity to hold ministers and their officials accountable for the performance of government programs. Scrutiny of the executive depends heavily on the efforts of the opposition parties, but they define this function primarily in the political terms of embarrassing the government. Only a few MPs are interested in the difficult and politically unrewarding toil of monitoring administrative performance. Rhetoric to the contrary notwithstanding, the abstract idea of contributing to the effectiveness of programs or the efficient management of the public service holds little political attraction for most opposition Members. And, for their part, ministers and their backbench supporters normally will not want or seek to encourage a closer inspection

Abridged from Paul G. Thomas, "Parliamentary Reform Through Political Parties," in *The Canadian House of Commons: Essays in Honour of Norman Ward*, ed. John C. Courtney (Calgary: University of Calgary Press, 1985), 43-66. Reprinted by permission of the publisher.

of government performance by opposition Members who, in most circumstances, can be counted on to interpret every revelation in the worst possible light. In short, reform schemes will not enjoy great success if they ignore or serve to stifle the partisanship that supplies much of the institution's political energy.

The role of political parties within Parliament cannot be understood in isolation from the wide constitutional and political context. Responsible cabinet-parliamentary government presumes the existence of disciplined parliamentary parties and contributes to their existence. Strictly speaking, political parties are not part of the constitutional structure, although they have been increasingly recognized and regulated by public law. For many years the Standing Orders of the House of Commons were silent about the role of political parties in Parliament and formal procedural studies still tend to talk as if they did not exist. In addition to formal arrangements, social, economic and political trends occurring beyond the reaches of Parliament Hill obviously exert great influence on the nature and role of party politics within the House of Commons. However, parliamentary parties should not be seen as mere captives of structural arrangements and outside forces; they are themselves important conditioning agents of the patterns and the quality of institutional life.

It is on the basis of this assumption that parliamentary reform can be examined through the vehicle of political parties. The first section of this chapter describes briefly the central importance of parties to the modern House of Commons and offers the suggestion that recent procedural reforms have delivered less than was promised because of the inhibiting factor of partisanship. The second section describes briefly the nature and role of party organizations within the institution of Parliament. The importance of party in Parliament is reflected and reinforced by the rise of more structured organizations and relations between party leaders and their backbench followers. The popular image of ordinary MPs as a servile group who regularly yield to the wishes of their leaders is a misleading one because it ignores the substantial measure of private, intraparty discussion and dissent which exists. The final section of the paper looks at how the internal functioning of the parties might be improved and how this might contribute to a better quality of partisanship within the House of Commons.

Party organization tends to be fluid, depending upon such factors as the traditions of the party, whether it has been mainly in or out of office, the size of its parliamentary contingent, the approach favoured by its leader and the issues before the House at a particular time. These factors contribute to an internal culture for each of the parties represented in the Commons. This culture sets limits on the types of reforms which any leader can contemplate in terms of party operations. As adaptive, human institutions whose practices express shared norms the parliamentary wings of political parties are less malleable than rational reformers usually presume. Furthermore, party leaders must worry about providing incentives, both material and psychological, to individual Members of Parliament in order to induce them to contribute actively and constructively to the party's goals. The modest nature of the reforms proposed in the final section of the paper reflects the assumption that as organic entities parties do not lend themselves to drastic social engineering.

"PARTY IS KING"

Party is the means by which the public holds governments politically accountable. It is also the means by which governments achieve coherence and parliamentary endorsement of their policies. Party serves as the basis for the aggregation and expression in an organized way of the various opinions within society through the presentation of policy ideas to be translated into legislation and spending. It helps to give shape and meaning to the votes of over 15 million electors. Parties serve as giant personnel agencies for the recruitment and election of members. It is on the basis of party and party leadership that most electors vote. The party (normally the one with the largest representation in the House of Commons following an election) provides leadership and direction to government, including the formulation of almost all the legislative and financial measures enacted by Parliament. The other parties perform the function of providing a visible, institutionalized and responsible opposition to the party in office, something which is considered valuable as a check on the possible abuse of executive power, as an outlet for minority opinions and as a means of ensuring peaceful alternation of office.

Party cohesion and party discipline ensure the endorsement of most government measures, but the success rate of Canadian governments appears to be less than their British counterparts. From 1945 to 1978, a British government could expect to see over 95 percent of all the bills it introduced enacted into law during a session of Parliament. For Canada, during the parliamentary sessions from 1966 to 1978, the government's success rate was approximately 70 percent on average. The greater frequency of minority government in Canada accounts for part of this difference. However, even majority governments appear to experience "power failures," usually towards the end of the life of a parliament. . . . Virtually every vote in the House of Commons occurs along party lines. Defections have become a rare, though not unheard of, occurrence. . . .

Many factors contribute to party solidarity. Under "normal" political conditions, socio-psychological factors appear to be the most important. Members of Parliament are conditioned to see party voting as an essential feature of the parliamentary system. They believe that the media and the public have come to expect party unity and will misinterpret acts of defiance of the party leadership. This view is held despite the findings of an August 1983 Gallup Poll: only 7.9 percent of the respondents felt that MPs should vote as their party directs them. Thirty-two percent believed that loyalty to their party was the priority of MPs. This difference in outlook between politicians and the public will be explored elsewhere in this chapter.

Members of parliamentary parties share collective goals, both instrumental and ideological. They are united in a desire to see their party in office or to increase their parliamentary strength at the next election. Open divisions are not likely to contribute to this goal. As pragmatic as the two main parties may be, there is at least some commitment to shared values and most MPs see their own party as representing a distinctive approach from their opponents. For the NDP Members, the ideological bond is more important, partly because the attainment of office is not an immediate prospect. Moreover, party politics are not simply a matter of tactics and debating policies. It is as much a matter of party loyalty, seeing the party through the rough spots, of belonging, enthusiasm and camaraderie. The belief that Parliament is a "team sport" runs deep among MPs.

If MPs define their role primarily as serving as part of a cohesive team, they are encouraged to do so by the wider trends in party politics. In an era of television politics, electoral success depends greatly upon the effectiveness and appeal of the party leader. Leaders are now chosen at large conventions where the party caucus is no longer in position to control the outcome. The rise of political consultants, the adoption of new techniques of campaigning and the increasing reliance upon public opinion polls threaten to make parties less programmatic in their concern and serve to undermine the role of the MP as a source of political intelligence and channel of communication. Party backbenchers have limited exposure in the media, they are elected as part of a team committed to support the existing leader and his policies; only occasionally is an individual politician able to build up an independent base of political support.

The rise of the so-called "administrative state" and the proliferation of pressure groups maintaining continuous contact with the bureaucracy also has implications for political parties in their parliamentary roles. The trends challenge the traditional democratic assumption that the individual elected representative is the main communication link between the interests of his constituency and government. Many years ago, S.D. Clark noted that during the 1920s emphasis began "to shift to influencing the policies and activities of government boards, commissions and departmental officials, and to the extent that parliamentary leaders become dependent upon such agencies, these influences were more effective than pressure exerted upon the party organization."[1] The focus of much pressure group activity within the executive arena is a recognition of where power is concentrated. Although reforms to Parliament have increased the attention paid to the House of Commons and the Senate, mainly to their committees, politically sophisticated groups still recognize the value of having their input earlier in the policy cycle. The interaction between pressure groups and cabinet ministers and/or their public servants is prior in time, and usually more decisive, than the parliamentary stages of the policy cycle. These pre-parliamentary discussions and negotiations often eliminate the more contentious features of legislation and thus help to account for the lack of dissent within the governing party. Unaware of the nature of such negotiations, and anxious not to cause harm to the government's reputation, government MPs will be reluctant to challenge ministers, even within the privacy of party meetings. Completely excluded from such preliminary discussions are the opposition parties. Unaware of the nature of the bargains struck, they are often reduced to challenging the process of decision-making, not its substantive results.

Within the caucus of the governing party, the leadership has available considerable powers of persuasion. The fact that the political fate of the government supposedly rides on every vote is often seen as the main source of party cohesion within the House of Commons. In fact, the rules on what constitutes a government defeat are vague and hence flexible. In general, when a government is defeated on an "important matter," it must resign or call an election. But what constitutes an important matter remains subject to dispute. Defeat of a major piece of legislation, perhaps central to a party's platform, is sometimes held to constitute a serious political setback. But governments in the past have stayed in office despite such defeats. Rejection of financial measures—both the raising and the spending of tax dollars—has traditionally been treated more seriously, but again the precedents (including the defeat of a clause of a money bill in December 1983) suggest that resignation or an election need not be automatic in every instance. Apart from explicit votes of non-confidence, therefore, the prevailing constitutional convention seems to be that the government decides how it will view any defeat in the House. A distinction is emerging between the loss of a bill and loss of confidence. Under prevailing conventions, governments could allow more "free votes" on legislation, but they have chosen not to do so because they want to maintain the high degree of party unity expected by the press and the public. There have not been more than six times since 1945 where the government has declared in advance that confidence in the government was not at issue in the outcome of a vote.

The votes of backbench MPs are a relatively weak resource during times of majority government. But things change when minority governments are elected, as has happened in six of the eleven elections since 1957. Party discipline generally becomes tighter during such periods, but there is additional pressure on the party leadership to bring its followers along by means of advance consultation. The Liberal party has been most adept at identifying the minimum conditions for political survival in a minority situation by carefully planning its legislative agenda to win the support of one or more opposition parties. The full story of how the Liberals stayed in office from 1972 to 1974 and then arranged, when the political omens were right, for their own defeat is worthy of a study.

The timing of elections within the normal five-year life of a Parliament rests with the Prime Minister. It is often suggested that the threat of an election can be used by the Prime Minister to stifle dissent within his cabinet and caucus. But the power to request a dissolution of Parliament is a two-edged sword in the hands of the Prime Minister. He has more to lose than his backbench followers and going to the country when his party is divided is not likely to enhance the chances for re-election. Control over the timing of an election represents more of a partisan advantage in relation to the opposition than a device to enforce conformity.

In addition to the threat of an election, the sanctions available to the government leadership include the refusal to appoint a Member to the cabinet, failure to reward a Member with an appointment as a parliamentary secretaryship or a committee chairmanship, and a campaign to deny a Member renomination by his constituency association. The provision in the *Canada Elections Act*, which requires the party leader to provide written authorization before a candidate can use the party label on the ballot, reinforces this latter power. Opposition parties have fewer immediate rewards and punishments, but the prospective use of such inducements at some future date may still be effective. It is difficult to discover how many members stifle their dissent out of fear that they might ruin their career chances by antagonizing those in authority. For those MPs who do not aspire to leadership positions, and such individuals do exist, the material incentives will be largely ineffective. In any case, the testimony from party whips suggests that the use of sanctions is not common and that threats of retribution will not work when a member is determined to break ranks.

A corollary of more active government and increased emphasis on competition among parties was the tightening of government control over the procedures of the House of Commons. Gradually during this century, governments used changes to the rules to ensure completion of its expanded workload without undue delay. . . . The net effect of most changes prior to the late 1960s worked in the direction of increased parliamentary "efficiency" and placed restrictions on the traditional rights of private Members which existed largely on the basis of conventions. The reform process begun in the mid 1960s offset this trend to some extent. In particular, the growth after 1968 of a more active and influential committee system provided more meaningful opportunities for backbench involvement. Younger, professional, full-time MPs still express disappointment with the extent to which the system underutilizes (more cynical observers would say "wastes") their talents. A tightening up of the rules was probably a necessary step if Parliament was not to become a bottleneck in an era of more active government. As the recent bell-ringing episodes revealed, the rules have not become instruments of complete political control in the hands of the governing party.

Partisanship is a large part of the reason why changes to the Commons' committee system adopted in December 1968 led to less parliamentary influence on legislation and spending than the reformers had anticipated. The evolution of the committee system owed little to abstract theorizing and much to political pragmatism. A desire by the Liberal government to increase parliamentary productivity was the principal motivation behind the 1968 reforms; enhancing the influence of backbench MPs was a secondary consideration. As the committees became active, disagreements arose over the amount of independence from government control they should enjoy and over the extent to which partisanship should govern the behaviour of MPs in committees. Since the committees were assigned several functions—the scrutiny of legislation, the review of spending and the conduct of investigations—it is not surprising that no single view on these questions emerged.

Any government has an interest in minimizing opposition to its legislative proposals. Advance consultations with affected interests are undertaken in part for this purpose. Forestalling parliamentary controversy enables the ruling party to claim that it is governing by a consensus. For their part, the opposition parties, if they are not to appear redundant, feel obliged to criticize government bills, particularly in the case of unpopular legislation. Since opposition parties in a majority situation do not control the content or the fate of proposed legislation, the chief question they face is whether to oppose a government bill. The decision can be based almost entirely on strategic, political grounds. Even when the opposition parties cannot bring themselves to say they would do things differently, they often insist they could do things better. Opposition attacks in the House tend typically to emphasize process rather than substance, and, in relation to substance, the speeches tend to be long on rhetoric and criticism and short on constructive alternatives. After all, why should a party add to the political reputation of its opponent by improving its legislation? Moreover, the opposition parties may not be in a good position to offer policy alternatives. Opposition backbenchers in particular may be more inclined than the leadership to emphasize party disagreements because they are not as conscious of the constraints of office. Although most bills could be characterized as "administrative" in nature, in a country like Canada with strong regional and cultural differences this does not mean that they are empty of political controversy. On major legislation, it is clearly unrealistic to expect MPs to drop their partisan orientations, even after a bill has been transferred to the appropriate standing committee.

It was the hope of the reformers that committee work on the estimates could be approached relatively objectively. Instead, the partisan approach which prevails in the House during Supply debates is often carried over into the committee setting. When the committees began to exploit the opportunity of estimates study to comment on specific programs and to make recommendations for future action, the government tightened its control. In 1974, following several incidents in which concurrence of the House was sought for substantive committee reports on the estimates, the Parliamentary Secretary to the Government House Leader wrote to all committee chairmen forbidding the practice. "Reports of a substantive nature," he wrote, "including recommendations on items relating to or contained in the estimates, are clearly not allowed."[2] The fact that there appears to be no procedural grounds for this assertion did not detract from its inhibiting effect on committee activity. Since 1973 only one committee has made observations and recommendations when reporting its estimates to the House.

Inquiries offer the best prospect for committee and backbench influence. But even in relation to this function a fortuitous combination of circumstances is usually required for success. Such inquiries work best when the government has not declared a position and is genuinely seeking advice for a committee. Topics which are guaranteed to divide committee members strictly along party lines should be avoided since a constructive inquiry will be almost impossible. Therefore, even inquiries are constrained by the fact of partisanship. Prior negotiations with the responsible minister and an avoidance of controversial topics are requirements for success. To avoid political confrontations, there has been a tendency in certain parliamentary inquiries to emphasize evidence rather than conclusions, and to produce reports which are bland almost to the point of being useless. Even a report reviewing a policy issue can serve the useful function of public education and wider debate, but this is different from saying that it will serve as a stimulant to executive action.

Committees are often seen as the best hope for greater parliamentary influence within the policy process. However, the autonomy of committees should not be the sole gauge of the political vitality of the Commons generally. Nor should they be seen as the sole avenue of reform. The drive for a stronger committee system during the last decade and half ignored (or at least underestimated) one of the most basic findings of comparative legislative research—namely, that the strength of a legislative committee system varies inversely with the strength of the party system. Strong parties and strong committees cannot coexist. Reform-minded individuals (like the present author) sought to avoid this political reality by suggesting that MPs could be more partisan in relation to certain activities than others. It was recognized that partisanship supplied the political energy necessary to move policy ideas forward and produced the incentive for much of the routine activity of the Commons. Important legislation and broad economic statements, it was usually agreed, should be the subject for party disagreements. But with regard to minor bills, administrative issues and emerging policy issues, the parties were urged to drop their usual adversarial postures and approach the subject matter more objectively. To some extent this already takes place. However, it was felt that more could be done in terms of the relaxation of party discipline. Finding the right balance between partisanship and more cooperative approaches proved more difficult than most of us imagined. We also tended to denigrate the value of partisan debate. The remainder of this paper looks at certain sources of partisanship and how the quality of partisanship might be improved as a contribution to the overall goal of improved parliamentary performance.

PARTY ORGANIZATION IN PARLIAMENT

The importance of party in Parliament is reflected and reinforced by the development of structured party organizations within the institution. While parties were the vehicle during earlier decades for the transfer of control to the executive, they could in the future become an important means for strengthening the role of elected Members. Recent developments in party organization have served to give Members, through their positions as party members, greater influence over the party leadership, and hence when in office greater input into government decision-making. We will examine the role of party caucuses, including the role of regional caucuses and caucus committees; the role of the "shadow cabinet" within the official opposition; and the role of the party whips.

The Government Caucus

The caucus in Canada is a private meeting involving all Members of Parliament and Senators from a given political party. National party caucuses continue to meet weekly on Wednesday mornings when Parliament is in session. Such meetings have usually focused on parliamentary business and strategy. In addition, all parties have met once or twice during parliamentary recesses, with each meeting lasting a couple of days, to discuss general problems and policies, including the party's standing in relation to public opinion. In addition to the national caucus all parties have operated a series of regional caucuses and a number of policy committees. Regional caucuses met on Wednesdays prior to the national caucus to discuss regional concerns and on occasion to work out common positions.

　　Caucuses serve a number of functions. Since parliamentary government has become government by party, the most important function of caucus is to provide for interaction between leaders and their backbench supporters. Precise conclusions about the patterns and nature of caucus influence are difficult to construct because of the secrecy which surrounds caucuses, the informal and variable nature of caucus operations, the differences among parties and the unpredictable impact of the interaction of personalities. There is no doubt, however, that caucus has become more important. In recent years, caucuses have met regularly, devoted more attention to legislation and were consulted more continuously by the party leadership.

　　The government party caucus stands the greatest chance of exerting influence on the content of legislation and the direction of spending. Since the Liberal party was in office for most of this century, its experience must serve as the basis for the discussion of the government caucus. Reports of caucus meetings during the time of Prime Ministers Mackenzie King (1935–48) and Louis St. Laurent (1948–57) tell of a quiet and acquiescent group. . . .

　　During the 1960s, Prime Minister Pearson sought to strengthen caucus input by encouraging his cabinet colleagues to consult groups of interested caucus Members before introducing legislation into the House. In addition, a pre-session meeting of caucus was instituted to allow Liberal MPs an early chance to discuss the government's legislative plans. While these changes were sold as representing a desire for closer relations between the government and the caucus, they also reflected the minority situation of the Pearson government and the desire to ensure as far as possible that the party would remain united on the floor of the Commons in order to survive. The practice of previewing legislation with caucus was not followed by most ministers, and was abandoned within a few years, allegedly because Liberal MPs had violated the requirement of confidentiality. Surveys of government MPs done at that time reflected the fact that most of the communication taking place was one way, with the cabinet presenting caucus members with *fait accomplis* and looking for their support.

A year after Mr. Trudeau became Prime Minister a special caucus grievance session was held. The two-day meeting in June 1969 was prompted by a number of backbench concerns. Liberal MPs were seeking clarification of how much independence they would be granted within the new committee system. In its first Throne Speech (September 12, 1968) the government had promised financial assistance to the opposition parties to enable them to establish caucus research offices, but a similar provision had not been arranged for government MPs. Advisory groups at the provincial level, consisting of a representative of cabinet, a representative of caucus and a representative of the provincial party membership, had been established to advise on the political aspects of party affairs in the province and to provide a channel of communications between the provinces and Ottawa. Many Liberal MPs regarded the new bodies with suspicion: "Rather than seeing the advisory groups as a means of improving communication within the party, some MPs saw them as a threat to the traditional personal relationships which they had been able to build up over the years with individual cabinet ministers."[3] The creation of Regional Desks within Trudeau's office at the same time convinced many Liberal MPs that caucus was being supplanted as the main source of political intelligence on the regions and they used the June 1969 meeting to complain about the trend.

A series of reforms to caucus operations was accepted as a result of the meeting. In theory ministers were required to discuss the subject matter of proposed legislation with interested Members before a draft bill was discussed in the appropriate cabinet committee and further consultations take place before second reading in the House of Commons. To take advantage of this opportunity, the Liberal caucus established six functional committees, with terms of reference corresponding to the cabinet's subject-matter committees and the standing committees of the House of Commons. Each committee consisted of a chairman and vice-chairman (elected annually by caucus), a secretary, the chairman of the parallel committees in the Commons, the appropriate Parliamentary Secretaries, a whip, and interested caucus members.

After 1970 when a caucus Research Office was established, a research assistant was assigned to each committee. Also in 1969 a national caucus executive was established consisting of an elected chairman and vice-chairman, the chairmen of the caucus committees, the House Leader, and the whips. Prior to 1970 the caucus chairman had been appointed by the leader. There were also regular regional caucuses and a place on the agenda of the national caucus when they would report.

Despite these improvements, discontent persisted. Time was always at a premium in caucus meetings. Not all ministers complied with the requirement of previewing legislation. During the minority government period (1972–74) the emphasis in caucus shifted to the short-term tactical requirements of political survival. Caucus met weekly rather than bi-weekly and the previous system of standing committees was replaced by *ad hoc* legislative committees, with the minister sponsoring a bill meeting with interested MPs. During the majority government (1974–79) the Liberal caucus convinced ministers to accept significant revisions to legislation on electronic eavesdropping, immigration, and unemployment insurance. In addition to these changes to legislative proposals, a special caucus committee on industrial policy met for over a year and brought enough pressure on the cabinet to move it in the direction of an industrial strategy. One of the committee's major proposals, the creation of the Board of Economic Ministers, was adopted late in 1978. The pattern of caucus involvement did not change much following the Liberals' return to office in 1980. The caucus' role in policy formulation, although limited and mainly reactive, was not unimportant.

The role of the government caucus was not formal decision-making; rather, it was communication and consultation. Caucus meetings represented an opportunity for ministers to explain and to gain support for their plans. Such efforts are crucial to the maintenance of party unity and in the parliamentary system party cohesion is necessary for the government to carry out its proposals. Caucus also represented an opportunity for the party leadership to listen to the views of backbenchers on legislation and other matters. Caucus reflected public opinion and helped to set the political agenda of government. It is true, as critics suggest, that caucus opinion was at times ill-informed, incoherent, inconsistent and variable, but in this regard it rather neatly reflected public opinion.

Consistent with the consultative nature of caucus operations, no agenda was circulated, almost all of the discussion was based upon oral reports, no votes were held, no formal announcements or press releases were issued, and it was left to the Prime Minister and the cabinet to determine the nature of the consensus, if any, expressed on the issues under discussion. Meetings were held on Wednesdays from 10:30 a.m. to 12:30 p.m. Caucus executive set the agenda, which typically included the following items: announcements; reports from regional caucuses; reports on parliamentary activities from the government House Leader and Chief Government Whip; miscellaneous subjects or the Topic of the Day; and the summation by the Prime Minister. In the caucus room the cabinet, including the Prime Minister, along with the officers of caucus, sat at the front. Unless they were making a presentation, cabinet ministers normally listened then responded to questions and comments. As Prime Minister, Mr. Trudeau would often use his closing remarks to debate points raised in the meeting, but there was no real give-and-take because he was the last to speak.

Consensus was not always easy to find. If the caucus appeared divided and if the minister in charge of a bill was not determined to proceed, the Prime Minister might indicate a delay until a consensus emerged. Even when caucus was united, ministers did not always feel bound to act on the apparent agreement. Most Liberal MPs accepted that cabinet should be free to reject or to accept caucus advice because only ministers, it was felt, had the necessary factual background to be aware of all the implications of a given action. Along with the handicap of inadequate information, time was another constraint on the government caucus. Only a half dozen topics of concern to MPs were raised in the weekly meetings; even fewer when a Topic of the Day occupied the bulk of the available time. Limitations of time meant that individual MPs were given three to five minutes to present their point of view.

During the 32nd Parliament, the rule continued to be that Liberal ministers would preview legislation with interested MPs at "pink slip" meetings (so-called because of the colour of the notice) convened for this purpose. Not all ministers honoured the rule. Most, however, recognized the advantage of gaining prior caucus approval as a way to forestall intraparty disagreements when the bill reached the Commons. Caucus was regularly successful in blocking, delaying, or amending proposed legislation. Examples were Bill S-31 (which sought to limit provincial ownership of transportation companies), the Crowsnest Rates Bill and the *Canada Health Act*. In all cases, controversy and outside pressures contributed to caucus influence. In connection with such measures, caucus will want to have its say and the cabinet will want to hear it.

Whether there is a majority, and the size of its majority, affects caucus' influence. In a minority situation, the requirement for outward public unity is greater, but there is greater pressure on the cabinet to consult in advance. A large government majority means that the non-ministerial element is larger and likely to contain more people with ability and political standing. On the other hand, dissent can be tolerated without adverse consequences. During smaller majority governments, ministers tend to loom larger and the fear of political mistakes is greater.

Different ministers approached caucus differently. Some clearly regard it as a nuisance to be tolerated. Other ministers genuinely wanted caucus advice. Weaker ministers were not accorded the same respect from caucus as their stronger colleagues. Some ministers sought to mobilize support in caucus for their legislative proposals as a way to overcome opposition within cabinet or to advance bills in the crowded legislative lineup controlled by the Government House Leader. Caucus influence was also indirect. Ministers who were exposed to weekly caucus discussions were made keenly aware of the feeling in the party. This created constant pressure to formulate policy with party attitudes in mind. Both astute and timid ministers were unlikely to propose legislation which was too far out of line with caucus opinion.

In addition to full caucus, the Liberals operated a series of *ad hoc* policy committees open to all members. Chairmen of the policy committees were selected by the caucus executive from a list of volunteers. The policy committees were transitory bodies so that it is difficult to know exactly how many were active at any point in time. During the 32nd Parliament, committees were established on agriculture, youth employment, forestry, social policy and economic policy. Four to six weeks prior to the budget being presented, an economic policy committee was established. A series of meetings were held and two reports were brought to caucus. The Minister of Finance, Mr. Lalonde, encouraged these exercises, not so much for the detailed input MPs could provide (which was limited), but for the broad, political advice received. Even more important was a desire to involve all MPs in the "selling" of the budget. To this end, MPs were supplied with a budget kit containing "good news" economic indicators, sample questions and answers, summaries of media commentaries, and model speeches.

In addition to these policy committees, the Liberals also operated four regional caucuses: Atlantic (nineteen MPs); Quebec (seventy-four MPs); Ontario (fifty-two MPs); and the West (two MPs). Regional caucuses met weekly before the national caucus. Meetings focused on the implications of national policies for their areas and on matters of a provincial nature. Oral reports from regional caucuses were presented during a time set aside for this purpose at national caucus. If a regional caucus feels particularly strongly about an issue, its chairman may request that other representatives from the region be allowed to speak.

Regional caucuses varied in size, level of activity, cohesion and the quality of their members. With seventy-four MPs, the Quebec caucus represented nearly half of the national caucus. There were a series of four sub-regional caucuses, but Quebec still presented a united stand on most issues. The presence of several powerful ministers, particularly Mr. Lalonde as the "lead minister," undoubtedly added to the strength of the Quebec caucus. Unlike Quebec, the Ontario Liberal caucus was far less hierarchical and cohesive. It was divided into three sub-regional caucuses. The overall political minister for Ontario was Mr. Herb Gray, but he was forced to compete with several regional "barons" within cabinet.

Individual MPs from all regions indicated that working through regional caucuses could be an effective way to gain influence. Numbers were not the sole, or even the main, basis for regional influence within caucus. The nature of the issue, the intensity of the regional feeling, the strength of the case being presented, the political skills of the regional representatives (particularly the regional minister), the cohesion of the regional grouping and the presence of outside pressures or support, were all important variables. Regional ministers were expected to play a lead role in organizing their regional caucuses. They were expected to ensure that there was regional understanding and support for government policies. They were expected to supervise party affairs and to keep in touch with opinion leaders in various fields from their region. They lobbied with other ministers to obtain benefits for their regions and are consulted on the distribution of patronage. A powerful minister could often compensate for numerical underrepresentation within cabinet and caucus.

In an earlier historical period, discussion of the government caucus would have concentrated on its impact in terms of party unity. Critics concentrated on the monolithic voting habits it produced. Undoubtedly caucus meetings contributed to keeping government backbenchers contented and working as a team. This function should not be denigrated since party loyalty and morale are essential to this system. Future discussions of the government caucus should take this point for granted and concentrate on the influence which backbenchers exert on government through caucus. What has been suggested in the above account is that caucus has grown in importance. Its meetings are more numerous, it is consulted more continuously, and it has an impact on proposed legislation. It does not dominate Cabinet, nor is it usually ignored.

The Official Opposition Caucus and the "Shadow Cabinet"

For most of this century the Progressive Conservative party has occupied the opposition benches. A not unrelated development is that the party has been wracked by internal conflict usually focused on the party leader. Recurrent conflict has meant that the party projected an image of factionalism, which has further weakened its appeal to the voter. The party has tended in the past to attract "outsiders," individuals who see themselves fighting an establishment in the form of the Liberal party. There has been speculation that some of these individuals actually prefer a role in opposition because they find an emotional outlet for their status insecurity by criticizing those in power. Undoubtedly, therefore, repeated rejections by the Canadian electorate and a history of internal divisiveness have affected the organizational effectiveness of the Conservative Party within Parliament.

Unlike the leader of a party in office, an opposition leader has fewer and less valuable rewards to bestow. The leader appoints party spokespersons, the party House Leader, the whips and, until recently, the Chairman of Caucus. In formal terms, these appointments are made by caucus, but in practice the leader's list is simply presented to caucus and not discussed or voted on. Historically, the leader of the Progressive Conservative party had the prerogative of declaring policy unilaterally and was responsible for determining the sense of caucus discussions. While in formal, constitutional terms the party is leader-dominated and this had tended to focus resentment on the leader, in practice the relationship between the leader and his parliamentary followers is more complicated.

Appointment to opposition positions may hold the promise of future preferment should the party gain office, but such advancement does not have the same impact as actual cabinet appointments. In opposition, dissent, though never welcome, is regarded less seriously because there is not the pressure to get the party's programmes enshrined in legislation and spending. An opposition leader makes appointments to his own office and appoints the National Director of the Progressive Conservative Research Office. These resources do not come close to matching those available to the Prime Minister and therefore the information advantage of the opposition leader in relation to his backbench followers will never be as great.

Another difference is that the orientation within the opposition caucus is far more strategic and tactical. Since the party does not control the levers of power, the principal issues faced are how to react to government plans. The stress will be on the daily and weekly routines of Parliament and how best to exploit the opportunities available to the opposition to attack the government. The long-term problems of governing the country necessarily take second place to these strategic issues because there is nothing an opposition party can do in the immediate future. Moreover, front-bench opposition spokesmen (so-called shadow cabinet ministers) have no firsthand knowledge of programs and lack the public service resources that provide ministers in a government caucus with an advantage in relation to backbenchers.

Opposition parties in the House of Commons since Confederation have recognized the need to pay some attention to organizing for purposes of parliamentary business. But the requirements of this task became more demanding during the twentieth century as parliamentary sessions lengthened, the volume of legislative work increased, public policy became more complicated and the administrative apparatus of government became more extensive. Some division of labour and a measure of specialization within the opposition became necessary. The growth in importance of the mass media as a means of political communication with a better educated electorate meant that there were electoral benefits to be won by conveying the image of a unified team of possible cabinet ministers. It was in the opposition's interest to appear credible as an alternative government by having official spokesmen ready at short notice to provide the media with commentary. Finally, the appointment of shadow cabinet ministers was seen as one way to combat some of the frustrations of being in opposition.

The term "shadow cabinet" refers to the opposition practice of assigning individual MPs to scrutinize particular departments, to question ministers in Parliament, to coordinate the study of subject areas within caucus committees and to deal with outside groups, including the media. . . . Gradually the concept became institutionalized within both parties, but only during the 1960s did it receive full expression.

After the forced departure of Mr. Diefenbaker as Progressive Conservative leader in 1967, Robert Stanfield inherited a deeply divided caucus with a significant element still loyal to the former leader. Stanfield's approach was to seek to appease the disgruntled group. As a price of obtaining party unity, he allowed the number of caucus committee chairmen, who served as designated spokesmen for the party on various topics, to increase from twenty-four in September 1968 to forty-two by December 1974. While chairmen had been elected by full caucus during the Diefenbaker years, Mr. Stanfield had caucus create a committee to advise him and he in turn recommended appointments, which in all cases were approved by caucus. Among his early appointments were noted Diefenbaker loyalists. The chairmen met weekly with the leader. Throughout his term as opposition leader, Mr. Stanfield stressed that these meetings did not constitute a shadow cabinet:

> They [caucus committee chairman] have not in fact constituted a shadow cabinet for at least two reasons. A committee chairmanship has not implied a commitment to a cabinet post in the event of the party forming a government and the committee chairmen have not constituted an inner-circle or decision-making group.[4]

While the chairmen's group was responsible for allocating work to the committees, they did not review the recommendations of caucus committees before those recommendations went to full caucus. A review at that stage would have been both "time-consuming and tension-creating" according to Mr. Stanfield. A strong shadow cabinet of the ablest twenty or so members might have been impressive to the media, but it would likely have led to resentment and rebellion by the remainder of the caucus. "An opposition," wrote Mr. Stanfield, "cannot work effectively if a small group makes the decisions and struts its stuff while the great majority have no role to play except to applaud."[5] Uniting a divided caucus was the primary goal of the caucus arrangements under Mr. Stanfield, but he was not entirely successful since there were fairly constant challenges to his leadership, especially from the western wing of the party.

When Joe Clark took over in 1976 he was determined to change the fractious and ragged image of the party. He retained the caucus committee structure and stressed that the committee chairmanship[s] were crucial to ensuring continuous scrutiny of the government and to demonstrating that the party had a "team" ready to provide a competent alternative. Starting with thirty-seven committee chairmen in April 1976, by December 1978 Mr. Clark had increased the size of his shadow cabinet to forty-five members, which made it larger than the actual Liberal cabinet. The large membership reflected Clark's desire to involve as many MPs as possible together with his belief that a single MP, with limited resources, could not monitor such extensive and technical fields as agriculture or transportation. An innovation by Mr. Clark was the introduction of an executive group of six policy coordinators, who stood above the forty-three chairmen and a chairman of chairmen, who was responsible for overseeing the work of policy coordinators and committee chairmen.

This rather elaborate structure was intended to work as follows. Caucus committee chairmen were expected to prepare recommendations on bills (whether to accept, oppose or seek to amend) for approval first in their coordinating group and then in full caucus. They were expected to lead debate on such bills and to arrange for other speakers. They were expected to question ministers, respond to ministerial statements, organize the opposition's examination of departmental estimates and provide a clearinghouse for information within their policy fields. The six policy coordinators were to perform essentially three functions. They were to supervise the work of committee chairmen to ensure consistency in the positions taken by the party. In addition, they directed research being done by caucus committees. Finally, each coordinator also served as a departmental critic in the House. This dual responsibility helped coordinators to understand their policy fields and enabled them to maintain some profile in the House and in the media. Coordinators met weekly with the party leader, several members of his staff, the House Leader, the Deputy House Leader, and the Chairman of Chairmen. Full shadow cabinet meetings of all forty-five chairmen were convened on a bi-weekly basis to provide opportunities for chairmen to preview recommendations they intended to present to full caucus on government bills.

While these and other steps were designed to ensure coordination and consistency within the party, Mr. Clark was acutely conscious of the resentment that too much centralization would create. Full caucus continued to meet weekly, notices of caucus committee meetings were sent out to all MPs, House bulletins on the status of various items on the parliamentary agenda were issued regularly, and both the House Leader and the whips sought to ensure that all members knew what was happening throughout the caucus structure. Final positions on government bills had to be approved by full caucus, as did position papers developed by caucus committees. The practice under both Mr. Stanfield and Mr. Clark was to rotate shadow cabinet ministers frequently and to pay close attention to the principles of representation followed in the construction of actual cabinets. While the rapid turnover among the party critics ... [militated] against the development of serious specialization, it served to promote a modest range of policy expertise throughout the entire caucus and, more important, it was a way to prevent a falling out in the party over personalities or policies.

Serious challenges to Mr. Clark's leadership emerged after the party lost power. In 1982, with the consent of Mr. Clark, a committee chaired by Mr. Frank Oberle, MP, was established to study the caucus structure, identify problems, and recommend reforms. The final draft of the committee's report was presented to caucus in August 1983 after Mr. Mulroney had replaced Mr. Clark as leader. The Oberle Report made a total of eleven recommendations, many (but not all) of which were accepted by the new leader and his caucus. The changes to the Progressive Conservative caucus had been in place for only a short time before the 1984 change in government so that it is premature to say definitely how effective they might have been.

The four goals of the reforms were to improve morale and the perception of unity within caucus, to make more effective use of caucus time, to utilize better the talents of backbenchers, and to establish a system of frontbench accountability. While the Oberle Report characterized the caucus as "under-developed," it actually resembled, on paper at least, an elaborate bureaucratic structure. As of June 1984 there were ten positions involved with the operation of the full national caucus. There were thirty-four designated spokesmen who monitored the performance of a government minister, and each of these critics was assigned a deputy. There were nine caucus committees, each with a chairman. In total, close to ninety of the 101 Conservative MPs held caucus jobs. The large number of positions seemed designed to avoid the appearance of a dominating elite and as a way to combat potential unrest.

To coordinate this cumbersome apparatus, Mr. Mulroney announced in September 1983 the creation of a Planning and Priorities Committee of caucus. Chaired by the party leader, the Committee consisted of the chairmen of the nine policy committees of caucus, the Opposition House Leader, his deputy and the Chairman of Caucus. Party positions were to be worked out initially in the policy committees. . . . Any MP who was interested could serve on a caucus committee. A policy coordinator from the party's Research Office served with each committee. Policy positions developed within committees were sent first to the Planning and Priorities Committee and then to full caucus. In addition, the caucus committees were each instructed to review the government's "spending envelopes" and to fit proposed policies within the financial limits of the envelopes. A two-day caucus meeting at Mont St. Marie, Quebec, was used to finalize this complicated process of policy development. The process did not override the short-term tactical considerations which normally dominate caucus discussions, but it represented the furthest extension to date of a policy role for an opposition caucus.

It was recognized that the new process reduced the party leader's traditional right to declare policy unilaterally. The optimistic hope was that the leader's authority could be preserved while still encouraging more MPs to contribute to policy formulation. On the matter of the autonomy of the leader, Mr. Mulroney made several statements after his leadership victory that conflicted with existing caucus policy. On the other hand, the process produced intelligent and innovative policy documents in the fields of agriculture and transportation. Along with the standing policy committees of caucus, Mr. Mulroney also appointed, in September 1983, four party task forces dealing with youth employment, accountability of Crown corporations, productivity and technological displacement. Later a task force on the collection practices of Revenue Canada was added. Not surprisingly, the task forces were uneven in the level and quality of work completed, but they brought additional MPs into contact with public servants and outside experts.

One of the recommendations of the Oberle Report was that caucus elect its own executive, including the chairman of caucus, and this was agreed to. The report also noted that an "overwhelming majority" of caucus favoured the adoption of a formal shadow cabinet system. Successive leaders had preferred the term "designated spokesmen" to describe the caucus assignments so as to avoid any implied commitment to an actual cabinet post should the party gain office. The Oberle Report disagreed. Only the understanding that an individual would become the corresponding minister justified the efforts he would make to understand a department's operations. It went further to suggest . . . [the] adoption of an annual secret rating sheet to evaluate the performance of shadow cabinet ministers.If 25 percent of the caucus membership requested it, a review of the individual's performance would be conducted, with the leader left to decide what to do with the results. Despite the assertion of majority support, the assumption of automatic cabinet posts and the rating system were seen as too extreme and were replaced by the assurance of more adequate consultation with caucus over appointments by the leader.

Caucus definitely gained ground when the Progressive Conservatives were in opposition. As part of the package of reforms in August 1983, it was agreed that when in office ministers would be obliged to preview the outlines of legislation with caucus before presenting an actual bill to the House of Commons. It will be interesting to see whether this rule is followed by the Mulroney government. The new system may provide involvement for the enormous backbench contingent elected in September 1984. Even with the new arrangements and the best political will not to ignore backbench opinion, it seems unlikely that the Mulroney cabinet can avoid completely the perennial complaint that a communications gap has developed between caucus and harried ministers. Perhaps the first sign of tighter government control was the move by Prime Minister Mulroney to select personally the chairman of the government caucus in November, 1984 rather than to allow the 210 Conservative MPs to elect their own chairman.

The Party Whips

A little-known and much misunderstood office is that of party whip. With the exception of the NDP, party whips are appointed by the party leader. Since 1963 the chief whips of all parties have been paid a sessional allowance. On the government side there is always a Chief Government Whip, at least one Deputy Whip and usually a number of regional whips depending upon the party's electoral success across the country. Unlike Great Britain, the Chief Government Whip is not normally a member of the cabinet.

The principal activities of the whip can be divided into three categories: management of the party in the Commons, liaison between the caucus and the leadership, and the development of party solidarity. The relative importance of these three functions depends on the party and whether it is in government or in opposition.

In relation to management of the House, this responsibility is now shared with the House Leader for each party. House Leaders have taken over the scheduling of parliamentary business, the negotiation of inter-party agreements and the development of party strategy. The decreased power of the whips means they are less important as a channel of communication with the party leader. Their essential task in terms of House management is to get their members out for votes. In the case of the governing party, the House Leader is seen as being in control of the whip, whereas in the opposition the relationship is more one of equality.

In his management role, the whip performs a number of administrative tasks directly related to the functioning of the caucus and the party's performance in the House. These activities include: the assignment of offices; the development of a seating plan for the Commons; the selection of Members to serve on parliamentary committees (usually done jointly with the House Leader); the monitoring of attendance and preparation of a duty roster to ensure a parliamentary quorum (the onus for this rests more with government whips); the organization of a speakers list; the arrangement of parliamentary pairs; and recommending which Members will join parliamentary delegations.

The second broad function performed by the whips is to serve as a channel for two-way communication between party leaders and backbenchers. To have a sensitive grasp of caucus opinion, the whip must have the confidence of Members. He must listen to their grievances and personal problems. He must not be seen as a tool of the leadership, although he is expected to convey their views and to persuade backbenchers on their behalf. The difficult task as the intermediary is to cultivate the confidence of Members without reciprocating in a way that would undermine the leadership's position. Each performs the liaison role somewhat differently, depending upon his own personality, the nature of his caucus and the relationship which emerges among himself, the party leader and the House Leader, who may also claim to be a sounding board for backbench opinion.

The final responsibility of the whip is to ensure party discipline. The term is used frequently, but seldom defined precisely. It refers to the process of obtaining, and the behaviour reflecting, party solidarity. For the reasons mentioned earlier, few MPs are prone to revolt. Sanctions are much overrated as means to contain dissent. Individual acts of rebellion are usually the product of frustrated personal ambitions rather than policy or ideological disagreements. The only full-scale backbench revolt in recent decades occurred among the Progressive Conservatives during the 29th Parliament (1963–65) when sixty-one members broke with their party, sixteen of them on five or more occasions.

Issues such as the new Canadian flag, bilingualism and opting out of shared-cost programs divided the party, but more important, Mr. Diefenbaker's leadership was under serious challenge. It is a reflection of the ultimate loyalty to party and the force of Mr. Diefenbaker's personality that he was able to retain the support of the vast majority of Conservative MPs. Less drastic forms of protest than breaking party lines are more common. Abstentions and absenteeism are examples of milder means of dissent which the whips must deal with through persuasion, perhaps by arranging for the regional minister to talk with disgruntled members if the party is in office. Absenteeism grew among the Liberals in the final months of the last Parliament. A certain amount of peer pressure also contributes to party solidarity. Most party discipline, however, consists of self-discipline. Also, as was indicated earlier, the party leadership works constantly to keep in touch with the opinions and sentiments of Members to guarantee their support and to help gauge how party policies and approaches are being accepted throughout the country.

FUTURE DIRECTIONS

Because of the wider political context described earlier and because of the caucus arrangements described in the preceding section, party will remain central to the beliefs and the behaviour of most MPs. Caucus has become more important in the two main parties. It has more opportunities and organizational capability to register its opinions and to call the leadership to account. It does not dominate, but it sets limits on the actions of the party leadership. The relationship is a working partnership. Caucus needs leadership and guidance which the cabinet supplies when in office. The party leadership needs a sounding board and confidence in party unity. Above all, caucus is a human institution. Its arrangements may not impress organizational theorists, but they reflect the need to provide incentives to members, strengthen morale and gain support for party positions. As long as caucuses operate democratically and party leaders heed their advice, backbench MPs will continue to favour party discipline.

Approaches to parliamentary reform must recognize the importance of parties. Rather than seek to stifle partisanship, we should strive to improve its quality and then provide opportunities for it to have an impact. In designing plans for reform we must pay some attention to the impact of change on the role of different parties in the House and on the relationship between party leaders and their backbench followers. Without acquiescing in the prevailing political practices as the only possible arrangement, we must pay some attention to the political feasibility of our proposals and the balancing of interests involved. Reform must occur on several levels—the organization and procedures of the House of Commons, the operations of parliamentary parties and the attitudes of Members. It is difficult to know what should, or must, come first, attitudinal changes or reforms to the structure of Parliament. Likely they will have to go hand-in-hand.

Various types of procedural reforms within the House of Commons could have an impact on party caucuses or provide public forums for the expression of the improved quality of partisanship. Not all of these changes can be discussed here. Recently there has been considerable talk about the desirability of allowing more free votes on legislation. Presumably this would allow MPs to act freer of party discipline and would enhance Parliament's reputation with the public who regard party voting negatively.

The ideology of cabinet-parliamentary government which stresses the need for a strong initiating executive, supported by responsible political parties, inhibits MPs from asserting themselves in the policy process. There is a fear that to allow more independence leads us down the slippery slope to congressionalism. There needs to be more acceptance of the idea that pushing alternative policy options in caucus is not subversive to the system. Nor are occasional shows of independence outside caucus. The electorate needs to see and appreciate that there is more diversity of opinion, along regional, ideological and other lines, than the monolithic voting statistics reveal. Some MPs invoke the principles of party government to justify their obsession with constituency work and their inaction in various policy forums. A self-fulfilling prophecy is established. Members of Parliament believe that the outcomes are inevitable and therefore do not participate. Their non-partisanship ensures that the government and the party leadership will prevail.

A number of specific reforms to caucus might encourage greater backbench involvement. There is a strong oral tradition within both caucuses. Minimum use is made of minutes and reports. However, when major reports are forthcoming from policy committees or regional caucuses, they could be printed and circulated in advance to all members. For substantive reports of this kind, extended caucus sessions could be arranged in order to allow enough time for serious discussion.

The use of party task forces, paid for out of party funds, was a useful innovation by the Progressive Conservatives. Travel to regions where the party is underrepresented could ensure better balanced policy recommendations and help a party's rebuilding efforts. Well publicized itineraries and arrangements for press coverage would help to publicize such activity. The emphasis in task force meetings should be on consultation and dialogue, not on making political speeches. Task force reports should be published and made available to interested Canadians.

Greater use should be made of public servants as a source of background information for caucus policy development. In Australia the practice of having public servants brief opposition caucus committees has existed for many years and has not been destructive of the neutrality of the public service. It is only beginning to emerge in Canada, with the Progressive Conservative party having taken considerable advantage of the government's offer to consult officials before the last election. Guidelines would have to be developed to govern appearances by public servants before caucus committees and party task forces. Prior ministerial approval and prohibition on policy debate would be necessary.

On the government side, caucus input to cabinet decision-making might be increased by making the Whip a member of cabinet or by having the chairman of the national caucus serve on the cabinet committee on Legislation and House Planning. Placing the Whip in cabinet as is done in Great Britain could have two contradictory effects in terms of caucus autonomy. It could improve two-way communication since the Whip would actually be present in cabinet deliberations. On the other hand, the Whip would enjoy additional leverage in relation to caucus colleagues because of his position in cabinet. Including the chairman of caucus on the legislation committee might improve communication links, but raises the constitutional question of whether the individual would be bound by the cabinet oath. The arrangement has been followed in Manitoba by the New Democratic government under Premier Pawley. The appointment of an individual in Prime Minister Mulroney's office responsible for caucus liaison may be sufficient to ensure that the cabinet does not lose touch with caucus opinion.

In terms of attitudinal changes, MPs are constrained from making a more meaningful contribution by certain prevailing norms perpetuated by the parties, the media, the electorate and even parliamentarians themselves. Many MPs spend a great deal of time on "constituency service." This function is important in terms of putting a human face on "big government" and can be used creatively to work inductively towards wider judgements about efficiency, effectiveness and fairness of programs. On the other hand, neglect of the policy development and scrutiny functions by sizeable number of MPs limits the capacity of the system—both the House of Commons and the parties—to cope with the growing workload. The problem is reflected in the failure by many MPs to take advantage of the opportunities available through Commons' committees. Talk of the "quality" of MPs is notoriously subjective. There has been more professionalization among members in the past two decades. There needs to emerge more members who are sufficiently educated to assimilate information quickly and who are committed to using the opportunities available to them.

Reliance upon parties to structure parliamentary behaviour has both costs and benefits. Most reformers would like to see less partisanship without going all the way over to free-wheeling congressionalism. Like baby's porridge in the famous fable, partisanship should be neither too "hot" nor too "cold." Whether we can create the institutional arrangements to promote this moderate partisanship remains an open question. Finally, it must be reiterated that wider constitutional and political forces will have more impact on the nature of party politics within Parliament than internal structures.

NOTES

1. S.D. Clark, *The Canadian Manufacturer's Association* (Toronto: University of Toronto Press, 1939), 71–72.
2. Canada, House of Commons, *Debates*, April 10, 1974, 1319.
3. Joseph Wearing, *The L Shaped Party: The Liberal Party of Canada 1958–1980* (Toronto: McGraw-Hill Ryerson, 1981), 155–57.
4. Robert Stanfield, "The Delicate Task of Molding the Opposition," *The Globe and Mail*, 22 November 1975, p. 7.
5. Ibid.

FURTHER READINGS

Atkinson, M.M. "Parliamentary Government in Canada." In M.S.Whittington and G.Williams, eds. *Canadian Politics in the 1980s*. 2nd ed., 331-350. Toronto: Methuen, 1984.

Clarke, H.D., C. Campbell, F.Q. Quo, and A. Goddard, eds. *Parliament, Policy and Representation*. Toronto: Methuen, 1980.

Jackson, R.J., and M.M. Atkinson. *The Canadian Legislative System*. 2nd rev. ed. Toronto: Macmillan, 1980.

Kornberg, A., and W. Mishler. *Influence in Parliament: Canada*. Durham, N.C.: Duke University Press, 1976.

Report of the Special Committee on Reform of the House of Commons. Ottawa: Supply and Services Canada, June, 1985.

22

The Changing Role of the Privy Council Office

R. GORDON ROBERTSON

Four years ago, before this Institute, Arnold Heeney gave a survey of the changes that had overtaken the Privy Council Office when Mackenzie King, faced by the pressures the second world war brought to the cabinet, decided that Canada had to do what Britain had done in 1914: establish a cabinet secretariat. Perhaps Mr King did not really decide quite that much. As Heeney pointed out, Mr King had only the vaguest idea what the cabinet secretariat in Britain did. What he really wanted was something—or more probably someone—to make it more possible for him, as prime minister, to cope with the new scale of government operation. However accidental some of the results may have been in relation to Mr King's initial expectations, the Cabinet Secretariat was grafted on to the Privy Council Office, which had discharged largely formal and legalistic functions since Confederation, and the entire nature of the Office changed. With it gradually changed the operation of cabinet government in Canada. It is now just over thirty years since Arnold Heeney was appointed as the first secretary to the cabinet. Mr King would be astonished—and possibly horrified—if he could see where his 1940 decision has led. Yet the changes have been exactly what his original step was: development "under the pressure of events and in response to actual need."[1]

In the role of the cabinet today, Mr King would find none of the fundamentals altered. It is still the place where the final decisions of government policy are taken, and they are taken by ministers in the exercise of their collective responsibility for that policy. He would be gratified, but not surprised, to note that the prime minister still is the master of the cabinet. But nearly every aspect of operation he would find quite different from those he had known, especially in the years before 1940. By 1945 he had, with some reluctance, agreed to having an agenda for cabinet meetings and to the recording of decisions—and even to their temporary communication in writing to ministers. These were concessions to necessity made grudgingly. Mr King would have preferred to hold everything close to his chest to be brought out for consideration as, when and how he preferred, with his ministers taken by

Abridged from R. Gordon Robertson, "The changing role of the Privy Council Office," *Canadian Public Administration* 14, No. 4 (Winter 1971), 487-508. Reprinted by permission of The Institute of Public Administration of Canada.

surprise and at maximum disadvantage. Today he would find not only the agenda circulated well in advance, but for every meeting a dossier of cabinet memoranda and reports of committees two to three inches thick. He would be relieved to know that some of the prime minister's former advantage had been restored through a system of briefing to inform him of the main issues involved in every question under discussion; to draw to his attention any differences of view between ministers or departments; and to suggest any implications that required consideration in arriving at a decision. However, I suspect Mr King would be more disturbed than comforted when he realized that the briefing papers were based on a meticulous recording by officials of discussions by ministers in all the cabinet committees. Mr King had a due and proper regard for the privacy of ministerial discussion, and the way in which system and secretariat have invaded it would worry him.

THE DEVELOPMENT OF THE
CABINET COMMITTEE SYSTEM

Arnold Heeney depicts graphically the informal way in which the cabinet operated when he became its Secretary in 1940. There was no agenda, no secretariat, no official present at meetings to record what went on, no minute of decisions taken, and no system to communicate the decisions to the departments responsible to implement them. Subjects to be discussed at each meeting were settled by the prime minister with no advance notice to ministers. As ministers had no notice of what was going to come up, they were normally quite unprepared for the discussion or for the decisions expected of them. It was obviously a system that could operate only where the pace of events was relatively slow and where the matters requiring decisions were not overly intricate or complex. Even so, it was a singularly inefficient and unfair way for a collective executive to reach decisions for which all would share responsibility. After a meeting few knew precisely what had been decided; there could be no confidence that all relevant information had been available or considered; and the accurate transmission of decisions, if it occurred at all, was a happy accident.

By March of 1940, "conditions of government had become such that sheer necessity compelled the introduction of systematic procedures for the conduct of ministerial business."[2] Ten cabinet committees had been set up in December 1939, each one theoretically responsible for an aspect of wartime operation. In actual fact, of these ten only the War Committee of the Cabinet had any continuing and active existence early in the war. It was for that committee that the small initial cabinet secretariat worked. There, the procedures for agendas, documents and the recording of decisions were developed. At the end of the war, it had become apparent that having cabinet committees served by a secretariat was an enormous advantage. A number of new committees were established and the secretariat was permitted to begin to serve the cabinet itself.

The nature of the evolving committee system becomes clear from the names of the committees and from Arnold Heeney's comments concerning them. He refers to them as being directed primarily toward particular problems; as being ephemeral and tending to come to an end when their purpose had been served; and as being flexible in their structure and objects.[3] The committee system retained this nature with only minor variations for nearly twenty-five years.

A third stage in the development of the cabinet committee system began with a reorganization instituted by Mr Pearson and announced on January 20, 1964. In his statement, Mr Pearson said:

> Since September, the use of Cabinet committees has been developed to a greater extent than in the past. This development will now be carried farther in order that the Cabinet form of administration may be effectively adapted to the needs of modern government in Canada. Greater use of committees is the best way to obtain, under the Prime Minister's leadership, thorough consideration of policies, co-ordination of government action, and timely decisions in a manner consistent with ministerial and Cabinet responsibility.[4]

Nine cabinet committees were established. Rather than being oriented toward specific *ad hoc* problems or operations, they were for the first time directed toward defined areas of the total governmental process.

A change in procedure was also initiated. Previously things had gone to the cabinet first and had been referred by it to cabinet committees when special consideration and report were required. The new procedure provided that matters requiring cabinet decision in most cases be first brought to the appropriate standing committee by the minister concerned. The committee thus became a normal and formal part of the decision-making process: a stage before consideration in the cabinet itself. In addition to the nine committees listed in Mr Pearson's announcement, there was a tenth — the Treasury Board — which has functioned since 1867. It was established by statute; at that time was regarded as a committee to aid the minister of finance; and was scarcely recognized as a committee of cabinet at all. It continued its powerful and quasi-independent existence; setting administrative standards in departments, improving management in the public service, dealing with contracts, departmental programs and estimates and the expenditures of government in general.

The system established by Mr Pearson in 1964 lasted throughout his regime. The only important change was the addition in January, 1968 of a Cabinet Committee on Priorities and Planning. The government found itself in recurring financial difficulties and crises and it became apparent that there was serious need of a systematic assessment of over-all priorities of expenditure with a view to better long-term planning. It is true that program priorities were set implicitly in the annual estimates, the annual expenditure plans, but this was done by the Treasury Board in the absence of any broad direction from cabinet as to over-all objectives or priorities.

When Mr Trudeau became prime minister, one of his earliest actions, announced on April 30, 1968, was a modification of the cabinet committee system. He said:

> This system has worked well for the past five years and greatly improved the efficiency of government. It has, however, become apparent that further changes are now required to permit a greater centralization of functions and the delegation of certain powers of decisions to the committee. To meet these difficulties, I have revised the system of Cabinet committees to reduce the number of committees and to provide for a regularity in their meetings.[5]

While the establishment of regular times each week for the meeting of each of the standing committees of the cabinet may seem a small change, experience has demonstrated that it produced the major improvement that it was designed to achieve. Ministers are overwhelmed by the obligations, engagements and pressures that throng upon them. Time is committed weeks and even months in advance. With no regular schedule for the meetings of their committees, attendance was poor and spasmodic. Continuing attention to areas of policy by the committee members was impossible. With regular meetings over the entire year, it became possible to have systematic and orderly consideration of problems for submission to the cabinet.

The second important change in 1968 was to give the committees the power, not simply to recommend courses of action to the cabinet, but to take specific decisions. The main object was to remove as many questions from the over-burdened cabinet. It was recognized, however, that there would have to be some means by which ministers who were not on a cabinet committee, or who did not attend a meeting, could re-open discussion or could register a view that differed from the decision of the committee. Without such a capacity, they could not reasonably be expected to assume their share of collective responsibility for policy. Two provisions were made: one was that all ministers, whether members of a committee or not, would receive agendas and documents. They would then know the questions to be discussed and decide whether they had an important interest or view. They could attend any meeting they wished to attend, with the exception of the Cabinet Committee on Priorities and Planning which the Prime Minister wanted to keep relatively small. The second provision was that decisions of the committees would not become effective simply by reason of such decision. They would be listed on an annex to the cabinet agenda for its next meeting. Any minister could notify the deputy secretary to the cabinet before the meeting of the cabinet that he wished to have any particular committee decision discussed. However, if no such notice were given, items on the annex were to be taken as approved by the cabinet and became its own decisions. At that point they were operative and became part of government policy.

Of the standing cabinet committees that now exist, five deal with areas of government activity: External Policy and Defence; Economic Policy; Social Policy; Science, Culture and Information; Government Operations. Four are co-ordinating committees: Priorities and Planning; Treasury Board; Legislation and House Planning; Federal-Provincial Relations. In addition, the Special Committee of the Cabinet handles regulations and other proposed orders in council that do not require the attention of the full cabinet. Other special committees deal, at irregular intervals as required, with questions relating to security and intelligence, the public service, and a few other matters. From time to time special problems assume an importance that require *ad hoc* committees that are abandoned when a satisfactory solution is reached.

One result of the changes introduced in 1968 was to increase greatly the number of cabinet committee meetings. The other was to reduce equally sharply the number of meetings of the cabinet. A statistical comparison of several recent years is of interest: see Table 1.

Table 1

	July 1, 1966 to June 30, 1967	July 1, 1968 to June 30, 1969	July 1, 1969 to June 30, 1970	July 1, 1970 to June 30, 1971
Number of cabinet documents	780	1287	1307	1367
Number of cabinet meetings	139	72	78	75
Number of cabinet committee meetings	120	317	310	311

The number of cabinet documents indicated for the last three years has to be adjusted since about one-third are reports by the cabinet committees of their recommendations or decisions on the substantive documents considered. Excluding such committee reports, the number of cabinet documents has averaged 818 for the last three years against about 700 for 1966–7 on a similarly adjusted basis. The interesting thing is that, as compared with the situation before the revisions in the system were made in 1968, cabinet is dealing with a large volume of business but taking only half as many cabinet meetings to do it. The number of cabinet committee meetings has more than doubled and, according to calculations in the Privy Council Office, the number of "minister-hours" devoted to the total executive function has remained about the same as in 1966–7. The difference is in the more probing, searching and formative nature of discussion that the committees permit, with both Ministers and officials present. I shall deal with this further.

ORGANIZATION OF THE PRIVY COUNCIL OFFICE

Making the cabinet and cabinet committee system work effectively has involved a substantial development of the cabinet secretariat begun in 1940. Heeney records that there were ten officers in 1945. In 1971 there are 55 officers engaged in work relating to the secretariat proper, and there are 13 officers providing the key services in relation to cabinet documents, orders-in-council and administrative and financial services. There is, of course, in addition, the normal complement of clerical and secretarial staff. But it is not a large office to attempt the tasks that are involved in relation to the entire range of government activities.

As shown in Figure 1, the Office is divided into three main divisions: the Operations Division, a Plans Division and a Federal-Provincial Affairs Division, each headed by a deputy secretary to the cabinet. The Operations Division has five secretariats, each under an assistant secretary to the cabinet and each responsible for the work of one of the standing committees which, together, are designed to cover all the fields of government operations. Each secretariat is responsible for moving forward, to and through the cabinet, the proposals that must be considered and decided in relation to the "operations" of government coming within its area of responsibility. The division also services a number of other special and *ad hoc* Cabinet committees with assistance from the other divisions, and has the primary responsibility of providing service to the cabinet itself.

The other main divisions of the Office are responsible for the coordinating committees of the cabinet other than the Treasury Board, which continues to be served by a separate department of government under its own minister, the president of the Treasury Board. The secretary and deputy secretaries of the Board maintain close collaboration with the secretary of the cabinet and the several deputy and assistant secretaries. In the Privy Council Office the Plans Division services the Cabinet Committee on Priorities and Planning as well as the Cabinet Committee on Legislation and House Planning. The Federal-Provincial Affairs Division has a general responsibility for federal relations with the provinces, including constitutional questions, and serves the coordinating committee where policies on matters affecting the provinces are considered. It is, significantly, two of these coordinating committees that are chaired by the prime minister: the Cabinet Committee on Priorities and Planning and the Cabinet Committee on Federal-Provincial Relations. All other standing committees are chaired by designated ministers and are not attended by the prime minister unless some quite unusual circumstance makes it desirable.

The scope of the Cabinet Committee on Priorities and Planning is now more inclusive than the mainly financial aspects of policy toward which it was directed in 1968. It gives special attention to the broad objectives of the

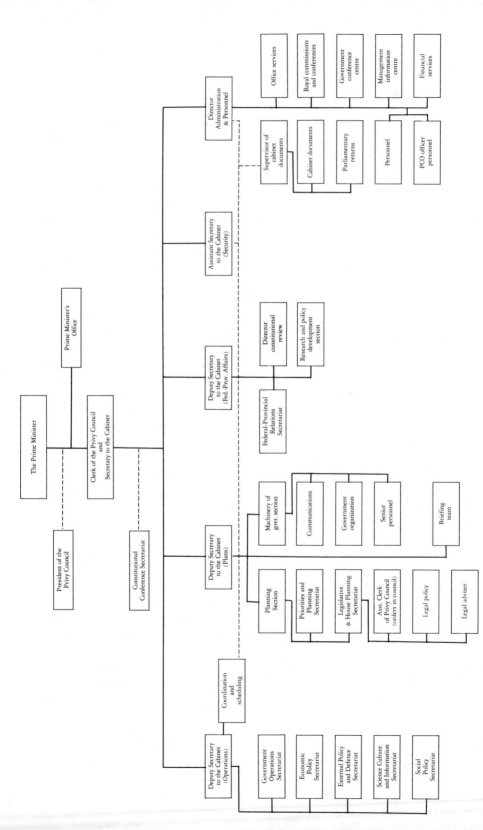

Figure 1 Organization Chart

government and to major questions of policy having long-term implications. It is in that committee that the basic decisions on objectives and strategies are taken, for recommendation to the cabinet. A very important aspect of these is, of course, deciding the general priorities of the government for the allocation of financial resources, and in the policy discussion of other cabinet committees the determination of such priorities is obviously related to and conditioned by the decisions as to policies and strategies. The priorities are set in broad terms: objectives to be achieved, the amount of effort and resource to be directed toward each, the increase or decrease in the emphasis to be accorded to general areas of government action. It is on the basis of such broad decisions that the Treasury Board determines in detail the funds to be made available for specific programs administered by the various departments and fixes the personnel establishment to be allocated to them.

Despite its key role, it is quite wrong, as some have done, to call the present Cabinet Committee on Priorities and Planning an "inner cabinet." Like other committees, its decisions or recommendations go to the cabinet for confirmation or for debate and final decision. They have no status without that confirmation. Moreover the committee is intended to deal with matters of long-term and broad scope. It is not a committee intended to cover any and all areas of government action or to take quick decision on urgent matters.

FEDERAL-PROVINCIAL RELATIONS

It may seem curious that in a federal state, where relations with the provinces are now so important, it was not until Mr Pearson's changes of 1964 that a concerted effort was made to achieve real coordination of them within the Government of Canada. It was, perhaps, because the activities of government hitherto had been more limited in scope and tended more readily to stay within allocated heads of federal or of provincial jurisdiction. Close and frequent relations were less necessary than they are now and they did not, in fact, exist as we now know them. Coordination poses a problem. Relations with the provinces may be and for some years now have been in respect of virtually any subject-matter of government. To assign them to a single minister would create difficulty in defining his responsibilities of a "horizontal" character as distinct from those of his colleagues under whom the various subjects fall. The Privy Council Office and the Department of Finance, which had a specialized group dealing with federal-provincial fiscal policy and economic relations, did try before 1964 to achieve some coordination but, in general, each department conducted such relations as there were in its own areas of responsibility. It became clear that this was not adequate. Programs that were logical and reasonable in relation to one aspect of government—health, transport, agriculture, or whatever it might be—often involved principles that were at conflict with those that had to be applied or developed for other areas or for general application. Action in one program area might unconsciously but fundamentally affect policy or action in another without the responsible federal department—or any minister—realizing it. After 1964, the task of coordination was placed more specifically with officers working as part of the general cabinet secretariat and in 1968 a special division was established headed by a deputy secretary to the cabinet.

The Federal-Provincial Affairs Division, in developing a uniform and consistent policy in relations with the provinces maintains liaison with government departments and tries, within the limits of its resources, to keep contact with the provinces as well. It coordinates preparations for major federal-provincial conferences and for constitutional review meetings.

It has become a common theme of public comment that federal-provincial relations should be more constant and intimate, and that this would remove the disagreements that have been, and continue to be, a feature of our national life. I must confess to a certain scepticism. At times one could be led to wonder whether it is not the very plethora of meetings that has provided the occasions for the disagreements and for the wide reporting of them. A Canadian Parkinson could probably demonstrate that the number of federal-provincial disputes in any one year varies in direct proportion to the number of federal-provincial meetings multiplied by the cube of the number of federal-provincial coordinating agencies in the respective governments. The following list indicates the number of formal committees as of June, 1970 that meet at the ministerial or deputy ministerial level: federal and all provinces, 28; federal and all provinces plus outside groups, 9; federal-provincial-municipal, 2; inter-provincial, federal representatives as observers, 12; federal and provincial-regional representatives, 6; total, 57. On the same date the total number of multilateral committees and sub-committees involving officials was 260. There were another 150 bilateral committees of the same type. Whatever the source of problems may be, it is not the lack of meetings to talk about them.

CABINET GOVERNMENT—
SOME MODERN ASPECTS

The organization and the activities of cabinet committees and of the cabinet secretariat are directed to one essential purpose: the more effective operation of our cabinet system, in which a collective executive decides the objectives, policies and programs of government and in which its members take a joint responsibility for the result. From the nature of our executive, so different from that in countries like the United States where it is a single person, there flow a number of implications and consequences. The first and most obvious is that each member of the executive must know what is involved in the policy and program decisions for which he shares responsibility, whether they are his direct concern or that of a colleague. The second is that each must have an opportunity to participate in those decisions. Participation is at its most rudimentary if it is simply to approve or disapprove a fully developed proposal. To be real and substantial it should involve awareness of problems and relevant consideration and discussion of lines of solution at a stage early enough that a minister can share in shaping the final result. Either to accept or to reject a finished product may be totally unsatisfactory and, indeed, the wrong decision so far as the government as a whole is concerned: some unknown and unconsidered alternative might have been the preferred and much better course if participation could have been effected at an earlier stage.

The cabinet before 1940 failed adequately to meet either of these needs for a collective executive. Ministers usually did not know in any real sense the full nature or implications of decisions they took on matters coming under the direct responsibility of their colleagues, and usually they had no involvement in the development of the proposals. A line of policy or a program would normally have been worked out between the responsible minister and his officials. There might have been discussion with the officials of other departments and possibly, though more rarely, with another minister whose interest was very obvious or whose power to oppose might be feared. Because the pressures on ministers were less, there were too, discussions of general issues of policy in the cabinet from time to time. Essentially, however, the collective executive operated on confidence, often justified and sometimes not, that a minister knew what he was doing in his own field and that a capacity to approve or disapprove a final proposal developed in and for that field was sufficient for the government as a whole. It was a system in which each minister had his own empire, big or small. He and his officials worked out policy and program that seemed sensible for it. The prime minister, within the limits of his information and knowledge, had a general influence and control. The rest of the cabinet 'participated' at the final stage, with a "yes" or a "no," or with limited modifications on the edges of a developed proposal. It was workable only when issues were such that the general information and common sense of politically sensitive men could be reasonably sufficient to decide whether a proposal was practical and acceptable or not.

The situation changed somewhat during the first period of the cabinet committee system: the very fact of having committees meant more discussion of at least designated subjects. But C.D. Howe, J.G. Gardiner and other monarchs of sovereign areas brooked little interference with what was theirs. The evolution did not go far. It became progressively apparent that methods were neither adequate for the inter-related complexity of problems with which modern government has to cope, nor satisfactory to the ministers who wanted a real share in developing the total policy for which they were responsible. The system as it now exists was gradually developed in an effort to meet both these needs. The changes of 1964 brought a greater measure of real consideration beyond departmental boundaries than in the past, but the situation was still one of discussing the end result rather than of participating in its production. The 1968 reforms brought that further stage. Discussions now on broad policy and general priorities mean that all ministers have an opportunity to share in giving shape to government in general and to the areas of policy for which others of their colleagues are directly responsible.

The second feature of today's system has already been pointed out. In all but the most exceptional circumstances, matters go to a cabinet committee *first* before coming to the cabinet. The essential officials of all interested departments are normally present. There can be, and is, probing of the information by any minister, reasoning and views of officials serving the minister putting forward the proposal. This is something that never happened before 1940 and was rare, except with regard to war policy and certain specific subjects, until recent years. Now it is constant and is a valuable addition to the total process of policy development. Ministers talk to other deputies than their own, and deputies to other ministers. Advice is less monolithic and discussions much more real. Frequently the result is to refer a matter back to officials or to the originating department for further work or for development of a different proposal. At the very least, significant modifications may be suggested in the report to the cabinet for further discussion and final decision.

The positive results of the new system are many. Ministers have the opportunity to learn more of what their colleagues are doing and to be better informed about all aspects of government activities than under the previous methods. Policies and programs are related more consciously and more constantly to the totality of problems and less to partial or sectional aspects. Ministers have more influence on the shape of policy as a whole, and on its development, and officials have proportionately less than they used to. This judgement is at variance with the conventional wisdom but, after thirty years in the operation of government, more than half of it at the centre, I feel confident that it is correct. Finally, there is a more planned attempt to assess in advance the probable nature of developments of broad national and social moment before they arrive as immediate problems for urgent action. Such things rarely fall within the boundaries established for administrative convenience, and, when plans were confined within these tidy limits, some quite major questions remained neglected. Obviously the success of such efforts is only partial, but they do constitute important gains. They have, however, had their price.

One price is in ministerial time: the rarest of government commodities. Better understanding and analysis of complex interrelated problems and policies takes time. Discussion that leads to mature decision-making takes time. All this time, and the energy that is expended in the decision-making process, is subtracted from the finite capacity and endurance of the minister. If a minister works a five-day week of eleven hours a day, plus a good part of each week-end, what competition is there for those hours? There is attendance in the House, executive work in his department, constituency business, general work for the party, general work for the government; consultation with businessmen, representatives of public organizations and others to keep him informed and to learn their views; ceremonial duties, travel to and from the constituency, travel to and from departmental assignments away from Ottawa; personal business; and finally, as part of the collective executive, reading cabinet documents, attending cabinet committees and attending cabinet. To do these last three thoroughly in the face of all the other demands is almost impossible. Something must suffer if more time goes into the process of executive decision. It is quite possible that the improvements in the cabinet system may have been at too high a cost in the time ministers can devote to the total political role that they fill. The right balance will never be final or certain: it will change with prime ministers, governments and the stages in their four- or five-year life cycles.

I have mentioned that the old days of fiefdom are passing. To work efficiently, a complex system requires some elements to give something to other elements to maintain a balance. Ministers now, in many cases, have to give up some share of their authority and control to other ministers if the totality of policies is to be coordinated. This is unpleasant, frustrating and can cause natural resentment when the minister thinks he sees clearly what is needed, wants to make a success of his particular portfolio and is anxious to fulfil perfectly natural ambitions. Understandably, some ministers feel their new share in the policies and programs of others to be unequal compensation for the subtraction they suffer in their individual capacity to decide and to act. Speed of action is certainly less in the new system, and ministers have less chance to appear in roles of clear and firm decision.

Another resentment which ministers must feel is that caused by the ubiquity of officials, including Privy Council officers. This, too, is a part of the price for a system that in total gives broader and more real ministerial participation in policy as a whole. Without the documents, reports and interaction between ministers and officials, it could not work as well—if it could work at all.

The relationships between ministers and officials are seen in interesting and sensitive focus at cabinet committee meetings. Ministers in general carry the discussion, but officials participate actively, especially on factual and operational aspects. They are conscious that policy decision[s], and therefore the main aspects of policy assessment, are for ministers. There are, however, occasions when a deputy must objectively review the full policy and public implications of proposed action. There are times when the responsible minister lets the deputy explain: there are equally times when the deputy remains silent while the minister explains. Both normally participate in active discussion. It is a blending of roles that requires mutual confidence and an awareness of their differences. The seasoned public servant will recognize that what are at issue are the policies of the government, to be decided by the judgment of the ministers, even though this means accepting gracefully decisions that may be personally distasteful. The advantages in decision-making are clear. There are equally advantages in administration. The exposure of senior officials to the thinking and policy concerns of ministers helps them to explain to their departments the logic of decisions that might otherwise seem wrong, incomprehensible or "petty politics."

During policy discussion there comes a time when the ministers must be alone. Candour is required. There must be no restraints on frank talk. This occurs at cabinet where the ultimate decision is taken. The ministers are responsible. It is their government. There must be no inhibition caused by the presence of an advocate official. He advises, he has full opportunity to be heard in the appropriate forum, but the cabinet decides, not the senior officials or any group of them.

Our decision-making process differs from that in Britain in several respects. One is in the degree to which ministers and officials are brought together in meetings. The British depend on inter-departmental committees of officials for the preliminary analysis and for the development of policy recommendations. There are cabinet committees, but none are attended by both ministers and officials. We borrowed British techniques and experience in 1940, and for a decade or more we relied more heavily than we do now on the recommendations of senior interdepartmental committees. Since then the two systems have developed independently and somewhat differently. Canadian ministers prefer to hear at first hand the differing views of senior officials from whatever departments may be involved, rather than to receive a report in which these differences have been compromised or suppressed. The problem is to have enough of such argument and difference at the ministerial stage without consuming undue amounts of time. Interdepartmental committees may have to be rélied on rather more in future, but the valuable blend of ministers and officials at committees will undoubtedly be retained.

The changes in the operation of our cabinet, and the advantages I have suggested for the system today, do not mean that those governing today are somehow possessed of greater wisdom than those who did so under other arrangements. It is rather that the conditions and the problems are very different, mainly in complexity and in scale. The change in thirty-odd years from a country relying essentially on a few primary products to an advanced, technological society is manifest. That alone would be a significant development. Equally complex and difficult for government has been the increased expectation that the state should achieve a more rapid growth and a more equitable distribution of both means and products so that a better share in the good life can be obtained by the greatest number. Social policies and social programs are complex and difficult in themselves: the added dimension of integration with provincial policies and programs multiplies the difficulties. New problems are added as personal and social expectations reach higher and higher. New policies must be devised to meet the relentless growth of the large urban areas. Other contributions to complexity are added continually: the revolution of rising expectations; ceaseless innovation and technological change; increasing mobility of people and rapidly changing social and moral values; feelings of alienation and disorientation; the demand for better protection of the consumer—and dozens of others: new, demanding, urgent.

Governing Canada has some special complications: the fact of our bilingual national character, our multicultural nature; our sheer size; the regional differences in economic growth and prosperity; the geographic, economic and cultural bonds that fuse us to the United States of America while we struggle to be different. All of these social, economic, physical, psychic and systemic factors and forces produce stress. Much of the task of regulating these stresses and strains, assuaging the pain and balancing the growth, falls upon the federal government.

With this increasing complexity, and partly as a result of it, comes the new scale of operation for those who must decide. The problems involved in tax reform, foreign ownership, the respective powers of the provinces and the federal government, the balance between environmental protection and resource development, inflation and unemployment, to name only a few that have been with us in recent months, come at a speed and with a level of expectation as to results that create a governmental load quite new in our history. For ministers to know the factors, the possible courses of action and the implications of alternative policies with respect to a single problem—or even to one part of a single problem—requires a thorough presentation of all the issues, time to weigh and analyse them, and adequate opportunity to discuss and to decide. Ministers today have a load that tries the limits of physical and intellectual powers.

ON PLANNING

Ministers would be justified in asking whether some of the things done in recent years have not added to their agonies rather than reduced them. This would especially be understandable in relation to planning, for there, something quite new has been added.

The principal planning objective of the past three years has been to increase the time available between the perception of a problem by ministers and the necessity of action with regard to it. An effort has been made to identify ministerial responsibility for the problem as clearly and as soon as possible and to marshal whatever is required to examine and prepare a plan to try to manage it, and finally, to allow time to organize for action.

What is urgent will always clamour for attention and probably get it. What is important must receive attention well in advance and be given lots of time for organization for action. If this does not happen—and if it is not insisted on whatever the pressures may be—the urgent pushes out the important. The consequence is to be overtaken by crises and to let events, rather than choice, determine the direction we take.

A good deal is being written about "normative planning" and what is taken by some to be the converse, "incrementalism." Considerable improvement has been made in the Privy Council Office in the last four years in methods of analysis, using general systems theory and to some extent general communications theory. Understanding the governmental system and the social system better, due to the insights of these theories, is one thing, but successful application of the theories by the central executive in a rational, creative way is another. The policy sciences taken together constitute a frontier field, and applying policy science to cabinet government is still a frontier effort. From our experience it might be said that "top down" policy determination works part of the time, "bottom up" policy determination works much of the time, and that, despite all efforts, many government decisions will continue to be in response to problems arriving at a different time and in a different form from what was anticipated. The process of integrated planning has, however, made great strides in the last few years at all levels of the government.

I have said that the time of ministers is finite, that it is already overburdened, and that more can be done in one place only at the cost of less in another. Integrated planning would be the easiest thing to shove aside. It would probably not show in the immediate future. Where it would show, in the longer term, would be in allowing drift and accident, the *ad hoc*, the technological jungle and the opportunity for individual profit to determine the shape of our national and social future. It is in response to a recognized need to do what is reasonably possible to foresee and to plan, however inadequate and imperfect the results, that ministers have added this new dimension to our governmental operation.

CABINET, PRIME MINISTER AND DEPARTMENTS

In the complex operation of the cabinet system, with ministers together deciding the policies and the strategies of government, it is obvious that the role of the prime minister is crucial. He alone of the cabinet is responsible for no one aspect of government. He alone looks constantly at the total picture. He it is who has chosen his colleagues; he is recognized by the country and by parliament as the person generally responsible for the success or failure of government in meeting the problems of the state. Within the cabinet he must be the master of his administration but he must recognize its collective nature and avoid autocracy. Where necessary he must change the functions of his colleagues and, when necessary, invite or require a departure. He is the only one with the authority to police and to change the boundaries between them. The many-sided role of the prime minister is nowhere more difficult or more demanding of a sensitive balance of intellectual and human qualities than when he is chairman of the collective executive. Assisting the prime minister in ensuring a coherence of policy and giving support in the total process of decision-making are two of the main functions of the Privy Council Office.

As a department provides its ministers with analysis, advice and recommendations on the objectives of the department, so the Privy Council Office gives the prime minister information, analysis and advice on the totality of policies. The probability of a coherence of policy is thus enhanced.

It will be readily apparent that the information, analysis and advice for the prime minister ties in completely with the broader function of the Privy Council Office in servicing the entire system of cabinet and cabinet committees which I have described. Programs and policy proposals come to the Office as submissions to the cabinet and are immediately circulated to all ministers. At the same time they are allocated to one or another of the cabinet committees. The appropriate secretariat picks it up at that point. If more information is needed, that is secured. If it has aspects that relate to another committee or secretariat, there is consultation to see how best to cover all aspects of consideration. When the matter goes to the committee, the secretariat records the discussion, prepares the minutes and draws up the report of decision, or recommendation to go on to the cabinet. All of this provides the information for a briefing document to the prime minister covering all essential aspects of every question on each cabinet agenda. It provides too the basis for the information system of the office on the operations of government as a whole.

When decisions are taken by the cabinet, or when committee recommendations or decisions are confirmed, the next stage in the Privy Council Office function is to inform departments and agencies with speed and precision so that action may follow. This may be done orally if the need for speed is great, but the standard procedure is communication by a 'Record of Decision' within twenty-four hours. Orders in council may or may not be involved: usually not. It is only when a formal, legal instrument is required that they enter the picture.

This, in essence, is the role of the Privy Council Office: one of information, coordination, follow-up and support provided to the prime minister and the cabinet as a whole with, as a vital aspect, constant relations with all departments of the government. It is a role that is replete with possibilities for misunderstanding, bruised feelings and grievances, and it has been necessary to develop principles to avoid them as much as possible. I might mention a few.

The first is the "stay-off-the-field" principle. The Privy Council Office operates no programs and administers no projects except those which are related to its own housekeeping. Administration and action are with the departments. It is the minister who is responsible and his department that acts. The ball does not stay in the Privy Council Office: it is passed to the team that is to make the play. The Privy Council Office remains aware and is frequently informed or consulted, but enters the game, only if inter-agency operation is required where a "neutral" can provide a coordinating service, or where there is a requirement for counsel and assistance that can only be provided by those with a general view.

With regard to planning as we define it, a similar principle applies. The goals of the government, as perceived by the cabinet, are stated as clearly as possible, but departments are left to act and to be guided by the principles laid down. This does not, however, mean that the roles are carried through in isolation. One of the benefits of the central planning process, with a longer look ahead and a broader look around, has been to help departments to anticipate new needs and new developments. This stimulates departments to respond and from the interaction emerges better integrated policy and, on the whole, a greater awareness of inter-jurisdictional problems. The basic principle, however, remains: the Privy Council Office tries to know, to discuss and to communicate, but execution is for departments.

The second principle, that supports the first, is that "Plans works through Operations." The Operational Division and the Federal-Provincial Affairs Division have the major portion of the workload relating to the various secretariats and cabinet committees. The Plans Division does not have a parallel structure covering the various areas of government activity but works through the other divisions, using their expertise, their contacts and their channels of communication. Thus planning is not divorced from operational insight and a duplication of contact with departments and agencies is avoided as much as possible.

A third principle is that there are virtually no officers making a career within the Privy Council Office. It is apparent that should a Privy Council Officer become an advocate of any policy or program, the objective and integrating character of his advice could be jeopardized. Further, if a Privy Council officer begins to feel authoritative, as opposed to possessing a proper and healthy appreciation of the limits of his role, his function is out of phase with the spirit of the Office. There can be no tendency to usurp the authority and the control which belongs to ministers and to the prime minister. Recognizing the fact of human frailty, it is unwise to permit too long a time in the sensitive work of the Privy Council Office. Conscious identification with a particular line and the wish to see action follow a course one believes to be wise, are subtle forces that can limit usefulness in this peculiar organization.

The term of appointment is purposely kept short, three to five years with personnel on loan from all departments. Vigour and integrity are maintained, but an elite with any sense of separateness or difference is not permitted to form. Privy Council Office service is part of broader career development. When alumni leave the Office to enter other parts of the system it is with an intimate appreciation of the central decision-making process, and the working of the total system. They are, or should be, much better equipped, in whatever department they enter, to analyse problems, develop programs and administer operations with a sense of the inter-relations that are vital, even in quite specialized areas.

Principle four is that the Privy Council Office is deliberately kept small. By recruiting versatile officers who work hard *not* to be encumbered by program responsibility, a large staff is avoided: I have indicated their present number. To expand beyond a certain critical size would be to deny the other principles that help control the Privy Council Office.

One other matter that must be referred to is the relationship between the Privy Council Office and the Prime Minister's Office. It is one that calls for a greater harmony. Given the prime minister's functions as leader of a political party, leader of the government in the House of Commons, and chairman of the cabinet, the prime minister's own staff are constantly securing information, analysing and recommending on matters that relate to policies and objectives of the government. The Prime Minister's Office is partisan, politically oriented, yet operationally sensitive. The Privy Council Office is non-partisan, operationally oriented yet politically sensitive. It has been established between the principal secretary to the prime minister and his senior staff on the one hand, and the clerk of the Privy Council and his senior staff on the other, that they share the same fact base but keep out of each other's affairs. What is known in each office is provided freely and openly to the other if it is relevant or needed for its work, but each acts from a perspective and in a role quite different from the other.

Obviously each office requires a knowledge of the areas of action of the other and the actions of the two must, to the extent that they affect the total policy for action of the government, be consistent. To aid in information and coherence two sets of meetings with the prime minister, involving both offices, have been established. The first, a daily meeting, with two officers from the Privy Council Office and two from the Prime Minister's Office, has been a constant base for coordination for many years. It started with one officer from each place and, as life became more complex and difficult, became the two from each that now attend. It deals with the day-to-day flow of affairs that the prime minister must know, consider, prepare for or decide. The second meeting is on planning, and occurs once a week with an additional person from each office who has responsibility in the longer term development and direction of policy.

It goes without saying that mutual confidence and mutual respect—and mutual understanding of the basic difference between the two roles—are the foundations of cooperation between the Prime Minister's Office and the Privy Council Office. All have been present, in my experience, and without them the operation of government under the stresses of today would be difficult indeed.

OF POLITICS AND PUBLIC SERVICE

Finally, a word about politics and liberty. The popular will is expressed through politics. Ideology, technology and bureaucracy have to be restrained so that politics may rule, otherwise theories, inventions and organizations would smother life. The elected representative of the people, who makes a trade of politics, but who makes no claim to total knowledge or wisdom, must be provided with optimum liberty to decide what set of relationships ought to prevail, stabilized at a chosen level, to constitute the goals of government. Providing this liberty to the politicians is exceedingly difficult. From the standpoint of the cabinet minister, the complications start with the catalogue of complexities of existing policies, programs and activities. To ensure that responsible politicians and not civil servants have the final say, the cabinet has the responsibility of decision. For what it does, it is responsible to parliament. It would be entirely unrealistic to expect the larger body of politicians to be quiescent and, in fact, our democratic system would be failing if they were. Thus the desired freedom of ministers to consider and to decide is conditioned by a torrent of observations, questions, and advice all proclaimed publicly from committees of the House of Commons and senate, backbenchers of all parties and from party conventions.

Further constraints on freedom of decision come from the fact of instant communications. Opinions and reactions, relevant or irrelevant, tumble in without ceasing. The speed with which society moves has conditioned the public to expect instantaneous decision and action on matters of public policy. Unrealistic expectations clamour for action at once. The final complication is the most serious of all. There is an unrecognized inconsistency in the demand for both speed and participation in difficult decisions on complex issues.

Conscious of the catalogue of complexities in the society which they have been elected to regulate, surrounded by the reality of the existing amalgam of policy programs and activities, sensitive to the clamour of friendly and unfriendly voices and often urged to act boldly but with due regard, in the light of all considerations but at once, cabinet ministers can only feel more captive than free. The staff of the Privy Council Office has, as its duty, to provide whatever aid and assistance it can to permit individual and collective judgment to prevail in the cabinet chamber and, through its wise application, sound policy to emerge to meet the problems of the present and the future. To assist government in this way is demanding employment, but for sheer interest and intellectual challenge it would be hard to match. The agenda of cabinet, week by week, reflects the problems, interests and aspirations of the Canadian people. To understand, to inform, to advise and to share in the discussion of such meetings is a reward in itself. For an official to feel that he has contributed, however modestly, to constructive decisions for a better country in a better world brings no glory, but a great sense of participation in events that count.

NOTES

1. A.D.P. Heeney, "Mackenzie King and the Cabinet Secretariat," *Canadian Public Administration*, vol. 10, September 1967, p. 370.
2. Ibid., p. 367.

3. A.D.P. Heeney, "Cabinet Government in Canada: some recent developments in the machinery of the Central Executive," *Canadian Journal of Economics and Political Science*, August 1946, p. 288.
4. Press release, Office of the Prime Minister, January 20, 1964.
5. Press release, Office of the Prime Minister, "Statement by the Prime Minister on Cabinet committee structure," April 30, 1968.

FURTHER READINGS

See "Further Readings" at end of Reading 23.

23

Recent Changes in the Cabinet
Decision-making System in Ottawa

Ian D. Clark

This paper describes the cabinet decision-making system instituted by Prime Minister Mulroney and some of the ways in which it differs from that of previous governments. For the purposes of the paper, the decision-making system includes the cabinet committee structure, the support provided to it by the central agencies, and the procedures for securing cabinet approval of a proposal.

HISTORICAL EVOLUTION

Constitutional and political realities impose a certain number of functions on any cabinet system. These include:

- securing agreement among ministers on government priorities (e.g., on expenditures, taxation and legislation) and on actions which extend beyond the bounds of a single ministerial portfolio;
- securing agreement on parliamentary actions by the government required to obtain passage of the government's program while retaining the confidence of the House;
- providing a forum for ministerial debate on issues of general interest;
- providing adequate information to ministers relative to decisions for which they will be held collectively responsible and which may impact on their individual responsibilities; and
- providing adequate information to the prime minister to carry out his responsibilities and his leadership role.

Although these cabinet functions do not differ from government to government, other factors obviously do. Any prime minister must take account of specific parliamentary, economic, regional and personal factors in designing a cabinet system in which ministers can make policy and expenditure decisions in a manner which is both timely and makes best use of their time, in a way which ensures that the ministry commands the support of Parliament and

Abridged from Ian D. Clark, "Recent changes in the cabinet decision-making system in Ottawa," *Canadian Public Administration* 28, No. 2 (Summer 1985), 185-201. Reprinted by permission of The Institute of Public Administration of Canada.

maintains cabinet solidarity. The cabinet system is, therefore, a very personal choice of the prime minister. No ideal system exists which would suit the needs of all prime ministers and all governments. Indeed, a cabinet system tends to evolve over the life of a government as the prime minister makes adjustments to adapt it to changing circumstances.

In attempting to describe the present cabinet decision-making system, it is useful to keep in mind the caveat provided by Arnold Heeney in his description of the federal cabinet system in 1945:

> . . . the practices and procedures of which I give some account are by no means immutable; the functions and composition of the committees, which I shall describe, are by no means rigid. Quite the contrary. These are rules and forms honoured frequently in the breach. They are always subordinate to the circumstances of the case and the conveniences and necessities of the Prime Minister and his colleagues.[1]

Figure 1 summarizes the changes made in the cabinet structure and the central agencies by successive prime ministers in the last half century.

Mackenzie King's cabinet had sixteen ministers in 1935 and nineteen in 1948. Prior to the Second World War, the only standing committees were Treasury Board and the Defence and Wheat committees. During the war ten new committees were established, by far the most important of which was the Cabinet War Committee chaired by the prime minister. After 1945 the use of committees was more ad hoc, with issues being referred to a committee by cabinet and the committees coming to an end when they had finished their work. In 1940 the clerk of the Privy Council was given the additional title of secretary to the cabinet, and a cabinet secretariat evolved within the Privy Council Office. Written agendas, minutes and decisions came into use, first for the War Committee and after June 1945 for the cabinet itself.

Louis St. Laurent's cabinet had twenty ministers in 1948 and twenty-one in 1957. Most cabinet committees continued to be ad hoc and designed to accomplish a particular task assigned by cabinet. Cabinet met about three times a week and handled a good deal of detailed business (such as contracts), particularly before the Financial Administration Act of 1951 gave the Treasury Board final authority over government contracts as well as routine financial and administrative items and gave the Governor-in-Council authority to delegate further powers to the board.

John Diefenbaker's cabinet had seventeen ministers in 1957 and twenty-three in 1963. Less use was made of committees, and cabinet met two or three times a week. The cabinet paper system that had evolved since the war was retained, but less use was made of committees of officials, and fewer officials attended cabinet and cabinet committee meetings.

The Pearson cabinet had twenty-six ministers in 1963 and twenty-five in 1968. The committee system was reorganized in 1964 to replace the ad hoc committees with nine standing committees. The Priorities and Planning

Committee was established in 1968 to develop government priorities in relation to the overall fiscal situation. In addition, over time, several other standing and special committees were established as the need arose. For the first time the cabinet procedures required issues to be dealt with in committee before going to full cabinet, but a certain amount of the committee work was still tasked by cabinet. Attendance of officials at cabinet committee meetings increased. Following the Glassco Commission recommendations, much of the responsibility for detailed expenditure decisions was transferred to the Treasury Board from the minister of finance, and in 1966 the Treasury Board Secretariat was split off from the Department of Finance and a separate ministerial portfolio, president of the Treasury Board, was created.

Figure 1
Evolution of Cabinet Structures and Central Agencies

Prime Minister	Ministry	Cabinet and Central Agencies
King (1935–1948)	16–19	— several committees during War, fewer after
		— recorded minutes and decisions of the War Committee from 1940 and of Cabinet from 1945
		— several Cabinet meetings weekly
St. Laurent (1948–1957)	20–21	— committees generaly tasked by Cabinet
		— several Cabinet meetings weekly
		— TB delegated significant powers through FAA (1951)
Diefenbaker (1957–1963)	17–23	— Infrequent meetings of committees
		— several Cabinet meetings weekly
Pearson (1963–1968)	26–25	— 9 standing committees (1968); issues generally to committee before Cabinet
		— Cabinet meetings weekly
		— Priorities and Planning (1968)
		— TBS split from Finance (1966) with separate Minister
Trudeau (1968–1979)	27–33	— fewer committees with more authority
		— FPRO split from PCO (1975)
		— OCG split from TBS (1977)
		— MSED established (1979)
Clark (1979–1980)	30	— Inner Cabinet plus 12 committees
		— PEMS established
		— MSSD set up (proclamation 1980)

Figure 1
Evolution of Cabinet Structures and Central Agencies (Cont'd)

Prime Minister	Ministry	Cabinet and Central Agencies
Trudeau (1980–1984)	32–37	— Priorities and Planning with authority to issue decisions
		— PEMS elaborated
		— Ministry of State function in External
		— MSERD with FEDCs (1982)
Turner (1984)	29	— Communications, Labour Relations and Western Affairs Committees wound up
		— MSERD, MSSD and similar function within External wound up; FEDCs to DRIE
		— "mirror committees" wound up
		— Assessment Notes discontinued
Mulroney (1984–)	40	— Foreign and Defence Policy Committee wound up
		— Communications Committee established
		— Envelopes consolidated
		— PEMS rules simplified

Pierre Trudeau's cabinet had twenty-seven ministers in 1968 (after the election) and thirty-three in 1979. The cabinet committee structure was reorganized so that there would be fewer standing committees (eight) with more delegated authority. Most issues went to committee before going to full cabinet. The operation of the cabinet system during the early years of Prime Minister Trudeau's government has been described by Gordon Robertson.[2] In 1975 a branch of the Privy Council Office was split off to form a separate Federal-Provincial Relations Office. In 1977, following the recommendation of the auditor general, the Office of the Comptroller General, reporting to the president of the Treasury Board, was established. In 1978 the Board of Economic Development Ministers and a supporting Ministry of State for Economic Development (MSED) were established (proclaimed in 1979). The secretary of this ministry chaired a committee of deputy ministers and circulated "Assessment Notes" to all members of the Board of Economic Development Ministers on the issues coming before the board.

Joe Clark's cabinet had thirty ministers. An inner cabinet with final decision-making authority was established. The role of full cabinet was limited to political discussion and coordination. The Policy and Expenditure Management System (PEMS) was instituted and four policy sectors designated: economic development, social development, foreign and defence policy, and government operations. Each sector was the responsibility of a standing cabinet committee of the same name and each committee was responsible for two of the ten policy "envelopes" into which the expenditure budget was divided (inner cabinet had the remaining two). The result was that policy committees had both the means and the duty to consider the expenditure implications of the policy proposals brought before them. Ministerial submissions were discussed initially in committee and then ratified by inner cabinet which also provided overall coordination. The Ministry of State for Economic Development was given the role of providing policy advice to the Cabinet Committee on Economic Development, through its chairman, and a parallel Ministry of State for Social Development (MSSD) was set up (although not formally proclaimed by Parliament until after the next election). "Mirror committees" of deputy ministers were established in the economic development and social development sectors to coordinate public service support in the preparation of ministerial submissions to cabinet. The operation of the planning systems and the various committees of ministers and officials during the Trudeau and Clark governments has been described by Richard French and by Richard Van Loon.[3]

The Trudeau cabinet had thirty-two ministers in 1980 and thirty-seven in 1984. Both cabinet and the Priorities and Planning Committee had authority to take the final decisions. The PEMS was retained with the Cabinet Committee on Priorities and Planning assuming the coordinating role of inner cabinet and its procedures were spelled out in greater detail. In 1982 a policy coordination branch with "Ministry of State" functions (e.g., responsibility for sector-wide analysis in the foreign and defence policy sector, for providing Assessment Notes to ministers on items coming to the Cabinet Committee on Foreign and Defence Policy and for supporting the mirror commitee) was established within the Department of External Affairs. At the same time, the Cabinet Committee on Economic and Regional Development was reconstituted to ensure that regional concerns were better taken into account in economic development decisions. At the public service level, this change was reflected in the announced intention to convert MSED to the Ministry of State for Economic and Regional Development (MSERD) and the establishment in that ministry of a Federal Economic Development Coordinator (FEDC) in each province.

John Turner's cabinet had twenty-nine ministers. The number of cabinet committees was reduced to ten as the previously existing committees on communications, labour relations and western affairs were abolished. The committees that made up the Policy and Expenditure Management System (Priorities and Planning, Treasury Board and the four sectoral policy committees) were retained. MSERD, MSSD and the ministry of state functions within External Affairs were wound up as were the mirror committees of deputy ministers and the practice of circulating Assessment Notes. The FEDCS were transferred to the Department of Regional Industrial Expansion.

Figure 2
Cabinet Committees

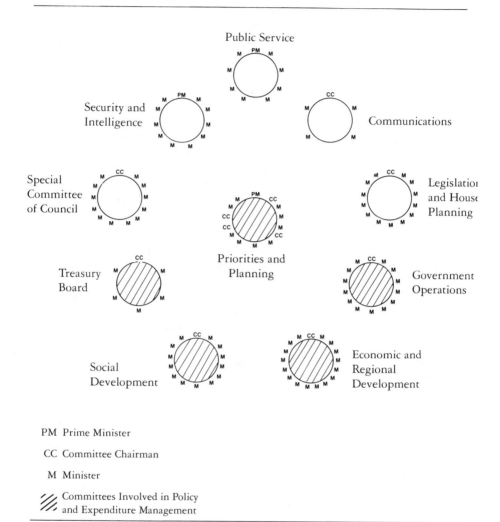

PM Prime Minister

CC Committee Chairman

M Minister

Committees Involved in Policy
and Expenditure Management

It is apparent from this brief historical review that each Canadian prime minister has adapted the cabinet structure to deal with the challenges he felt his government had to meet. This pattern is also seen in other countries with Westminster-style governments. Britain's Margaret Thatcher manages a cabinet system which is quite different from that of, say, Australia's Bob Hawke.

An important corollary of the political and personal imperatives in cabinet decision-making is that all cabinet systems are designed by prime ministers to suit their own personal styles and the particular circumstances of the time. The basic cabinet functions noted earlier can be performed with more or less involvement of officials, with more or less paper at the cabinet table, with more or less frequent meetings of cabinet and its committees, and with more or less reliance on formal procedures.

CABINET COMMITTEES AND ENVELOPES

In Brian Mulroney's government, the basic function of cabinet committees is, as previously, to work through the financial, policy and political implications of proposals for government initiatives, and to reach a decision which can be presented for ratification by full cabinet or by the Priorities and Planning Committee. As Figure 2 illustrates, Mr. Mulroney has provided for ten cabinet committees, three fewer than existed in the last Trudeau government and the same number as in the Turner government. There are four committees which, along with the Treasury Board, form the PEMS.

The Priorities and Planning Committee has an overall "executive committee" role, which includes establishing the government's broad priorities and policy direction and, in that context, setting envelope levels, ratifying committee decisions and, in general, coordinating the work of the other cabinet committees within the context of the overall government program. The Priorities and Planning Committee performs the policy committee function for those issues which the prime minister deems to be best dealt with in the cabinet committee that he chairs—including issues that would formerly have gone to the Cabinet Committee on Foreign and Defence Policy. In that latter connection, Priorities and Planning can be considered to be one of the sectoral policy committees, along with the Cabinet Committee on Economic and Regional Development, the Cabinet Committee on Social Development and the Cabinet Committee on Government Operations.

There are currently five other standing committees in Mr. Mulroney's cabinet system: Legislation and House Planning, Communications, the Public Service, Security and Intelligence, and the Special Committee of Council.

The expenditure envelopes have been reorganized. The current sturcture is illustrated in Figure 3.

The responsibility for the external affairs and aid and the defence envelopes now rests with the Cabinet Committee on Priorities and Planning. The former energy envelope was folded into the economic and regional development envelope. The previous justice and legal envelope and the social affairs envelope were combined to form the social development envelope.

Figure 3
Expenditure Envelopes
(Total $105.4 billion)*

GOVERNMENT OPERATIONS			SOCIAL DEVELOPMENT	ECONOMIC AND REGIONAL DEVELOP.	PRIORITIES AND PLANNING

GOVERNMENT OPERATIONS

PARLIAMENT
$201 billion

· House of Commons
· Parliamentary Library
· Senate

SERVICES TO GOVERNMENT
$4.1 billion

· Canada Post
· Central Agencies
· National Revenue
· Public Works
· Supply and Services

SOCIAL DEVELOPMENT

SOCIAL DEVELOPMENT
$44.8 billion

· Arts & Culture
· Canada Mortgage and Housing
· Employment and Immigration
· Environment
· Fitness and Amateur Sport
· Indian Affairs and Northern Development
· Justice
· National Health and Welfare
· Secretary of State
· Solicitor General
· Veterans Affairs

ECONOMIC AND REGIONAL DEVELOP.

ECONOMIC AND REGIONAL DEVELOPMENT
$13.0 billion

· Agriculture
· Communications
· Consumer and Corporate Affairs
· Energy, Mines and Resources
· Fisheries
· Forestry
· International Trade
· Labour
· Regional Industrial Expansion
· Science and Technology
· Transport

PRIORITIES AND PLANNING

FISCAL ARRANGEMENTS
$5.7 billion

EXTERNAL AFFAIRS AND AID
$2.7 billion

· External Affairs
· Foreign Aid

DEFENCE
$9.4 billion

· National Defence

PUBLIC DEBT
$25.5 billion

*1985–86 Estimates.

DIVISION OF RESPONSIBILITIES
AMONG THE CENTRAL AGENCIES

Whereas a line department is expected to focus on its own programs and its individual minister's objectives and responsibilities, central agencies exist to support the cabinet's corporate objectives and the collective responsibilities of ministers.

Figure 4 lists a number of the corporate concerns for which a lead minister has been assigned coordinating responsibility. The public service support to the coordinating ministers is provided by the three "traditional" central agencies—the Privy Council Office, the Department of Finance and the Treasury Board Secretariat—as well as five more sectorally focused coordinating agencies: the Department of External Affairs, the Federal-Provincial Relations Office, the Department of Justice, the Ministry of State for Science and Technology, and the Office of the Comptroller General.

In addition there are a number of ministers with coordinating responsibilities relating to particular groups (e.g., status of women, youth, small businesses) who are supported by secretariats within departments. As well, departmental ministers have coordinating or lead responsibilities within their sectors. The minister of regional industrial expansion retains special responsibilities for regional development through his responsibilities for the Economic and Regional Development Agreements and the Federal Economic Development Coordinators. Finally, there are a number of "common service agencies" providing service for other government departments. Examples include Public Works Canada, Supply and Services Canada and Statistics Canada.

The wind-up of the ministries of state for Social Development and Economic and Regional Development, and the ministry of state function within External Affairs, has been accompanied by a realignment of the roles and responsibilities of the three traditional central agencies. The revised responsibilities of the Privy Council Office, the Department of Finance and the Treasury Board Secretariat are summarized in Figure 5.

In operational terms, the wind-up of the ministries of state means that the Department of Finance has increased responsibilities for analysing the economic effectiveness of new proposals. In addition, the Department of Finance, of the central agencies, maintains the broadest socioeconomic analytical capability. The department advises both the minister of finance and, through the Privy Council Office, the chairmen of the policy committees on the overall economic impacts of proposals coming to cabinet.

The Treasury Board Secretariat's "chief accountant" responsibilities include regular reporting to the cabinet committees on the status of their envelope reserves as well as advice to the Treasury Board and, through the Privy Council Office, to the committee chairmen on the efficiency and management aspects of new proposals and on the effectiveness of existing programs. The secretariat needs to be highly knowledgeable about the expenditure patterns associated

Figure 4
Corporate Concerns and Lead Responsibilities

Areas of Concern	Lead Ministers
policy coherence	Prime Minister Committee Chairmen
resource limits	Min. of Finance, President of TB
administrative practices	Treasury Board
legislative program	Prime Minister, House Leader
decision-making process	Prime Minister
international relations	Sec. of State for External Affairs
federal-provincial relations	Prime Minister
legal interpretation	Attorney General
science policy	Min. of State for Science and Technology
financial practices	President of TB

with existing programs so that new proposals can be assessed in light of current operations.

The Privy Council Office has a responsibility to communicate with departments on items destined for cabinet and to prepare briefing notes for policy committee chairmen and the prime minister. It has a continuing responsibility to analyse issues in relation to prime ministerial and governmental priorities and in relation to the prime minister's prerogatives for governmental organization and ministerial mandates. It also has a "due process" responsibility for ensuring that adequate information is available for ministers when they consider an item and that ministers receive adequate notice of items to be discussed.

Policy development takes place in departments under the direction of the minister with statutory responsibility and the onus is on departments to ensure that appropriate consultation occurs. Where interdepartmental meetings are required, they are usually convened by officials reporting to the responsible

Figure 5
Roles of the Three Traditional Central Agencies

Privy Council Office	Treasury Board Secretariat	Department of Finance
• support for Prime Minister on prerogatives of government organization, ministerial mandates and senior personnel	• support for Minister and Treasury Board on statutory responsibilities, monitoring of delegated authorities, Estimates process	• support for Minister of Finance on statutory responsibilities
• secretariat support for Cabinet operations	• government's chief accountant (including reports on policy reserves)	• government's chief economist (including preparation of fiscal plan and economic outlook)
• briefing of committee chairmen (including Prime Minister) on relationship of new proposals to priorities and to other activities	• advice on resource implications and management aspects of proposals and of effectiveness of existing programs (to Minister, Treasury Board and, through PCO, to committee chairmen)	• advice on economic impacts of proposals and their relationship to macro-economic framework (to Minister and, through PCO, to committee chairmen)

minister. Only in rare cases—usually when another minister or department is not satisfied with the degree of consultation undertaken by the sponsoring department—would an official from a central agency convene an interdepartmental meeting relative to an item sponsored by a departmental minister.

The principal function previously performed by the ministries of state which is not being replaced is the ongoing provision of a "sectoral" analytical perspective in the economic development, social development, or foreign and defence policy sectors. In contrast to the situation prevailing in the early 1980s, there are no regular meetings of deputy ministers to review items destined for cabinet, no Assessment Notes or Assessment Reports, and no annual articulations of sectoral strategies in Sectoral Overview papers. The prime minister may, of course, call for such papers and meetings as the need arises including, if necessary, a new system for reviewing sectoral perspectives.

One major former capacity of the Ministry of State for Economic and Regional Development that remains intact is the provincial network of Federal Economic Development Coordinators (FEDCS) supported by an associate deputy minister and an Office of Regional Development in Ottawa. These groups are now in the Department of Regional Industrial Expansion, where they operate as a distinct unit within the department. The coordinators retain their provincial overview role, including the coordination of activities under the recently signed federal-provincial Economic and Regional Development Agreements. The coordinators and the Office of Regional Development provide support to cabinet committee deliberations through their minister, who has been appointed chairman of the Cabinet Committee on Economic and Regional Development.

In summary, the new alignment of responsibilities following the wind-up of the ministries of state is likely to continue to evolve in response to the emerging requirements of cabinet decision-making. Most but not necessarily all of the activities formerly undertaken by the ministries of state will be performed by the three traditional central agencies which, between them, are responsible for providing ministers with most of the necessary public service-based analytical and secretariat support for cabinet decision-making.

PRINCIPLES AND PROCEDURES
OF THE PEMS

The underlying principles of the PEMS have not changed. Sectoral envelopes have been retained, and the integration of policy and expenditure decisions remains a central feature of the system. The new description of the principles issued to departments in September 1984 places an even greater emphasis on the need to review existing expenditure priorities and reallocate resources within departments and envelopes in order to generate resources for new initiatives. The procedures have been streamlined, and can now be described in seven pages rather than in the twenty-odd pages of text in the previous documents.

Individual ministers now have greater discretion to make expenditure decisions within their approved departmental resources without cabinet approval, where they judge that the policy or political implications of the decision are not sufficient to warrant collective cabinet examination. This is intended to simplify decision-making and increase the ability of individual ministers to exercise their discretionary authority within broad corporate management standards. At the same time, the access to the policy reserves is intended to be more limited and ministers are encouraged to look to their own budgets rather than to "the centre" to finance new proposals. Minor expenditure initiatives are expected to be financed out of internal resources rather than the policy reserves. This does not, of course, imply that no proposals with low cost come to cabinet for policy approval. There are many proposals with few or no immediate financial implications which could have substantial policy and political implications and for which ministers want to ensure they have the collective support of their colleagues.

Figure 6
Process of Cabinet Approval

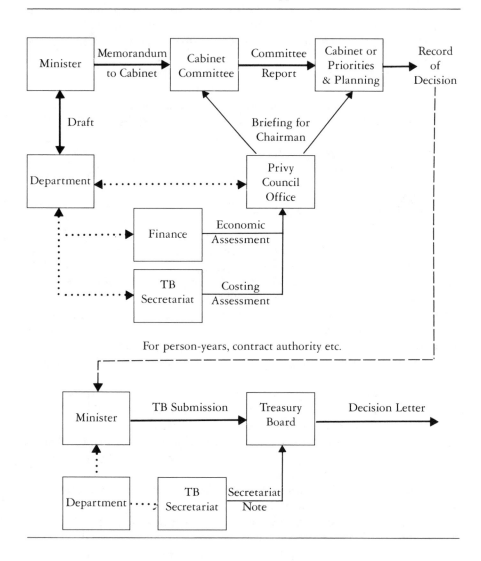

PROCESS FOR CABINET APPROVAL

The process for cabinet approval of a proposed course of action is illustrated in Figure 6.

Despite the number of dotted lines and boxes in Figure 6, the process of cabinet approval is straightforward. The process is based on two primary principles: first, that all ministers have the right to bring to their colleagues proposals for government action in their area of policy responsibility; and second, that all ministers should have the opportunity to express an informed view within the cabinet process on a proposal for which they will share collective responsibility.

The existence of the central agencies and the dotted interdepartmental consultation lines in Figure 6 do not compromise the first principle. A minister can sign a memorandum whose recommendations ignore comments made by officials reporting to other ministers. The second principle, however, requires that those aspects of the proposal which could be of concern to other ministers be brought to their attention in time for them to express their views to their colleagues. As noted earlier, the essential role of the three central agencies is to help ensure that ministers collectively have the appropriate information before them. It is the task of the chairmen of the cabinet committees and of the prime minister to ensure that all relevant views are expressed before the government's position is finalized.

There are several cabinet procedures designed specifically to support the second principle. One is the 4-day rule: the requirement that a memorandum to cabinet be signed early enough so that the Privy Council Office can circulate it to all ministers four working days before the cabinet meeting. There is an additional 7-day rule: a requirement that the relevant assistant secretary to the cabinet be made aware of a minister's intention to bring a subject to the committee a week before the meeting. There is also the provision that all ministers receive all memoranda to cabinet (except in the rare instance, usually pursuant to interim negotiating positions, where memoranda may be restricted to ministers on the Priorities and Planning Committee) and all committee agendas. Finally, any minister can attend any meeting of the Economic and Regional Development Committee, the Social Development Committee, the Government Operations Committee, the Communications Committee, the Legislation and House Planning Committee or the Special Committee of Council. (Invitations from the chairmen are required for non-members to attend other committees.)

Even though the Priorities and Planning Committee has the authority to make final decisions, most items of general interest (e.g., Throne Speech preparation, major foreign policy initiatives) that are brought initially to Priorities and Planning are subsequently taken to cabinet for discussion. These provisions ensure that all ministers have a chance to express their views on virtually all matters of general interest.

In most cases, where all the relevant views have been expressed in cabinet committee, the committee reports can be ratified with little or no discussion in cabinet or the Priorities and Planning Committee. The resultant Record of Decision is not a legal document; it merely expresses the collective will of the ministry to undertake a particular course of action. Where a statutory instrument is involved, a separate order-in-council is prepared which, after signature by the governor general, takes legal force.

In contrast to other cabinet committees, the Treasury Board is a statutory body created under the Financial Administration Act. Members are formally appointed by the Governor in Council. Treasury Board authorization is required for many departmental actions pursuant to cabinet decisions (e.g., to spend under particular legislation, to enter into certain contracts, to increase the use of public service resources).

MEETINGS OF OFFICIALS

The wind-up of sectoral mirror committees of deputy ministers means that there is no regular review of cabinet committee items by officials collectively in advance of ministerial discussion. This will require more reliance to be placed on meetings between representatives of the concerned departments. In particular, departments have an obligation to ensure that External Affairs is consulted where international relations may be affected, that the Federal-Provincial Relations Office is consulted where federal-provincial relations could be implicated, and that the Ministry of State for Science and Technology is consulted where science and technology policy issues are at stake in order that the relevant minister can be apprised of the proposal at an early point in the process.

Where there is a perceived need for interdepartmental consultation at the level of officials, meetings are called by the lead department or requested by another department concerned with the issue. This puts more responsibility on officials to consult with other concerned departments and to pay close attention to proposals being developed in other departments in order to ensure that ministers are made aware of any issues that will affect their portfolio responsibilities.

There are a number of regular forums for discussion of issues of general interest to deputy ministers. The Coordinating Committee of Deputy Ministers is chaired by the secretary to the cabinet and includes the deputies from Finance, the Treasury Board Secretariat, External Affairs, Justice and the Federal-Provincial Relations Office. Its purpose is to keep the heads of the central agencies informed of the collective concerns of the government. In addition, the secretary to the cabinet convenes meetings with all deputy ministers from time to time to keep deputies apprised of issues of concern to the prime minister and to discuss procedural issues relative to the operation of the cabinet system. Finally, there is a monthly deputy ministers' luncheon hosted by the secretary of the cabinet which provides an opportunity to conduct informal business and discuss issues of general interest.

CONCLUSIONS

The cabinet system in the federal government was changed significantly in 1984: there are now fewer Cabinet committees; several envelopes have been consolidated; ministries of state have been wound up; the roles of the three traditional central agencies have been realigned; the procedures of the PEMS have been simplified; and the mirror committees of officials have been discontinued. The basic purpose of the new set of arrangements is, however, the same as any cabinet system—to reach timely decisions in a way that will satisfy the government's priorities and needs while maintaining the collective responsibility of the cabinet ministers.

NOTES

1. A.D.P. Heeney, "Cabinet Government in Canada: Some Recent Developments in the Machinery of the Central Executive," *Canadian Journal of Economics and Political Science*, 12 (1946), pp. 282–301.
2. Gordon Robertson, "The Changing Role of the Privy Council Office." *Canadian Public Administration*, 14, no. 4 (Winter 1971), pp. 487–508.
3. Richard French, *How Ottawa Decides: Planning and Industrial Policy Making*, 1968–1984, 2nd. ed. (Toronto: James Lorimer and Co., 1984); and Richard Van Loon, "The Policy and Expenditure Management System in the Federal Government: The First Three Years," *Canadian Public Administration*, 26, no. 2 (Summer 1983), pp. 255–85.

FURTHER READINGS

Aucoin, P. "Organizational Change in the Machinery of Canadian Government: From Rational Management to Brokerage Politics." *Canadian Journal of Political Science* 19, 1 (March 1986): 3–27.

Campbell, C. *Governments Under Stress: Executives and Key Bureaucrats in Washington, London and Ottawa.* Toronto: University of Toronto Press, 1983.

Campbell, C., and G. Szablowski. *The Superbureaucrats: Structure and Behaviour in Central Agencies.* Toronto: Macmillan, 1979.

French, R.D. "The Privy Council Office: Support for Cabinet Decision Making." In R. Schultz *et al.*, eds. *The Canadian Political Process.* 3rd ed. 363–394. Toronto: Holt, Rinehart and Winston, 1979.

French, R.D., with R. Van Loon. *How Ottawa Decides: Planning and Industrial Policy-Making, 1968–1984.* 2nd ed. Toronto: Lorimer, 1984.

Van Loon, R.J. "Kaleidoscope in Grey: The Policy Process in Ottawa." In M.S. Whittington and G. Williams, eds. *Canadian Politics in the 1980s.* 2nd ed. 412–433. Toronto: Methuen, 1984.

24

Prime Ministers and Power

PATRICK WELLER

"The influence of the crown has increased, is increasing and ought to be diminished": this famous motion by Dunning was passed in the House of Commons in 1780. Two hundred years later similar comments are made about the power of prime ministers. Their influence is said to have increased to a level at which it cannot be checked; their control over government activities is regarded as excessive, and their accountability as far too limited. Observers complain that the system has changed from cabinet government to prime ministerial government, or that the office of prime minister has been "presidentialised." As a result the prime ministership has been the subject of proposals designed to limit its power. These views have been expressed most frequently in Britain, where debate on the subject has continued for twenty years, but similar feelings are noticeable in other parliamentary democracies like Canada, Australia and New Zealand.

Obviously the power wielded by prime ministers is substantial. They hold the key position at the "apex of power" in democratic governments. Governments are as often known by the names of the leader as by his or her party. . . . The media concentrate their attention on what prime ministers say and do. Prime ministers represent their countries overseas. Therefore knowledge of what they do, how they relate to other parts of the political system, what options are available to them, is essential to an understanding of the way we are governed.

How powerful are they? The question is of fundamental importance. In a parliamentary democracy the language of government is collective. We speak of collective ministerial responsibility and of party control of parliament. The main decision-making body is said to be cabinet; its decisions are authoritative. Prime ministers are not presidents, that is individuals at the top of the pile; they are the leaders of teams. The processes of government have been developed on the assumption that these constitutional doctrines are accurate. Ministers sit at the head of departments which they must run and for which they, not the prime minister, are constitutionally responsible. If this assumption is

Abridged from Patrick Weller, "Prime Ministers and Power," *First Among Equals. Prime Ministers in Westminster Systems* (London: Allen & Unwin, 1985), 1-17. Reprinted by permission of Allen & Unwin (Publishers) Ltd.

mistaken—and that has still to be proved—then the impact on government will be considerable. . . .

THE DEBATE ON PRIME MINISTERIAL OR CABINET GOVERNMENT

The view that prime ministers have become pre-eminent was first expounded in detail by John Mackintosh in his study of the British cabinet. It was then popularised—and at times in Mackintosh's opinion extended to an unwarranted degree—by Richard Crossman's introduction to Walter Bagehot's *The English Constitution*. Crossman restated his views, with the benefit of six years of ministerial experience, in the Godkin Lectures presented at Harvard in 1970 and later published as *Inside View*. He then provided massive (if at times contradictory) evidence in his three volumes of *The Diaries of a Cabinet Minister*. Mackintosh answered critics of his argument in a series of books and articles, although in the third edition of *The British Cabinet* he did not tackle them directly because he believed that "events since [1962] have done so much to confirm the general case argued in this book."

Reduced to simplified form, the argument of Crossman and Mackintosh is that the prime ministers' powers were exerted through their control over several important levers. The first two are traditional:

1 The right to select and dismiss ministers. All ministers are chosen by prime ministers and depend on them for their jobs. Even though some ministers may be chosen because of their position in the party, prime ministers can keep out those whom they do not want.
2 The right to control cabinet's structure and proceedings. Prime ministers control access to cabinet through the agenda, chair the meetings, summarise the decisions, decide the composition and subject matter of cabinet committees and may limit decisions to meetings of inner or partial cabinets.

These two levers have existed for over 150 years, although their value has been extended by the increase in the workload of cabinet and in the size of ministries. To these have been added four other factors:

3 The development of disciplined parties, which support prime ministers and try to guarantee that they can maintain a parliamentary majority.
4 The increased direct influences of the media. Since the media concentrate on the figure at the top, prime ministers can use that attention for their own purposes. The immediacy of access to the general public provided by the electronic media and the development of a mass, and manipulable, press have provided great opportunities for prime ministers to get their message across.
5 The increase in the levels of prime ministerial patronage.
6 The development of the new processes of co-ordination have provided sources

of intelligence and manipulation which allow prime ministers to control the large bureaucratic machines of which they are the head.

The general argument can be summarised by two passages. Mackintosh's original proposition, re-affirmed fourteen years later, stated:

> The country is governed by the Prime Minister who leads, coordinates and maintains a series of Ministers, all of whom are advised and backed by the Civil Service. Some decisions are taken by the Prime Minister alone, some in consultation between him and the Senior Ministers, while others are left to the heads of departments, the Cabinet, Cabinet Committees, or the permanent officials . . . There is no single catch-phrase that can describe this form of government, but it may be pictured as a cone. The Prime Minister stands at the apex, supported by and giving power to a widening series of rings of senior ministers, the Cabinet, its Committees, non-Cabinet Ministers, and departments. Of these rings, the only one above the level of the Civil Service that has formal existence and acts as a court of appeal for the lower tiers is the Cabinet.[1]

Crossman's formulation was slightly different. He relegated cabinet to join the other dignified, if unimportant, parts of the constitution and argued that the prime minister was "now the apex not only of a highly centralised political machine, but also of an equally centralised and vastly more powerful administrative machine." Then, adjusting Bagehot's view of cabinet to his own purposes, he wrote: "The post-war epoch has seen the final transformation of Cabinet Government into Prime Ministerial Government. Under this system "the hyphen which joins, the buckle which fastens," the legislative part of the state to the executive has become one man."[2]

These two passages indicate the degree to which Crossman extended Mackintosh's argument. Yet there is considerable similarity between the two in the predominance given to the prime minister as the centre of most action. Neither argues that prime ministers make *all* the decisions or that they can ignore their ministerial colleagues; but they do suggest that prime ministers have few limitations on their power, that they decide where decisions will be taken and often what they will be.

Critics of Crossman and Mackintosh argue that the picture they paint exaggerates prime minsterial power. George Jones has consistently argued that they underestimate the power of ministers who can have an independent influence; the prime minister is only as powerful as his or her colleagues allow; they are restricted in their choice of ministers and in their treatment of cabinet. Jones provides an epigrammatic summary of his counterview: "The British system of government cannot really be called prime ministerial government, nor cabinet government. The right term is ministerial government."[3] Patrick Gordon Walker, like Crossman writing with the benefit of considerable ministerial experience, is concerned with one basic question and its answer: "Where does political authority lie? Where can the great political decisions be made? I hope to have shown that the answer in Britain is in the Cabinet and in the Cabinet alone."[4] He argues that, despite obvious shortcomings as an efficient decision-making body—a function for which it was not designed—cabinet is never the creature of the prime minister. Ronald Butt has argued that parliament too is more influential than Mackintosh and Crossman suggest and that it cannot be taken for granted by the prime minister. Ian Gilmour suggests that the power of the great departments of state is such that they can act as a counterweight and that British government is thus self-limiting. In turn, these writers have tried to reinstate the power of ministers, cabinet, parliament and the civil service against the claims of prime ministerial power.

Prime ministers too have denied that they hold the excessive power attributed to them by Mackintosh and Crossman. Macmillan and Heath both declared that they would not take important decisions without consulting cabinet. (They did not indicate whether they felt certain of carrying cabinet with them when they did consult.) Wilson declared that the

> ... predominantly academic verdict of overriding prime ministerial power is wrong. It ignores the system of democratic checks and balances, in Parliament, in the Cabinet, and not least in the party machine and the party in the country . . . Cabinet is a democracy, not an autocracy; each member of it, including the prime minister, seeks to convince his colleagues as to the course to follow. The Cabinet bears his stamp, it is true, on each and every policy issue, but it is the Cabinet, not the prime minister, who decides.[5]

Of the people interviewed for this study, those closest to a prime minister were always most conscious of the limitations on prime ministerial power.

It is easy to overstate either side of the case. By extracting general propositions stated in absolute terms, and then testing them against empirical evidence and individual events, it is fairly easy to disprove any notion as broad and vague as prime ministerial dominance. An argument that prime ministers will always dominate their cabinet can be discredited by finding examples where they have been overruled, but a few instances do not disprove a general tendency concerned with the distribution of power. Obviously propositions about absolute authority serve little use: prime ministers are part of political systems, interaction is continuous, calculations of advantage and position are consistently re-evaluated. To present an argument on the grounds that one side will always win is too crude.

In 1975 Tony King was critical of the literature on both sides:

> Unfortunately, neither side has ever specified in any detail what it takes the term 'prime ministerial government' to mean and therefore what its empirical referents are; both sides, instead of analyzing the available evidence systematically, have resorted to proof by illustration . . . As a result most of the debate has been conducted at the level of a barroom brawl. Some good points have been made, just as at least a few good punches are landed in most barroom brawls. But remarkably little new evidence has been forthcoming and the terms of the debate in the 1970s are almost exactly what they were in the early 1960s.[6]

Little has changed; there has been no effort to define the terms, in part, perhaps, because of the inherent difficulty of doing so within the confines of a single country.

The argument has been contested most fervently in Britain, but it has been joined on similar lines in other countries with parliamentary systems of government. In Canada the long terms that many prime ministers have served may have helped the case; Trudeau, after all, was prime minister for fifteen years, with only one break of nine months; Mackenzie King held office for twenty years, thirteen of them unbroken. Following the development of the British argument, in 1969 Denis Smith argued that Trudeau was clearly trying to presidentialise the system and spoke of his "unerring presidential instincts": he concluded that Canada has "created . . . a presidential system without its congressional advantages." His summary is worthy of inclusion alongside those of Mackintosh and Crossman:

> Before the accession of Pierre Trudeau, our presidential system, however, was diffuse and ill-organized. But Pierre Trudeau is extraordinarily clear-headed and realistic about the sources of political power in Canada. On the one hand, he has recognized the immense power of initiative and guidance that exists in the federal bureaucracy; and he has seen that this great instrument of power lacked effective centralized political leadership. He has created that coordinated leadership by organizing around him a presidential office, and by bringing order and discipline to the Cabinet's operations. He has made brilliant use of the public opportunities of a party leader, in convention, in the general election, and in his continuing encounters outside Parliament. He has recognized that the public responds first to personalities, not to issues, and so he campaigns for the most generalized mandate. And now, finally, he has successfully altered the procedures of the House of Commons so that it may serve the legislative purpose of an efficient presidential administration.[7]

Others have emphasised Trudeau's dominant, if changing, role. Yet this has also been challenged by arguments similar to those espoused in Britain. . . . One senior official commented that the presidential image was a "figment of the non-accountable media's imagination, nurtured to the point of a vendetta." He argued that Canadian prime ministers, and particularly Trudeau, were usually powerful but patient.

In New Zealand, writers in the late 1960s and early 1970s were careful to point out that their country had *not* followed British trends and they deliberately repudiated the idea of prime ministerial government. . . .

In Australia there is less academic literature on the question. Several journalists emphasise the central role of prime ministers, particularly of Menzies, Whitlam and Fraser . . ., and attribute to them considerable power. While the discussion is seldom systematic, belief in over-powerful prime ministers has become orthodox. . . .

In all four countries the argument has two interrelated parts: the first is that the power of the prime minister has *increased*; the second tries to identify how much power a modern prime minister *actually has*. Both issues have been debated at some length, but more recently debate has concentrated on the second—which raises questions of more immediate importance.

The argument for the increase in power is that when changes in the party and media are coupled with the existing controls over cabinet and patronage, the prime ministers' powers must be enlarged. Whether that growth has been gradual or spasmodic is disputed . . ., and there are problems of comparisons of historical material. Given that the scope of government has increased dramatically, that modern economic management has extended the government's tentacles and public expectations, and that many of the processes have altered, it is questionable how realistic historical comparisons are. It might be possible to argue that Sir Robert Peel had greater control over his ministers than Douglas Home, while still being able to argue that his national influence over the people was much less. But that would be as much a comment on the impact of government as on the power of the prime minister. Some of the political conventions and institutions may have remained, but the environment in which politicians work has become very different. Comparing the actions of prime ministers across a century . . . understates the pressures of modern society. . . .

The second theme in the debate concerns the power of modern prime ministers. What capacity do they have to get their own way? The immediate problem that confronts such a debate is one of personality. The important factor, it is argued, is not institutions but individuals. Modern prime ministers are uncommon creatures. In the 1945–82 period there were nine prime ministers in Britain, six in Canada, eight in New Zealand and nine in Australia. Those small numbers make classifications difficult and allow considerable scope for differing explanations on the basis of style.

Obviously personality and style do make a difference. As Rose comments, "In the most trivial sense there *is* a difference in personality and style between Prime Ministers. Clement Attlee was not Winston Churchill, nor was Edward Heath the same sort of politician as Harold Wilson."[8] The influence of particular individuals also changes over time: electoral success, public prestige and high professional reputation give prime ministers authority that can easily be diminished when those temporary advantages disappear. The Attlee of 1945, fresh from a great victory and surrounded by powerful lieutenants, was in a different position from the tired man of 1951. So too the Trudeau of 1968 from the withdrawn leader of 1975, or Holyoake in 1960 and 1971. Political circumstances and individual energies lead to variations in prime ministerial power that are perhaps as great as changes of people. Of course the final policy outcomes would be different if the prime ministers were to be changed; no-one would seriously argue that prime ministers have no influence. Yet systematically relating personality to patterns of outcome is probably impossible.

Research on prime ministerial power can be concerned with identifying the framework and processes which *do* limit or assist the influence of personalities and which shape those outcomes. Rose argues that prime ministers are inevitably constrained by traditional expectations:

> There are certain roles that all Prime Ministers must undertake. While individual Prime Ministers may respond differently to the demands of office, the imperatives tend to remain constant.
>
> The high degree of institutionalization in British government—encompassing informal Whitehall norms even more than formal organizations—is the most powerful determinant of what a Prime Minister can or can not do. Personal style influences how a Prime Minister carries out the demands of office, but it does not determine what is to be done. The first priority of a Prime Minister is to do what is expected of him or her.[9]

To examine institutions rather than personalities is not to deny the importance of the latter, but rather to concentrate on the framework within which they must work.

Institutional arrangements make demands on prime ministers, who have a limited amount of time. If they first do what they must, that is if they first obey the institutional and normative imperatives of office, only then do they have the scope to make choices of what to do with the remaining time. Imperatives may be created by the demands of the job or by the expectations of their colleagues and the wider public. It is important therefore to understand these norms and imperatives, to be aware of what the expectations are and how they work. A systematic study of prime ministerial power must be concerned with the institutional and conventional sources of authority, within which personalities can operate. An understanding of those structures provides initial insights; an awareness of how they can be or have been changed can show what opportunities also exist for prime ministers to extend their positions. Norms can be challenged or examined, their strength analysed and the alternative options sketched out.

Yet even such an apparently obvious process has its problems. The first is concerned with the identification of prime ministerial influence. Cabinet government is collective government. Some decisions may be made individually by prime ministers; many more are formally made, or at least endorsed, by cabinet. It is often difficult to identify the impact of prime ministers, or to discover who makes the important decisions. In a presidential system the issue is more straightforward. The question is not whether the president has the constitutional power, but how that power can be used. Richard Neustadt's most celebrated finding—that the presidents' power is the power to persuade—was important in that it emphasised the limitations of presidential power and the means that have to be adopted to get things done. His interpretation of 'persuade' was broad; its usefulness was to show how limited was the presidents' power to command, though some of their tools of persuasion would be hard to resist. That conclusion was within the context of a system where, at least formally, the president is assumed to have the power to command. In a prime ministerial system such a distinction tells us little. Prime ministers *only* have the power to "persuade." Statutory responsibility is usually vested elsewhere, with departmental ministers. Prime ministers generally act through their colleagues—at least nominally.

To agree that prime ministers only have the power to persuade is not a very useful conclusion, though it is useful as a general reminder. We also need to know *how* prime ministers persuade. If they are dominant, what levers of power can they use? Why do ministers often accept directions, if they are not constitutionally required to?

This question goes to the basis of the prime ministerial position. To adopt the term used by Burns, it is *transactional* leadership. Prime ministers are party leaders; they hold the former position only as long as they hold the latter. They have been chosen or elected in order to deliver political success, ideological satisfaction or party unity—or combinations of these and other aims. They survive as long as they lead their party and maintain a parliamentary majority. Of course their position is more powerful than that of a party leader— the resources available to a national leader are both material and psychological— but their position is still based on that original transaction with the party. What is more, the troops in the army need to be led; the prime minister needs to understand what they want and how they feel. One Australian senator once criticised Malcolm Fraser's style: "You confuse leadership with command."[10] Prime ministers cannot act purely as dictators. They may get away with what they can; but they cannot habitually ignore their supporters and expect to survive. It is therefore crucial to discover how extensive that freedom to act is and in what circumstances it can be used.

These problems of studying the power of prime ministers are increased by the difficulty of examining political figures who play many roles at once— as party leader, public figure, cabinet chairman and so on. In his book on *Presidential Power* Neustadt criticises studies that examine the president separately in each of his various hats; he is more concerned to describe how the president protects his power stakes. Obviously he has an important point: to discuss in isolation the role of a prime minister as chairman of cabinet and the powers that that position might give is essentially artificial. Prime ministers play all their roles at once; they are aware in cabinet of public image and of party pressures. Yet for the observer to approach prime ministers as integrated individuals also limits the analysis. Obviously prime ministerial influence may be ubiquitous. Obviously prime ministers are concerned to protect their power stakes (to use Neustadt's term). Obviously power is a limited resource to be husbanded, to be used sparingly at the most apposite moments. Prime ministers will fight hard for some policies, not for others. What is required is an understanding of how, on those occasions they choose to fight, they can win, what factors or patterns of behaviour assist them and why they make *those* choices. Power suggests a relationship. Prime ministers have the power to get others to do what they want. Relationships will change from institution to institution as the resources are different in each case, but resources and relationships must be at the centre of any discussion of prime ministerial power.

These factors become particularly important when the decision *not* to use power that might exist is made, when restraint is exercised. Is that an indication of actual limitations on prime ministerial power or merely a tactical means of gaining a consensus? Crossman has argued for the second explanation. A decision of a prime minister not to exert full authority is a conscious refusal "to make use of the powers which now constitutionally belong to his office," even though Crossman did agree that the decision might be "of his own volition or by force of circumstances." Rose has argued that "Prime Ministers accept without hesitation the self-restraint of cooperative government. It is part of the job description." Yet if that self-restraint is exercised by "force of circumstance" or as "part of the job description," one wonders how much it is indeed *self*-restraint. Presumably it is not simply a decision to be less powerful that day but a calculation about costs and values. To say that a prime minister does not have the political will (an over-used catch-all phrase) to impose his or her view might be to suggest that other political factors make the costs too high. The prime minister's political will is shaped by the influence of those other factors. These, then, are constraints that need to be understood. It is not that prime ministers, often hungry for power, choose to limit themselves; rather the position they are in requires limitation.

It is therefore necessary to be conscious of the different ways in which prime ministers can influence decisions. They can *initiate* or *respond*; that is, the ideas may come from the prime minister and be fed to the minister, or the prime minister may react to other people's proposals. They can be *positive* or *negative*; that is they can support or stop the proposals that other people are presenting. Prime ministerial support is often seen as important, if not crucial, to the success of a minister's project. Influence can also be *direct* or *indirect*. A prime minister's power does not have to be used directly in order to exist; people may decide not to act because they anticipate prime ministerial opposition.

If precision is impossible (there are too many variables to predict how a particular individual will react in a given situation), to discuss capacity is not. We can undertand what factors/institutions/traditions will assist prime ministers. A basic test can be applied: what is a prime minister's capacity, faced with a problem of any sort, to take *independent* action or, by whatever means, to *influence* or *direct* outcomes. The emphasis is then on intention and capacity. If we can discover the impact of the relationship between prime ministers and various parts of the political systems, the opportunities that they provide or the problems they create, then it may be possible to understand better the prime ministerial job.

It is necessary to add one rider. In this concern to establish who has power, we are concerned to determine who is influential *within* the political system, who decides what the government will try to do. We judge prime ministerial success by its impact on colleagues and the system of government, not on its capacity to make government policy work in society. The latter would bring into play a whole range of questions about the effectiveness of governments in the modern state. In that discussion, the individual influence of prime ministers becomes impossible to isolate. . . .

Yet power must be relative; one person or institution has power over another. How then can it be identified? When considering the best way to identify the influence of prime ministers, three strategies can be adopted: to compare the power of prime ministers with that of other parts of the political system; to compare the impact of different prime ministers in the same political system; and to compare prime ministers in different political systems. Each has its own problems.

First, it is difficult to compare the power of different institutions. The questions only have to be posed to indicate the problems. Are prime ministers more powerful than cabinet; can they control cabinet? To what degree does the executive dominate parliament? Analyses of these questions in a parliamentary system seldom lead to clear conclusions. The prime minister is part of cabinet, the executive part of parliament. This inconclusiveness of such debate is perhaps inevitable when institutions that derive their power from different sources are compared. It is better to compare like with like; if prime ministers are to be analysed, then surely it is preferable to consider the roles of different prime ministers.

A similar point can be made about advancing the argument within the constraints of a single system. As Rose argued, every prime minister is limited by institutional arrangements and normative expectations. Often these are created by historical traditions or constitutional conventions which are taken for granted as part of the political framework within which actors must work. They are regarded so much as part of the political environment that their political influence is underestimated.

Yet there is nothing sacred about historical traditions; in different countries the parliamentary machinery has developed substantially different traditions, leading to a wide range of practices that are all legitimate. There is nothing inherently rigid in any of the systems that need prevent one adopting the procedures of another. Nor is there anything binding about conventions. A convention is a generally accepted practice that helps make a system work smoothly. Once that general acceptance declines, so that its maintenance is no longer of benefit to all practitioners, its lifespan is limited. If the benefits to be gained from breaking conventions outweigh the costs incurred by the condemnation for ignoring them, conventions will be of little value. Besides, prime ministers will often regard such limitations as liable to amendment. They will often try to adjust the rules in mid-stream, to their own advantage. We need therefore to be conscious of the implications and importance of traditions and conventions, of the way they limit and shape our thinking about practical problems, and of their capacity for change. That is difficult to achieve in looking at the one system where, so far, particular conventions are regarded as binding.

A second problem is that, in stable constitutional systems, changes are likely to be marginal and often reversible. Yet because they are the *only* changes, they are credited with great significance, perhaps deservedly, as long as it is realized that they occur *within* the established framework.

Difficulties that occur when that perspective is not maintained can be illustrated by British and Canadian examples. In Britain "the most significant, though as yet relatively small, institutional change in the political direction of government . . . since 1945 has been the introduction of political advisers into Whitehall offices, including 10 Downing Street."[12] Though significant for Britain because of its traditions, this change is not new or unusual for a parliamentary system or a prime minister. . . . Institutional assumptions make what may be seen as marginal from other perspectives into a major change within a single system.

For Canada, Denis Smith gives as an indication of presidential tendencies the new rules on the guillotine introduced in 1970: "the provision meant that if necessary a determined Government could guide a piece of controversial legislation through the House in a minimum of four days of debate over a period of ten sitting days against the protests of the minority."[13] That change may have appeared to be a dictatorial limitation of parliamentary freedom to debate in Canada, but other parliamentary oppositions would be delighted to be granted so much time to discuss important legislation.

How then can the strengths and weaknesses of prime ministerial positions be more effectively estimated? A third strategy is to compare like with like. King has argued:

> There are two reasons for studying institutions comparatively which, taken singly or together, strongly suggest that single-instance studies are almost bound to be defective. The first is that observing several instances almost invariably leads one to ask questions of each single instance that one would not have asked otherwise . . . The second reason . . . is that unless one does, one has no 'control' in the scientific sense. One does not know what is peculiar to a specific country, what general to a number of countries; one has no means of discovering which correlation among phenomena are accidental or spurious, which are genuinely causal.[14]

It is of course necessary to compare systems that are sufficiently similar for the impact of established factors to become more obvious. By looking at four similar systems, we can throw the differences that exist into greater relief and assess their importance.

Comparative studies also have their difficulties. The most obvious one might be termed "trial by anecdote." Those who have a detailed knowledge of one system can indicate instances where a broad generalisation does not hold and argue that the situation in the country can only be properly understood by reference to the unique features of political tradition and personality. . . .

The four parliamentary systems studied . . . [here]—those of Australia, Britain, Canada and New Zealand—developed from the nineteenth-century British parliamentary model. They have all—including that of Britain—developed away from that model in their own way. Yet each has a similar political heritage, similar constitutional assumptions, and similar terminology. In each, cabinet means the same thing and the roles of the prime minister are similar, although by no means identical. As a result, the more subtle differences are easier to identify and their impact is easier to assess.

Consider first the similarities. In all four parliamentary systems prime ministers are heads of political parties whose tenure of office depends on maintaining a majority in parliament. Cabinet contains only parliamentarians. Collective and ministerial responsibility is still regarded as the corner-stone of the constitutional system, even if there is some doubt about how it is to be applied. The bureaucracy is largely anonymous, non-partisan and career-oriented. The constitution—whether or not in written form—leaves a large amount to convention. There are no formal rules prescribing how prime ministers acquire or lose their office. . . . The prime minister and cabinet may have no formal legal existence; they exist by virtue of tradition and convention. Elections are regular and free. Governments for the past 30 years have been formed from a single party or by the very tight coalition between the Liberal and National (formerly Country) parties in Australia (there was never any serious question of them not combining); more flexible coalition governments are unknown. Many of the symbols and practices are thus the same. To remove any of these common factors would make the process of comparison far more difficult.

The differences are also substantial. Australia and Canada are federations; Britain and New Zealand have unitary systems. Britain and Canada have powerless upper houses; Australia has an immensely powerful Senate; New Zealand has neither. Australian, New Zealand and British parties are class-based and national in coverage; Canadian parties are not. All four countries differ in the methods they use for choosing prime ministers. The size of each population ranges from 3 million to 60 million. And so on.

The point is not that one model is somehow 'correct' and that others should be judged against it. It is as valid and as useful to talk of the Canberra model or the Ottawa model as it is to refer to the Westminister model. It is also valid to assume that there is no one proper way of making systems of parliamentary government work. It would be incorrect to argue that the way the British prime minister works is the way prime ministers *should* operate. The Westminster system has always been sufficiently flexible to allow multiple interpretations of what is proper. There is no theoretical model to be adopted. Rather the four systems have sufficient factors in common to allow them to be used to compare and contrast their procedures in such a way as to emphasize the importance of the structural and traditional as well as the changing balance of power. A comparative study thus allows us to get away from normative ideas of how prime ministers ought to behave.

Systematic and comparative study of the prime ministers in four similar but not identical systems may therefore throw some light on the relationships that prime ministers have with different parts of the political system, on the importance of institutional and traditional forces in forming those relationships and thence on the capacity of prime ministers to use their powers. The test of prime ministerial power must be related to capacity and intent. Even if that test may be impossible to apply rigidly, it provides pointers for discussion. . . .

NOTES

1. J. Mackintosh, *The British Cabinet* (London: Stevens, 1962), 451–2; 3rd ed., 1977, 541–2; for the reaffirmation see J. Mackintosh, ed., *British Prime Ministers in the Twentieth Century* (London: Weidenfeld & Nicolson, 1977), 6–7.
2. R. Crossman, Introduction to W. Bagehot, *The English Constitution* (London: Fontana, 1963; first printed 1867), 51.
3. G. Jones, "The Prime Minister's Aides," *Hull Papers in Politics* 6 (1979): 1.
4. P. Gordon Walker, *The Cabinet* (London: Cape, 1972), 162.
5. H. Wilson, *The Governance of Britain* (London: Sphere, 1976), 20–21.
6. A. King, "Executives," in N. Polsby and F. Greenstein, eds., *A Handbook of Political Science*, vol. 5 (Reading, Mass.: Addison Wesley, 1975), 232–3.
7. D. Smith, "President and Parliament: The Transformation of Parliamentary Government in Canada," in T. Hockin, ed., *Apex of Power: The Prime Minister and Political Leadership in Canada* (Scarborough: Prentice-Hall, 2nd ed., 1977), 323.
8. R. Rose, "British Government: The Job at the Top," in R. Rose and E. Suleiman, eds., *Presidents and Prime Ministers* (Washington: American Enterprise Institute, 1980), 43.
9. Ibid., 44.
10. R. Schneider, *War Without Blood: Malcolm Fraser in Power* (Sydney: Angus & Robertson, 1980), 6.
11. R. Rose, "Government against Sub-Governments: A European Perspective on Washington," in Rose and Suleiman, op. cit., 340.
12. R. Rose, "British Government: The Job at the Top," in Rose and Suleiman, op. cit., 45.
13. D. Smith, in Hockin, op. cit., 322.
14. A. King, in Polsby and Greenstein, op. cit., 248.

FURTHER READINGS

Courtney, J.C. "Has the Canadian Prime Minister Been 'Presidentialized'?" *Presidential Studies Quarterly* 14, (Spring 1984): 238–241.

Hockin, T.A., ed. *Apex of Power: The Prime Minister and Political Leadership in Canada.* 2nd ed. Scarborough: Prentice-Hall Canada, 1977.

Matheson, W.A. *The Prime Minister and the Cabinet.* Toronto: Methuen, 1976.

Punnett, R.M. *The Prime Minister in Canadian Government and Politics.* Toronto: Macmillan, 1977.

25

Power, Politics, and Bureaucracy

KENNETH KERNAGHAN AND DAVID SIEGEL

BUREAUCRATIC POWER

Power [is defined] as "the capacity to secure the dominance of one's values or goals." In this sense, public servants wield substantial power by virtue of their role in policy development and execution. If the machinery of government could be so arranged that bureaucrats simply implemented laws spelled out in very specific terms by the legislature, enforced judicial decisions interpreting these laws, and administered policies and programs under the close supervision of political executives, few value problems would exist for most bureaucrats. The realm of politics and policy would belong to elected representatives and would be sharply delineated from the administrative sphere. The value issues in any situation would be worked out by others so that the bureaucrat's primary concern would be to adhere to those values emerging from the legislative, executive, and judicial spheres of government.

The historical record shows that an era of such bureaucratic innocence has never existed in modern democratic states. There is in reality much room for the injection of public servants' values into decisions and recommendations. It is generally acknowledged that public servants exercise significant power in both the development and execution of policy. In a lecture on the threat to parliamentary responsible government, Robert Stanfield, a former leader of the federal Progressive Conservative Party, stated that, "while the House of Commons has been losing control, so also has the Government. The ministers just do not have the time to run such a vast show and make such a vast range of decisions. Consequently, more and more is for all practical purposes being decided by and implemented by the bureaucracy."[1] And in a reminiscence on thirty years as a senior public servant and minister, Mitchell Sharp observed that "top public servants are powerful persons in the machinery of government at the federal level. They wield great influence. They do so because they are, in the main, professionals who have been selected for their proven administrative ability and who devote their full time to government. In many cases,

Kenneth Kernaghan and David Siegel, "Power, Politics, and Bureaucracy," *Public Administration in Canada: A Text* (Toronto: Methuen Publications, 1987), 267-89. Copyright © 1987 by Methuen Publications. Reprinted by permission of the authors and publisher.

they have a greater influence upon the course of events than have Ministers, particularly the weaker and less competent."[2] The extent of this bureaucratic power clearly varies in accordance with such factors as the government's view of the proper role of public servants in the political process, the policy or program under consideration, the department or agency involved, and the style and competence of ministers and their officials.

The Concept and Practice of Political Neutrality

A framework for examining the power of public servants may be devised by utilizing the concept of political neutrality. Political neutrality is a constitutional doctrine or convention according to which public servants should not engage in activities that are likely to impair—or appear to impair—their impartiality or the impartiality of the public service. The several interrelated ideas traditionally associated with the notion of political neutrality provide a useful model for examining the nature of interaction between public servants and other actors in the political system. The model also permits a consideration of the changing nature of bureaucratic power and the role of public servants in the policy process. The major elements of the traditional model may be summarized as follows:

1. politics and policy are separated from administration: thus politicians make policy decisions; public servants execute these decisions;
2. public servants are appointed and promoted on the basis of merit rather than of party affiliation or contributions;
3. public servants do not engage in partisan political activities;
4. public servants do not express publicly their personal views on government policies or administration;
5. public servants provide forthright and objective advice to their political masters in private and in confidence; in return, political executives protect the anonymity of public servants by publicly accepting responsibility for departmental decisions; and
6. public servants execute policy decisions loyally irrespective of the philosophy and programs of the party in power and regardless of their personal opinions; as a result, public servants enjoy security of tenure during good behaviour and satisfactory performance.

As a means of explaining the nature and extent of bureaucratic power in the Canadian political system, each of these six elements of political neutrality will be examined separately below. Special attention is centred on the degree to which actual practice has departed from the requirements of the traditional model.

(1) Politics and Administration

The politics-administration dichotomy. The political neutrality of public servants has traditionally rested on the possibility of a separation between politics and administration and on a related distinction between policy and administration. Frequently, the two dichotomies are treated as synonymous—as if the terms politics and policy are interchangeable. The scope of activity covered by the term politics is, however, much broader than that embraced by the term policy. "*Politics* is concerned, throughout the sphere of government, with the whole business of deciding what to do and getting it done. *Policy* is the decision as to what to do; *administration* is getting it done."[3] According to the politics-administration dichotomy, political executives and legislators are concerned with the formation of policy and public servants are concerned with its implementation. Policy decisions are political; administrative decisions are non-political. However, abundant evidence points to the important political and policy-advisory roles of public servants.

The distinction between politics and policy on the one hand, and administration on the other, has been central to the evolution of both the study and the practice of public administration. V. Seymour Wilson, who uses interchangeably the terms politics-administration dichotomy and policy-administration dichotomy, states that the dichotomy

> remains a powerful philosophy . . . It has guided, and will continue to guide, many aspects of the actions and perceptions of politicians, public servants and the public . . . The policy/administration dichotomy has a profound influence on just about every aspect of theory and practice in public policy and administration.[4]

From 1887 up to the end of the Second World War, most prominent writers on public administration wrote within a framework of a dichotomy between politics and administration. Woodrow Wilson's celebrated essay of 1887 on "The Study of Administration"[5] is usually taken as the point of departure for academic and theoretical writing on public administration in North America. In his essay, Wilson asserted that

> the field of administration is a field of business. It is removed from the hurry and strife of politics . . . administrative questions are not political questions . . . "Policy does nothing without the aid of administration," but administration is not therefore politics.[6]

Wilson's distinction between politics and administration was accepted and perpetuated by such other pioneers as Frank Goodnow (1914), L.D. White (1926), and W.F. Willoughby (1927). In their writings, "the politics-administration dichotomy was assumed both as self-evident truth and a desirable goal; administration was perceived as a self-contained world of its own, with its own separate values, rules and methods."[7] Set in proper historical perspective, these questionable views are more comprehensible.

During the late nineteenth and early twentieth centuries, administrative reform efforts in both the United States and Canada were devoted to eradicating patronage from the government service, with a view to promoting efficient administration. A separate, but overlapping, development which had its origins in industrial organization in the United States was the "scientific management" movement. This movement, which pursued efficiency in large-scale organizations by seeking the most rational means—the "one best way"—of performing any organizational task, had an enormous impact on the civil service reform movement in the United States. The tenets of the scientific management movement spread not only throughout the United States, but also to Canada and several European countries.

In both the United States and Canada, the two elements of the reform movement—efficiency through the elimination of patronage and efficiency through scientific management—reinforced one another and became integral components of the merit system. In Canada, the 1917–18 Report of the Civil Service Commission noted that the merit system in the Canadian civil service "consisted of two distinct parts: the first is concerned with the selection and appointment of individuals 'without regard to their politics, religion or influence'; the second is concerned with 'applying the methods of scientific employment to maintain the efficiency of these selected employees after they enter the service.'"[8] While the Civil Service Act of 1918 was a landmark event in establishing a merit system for the Canadian public service, political interference with the application of the system hindered efforts to eliminate patronage appointments.

Although there were no Canadian counterparts to American writers on public administration who articulated the notion of a separation between politics and administration, Canadian reformers operated within a similar framework. Implicit in their efforts to remove partisan political considerations from appointments to the public service was acceptance of the possibility and desirability of separating politics from administration—at least in so far as staffing the service was concerned. For example, the 1917–18 Report of the Civil Service Commission stated that the purpose of the 1918 Civil Service Act was to promote "efficiency and ecomony in the *non-political* Civil Service."[9]

Concurrent with this pursuit of impartial and efficient administration was a steady growth in the discretionary powers of public servants. While efficient staffing of the service required the separation of politics and administration, the need for effective development and execution of public policy drew administrative officials into the political maelstrom—not in the sense of partisan activity, but in the sense of involvement in the authoritative allocation of values for society. Public servants formulated rules and regulations to put flesh on the skeleton of vaguely worded statutes, enforced these rules and regulations, and adjudicated disputes arising from this enforcement. Moreover, the complicated and technical nature of public policy issues meant that political executives had to rely increasingly on public servants for policy advice and for the management of large-scale public organizations.

During the 1930s, writers on public administration who recognized the significant and growing political role of the bureaucracy lived uncomfortably with the textbook dichotomy between politics and administration.[10] The dichotomy came under increasing attack during the war years as many scholars gained practical administrative experience in government. Shortly after the war, a number of political scientists launched a devastating assault on the notion that politics and administration were or could be separated. Among this group of post-war authors, Paul Appleby stands out for his defence of the proposition that "public administration is policy making . . . Public administration is one of a number of basic political processes."[11] In less celebrated and more broadly focussed works than those written by American authors, British and Canadian writers demonstrated during this same period a growing recognition of the blurring of the traditional constitutional line between politicians and bureaucrats in the parliamentary-Cabinet system of government.

By 1960, the interdependence of politics and administration had been enshrined in the theoretical literature on public administration and accepted by the major actors in the political system. By this time, however, recognition of the reality of bureaucratic power in the political process led to suggestions that public servants should assume the task and the orientation of "agents of social change." Public servants were encouraged to promote new and creative innovations and solutions in social policy by aggregating and articulating the needs of unorganized and disadvantaged groups (for example, consumers, the poor), and by stimulating groups and individuals to make demands on government for remedies to their social and economic ills. It was clear that public servants who undertook such activities were likely to clash on occasion with political and administrative superiors who did not perceive the proper role of a public servant to be an active initiator of social change. The basic question was the extent to which appointed public officials could or should share with elected representatives the responsibility for stimulating and responding to social change. Discussion of public servants as social change agents was intermingled with the movement for increased citizen participation in government decision making. This movement brought both politicians and public servants into more direct contact and confrontation with the general citizenry.

In the United States, these and other developments culminated in the late 1960s in a loose confederation of scholars and practitioners seeking a "new public administration."[12] Among the major concerns of the advocates of this movement were social equity, sensitivity to and representation of disadvantaged minority groups, increased citizen participation in government decision making, and new forms of public organization.

The relevance of the new public administration movement for the relation between politics and administration is that some of its supporters called for a reformulation of the traditional roles of politicians and public servants.[13] It was argued that public servants, because of their expertise and experience and their close contacts with members of the public, are better qualified than political executives or legislators to determine the public interest. Public servants must, however, establish a value system with a focus on human dignity or administrative humanism; they should not simply reflect the values of their political masters. Implicit also was a resistance to political control over public administration. The new public administration movement drew attention to the actual and potential power of public servants and to the importance of their value system for decision making in government; however, it did not resolve—indeed, it complicated—the issue of finding an appropriate balance between the power of public servants and that of elected representatives.

Thus, the scholarly literature on public administration records an evolution since 1945 from a situation where only a few writers recognized the necessary involvement of public servants in politics to a situation where a few writers suggested that leadership in policy development rightly belongs to public servants rather than to politicians. The new public administration movement had little spillover effect on the study and practice of public administration in Canada. Nevertheless, scholars and practitioners in Canada are acutely aware that the line between politics and administration has become increasingly indistinct as both politicians and public servants participate actively in policy development. Moreover, the line is a fluctuating one, characterized by the expansion of bureaucratic power and the gradual politicization of the public service.

Policy development and policy implementation. Since the political role of public servants is attributed primarily to their contribution to policy development, much attention in the literature has focussed on the intermingling of policy and administration. The conventional view that a clear division may be made between policy and administration has always been a fiction, but has become increasingly untenable with the continuing growth of government activities and of bureaucratic power. The terms policy and administration are of limited use in distinguishing between the roles of political executives (i.e., Cabinet ministers) and public servants, because political executives and public servants are jointly involved in the administration of policy. Gordon Robertson, former clerk of the Privy Council, observed:

> I can hardly claim to be capable of complete objectivity. It would be easier to achieve such detachment if I could shelter behind the dictum so solemnly delivered from editorial pages and professorial podia that politicians, and not civil servants, make policy and civil servants, and not politicians, apply it. It is unfortunate that so clear and helpful a distinction should have so little truth about it.[14]

In the late 1970s, public administration scholars began to study more vigorously "the missing link" in the policy-making process, namely policy implementation. It is now widely recognized that the power of bureaucrats is greatly enhanced by their dominant role in program implementation and service delivery. Subsequent discussion will, therefore, examine in turn the exercise of bureaucratic power in both policy formation and policy implementation.

Writers on bureaucratic power have long recognized the enormous influence of bureaucrats on policy *formation*. Senior public servants in particular make significant discretionary decisions as to the policy options to be set before their political masters. Moreover, in the development and presentation of policy proposals, these public servants are expected to be attuned to the *political* as well as the administrative, financial, and technical implications of their recommendations. By the late 1960s, the power of public servants in policy development was perceived to be so great that Prime Minister Trudeau endeavoured to place more policy-making power in the hands of politically accountable authorities, especially Cabinet ministers. To this end, the Cabinet committee system and the parliamentary committee system were reformed, the coordinating capacity of the Privy Council Office was strengthened, and the policy influence of the Prime Minister's Office was expanded. The use of such alternative sources of policy advice as task forces, white papers, and advisory councils provided a competing influence to departmental advice. . . . [It is notable] that these changes did increase the role of ministers in policy formation. Moreover, during the late 1960s, the power of the so-called "public service mandarins" (a small group of influential senior bureaucrats) was diffused among a broader range of political actors and among a greater number of senior public servants.[15]

Despite these reforms, certain public servants continue to exercise significant power by virtue of their central positions in the policy process (for example, the deputy minister of finance, the clerk of the Privy Council). Furthermore, despite the greater variety of available sources of policy advice, the very technical, complex and time-consuming nature of certain policy issues obliges ministers to continue to rely heavily on the advice of their officials. Robert Bryce, a former deputy minister of finance and clerk of the Privy Council, has observed that during the Trudeau years senior public servants had a great deal of influence on their ministers because they were "in day-to-day contact with them. It is this contact, the continued relationship, that develops into the kind of influence that is important and leads . . . to power."[16]

In the sphere of policy *implementation*, public servants also exercise substantial power. The extent of bureacratic power in policy implementation depends largely on the specificity of the statute enacted by the legislature. In an early, but very perceptive, discussion of administrative discretion, the philosopher Wayne A.R. Leys developed a three-fold classification of discretion depending on the willingness and capacity of elected representatives to set down in statutes the criteria on which administrative decisions are to be based. Leys's classification of discretionary powers distinguishes among: (1) merely technical discretion, where the legislature has stated or assumed that the administrator knew the results which it desired; (2) discretion in social planning, where the legislature does not know exactly what it ultimately will want in the way of results; and (3) discretion in the work of reconciliation, where the legislature has, in effect, asked the administrator to break a political deadlock.[17] The first category, where discretionary judgement is limited, illustrates that care must be taken not to exaggerate the number of heavily value-laden issues confronting officials. A large percentage of thousands of administrative decisions made each day present value problems of such minor significance that officials are scarcely aware of any value content in the decisions made. The second and third categories demonstrate the discretionary powers exercised by officials, either because of the complexity of the issue or of the inability of the executive or legislature to resolve the political conflicts involved. Both situations shift the burden of decision making from political executives, legislators, and judges to public servants. The making of decisions and recommendations on complex and technical matters of "social planning" requires the exercise of discretionary powers of a legislative and judicial nature. And the participation of officials in negotiation, bargaining, compromise, and reconciliation in order "to break a political deadlock" is undeniably *political* activity.

In the course of interpreting, clarifying, and applying policy, public servants can significantly influence the success of policy decisions taken by ministers and legislators. The care and enthusiasm with which public servants administer policy determines to a large extent the success of that policy. A series of individual, relatively minor decisions in a particular policy area can have a significant cumulative impact on the extent to which the original intent of Cabinet and Parliament is realized. Moreover, such decisions can help to determine the content of subsequent changes in existing policy. In wielding such discretionary powers, public servants are, of course, expected to ensure that their decisions are broadly attuned to the general policy of their minister and their department.

The discretionary powers of public servants in policy implementation are especially evident in the making and enforcement of regulations under authority delegated to them by Parliament or subdelegated to them by a minister or by Cabinet. The statutory provisions authorizing the making of regulations are often phrased in general or imprecise language which permits public servants to exercise significant discretion, both in the wording of the regulations and in the application of their provisions to particular cases. Eric Hehner has repeatedly warned of the danger of "dispersed discretions." He argues:

> If regulations extend only to details of mechanical procedures, no real discretionary powers are delegated. However, where the statutory provisions are only a skeleton and it is left to regulations to say "what, where, when, why, how and who," then we have created meaningful discretionary powers . . . When regulations are issued by the governor-in-council, or even by a minister of the Crown, there is at least a degree of accountability for the first step. Where the power is conferred upon

a board or commission, review of its exercise becomes more difficult and remote
. . . If persons or bodies possessed of delegated powers redelegate them, we come
to a state that may be described as "dispersed discretions."[18]

The delegation by Parliament of power to make regulations is now very
common, and a large number of regulations has been made. The Special
Committee on Statutory Instruments reported in 1969 that 420 of 601 statutes
perused by the committee provided for delegated legislation, and that an annual
average of 530 regulations had been passed between 1956 and 1968.[19] Then,
in 1977, the Senate-House Committee on Regulations and Other Statutory
Instruments, on the basis of its inquiry into "the subordinate law made by
delegates of Parliament," provided examples not only of the substantial volume
of subordinate law, but also of cases where public servants had exceeded the
regulation-making authority granted to them by Parliament.[20] The committee
recognized the need for subordinate legislation, but made a number of
recommendations to ensure more effective parliamentary scrutiny of this
legislation and more attention to the rights of individuals affected by it.

The exercise of discretionary powers is also pervasive in that these powers
are dispersed to various levels of the hierarchy. Both the scope and importance
of discretionary powers increase, however, as one moves up the administrative
pyramid into the upper echelons of the bureaucracy. It is, therefore, among
senior public servants that value problems and priorities are most crucial for
the determination of public policy and the state of administrative responsibility.
It is important, however, not to overestimate the value problems of the most
senior bureaucrats and thereby to minimize the substantial, sometimes critical,
significance of value choices made by professional, technical, and administrative
personnel at lower levels of the hierarchy. The failure of such officials to act
responsibly, particularly by making decisions that are efficient, effective, and
responsive, may seriously jeopardize policies and programs determined at the
top executive levels of the organization. Decisions judged to be irresponsible
may be taken with the best of personal intentions; other irresponsible decisions
may constitute deliberate efforts to obstruct or sabotage the implementation
of government policies. Instances of this latter type of irresponsible administrative conduct are difficult to document, but there are numerous opportunities
for such conduct. In a large organization—whether in the public or the private
sector—the decision-making process may involve inputs and judgements by
so many individuals that the persons guilty of irresponsibile behaviour, whether
unintentional or deliberate, are extremely difficult to pinpoint. This is the
condition Robert Presthus describes as "organized irresponsibility."[21]

The role of provincial public servants in policy development and in
implementation is very similar to that of federal public servants. Kornberg,
et al. have noted that "provincial bureaucracies exercise legislative powers in
various ways. Some bureaucratic officials identify problem areas requiring the
action of cabinets. They marshall the information ministers require to decide

among competing priorities . . . and they either draft or assist in the drafting of legislation." In addition, these provincial public servants "formulate general and specific rules having the force of law as part of the process of implementing legislation which assemblies have enacted."[22] Clearly, policy implementation has a significant effect on the development and content of policy in all spheres of government.

Despite the fact that politics and policy cannot be easily separated from administration, the distinctions commonly made between politics and administration, policy and administration, and policy formation and implementation serve an extremely useful analytical and practical purpose. They enable political theorists to distinguish—not in an absolute sense, but as a matter of degree and emphasis—between the constitutional and legal functions of political executives and public servants. While the policy role of public servants has led some writers to refer to them as "permanent politicians" and "ruling servants," they remain, in fact and in democratic theory, subject to the overriding authority of elected representatives and the courts. It is useful then to refer to the *predominance* of ministers in policy formulation and the *predominance* of public servants in policy implementation, while acknowledging that both ministers and public servants are involved in both policy formation and implementation.

These dichotomies also serve a very practical end in that they enable politicians to preserve the appearance before the public that they, not the public servants, are the policy makers. Elected representatives have a stake in preserving the notion that public servants are neutral instruments of political masters. This notion in turn supports the doctrine that ministers must accept responsibility for the decisions of their administrative subordinates. Public servants also have an interest in preserving these convenient fictions so that they may retain their anonymity and be sheltered from public attack.

(2) Political Appointments

Merit and patronage. A second component of the traditional model of political neutrality is the practice whereby "public servants are appointed and promoted on the basis of merit rather than of party affiliation or contributions." *Political patronage* involves the appointment of persons to government service on the grounds of contributions, financial or otherwise, to the governing party; it is a blatant violation of the doctrine of political neutrality. Indeed, the appointment is made on the basis that the appointee is *not* politically neutral, but rather is politically partisan. Such appointments clash with the merit *principle* according to which

(1) Canadian citizens should have a reasonable opportunity to be considered for employment in the public service.
(2) selections must be based exclusively on merit, or fitness to do the job.[23]

The merit *system*, on the other hand, "is the mechanism in use at any time by which these goals are achieved." It is "an administrative device which can and should be adapted to changing circumstances."[24]

The merit system established by the Civil Service Act in 1918 greatly diminished, but by no means eliminated, patronage appointments. As late as 1944, H.M. Clokie claimed that Canada had not "fully emancipated herself from the laxness of appointment by favour which tends to paralyze all efforts to attain a sound merit system."[25] By 1945, however, the number of patronage appointments had been greatly reduced, and by 1962 the Glassco Commission was able to conclude that "for all practical purposes . . . the Civil Service Commission [now the Public Service Commission] has managed to eliminate political patronage appointments to those positions falling within its jurisdiction."[26]

Recipients and effects of patronage. Patronage appointments have certainly not disappeared altogether. A review of debates in the House of Commons in recent decades reveals numerous allegations and denials regarding the use of patronage in staffing the public service. Many of the alleged patronage appointments have been to lower-level or part-time positions, where the appointees are so far removed from policy development that their appointment has negligible effect on the status of political neutrality. Opposition parties, the news media, and the general public have shown greater interest in *senior* positions that are filled by patronage appointees rather than on a competitive basis by persons from within or outside the public service. The Cabinet has the authority to appoint deputy ministers, heads and members of agencies, boards and commissions, ambassadors, high commissioners, consuls general and certain other diplomatic representatives, and federal judges. Moreover, officials in the Prime Minister's Office are selected by the Prime Minister, and Cabinet ministers choose their assistants. All these appointments are exempt from the appointing power of the Public Service Commission.

Among the persons who may be, and frequently are, appointed to exempt positions are retired legislators, defeated candidates of the governing party, and party supporters who have made significant financial or other contributions to the party's fortunes. For example, in the period following the 1972 general election, more than two-thirds of the thirty-eight retired or defeated Liberal politicians were appointed as heads or members of government agencies, contract employees in government departments, judges, or assistants to the Prime Minister or to ministers. An Opposition member was stimulated to propose a motion to the House of Commons "that this House request the government to table a list of all Liberal candidates defeated in the last election who have not yet been appointed to government positions, together with a list of the positions to which they will be appointed."[27] Defeated or retired Cabinet ministers have enjoyed particular success in finding a comfortable niche in government service.[28] Finally, the expansion of the personal staff of Cabinet ministers since 1960 has increased the importance of this group as a source of patronage appointments.[29]

Such appointments are often denounced on the grounds that they are made more on the basis of partisanship than merit. Nevertheless, the government has the authority to make these appointments on whatever basis it deems appropriate. A measure of merit is achieved with respect to the most senior posts because the government is not usually willing to bear the embarrassment that the appointment of an incompetent partisan may bring. Moreover, party supporters are more likely to find their reward in appointments to Crown agencies, boards, and commissions than to the regular departments of government. There are few partisan appointments to deputy ministerial posts.

The number of patronage appointments in each of the categories examined above is relatively small, but taking all the categories together, the number of *senior* positions filled by patronage appointees is substantial. The impact of these appointments on bureaucratic power is difficult to measure with any precision. Appointments to public service posts without competitive examination and on grounds of partisanship violate the merit principle, but not the merit system. Such appointments limit the influence of career public servants by blocking their access to some of the highest positions in government. Moreover, longserving officials are obliged to share their influence in the policy process with newcomers who may have fresh ideas and unorthodox approaches, and who may not share the administrative values to which most public servants have become socialized.

Patronage in the provinces. The evolution of political patronage in Canada's provinces has been very similar to that of the federal government. Civil service acts were passed and civil service commissions or their equivalent were created to promote public service neutrality and efficiency through a merit system of personnel management.[30] The timing of these reforms varied greatly from province to province, but in all cases effective reforms occurred more slowly than on the federal scene. Hodgetts and Dwivedi note that "until the early '60s, most provinces continued to present only the facade of a merit system, while combatting charges of patronage and personal favouritism in their public services." However, "by the mid-'60's nearly all provinces had made their central personnel agencies powerful enough to implement the merit principle."[31] Patronage appointments to agencies, boards, and commissions and to lower-level positions in certain operating departments remain a common practice in provincial governments. The Ontario government has available for political appointments more than three thousand full-time and part-time positions in agencies, boards, and commissions.[32] Some provinces (e.g., Saskatchewan)[33] are more inclined than others to make political appointments to senior posts in *departments* as well as in semi-independent bodies.

(3) Political Partisanship

Political sterilization. The traditional model of political neutrality requires that public servants not "engage in partisan political activities."[34] During the first fifty years of Canada's political history, the issues of political partisanship and political patronage were intimately linked. Patronage appointments were rewards for service to the governing party. Many of the appointees sought to enhance their progress within the service by continuing their partisan support of the governing party after their appointment. Thus, when a new party came into power, it replaced these persons with its own supporters.

In an effort to eliminate this practice, legislators provided in the 1918 Civil Service Act that no public servant could "engage in partisan work in connection with any . . . election, or contribute, receive or in any way deal with any money for any party funds." Violations were punishable by dismissal. The penalty was so severe and so clearly stated that, with the exception of the right to vote, the impact of the Act was the political sterilization of Canada's federal public servants. Despite this effective weakening of the link between patronage and political activity, the rigid restraints imposed in 1918 remained virtually unchanged until 1967. The primary explanation for those enduring restraints was the desire to ensure the political impartiality of public servants in the performance of their advisory and discretionary powers.

The Public Service Employment Act of 1967 liberalized the long-standing restrictions on political activity. Section 32 of the Act provides that public servants, unless they are deputy heads, may stand for election to public office if the Public Service Commission believes that their usefulness would not be impaired by their candidacy. Employees who are elected must resign from the public service. The decisions of the Public Service Commission suggest that roughly 90 per cent of all public servants will be permitted to seek election if they wish. This liberalization of restraints on political candidacy has attracted a small number of public servants to the hustings for each federal election. Employees are not permitted to work for or against a candidate for election to a federal or provincial office, or for or against a political party; they are permitted, however, to attend political meetings and to make contributions to the funds of a political candidate or party.

Political activity in the provinces. In provincial governments, a common pattern has emerged with respect to public servants who wish to become candidates for public office. Although the number of senior and other officials who are prohibited from such activity varies from province to province, most public servants seeking candidacy and election may receive a leave of absence for a period preceding the date of the election. Employees who are elected must resign their public service position. In several provinces, however, an employee who is elected, but who ceases to be a representative within five years, will be reinstated to government service.

In regard to other forms of political activity (e.g., membership in political parties; attendance at political meetings, rallies, and conventions; making and soliciting financial contributions; canvassing for a political candidate), provincial governments vary greatly in their rules. In virtually every province, the right of public servants to support the party of their choice or no party at all is specifically protected by statute. For example, the Saskatchewan Public Service Act provides that no public servant (1) shall be obliged to contribute to a political party or to participate in political activities; (2) use his or her authority or influence to "control or modify" political action of another person; (3) engage in political activities at the workplace; or (4) participate in political activities likely to impair his or her usefulness in the public service.

The fact that most public servants may now stand for election and engage in a broader spectrum of political activities has heightened the general level of partisan activity and consciousness in Canada's public services, especially among younger employees. However, officials in senior and sensitive posts are usually required to refrain from partisan activity; thus those officials most actively involved in policy formation and in the discretionary application of policy retain their impartiality. Also, officials with many years of government experience seem to have difficulty overcoming their ingrained avoidance of political activity. Some public servants may justifiably perceive overt partisanship as an obstacle to promotion to the senior ranks of what is substantially a politically neutral public service. Moreover, one of the attractions of government employment at the senior levels is the opportunity to exercise influence in relative privacy and anonymity. While there have been some notable examples of public servants being transformed into Cabinet ministers, a Cabinet post is by no means a sure reward for a public servant who is elected to public office. Thus, the broadening of the permissible limits of political activity has modified the traditional doctrine and practice of political neutrality, but it has not had a significant effect on the exercise of bureaucratic power.

It is notable that the restrictions on the political partisanship of public servants, in both the federal and provincial spheres of government, have been challenged in the courts under the Canadian Charter of Rights and Freedoms. The issue is for the most part framed in terms of the need to strike the most appropriate balance between the political rights of public servants and the political neutrality of the public service. Section 2 of the Charter guarantees the fundamental freedoms of expression, peaceful assembly and association, and section 1 provides that the guarantees to rights and freedoms under the Charter are subject to "such reasonable limits prescribed by law as can be demonstrably justified in a free and democratic society." The issue before the courts then is whether the limits on the political partisanship of public servants can be demonstrably justified to be reasonable limits in contemporary Canadian society.

(4) Public Comment

Restrictions. The admonition that public servants "not express publicly their personal views on government policies or administration" is an integral component of the traditional model of political neutrality. The prime reason given by contemporary governments for restrictions on public comment is the need to preserve the confidence of the public and of political superiors in the impartiality of public servants.

Strict interpretation of this rule of official reticence requires that public servants not express personal opinions on government policies, whether they are attacking or supporting those policies. As explained below, this convention has been supplemented by statutory prohibitions relating to political partisanship and to the use of confidential information, by decisions of administrative tribunals, and by written guidelines.

Section 32 of the federal Public Service Employment Act restricts public comment by providing that "no employee shall engage in partisan work in connection with any . . . election." A few provincial governments accompany their regulations on political activities with guidance on partisan public comment. Section 14 of the Ontario Public Service Act, for example, states that "except during a leave of absence . . . a civil servant shall not at any time speak in public or express views in writing on any matter that forms part of the platform of a provincial or federal political party." Public servants on leave on absence to seek election are, of course, obliged to express personal and partisan views on campaign issues. Those who wish to return to government service if they are defeated may find it prudent to show discretion in their public statements, especially with respect to the policies and programs of the department to which they may wish to return.

Public servants, whether seeking election or not, are normally prohibited by an oath of office and secrecy and by the Official Secrets Act from disclosing or using for personal gain confidential information acquired by virtue of their government position. It is a serious offence to criticize publicly government policy or administration; the use of confidential information for this purpose would greatly compound the offence.

Formal written guidelines on public comment are so sparse that considerable uncertainty exists as to the rights of public servants in this area. It is well established in the civil service legislation of modern democratic states that the role of public servants in policy development and implementation requires that they enjoy fewer political rights than other citizens. In the area of public comment, the difficulty is to strike an appropriate balance between freedom of expression and political neutrality. The dilemma for a public servant who engages in public criticism of government is illustrated well by the celebrated Fraser case.

Mr. Fraser, an employee of the Department of National Revenue, began his public protest with attacks on the government's compulsory imposition of the metric system; he then extended his criticism to the proposed Charter of Rights. When Mr. Fraser's appeal against his subsequent dismissal was being heard by an adjudicator of the Public Service Staff Relations Board, Mr. Fraser said that if he discontinued his protests, he would be breaking "the common law that the citizen has a duty to speak out against a Government that lies to the people."[35] The adjudicator's decision that Mr. Fraser's dismissal was appropriate was upheld by the Supreme Court of Canada. The court stated that

> public servants have some freedom to criticize the government. But it is not an absolute freedom. . . . In some circumstances a public servant may actively and publicly express opposition to the policies of a government. This would be appropriate if, for example, the Government were engaged in illegal acts, or if its policies jeopardized the life, health or safety of the public servant or others, or if the public servant's criticism had no impact on his or her ability to perform effectively the duties of a public servant or on the public perception of that ability.[36]

Beyond public criticism. The decisions of the adjudicator and of the Supreme Court are of limited value in dealing with forms of public comment other than criticism of government. The issue of public comment is much more complex than the conventional rule suggests. This rule does not take adequate account of the extent to which public servants are inescapably involved in public comment in the regular performance of their duties. In speaking or writing for public consumption, public servants may serve such purposes as:

1. providing information and analysis of a scientific or technical nature for consideration primarily by their professional colleagues within and outside government;
2. describing administrative processes and departmental organization and procedures;
3. explaining the content, implications, and administration of specific government policies and programs;
4. discussing, within the framework of governmental or departmental policy, the solution of problems through changes in existing programs or the development of new programs;
5. discussing issues on which governmental or departmental policy has not yet been determined;
6. explaining the nature of the political policy process in government;
7. advocating reforms in the existing organization or procedures of government;
8. commenting in a constructively critical way on government policy or administration;
9. denouncing existing or potential government policies, programs, and operations; and

10. commenting in an overtly partisan way on public policy issues or on government policy or administration.[37]

This list moves from types of public comment which are generally expected, required, or permissible to those which are questionable, risky, or prohibited. Few public servants have ventured beyond the first four categories. The fourth category often involves public servants in bargaining, accommodation, and compromise on behalf of their political superiors. It is on these occasions that members of the public may see most clearly the nature and extent of bureaucratic power in the policy process. These meetings usually take place in private, but public servants are sometimes required to make presentations and answer questions in public forums where a larger measure of risk exists.

The extent to which public servants may venture beyond the first four categories of public comment was clarified in 1979 by the Clark government. To complement the government's freedom of information bill, Prime Minister Clark issued guidelines on communications between public servants and the public.[38] Public servants were advised that they "should be prepared to discuss frankly information within their areas of responsibility that describes or explains programs that have been announced or implemented by the government." Public servants were counselled not to go "beyond this discussion of factual information" and not "to discuss advice or recommendations tendered to Ministers, or to speculate about policy deliberations or future policy decisions." The guidelines stated that "it will be normal for public servants to be quoted by name, and to be interviewed" for both the electronic and print media. Finally, the guidelines prohibited the disclosure of information which was specifically prohibited by law. However, public employees *"acting in good faith"*[39] under the guidelines were not to be "be considered as having violated their oaths of secrecy." The new Trudeau government elected in 1980 retained these guidelines, but the Mulroney government elected in 1984 amended the guidelines by requiring that interviews with the public or the media "shall be on the record and for attribution by name."[40] While this amendment was made in the name of "open government," the view was widely expressed that it would have the effect of discouraging public servants from giving out even factual information.

As a result of the intimate links among politics, policy, and administration described earlier, public servants often enhance understanding of the political and policy process through their speeches and writings on the machinery of government and the administrative process. The major burden of explaining the political system to the public is, however, likely to remain with politicians and academic scholars.

Public advocacy of administrative reform and constructive criticism of government activities may complement the public servants' information and conciliation functions. However, the participation of public servants in these forms of public comment is restricted by their political superiors who bear public responsibility for the operations of government.

Denunciations and overtly partisan assessments of government policy or administration tend to be clearer than other forms of public comment in their manifestation and in the certainty of their punishment. Both the traditional admonition against public comment and recent decisions by administrative tribunals prohibit such activity unless public servants are on leave of absence to seek election.

The unwritten rule against public comment is subject to varying inter-pretations and applications in contemporary society. Public servants are now involved in forms of public comment not explicitly covered by the conventional rule, and the nature of this involvement constitutes a significant departure from a position of political neutrality. It appears that public servants will increasingly be required to attend public meetings to provide information about the substance and implementation of government policies and programs. As a result, the public will become more aware of the influence that public servants bring to deliberations on public policy matters. It is often difficult for public servants to discuss government policy without indicating, inadvertently or otherwise, some measure of the influence they have—or could have—over the content of policy.

(5) *Anonymity and Ministerial Responsibility*

The traditional model of political neutrality requires that "public servants provide forthright advice to their political superiors in private and in confidence. In return, political executives protect the anonymity of public servants by publicly accepting responsibility for departmental decisions." The anonymity of public servants depends in large measure on the vitality of the doctrine of individual ministerial responsibility according to which ministers are personally responsible to the legislature both for their own actions and for those of their administrative subordinates. Thus, public servants are not directly answerable to the legislature, and their minister protects their anonymity. Recent events have shown, however, that ministers will not invariably protect the anonymity of their officials by refusing to name or blame them publicly. . . .

The decline of official anonymity. Public service anonymity depends sig-nificantly on factors other than the operation of ministerial responsibility. Departures from political neutrality in the areas of patronage and political activity also diminish official anonymity, but the greatest threat is probably the expansion of public comment described earlier. The increased interaction of public servants with both individual citizens and specific "publics" or clientele groups reveals the nature of official involvement in policy development. The cumulative impact of the growing information and conciliation functions performed by public servants is a gradual, but significant, decline in official anonymity.

The anonymity of public servants has been diminished also by their more frequent appearances before legislative committees. Their diplomtic skills are often severely taxed as they strive to describe and explain their department's program fully and frankly, while preserving their loyalty to their minister and their reputation for impartiality. On occasion, however, legislators, pressure groups, journalists, and others concerned with the committees' deliberations can discern the actual or potential power of public servants in the policy process. . . .

The pervasive role of the news media in contemporary society has been reflected in increased media coverage of the activities and identities of public servants. . . . [The] media and public servants share a mutual desire to inform the public about government programs. Public servants utilize the media for public relations and publicity—to tell their department's story and to sell their department's programs. The media serve as excellent channels of communication to the public for officials engaged in public comment requiring the description and explanation of government programs. The media in turn analyse the purposes and, whenever possible, identify the personalities involved in the development and administration of programs. This media coverage helps to limit bureaucratic power by exposing the activities of public servants to public questioning and criticism.

The extent to which public servants are exposed to the public's gaze through the news media depends largely on the position they occupy, on current interest in their department's activities, and on their personal views and their minister's views on anonymity. Certain public servants (for example, a deputy minister of finance) are better known because of the enduring importance of their position; others receive publicity during periods of public controversy in their sphere of responsibilities.

Although the tradition of anonymity remains strong among public servants, their visibility has been heightened by changes in political institutions and practices, and by the media's response to demands for more public information. This gradual decline in official anonymity is likely to continue and to reveal the expanding role of public servants in the political process.

(6) Permanency in Office

The case for security of tenure. The preservation of political neutrality requires that "public servants execute policy decisions loyally irrespective of the philosophy and programs of the party in power and regardless of their personal opinions. As a result, public servants enjoy security of tenure during good behaviour and satisfactory performance." Thus, in the event of a change of government, official neutrality helps to ensure continuity of administration by competent and experienced public servants, as well as the provision of impartial advice on policy options and the loyal implementation of policy decisions. Security of tenure enables a career public servant not only to establish and wield influence in the policy process, but also to continue to exercise such influence even if there is a change in the governing party. Long tenure in office enables public servants to acquire knowledge and experience both in specific policy fields and in the political-administrative system within which policy decisions are made. Permanence in office for public servants increases their power vis-à-vis politicians. Ministers cannot match the expertise of their senior officials, and the frequent rotation of ministers among departments prevents them from accumulating much experience in particular policy areas.

As public servants, especially at the senior levels, become more overtly or apparently political, the argument for political appointments to senior posts is strengthened. Thus, permanence in office depends largely on adherence to the elements of political neutrality already described. The merit system is designed to bring about a career public service by minimizing the number of patronage appointments and avoiding a turnover of personnel following a change of government. Senior public servants are not permitted to engage in partisan political activity or public criticism of government. Finally, the preservation of ministerial responsibility and public service anonymity helps to protect officials from public identification as supporters or opponents of particular policies.

Despite these efforts to achieve the fact and the appearance of administrative impartiality, Opposition party leaders have frequently promised, if elected, to turf out senior officials because of their assumed contribution to government policies to which these leaders are opposed. Public servants must be able to demonstrate, therefore, the capacity to adapt quickly and effectively to the requirements of a new governing party. Easily the best test of these adaptive qualities is the behaviour of public servants when a different political party comes into power.

When permanence in office for public servants has been combined with longevity in office by a particular political party, a change of government presents an especially difficult challenge to the capacity of public servants to serve impartially different political masters. It is understandable that senior officials who have worked closely with ministers in the development of existing policies should be apprehensive about the arrival of a new governing party. Shortly before Mr. Diefenbaker and the Progressive Conservatives ended the twenty-two-year reign of the Liberal Party in 1957, J.E. Hodgetts wondered about the effects of such a change: "Could we expect impartial service from the permanent servants or would we have to face some form of the American system of turning out the top ranking officials?"[41] During the Diefenbaker period, unhealthy tension often existed between senior public servants and the government. J.R. Mallory has observed, however, that "there were few resignations and few drastic changes in policy. The new ministers soon discovered that a good civil servant conceives it his duty to serve his political master to the best of his ability, and that the higher civil service was as effective at advising the new government as it had been the old."[42] In general, subsequent new governments have come to the same conclusion.

During the brief Clark period, few senior officials were invited or decided to resign. But ministers in the Clark government disagree as to whether they were well and faithfully served by senior bureaucrats. Flora MacDonald, the Secretary of State for External Affairs, stated[43] that her efforts to seek advice from persons outside government were resisted almost entirely by "those who really have their hands on the levers of power—the senior mandarins." She also complained about the use by senior bureaucrats of such "entrapment devices" as the many "crisis corridor decisions" with which she was faced, unduly lengthy and numerous memos, the late delivery of her submissions to Cabinet, and "the one-dimensional opinions put forward in memos." She noted that she "was expected to accept the unanimous recommendation of the Department" and that she was "seldom, if ever . . . given the luxury of multiple-choice options on matters of major import."

Miss MacDonald's experience was shared by Alan McKinnon, the Minister of National Defence and of Veterans Affairs.[44] He was especially critical of the "extraordinary influence" of the Prime Minister's Office and the Privy Council Office, sometimes in concert with departmental officials, on the "content" of Cabinet business. He asserted that the Clark government "met a form of passive, but inspired, resistance to change which proved highly effective, since it was presented with all the skill, and sometimes charm, that a group of highly intelligent men and women can muster when faced with a neophyte Cabinet, and a minority situation." He stated further that senior bureaucrats seemed unable to believe that he "was interested in, or even capable of understanding the immense subtleties of the problems that they had to solve. It was clearly something of an eye opener to them that any minister should wish to originate policy himself." Mr. McKinnon was dismayed at the bureaucrats' "entrenched hostility to the concept of the minister actually having both the *power* as well as the *responsibility.* . . ."

The experience of other ministers was different.[45] One minister stated that his experience with officials in his own department and "indeed, generally, was not similar to Miss MacDonald's. I am not suggesting there might not have been some incidents where public servants with deep political or policy convictions which differ from mine, might have endeavoured to frustrate or mislead me. However, generally I found them to be hard-working, dedicated and professional."[46]

These differing views support the argument earlier in this chapter that the extent of bureaucratic power varies according to such factors as "the policy or program under consideration, the department or agency involved, and the style and competence of ministers and their officials." Prime Minister Clark stated that he and his government had no complaint regarding the treatment they received from the senior public service. He did ask, however, whether "a large and diverse country like ours can be as well served as Britain is by the exclusive reliance upon a professional Public Service, or whether we should be leaning more towards elements of the American system which allow a new government to bring in people who agree with its point of view."[47]

The case for politicization. There is some support in Canada for a system of political appointments similar to that in the United States. Supporters of a politicized public service usually cite the following benefits from political appointments to senior public service posts:

- a strong commitment to implementing the policies of the new government;
- a breath of fresh air in the form of new ideas and approaches towards government policies and processes;
- the restoration and preservation of political (ministerial) control over permanent officials and the decision-making processes of government;
- advice on policy issues that is more sensitive to their partisan political implications;
- greater trust by ministers in their policy advisors.

Under this system, the incumbents of the most senior public service positions would be replaced whenever a change in government occured. Some senior appointments would thus be held on a temporary rather than a permanent basis. The power of career public servants would be reduced, because they would not normally be appointed to the highest administrative posts in government. However, assuming regular changes in the governing party, the tenure in office of senior political appointees would be too brief to enable them to exercise as much power based on experience and expertise as career public servants do.

At present, a shift to a system of political appointments either in the federal government or in most provincial governments is unlikely. Career public servants in Canada can normally expect security of tenure during good conduct, adequate performance, and political neutrality. Note must be taken, however, of a gradual politicization of the senior bureaucracy in a few provinces, and of the fact that the Conservative government that came to power in Saskatchewan in 1982 dismissed about two hundred senior public servants. The Saskatchewan experience appears to be an aberration. Certainly the rationale for the sweeping nature of the dismissals is unclear; many of those dismissed were career public servants with no partisan affiliation.

Political Neutrality and Bureaucratic Power

The present operations of Canada's public services are not in accord with a strict interpretation of the traditional doctrine of political neutrality. Some of the requirements of the traditional doctrine remain substantially unchanged, but some have never been met, and others have been altered to keep pace with changing political, social, and technological circumstances. The elements of the doctrine may be updated and restated as follows:

1. Policy, politics and administration are intertwined.
2. Most public servants are selected and promoted on the basis of merit, but some positions are filled by partisans of the governing party.
3. Public servants may participate in a number of partisan political activities unless they occupy senior or sensitive positions.
4. Public servants are usually not permitted to criticize publicly their government's actions, but are involved in various other forms of public comment in the normal course of their duties.
5. Public servants provide confidential advice to ministers; ministers usually protect the anonymity of public servants, but this anonymity is gradually declining for other reasons.
6. Public servants usually execute policy decisions loyally regardless of their personal views and of the political complexion of the governing party.

Thus, public servants are actively involved in the political system both by necessity in the areas of policy development and execution, and by choice in the sphere of political partisanship. This involvement accounts in large part for the nature and extent of bureaucratic power in contemporary Canadian governments. . . .

NOTES

1. The George C. Nowlan Lecture, Acadia University, February 7, 1977. Reprinted in *The Globe and Mail*, February 8, 1977.
2. Mitchell Sharp, "Reflections of a Former Minister of the Crown," address to the Toronto Regional Group of the Institute of Public Administration of Canada, November 29, 1976, pp. 6–7.
3. R.J.S. Baker, *Administrative Theory and Public Administration* (London: Hutchinson, 1972), p. 13.
4. *Canadian Public Policy and Administration* (Toronto: McGraw-Hill Ryerson, 1981), p. 99.
5. Woodrow Wilson, "The Study of Administration." Reprinted in Peter Woll, ed., *Public Administration and Policy* (New York: Harper and Row, 1966), pp. 15–41.
6. Ibid., pp. 28–29.
7. Wallace S. Sayre, "Premises of Public Administration: Past and Emerging," *Public Administration Review*, vol. 18 (1958), p. 103.
8. Quoted in J.E. Hodgetts, et al., *The Biography of an Institution: The Civil Service Commission of Canada*, 1908–1967 (Montreal: McGill-Queen's University Press, 1972), p. 56.
9. Ibid. (Emphasis added.)
10. See for example, Luther Gulick, "Politics, Administration and the New Deal," *Annals of the American Academy of Political and Social Science*

(1933), and Pendleton Herring, *Public Administration and the Public Interest*, 1936. (Reprinted in 1967 by Russell, New York.)

11. Paul Appleby, *Policy and Administration* (University, Alabama: University of Alabama Press, 1949), p. 170. See also Dwight Waldo, *The Administrative State* (New York: Ronald Press, 1948) and Harold Stein, *Public Administration and Policy Development: A Casebook* (New York: Harcourt, Brace, 1952).

12. See Frank Marini, ed., *Toward a New Public Administration: The Minnowbrook Perspective* (Scranton, Pa.: Chandler, 1971).

13. See especially Eugene P. Dvorin and Robert H. Simmons, *From Amoral to Humane Bureaucracy* (San Francisco: Canfield Press, 1972) and Louis C. Gawthrop, *Administrative Politics and Social Change* (New York: St. Martin's Press, 1971).

14. "The Coming Crisis in the North," *Journal of Canadian Studies*, vol. 2 (February 1967), p. 3.

15. See Kenneth Kernaghan and T.H. McLeod, "Mandarins and Ministers in the Canadian Administrative State," in O.P. Dwivedi, ed., *The Canadian Administrative State* (Toronto: University of Toronto Press, 1982), pp. 17–30.

16. Quoted in Douglas Fisher, "A Mandarin Reflects on the Bureaucracy," *Executive*, December 1979, p. 90.

17. Wayne A.R. Leys, "Ethics and Administrative Discretion," *Public Administration Review*, vol. 3 (Winter 1943), p.23.

18. Eric Hehner, "Growth of Discretions—Decline of Accountability," in Kenneth Kernaghan, ed., *Public Administration in Canada: Selected Readings*, 5th ed. (Toronto: Methuen, 1985), p. 342.

19. House of Commons, *Special Committee on Statutory Instruments*, 3rd Report (Ottawa: Queens Printer, 1969), p. 4.

20. Senate and House of Commons, *Standing Joint Committee on Regulations and Other Statutory Instruments*, 2nd Report (Ottawa: Queen's Printer, 1977), esp. pp. 2–12.

21. Robert Presthus, *The Organizational Society* (New York: Vintage Books, 1962), p. 53.

22. Allan Kornberg, William Mishler, and Harold D. Clarke, *Representative Democracy in the Canadian Provinces* (Scarborough: Prentice-Hall, 1982), p. 184.

23. R.H. Dowdell, "Public Personnel Administration," in Kenneth Kernaghan, ed., *Public Administration in Canada*, 4th ed. (Toronto: Methuen, 1982), p. 196.

24. Ibid.

25. H.M. Clokie, *Canadian Government and Politics* (Toronto: Longmans, Green, 1944), p. 190.

26. Canada, *Royal Commission on Government Organization*, vol. 1 (Ottawa: Queen's Printer, 1962), p. 371.

27. Stanley Knowles, House of Commons, *Debates*, April 11, 1973, p. 3176.
28. Between 1948 and 1972, 12.1 per cent of retiring or defeated ministers were appointed to patronage positions. See W.A. Matheson, *The Prime Minister and the Cabinet* (Toronto: Methuen, 1976), p. 121.
29. See Chapter 14 [of K. Kernaghan and D. Siegel, *Public Administration in Canada: A Text* (Toronto: Methuen, 1987)] for elaboration on the role of ministerial staff.
30. See J.E. Hodgetts and O.P. Dwivedi, *Provincial Governments as Employers* (McGill-Queen's University Press, 1974), ch. 2.
31. J.E. Hodgetts and O.P. Dwivedi, "Administration and Personnel," in David J. Bellamy, Jon H. Pammett, and Donald C. Rowat, eds., *The Provincial Political Systems: Comparative Essays* (Toronto: Methuen, 1976), p. 347.
32. *The Globe and Mail*, August 6, 1985, p. 1.
33. See S.M. Lipset, *Agrarian Socialism: The Cooperative Commonwealth Federation in Saskatchewan* (Berkeley: University of California Press, 1959); Evelyn Eager, *Saskatchewan Government* (Saskatoon: Western Producer Prairie Books, 1980), pp. 164–167; and Hans J. Michelmann and Jeffrey S. Steeves, "The 1982 Transition in Power in Saskatchewan: The Progressive Conservatives and the Public Service," *Canadian Public Administration*, vol. 28 (Spring 1985), pp. 1–23.
34. For a definition of political activity and an account of the arguments usually raised for and against the political activity of government employees, see Kenneth Kernaghan, *Ethical Conduct: Guidelines for Government Employees* (Toronto: Institute of Public Administration of Canada, 1975), pp. 26–28.
35. *Neil A. Fraser, Grievor, v. Treasury Board (Department of National Revenue, Taxation), Employer*, Public Service Staff Relations Board Decision, May 31, 1982, p. 16.
36. Supreme Court of Canada, *Neil Fraser and Public Service Staff Relations Board*, [1985] 2 S.C.R., pp. 468, 470.
37. This classification is an expansion of that set out in Kernaghan, *Ethical Conduct*, p. 36.
38. *Policy Guidelines for Public Servants: Communications with the Public*, November 23, 1979, reproduced in *Debates* (Commons), November 29, 1979, p. 1875.
39. Emphasis added.
40. Office of the Prime Minister, *Policy Guidelines for Public Servants: Communications with the Public*, November 23, 1984.
41. J.E. Hodgetts, "The Liberal and the Bureaucrat," *Queen's Quarterly*, vol. 62, (1955), pp. 176–183. Following the 1957 election, John Meisel observed that the Liberal program "had, in the main, evolved gradually as the consequence of the continuous interaction of the cabinet and the leading experts in the civil service . . . Much of what had, in the years immediately before the election, been called Liberal policies or the Liberal programme

was actually the product of the inimate co-operation of leading civil servants and their ministers." John Meisel, *The Canadian General Election of 1957* (Toronto: University of Toronto Press, 1962), pp. 37–38.

42. J.R. Mallory, *The Structure of Canadian Government* (Toronto: Macmillan, 1971), p. 116.
43. See "The Ministers and the Mandarins," *Policy Options*, vol. 1 (September-October 1980), pp. 29–31.
44. "An Address to the Rotary Club of Victoria," August 1980.
45. Reported in confidential communications with Professor Kernaghan in October 1980.
46. Ibid.
47. Transcript of An Address (Including Question and Answer Period) to the 11th Annual Leadership Conference Sponsored by the Centre for the Study of the Presidency, Ottawa, October 19, 1980, p. 14.

FURTHER READINGS

d'Aquino, T. "The Public Service of Canada: The Case for Political Neutrality." *Canadian Public Administration* 27, 1 (Spring 1984): 14–23.

Atkinson, M.M., and W.D. Coleman. "Bureaucrats and Politicians in Canada: An Examination of the Political Administration Model." *Comparative Political Studies* 18, 1 (April 1985): 58–80.

Doern, G.B., and R.W. Phidd. *Canadian Public Policy: Ideas, Structure, Process.* Toronto: Methuen, 1983.

Doerr, A.D. *The Machinery of Government in Canada.* Toronto: Methuen, 1981.

French, R.D., with R. Van Loon. *How Ottawa Decides: Planning and Industrial Policy-Making, 1968–1984.* 2nd ed. Toronto: Lorimer, 1984.

Hartle, D. "Techniques and Processes of Administration." *Canadian Public Administration* 19, 1 (Spring 1976): 21–33.

Kernaghan, K., ed. *Public Administration in Canada: Selected Readings.* 5th ed. Toronto: Methuen, 1985.

Kernaghan, K., and D. Siegel. *Public Administration in Canada: A Text.* Toronto: Methuen, 1987.

Norman, R. "Les relations entre les hauts fonctionnaires et le ministre." *Canadian Public Administration* 27, 4 (Winter 1984): 522–541.

26

The Federal-Provincial Decision-making Process

RICHARD SIMEON

Two central facts characterize the relationship between federal and provincial governments. The first is that they are *interdependent*: functions and responsibilities are not neatly divided between Ottawa and the provinces. In virtually every important policy field one finds two and often three levels of government deeply involved. Social policy, environmental policy, economic policy, and many others are all shared: effective policy requires joint action. What one government does will affect the ability of others to achieve their goals. Watertight compartments of sharply defined responsibilities no longer exist, if, indeed, they ever did. The second fact is that governments are in some policy fields *autonomous*: none can dictate to the others. Each has extensive resources— political, constitutional, and financial—with which to pursue its own goals and influence others. Hence, in order to achieve coordination and collectively deal with the problems facing Canadians, governments must find ways to resolve conflicts, coordinate their activities, and jointly make policy. An elaborate framework of intergovernmental bargaining and negotiation (which has been described variously as "cooperative federalism," "executive federalism," "administrative federalism" and "federal-provincial diplomacy") has therefore arisen. It has become one of the most important processes, if not the most important process, within which policy is developed in Canada.

This paper will examine the nature and extent of the collaboration and sharing between governments, describe the structure and operation of the machinery for coordination which has developed, assess some of the problems and criticisms which have developed, and consider some alternative means of rationalizing the processes of federal-provincial decision-making.

SHARED RESPONSIBILITIES

In few policy areas—except perhaps defence, the post office or garbage collection—does one government act alone. Social welfare policy, for example, encompasses purely federal programs (family allowances, old age pensions, unemployment insurance); shared cost programs (the Canada Assistance Plan);

Richard Simeon, "The Federal-Provincial Decision Making Process," *Intergovernmental Relations* (Toronto: Ontario Economic Council, 1977), 25-37, Reprinted by permission of the Ontario Economic Council.

purely provincial activities; and often municipal financing and administration of welfare. The amount, cost and quality of housing available to Canadians is affected by local zoning and building standards, provincial land use policies, grants to home buyers, landlord-tenant regulations and a host of other measures; and federal policies such as sales taxes, interest rates, use of federally controlled lands, and the programs of Central Mortgage and Housing Corporation with respect to public housing, neighbourhood renewal, and the availability of mortgage funds. A similar pattern repeats itself over and over again.

Why has this pattern developed? The first reason is constitutional. The framers of the British North America Act could not anticipate the new responsibilities—such as the welfare state or environmental quality—that government would undertake in the twentieth century. Hence, as old functions changed in importance and as new functions arose, they did not neatly fit into the constitutional categories set out in Sections 91 and 92 of the Act. The number of constitutional grey areas, and of effective concurrent jurisdiction, multiplied. Under the twin impact of the Depression and wartime centralization, the federal government, with the general support of the provinces, moved strongly into areas of provincial jurisdiction. In part this was achieved by a transfer of jurisdiction but much more commonly it involved the federal government's use of its unrestricted spending power in order to develop new transfer programs to individuals and to influence provincial policies through the device of shared-cost programs. As new policy concerns arose, both levels of government found that they possessed the constitutional powers to become involved. New issues almost inevitably cut across jurisdictional lines, making a comprehensive attack on them difficult. Policy tends to be a seamless web: political institutions are sharply divided within and between governments.

Two more specific factors also account for the sharing of responsibilities. First, citizens make demands on governments with little understanding of constitutional divisions: both levels of government are under pressure on consumer issues, women's rights, the environment and so on. Both therefore try to respond. This is linked to the phenomenon of bureaucratic expansionism. Governments—and individual agencies within them—seek to move into those policy areas in which they perceive political credit to be gained. The federal government established a Ministry of State for Urban Affairs: provinces became involved in manpower training; both established consumer protection bureaus.

Frequently governments compete for primacy, especially in new problem areas. In the immediate postwar period, the federal government was most expansionist: its bureaucracy had vastly grown in size and competence during the war; it had centralized the tax system; Keynesian economics gave a new rationale and new tools for economic management; and public opinion seemed receptive to the welfare state and a more dominant central government. The result was massive federal intervention into many areas of provincial jurisdiction under the rubric of "cooperative federalism." More recently, the growth in importance of provincial matters, the increasing size and competence of provincial governments, the inability of the federal government adequately to reflect regional diversity and other factors have contributed to more expansionist provincial governments. They have sought not only fewer federal controls and more taxing powers but also a greater voice in economic, transportation, trade and other policies over which Ottawa has primary jurisdiction. This may be seen as a shift from federal dominance to the "attenuation of federal power." But it can also be seen as an expansion of the roles of both levels, with a resulting increase in overlapping and joint responsibilities.

A list of joint federal-provincial programs in 1975 included almost 300 different programs. And, in addition to these programs, both levels were simultaneously involved in many other policy areas. At some times there have been explicit attempts at coordination. At others, the two levels of government have operated independently of each other.

The growth in shared responsibilities—together with much increased provincial shares of spending and revenues in recent years—poses many questions.

The most general problem has been called "entanglement" by the Ontario Government. Entanglement takes several forms. Some programs simply *duplicate* each other: for example, Ontario's Home Ownership Made Easy Plan and Ottawa's Assisted Home Ownership Plan. Both provide cash grants to first-time home buyers. Similarly, both levels pursue active programs for economic development, often in competition. Some programs are *fragmented* between two levels. Ontario's Guaranteed Annual Income Supplement is added on top of the Federal Old Age Security Program. Provincial welfare systems come into play when Unemployment Insurance Benefits run out. A change in one affects the other. *Incursion* occurs when a government makes a policy which affects the existing programs provided by the other level. Recent federal competition policies, for example, may well run up against provincial regulation of the legal profession, or of realtors. *Spillovers* occur when one government in its attempt to deal with a problem, creates new burdens for the other level. For example, the proposed federal Young Offenders Bill may create additional administrative and financial difficulties for the administration of justice by Ontario. Often governments will seek to *neutralize* the effects of policies by one level which are seen to be harmful to the other. Ottawa altered its corporation tax regulations to counteract the effect of provincial changes in mineral royalties and taxation in 1974, to illustrate the point.

The problems are not merely administrative. There is also more substantial conflict as governments compete with each other both for resources and political support. Given their different perspectives and constituencies, they have different priorities and goals. Intergovernmental relations therefore are a mixture of conflict and collaboration. Disagreements arise both about the substance of policy—what should be done—and jurisdiction—who should have the power to do it.

Finally, underlying much federal-provincial conflict are the considerable regional differences in wealth, economic structure, and ethnic make-up and the like. Conflicts between Ontario and Ottawa are primarily over administrative difficulties, and disagreements over how best to achieve development goals. But in the West, Atlantic Canada and Quebec, these are less important than are sometimes profound differences in basic social and economic goals.

One result of this overlapping and duplication is greatly to increase decision costs. Coordination itself requires a great deal of time and effort and involves the energies of a host of officials serving on a multitude of federal-provincial committees. Decisions are likely to take longer to reach when the interests of many governments must be reconciled.

It is impossible to measure the extent of these costs. But they are high. Related to these decision costs is the danger that, in the preoccupation with competition and coordination, policy discussions turn primarily on questions of organization, financing and jurisdiction; less attention is available for discussion of the substance of the actual policies to be pursued. Programs are likely to be contradictory or inconsistent with each other. Alternatively, other policy problems may be neglected because they fall between jurisdictional stools.

From the viewpoint of the citizen affected by policy the existing system also has costs. It is often difficult for citizens to know which level of government is responsible for what. Thus it is difficult to know where and how to intervene in the policy process. When governments share responsibility, or one level of government pays for programs administered by another, it is much more difficult to achieve accountability. The citizen does not know whom to praise or to blame. Intergovernmental argument about jurisdiction often seems irrelevant to citizen needs. It is difficult to anticipate what a change, such as ending shared cost programs in the health field, means for the cost and quality of care.

Against these costs of overlapping and duplication, however, must be set some advantages. Given the division of powers in the BNA Act, and the difficulty of amending it, joint action (largely through the device of shared cost programs in welfare, health, and post-secondary education) was essential if the new needs of Canadians were to be met. Despite many difficulties, the welfare state has been firmly set in place through such collaboration. Intergovernmental sharing of responsibility also allows the accommodation and reconciliation of the twin goals of achieving national purposes and responding to regional diversity. It permits variation and experiment in policies across governments.

THE MACHINERY OF
INTERGOVERNMENTAL RELATIONS

An elaborate machinery of intergovernmental negotiation and decision-making has developed outside the former Canadian constitution. Yet it is now an essential part of the effective constitutional framework. The central element is "executive federalism": a pattern of bargaining between the executives of federal and provincial governments similar in many ways to international negotiations.

The primary institution is the Federal-Provincial Conference or the Conference of First Ministers, at which the Prime Ministers and Premiers, together with large delegations of Ministers and officials, meet to discuss the broad issues of federal-provincial relations. The meetings provide an opportunity to exchange information, exercise mutual influence, and occasionally to make joint decisions. The Conference is not, however, a formal decision-making body. The decisions reached there mut be ratified by the individual governments. The agenda varies but tends to focus on the immediate issues of current federal-provincial conflict. Increasingly the atmosphere has been one of confrontation, as provinces have sought to influence federal policies and gain a greater voice in many policy areas. Most conferences involve all eleven governments. But there has recently been more bilateral diplomacy in which federal representatives travel the country preparing the ground for coming negotiations. The Western Economic Opportunities Conference, called to discuss Western grievances, represented the first recent conference at which Ottawa sat down with a group of provinces.

During the constitutional conferences between 1968 and 1971, a Secretariat was established to provide support services and coordination for the governments. That has been succeeded by the Canadian Intergovernmental Conference Secretariat. Its role is primarily that of administration and house-keeping. Canada has no joint intergovernmental body of officials comparable to the Commission of the European Common Market.

One of the chief objections to these conferences is that they are secret. Several of the constitutional conferences were open to press and television but the normal pattern is for *in camera* discussion. To the extent that the meetings are a forum for detailed negotiation, secrecy is probably justified. But to the extent that they are increasingly a setting for basic debate about the nature of Canadian federalism and broad policy options—with more detailed negotiation going on elsewhere—then this role is more akin to that of Parliament. Openness should be increased.

In the past, provincial governments seldom developed a common position before sitting down with federal representatives. In many cases provincial positions differed. "Ganging-up" was considered not only a violation of the informal rules of the game, but was difficult to achieve. One of the most important recent developments in federal-provincial relations has been an increasing tendency for the provinces to develop joint positions, and to negotiate with each other, without federal participation. Thus regional groupings, such as the Atlantic Premiers and the Prairie Economic Council, have played a greater role. In the renewed constitutional discussions in 1976 the provinces met alone to discuss patriation and other issues. And in the discussions on financial arrangements in 1976 the Premiers went to Ottawa with a common front on many issues. Provinces are thus tending to negotiate their differences among themselves, and present Ottawa with an agreed position. This could greatly increase their bargaining power, making it harder for Ottawa to pursue a policy of divide and rule. Provincial unanimity is likely to be limited, however. Interprovincial differences on many issues—between oil consumers and oil producers, between richer and poorer provinces and between Quebec and other provinces—are likely to remain.

Interprovincial conferences have another purpose as well: to permit provinces to exchange information and coordinate policies which are not immediate issues of federal-provincial debate: for example, the agendas of these conferences, now held annually, have included such matters as interprovincial trucking and securities legislation.

Below the Conferences of First Ministers are meetings of groups of Ministers. Some, such as conferences on housing, are *ad hoc*. Some, such as those established during the Constitutional Conferences, are sub-committees reporting to the First Ministers. Others have been held more regularly. One of the most important is the Conference of Finance Ministers which is not only a forum for discussion of fiscal issues but also for exchange of information and plans concerning general economic policy. The increased fiscal weight of the provinces make such meetings especially important.

Other, more formal, ministerial meetings include groupings of Ministers in particular areas, such as the Council of Resource Ministers and Council of Ministers of Education, which meet regularly, and have had their own secretariats and research staffs. This whole structure could be formalized and rationalized to cover more systematically the major policy areas.

Finally, there is a host of meetings of officials. Again, some are *ad hoc*, while others meet regularly. The range of such meetings is broad. Some are devoted to coordination of relatively detailed and non-controversial matters: others are devoted to more general issues of policy and strategy, primarily as backup for the more political meetings of ministers and premiers. The most important of these have been the Continuing Committee on Fiscal and Economic Matters and the Continuing Committee on the Constitution.

In general, the more specific the policy areas the more harmonious have been federal-provincial meetings. Often officials concerned with specific program areas, such as welfare, share common professional goals. To some extent they have more in common with each other than with their respective political masters. Recent events, however, have undermined this pattern of harmonious relationships, which developed after World War II, in the heyday of the adoption of many shared cost programs. Federal-provincial discussion is increasingly "political" and devoted to the broad issues of overall governmental strategy. Conflict is less contained at the official level, and more likely to find expression in disagreement among politicians.

There are several reasons for this development. In part it reflects the general increase in regional differences and the desire of provincial governments for more autonomy and power. In part it reflects governmental desire to achieve much greater control over their own patterns of spending and policy priorities. Hence, most governments have now moved to exert greater central coordination, through cabinets, treasury boards and other agencies, over the cooperative activities of program officials. Governments have sought to ensure that official relationships will be subordinate to overall political strategy. Thus Ottawa has established a cabinet committee on federal-provincial relations and the Federal-Provincial Relations Office alongside the Privy Council Office. Quebec was the first province to establish a ministry of Intergovernmental Affairs. Ontario has established strong control through the Department of Treasury, Economics and Intergovernmental Affairs. Alberta has established a ministry of Federal and Intergovernmental Affairs and other provinces have followed suit.

The development of new techniques for policy analysis and political control within governments has, perhaps ironically, had the effect of sharpening intergovernmental conflict and rendering policy coordination more difficult. One important consequence of these developments is to ensure that political disagreement, especially the competition for status and power, may override concern for the substance of policy. The central actors are Premiers, Treasury Departments and the like. For example, the Canada Pension Plan was discussed by these participants primarily as a problem of intergovernmental finance, not as a problem in social policy. Similarly the recent discussion of the future of shared cost programs in higher education and health care subordinated the discussion of the content of these programs. Financial and jurisdictional concerns were overriding.

Carrying out intergovernmental negotiations is a major preoccupation of Canadian governments. A 1957 study discovered 67 federal-provincial committees. In 1967, 119 such committees were identified. In 1973, representatives of Alberta participated in 118 meetings and conferences: 25 were bilateral, 73 included all governments, and 20 were regional. Twenty-three occurred at the ministerial level, 24 at the level of Deputy Ministers, 14 at the assistant Deputy level, and 14 at other levels. The decision-making process is obviously complex.

In the 1940s and 1960s cooperative federalism was a vehicle for federal leadership. In the 1970s, the same machinery has become the mechanism through which the provinces have become much more important political actors. The bargaining power of the various governments varies greatly from issue to issue and from time to time. Most fundamentally, power depends on the extent of the political support a government enjoys. The growth of regional feeling and the erosion of electoral support for the present federal government in many areas seems to account for increased provincial assertiveness. In addition, the constitutional allocation of responsibilities affects bargaining power. Provinces remain little more than pressure groups in a federal area like transportation or in seeking more generous equalization. Influence also depends on skill and competence. While it is difficult to measure, it appears that the technical and administrative resources of provincial governments have increased greatly in recent years. They are less willing to defer to federal expertise. The mechanisms of federal-provincial negotiations have also played a significant role. Provincial governments now play a major part on the national stage and have come to be seen as integral parts of national policy-making mechanisms. The forum provided by federal-provincial machinery also allows provinces to act together against the federal government.

It should not be thought, however, that power has shifted decisively away from Ottawa. While deferring to the provinces in some areas, the federal government has been acting more aggressively in others—especially in economic policy and regulation. The heightened conflict stems from the existence of two levels, both of which are innovative, aggressive and self-confident.

This process also suggests that the distinction between national purposes and provincial purposes is not sharp. The federal government can be heavily involved in provincial development. On the other hand, it is possible that national purposes can be attained through federal-provincial negotiation, or even by the provinces acting together without much federal involvement.

The range of issues debated in this federal-provincial forum is wide. A quick summary of the current issues under negotiation will illustrate this point:

- Public finance: equalization, shared cost programs, the revenue guarantee, and tax collection agreements;
- Transportation: conflict over the federal move towards "user pay" as a principle, prairie freight rates, regulation of trucking, the federal worry about provincial ownership of Pacific Western Airlines, the Pickering airport, passenger rail transport;
- The constitution;
- Justice: legal aid and family law reform;
- Immigration: the demand for a greater provincial role;
- Energy: oil and gas pricing, subsidy to the east coast, energy exports, interprovincial transmission of electricity, supply and refining of uranium, intergration of federal and provincial coal development strategies, conflicts over pipelines and energy exploration, off-shore minerals, the need for cooperation in energy conservation:
- Other economic matters: closure of armed forces bases, foreign investment, alterations on federal banking policy, securities legislation:

- Native peoples: tribal land claims, provision of social services to Status Indians;
- Parks;
- Communications: the provincial desire for regulatory authority over cable TV and for public ownership of communications networks;
- And so on . . .

The agenda is a long one, and it is always changing.

ASSESSMENT OF THE PROCESS

The mechanisms for intergovernmental consultation can be assessed from various points of view: the federal government might assess them differently from provincial governments and both differently from citizens.

Federal-provincial conferences have been the vehicles for increasing provincial criticism of the federal government. It is sometimes argued that federal policies in such areas as transportation, trade and economic policy do not adequately take account of provincial needs and interests. The provinces have sought greater influence in these areas with mixed success. Provinces have also acted more aggressively on their own on matters such as agricultural marketing, trade, foreign ownership and economic development.

It is also argued that the federal government controls too great a share of the more elastic and lucrative revenue sources. This, it is said, encourages the federal government to move more aggressively into areas of provincial jurisdiction, such as municipal affairs, while starving the provincial public sector. In part this is a purely political argument. The provinces have every right to increase taxes and Ottawa argues quite rightly that they simply wish the federal government to take the blame for raising taxes.

Finally, it is argued that the federal government moves indiscriminately into areas of provincial jurisdiction without adequate consultation. The federal government responds to its own political environment and its own policy goals of which the provinces form only a part. This complaint is frequently justified but it must also be noted that "adequate consultation" is in the eye of the beholder. Frequently the issue is not whether or not there was consultation but rather whether or not Ottawa acceded to provincial requests.

Shared cost programs have become the primary focus of discontent. Provinces complain that such programs have been introduced and terminated without full discussion; the conditions attached to them have been onerous and have increased administrative difficulties; that the lure of 50-cent dollars represented in cost-sharing formulae has skewed provincial priorities. They have also complained that sharing formulae have led to irrationalities. For example, it is claimed the hospital insurance program has encouraged over-production of acute-care hospital beds but done nothing to increase availability of cheaper extended-care facilities that are badly needed.

Shared cost programs have also been criticized from the federal side.

Ottawa was helping to pay for programs for which it got no credit. The fact that Quebec had opted-out of many such programs in 1964 implied a form of special status. But most important, the costs of the most important programs were rising faster than either governmental revenues or GNP. Ottawa has little control over a large part of its own spending budget. With the growing concern with restraining growth in government expenditures, Ottawa first moved to put a limit on year-to-year increases in the most important programs. It then proposed that medicare, hospital insurance and post-secondary education be turned over to the provinces completely, along with a fiscal package including cash payments and further tax shares. The new federal-provincial Fiscal Arrangements Act, negotiated in 1976, embodies this important policy change. It represents a substantial disengagement of federal and provincial activity. While it does not rule out additional shared-cost programs in the future, it does suggest the device will have only limited use and, indeed, Ottawa itself has suggested its willingness to limit use of the federal spending power to circumstances in which there is prior provincial consensus.

This should reduce some of the problems of overlapping and joint administration, and give the provinces increased freedom to adjust these policies in light of provincial needs. It has some costs, however. It means that the poorer provinces will be even more dependent on the revenue equalization program to alleviate regional disparities and thus will be highly vulnerable to changes in it. It also means that program differences between provinces are likely to increase. The dilemma remains: can policy simultaneously achieve national goals and be responsive to differing provincial needs and priorities?

From the point of view of the public, the process we have described has other consequences. The secrecy and complexity of the negotiations makes public awareness of the issues and alternatives extremely difficult. The arcane technical language with which questions of tax points, shared cost programs, the spending power and others are discussed by governments renders public understanding even harder. Governmental concern with the federal-provincial bargaining game may well lead to policy competition in which citizen groups are caught in the cross-fire: the experience of mineral and petroleum companies in the conflict over mineral revenues is a recent example.

More generally, the process ensures that issues of intergovernmental concern—structural, jurisdictional and financial—will always be to the fore. It increases the Canadian tendency to see policy in regional terms and to force even issues that are not on the surface obviously "regional"—like poverty—into a regional mould. Other definitions of the situation and other policy alternatives tend to be neglected because of the dominance of intergovernmental relations in policy debate. The process does make it difficult to deal with "national" policy problems, because jurisdiction with respect to them is divided.

On the other hand, it could be said that the process is an effective accommodation both to the constitutional rigidities and to the obvious fact of the importance of regional divisions. From this point of view it could be said that the process permits reconciliation of conflicting interests, that it adjusts effectively to the varying strength of provincial and national demands and that without it the problems of policy-making in the federal state would be even more difficult. In a real sense the problems of contemporary Canadian federalism are not so much the problems of the machinery of intergovernmental discussion but are rather the consequences of the sharp regional conflict in the country, the kinds of policy problems it faces and the inability of any constitution unambiguously to divide responsibilities.

REFORMING THE SYSTEM

In considering reform of the mechanisms of intergovernmental relations, two sets of alternatives can be raised. First, what can be done to minimize the overlapping, duplication and inconsistencies which characterize so many areas of public policy in Canada? Second, how can the formal machinery of federal-provincial decision-making be modified so as to promote public awareness, facilitate compromise and increase the capacity of governments jointly to deal with major societal problems?

The first strategy might be called "disentaglement," the search for ways to identify policy or program areas in which both levels of government are operating, in order to identify overlaps. This could be done on an area by area basis. In each, then, the governments should ask to what extent are the activities complementary, competing, redundant, and so on. Once these areas are identified, it may be possible to disengage: to allocate some to each level of government, in which it would be able to act alone.

Such an administrative procedure could usefully rationalize many areas which have grown up on a piecemeal basis without much rational consideration.

It would not, however, alleviate the more fundamental problems we have identified as leading to joint action. Competition for credit would remain. Public demands for both levels to intervene would not abate. Governments would still want to intervene in ways which would spill over to other governments. The preferred programs and priorities of the two levels of government would still differ. Nevertheless, as a first step to rationalization governments should search out and identify these areas of overlap. More fundamentally, it might be possible to think of a wide-ranging redistribution of responsibilities between federal and provincial governments. Rather than joint action through shared cost programs, the responsibility and the funds would be allocated unambiguously to one level of government. This is the implication of the recent transfer of shared-cost programs to the provinces. Other redistributions might involve formal change in the constitution. The logic here is that of watertight compartments. The difficulty is to identify any important policy area in which one level of government would be content to allow the other to operate alone. Many have suggested that overall economic management is one of the primary federal roles; but provinces may also have a role to play in stabilization policy and have strong views about it. Environmental policy, to take another example, similarly has local, provincial and national dimensions, inextricably intertwined. Policy sharing is a permanent feature of Canadian federalism.

Even if the present policy concerns of government could be rationalized in this way, new policy areas would inevitably arise to cut across whatever new policy boundaries had been devised. Hence, while it would be useful to study policy areas in this light, high expectations should not be placed on a general reorientation of overall governmental responsibilities.

There have been many suggestions for improving the machinery of intergovernmental consultation. Some such improvements are probably necessary but it must be remembered that the machinery is less important to success in negotiations than are the attitudes and orientations of the participants and the nature of the problems facing them. Conflict stems not just from administrative weaknesses, but from real differences in goals and priorities.

It is, however, vital to make a sharper distinction between those elements of the machinery which should be open to public view and those which should remain private. The Victoria Charter restricted its proposals about machinery to the requirement of a yearly meeting of First Ministers. This should be retained with the additional stipulation that at least one such meeting be open to the press and provide an opportunity for general public discussion of major issues facing the federation.

Consideration should be given to strengthening the role of the Intergovernmental Secretariat, so that in addition to its housekeeping activities, it would undertake research and other activities at the direction of the eleven governments.

In addition to the regular First Ministers Conferences, it would be useful to have permanent standing committees of ministers, supported by relevant officials' groups, in the most important policy fields. This could permit a more regular exchange of information.

The intergovernmental bargaining process has grown up largely separate from Parliamentary institutions, and without adequate mechanisms for scrutiny and ensuring accountability. Hence, in order to facilitate greater public awareness of the issues and alternatives in intergovernmental relations it is important that the federal Parliament and provincial legislatures have greater opportunity to study and assess them. Specific responsibility for the oversight of intergovernmental activities—municipal-provincial as well as federal-provincial—should be assigned to permanent committees of the legislatures and federal Parliament.

FURTHER READINGS

Gibbins, R. *Conflict and Unity. An Introduction to Canadian Political Life*, Chapter 7. Toronto: Methuen, 1985.

Simeon, R. *Federal-Provincial Diplomacy: The Making of Recent Policy in Canada*. Toronto: University of Toronto Press, 1972.

————, ed. *Intergovernmental Relations*. Toronto: University of Toronto Press, 1985.

Smiley, D.V. *The Federal Condition in Canada*, Chapter 4. Toronto: McGraw-Hill Ryerson, 1987.

Stevenson, G. "Federalism and Intergovernmental Relations." In M.S. Whittington and G. Williams, eds. *Canadian Politics in the 1980s*. 2nd ed., 371–390. Toronto: Methuen, 1984.

27

The Anti-inflation Case:
The Anatomy of a Constitutional Decision

PETER H. RUSSELL

The Supreme Court of Canada's decision[1] in July 1976 on the constitutional validity of the federal Anti-Inflation Act was probably the Court's most heralded decision since it became Canada's final court of appeal in 1949. For the first time since 1949 a major national policy, upon which the federal government placed the highest priority, was challenged before the Court. Also, this was the first clear test of whether the Supreme Court would "liberate" the federal Parliament's general power to make laws for the "peace, order and good government of Canada" from the shackles placed upon it by the Privy Council's jurisprudence and thereby provide the constitutional underpinning for a revolutionary readjustment of the balance of power in Canadian federalism. And it was the first major constitutional case for a Supreme Court headed by Chief Justice Bora Laskin, who during his academic career had earned a reputation as Canada's leading authority on constitutional law and as an articulate critic of the Privy Council. All in all, the case appeared to be a showdown.

The outcome may seem rather anti-climactic. The federal government's wage and price control policy escaped a judicial veto. But the Court's decision gave it only a temporary and conditional constitutional mandate. More importantly, the Court did not endorse the expansive interpretation of Parliament's general power which a generation of centralist-minded commentators had hoped for as much as a generation of provincially-minded Canadians had feared. Instead, the Court as a whole could agree only on the Judicial Committee of the Privy Council's "emergency doctrine," while its majority appeared to endorse a novel and unLaskin-like way of interpreting the peace, order and good government clause.

To understand the significance of these results, the case must be placed in both its legal and political settings. By so doing we may learn something about the nature of judicial review in Canada. Among other things, the case demonstrates the limited importance of judicial review in the politics of

Abridged from Peter H. Russell, "The Anti-Inflation case: the anatomy of a constitutional decision," *Canadian Public Administration* 20, No. 4 (Winter 1977), 632-65. Reprinted by permission of The Institute of Public Administration of Canada.

Canadian federalism. The court's decision may signal that a constitutional revolution is not about to occur, but the decision itself is far from being the major factor in preventing such a centralizing shift in the balance of power. The case also reveals how paradoxically political the process of judicial review can be in Canada even though the end product—the opinions of the judges— is cast in a relatively legalistic style. Above all, the case teaches us a good deal about the interaction of law and politics. The main lesson is clear: politicians and interest groups will risk losses in terms of long-run constitutional doctrine in order to secure important short-run policy objectives, although in the process they may try their best to minimize or obscure their constitutional losses.

THE CONSTITUTIONAL STAKES

On 14 October 1975 the federal government unveiled the new anti-inflation program. The program had four main prongs, only one of which was highly controversial and required new legislation. This was a scheme to control prices and wages in certain key sectors of the economy. The Liberal party had vigorously opposed a Conservative party proposal for wage and price controls in the federal election fifteen months earlier. But now Mr. Trudeau's government was apparently convinced that this was a policy whose time had come. Legal authority for the wage and price control policy was contained in the Anti-Inflation Act which became law 15 December 1975 (with retroactive effect to 14 October 1975) and in the detailed regulations or 'guidelines' promulgated on 22 December 1975.

It was clear from the start that there was a good deal at stake constitutionally in the enactment of this legislation. The Anti-Inflation Act purported to give the federal government regulatory authority over prices, profit margins and wages in selected areas of the private sector: construction firms with twenty or more employees, other firms with five hundred or more employees, and professionals. The Act applied directly to the federal public sector, and it authorized the government to enter into agreements with the provinces to apply the program to the provincial public sectors. Normally most of the economic relations which the federal Act purported to regulate in the private sector are under exclusive provincial jurisdiction. Since the *Snider* case in 1925, labour relations has been treated as a field of divided jurisdiction, with federal authority confined to the limited number of activities which can be brought under specific heads of federal power. A long series of judicial decisions, beginning with the *Parsons* case in 1881, gave the provinces the lion's share of regulatory power over business and commercial transactions in the province. The only earlier peacetime attempt to control prices and profit levels on a national basis had been ruled unconstitutional by the Judicial Committee of the Privy Council in the *Board of Commerce* case.

On what constitutional basis then could the federal government hope to rest the Anti-Inflation Act? The federal trade and commerce power which would be the basis of federal authority for such legislation in the United States was not a very likely possibility in Canada. "Interprovincial or international" as the main criterion of the trade and commerce which the federal Parliament can regulate has been narrowly interpreted in Canada, and the Act made no gestures toward focusing its impact primarily on activities of an interprovincial or international character. Thus, it was the federal Parliament's general power "to make laws for the peace, order and good government of Canada" which appeared to be the only constitutional basis for the Act, and it was in the possibility of successfully invoking the general power for this purpose that a revolution in constitutional doctrine was in the making.

Constitutional case-law had produced two rival conceptions of what could sufficiently magnify legislative matters normally subject to provincial jurisdiction to bring them under the general or residual power of the national Parliament: the emergency doctrine and the test of inherent national importance. The emergency doctrine was authored by Viscount Haldane of the Judicial Committee of the Privy Council in the 1920s, and, with but one clear exception, consistently followed by that tribunal until the end of its regime as Canada's highest court. The doctrine's only positive application was to justify the virtually unlimited scope of national power in time of war and postwar transition. Beyond war, the Judicial Committee's vision of emergencies serious enough to set aside the normal distribution of powers and invoke the general power had been limited to such possibilities as "famines," "epidemic of pestilence" or a drastic outbreak of the "evil of intemperance." Economic crisis—even the need for a national scheme of unemployment insurance during the Depression—failed to meet the Judicial Committee's standard of necessity. Further, it appeared that the presumption of constitutionality which attached to war-related legislation did not apply to *permanent* peacetime measures. With the former, the onus of proof rested with the opponents of the legislation who would have to adduce ". . . very clear evidence that an emergency has not arisen, or that the emergency no longer exists . . . ,"[2] whereas, with the latter, the supporters of the legislation would have to provide "evidence that the standard of necessity . . . has been reached."[3]

In 1946 Viscount Simon in the *Canada Temperance Federation* case wrote an opinion which offered a much wider conception of peace, order and good government than Haldane's emergency test. In dismissing Ontario's attempt to have the Privy Council overrule *Russell v. The Queen* (the Privy Council's earliest decision finding federal legislation constitutional on the basis of peace, order and good government), Viscount Simon held that the Dominion Parliament could not legislate in matters which are exclusively within the competence of the provincial legislature "merely because of the existence of an emergency." The "true test" for determining whether the national legislature may assume jurisdiction over matters which are normally provincial ". . . must be found in the real subject matter of the legislation: if it is such that it goes beyond local or provincial concern or interest and must from its inherent nature be the concern of the Dominion as a whole . . . , then it will fall within the competence of the Dominion Parliament as a matter affecting the peace, order and good government of Canada. . . ."[4] This holding seemed to return the interpretation of peace, order and good government to the pre-Haldane formula of national dimensions and concern enunciated by Lord Watson in 1896, namely ". . . that some matters, in their origin local and provincial, might attain such dimensions as to affect the body politic of the Dominion, and to justify the Canadian Parliament in passing laws for their regulation or abolition in the interest of the Dominion."[5] On its face, this inherent national importance or national dimensions conception of peace, order and government appeared to offer the federal government a much wider opportunity to exercise regulatory power in peacetime on more than a temporary basis in areas normally reserved to the provinces.

Court decisions after 1946 were not conclusive as to whether the Haldane emergency doctrine had been superseded by the wider notion of national dimensions. On the two occasions after 1946 when the Privy Council dealt with peace, order and good government it ignored Simon's opinion. The Supreme Court's decision in the *Johannesson* case in 1952 provided the only strong endorsation of Viscount Simon's national important test. On two subsequent occasions in the 1960s, the Supreme Court employed the vocabulary of "national importance" in upholding federal jurisdiction over the national capital and offshore mineral rights. But in neither case was the Court reviewing a major scheme of federal regulation in an area normally under provincial jurisdiction. Even in *Johannesson*, though the court sustained the paramountcy of federal control over aeronautics in part on national importance grounds, it was dealing with a regulatory scheme which had been in place for several decades and which could find a large measure of constitutional support in other heads of federal power.

So, coming down to the *Anti-Inflation* case, a large question mark still hung over the peace, order and good government power. That for three decades there had been so little Court action on this issue had much to do with the fact that even during the most centralist years of this period the federal government had relied primarily on its spending power rather than regulatory schemes for carrying out policy initiatives in areas normally under provincial jurisdiction. But inflationary pressures in the 1970s might force the federal government to shift from spending programs to regulatory schemes. Such a shift, . . . would increase the occasions for judicial review. Thus, as the federal government in the fall of 1975 moved toward the implementation of a fairly comprehensive scheme of price and wage controls, the question in constitutional law of whether the peace, order and good government would provide a basis for national regulation of broad areas of economic and social activity took on more than academic importance.

POLITICAL AND LEGAL STRATEGIES
OF THE PARTIES

With these constitutional stakes in the background, it is interesting to examine the approach taken by the federal and provincial governments and the major interest groups to the constitutional implications of the anti-inflation program. Turning first to the federal government, we find a significant difference between the political and legal aspects of its behaviour. Politically, Prime Minister Trudeau endeavoured to present the program as an exercise in cooperative federalism. The day before the program was presented to Parliament, the ten provincial premiers came to Ottawa to discuss the program. That night, in his address to the nation on radio and television, Mr. Trudeau said that he had asked the premiers "to join as full partners in the attack upon inflation."[6] During this period Mr. Trudeau tended to be somewhat on the optimistic side in referring to the extent to which the provinces supported federal wage and price controls. Following the first ministers meeting on 13 October, a number of premiers reserved any commitment of support for the program until they had reviewed the matter with their provincial cabinets. Ten days later federal and provincial finance and labour ministers met in Ottawa and following their meeting, Mr. Macdonald, the federal Minister of Finance, announced that "No province declared that it is opposed to the programme or will refuse to co-operate."[7] The next day Mr. Macdonald reported in a more positive vein to the House of Commons: apparently all of the provincial governments were now "prepared to support the programme and co-operate."[8]

While, on the political front, the federal government proceeded on the assumption that provincial cooperation was a political imperative, the Anti-Inflation Act was drafted as if the federal Parliament had full legislative power to proceed with such a program on its own. Section 3 of the Act authorizing the federal government to establish guidelines for the restraint of prices and wages in the private and public sectors made no concessions to any constitutional limitations on the scope of Parliament's regulatory power. It is true that the next section of the Act exempted a province's public sector unless the provincial government entered into an agreement to apply the Act to its public sector. But the implication was that this "opting in" device was entirely dependent on the will of the federal Parliament, and that Parliament, if it had preferred, could have applied the program directly to the provincial public sectors. This implication became explicit later on when the federal government came to defend Ontario's "opting in" Agreement before the Supreme Court. In the absence of any provincial legislation authorizing this Agreement, the only legislative authority for the Agreement was provided by the federal Act and, indeed, federal lawyers asserted the power of the federal Parliament to bind the provincial Crown and regulate the provincial public service.

More important than this is the evidence that the Anti-Inflation Act was drafted so as to preserve the possibility of basing the legislation on a constitutional foundation wider than the emergency doctrine. Nowhere did the Act speak the language of national emergency. Instead, the preamble referred to inflation as "a matter of serious national concern," language clearly suggesting Viscount Simon's approach to peace, order and good government in the *Canada Temperance Federation* case. The only mark of emergency or crisis legislation on the face of the Act was its penultimate section limiting its duration to three years unless Parliament agreed to an extension. Statements by government spokesmen in Parliament made it clear that the omission of any reference to a state of emergency was deliberate. . . .

Now, with the federal government playing something of a double game, how did the provinces respond to the constitutional issue? Briefly, because they saw that it was not in their political interests at the time to oppose the federal program, they agreed not to raise the constitutional issue. However, because they wished to avoid conceding constitutional power to Ottawa, they were careful not to commit themselves to any particular view of the Act's constitutional validity. At this stage it was in the interests of both levels of government to suppress the constitutional issue. Apparently the constitutional issue was discussed at the federal-provincial meetings concerning the anti-inflation program, and the federal leaders felt free to declare after these meetings that the provinces would not challenge Parliament's jurisdiction to enact the Anti-Inflation Bill. But, as with so much that happens at meetings of this kind, we do not know in what terms the constitutional issue was discussed. My own guess is that the constitutional discussion was kept at a pretty vague level and that there was just enough reference to the temporary nature of the legislation and provision of an opting in mechanism for the provinces to set aside, at least for the time being, any reservations of a constitutional nature.

The provinces kept their word. They did not exercise the right which all of them have to refer the question of the Act's constitutionality directly to the courts. All, in varying ways, took steps to bring their public sectors into the program. But, nonetheless, they kept their constitutional options open and, as we shall see, when the constitutional issue was forced before the Supreme Court, a number of them attacked the broad grounds upon which the federal government tried to defend its legislation. In the legal instruments authorizing provincial participation, it is notable that Quebec, of all the provinces, was most careful to concede as little as possible to federal legislative authority. Thus, Quebec's Agreement not only established the province's own Inflation Control Commission to administer guidelines for the public sector 'in consultation with' the federal Anti-Inflation Board, but further gave the province's consent to have the guidelines apply to the private sector. Quebec's submission to the Supreme Court subsequently made it clear that in the province's view, even in the context of an emergency, federal regulation of the provincial private sector of the economy could not take effect without provincial consent.

If the federal and provincial governments were the only agencies for initiating judicial review, there would probably not have been an Anti-Inflation case. In Canada only the federal and provincial governments have access to the most direct means of bringing questions before the courts—the reference procedure. Private litigants can raise constitutional issues in the courts only when they are plaintiff or defendant in normal litigation, and Canadian courts have tended to be relatively stringent in granting "standing" to raise such issues. One of the interesting features of the *Anti-Inflation* case is that it was the persistence of private interest groups, namely a number of trade unions, in trying to challenge the constitutional validity of the anti-inflation program through normal litigation which eventually persuaded the federal government to resort to the reference device and bring the issue directly before the Supreme Court.

It is particularly interesting that organized labour rather than business interests were responsible for initiating the constitutional challenge to the anti-inflation program. Traditionally, organized labour has favoured strengthening rather than weakening the capacity of the federal government to deal with national and international economic forces. But once labour representatives perceived what in their view was the unjust character of the federal program they began to oppose it vigorously, and soon after its introduction officials of the Canadian Labour Congress announced their intention to challenge the program in the courts. There is no indication that union leaders had any qualms about the long-run constitutional consequences if their court action was successful. The attack through the courts was adopted as simply one of the means for conducting the anti-controls campaign. However, it should be noted that the grounds upon which the CLC initially proposed to base its challenge were that the controls program was too selective to meet the national dimensions test and that provinces could not turn over their legislative jurisdiction to the federal authority by order-in-council. While these arguments did not so clearly threaten the scope of federal authority, those which union counsel subsequently used before the Supreme Court were much more anti-centalist.

It was not easy for those labour groups who wished to challenge the constitutional validity of the anti-inflation program to gain access to the courts. The most direct means of appealing an order of the Anti-Inflation Administrator to the Appeal Tribunal (and from there to the Federal Court of Canada) was available only to employers. This deficiency in the Act was eventually remedied but not until after the federal government had made the reference to the Supreme Court. The legal actions which eventually provoked the reference all involved unions in Ontario resisting the application of the controls to collective agreements they were in the process of negotiating. The most significant of these, in terms of bringing the constitutional issue before the courts, was that of the Renfrew County branch of the Ontario Secondary School

Teachers Federation. In November 1975 the Renfrew teachers had signed a collective agreement with the Renfrew County Board of Education for an amount considerably in excess of the anti-inflation guidelines. This settlement was made pursuant to the result of binding arbitration under Ontario legislation. The arbitration award had been made two weeks after the introduction of the anti-inflation program. On 10 February 1976 the Anti-Inflation Board notified the teachers and the Board that the settlement should be reduced. Six days later the teachers' federation applied to the Divisional Court of the Supreme Court of Ontario for a declaration that Ontario's Agreement with the federal government bringing its public sector under the anti-inflation program was invalid on the ground that the Order-in-Council authorizing the Agreement had been made without the necessary legislation by the province. It is doubtful whether this legal stratagem would have worked because the Federal Court of Canada has exclusive jurisdiction to review the actions of federal administrative agencies including jurisdiction to grant declaratory relief. On the same day that the Renfrew teachers submitted their application to Ontario's Supreme Court, a Board of Arbitration in another Ontario labour dispute (this time involving the University of Toronto and a local of the Canadian Union of Public Employees representing the University's library technicians) ruled that it was not bound by actions of the Anti-Inflation Board.

Apparently it was these two developments which convinced the Attorney General of Ontario, Mr. Roy McMurtry, that in order to avoid a lengthy and uncertain period of litigation he should ask the federal Minister of Justice to refer the issue to the Supreme Court. There were possibly other factors which influenced Mr. McMurtry. The Ontario government had entered into its Agreement with the federal government without any approval from the provincial legislature. The Agreements of all the other provinces except Newfoundland's had some legislative sanction. The Davis government wished to avoid the legislature because it was in a minority there and both opposition parties indicated they would oppose the government on the controls issue. But by February of 1976, the Ontario Liberals under Mr. Stuart Smith's leadership had shown that they did not want an election in the near future and so for the time being they would not use their balance of power in the legislature to defeat the government. Thus, Mr. McMurtry had some assurance that if the Ontario Agreement was ruled invalid by the Supreme Court he could go back to the legislature and with support from a compliant Mr. Smith obtain the necessary approval for the Agreement. This assurance was important, as the validity of the Ontario Agreement was a much more dubious proposition than was the validity of the federal Act.

On 12 March, the federal Minister of Justice, Mr. Basford, announced that the federal cabinet had approved an order-in-council referring the question of the federal Act's constitutional validity and of the Ontario Agreement's validity to the Supreme Court of Canada. It was, he said, the Renfrew teachers' action which prompted this decision,

Because the whole thing (the anti-inflation programme) is vulnerable to such challenges and because the work of the nation must go on we have decided to avoid time-consuming litigation over issues like this which ultimately would have to be decided by the Supreme Court anyway.[9]

We might also speculate that Mr. Basford's government, with its program well in place and having secured the cooperation of all the provinces, could now contemplate judicial review of the Anti-Inflation Act with a fair degree of confidence.

THE REFERENCE:
THE PARTIES AND THEIR SUBMISSIONS

The use of Canada's extraordinary reference procedure in the circumstances outlined above illustrates one of the advantages of this device. Once it was reasonably certain that judicial review would occur through private litigation, it was in the government's interest to remove as quickly as possible the legal clouds surrounding the program—especially a program which was encountering considerable resistance from those whose behaviour it was supposed to regulate. In the alternative, if the unions had found their access to the courts completely blocked, the reference would compensate for the relative disadvantage which citizens or private groups are under in obtaining judicial review in Canada and give the unions an opportunity to establish their constitutional rights before the country's highest tribunal.

But the disadvantages of the reference procedure have been advertised just as much as its advantages. The primary criticism has been that the procedure forces judges to make decisions about the constitutional validity of government policies in a highly abstract and hypothetical manner divorced from any consideration of the factual context which gave rise to the legislation and in which the real effect of the legislation may be revealed. Added to this is the fear that such a procedure, by bringing statutes to court "... in the very flush of enactment, while the feelings that produced them were at their highest pitch ... "[10] may unduly politicize the process of judicial review and force the judges to participate in a political controversy in a way which will ultimately weaken their authority. It is instructive to review the conduct of the *Anti-Inflation Reference* in the light of these criticisms and concerns.

Certainly, the questions submitted to the court by the Reference Order were presented in the barest possible way:

1. Is the Anit-Inflation Act *ultra vires* the Parliament of Canada either in whole or in part, and, if so, in what particulars and to what extent?
2. If the Anti-Inflation Act is *Ultra vires* the Parliament of Canada, is the Agreement entitled 'Between the Government of Canada and the Government of the Province of Ontario', entered into on January 13, 1976 effective under the Anti-Inflation Act to render that Act binding on, and the Anti-Inflation

Guidelines made thereunder applicable to, the provincial public sector in Ontario as defined in the Agreement?

The reference itself was not accompanied by any factual material describing the situation which gave rise to the legislation or details concerning the implementation of the Anti-Inflation program. However, procedures were soon set in motion to provide the basic ingredients of a law case—adversaries and their submissions—and make the decision-making process less like an academic seminar and more like the adjudication of a concrete dispute.

There was no difficulty in obtaining parties to argue all sides of both questions. The federal government, of course, would appear in support of the legislation. All the provinces were notified of the hearing but only five decided to participate: Ontario, Quebec, British Columbia and Saskatchewan in support of the legislation (although for the latter three this "support" turned out to be qualified indeed) and Alberta in direct opposition. Alberta would be joined by five unions (or groups of unions) who were considered to have distinct interests at stake in the proceedings. This labour representation included the Ontario teachers and public service unions which had been attempting to litigate the constitutional issues in Ontario courts, the Canadian Labour Congress which had been pressing for judicial review since the introduction of the Act and one major international union, the United Steel Workers of America. Thus, the reference procedure, compensating for the relatively cautious policy of Canadian courts in granting access to the judicial process, enabled the major political contestants to do battle in the judicial arena. But the Supreme Court was not prepared to go all the way in the "politicization" of its process and drew the line at political parties, declining to give permission to the Ontario NDP to appear as an interested party.

The material submitted by these parties compensated, in part, for the bareness of the reference questions. Some of it also posed a severe challenge to the Supreme Court's jurisprudential style. Non-legal material such as the "Brandeis brief" prepared by social scientists and designed to support propositions about the social or economic background and implications of legislation has not played an important role in the Canadian Supreme Court's decision-making. This is not because there is any rule formally proscribing such material. It has stemmed primarily from the character of jurisprudence favoured by Canadian judges and lawyers.[11] In constitutional interpretation, as in other areas, Canadian jurists have been most comfortable with a highly conceptual approach in which the focus is on applying definitions of legal categories to the words of the statute with little or no reference to the empirical meaning of this exercise. But in the *Anti-Inflation* case some of the counsel came from a younger generation of lawyers imbued with the example of modern American constitutional jurisprudence which has been far more receptive to social science material. The Chief Justice of the Court both as an academic and a judge had stressed the importance of empirical evidence in constitutional interpretation.[12]

Also, one of the basic questions in the case—whether inflation in Canada had become a matter of inherent national importance or a national emergency— seemed to be essentially an empirical issue. Thus, it is not surprising that the Court's reception and use of socio-economic material as an "extrinsic aid" to constitutional interpretation became one of the most significant features of the case.

About a month after the Reference Order was issued, Chief Justice Laskin met with counsel for the various parties to consider some of the procedural issues. On 6 April, at the conclusion of this hearing, the Chief Justice made a number of rulings: applications to join the proceedings as an interested party would be accepted up until 15 April; the Attorney General of Canada was to prepare the "case" (the material submitted by the appellant in an appeal which would normally include full documentation of the proceedings in the lower courts), which here was to include the federal government's White Paper and any other material the Attorney General considered appropriate; the parties were to file their factums (the written briefs setting out each party's arguments on the various issues) by 10 May, and could "annex supplementary material" to their factums; parties would have a short period (until 21 May) in which to submit additional material in reply to material filed by other parties; the oral hearing of the case would begin on 31 May 1976. These rulings gave an opportunity to all the parties to submit whatever empirical argumentation they wished and met one of the traditional complaints against this type of material by giving the parties an opportunity to prepare written replies to their adversaries' submissions. However, the Chief Justice could not make any commitment as to the weight which the Court would give any of this material in reaching its final conclusion.

It is interesting to see how the various parties responded to this opportunity. Only the Canadian Labour Congress annexed supplementary material to its factum. This took the form of a 64-page brief written by Richard G. Lipsey, professor of economics at Queen's University. A group of thirty-eight economists who had been attacking the controls program outside of the judicial arena supported the Lipsey brief. Their telegrams of support were added to the CLC material. Professor Lipsey's study advanced the argument that it was very far-fetched to regard the state of the Canadian economy when controls were introduced as an "economic crisis." This argument was supported both by absolute considerations (inflation is primarily redistributive in its effects so that *average* living standards are not lowered) and, perhaps more impressively, by comparative data showing, for instance, that compared both with other periods in Canadian history and with the economic situation of Canada's major trading partners the level of inflation in the fall of 1975 was not extraordinary. Professor Lipsey concluded that:

> It seems hard to believe that the inflation-unemployment problem is unique in its degree of seriousness. . . . If it is held that this problem constitutes an economic

crisis, then it is hard to avoid the conclusion that economies are nearly always in states of 'economic crises'. If this kind of 'economic crisis' justifies the use of extraordinary measures, these extraordinary measures may be nearly always justified.[13]

In the light of the Supreme Court's final holding, this is a very significant conclusion. Professor Lipsey's study also attacked the efficacy of the controls program in reducing inflation. Given the strict taboo in our legal tradition against courts reviewing the wisdom of legislation, this, I believe, was a serious tactical mistake and made it easier for the judges to discount the Lipsey brief.

The only other material of this kind was submitted by the federal government and the Province of Ontario. The "case" material prepared by the Attorney General of Canada included, in addition to the White Paper requested by the Chief Justice (which nowhere referred to the existence of a "crisis" or "emergency"), the monthly bulletin of Statistics Canada showing fluctuations in the consumer price index up to September 1975. In reply to the Lipsey brief, the Attorneys General of Canada and Ontario both submitted additional material. The federal submission was a copy of an after-dinner speech delivered by the Governor of the Bank of Canada, Gerald K. Bouey, a month before controls were introduced. The speech stressed the seriousness of inflation but was in no sense a counter-analysis to Professor Lipsey's brief. But Ontario's additional material, prepared by the province's Office of Economic Analysis, did attempt a direct rebuttal of Lipsey's main argument. It challenged neither the accuracy of his data nor his technical economics, but (on Galbraithian grounds) it questioned his judgment that the severity of Canada's existing economic problems could be expected nearly always to prevail from now on. Perhaps most significantly, it argued that the question of whether or not a "crisis" exists cannot be answered by technical economics but by public opinion polls (although it cited no actual poll results on this question).

While empirical considerations were more prominent than is usually the case in constitutional references, the arguments which predominated in both the written factums and the oral hearing were still essentially legal in character. These arguments were put to the Court by as impressive an array of legal talent as has ever been assembled for a constitutional case. . . . Certainly it would be difficult to contend that the outcome of this case was influenced by the fact that one or other side was badly argued. This is important because the strictly adversarial dimension of the proceedings is probably more significant in the Canadian Supreme Court than it is, for instance, in the United States Supreme Court, where the time allowed for oral argument is very limited. In typical Canadian fashion our Supreme Court procedure combines the written American brief (called factums in Canada) with the English emphasis on virtually unlimited time for oral argument. In this case the oral hearing ran for a full week and it is likely that the way in which the adversarial exchange in the courtroom structured the issues had more to do with the Court's final decision than would be the case in the United States.

The Ontario Agreement was defended only by counsel for Ontario and the federal government. The other provinces did not make submissions on this question. The unions all vigorously attacked the Agreement's validity. The Ontario unions were able to use the concrete situations which had been the original basis for their litigation as illustrations of the extent to which the Agreement altered the basic law regulating collective bargaining in Ontario. This added considerable strength to their proposition that an executive Agreement without any legislative sanction which purported to set aside existing legislation was a clear violation of the principle of responsible government. The main defence of the Agreement did not contend that the federal Act had actually provided the legislative sanction for the Ontario Agreement. Instead it relied primarily on precedents of executive agreements and contracts for which there had been no specific legislative authorization. Nonetheless, one of the Canadian Labour Congress counsel, P.W. Hogg, argued that in a federal system of dual sovereignty there must be a basic immunity of the Provincial Crown which would set some limit on federal authority to regulate the remuneration of the provincial civil service directly under ministers of the Crown—even in an emergency, and yes, even during a war. This contention clearly shocked a number of judges, and one was heard to exclaim that "if the argument had any validity it would ultimately deny the existence of a Canadian Nation."[14]

On the issues associated with the first question concerning the Anti-Inflation Act's constitutional validity, the alignment of the parties was revealing. The federal position before the Court was the most predictable. It reflected the double game which the federal government had been playing from the start on the peace, order and good government issue. Ottawa was fairly confident that the Act could at the very least be sustained as emergency legislation and its counsel now put forward the emergency use of the general power as a basis for the legislation—*but only as a fall back position*. The primary argument advanced by federal counsel was that "because inflation is a subject matter going beyond local or provincial concern or interests and is from its inherent nature the concern of Canada as a whole,"[15] the Anti-Inflation Act should be upheld as a proper exercise of the peace, order and good government power. To this was added reference to several specific heads of federal power—trade and commerce, taxation, the power to borrow, currency, banking, interest, legal tender—all of which were closely related to the aims and effects of the anti-inflation program and hence, it was argued, provided evidence of the inherently national character of the legislation. Obviously, the primary federal argument was designed to do more than save the Act: if it were accepted by the Court it would consolidate the gains in constitutional law which the federal government hoped would flow from Viscount Simon's decision in the *Canada Temperance Federation* case. Surprisingly, Ontario endorsed the federal position. In fact, Mr. McMurtry in one respect went further in that he did not advance the emergency doctrine even as an alternative argument. For Ontario, Viscount Simon's test of inherent national importance was the only test for invoking peace, order and good government.

But the other provinces and the unions all argued that the only possible way of supporting such legislation was on emergency grounds. The constitutional issue which it had been convenient to suppress in October now came out in the open. The most important constitutional arguments were advanced by Mr. Lysyk, the Deputy Attorney General of Saskatchewan and Professor Lederman for the Renfrew teachers. They put forward a new thesis on the meaning of previous decisions dealing with peace, order and good government. The gist of this thesis was that outside of emergencies, peace, order and good government can be used only in a residual sense to support federal legislation in discrete, narrowly defined areas of legislation which clearly fall outside provincial jurisdiction. Legislation in an area defined as broadly as "inflation" and clearly intruding on matters which are normally subject to exclusive provincial jurisdiction fails to meet this test. This interpretation of peace, order and good government was a clear alternative to the views expressed by Chief Justice Laskin in his academic writings—views which his frequent interventions from the bench indicated he might still hold.

Even on emergency grounds the federal position received meagre support from the provinces. Alberta along with the unions went all the way and argued (in the CLC's submission on the basis of the Lipsey brief) that the Act should be found unconstitutional as there was no economic emergency. Quebec, British Columbia and Saskatchewan remained on the federal government's side of the courtroom nominally in support of the legislation. But their support, at times, must have reminded federal counsel of the old saying, "With friends like that— who needs enemies?" In their factums, they were at best agnostic as to whether an emergency existed sufficient to justify the use of the general power. Mr. Vickers, the Deputy Attorney General for British Columbia, concluded his oral presentation by submitting that the burden of proof (on the existence of an emergency) lay with the federal government, and that "on the evidence now before the court I do not feel one could conclude that there was a national emergency."[16] Counsel for the federal government did not try to meet this burden of proof nor parry the economic arguments of the Lipsey brief. Mr. Robinette's position was that the Court had only to find that it was not unreasonable for Parliament to believe that there was an emergency or "a generally apprehended crisis."

The submissions of the parties in the *Anti-Inflation* case contrast in some important ways with those of counsel in the New Deal references of the 1930s— the last occasion on which there was a serious challenge to federal power through judicial review. In those cases a foreign tribunal witnessed a strong provincial attack on federal legislation rather weakly defended by a government whose political opponents had actually introduced the legislation. Here, a Canadian court in the national capital was considering the constitutional validity of what at the time was the federal government's most important domestic policy initiative. The judges knew that all of the provinces had in fact agreed to cooperate with the federal program. In the courtroom they *saw* on the federal side four provinces (including the three largest) with governments covering the entire Canadian political spectrum supporting the legislation. But they also heard that the only common denominator of constitutional support was the emergency doctrine. In these circumstances it would have taken an exceptionally bold court either to have found the federal Act *ultra vires* or to have based its constitutional validity on a wider footing than the emergency use of peace, order and good government.

THE COURT'S DECISION

Five weeks after the conclusion of the hearing the Supreme Court pronounced its judgment. The Court unanimously found that the Ontario Agreement did not render the Anti-Inflation program binding on the provincial public sector. On the question of the Anti-Inflation Act's constitutional validity, the Court split seven to two: seven judges found that it was constitutional on emergency grounds, but Justices Beetz and de Grandpré, both from Quebec and the most recently appointed judges, dissented. That is the bare bones of the decision, but as is always the case with appellate decisions, the reasons of the judges are more important than their votes.

First, the Court's decision on the validity of the Ontario Agreement, while constituting a small portion of the judgment quantitatively, is not without its constitutional significance. Chief Justice Laskin wrote the Court's opinion on this question. Because the federal Act did not spell out precisely how the guidelines should apply to the provincial public sector, the Chief Justice found that the Act itself did not provide the necessary legislative sanction for the Ontario Agreement. The Agreement could not be regarded as sanctioned by conditional legislation for which action by the provincial government was merely a "triggering device." However, it is significant that in reaching this conclusion he went out of his way to indicate that he did not accept the view that it would have been beyond federal power to regulate the provincial public service. Assertions of immunity for the provincial public service, he wrote, "misconceive the paramount authority of federal legislative power . . . and the all-embracing legislative authority of the Parliament of Canada when validly exercised for the peace, order and good government of Canada."[17] But, in the absence of federal or provincial legislation *clearly* authorizing the Agreement, he ruled that the executive Agreement could not make new labour legislation binding on the citizens of the province. The Chief Justice seemed bent on de-emphasizing the constitutional significance of this holding: the issue, he said, did not engage "any concern with responsible Government and the political answerability of the Ministers to the Legislative Assembly." Nonetheless, by holding that:

> There is no principle in this country, as there in not in Great Britain, that the Crown may legislate by proclamation or Order in Council to bind citizens where it so acts without the support of a statute of the Legislature: see Dicey, *Law of the Constitution*,[18]

he at least confirms an essential element of our "unwritten constitution." Those concerned about the increasing erosion of the role of the legislature and the trend in Canada toward policy-making within the closed confines of federal-provincial negotiations, should welcome this judicial recognition of an important constitutional principle.

The Court's decision on the primary question concerning the constitutional validity of the Anti-Inflation Act can be analysed by breaking the question into two components: (1) the interpretation of the peace, order and good government clause and (2) the judgment as to whether the Anti-Inflation Act could be upheld as emergency legislation. The court split in quite different ways on these two aspects of the question. Three opinions were written: Chief Justice Laskin's reasons were supported by three Justices, Judson, Spence, and Dickson; Mr. Justice Ritchie's were concurred in by Justices Martland and Pigeon; Mr. Justice de Grandpré concurred in Mr. Justice Beetz's opinion. On the second aspect of the question, Chief Justice Laskin's group of four and Justice Ritchie's group of three formed the majority which found the Act *intra vires*. But on the first issue—the fundamental question of constitutional doctrine—the reasoning of Mr. Justice Beetz's dissenting opinion was adopted by the Ritchie threesome and so became, in effect, the majority position of the Court.

The short 5-page opinion of Mr. Justice Ritchie at least has the merit of highlighting the Court's division on the meaning of peace, order and good government. Ritchie rejects broad considerations of national concern or inherent national importance as the framework within which to test whether Parliament can exercise its peace, order and good government power in areas normally under provincial jurisdiction. For him the relevant precedent is not Viscount Simon's judgment in the *Canada Temperance Federation* case, but the decisions following it, especially the *Japanese Canadians* case, in which the Privy Council returned to the emergency doctrine. Since then, Justice Ritchie takes it to be established "that unless such concern (i.e., national concern) is made manifest by circumstances amounting to a national emergency, Parliament is not endowed under the cloak of the "peace, order and good government" clause with the authority to legislate in relation to matters reserved to the Provinces under s. 92. For more elaborate jurisprudential reasons he defers to Mr. Justice Beetz with whose reasons he is "in full agreement."[19]

Justice Beetz provided a re-interpretation of previous judicial decisions on this constitutional issue. This re-interpretation followed the main line of argument submitted to the Court by Mr. Lysyk and Professor Lederman. The essence of this approach is to draw a radical distinction between the "normal" and the "abnormal" uses of peace, order and good government. The normal use of the clause is as a national residual power to cover ". . . clear instances of distinct subject-matters which do not fall within any of the enumerated heads of s. 92 and which, by nature, are of national concern."[20] Thus, it has been invoked successfully in the past to support such fields as radio, aeronautics, the incorporation of Dominion companies and the national capital, all of which in Justice Beetz's view display the requisite "degree of unity," "distinct identity" or "specificity." But the containment and reduction of inflation fails to meet this test of specificity: "It is so pervasive that it knows no bounds. Its recognition as a federal head of power would render most provincial powers nugatory."[21] The normal application of peace, order and good government has the effect of adding, by judicial process, new subject matters of legislation to the list of exclusive federal powers in Section 91 of the BNA Act. National concern, national dimensions are still relevant in determining whether such unforeseen, discrete, new subject matters should be brought under the federal residual power or under its counterpart on the provincial side, Section 92(16)—"Matters of a merely local or private nature in the province." But the only constitutional basis for federal legislation cast in such broad terms as the Anti-Inflation Act is the abnormal use of peace, order and good government—the emergency doctrine. It is abnormal precisely because it "operates as a partial and temporary alteration of the distribution of powers between Parliament and the provincial Legislatures." Once the Court agrees to apply this doctrine no longer is the power of Parliament limited by the identity of subject matters but solely "by the nature of the crisis."[22]

This then was the new constitutional doctrine fashioned by Justice Beetz and supported by a bare majority of the Court. Against it—but by no means in total opposition to it—was Chief Justice Laskin's opinion supported by three other judges. The Chief Justice wrote a long review of all the major cases bearing upon peace, order and good government. While it is not always clear just where this review is going, it contains one basic point of contrast with the majority position. Instead of driving a wedge between the normal and abnormal uses of the general power, Chief Justice Laskin tries to weave a single piece of cloth out of all the strands to be found in previous decisions. The key to this approach, the central idea which gives the multi-coloured fabric some shape and pattern, is Lord Watson's proposition in the *Local Prohibition* case that ". . . matters in origin local or provincial . . . might attain national dimensions."[23] Since then Laskin sees the jurisprudence moving in two directions—under Viscount Haldane narrowing to the point of "studiously ignoring" Lord Watson's "national dimensions," but then returning to it, at first cautiously in judgments written by Lord Atkin and Chief Justice Duff followed by the more expansive views of Viscount Simon. The Chief Justice's response to this legacy of competing emphases is not to pick his own favourite strand and discard the others but to identify the extremes which clearly lie beyond the main body of jurisprudence. Thus, at one extreme, basing the use of peace, order and good government on the mere desirability or convenience of national regulation (a possible interpretation of the first Privy Council decision on this issue, *Russell v. The Queen*) is ruled out. But at the other extreme, a pure Haldane approach which ignores "national dimensions" and confines the use of peace, order and good government to war-related emergencies is equally beyond the pale. In between these extremes there are many possibilities, and the Chief Justice warns against fixing constitutional doctrine so tightly as to prevent the constitution from serving ". . . as a resilient instrument capable of adaptation to changing circumstances."[24]

In the case at hand, because all of the parties accepted as constitutional doctrine the use of peace, order and good government to deal with a national emergency, ". . . it becomes unnecessary to consider the broader ground advanced in its support. . . . "[25] So the Chief Justice was willing to rest his decision on the narrow grounds of emergency (semantically softened to "crisis"). But unlike the majority he did not rule out the broader grounds advanced by the federal government.

For those who have admired the Chief Justice's contribution to Canada's constitutional jurisprudence, the opaque, open-ended quality of his reasoning in this case may be a disappointment. But it is reasonable, I think, to regard his opinion as that of a Chief Justice endeavouring to build a majority around the widest common denominator on his Court without foreclosing jurisprudential possibilities which he personally favoured. That he failed is not too surprising. Since joining the Court in 1970 he has been its most frequent dissenter. The available statistical data (based on the *Supreme Court Reports* from 1970 to 1974 inclusive) reveal that of the 196 dissents recorded during this period more than half (109) were attributed to three justices: Laskin (45), Spence (34) and Hall (30). The relative isolation of these justices is not tied to issues of federalism. Between the time the present Chief Justice joined the Court and the Anti-Inflation Reference, the Court rendered 20 decisions on the division of powers in the BNA Act. Fifteen of them were unanimous, and although the Chief Justice was on the dissenting side in three of the split decisions, an examination of these cases does not suggest a division on provincial rights/centralist lines. Chief Justice Laskin's differences with a majority of his colleagues more likely stem from general questions of judicial philosophy and style. If there is a consistent pattern of division on matters of substance, it is more likely to be found in cases dealing with criminal law and the Bill of Rights.

Given the clear consensus both on the Court and amongst the litigants concerning the power of Parliament in a national emergency (or crisis) to override the normal division of powers, the second dimension of the constitutional question—whether in fact the Anti-Inflation Act was emergency legislation—may become more important than the general doctrinal issue of the meaning of peace, order and good government. The Supreme Court's handling of this issue indicates a significant shift to a more deferential attitude to the exercise of emergency powers in peacetime by the national government.

The Court's split on this issue—Chief Justice Laskin's group of four plus Justice Ritchie's group of three versus Justice Beetz and de Grandpré in dissent—did not turn on the empirical question of whether in fact there was an emergency. It concerned the prior question of whether emergency legislation must be clearly identified as such by Parliament. The dissenters took the position that a necessary but by no means sufficient test of valid emergency legislation is a clear, unambiguous indication by Parliament that it is enacting the legislation on an emergency basis. Justice Beetz emphasized that responsibility for declaring an emergency must lie with the "politically responsible body," not the courts.[26] The courts' responsibility begins after the affirmation by Parliament that an emergency exists. In this case not only was there no acknowledgment on the face of the federal Act (as there had been with other recent exercises of the emergency power), but there was clear evidence to show that this was no accidental oversight. Breaking the convention which precludes Canadian judges from considering parliamentary history, Justice Beetz referred to the numerous passages in Hansard where government spokesmen refused to be pinned down on the constitutional basis of the legislation and refused to preface the Bill with a declaration of an emergency. Further, the large gaps in the Act's coverage—the omission of farmers and small businesses, the optional nature of the provincial public sector's inclusion—were, in Justice Beetz' view, not easily reconciled with an emergency characterization of the Act. He was also impressed by the lack of provincial support for the view that it was emergency legislation.

For the majority, Parliament's failure to declare an emergency or stamp "emergency" on the face of the Act was not fatal. The reference in the Act's preamble to a level of inflation "contrary to the interests of all Canadians" which had become "a matter of serious national concern," combined with similar statements in the government's White Paper, were enough to indicate how serious the situation must have appeared to Parliament. The omissions from the Act's coverage and the opting-in approach to the provincial public sector, in Chief Justice Laskin's view, could be accounted for in terms of administrative convenience and need not be regarded as indicating a lack of any sense of crisis. Since there were no formal deficiencies in the federal Act, the only ground upon which its validity as emergency or crisis legislation could be impugned was the factual question: did an emergency exist? Here, for at least three of the justices, the onus of proof was placed squarely on the Act's opponents. The peacetime exercise of the federal emergency power was put on the same footing as its use in time of war. Justice Ritchie cited Lord Wright's statement in the *Japanese Canadians* case:

But very clear evidence that an emergency has not arisen, or that the emergency no longer exists, is required to justify the judiciary, even though the question is one of ultra vires, in overruling the decision of the Parliament of the Dominion that exceptional measures were required or were still required.[27]

In Justice Ritchie's opinion the evidence presented by the opponents of the legislation failed to meet Lord Wright's test—period.

Chief Justice Laskin approached the issue in terms of assessing the rationality of Parliament's judgment. The Court would be justified in overruling the Act as emergency legislation only if it found that:

> . . . The Parliament of Canada did not have a rational basis for regarding the *Anti-Inflation Act* as a measure which, in its judgment, was temporarily necessary to meet a situation of economic crisis imperilling the well-being of the people of Canada as a whole and requiring Parliament's stern intervention in the interests of the country as a whole.[28]

In assessing rationality Chief Justice did not place the burden of proof solely on the Act's opponents. He took into consideration statistics showing the rise in the Consumer Price index submitted by the federal government as well as the arguments advanced in Professor Lipsey's brief. He noted Professor Lipsey's candid admission that whether "a problem is serious enough to be described as a crisis must be partly a matter of judgment," and added that the Court cannot be governed by the judgment of an economist however distinguished he may be in the opinion of his peers. Positive evidence of the rationality of Parliament's judgment could be found in the connection between rising inflation and Parliament's clear constitutional responsibilities in monetary policy and areas of trade and commerce which "the extrinsic material does not reveal" could be treated in isolation from those economic areas ordinarily beyond federal regulatory control.[29]

Thus, the Chief Justice concluded that the Court would be unjustified in finding Parliament lacked a rational basis for its judgment that the legislation was needed to meet an urgent crisis. But we should note how in this part of his opinion he attempted to retain as close a link as possible between the emergency use of peace, order and good government and broad considerations of national dimensions or national aspects. With severe inflation impinging so heavily on areas of federal responsibility, the subject matter of the Anti-Inflation Act—the regulation of prices and wages—loses its ordinary parochial or local character and becomes a matter sufficiently urgent for the well-being of all Canadians as to require national action.

THE SIGNIFICANCE OF THE DECISION

Normally a judicial decision in our system of government "settles" one aspect—the judiciable aspect—of what is usually a larger dispute. In the context of this large dispute a court's role is perhaps better described as "dispute processing" rather than "dispute settlement." In assessing the political importance of a judicial decision it is important to see how it affects the political interests involved in the larger area of conflict. The political impact of a constitutional decision by the national court of appeal will usually be felt much more in terms of the long-run significance of the new rules of law it produces than in terms of the immediate outcome of the adjudication.

This is certainly true of the Supreme Court's decision in the Anti-Inflation case. For the labour organizations which provoked the case as part of a general anti-controls campaign the immediate outcome was a loss. The controls would continue. Even that part of the decision which invalidated the Ontario Agreement was quickly overcome. The ink was scarcely dry on the Court's judgment when the Ontario government went back to the legislature and obtained retroactive sanction for its participation in the anti-inflation program. The government's minority position in the legislature proved to be no problem, as Mr. Smith, the Liberal leader, was as compliant as predicted. But the "loss" for labour was probably not a very serious one. Labour opposition to the controls program, if anything, intensified rather than diminished after the decision. It is doubtful that the Supreme Court's validation of the Anti-Inflation Act added to the program's political legitimacy. In fact, a judicial veto of the Anti-Inflation Act might have provided the immediate benefit to the Trudeau government of a politically safe exit from a potentially unpopular program. Besides, the grounds of the Court's decision meant that the door was far from closed on future constitutional challenges to the program. If the inflationary situation significantly eased, it would always be possible to argue that the circumstances which made it reasonable to regard the Act as an emergency measure no longer existed. Indeed, shortly after the Parti Québécois took over in Quebec City, Mr. Parizeau, Quebec's Finance Minister, announced that he was considering a challenge on precisely those grounds.

The rules of law and the constitutional doctrines which emerge from the decision bear more directly on the interests of the two levels of government in the Canadian federation than upon the labour-capital axis. Indeed, one of the interesting features of the case is the apparent indifference of organized labour to the division of powers question. The federal and provincial governments cannot be indifferent because Supreme Court rulings on the constitution directly increase or diminish their political resources. From this perspective, the Court's judgment on the Ontario Agreement entails a slight decrease in the resources of both levels of government. The decision reduces the freedom of provincial and federal governments to collaborate in making policy through the mechanisms of cooperative federalism without obtaining support from their respective legislatures. This modest restraint on "executive federalism" is a boon for citizens and interest groups (like labour unions), not to mention old-fashioned democrats who believe that major changes in the law should be approved by the legislature. But its significance must not be over-rated. Chief Justice Laskin's decision clearly implies that federal legislation upheld on emergency grounds could, if properly worded, regulate all aspects of a field normally under provincial jurisdiction and eliminate any need for provincial legislative sanction.

As for the meaning of the peace, order and good government clause in the BNA Act, the decision did not yield the particular benefit sought by federal legal strategists. The legislation was not sustained on broad grounds of inherent national importance or concern. Viscount Haldane was not put away in mothballs. The jurisprudence of Viscount Simon and the *Johannesson* case, which Mr. Macdonald said his government was counting upon, was not accepted by the Court's majority as the key to interpreting peace, order and good government. But the federal government did not come away from the decision empty-handed. To begin with, what I shall call the "Lederman doctrine" on peace, order and good government, adopted by Justice Beetz and supported by a majority of the judges, means that when new matters of legislation are considered distinct and specific enough to justify the residual or "normal" use of peace, order and good government, they are added to the list of *exclusive* federal powers. The exclusiveness of federal jurisdiction in areas such as aeronautics and radio communications, which are cited as instances of this normal use, was not clear in the past. The Lederman doctrine, while apparently not as favourable to federal power as Viscount Simon's dictum, still is not necessarily unfavourable. While it may have seemed relatively easy to Justice Beetz and his colleagues to apply the criterion of "specificity" retrospectively, I would contend that it is not an easy test to apply prospectively. In the hands of a nationally-minded court it may be surprising what turns out to be specific enough to come under the federal residual power. Besides, it should be noted that considerations of national concern and importance have not been discarded by the Court. Under the Lederman doctrine, national concern is the test for determining whether a new subject with the requisite degree of specificity should be brought under the federal rather than the provincial residual power. Also, as I have tried to explain above, Chief Justice Laskin's opinion, which after all spoke for four of the Court's nine judges, kept Viscount Simon's jurisprudence alive and, in deciding whether the legislation was valid on emergency grounds, made the national dimensions of the economic crisis a prime consideration.

But the Court's handling of the emergency question constitutes a more distinct gain for the federal authorities. The majority's ruling that Parliament does not have to proclaim an emergency or crisis in order to be able to defend legislation successfully in court as emergency legislation increases the manoeuvrability of federal government leaders. This is especially important with regard to crisis situations related to peacetime economic management when the open admission in Parliament that an emergency or urgent crisis exists might be politically embarrassing to the government. The majority's position means that the federal government does not have to pay the price of that embarrassment in order to secure the emergency argument as the basis for an Act's constitutional validity. To put the matter bluntly, temporary federal legislation may be upheld on emergency grounds if federal lawyers can persuade the Court that there is not enough evidence to conclude that it would have been unreasonable for Parliament to have regarded a matter as an urgent national crisis at the time it passed the legislation. Given the probable deference of most Supreme Court Justices to the judgment of Parliament, this is at least a small gain for federal authority.

It may, however, be a significant loss to those Canadians who care about maintaining parliamentary democracy and constitutionalism. For it must be remembered that all of the judicial decisions upholding federal legislation on emergency grounds (as well as those denying it on these grounds) indicate that "the rule of law as to the distribution of powers"[30] is set aside for the duration of the emergency. One can understand the need for an overriding emergency power to protect the state against threats to its very survival, as well as the reluctance of judges to question a clear determination by Parliament that such an emergency exists. But the constitution as a limit on governmental authority will come to mean very little if it is set aside too easily. At the very least, the better constitutional policy might be to insist, with Justice Beetz, that it should be the responsibility of Parliament rather than the courts to proclaim an emergency.

Finally, what does the *Anti-Inflation* case indicate about the future of judicial review in Canada? First, I think it is likely that the frequency with which constitutional issues are brought before the Court will increase rather than decrease. The Supreme Court's almost perfect record in upholding federal laws will not be a serious deterrent to those who wish to challenge federal legislation. For provincial governments, and even more, for private interest groups, constitutional litigation is just one weapon that can be used to fight a larger campaign. Even the Parti Québécois, for instance, although it has no respect for the Supreme Court as an institution of national government, contemplates constitutional litigation as a tactic in its larger constitutional warfare. If it loses it can portray the decision as yet further evidence of the hostility of federal institutions to Quebec's interest; if it wins this would vindicate the charge that the federal government is encroaching on areas of provincial jurisdiction. But private individuals and groups may be even more likely to provoke constitutional litigation. The rapid growth of the legal profession, more generous rules of standing , the influence of the American example and the new jurisdictional rules under which the Supreme Court's docket is shaped primarily by judicial selection of nationally important cases— all of these factors are likely to generate more privately-initiated constitutional cases. And, as labour's approach to the *Anti-Inflation* case indicates, when these pressure groups litigate constitutional issues they may be inclined to let the constitutional chips fall where they may for the sake of pursuing some short-run advantage on an immediate policy issue.

So the Supreme Court's decision in this case will not deter resort to judicial review in the future. Nor, despite the scant attention given Professor Lipsey's brief, should future litigants in constitutional cases be deterred from supporting their arguments with this kind of social science evidence. None of the judges denied that Professor Lipsey's brief was admissible evidence, and the Chief Justice explicitly acknowledged its relevancy even though he did not find it completely persuasive. Further, where the question of constitutionality turns on the reasonableness of regarding a situation as an urgent national crisis requiring national legislation, what other than empirical arguments can lawyers who wish to challenge the legislation use? I am not suggesting that there will be a sudden revolution in the Supreme Court's style of jurisprudence, but that we will likely see more lawyers using this type of material in future constitutional cases. One leading constitutional scholar has suggested that "... the admission of social science briefs in constitutional cases where legislative facts are in issue . . . may prove in the long run to be the most influential point of the case."[31]

On a more fundamental plane, the Court's majority in subscribing to Professor Lederman's approach to peace, order and good government, rather than Professor Laskin's (as he once was), have opted to maintain a more traditional style of opinion-writing. The central concern apparent in this style of reasoning is "distilling the essences" of legal categories and characterizing the subject matter of legislation. It is basically the old game of sticking the legislation in the right pigeon-hole. Most of our judges (and probably, still) most of our lawyers find this a more congenial exercise than reasoning about legislative schemes in terms of the necessary requirements of effective national policy-making.

Judicial decisions based on the majority's approach have the *appearance* of being based on narrow, technical, purely legal considerations. But the preference for this style of jurisprudence is based on larger considerations of constitutional policy. Only Justice Beetz gave a clear expression of the underlying policy reason for rejecting the federal government's first submission that the Anti-Inflation Act should be sustained under peace, order and good government as a matter of inherent national importance. "It is not difficult to speculate," he wrote "as to where this line of reasoning would lead: a fundamental feature of the Constitution, its federal nature, the distribution of powers between Parliament and the provincial legislatures, would disappear not gradually but rapidly."[32] So, for policy reasons, a jurisprudential style which would make policy reasons more transparent, is rejected. As a result, Canadians cannot expect judicial reasoning to add very much to the country's stock of constitutional wisdom. The question remains whether this masking of judicial power is in itself a kind of constitutional wisdom.

NOTES

1. *Reference re Anti-Inflation Act*, [1976] 68 D.L.R. (3rd) 452. (1976) 2 S.C.R. 373. Hereinafter referred to as the *Anti-Inflation Reference*

2. *Co-operative Committee on Japanese Canadians v. A.-G. Canada*, [1947] A.C. 87, at p. 101.
3. *In re Board of Commerce Act* [1922] 1 A.C. 191, at p. 201.
4. *A.G. Ontario v. Canada Temperance Federation* [1946] A.C. 193, at p. 205.
5. *A.G. Ontario v. A.G. Canada* [1896] A.C. 348, at p. 361.
6. *Globe and Mail* (Toronto), 14 October 1975, p. 13.
7. Ibid., 23 October 1975, p. 9.
8. *House of Commons, Debates*, 1st Session, 30th Parliament, 24 October 1975, p. 8519.
9. *Toronto Star*, 12 March 1976.
10. Alexander M. Bickel, *The Least Dangerous Branch* (Indiannapolis, 1962), pp. 116–17.
11. For a valuable analysis of this issue in Canadian constitutional law, including a review of this aspect of the Anti-Inflation case, see P.W. Hogg, 'Proof of Facts in Constitutional Cases,' *University of Toronto Law Journal*, 26 (1977), p. 386.
12. See his 'Tests for the Validity of Legislation: What is the Matter?' *University of Toronto Law Journal*, 11 (1955-56), and his opinion in *A.G. for Manitoba v. Manitoba Egg and Poultry Association*, [1971] S.C.R. 689, at pp. 704–6.
13. *Appendix to Factum of the Canadian Labour Congress*, pp. 62–63.
14. *Globe and Mail*, 4 June 1976, p. 1.
15. *Factum of the Attorney General of Canada*, p. 4.
16. *Globe and Mail*, 2 June 1976, p. 1.
17. *Anti-Inflation Reference*, p. 502.
18. Ibid., p. 504.
19. Ibid., p. 507.
20. Ibid., p. 524.
21. Ibid.
22. Ibid., p. 527.
23. Ibid., p. 487.
24. Ibid.
25. Ibid., p. 493.
26. Ibid., p. 529.
27. Ibid., p. 509.
28. Ibid., p. 498.
29. Ibid., p. 499.
30. This is the phrase used by Lord Wright in *The Japanese Canadians* case, at p. 101.
31. P.W. Hogg, "Proof of Facts in Constitutional Cases," p. 386.
32. *Anti-Inflation Reference*, p. 514.

FURTHER READINGS

Bernier, I., and A. Lajoie. *The Supreme Court of Canada as an Instrument of Political Change*. Toronto: University of Toronto Press, 1985.

Cheffins, R.A., and P.A. Johnson. *The Revised Canadian Constitution: Politics as Law*. Chapters 8 and 9. Toronto: McGraw-Hill Ryerson, 1986.

Russell, P.H. "Judicial Power in Canada's Political Culture." In M.L. Friedland, ed. *Courts and Trials: A Multidisciplinary Approach*, 75-88. Toronto: University of Toronto Press, 1975.

————, ed. *Leading Constitutional Decisions*. 4th ed. Ottawa: Carleton University Press, 1987.

———— "The Supreme Court's Interpretation of the Constitution." In P.W. Fox, ed. *Politics: Canada*. 5th ed. 562–620 Toronto: McGraw-Hill Ryerson, 1982.

———— "The Supreme Court and Federal-Provincial Relations: The Political Use of Legal Resources." *Canadian Public Policy* 11, 2 (March 1985): 161–170.

Printed in Canada